ARTEFACTS OF LEGAL INQUIRY

What is the value of fictions, metaphors, figures and scenarios in adjudication? This book develops three models to help answer that question: inquiry, artefacts and imagination.

Legal language, it is argued, contains artefacts – forms that signal their own artifice and call upon us to do things with them. To imagine, in turn, is to enter a distinctive epistemic frame where we temporarily suspend certain epistemic norms and commitments and participate actively along a spectrum of affective, sensory and kinesic involvement.

The book argues that artefacts and related processes of imagination are valuable insofar as they enable inquiry in adjudication, ie the social (interactive and collective) process of making insight into what values, vulnerabilities and interests might be at stake in a case and in similar cases in the future.

Artefacts of Legal Inquiry is structured in two parts, with the first offering an account of the three models of inquiry, artefacts and imagination, and the second examining four case studies (fictions, metaphors, figures and scenarios).

Drawing on a broad range of theoretical traditions – including philosophy of imagination and emotion, the theory and history of rhetoric, and the cognitive humanities – this book offers an interdisciplinary defence of the importance of artefactual language and imagination in adjudication.

Artefacts of Legal Inquiry

The Value of Imagination in Adjudication

Maksymilian Del Mar

•HART•

OXFORD • LONDON • NEW YORK • NEW DELHI • SYDNEY

HART PUBLISHING
Bloomsbury Publishing Plc
Kemp House, Chawley Park, Cumnor Hill, Oxford, OX2 9PH, UK
1385 Broadway, New York, NY 10018, USA
29 Earlsfort Terrace, Dublin 2, Ireland

HART PUBLISHING, the Hart/Stag logo, BLOOMSBURY and the Diana logo are trademarks of Bloomsbury Publishing Plc
First published in Great Britain 2020

First published in hardback, 2020
Paperback edition, 2021

A catalogue record for this book is available from the British Library.

Library of Congress Cataloging-in-Publication Data

Names: Del Mar, Maksymilian, 1979- author.

Title: Artefacts of legal inquiry : the value of imagination in adjudication / Maksymilian Del Mar.

Description: Oxford ; New York : Hart, 2020. | Includes bibliographical references and index.

Identifiers: LCCN 2019049495 (print) | LCCN 2019049496 (ebook) | ISBN 9781849468138 (hardback) | ISBN 9781509936199 (Epub)

Subjects: LCSH: Law--Language. | Law--Methodology.

Classification: LCC K213 .D45 2020 (print) | LCC K213 (ebook) | DDC 340/.14--dc23

LC record available at https://lccn.loc.gov/2019049495

LC ebook record available at https://lccn.loc.gov/2019049496

ISBN: HB: 978-1-84946-813-8
PB: 978-1-50995-504-6
ePDF: 978-1-50993-618-2
ePub: 978-1-50993-619-9

Typeset by Compuscript Ltd, Shannon

To find out more about our authors and books visit www.hartpublishing.co.uk. Here you will find extracts, author information, details of forthcoming events and the option to sign up for our newsletters.

Dla Mamy, Babci, i ich bajki

My mind now turns to stories of bodies changed into new forms.

Ovid, *Metamorphoses*

… in a complex society, civic life and civic virtues consist in the continuous struggle to live through, to be actively and imaginatively engaged in the ingenious practical work of attempting to preserve multiple and often competing values. In that sense, the skills of preserving appropriate, constructive ambivalence – the skills of a resourceful and epistemically constrained imagination – are the virtues of civic engagement.

Amélie Rorty, 'The Ethics of Collaborative Ambivalence'

ACKNOWLEDGEMENTS

Although a single authored work requires considerable individual will and effort, with all its requisite mixtures of delight and anguish, attributing a book to just one author is in many ways misleading. It seems more accurate to say that the author is a vector for so many influences, most the result of serendipity rather than design. This book is no exception. I owe enormous debts of gratitude to many people. Some were directly instrumental: without them, I could not have written this book. Others, no less important, provided pointed criticism of particular parts. Others still, and again just as importantly, gave their support through words of encouragement. Standing back now, and seeing the book complete, I appear to myself as a mere, and inadequate, conduit for these many wise, kind and generous acts.

I began conceiving of writing something like this book soon after I arrived at Queen Mary University of London in 2011. I was enormously lucky to have very supportive Heads of School: Peter Alldridge, Valsamis Mitsilegas and, more recently, Penny Green. For most of this period, Valsamis was my Head of School, and I am especially grateful to him for the freedom he gave me and the resources he made available to the Centre for Law and Society in a Global Context.

I have been blessed at Queen Mary with wonderful colleagues. I cannot possibly mention them all, but I would like to especially thank a few. Both Roger Cotterrell and Michael Lobban have been incredibly kind and generous to me, and I have learnt a lot from collaborating with them. Malgosia Fitzmaurice has been a great colleague. Even when I was at my most anti-social, which happened often, Malgosia always came to visit and chat. I have learnt a lot from, and enjoyed the company of, my fellow directors at the Centre for Law and Society in a Global Context: Sionaidh Douglas-Scott, Isobel Roele, Eva Nanopoulos, and Noam Gur. I have also enjoyed discussions with colleagues who have taught jurisprudence, always broadly conceived at Queen Mary, including Richard Nobles, David Schiff, Wayne Morrison, Rosemary Hunter, Susanna Lindroos-Hovinheimo, Richard Ashcroft, Eric Heinze, Ralf Michaels and Hans Lindahl. I would also like to thank Kenneth Armstrong, Stavros Brekoulakis, Matthieu Burnay, Eyad Dabbah, Ruth Fletcher, Jessie Hohmann, Phoebe Okowa, Prakash Shah, Mira Siegelberg and Mark van Hoecke. A number of Visiting Professors have also greatly enriched the research culture at Queen Mary and have offered support and encouragement to me. I thank especially Wibren van der Burg, Paul Schiff Berman, Brian Tamanaha and Christopher Tomlins.

In addition to colleagues, I have been lucky to have had the opportunity to teach classes in Contract Law, Jurisprudence and Legal Theory, and, most importantly with respect to this book, Imagination and Legal Cognition and Common Law Reasoning. Discussions in these latter two classes, which were both in our LLM program, have been incredibly helpful and have contributed directly to the ideas canvassed in this book. In addition to the teaching at Queen Mary, I have also had the pleasure of teaching some of the material in this book in Poland and Mexico. In Poland, I am grateful to Michał Paździora and Michał Stambulski for hosting me at the University of Wroclaw in 2016. In Mexico, I am grateful to Amalia Amaya for hosting me at UNAM. Teaching a 3-day intensive graduate workshop on 'Imagination and Practical Reason' in the summer of 2016 in Mexico was both very enjoyable and very helpful. I thank all my students very much.

I have presented the material developed in this book in a wide number of institutions, and before some very different audiences. I am enormously grateful to the organisers and the audiences at these events. These have included: the University of Durham, Personification Across the Disciplines conference, 17–19 September 2018; University of Utrecht, New Perspectives on Active Learning and Teaching in Legal Education conference, 3 November 2017; Aesthetics Research Centre, University of Kent, 18 October 2017; Conference on Comparative Legal Reasoning in Honour of Geoffrey Samuel, School of Law, University of Kent, held in Reid Hall, Paris, 3 December 2016; Lecture, The Honourable Society of the Inner Temple, 10 October 2016; Compassion and Legal Reasoning, IVR Congress workshop, Washington, 31 July – August 2015; Exemplary Narratives, IVR Congress workshop, Frankfurt, 15–20 August 2011; Legal Fictions, IVR Congress workshop, Frankfurt, 15–20 August 2011; Seminar, Centre for Legal Theory, National University of Singapore, 25 May 2015; Seminar, Edinburgh Legal Theory Research Group, 25 February 2015; and Seminar, UCL Legal Philosophy Forum, London, 4 June 2014.

I would like especially to highlight the Honourable Society of the Inner Temple: being an Academic Fellow, and now an Associate Academic Fellow, has made a great difference to me, and delivering the Inner Temple lecture on the topic of this book in 2016 helped enormously in organising and disciplining the material. In addition, the Inn sponsored a major international workshop on 'Imagination and Legal Reasoning', held at Queen Mary on 15 June 2016. I am very grateful for the Inn's support.

Beyond Queen Mary and these events, there are many people who have been incredibly important, not only to this book, but also to my academic and personal life. Zenon Bańkowski has not only been an enormous influence on me intellectually, but he has also been the most supportive and kind friend and advisor anyone can ever wish for. I owe him more than I can say: dziękuję kochany. William Twining has also been supportive for many years and in many different ways, and I have learnt a lot from my discussions with him, about fictions and much else besides. Neil Walker has been a friend and his words of encouragement have meant a lot to me. As anyone who knows him will agree, Simon Stern is a fountain of knowledge and enthusiasm, and I am grateful for his friendship and for discussions with him on law, history and aesthetics. I have learnt a great deal also from Amalia Amaya, who has been so generous in engaging with my work. Sanne Taekema has been a kind and generous presence. Andrew Halpin, who has been a friend throughout, supported this project from early on in its gestation, and this meant a lot to me. I cannot thank everyone, and I apologise in advance for omissions, but I would like to thank especially: Kristin Albrecht, Ruth Buchanan, Adam Czarnota, Julien Deonna, Luis Duarte D'Almeida, Dermot Feenan, Michael Giudice, Simone Glanert, Randy Gordon, Alex Green, Lorna Hutson, Susan James, Laurence Kauffman, Stephan Kirste,

Bart van Klink, Martin Krygier, Cormac MacAmlaigh, Paul Maharg, Elaine Mak, Bernadette Meyler, Claudio Michelon, Subha Mukherji, Paul du Plessis, Haris Psarras, Oche Onazi, Paul Roth, Nicole Roughan, Miri Rubin, Geoffrey Samuel, Quentin Skinner, Margrethe Bruun Vaage, Scott Veitch, Bald de Vries, Natasha Wheatley, Emily Kidd White and Benjamin Zipursky.

As one gets older, so many inspirations and friends depart. Some of them have been not only influential, but also enormously kind and generous to me, including Neil MacCormick and Patrick Glenn. I thank them and I remember them. During the course of writing this book, Fabian Dorsch, who I got to know when in Switzerland, died at the age of 42. In addition to being a brilliant scholar of imagination, he was also a kind and gentle soul, with many interests and so many exciting plans for the future. I salute him and his scholarship.

I wanted also to take the opportunity to thank my teachers at the TC Beirne School of Law, at the University of Queensland. It was while studying law in Brisbane as an undergraduate that I first became an addict of reading common law cases. I remain as ever grateful to my teachers there, including Ann Black and Jonathan Crowe. I am also deeply grateful to my teachers in Philosophy and Literature at the University of Queensland, including Aurelia Armstrong, Michelle Boulous Walker, Deborah Brown, Marguerite La Caze and Tony Thwaites. Before graduation, I had the opportunity to be a summer research fellow at the Centre for the History of European Discourses at the University of Queensland – I remember my time there very fondly, and I thank the staff at CHED, and especially Ian Hunter, for their kindness and support. Following graduation, I spent a wonderful year as Associate to the Hon. Justice Margaret White, then of the Supreme Court of Queensland. I was incredibly lucky to have been exposed to such a brilliant judge, and one so interested in art and literature. In writing this book, and thus in theorising adjudication, I have often reflected on my experience during that year.

There are two people without whom I would not have written this book, and much else besides: Alexandra and Tristan. Each, in their own way, taught me to slow down and enjoy life.

CONTENTS

PART II
CASE STUDIES

Introduction

I. The Claim

The central claim of this book is that artefacts and related processes of imagination are valuable in adjudication insofar as they enable activities of inquiry. In brief, as modelled in this book:

- Activities of inquiry are social, ie both interactive and collective, processes that: are not reducible to, but overlap with, the contexts of discovery and justification; occur in real time and over time; are experimental in their cognitive and expressive character; and the object of which is the making of insight into what values, vulnerabilities and interests might be at stake in a case and in cases potentially like it in the future.
- Artefacts are forms of language that: first, signal their own artifice, thereby also capturing our attention; and second, call upon us to participate, ie to do things with them.
- Imagination is a combination of two simultaneously exercised and active processes: first, we enter a distinctive epistemic frame, which is an active and deliberative process of constructing a certain epistemic attitude, including selectively suspending certain epistemic norms and commitments while retaining others; and second, we participate within that epistemic frame along a spectrum of affective, sensory and kinesic involvement.

This is, I readily acknowledge, an inelegant mouthful. It is the task of this book to elucidate and elaborate on this claim, I hope more elegantly. In order to do so, I construct what I call three 'models', which are all key to the above claim: inquiry, artefacts and imagination. Models, roughly for now, are theoretical devices that are designed to help us focus on some distinguishable object of study, while at the same time enabling and encouraging us to see its variability. Thus, this book is not a wholescale theory of adjudication. Instead, it seeks to construct three specific models that, I hope, help us to get a little closer to, and appreciate, certain hitherto neglected features of adjudication.

In fact, 'adjudication' is somewhat of a misleading label for another reason: the book is not concerned with adjudication in general, but with a specific context of adjudicatory practice, namely the practice of appellate courts in the English common law in the twentieth century. I consider this sensitivity to, and self-reflexiveness about, context to be an important part of the activity of theorising. Of course, I do not claim to be fully sensitive to or wholly self-reflexive about that context; far from it. It is inevitable that I make assumptions about features of that practice that I have not articulated or reflected upon: there are 'hinges' upon which this door swings (with apologies to Wittgenstein).[1] Nevertheless, my aim, which also marks the limitations of my claim, is to assist us to see and appreciate a little better certain features of the above-mentioned context of adjudicatory practice. Whether the models developed here are thought, by others, to be helpful in other contexts of adjudication – or indeed in this one! – remains to be seen.

The book is structured into two parts. The first part elucidates and elaborates the three models, namely inquiry in Chapter 1, artefacts in Chapter 2, and imagination in Chapter 3. The first part ends with Chapter 4, which serves as a bridge between the two parts, relating the three models to each other, with one eye on the case studies in the second part. The second part then examines four case studies, these being all examples of artefacts, and their related processes of imagination. In each case, the focus is on when, and if so how, these artefacts and related processes of imagination enable activities of inquiry. The four case studies are: fictions in Chapter 5, metaphors in Chapter 6, figures in Chapter 7 and scenarios in Chapter 8.

One feature of the book is that it makes distinctions between these different artefacts, and their related processes of imagination. Another feature is that the defence of the value of these is a contingent one, ie it depends on whether they enable, rather than obstruct, activities of inquiry. Thus, identifying what are the features of these artefacts, and their related processes of imagination, that assist inquiry is a vital part of the analysis.

As may already be evident from this brief description, this book is no wholescale defence of the inherent value of artefacts and the imagination. It is very much a contingent defence.[2] Nevertheless, and given especially the neglect and side-lining of imagination in theories of adjudication, this is an undoubtedly upbeat and positive book. Artefacts, and their related processes of imagination, deserve not only our theoretical attention: they also deserve a case to be made for their valuable contribution to adjudication. Making that case is the task of this book.

II. The Story of a Project

As I have presented the structure of the book, it may seem that theory, or what I call 'modelling', in part one precedes and drives the identification, description, analysis and evaluation of the case studies, which are presented in part two. That is not so and indeed was not so. In order to show this, and also to offer a perhaps more accessible way into the questions and issues explored in this book, I want to offer a brief and personal account of how this project began and describe some of its twists and turns along the way.[3] Far from being driven solely or even mainly by theoretical concerns, the real engines of

[1] On 'hinge epistemology', inspired by Wittgenstein, see Coliva and Moyal-Sharrock (2016).

[2] For a fascinating study of the very genre of defences, with a focus on defences of poetry in the Renaissance, see Ferguson (1983). It is interesting to ask, for instance, why do we (feel we have to) offer a defence of poetry, and not, say, of science?

[3] I do so deliberately, even if at the risk of sounding indulgent, as we do not often enough share our personal experience, including affective experience, of research. I do so also in the service of recognising the limits of theorising, which are set, in part, by the particular life and experiences of a theorist.

this project have been particular instances of language use, which I kept coming across when reading, and re-reading, common law cases, and which puzzled me, and which still very much puzzle me, often with equal measures of excitement and exasperation.

Although the roots of this project may lie in the pleasures of reading common law cases during my undergraduate studies, a reading that was very much informed by my also studying literature and philosophy at the time,[4] the more immediate beginning was a reading of Lon Fuller's series of papers on legal fictions.[5] Wonderfully generative and speculative, I still recall the excitement of reading these papers, initially in some dark bar in Berlin, now some seven years ago. Fuller's reflections took me quickly to the work of Hans Vaihinger, and his magnificent *As If*,[6] which although a little too in the vein of the Kantian tradition for my taste, could also be thought of in another way: as an aesthetically-sensitive pragmatism concerned with devices for thinking with, for trying things out, for experimenting. In Vaihinger's case, this was also a most expansive pragmatism, the objects of which appeared to have no bounds, for he found fictions in such a dazzling range of areas of human inquiry, from philosophy to mathematics to science to law, and beyond. I was attracted to the non-foundationalist, the delicately sceptical, but also the upbeat, tone of classical pragmatism. Unlike some contemporary versions of pragmatism, the classical pragmatist tradition, including not only Vaihinger, but also Charles Sanders Peirce and John Dewey, was still awash with enthusiasm if not enchantment. The human mind, and human minds together, could, in the eyes of these classical pragmatists, do so much, and they were giddy with the pleasure of showcasing those possibilities. I too, in truth, was giddy.

I began to think seriously about fictions, or at least as seriously as my then new-job at Queen Mary University of London allowed. I was reading all I could about them, especially in the common law tradition. At the same time, I was reading cases that could be said to have deployed them. My enthusiasm, informed as it was by Vaihinger and his defence of fictions, kept jarring up against a disjuncture between theory and practice: on the one hand, courts were clearly using fictions, finding them useful in a whole range of different areas of the law, and perhaps especially private law; on the other hand, the theory on fictions in the common law, both by scholars and in extra-judicial writings by judges, was passionately critical of fictions. At times, it seemed like scholars were in competition to see who could be most critical about them. Jeremy Bentham's infamously colourful critique, characterising fictions as the pestilential breath of the law, and so on,[7] seemed to have infused common law scholars to the point of blindness. They could no longer see, or were so unwilling to admit, the possibility that fictions could be valuable.

I turned to the historians, and this helped enormously, though only partially. Sir Henry Maine, for example, had argued that modern law no longer needed fictions,

[4] One of the most formative, but also pleasurable, aspects of my experience as an undergraduate student at the University of Queensland was moving, often in the same day, from a class on Victorian literature, to a class on epistemology, and then to a class on contract law. During this period, and increasingly so as I focused more and more intensively on law, I was also influenced by less mainstream views on common law reasoning, especially the work of Julius Stone (1985), Geoffrey Samuel (2003), Bernard Jackson (1988) and William Twining and David Miers (1976).

[5] Fuller (1930–31). I engage with these three papers in more detail in ch 5.

[6] Vaihinger (1925) [1911].

[7] See Ogden (1932).

but he nevertheless found an important place for them in the history of legal development: they were the first mode of legal change, followed, in ever-higher degrees of rationality, by equity and finally by legislation.[8] So, for Maine, fictions were irrational and no longer needed, but still, there was a begrudging sort of recognition that they may at a certain point have been valuable. What if, I thought, Maine, and others since,[9] had over-estimated the so-called 'rationality' of the modern age? What if fictions were still valuable today, and it was an illusion to think that we, in the present, were so much more enlightened that we no longer needed them?

This possibility raised other questions: for instance, the vexing problem of just how to define fictions. Scholars had given so many different examples of fictions, and some of these seemed to mix up fictions with other kinds of devices, like metaphor or figuration, which I had a sense were doing different sort of work. Partly in order to deal with these difficulties, and in order to begin a conversation from which I could also learn, I convened a workshop on legal fictions at the IVR Congress in Frankfurt in 2013, and this led eventually to a special issue and a large edited volume.[10] It was in this period, and thanks to conversations with William Twining and others, that I began to develop my own view of fictions, offering my own defence of their value in enabling common law change.[11] Legal fictions, as I came to define them, were a means of temporarily suspending operative requirements of an existing rule, while still applying the normative consequence of that rule, thereby signalling to future courts that either the rule ought to be abandoned and a new one created, or that an exception ought to be introduced. Importantly, fictions were not a means of changing the law. They were, instead, a means of deciding the case without changing the law, but nevertheless communicating the potential need for change in the future.

One of the vital shifts of perspective that this defence of fictions required was that one could not hope to see the value of fictions if one focused only on their use in the instant case. If one focused only on the instant case, fictions were indeed a failure, eg of rationality, of principled justification, of transparent reason-giving in adjudication. If, however, one thought of reasoning as something that occurs over time, then what looks initially like a failure may in fact turn out to be a blessing, for the extra time that a fiction enabled gave courts the opportunity to explore, by reference to a greater range of factual scenarios, how to respond to the alleged inadequacy of the rule that the fiction signalled.[12] There was another crucial point: the extra time that fiction bought, so to speak, was not only extra time for that judge or that panel of judges, but for a whole range of future readers of the case, including other judges, advocates and scholars. Thus, fictions enabled a mode of interactive and collective reasoning, deliberation and experimentation. And, I wondered, what if we looked at legal reasoning, and adjudication in general, in much more social terms than mainstream theories of legal

[8] See Maine (1931) [1861].

[9] In contemporary scholarship, Peter Birks had made a similar argument: see Birks (1986).

[10] See Del Mar and Twining (2015).

[11] See Del Mar (2015a).

[12] There was a parallel interest that kept reminding me of the importance of approaching legal reasoning diachronically: an interest in the relations between legal theory and legal history. See Del Mar and Lobban (2014) and Del Mar and Lobban (2016).

reasoning appeared to do? What if we shifted the perspective entirely, and instead of examining the rationality of justification offered by a single judge in an instant case, we instead explored the practices of signalling, communicating, and experimenting over time by a community of different actors in the adjudicatory process?

It is these questions, driven as they were by shock and frustration with the negativity of common law scholars about fictions, especially given their long and continued role in practice, that formed the crucible within which this project was born. Having made the defence of fictions, I began to think whether a similar kind of defence could be made of other devices, also often derided or side-lined by mainstream theories of legal reasoning. The derision, with respect to these other devices, was often not as passionate or exaggerated as it was in the case of fictions. Some of these other devices, such as the ones I study in this book, ie metaphors, figures, and scenarios, were less often said to be wholly irrational; more often, they were simply characterised as either unhelpful or unnecessary, or as the flotsam and jetsam of the common law. In keeping with mainstream attitudes to rhetoric and rhetorical language, many of these devices were said to be but superfluous embellishments, at worst vain flights of whimsy, and at best powerful means of persuasion, but really in the end unbecoming of the gravity of the law. Adjudication, it seemed, had to be a sober affair: not only rational, with transparent and principled reasons given for decisions, but also objective, neutral, and universal, operating in the realm of a heaven of concepts, held together securely by logic and untainted by anything as messy as an experiment.

As will be obvious to the reader, I was taken aback by such attitudes. Surely, given that it was impossible to escape the contingent genealogies of our language, we needed to confront the rhetorical dimension of communication rather than hide it away. The very idea of a language that was sober, objective, neutral, universal, and so on, was itself a style, a genre, with its own forms and their genealogies. The attack on rhetoric was a form of self-delusion, a noble dream for some perhaps, but really a nightmare. Similarly so with the idea that language was something we could master, or that meaning was something we could control: to think like this was to forget about the deeply social character of language and meaning.

All this was well and good, but also said many times by those who came to the defence of rhetoric and the social character of language, both past and present, from Vico to Derrida, and even more so, feminist epistemologists and feminist theorists of legal reasoning and legal language. How could we, how could I, move beyond mere critique? If rhetoric was not reducible to optional ornament or to powerful persuasion, what exactly was valuable about it? This question has animated this project throughout. In a thirst for possible ways of defending rhetoric, and, in particular, to eventually thinking of it as a form of inquiry, I turned to a whole range of scholarship from many different fields. This has included, naturally, the theory and history of rhetoric itself; literary theory and history,[13] some of which explicitly involved defences of rhetorical forms, such as those given by IA Richards,[14] and some of which was in a different

[13] I was, and remain, especially taken with the work of Wesley Trimpi, Joel Altman, Kathy Eden, Lorna Hutson, Quentin Skinner, Peter Mack, and others working on rhetoric in the early modern period.

[14] See Richards (1936).

vein, informed by more recent developments in cognitive science and philosophy of mind, such as work in cognitive literary studies;[15] psychology, including developmental psychology, as in Paul Harris' work on imagination;[16] the history and philosophy of science, where rhetoric too was defended, eg by Jeanne Fahnestock;[17] and to philosophy, eg within epistemology, in the work of Catherine Elgin, and, within methodology, in feminist accounts of the aesthetics of philosophical discourse, such as those by Michèle Le Doeuff or one of my teachers in philosophy, Marguerite La Caze.[18]

Throughout this time, in what has seemed like endless reading, across many different disciplines, I continued to teach and think about common law cases, including mainstream theories of legal reasoning. One of the key sources for me was Neil MacCormick's work on legal reasoning, which, though mainstream, was also always responsive to less mainstream views, eg Chaim Perelman's rhetorical accounts of legal argumentation. MacCormick's *Legal Reasoning and Legal Theory*[19] was crucial for me, in part because it was packed with examples. For instance, it was by trying to make sense of MacCormick's reflections on consequential reasoning in law, from his 1978 book, but also beyond to his Dewey lecture on the subject,[20] that I began to think seriously about what I call in this book 'scenarios', ie short, fictional narratives, which play a variety of roles, eg testing and refining possible ways of justifying a decision in a particular case and others like it in the future. Somewhat to my surprise, one could think about universalisation, as MacCormick deployed it, but also Kant and Hare, as a kind of thought experiment, ie a mode of 'what-if' thinking, which was not possible wholly in the abstract, but which needed the stimulus of specific and sometimes exaggerated facts. In other words, MacCormick's defence of the role of consequences in legal reasoning,[21] as based not on probabilistic reasoning, ie trying to predict the outcome of certain rules, but instead on hypothetical reasoning, ie based precisely on reactions, in part emotional, to hypothetical cases, emerged, slowly, as another kind of device to think with. In this respect, I thought, hypothetical cases, or, as I call them in this book, scenarios, resembled fictions, though they were processed in different ways and performed different kinds of functions.[22]

Crucial in all this was not only research, but also teaching. This included teaching Contract Law to first year undergraduates when I first arrived at Queen Mary. Readers will notice that quite a few of the examples discussed in this book are contract law cases. Of particular, direct importance was the experience of teaching a Masters course on 'Imagination and Legal Cognition' and later 'Common Law Reasoning'. I taught fictions, certainly, but also began to incorporate other devices: scenarios and metaphors, as well as what I then-called 'personification', or the use of imaginary figures, such as the reasonable person. Teaching allowed me to work in detail through examples, driven as

[15] Scholarship by Terence Cave and Ellen Spolsky was especially important for me, as was Lisa Zunshine's *The Oxford Handbook of Cognitive Literary Studies* (2014).

[16] Harris (2000).

[17] Fahnestock (1999).

[18] See Elgin (1996); Le Doeuff (1989); and La Caze (2002).

[19] MacCormick (1978).

[20] See MacCormick (1983).

[21] See Del Mar (2015c).

[22] Dewey too was important for me here, eg in his notion of dramatic rehearsal, as well as various interpretations of him, eg see Fesmire (2003).

the course was by cases and discussion of those cases. I also began to experiment with different ways of theoretically framing what I was interested in; hence the reference to 'imagination' and to 'cognition' in the title of the course, which were attempts to get beyond narrow and rigid uses of 'reasoning' or 'rationality'.

I will, of course, be saying a great deal more about imagination in this book. At times in this project I was overcome by the immensity of the literature on imagination, which has also mushroomed in recent years, constituting new-found interest amongst analytical philosophers.[23] At times, too, I got, and still get, lost in various thickets of discussions of imagination, such as the debates over mental imagery, or debates about the role of imagination in perception, eg the seeing-as way of understanding imagination. One of the important turning points in this respect was the sudden realisation that it was vital not to lose sight of two things when thinking about imagination: first, the complex and dynamic relations between imagination and forms of expression and representation, especially in language; and second, that imagination was not something that occurred only in the mind of an individual, but that there were important social dimensions to imagination, including both interactive and collective modes of imagining. Both of these realisations helped a great deal, if only to rescue me a little, though I am by no means wholly free, from endless perplexity at just what goes on in the mind of an individual when imagining.

There are three other influences on this project that have informed it throughout and that have shaped it and continue to shape my work in general. They are: emotion; morality; and education.

Like imagination, emotion has been one of the most side-lined, derided and neglected dimensions of legal thought, at least until relatively recently, when there has been an outpouring of works, both philosophical and historical, on the importance of emotion for law in a whole range of ways.[24] There is no serious discussion of emotion, and its epistemic significance, in mainstream theories of legal reasoning, certainly not in the positivist, analytical tradition, eg in HLA Hart or Joseph Raz, nor in the interpretivist tradition of Ronald Dworkin. Realist and other naturalist-inspired theories of adjudication had and have more reference to emotion, though these references have often struck me as being too narrowly focused on the psychology of decision-making. For all the emphasis placed on the importance of psychology in legal realist writings, eg in Jerome Frank, there was little to be found on the epistemic role of emotion, or on the entanglement of emotion with deliberation and reasoning.[25] Indeed, it was partly in order to engage properly with the role and value of emotion that I began to get increasingly frustrated with the division of labour mandated by the justification-discovery dichotomy (imported from the philosophy of science), which was advocated so eagerly especially by analytical legal philosophers. This dichotomy, about which I say more in Chapter 1, has had the effect of splitting research between empirical studies of how one came to a decision on the one hand, ie discovery, and analytical or normative studies

[23] See, eg, Kind (2016) and Kind and Kung (2016).

[24] Work on affective histories of law is especially important: see, eg, the essays collected in Bailey and Knight (2017); and Holmes and Johnson (2018).

[25] An exception is the work of Leon Petrażycki, who remains greatly under-valued in this area. See Petrażycki (1955), and for a helpful discussion, Motyka (2007).

of practices of giving reasons, ie justification, on the other hand. The problem with this is that a serious engagement with emotion, or, for that matter, imagination, and its epistemic importance, including its role in deliberation and reasoning, simply has to cut across these divisions. Put another way, the kind of division of labour engendered by the dichotomy between discovery and justification was, I found, not helpful when seeking to understand the multifarious and vital roles of emotion and imagination in adjudication.

In fact, the more I engaged with imagination, the more often I kept coming across emotion. The two, I kept finding, were more closely related than one might at first think. If we looked more carefully, we could see that many acts of imagining involve emotion, and many emotions have an imaginative component, eg think only of how much we imagine when experiencing fear or jealousy. I began to crave scholarly literature on the complex and rich relationship between emotion and imagination, which, in the legal context as in any other context, calls for and requires interdisciplinary research. It helped me enormously to think through these issues with Amalia Amaya, and the group of scholars we invited to our joint project on 'Virtue, Emotion and Imagination in Law and Legal Reasoning'.[26]

Most of the study of emotion in adjudication that I came across was via the concept of empathy. I came to think there were important distinctions to be made between empathy, sympathy and compassion,[27] and that, again, some of what is defended under the canopy of emotion, and especially empathy, is perhaps better defended under the canopy of imagination.[28] Work on these emotions is important, but I also came to feel frustrated by the very narrow focus on just these processes, and the lack of engagement with other kinds of emotions in adjudication, eg with epistemic emotions, such as those of doubt or satisfaction, or what Hume called the 'calm passions'. I also began to think that there was another story to tell about the role of simulated emotions, ie the process of imagining one's emotional reactions, for instance to the actions of imaginary figures (like the reasonable person) or to hypothetical scenarios. I shall be returning to these issues later in the book.

The interest in emotions, and most obviously empathy, sympathy and compassion, was intimately related to morality, and the vexed issue of whether, and if so how, moral reasoning features in legal reasoning. On this, of course, there is no shortage of debate in mainstream theories of adjudication. But my approach to these issues has always been from less-frequently opened doors, or via less-well-travelled paths: precisely via emotion and imagination, or indeed via education. Thus, the moral imagination has been an interest for me for a long time, certainly ever since encountering the work of my other doctoral supervisor (in addition to Neil MacCormick), Zenon Bańkowski. It was thanks to Bańkowski, and his work on the anxiety and moral perception of the judge,[29] that I began to think about the presence of morals in adjudication. It was also thanks to Bańkowski that I thought and wrote about vulnerability, and about the inevitable difficulties, and yes, anxieties, of being able to see the suffering and vulnerability of

[26] This has recently culminated in an edited collection: see Amaya and Del Mar (2020).
[27] See Del Mar (2017a).
[28] A point made also by Kind (2020).
[29] See Bańkowski (2001), Bańkowski (2006), and Bańkowski (2013). See also Del Mar and Michelon (2013).

those who come before the courts, especially where that suffering and vulnerability may be distinctly unfamiliar to, in part because it was distant to the personal experience of, the judge or judges in question.[30]

The key questions that emerged for me out of engagement with Bańkowski's work, and his references, including Iris Murdoch, Simone Weil, and Martha Nussbaum, included: what helps a judge to have the requisite attention, and be able to encounter, the suffering and vulnerability of others that he or she has not experienced? How can judges, and other legal professionals, loosen the hold of their professional habits so as to, again, better see what ought to be seen, and what may be beyond the scope of a rule as conventionally understood? And how should the 'ought' be understood here? 'Ought to be seen' according to whom? Here, I kept coming back to the basic existential situation of moral difficulty, of the sheer effort required to, for a start, recognise the limitations of one's own moral outlook and intuitions about the right and the good, and, then, of seeking to go beyond oneself, as it were, and out towards the people coming before the court and their experiences and plights. This included reflection on my own stance as a theorist examining the work of judges: could I theorise that work, including sometimes be critical of it, in a way that was also respectful of the moral difficulties the judges faced? Could I find a way of being mindful of those difficulties, and the various inevitable epistemic and institutional limitations, while not falling into mere apology? Could I practice a form of respectful critique of judicial work? Could I do so not from a position of the superiority of hindsight, with unshakable confidence in the correctness of my moral beliefs, but instead from a hermeneutic perspective that recognised the difficulties, the fragility and incompleteness of any moral knowledge, but nevertheless insisted upon certain duties and standards?

And I began to think: is there a connection between the devices I was interested in and teaching, especially fictions, metaphors, figures, and scenarios, and this experience of moral difficulty and normative uncertainty, and the process, indeed the duty, of being responsive to suffering and vulnerability? My answer is that yes, there is a link. In this book I seek to articulate that link via the model of 'inquiry', and especially its normative dimension. It is, I shall argue, at least in part, via artefacts and related processes of imagination, that we can make insights into potential normative relevance, ie better sense, the values, vulnerabilities and interests that may be at stake in a case and in cases potentially like it in the future.

The reader has probably already discerned how concerns with education permeates much of the above. Indeed, my first way in, broadly speaking, to these issues of imagination, emotion, morality, and their connections to law and adjudication, was via reflection on pedagogical practices, and ultimately also on my role and duty as a teacher. Beginning with a collaboration with Bańkowski in Edinburgh, when I was a PhD student and a tutor in jurisprudence, and during which we thought together about the possible role and value of visual and dramatic arts for teaching legal professional ethics,[31] I have throughout the last ten years often returned to and grappled with questions about moral education in law schools. And, as I did so, while developing the

[30] I have wrestled with the issues in numerous places, see, eg, Del Mar (2012), (2013) and (2014).

[31] See Del Mar (2010a); Bańkowski and Del Mar (2013); and Bańkowski, Del Mar and Maharg (2013).

above interests in emotion and imagination, I began to write about their roles in legal education.[32] Indeed, as originally envisaged, an important part of this book was to be a discussion of imagination in legal education. That is no longer the case – the principal reason being that I could not do this topic justice in a part of a book – but I want to emphasise that it has greatly informed the arguments and claims made in this book. Pedagogical reflection, for me, has never been a side-line or a soft subject that is of no philosophical significance; on the contrary, reflection on pedagogy has been, for me, one of the most important matters to think carefully about, both philosophically and existentially.

And so the many braids of one's work, and one's life, too, as a colleague, as a teacher, as a member of an institution, come together, mostly in unpredictable and often accidental ways, to inform a project, and here a book.

III. Limits and Scope of this Book

It is important that I outline more explicitly the limits and scope of this book. I do so in three steps: first, I highlight the very specific context of the examples drawn on in this book, namely contemporary common law adjudication in English appellate courts; second, I discuss the broad attitude I take to the ethics and politics of adjudication; and third, I say a little more about what I mean by 'modelling' as a theoretical practice.

A. Common Law Adjudication

Almost all the examples drawn on in this book come from the common law tradition. They are also almost all from the late twentieth and twenty-first century, and thus largely contemporary examples. The contemporary focus does not mean, however, that one can simply take features of common law practice for granted. Indeed, an important part of any theory of legal reasoning, and this may be all the more important when one's focus is contemporary, is just what features of practice are deemed important as the institutional setting for that investigation. Indeed, I take it to be a duty and virtue of theorising to be as reflexive as one can about the construction of one's object of theorising.

At first blush, this may seem surprising. Is it not the ambition of theorists to apply to wherever and whenever one finds practices of legal reasoning? But that's just the rub: exactly *where* and *when* does one find them? And what does one mean by 'practices of legal reasoning'? The moment one asks this question one also quickly realises how many different kinds of adjudicatory institutions there are, and have been, operating in very different institutional environments, with very different histories and influences.[33] Indeed, one very quickly realises that one needs an account of what are

[32] See Del Mar (2011), (2016a), (2018a) and (2018b).

[33] In addition, as William Twining has often insisted, there is the issue of practices of legal reasoning outside the adjudicative context. Hence, Twining urges us to think more broadly of 'reasoning in legal contexts': see recently Twining (2019), 116–135.

the differences between adjudicatory institutions that matter, and which, in one's view, do not. For example, does it matter whether we are talking about a domestic court as distinct from an international one, and is the domestic/international distinction the most, or even a, relevant distinction? Does it matter that we are talking about an appellate court rather than, say, a magistrate's court? Does it matter that we are talking about a court dedicated to a very specific area of the law, say a tribunal dealing only with patent applications, or a generalist court, hearing appeals from all areas of the law, or perhaps a constitutional court? Does it matter whether the court is sitting in its contentious or advisory jurisdiction? Does it matter who the judges are, eg is there a relevant difference between, say, Supreme Court Justices and arbitrators, and are differences in typical career progressions of judges significant? Does it matter whether the judges form a tight-knit, long-term community, or are more ad hoc appointments? Does it matter what kind of assistance judges receive, say from judicial clerks, or what resources they have easy access to, eg libraries, databases and other archives? Does the procedure before the court matter, eg whether it is adversarial or inquisitorial, or what style of advocacy it facilitates and encourages? Is it important what options judges have to express their views, eg whether they do so orally or in writing, and if in writing, whether there are only ever single, collective judgements or also separate and dissenting opinions?

These questions are just the tip of the iceberg, but the moment one turns to them, even in a superficial way, one quickly sees that one can hardly avoid asking them. These questions also illustrate the close relationship there is between comparative law and legal theory, for all the above questions, if they are to be asked properly, can only be done with sensitivity to the difficulties and opportunities of comparison.[34] Similarly so as to the relations between legal history and legal theory: important insights as to peculiar institutional features of the practice one is focusing on often only come into view when one compares, say, the contemporary instantiation of a tradition with its past lives, but also in terms of its relations with other traditions across time.[35]

I cannot here perform this task with the rigor and discipline it requires. Nevertheless, I shall attempt to be as reflexive as I can about the features of the contemporary practice of the common law that I have taken as important for this book. To reiterate, to articulate such features is not an optional matter. I take to be an essential part of what it means to theorise legal reasoning. In this respect, then, comparing and historicising are distinct and important aspects of any theoretical project.

Needless to say, I am hardly the first to attempt the identification of important institutional features of common law reasoning. Some theories of legal reasoning have presented themselves not as general theories but precisely as theories of common law practice.[36] This literature itself has many divisions which are often un-mentioned,

[34] See, eg, John Bell's work on judicial cultures (2006). See also Bell (2016).

[35] See, eg, Patrick Glenn's scholarship on legal tradition (2014) and on common laws (2007). See also Samuel (2018a) and (2018b) on the importance of studying legal reasoning historically; and, generally, Gordley (2013); and Thomas (2011).

[36] An important challenge to the abstractions of analytical jurisprudence in this respect, ie from the perspective of the particularities of the common law, was made by Brian Simpson in his influential 'Common Law and Legal Theory' (1973). See also Twining (1986); Edlin (2007) and Edlin (2016); Postema (2002) and Postema (2003); Eisenberg (1988); Schauer (2009), chapter 6; and Jaffey (2017).

as for instance between mainly US-based theories and mainly UK-based theories,[37] or as between theories that take the colonial and imperial context of the common law seriously and those that do not.[38] Similarly so with respect to theories, even, say, within the UK, that are historically sensitive, and thus seek to theorise common law reasoning as it has changed and developed over time, and those which focus, largely un-reflexively, on contemporary common law.[39] One can multiply such divisions further, depending on whether the focus is mainly on appellate courts or lower courts and other tribunals, or on reasoning with law or reasoning with fact,[40] or on case-based reasoning or statutory interpretation.[41] All these divisions can be contested. The differences between, say, appellate and first-instance reasoning, or between case-based reasoning and statutory interpretation, may be argued to be irrelevant. The point, once again, is that it is important to be as reflexive as one can about the differences one endorses and those one does not insist upon.

My focus here is on twentieth and twenty-first century common law in English appellate courts. I do attempt to take seriously the imperial and colonial context of the common law, though, to my regret, this really only surfaces in one of the case studies in the second part of the book (in Chapter 6 on metaphor). I generally also focus on reasoning with law, although I do not accept a very rigid distinction between reasoning with fact and law. But even if one limits oneself in this way, there is still very considerable scope for differences as to which institutional features of common law practice one takes as important, and which one does not.

To illustrate this briefly, consider Grant Lamond's approach to one of the nuggets of theorising about common law practice: precedent.[42] Lamond makes clear that there are some features of common law practice that, for the purposes of theorising precedent, are relevant and that he takes seriously, ie he takes them to be constraints on any plausible theory of precedent. These include: the absence of canonical formulation of rules or principles; the significance of the facts of cases and the extensive attention paid to those facts, eg in the practice of distinguishing; and the persistence of disagreement as to the legal significance or ratio of a past case.[43] On the other hand, and it is laudable that

[37] There are many significant institutional, cultural and other differences between these two legal traditions, and yet scholars of common law reasoning often mix them. Sometimes, though, the differences do come to the surface, often unwittingly, as became evident in some responses from UK scholars to Dworkin's mainly US-based theory of legal reasoning. See, eg, Priel (2016). There is important comparative work to be done within common law traditions; in other words, even within the common law, there are important differences that affect the practice and normativity of common law reasoning.

[38] Although there are many important historical studies of common law in its imperial and colonial contexts, there are few theories of common law reasoning that take these contexts seriously. An exception is the work of Peter Fitzpatrick (2002).

[39] There have been a number of scholars who have stressed the importance of theorising common law reasoning historically and diachronically, critiquing the often atemporal, static, momentary and ahistorical theories of legal reasoning by contemporary analytical jurisprudence: see, eg, Lobban (1991); Samuel (2003); Waddams (2003); Hutchinson (2005); and Postema (2002), (2003), (2017). I return to the importance of diachronicity in Chapter 1.

[40] This importance of taking facts seriously in theories of legal reasoning has been a theme of Twining's scholarship; see, eg, Twining (1984).

[41] See the two volumes of the Bielefelder Kreis, one on comparing statutory interpretation and the other on comparing precedential reasoning: MacCormick and Summers (1991) and (1997).

[42] Lamond (2005).

[43] Ibid, 3.

Lamond is explicit about this, there are features that Lamond claims are not relevant to, and in this sense are not constraints on, a plausible theory of precedent in the common law. One such feature is whether or not the judgement delivered by a court is a single or a multiple one. Lamond asserts that he is 'not concerned with complications that arise in legal practice from cases where there is no agreed majority judgement in favour of the result, or the judgement gives two separate but individually sufficient grounds, or no reasons at all are given by the court'.[44] He adds: 'These questions are important for practitioners, but the key theoretical questions arise from the uncomplicated single judgement case'.[45] What should we make of this move? On what basis can one assert that only some features of practice, and not others, raise 'key theoretical questions'? Would not the fact that something is 'important for practitioners' be instead an argument for its prima facie theoretical importance? And when constructing a theory of legal reasoning in the common law, or even, in a more limited way, of its precedential dimension, can one really ignore a feature as prominent as the regular production of multiple, sometimes dissenting, judgements?

In answering these questions we have to keep in mind one crucial point: that no matter how reflexive we are about features of practices, there are always going to be some that we take for granted, and even where we are reflexive about them, there can always be disagreement between theorists as to what ought to be taken as relevant. Thus, although I disagree with Lamond that one can ignore the feature of the production of multiple, sometimes dissenting, judgements in the common law, I also wish to make clear that there is no neutral stance here, no stance above the practice. Instead, a theorist must articulate what they take to be relevant, while recognising that these choices are part of a theory, as are the less reflexive taken-for-granted features, either included or excluded as relevant.

What follows, then, are the features of contemporary common law practice I take to be especially relevant and important for this book. I recognise these are all theoretical claims that cannot be properly defended in this book. However, as noted above, I take it to be part of the ethics of theorising that one tries to be reflexive about them. There are four such features: individuality, multiplicity, discursiveness and restrained generalisation. I shall treat them briefly in turn.[46]

The first feature one may label 'individuality'.[47] To take this is as a feature, let alone the first, is already controversial. And yet, there are so many aspects of contemporary common law practice that signal its importance. One of these is that judgements in the common law are not anonymous but signed by the judge(s) that author them. Further, the judgements are referred to as 'opinions' or as 'speeches'. Common law judges present themselves and are treated as authors of opinions. They also often have public personas, eg, as scholars in their own right, and as speech-givers on public occasions. As authors,

[44] Ibid, 4.

[45] Ibid.

[46] The features identified here bear some similarity to others: see, eg, Postema (2003), 3–9, who identifies six features (by reference to the 'artificial reason' of the common law): it is pragmatic; it has a public mission; it is a contextual competence (involving long years of immersion in the particularity of cases); it is non-systematic; it is discursive (meaning that it is argumentative and contested); and it is common or shared.

[47] I prefer this term to 'subjectivity', which carries a heavy philosophical baggage. For an important recent defence of the role and value of subjectivity in common law adjudication, see Edlin (2016).

judges have their own styles and temperaments, eg some are known for their dissenting judgements. An outstanding example is Justice Michael Kirby, known as the Great Dissenter in the High Court of Australia. Others are known for their distinctive style: Lord Denning is the most obvious example in the English context. Or they are said to have a distinctive voice and temperament: Justice Ruth Ginsburg of the US Supreme Court is, again, a standout example. Some judges are known, too, to be especially sensitive to certain sources or to certain issues, eg some take it to be an important feature of any domestic judge to take seriously the sources of international law or the practice of so-called 'foreign' courts, while others resolutely do not. Here, one need only contrast the jurisprudence of Justice Kirby with the late Justice Anthony Scalia of the US Supreme Court. Another way in which the presence of individuality is made visible in the contemporary common law is that judges are not discouraged from the use of the first person. Indeed, the first person may be found more often than the royal third person.[48] Judges will often say 'I confess to the difficulties of this case' or share other aspects of their experience of the case before them. This sharing of individual experiences is important, eg it serves to communicate attitudes of an individual judge to certain issues. It matters, for example, whether judges express confidence in, or, equally, doubt or hesitation in applying, a certain rule or principle.[49]

To say that individuality is an important feature of the contemporary common law tradition is not, for the moment, to defend its role, or indeed to attack it. Nevertheless, I would like to make explicit that I think individuality is not only a central feature of common law practice, but also, on the whole, a valuable one. The presence of individuality allows for many of the other features I shall mention in a moment. But it is also important in its own right: for example, one could argue that the practice of judgement is, in some respects inevitably, one that involves drawing on one's own personal experiences. To see this is also to recognise the importance of diversity on the bench. Of course, the drawing on of one's personal experiences, including one's emotional knowledge, acquired as a member of a certain gender, a certain culture, and a certain community and social class, needs to be and is typically appropriately tempered by certain social and institutional practices. There are, appropriately, many forms of interpersonal review and constraint, including the duty to address the audience of one's peers, to deploy a common language, to draw on recognised sources, and other institutional constraints. Thus, what I take to be both relevant and important for common law adjudication is the presence of individuality, enabled by various processes, such as the signing of judgements, calling them 'opinions', noticing their distinctive styles, use of the first person, etc., as appropriately filtered and constrained by social and institutional practices.

Another important feature one may call 'multiplicity'. The fact that the large majority of appellate judgements in the contemporary common law are multiple, including some that are dissenting, is a central feature of that practice. Without the presence of

[48] I have no evidence to support this: it is my own impression from many years of reading cases.

[49] In this sense, attitudes are very much part of the law, and are as important as, say, rules, principles, concepts or doctrines. One can argue that one's knowledge of the law as a practitioner must include a pragmatic sense of judicial attitudes, eg how positively or negatively disposed they may be to certain rules, principles, concepts, doctrines or arguments. More work is needed on this altitudinal dimension of legal expression and legal knowledge.

such multiple judgements, each offering a slightly different construction of the relevant facts, and each taking their own opportunity to examine and respond to the arguments of counsel, and to offer their own further resources and views on the issues at hand, common law practice would be a great deal different from what it is. Again, this includes, but is not limited to, the capacity to give dissenting judgements. Just as important is the opportunity to contribute to a majority decision, but in one's own distinctive way. Multiple judgements in any case can differ in a bewildering array of ways: eg they can treat as relevant some rather than other cases, and even where there is agreement on which cases are relevant, there can be considerable disagreement on how to construe their legal significance for the present case or for future projected cases. Further, the justifications offered for the decision can be widely different, even if they agree on the result, and this includes diversity in how any agreed-upon rule or principle is articulated. In addition, judgements can also differ in their constructions of the relevant facts of past cases, or indeed the present case. Sometimes, this 'multiplicity' is the cause of frustration of law teachers or practitioners. There are two responses to this: one is that we cannot wish it away, for it is simply a feature of the practice; another is to consider how we can treat that multiplicity not as a bug, but as a feature, ie to ask, in other words, what are its benefits, as much as it may have some negative consequences. I shall not do that here, but we will see that I shall have occasion throughout this book to refer back to the presence of multiplicity, this being an important feature, for instance, of the treatment of certain artefacts, such as metaphors or scenarios.

A third, and related feature, is what we might call the 'discursiveness' of contemporary common law practice. To point to this feature is to recognise not only the sheer length of common law judgements, though this too is important and looms especially large when one compares it to the considerably shorter judgements one finds in other legal traditions. Length is important, but to speak of discursiveness is also to notice the wide variety of uses of language deployed in common law judgements, ie to begin to see the many different kinds of communication practices engaged in by judges. One way to see this is to notice the many different kinds of audiences judges are addressing: the parties before them, their legal representatives, the arguments of other judges (whether in the courts below or in the present court, or in anticipating the arguments of higher courts), courts in other jurisdictions, scholars, and the press and the general public. Another is to recall the oral dimension of common law judgement, ie the fact that judgements were delivered orally, some *ex tempore*, some after deliberation, and all this against the background of the long history in the common law of the art of dialogue;[50] and to recognise that, although this has been transformed in various ways, with judgements being written, and no longer delivered in full orally, vestiges of orality remain.[51] One such echo is the often un-structured, or more loosely structured, character of judgements. There is not one formula for how one composes a judgement. Another is the presence of side remarks, eg the inclusion of discussion that is not strictly speaking necessary to deciding the present case. The presence of this 'obiter dicta', as it

[50] The Yearbooks of the Common Law may be characterised as the greatest medieval repository of the art of dialogue. See, eg, Bolland (1925).

[51] See, eg, Tiersma (2007).

is often called, or, more generally, of digressions or tangents in a judgement, I take to be another central aspect of contemporary common law practice. It is important that common law judgements often read more like conversations than systematic and formal treatises. There are many other ways to bring out the discursiveness of common law judgements, eg, one could emphasise the absence of canonical formulation of rules or principles, while also noticing that certain formulations come to acquire the status of often-repeated 'sayings' or 'maxims', or even 'doctrines' or formulas'; one could also pay attention to the varying genres (tragic, comic, epic, lyric) as well as to the varying literary forms, eg parable, maxim, etc deployed; and one could begin to classify the different kinds of digressions and tangents entertained by judges.[52] As the reader will see, one of the aims of this book is to begin to point to the sheer variety of language uses, and thus also communication practices, in the common law tradition.

The fourth and final feature I shall call 'restrained generalisation'. This may equally be labelled in other ways, eg some have referred to the 'minimalism' of the common law,[53] or to its 'gradualism' or 'pragmatism',[54] or to its 'inductive' approach as signalled for instance by the central role of analogy,[55] and others, as Lamond above, have spoken of the significant attention bestowed upon facts, and the many practices of constructing and framing facts or patterns of facts.[56] I have long been fascinated by these practices. Indeed, in many respects, I could trace the pleasure I felt, and feel, reading common law cases to the realisation of, and hunt for, the importance of fact patterns in common law reasoning, and to how that patterning of facts in the common law overlaps with the various ways of making patterns with words in literary history. Another way to read this book, and especially the case studies in the second part, is to think of them as particular ways of making patterns of facts with language. Is that not a way we could classify, say, metaphors, figurations or scenarios?

In calling this feature 'restrained generalisation', though, I would like to signal the importance of not only patterning of facts, but also the presence of a tension between attention paid to facts of the present case, past cases as well as projected future cases with an equally fascinating and various array of practices of generalisation. In some respects, thinking of the common law as 'inductive' is helpful; in other ways, however, it hides from view the presence of generalising practices, and their relations with the more fact-anchored aspects of common law practice. There are occasions, even if relatively rare, in which common law judges go out of their way to assert, with varying degrees of confidence, a general rule, formula, doctrine or principle, these being themselves different genres or forms of generalisation. These varieties of generalisation, and their roles and consequences, cannot be wished away, as one might be tempted to, if committed to an all-out romanticised particularism.

[52] Examining the rich variety and value of 'obiter dicta', including how this has changed historically, would make for an exciting and important project. Indeed, there is a cultural, and perhaps especially literary, history to be told about digression: see, eg, Terry (1992); and Cotterill (2004). Interestingly, Anselm Haverkamp has recently suggested that 'Productive Digression' could be a good translation of the ancient term 'poeisis': see Haverkamp (2017).

[53] See Sunstein (1999).

[54] See, eg, Atiyah (1987).

[55] See, eg, Levi (1949), and Weinrib (2005).

[56] See, eg, Samuel (2003); and Jackson (1988).

Further, and this is of special significance to this book, as I shall expand on later, adjudication is not a mere matter of deciding a present case, or on 'applying' past 'sources' to 'present facts'. This language of 'identification' of 'sources', being 'applied' to make and justify a 'decision' is in many respects misleading[57] and occludes from view the variety of temporalities important to adjudication, the most obvious of which is the attention paid by judges to the future. The point here is that judges do engage in generalisation, but that this is often restrained in various ways, with judges often employing alternatives to statements of too general or universal scope.

Indeed, yet another way to think of the artefacts examined in this book is to see them as examples of restrained generalisation. But there are other examples of restrained generalisation, which I do not explore in this book, eg the use of the prefix 'quasi', as in 'quasi contract'. Such uses of language signal that some change may be necessary. They suggest that further reflection is called for, in ways that may challenge the currently conventionally accepted classification or taxonomy of concepts, and that may require the introduction of some new category (such as 'unjust enrichment'). It is true that the common law often finds ingenious ways of avoiding ever having to systematise or 'theorise' its classifications, eg by focusing on 'remedies' or 'interests',[58] or by insisting on its character as an always-moving classification system,[59] or by deploying policy-based rather than, or in conjunction with, principled justifications.[60] Nevertheless, to repeat, it is also the case that judges in the common law tradition do engage in practices of generalisation or abstraction, that there are a wide variety of such practices, and that these are often restrained in different ways. Much work remains to be done on these practices, including considering whether to see the patterning of facts as part of a spectrum of generalisation or abstraction, or whether to see these practices instead as in productive tension with various ways of attending to and constructing facts and patterns of facts.[61]

Individuality, multiplicity, discursiveness and restrained generalisation: these are the general features of common law practice that I take to be relevant and important for this book. Although I have not sought to defend their value, I do think they are valuable, even if they also have their drawbacks and dangers. For instance, a defence of these features could argue that they help to ensure the resourcefulness of the contemporary common law. Further, such resourcefulness may be argued to have moral and political value: it makes the law more contestable, and, at once, more accessible to argument, and thereby also creates a space in which more voices can contribute to the making of law in the endless pursuit of justice.[62] The common law, we might say, is always in the making, all of it always contested, though to different degrees at different times, and stabilised, though only ever provisionally and tentatively, by certain conventional commonplaces

[57] See also Swaminathan (2019).

[58] See Samuel (2017).

[59] See Levi (1949). See also Balganesh and Parchomovsky (2015) for an interesting attempt to show how the common law tradition combines stability and change via 'concepts', eg good faith, privity, duty of care, proximate cause, foreseeability, reasonableness, commercial fairness, unreasonable risk, offensiveness, substantial harm, wanton disregard, amongst others: (2015), 1125.

[60] See Waddams (2003).

[61] For a fascinating study along these lines in the context of Talmudic legal reasoning, see Moscovitz (2002).

[62] See MacCormick (2005) for a defence of the rule of law in this vein. We could characterise MacCormick's particular defence of the rule of law as part of a tradition of 'rhetorical jurisprudence'.

and common forms of argument. This relatively loose and dynamic normative world, which also allows it to remain open to absorbing resources from beyond itself, and thus other normative worlds, makes room for argument, for pleas of justice to be heard. To me, that sounds like an attractive prospective defence of the resourcefulness of the common law, but, again, not one I can make here.[63]

Another point to make is that these features may strike the reader as quite general and abstract. Indeed, I have not enumerated all the various institutional manifestations of these general features; nor have I, as indicated above, engaged in any comparative or historical examination of the personnel and procedures of adjudication in the contemporary common law tradition. Some of these will emerge in the course of this book. For the moment, the key point is that the claims I make in this book about the value of artefacts and related process of imagination are limited to the presence of these features, and their institutional manifestations, and to no doubt others that, despite my best efforts, I have not been reflexive about.

B. The Ethics and Politics of Adjudication

Theories of adjudication and legal reasoning are rife with ethical and political disagreement about the exercise of judicial power. Disagreements and divisions on this score are often passionate. They are also very complex. It would be impossible to avoid caricature in any summary. We could try to say, for instance, that some theorists have been divided to show either: 1) that judges exercise virtually no power at all, being mere mouthpieces of the law already made, mere declarators of law already there, or doing nothing but rather mechanically, or without great difficulty, deciding particular cases, say by merely applying laws with determinate meanings; or 2) that, appearances deceive, and that no matter how determinate legal language seems on the surface, or how easy the case seems, or is made to appear, and no matter how inevitable the justification in a case looks, or again, is made to look, judges are effectively exercising arbitrary power, making the law up as they go along, deciding on the basis of either a moral hunch or an ideological bias, and then cleverly constructing the appearance of a decision determined by reason and pre-existing laws.

Of course, this division is much too crude and does not correlate with the much more subtle positions of individual theorists. It also hides from view other vectors of disagreement. For instance, one might argue there is a subtler split between: 1) those who do think that judges exercise power, and at least a weak form of discretion, including making law, eg by interpreting it, but that this is for the best, eg because that is the best way to protect rights; and 2) those who think that, because judges never are merely mouthpieces, they always exercise either weak or, more often, strong discretion, which

[63] Of course, this picture is, in some respects, much too idealised, eg what appears as openness to other traditions to some, to others involves the exercise of epistemic violence. This is especially visible in the tragic treatment of indigenous traditions by common law courts, see, eg, Veitch (2007), Valverde (2015), ch 5 on 'the Honour of the Crown'; and Motha (2018). The common law, like other legal traditions, is also a site of epistemic violence, and has as many jurispathic as it has jurisgenerative techniques and dynamics: see Cover (1983).

is un-determined by pre-existing authoritative standards, so everything possible should be done to minimise that power and the role of judges in a legal system, eg there should be no expansive bills of rights, which would, so the argument goes, give judges too much power vis-à-vis the democratically elected legislature. Here, the positions may be taken to hover between seeing judges as heroes, ie protectors of our rights, and of liberty and equality, especially against encroachment by executive power, and between seeing them as villains, perhaps necessary for a system to operate but regrettably so, standing in the way of a truly democratically government. This second vector of disagreement correlates perhaps a little better to positions taken in the literature, but it, too, is too crude to be helpful.

Although both of these divisions cannot be relied upon as summaries of the stances taken, they do give a flavour of the debate and disagreement. My own impression in reading this literature is that it does sometimes feel like moving from one extreme to another, eg from characterisations of judges as exercising enormous, almost wholly unconstrained power and characterisations of them as almost like automatons, operating within strict confines of logic and form; and, equally, between great belief in judicial power and great suspicion of it.

The highly charged language of these debates is a sign, surely, that a lot is at stake, and that debates over the exercise of judicial power reach considerably beyond the issue of adjudication, to broader issues of method, ethics and politics. Indeed, one could argue that disagreement over the exercise of judicial power, including its reality, its desirability, and its justifiability, has been at the centre of debates within legal theory and jurisprudence generally, and certainly within the twentieth century. Legal positivism, argued Ronald Dworkin, fails as a theory in part because it leads to an untenable account of the power exercised by judges. Positivism, or at least the positivism propounded by HLA Hart, by focusing exclusively, Dworkin said, on law as a system of rules, identified by a conventional rule of recognition, ends up, in hard cases, where the rules do not dictate a result, with a picture of judges exercising what he called 'strong discretion', ie a discretion un-determined by pre-existing authoritative standards. Dworkin's solution – his interpretivism – in which judges exercise merely weak discretion, a discretion guided in hard cases by principles, is in part a defence of the exercise of judicial power and the role of judges in a democracy, but it is also in many respects a theory of law built upon a theory of adjudication. On this picture, the law is not merely a system of rules; it is an empire of principles, and it is Dworkin's allegedly more accurate theory of adjudication that allows us to see this.[64]

The ensuing debate – the Hart-Dworkin debate as it has come to be known – has dominated not only the late twentieth century literature on adjudication, at least in the English-speaking world, but also the general jurisprudential landscape. There have been any number of attempts to defend Hartian legal positivism, and to show that it is, or some version of it is, compatible with a tenable theory of adjudication and legal reasoning.[65] Equally, there have been other kinds of responses to Dworkin, eg defences of realist positions, which were also criticised by Dworkin, say on the role of consequences and

[64] See Dworkin (1986).

[65] These include the work of Joseph Raz and Neil MacCormick but extend considerably beyond to many contemporary analytical legal theorists.

policies in legal reasoning.[66] There have also been important critiques from critical legal scholars and feminist legal theory,[67] not to mention other approaches to adjudication from natural law theory[68] or from within law and humanities scholarship.[69] To say this is hardly to cover the field, for theories of adjudication and legal reasoning have been, as is suggested above, in many ways the central preoccupation of so many legal theorists in the twentieth century, both in the common law and beyond.[70] All these theories are shot through, sometimes more and sometimes less self-consciously, with methodological, ethical and political disagreements about judicial power, but also considerably beyond, extending to issues concerning relations between law and morality, and law and politics. And it would take considerably more than one book to try to map these disagreements, and to do the various positions justice.

For present purposes, what is important is that I give a sense of my own approach, while also pointing out the limits of what is undertaken in this book. In this respect, I would like to be especially clear: this book does not offer a fully worked-out and explicit ethical and political theory of adjudication; far from it. Nevertheless, the ethical and political dimension of adjudication is crucial to this book, and that can be seen in various ways, perhaps most obviously in the unpacking of the 'normative' dimension of inquiry in Chapter 1. What I would like to do here, in brief compass, is to articulate the attitude that informs my approach to the ethics and politics of adjudication in general.

My starting point is to begin not with the power exercised by judges, but with the power exercised by theorists when observing and evaluating the practice of adjudication. It is often easy to forget just how privileged the position of the theorist is when compared to that of the judge: the theorist is not the one with the burden and responsibility to decide, or to offer plausible and persuasive reasons for the decision; the theorist is also not the one placed, or not placed as much, under very considerable institutional constraints, eg of time and resources, including the quality of counsel submissions, keeping in mind that counsel too are subject to all kinds of constraints; and, just as, if not more, importantly, the theorist has the benefit of the passage of time, including having the judgement or judgements authored by the judges to work with, rather than having to construct them from scratch, and possibly even a longer passage of time, thanks to which she can have access to insights that are available now, but were not then. The privileged position of the theorist suggests to me the importance of trying, when theorising adjudication, to recreate as much as possible the vulnerable, constrained and uncertain position of the judge, faced with the dispute before her, and feeling the burden and pressure of deciding and producing a helpful judgement.

This starting point has some important consequences. It involves treating every exercise of adjudication as epistemically, morally and politically difficult. This is not merely because judges are themselves epistemically-limited creatures, like all of us, and

[66] Out of a large literature, see Greenawalt (1976).

[67] See, eg, Kennedy (2008), Goodrich (1986), and Conaghan (2013).

[68] See, eg, recently Crowe (2019).

[69] Work in law and humanities often approaches similar issues, but through other frames and problematics, eg exemplarity (see Lowrie and Ludemann (2015)).

[70] For an overview of the last 25 years of scholarship in the twentieth century, and one which encompasses also theorists beyond the common law tradition, see Feteris (1997).

also not merely because of the institutional pressures and constraints of time, resources, etc that they are under, which are, as noted above, considerable. It is also because of the central duty of a judge: to do justice. To do justice is always difficult; it has to be. This includes deciding, for instance, whether a case is easy or hard, this being a decision that, in itself, is a difficult one, even if it is sometimes presented as obvious. Adjudication has to be difficult because it involves judgement, and judgement, if it is to be exercised by a human being rather than by a machine, has to involve difficulty: hesitation, for example, is part of the phenomenology of judgment. It is also difficult because it involves caring, and expressing one's care, for the many addressees of any one judgement, as well as for the moral and political quality of the law, and the authority and legitimacy of the court and its procedures, including, for instance, its relations with other courts, within its own system and beyond. Furthermore, all these cares and concerns have to be balanced against each other: a sometimes almost impossibly difficult task.

Of course, recognising that judging is incredibly ethically and politically difficult does not mean that one needs to ignore or downplay the exercise of power by judges. Nor does it mean that one has to avoid holding the judges to account, upholding what one takes to be the standards and responsibilities of judgement. It does mean, however, that one approaches these tasks in particular ways. It means, for instance, taking seriously, as I try to in this book, the mechanisms and strategies developed by judges to cope with the difficulties of judging. One of these mechanisms and strategies is to work with language, and to deploy uses of language that call on others for assistance, either in the present case, eg by opening up dialogue between judges and advocates, say by way of a proposed metaphor or scenario, or in future cases, eg using a fiction and signalling to future courts that legal change is needed, but perhaps when better informed by a wider range of cases. Taking seriously these 'coping' mechanisms and strategies (a term I do not much like, for it casts a negative shadow over what may be better seen to be features, rather than bugs, of adjudicatory practice) does not mean that one cannot see them as exercises of power. To the contrary: to be in a position where one can introduce a metaphor that others will need to read and consider is a position of power; 'rhetorical' or 'discursive' power one may call it. It follows that such uses of power can be criticised, eg there may be better or worse metaphors: some that are more helpful than others, or perhaps some that have outlived their usefulness. However, what foregrounding the difficulties of judging does exclude is taking up a position in which one decries the use of 'coping' mechanisms and strategies altogether, say, by projecting the image of an ideal judge who, in all his impressive omniscience, can see the right answer or come up with the ideal universal justification.

Let me be especially clear: yes, judges do exercise very considerable power. Particular decisions, particular procedures for reaching them and other institutional features of adjudication, and the language of judgements in general, are, in themselves, exercises of power. They can also be seen to be violent, eg doing epistemic violence, for instance, to other languages and other normative worlds, with consequences that are often hidden from view, sometimes both for 'winners' and 'losers', but in any event always operating, as Robert Cover pointed out, in 'a field of pain and death'.[71] Recognising the power

[71] Cover (1986), 1601.

and violence of adjudication, however, does not exclude approaching, with humanity, the difficulties that judges face. Put more strongly, by foregrounding these difficulties, I think we, as theorists, owe it to the judges to treat their efforts in adjudication as sincere efforts to do, and to appear to do, justice. This includes approaching the above-mentioned 'coping' mechanisms and strategies not as judges falling short of some ideal, or as judges hiding their exercises of power, but as genuine attempts to care, ie to do justice in the instant case while also doing justice to other cares and concerns, such as the moral and political quality of the law, and the authority and legitimacy of the court. We can certainly disagree with the way that judges attempt to do justice. We ought not, however, unless we have very clear evidence to the contrary (eg corruption), approach judging as something other than exercising the very difficult task of doing justice.

There is another aspect to this attitude of foregrounding the difficulties of judging, while nevertheless recognising the power of judges, and insisting on certain standards and responsibilities of judging. One of the ways that theorists have taken that difficulty seriously is by shifting the critical lens away from judges, and the power they exercise, to the law itself, and the alleged blindness to suffering and vulnerability that it manufactures. To position matters in this way is to propose a tension between the universal pretensions of the law and the particular cases that come before judges.[72] To do this is to speak less of the violence of the judicial power, and more of the violence of law itself. The exhortations, under such an approach, are then to certain virtues of judging, eg, the virtues of attention to particulars, or the virtues of empathy, sympathy, compassion and mercy, which are then said to require education, eg via literature.[73] Although I recognise the importance of this approach to judging, this is not the approach I take in this book. One of the worries I have is that positioning matters in this way, ie as a tension between the universal and the particular, is that it makes us approach the language of law in certain ways, and more often than not, to see it as an obstacle to doing justice in some particular case. This can have the effect of making us too suspicious of legal language, and equally, too hopeful, if not too romantic, about the personal qualities and virtues of judges, as important as these are.[74] It also, I think, makes us focus too much on the instant case, and this can obscure from view the other temporalities at work in adjudication, eg the importance of caring for the future, including the implications a particular way of deciding the case can have for future potentially similar cases.

While recognising the importance of the literature that situates the issues of adjudication in this way, my approach in this book is different. Rather than seeing the language of law as either an obstacle or a guide, which is more or less determinative, to be applied or interpreted in a particular case, I wish instead, in foregrounding the difficulties of judging, to see legal language as a communicative and cognitive resource. To approach legal language in this way is to see it as something we think with, not only in the instant case, but also over time, and not only as individual judges but together with others, and

[72] For some great essays on this tension, see Bańkowski and McLean (2006). For more on particularity and singularity, see, eg, the essays in Lowrie and Ludemann (2015).

[73] See, eg, Nussbaum (1997).

[74] None of what I say here is intended as a critique of virtue jurisprudence. I do think, however, that talk of virtues, especially at an individual level, needs to be combined with attention to the qualities of legal language, and to other social and institutional features of adjudication.

as something we can draw on to communicate under conditions of uncertainty, in part by way of coping with the difficulties of judging. This does not mean that legal language is something that judges merely use. To the contrary: we cannot merely *use* language because we cannot predict or control its meanings. Language is too much of a social phenomenon to speak of controlling it or mastering it. Put another way, we may use language, but it also uses us, for it affects us in ways we cannot predict, control or master.

My title for this section is 'the ethics and politics of adjudication', but it could equally be 'the ethics and politics of theorising about adjudication'. I take this theorising to be epistemically, morally and politically difficult too; hence the insistence here on theoretical modesty in approaching the exercising of judging. Approaching judging, in this book, means foregrounding its difficulties, taking seriously its ways of coping with those difficulties, holding those ways of coping up to certain standards and responsibilities, and trying one's best to be neither too suspicious nor too hopeful about either judges or the language of law.

C. Modelling

I have been emphasising, throughout this introduction, the limits of theorising, and I want to return to this theme yet again. In this book, as noted already above, I propose three 'models': inquiry in Chapter 1, imagination in Chapter 2, and artefacts in Chapter 3. I use the terminology of 'modelling' for a number of reasons.

One such reason is the desire to move away from the terminology of 'concepts', and thus also away from the associated claims to capturing the nature or essence of something. Sometimes, if not typically,[75] when we speak of concepts, eg 'the concept of law', we mean to refer to the necessary and sufficient conditions of that something, eg with respect to law, the necessary and sufficient conditions that allow us to distinguish law from, say, social norms, morality and coercion. I acknowledge that an important part of theorising is constructing a distinguishable object of study. However, it is sometimes forgotten that any attempt to distinguish some object will always be contingent on what we think it is relevant to distinguish it from. Once we realise the contingency of our pools of comparison and contrast, eg social norms, morality and coercion with respect to the concept of law, we also come to see that any attempt to build a concept is necessarily incomplete, giving us a very specific view of what we, in some particular community, think is relevant and important to distinguish law from. Thus, it is in part to embrace, rather than hide, the contingency of theorising, and thus be mindful of its limitations, that I use the terminology of models rather than concepts. In that respect, I am conscious that the models I here propose, ie of inquiry, artefacts and imagination, are one of a number of possible ones, given that I have distinguished them, selectively, from certain other phenomena. I try to be as explicit as I can about what I compare inquiry, artefacts and imagination to and what I contrast them with, though I am also conscious that I cannot make all of this explicit, no matter how hard I try.

[75] I acknowledge that there are other traditions of characterising concepts, eg as prototypes. I also acknowledge that this is a very rough and crude characterisation of 'conceptual analysis'. I make no claims about what 'conceptual analysis' entails. Rather, my aim here is to clarify my own approach to the activity of theorising. For a sophisticated approach to what he calls 'constructive conceptual explanation', see Giudice (2015).

A second reason for preferring the terminology of models, eg to concepts, is that in addition to constructing necessarily contingent distinguishing marks or threshold criteria, and thus helping us to focus on some distinguishable object of study, models foreground variability. On the way I approach modelling, one proposes a relatively thin layer of distinguishing marks or threshold criteria, eg for imagination to count as imagination. One does so in order to make as much room as possible for variation. Thus, and especially with respect to artefacts and imagination, I have attempted to construct models of these that will allow us to capture some, though again, only some, of that variability. For instance, with respect to artefacts, the model seeks to make room for the many different ways in which we can signal artifice as well as the many different ways in which artefacts invite us to participate. Similarly so with the model of imagination: I have constructed this in such a way that we see that we can enter a distinctive epistemic frame in many different ways, suspending different kinds of epistemic norms and commitments, and that we also participate in many different ways, along a spectrum of affective, sensory and kinesic involvement. Models, then, not only help to signal limitations, and thus the contingency of any theoretical activity of making a distinguishable object of study; they also help us to foreground and emphasise variability.

A related point is that insofar as modelling involves constructing relatively thin layers of distinguishing marks or threshold criteria, placing more emphasis on variability, then this may also help us to forge links and build bridges between different disciplines and literatures. One of my aims, in constructing the models I do in this book, is that it will: 1) show scholars working in fields outside adjudication, eg literary theorists and historians, philosophers of mind and language, cognitive scientists and psychologists, just how rich, and ripe for the picking, are adjudicatory practices; and 2) show scholars working on adjudication just how much there is to learn, about adjudication, from scholars working in the above-mentioned fields. Accordingly, in the case of each model, I try to situate the models I construct by reference to a wide range of literatures about them. There is a danger, of course, in this practice, given that the literatures I try to relate to the models in question are so varied. Nevertheless, even if at the risk of being eclectic and superficial, I thought it important to design the models in such a way that they can attract a variety of disciplinary orientations and languages. This goes for all three models, but it is perhaps clearest in the case of the model of inquiry. I acknowledge the rich and complex history of the term 'inquiry', but I model it in a very specific way, namely in order 1) to loosen the hold of the dichotomy between justification and discovery, which I argue has led to unhelpful divisions and hierarchies of disciplinary labour; and 2) to enable more multi- and inter-disciplinary work on adjudication.

So far I have identified two reasons to prefer the terminology of modelling: first, to signal the limitations of one's theoretical work, especially with respect to the contingency of the distinguishing marks or threshold criteria that one uses to make a distinguishable object of study; and second, to foreground and emphasise variability, in part in order to enable multi- and inter-disciplinary research on that object of study.

There is also a third reason, namely that to use the terminology of modelling can help us remember the evaluative character of theorising. Thus, I include within the construction of a model the articulation of a certain attitude to what it seeks to make relevant, eg a certain kind of attitude to the imagination, namely that it is something worthy of our theoretical attention and that it may be important and valuable, eg that we can think of it as a distinctive kind of epistemic activity, which may be valuable to inquiry. Theorising is not just about constructing a concept of something or giving something hitherto-nameless a label. Theorising, and in this case modelling, is an evaluative activity: one does not point to something merely for the sake of it, but because one thinks it is something worthy of attention.[76] Further, to think of theorising as an evaluative activity is also to recognise that it is laden with emotion: theorists, too, after all, are affectively-embodied beings. To construct a model, then, is to signal one's attitudes, including emotions, to that which one is proposing as relevant and worthy of our theoretical attention. These emotions relate not only to what one claims for one's theory, and thus how reflexive one is of a theory's necessary limitations, but also to how one attempts to relate to different disciplines and literatures.

To speak of models, at least to my ears, helps to keep in mind that theorising is an activity, with inevitable and inescapable limitations, involving attitudes both to one's own claims and to one's relations with other theorists, including those from different disciplines and working in different theoretical languages and methods. Put another way, to think of theorising-as-modelling is to remember that theorising is an activity performed by affectively-embodied and socially and historically situated beings.[77]

IV. The Painting on the Cover

I end this introduction with a word about the painting on the cover of this book. It is a trompe l'oeil entitled 'Escaping Criticism', painted in 1864 by the Spanish painter Pere Borrell del Caso, who was well-known for trompe l'oeil paintings. It depicts a young boy, poised at the threshold of a painting frame, seemingly both eager and anxious to escape the frame. The boy is both inside and outside, on the doorstep if you will, and in a liminal state, in some respects within the world of art and in other respects in defiance of it. The boy is also both passive and active, waiting but also alert, still but at the same time full of movement. This is a balancing act in so many ways, and for me, when I first saw it, it struck me as an icon of imagination.

I saw it this way because imagination, as I model it here, is a combination, and indeed a balancing act, of two simultaneously exercised and active processes: first, the entrance into a distinct epistemic frame, in which we selectively suspend certain epistemic norms and commitments; and second, participation along a spectrum of affective, sensory and kinesic involvement. It is precisely both an inside and an outside, a mixture of passivity and activity, of distance and immersion, of being offline and

[76] This is not unrelated to points about the practice of theory that have been made by natural law theorists for a long time, most obviously Finnis (1981).

[77] It would be interesting to apply the same framework (of inquiry, artefacts and imagination), which I apply to adjudication in this book, to the making of legal theoretical insight. Of course, there would be specific cultural and institutional features of the practice of scholarship, in different times and places, and this would call for different artefacts, and different processes of imagination, than those found in adjudication. Nevertheless, some may well be very similar: eg uses of figures in legal theory (Dworkin's Hercules), scenarios (and thought experiments generally) and metaphors (eg Hart's core and penumbra, Kelsen's pyramid). See, eg, West (1985); Schlag (2002); and Del Mar (2013b).

online, of withdrawal and participation. Imagination has often been explained and described as a lack, ie as missing something, whether that be in terms of escape from reality, or by reference to creating a mental object of something that is not present, and that is part of the story. But imagination, as others have also noticed, is much more than that: it is also something active, in part a driver of action, as it was for Aristotle, both for animals and humans,[78] as something we actively perform, eg in seeing-as, but also in deliberating as-if, what-if or if-only, and something that draws on so many features of us as affectively-embodied beings, engaged and responsive to the world and others.

We can, then, see the painting as an icon of imagination. But the painting is, of course, also an artefact (a visual artefact, whereas I focus on linguistic artefacts). As modelled in this book, artefacts are forms that: first, capture our attention by signalling their own artifice; and second, call upon us to do something with them. An artefact is not fully definable by its formal properties. Its capacity to perform its functions is in part dependent on whether it actually does capture our attention and successfully calls upon us to do something with it. In this case, the painting was and remains an artefact for me. My attention was captured by the signalling of its own artifice, also triggered by its title 'Escaping Criticism'. But my engagement with it was by no means confined to some abstract reflection, as if in a state of withdrawal from my emotions, my senses and my body. I also engaged with it, and still do, when I spend time with it, simulating the movement of the boy (kinesic participation), simulating the boy's emotion (affective participation – here, that mix of anxiety and curiosity), and perhaps even simulating what the boy sees when he looks into the great beyond (sensory participation). This artefact, then, successfully called upon me to imagine.

[78] See Nussbaum (1986).

PART I

Models

1

Inquiry

One of the key models I construct in this book is that of inquiry. I use this as a term of art and build, albeit necessarily incompletely and imperfectly, my own understanding of the term. I do so in five steps, corresponding to the five sections of this chapter.

The first step is to situate inquiry beyond, but also overlapping with, a dichotomy that has dominated twentieth-century scholarship on legal reasoning: namely the dichotomy between justification, ie roughly, the conscious expression of reasons for a decision, and discovery, ie again roughly, the less-than-conscious causes leading to a decision. I argue that adoption of this dichotomy has: 1) led to the neglect and side-lining, especially within philosophical scholarship, of certain dimensions of legal reasoning that are crucial to it, including crucial to justificatory practices, with these features including emotion and imagination; and 2) resulted in an unhelpful division of scholarly labour, including often claims as to the hierarchy of disciplines, between the philosophical interest in justification and the empirical science interest in discovery.

This first step, then, is a ground-clearing exercise. I am, however, very conscious of the risk of throwing out the baby with the bathwater. I also recognise that a wholescale attack on this dichotomy requires much more than the short section I devote to it. Let me then emphasise: the critique of the dichotomy between justification and discovery is not meant to be a critique of the scholarship written under the guise of either category. My aim, instead, is to help create a space for future work, in ways that I hope open up prospects for collaborative and inter-disciplinary scholarship on unduly neglected, and yet vital, dimensions of legal reasoning, especially, as noted above, emotion and imagination. The critique of the dichotomy is made in that constructive spirit.

Having carved out a space for inquiry beyond, but overlapping with, the dichotomy of justification and discovery, I then go on in sections two to five to add four dimensions to the model of inquiry. These four dimensions are: first, the social dimension of inquiry, including its interactive and collective character (section II); second, the diachronic dimension, and thus the different temporalities at which inquiry is conducted (section III); third, the experimental dimension of inquiry (section IV); and fourth, the normative dimension, concerning the objects of inquiry, this being the process of making insight into potential normative relevance, ie sensing what values, vulnerabilities and interests might be at stake in a case and in potentially alike cases in the future (section V).

This model of inquiry is designed to assist us, as theorists of adjudication, to get a little closer to features of the practice of adjudication that we might not otherwise see or that, if we see, we might not treat as either important or valuable. Persons involved in adjudication engage in practices of inquiry. They do so within and across the different dimensions of inquiry: thus, they engage in inquiry interactively and collectively (the social dimension); in the instant case but also across time (the diachronic dimension); in a manner that is tentative, subjunctive, provisional, non-assertive and non-committal (the experimental dimension); and by making insight into potential normative relevance, ie seeking to identify what values, vulnerabilities or interests might be at stake in this case and in cases that may be like it in the future (the normative dimension).

Within the overall design of this book, inquiry plays a crucial part. To recall, the overall claim of the book is that artefacts and related processes of imagination are valuable when they enable practices of inquiry. Put another way: specific artefacts, like fictions, metaphors, figures, and scenarios, and their related processes of imagination are valuable when they assist interactive and collective practices of inquiry, in the instant case and over time, providing modes of experimentation that allow for the making of insights as to what values, vulnerabilities and interests might be at stake in the case and in cases potentially like it in the future.

I. Beyond the Dichotomy of Justification and Discovery

One of the frames that has structured theories of adjudication, including division of scholarly labour between disciplines, and is often accompanied by claims of disciplinary hierarchy, has been the dichotomy between justification and discovery. This distinction originated in a different context, namely the philosophy and history of science, but soon found its way, as did many analogues from scientific practice and theory, eg the 'elements' of a rule, into jurisprudence and legal theory. Here, and by way of situating the approach I take in this book, I want to suggest that the dichotomy has hampered much-needed interdisciplinary research on adjudication. Its most deleterious effect has been to split research in this area, distinguishing between but also separating out into, first, the allegedly more analytical and normative domain of reason-giving (or justification), and second, the allegedly more empirical study of judicial psychology and decision-making (or discovery).

In this section, I very briefly examine this dichotomy and argue that we ought to question it, and to find ways of moving beyond it. This is especially so if we want to make room for and to treat seriously phenomena that have been traditionally side-lined by theorists of legal reasoning, eg imagination and emotion. It is also important if we want to be more sensitive to, including keep in mind the possible value of, a much wider range of language forms and experiences within adjudication. The argument I present is not a full-scale attack on the discovery-justification distinction. It may well be that the distinction can remain useful for certain purposes. But, pragmatically speaking, I argue, we should avoid the dichotomy, and especially the resultant division, and sometimes also hierarchy, of scholarly labour between disciplines that the dichotomy enables, if not encourages. Topics like imagination and emotion, but ultimately also adjudication itself, demand collaborative multi- and inter-disciplinary work, and dichotomies like that between justification and discovery make it much harder, if not impossible, to collaborate across disciplines.

A. The Dichotomy in the History and Philosophy of Science

The dichotomy between contexts of justification and discovery has a long and complex history. Contemporary references to it are often traced back to debates in the history and philosophy of science, eg to Hans Reichenbach's *Experience and Prediction* of 1938, and thereafter through to Karl Popper's *The Logic of Scientific Discovery* in 1968.[1] Paul Hoyningen-Huene argues that 'the distinction can be traced back further', citing Rudolf Carnap, Moritz Schlick and Gottlob Frege, and claiming that the real starting point is probably 'Kant's opposition of epistemology to empirical psychology.'[2]

The history of this dichotomy is complicated by a number of other distinctions or dichotomies related to it. Candidates would include: distinctions or dichotomies between the natural and the normative, facts and values, the analytical and the empirical (or logical), as well as the more administrative and institutional distinctions made between, on the one hand, philosophy (of science), and the history, psychology, sociology (of science). Whatever the terms used, and however different these various distinctions may be, they are all bound up with the politics of scholarship: eg defences of these distinctions are often part and parcel of a claim to autonomy, if not superiority, of a certain philosophical method. Certainly, the dichotomy between justification and discovery has been used, as Hoyningen-Huene observers, 'to define the legitimate field of philosophy as set apart from other disciplines.'[3]

Of course, the dichotomy, whether under the guise of justification and discovery, or under any of the related distinctions, has also been subject to considerable critique. The debate has been especially heated in the philosophy and history of science:

> The distinction has … been undermined on different grounds. It has been argued that the kind of reasoning that is involved in generating a hypothesis is not fundamentally different from the kind of reasoning employed in justification. Moreover, hypothesis generation and theory construction are extended problem-solving processes with many stages, each of which involves (partial) justification. At each particular stage one's aim is to satisfy some of the constraints posed by the problem. The satisfaction of those constraints amounts to partial justification of the evolving solution. Furthermore, justification in science often takes the form of heuristic appraisal, ie of evaluating the future problem-solving potential of a theory. For someone who views discovery as an instance of problem-solving, this form of theory appraisal amounts to judging the capacity of a theory to generate discoveries and, therefore, it is closely linked with discovery itself. Finally, Nickles has stressed the importance of "generative justification" or "discoverability", namely a form of appraisal that justifies a claim by deriving it from already established knowledge. Justification in this case amounts to specifically a rationally reconstructed (not necessarily the actual) discovery path. Thus, it is reasonably established that justification and discovery are much more closely related than formerly thought.[4]

[1] Reichenbach (1938); Popper (1959). See, generally, Schickore and Steinle (2006). Reichenbach was explicit about the division of scholarly labour: he said we must 'distinguish carefully the task of epistemology from that of psychology. Epistemology does not regard the processes of thinking in their actual occurrence; this task is entirely left to psychology. What epistemology intends is to construct thinking processes in a way in which they ought to occur if they are to be ranged in a consistent system' (1938), 5. For a nuanced engagement with Reichenbach's distinction, see Siegel (1980).

[2] Hoyningen-Huene (1987), 502–3.

[3] Ibid, 503.

[4] Arabatzis (2006), 216. See also Nickles (1989).

Theodore Arabatzis, who offers this helpful summary, has his own argument against the divide. On the one hand, he argues that discovery is already laden with justification, for discovery 'is a term which refers to an epistemic achievement'.[5] To claim a 'discovery', one cannot merely hypothesise that some entity exists: rather, 'the justification of that hypothesis would be a constitutive characteristic of that discovery'.[6] On the other hand, Arabatzis says, 'justification itself is a constantly evolving process: it is rarely the case that the justification of a hypothesis retains its original form'.[7] Justification continually undergoes 'reconstruction'; rather than pointing to a 'logical' distinction, what the terms of justification and discovery may be picking up on are two different temporal dimensions of the same process.[8]

Arabatzis' attack is one of many in the history and philosophy of science. Indeed, as he acknowledges, his arguments are very much Kuhnian in character: for instance, like Thomas Kuhn, Arabatzis emphasises the social dimension of both discovery and justification processes.[9] For Arabatzis, the history of science cannot be understood without paying attention to collective dynamics of projecting possibilities into the future, defending them tentatively, testing them, and, at some point, accepting them, though even then only provisionally and by reference to a framework of beliefs that hold them up and hang together.

In addition to different ways of directly attacking the dichotomy, other strategies have also been employed to escape its grasp. Some scholars seek to expand our understanding of the process of discovery, incorporating what others might see as elements of justification into discovery.[10] Others propose a richer taxonomy, eg offering a trilogy of generation, pursuit, and acceptance,[11] or a quartet of generation, pursuit, test, and decision.[12] If one includes, as part of this debate, the wars over naturalism and normativity, and thus attempts either to naturalise epistemology, as in WVO Quine and those working within that tradition,[13] or to defend the space of the normative from the inroads of naturalism, as in Wilfred Sellars and arguably also Robert Brandom,[14] and one includes, in addition, the debates over the tenability of the fact-value distinction,[15] then the complexity of the various strategies and cross-cutting debates here is almost overwhelming.

[5] Arabatzis (2006), 217.
[6] Ibid.
[7] Ibid, 218.
[8] Ibid.
[9] Ibid, 219. See Kuhn (1970) [1962]. See also Devlin and Bokulic (2015); and Richards and Daston (2016).
[10] See, eg, the essays in Nickles (1980).
[11] As Hoyningen-Huene describes it: 'In the first phase a theoretical idea, a hypothesis, or a theory sketch is "generated". In the second phase the plausibility of the idea is assessed. It may be compared with alternative ideas, and / or it may be elaborated on. In other words, it is "pursued". Finally, the elaborated idea may be subjected to critical testing and, if it is successful, it may be "accepted"': (1987), 508. It is important to add to this that this process is not occurring, in a successive manner, in one mind, but is instead the work of many hands, involving a dynamic that moves back and forth between the different phases.
[12] See Goldman (1983).
[13] Which also includes legal scholars: a leading figure here is Leiter (2007).
[14] For a discussion, linking also to some debates within legal theory, see Turner (2010); and for a response, see Del Mar (2010b).
[15] Within the legal theory literature, see, eg, Taekema, van Klink and de Been (2016).

A proper, critical engagement with the dichotomy between justification and discovery would need to delve into these disagreements and possibilities.[16] I cannot offer that here. My strategy is considerably more modest. I do not seek a direct and full-scale attack on the distinction, but I do seek to make at least a prima facie case for a space that goes beyond, while still overlapping with, the contexts of justification and discovery. In other words, I would like to suggest that the dichotomy does not exhaust the terrain, and that holding onto it too rigidly, especially when accompanied by claims as to the hierarchy of scholarly labour, may have deleterious effects on our understanding of adjudication, including on the prospects of interdisciplinary research on adjudication. To do this, however, we need to first look briefly at how this dichotomy has operated in theories of adjudication.[17]

B. The Dichotomy in Legal Theory

A classic and influential statement of the dichotomy in twentieth-century theories of adjudication can be found in Richard Wasserstrom's *The Judicial Decision*.[18] Wasserstrom argued as follows:

> Placing the problem within the broader context of decision procedures in general, there are two quite distinctive procedures that might be followed before any particular decision is made or accepted. This is as true in science or ethics as it is in law. The way in which these two procedures operate can be indicated by reference to two types of questions that may be asked about any decision. One kind of question asks about the manner in which a decision or conclusion was reached; the other inquires whether a given decision or conclusion is justifiable. That is to say, a person who examines a decision process may want to know about the factors that led to or produced the conclusion; he may also be interested in the manner in which the conclusion was to be justified.[19]

The distinction seems very clear. On the one hand, within the context of discovery, we have the procedure by which a judge reaches a conclusion; on the other, we have the procedure by which the judge 'justifies' the conclusion. The process of discovery may 'generate' many 'more conclusions' than those that could 'be justified within the accepted logic of "justification".'[20] The 'logic of justification', then, continued Wasserstrom, provides the criteria 'by which both particular conclusions and the procedures of discovery may be evaluated.'[21] The other way does not work: discovery cannot generate criteria of evaluation, only justification can. Indeed, said Wasserstrom, the very idea of 'rational behaviour' consists in subjecting the results of one's discovery to the criteria of evaluation set by the logic of justification.[22]

[16] This is one of many promising intersections between debates in the history and philosophy of law, and the history and philosophy of science. It would be tremendous if these groups of scholars got together more often.

[17] For a more detailed overview of this dichotomy in legal theory, see Silveira (2014).

[18] Wasserstrom (1966).

[19] Ibid, 18.

[20] Ibid, 20.

[21] Ibid.

[22] Ibid.

For Wasserstrom, the tasks of investigating processes discovery and justification were very different and required very different methodologies. 'It is', he said, 'one thing to read a judicial opinion as a report of why or how the judge "hit upon" the decision and quite another thing to read the opinion as an account of the procedure he employed in "testing" it.'[23] There may well be various ways of articulating how it was that judges 'hit upon' the decision, eg 'judicial hunches, emotions and personalities',[24] but to speak of these was very different to speaking of procedures of 'testing' or justifying. Significantly, for present purposes, Wasserstrom continued from this observation to insist on the division of scholarly labour: 'Thus I do suggest that questions pertaining to justification can usefully be kept distinct from questions about discovery'.[25]

In the years since Wasserstrom's book, the dichotomy has continued to dominate philosophical, especially analytic, theories of adjudication. These sometimes begin with precisely this distinction and then go on to claim that they are concerned solely, and appropriately, with the context of justification. Thus, for example, Martin Golding's *Legal Reasoning* opens with the claim that 'this book is about legal reasoning in the narrow sense.'[26] In this narrow sense, said Golding, the study of legal reasoning 'refers to the arguments that judges give, frequently in written form, in support of the decisions they render. These arguments consist of the reasons for the decisions, and these reasons are intended as justifications for the decisions.'[27] This 'narrow sense' of legal reasoning contrasts with its 'broad sense', which 'would be a study of judicial psychology and biography.'[28] Studying legal reasoning in this broad sense would involve investigating the 'psychological processes undergone by judges in reaching decisions in the cases that are before them.'[29] Golding went on to identify what these processes could be and what character they have:

> These processes are comprised of ideas, beliefs, conjectures, hunches, feelings, and emotions. Loosely speaking, a judge's reasoning is what passes through his mind in the course of arriving at a decision, though in fact he may be barely conscious, or even not conscious at all, of many components of the process. In the broad sense, an occurrence of legal reasoning is part of the biography of some judge.[30]

Golding is thus clear that, on the one hand, we have processes of reasoning, of conscious reason-giving in justification, and hopefully, from the perspective of the judge, 'rational persuasion', all of which would characterise a 'legitimate exercise of authority';[31] and, on the other hand, we have 'hunches, intuitions, and flashes of insight', as well as 'feelings' and 'emotions', all of which 'may be barely conscious, or even not conscious at all.'[32] Golding also clearly relates these two processes to the contexts of justification and discovery, as they have appeared in discussions of the practice of science. For instance,

[23] Ibid.
[24] Ibid.
[25] Ibid.
[26] Golding (1984) 1.
[27] Ibid.
[28] Ibid.
[29] Ibid.
[30] Ibid.
[31] Ibid, 8.
[32] Ibid, 1.

he says that 'The process of scientific discovery', which, as above, includes 'hunches, intuitions, and flashes of insight', 'may be inspired by anything ranging from a scientist's religious beliefs to prior scientific knowledge to the stimulation of a drug.'[33]

Golding's equation of the processes of discovery to the stimulation of drugs may be quite an extreme one, but it generally exemplifies the largely dismissive tone of many philosophical, again principally analytical, treatments of what is put on the other, the dark side, of legal reasoning, including imagination and emotion.[34] Of course, examples can be found of a similar tone of dismissal with that which is placed in the category of justification from the other camp, that of the naturalists.[35] Thus, one could point to any number of attacks on the 'illusion of reason' and 'rationality', and on the mere sham or gloss of justificatory practices. Equally, though, just as there are more friendly analytical treatments,[36] so there are more moderate, temperate attempts at conciliation offered by, say, realists, naturalists, or critical legal scholars.[37] There is also evidence, perhaps especially in the domain of emotion, that the tide is slowly turning, and more and more analytical philosophers of adjudication are taking the emotions seriously, with ever more attempts at reconciliation between different philosophical traditions and attitudes to the emotions.[38]

To recall, my strategy here is not one of mapping the field of the literature; nor do I intend to construct easy and straw targets for critique. I do not even intend to question the viability of studies of adjudication in the 'narrow sense', as Golding characterised them. Instead, my aim is to suggest, much more modestly, that there is room for an approach that does not hold on, so rigidly, to the dichotomy, and that does not see it as exhausting the terrain of possible research methods or questions. Such an approach would, for instance, refuse the split between conscious and 'barely conscious'

[33] Ibid, 2.

[34] Many examples of this could be given, eg, Kelsen's sometimes very critical reaction to work in the psychology and sociology of law. See van Klink (2009).

[35] See Turner (2010).

[36] Consider the stance of Giudice (2015).

[37] See, eg, Roth (2006).

[38] See, eg, Sellers (2017); and Amaya and Del Mar (2020). In comparison to treatments of emotion, extended reference to imagination is rare in contemporary analytic jurisprudence. An exception, which I only discovered after completing this book, is Timothy Macklem's *Law and Life in Common* (2015). In that book, Macklem argues for the importance of imagination, together with reason and will, in the construction of a life in common, including that of a legal culture: see especially chs 4 and 5. Macklem's approach to the imagination places it within a tradition of theorising the relationship between law and practical reason, and in particular within the frame of an agent or a community deciding which, amongst a number of possible courses of action, is the most compelling. For instance, Macklem says: 'The role of imagination, in one life or many, and of the narrative power that the exercise of imagination finds expression in and through, is to foster the belief that one possible course of action possesses greater rational weight than its rivals': Macklem (2015), 95. Sometimes, Macklem suggests, neither will nor reason will be sufficient to make one possibility more appealing than another: imagination will be needed. If there is a difference between Macklem's approach and the one taken in this book, and I mention it only tentatively, for it would require a great deal more careful attention than I can devote to it here, it may be that I am less concerned in this book, as Macklem appears to be, with imagination as persuasion, ie as a matter of making one course of action more appealing and compelling than another. I am here more concerned with imagination as inquiry, and thus as a mode of making insight into which values, vulnerabilities and interest might be at stake. Imagination, on the approach I take, is a particular kind of epistemic activity, and more a matter of generating and communicating normative stakes, than it is deciding between competing courses of action. I am not denying imagination can play the role that Macklem argues it does; just that its value is not exhausted by that role.

or 'unconscious' processes, recognising instead that certain mental processes can be complex mixtures of both. Arguably, emotions and the imagination are precisely such mixtures: we can, for instance, engage in them deliberately and consciously, and yet, in the deliberate and conscious process of experiencing them, ie in the process of feeling or imagining, there are also likely to be elements of those experiences that are non-deliberate, and less-than-conscious.

To take a simple example: I can deliberately and consciously choose to remember my childhood home, and also even choose to do so in ways that will most likely generate feelings of happiness, and I can be largely successful in this. But it can also be the case that in the course of experiencing those memories, I may find myself having feelings and mental images that are non-deliberate, and that lead me to feel, in addition to feelings of happiness, feelings of sadness, eg missing certain aspects of my childhood, or, more strongly, resenting them. What begins as a deliberate and conscious process comes, in the course of being experienced, to be woven in with less-than-deliberate and less-than-conscious elements. Processes of emotion and imagination are, then, better investigated as complex mixtures of the conscious and less-than-conscious, or deliberate and non-deliberate processes. Accordingly, throughout this book, and especially in discussion of imagination, I return to these various mixtures of conscious and less-than-conscious elements.

What about the claim that, on the one hand, we have reasons for decisions, and on the other, causes of them? Does this distinction exhaust the terrain? Take, again, the case of emotion. Where exactly does it fall: on the reason side or the cause side? Those who hold on to the distinction, often place it on the side of causes: we experience emotions, and then we subject them to the discipline of reason. But, acknowledging that this is a structure that our experience can take, does it necessarily have to be so, and is it often so? Might it not be the case that, at least sometimes, if not often, emotions give us access to reasons, and themselves yield reasons, and that they do so in ways that cannot be achieved in any other non-emotional way? Further, is it not the case that we often deliberately and consciously trigger certain emotions in us, and maintain them, as we reason? Might emotions not be, at least sometimes, thoughtful, and largely deliberate and conscious, ways of engaging with the world and others?

Here, we could give any number of examples, which range from background emotions, such as cares, eg caring for the poor, to long-term emotional dispositions, such as love, eg love for one's child, to short-term emotional episodes, eg compassion or mercy. Although it requires much more of a defence than I can engage in here,[39] there is at least prima facie plausibility to the idea that caring for someone or something, loving someone, or feeling compassionate or merciful towards them, makes salient features of the world that we would otherwise not have access to and that, in themselves, without further evaluation by some independent faculty of reason, give us reason to do something, eg engage in a program or activity of relieving the plight of the poor. And if there is such prima facie plausibility to the reason-giving character of the emotions, then this, surely, suggests that we should keep the options open rather than shutting them down, for instance, by holding on too rigidly to the dichotomy between justification and discovery.

[39] I return to this topic throughout the book. See, especially, section III of ch 3.

By being too strongly committed to the dichotomy, then, we may be making it more likely than not that we will have deeply impoverished accounts of certain key mental processes, like emotion and imagination. This is especially so when, from the perspective of justification, we treat whatever is put into the box of discovery as less-than-conscious, or entirely unconscious, and almost inexplicable or otherwise mysterious, as has often been claimed for 'intuition' or 'hunches'. None of this is to exclude the possibility that there are less-than-conscious mental processes. Instead, the idea is to enrich rather than close down possibilities. It is to suggest that at least some of the mental process placed traditionally in the discovery box may be more complex than we thought. It is also to suggest that most, if not all, of our mental processes are more profitably examined as mixtures of conscious and less-than-conscious elements.

But it is not only the discovery side that suffers from holding on to the dichotomy too rigidly. The justification side suffers too. For instance, we are then led to offer very thin and under-nourished concepts of reason or rationality. On the back of the dichotomy, our approach to reason and rationality is simply too divorced and too distant from our lives as embodied, imagining, feeling beings. One way of getting at this is to notice the difficulties with attempts to include, under the canopy of the dichotomy, other processes, such as generation of hypotheses and the testing of them. As the quote from Golding above illustrates, it is sometimes said that the process of discovery leads to more than one possibility, and instead generates multiple possibilities. This, however, is not very easy to square with certain other characterisations of the process of discovery, especially the idea that these processes are less-than-conscious or even wholly unconscious. For instance, do we not need to be aware, at some level, that these are indeed multiple possibilities, relevantly grouped and considered together? And if this is so, then is this awareness part of the process of discovery or some other process? It seems that the idea of including generation under discovery raises problems for the very coherence of the category of discovery. Similarly so on the other side of justification. Here, what is sometimes included under the canopy of justification is the procedure of testing. And yet it is not clear how testing relates to justification, which, with its focus on articulating reasons for decision or action, does not seem to admit much ambivalence or the kind of provisionality and suspension of judgement that testing to some degrees requires.

The point is not that generation and testing do not deserve a place in the mental processes engaged in during adjudication. The point is quite the contrary: surely they do, or something like them does. And yet, if we want to include them, it is not entirely clear how they fit into either category of justification or discovery. Further, if we would want to include them under the practices of justification (and the seeming necessity for some consciousness with respect to generation would give us reason to do that) then, again, would we not risk giving an all-too impoverished account of the procedures of generation and testing by forcing them into the strictures of a dichotomy between justification and discovery? There does not seem to be much to gain by blocking from the outset the possibility that processes of generation and testing involve a mixture of conscious and less-than-conscious elements of experience, as well as mixtures of, say, emotion, imagination and rationality.

The dichotomy between justification and discovery simplifies the mental processes involved in adjudication in another way. In many respects, and as also suggested by Arabatzis above, the dichotomy is founded on a very simplistic temporality: first we discover, then we justify. But we know from reflection on our experience of practical reason, as well as from accounts, such as John Rawls' on reflective equilibrium,[40] that the temporality of mental processes is much more complex than that. Being unsatisfied with the justificatory resources available at our disposal, we push further, to investigate what we may be missing. In the process of constructing possibilities, eg rehearsing possible consequences of some decision, we link them and our evaluations of them up with what we have so far taken ourselves to care about, and we consider whether we should revise those justificatory resources. We zig-zag our way through dilemmas, experiencing the uncertainty that they provoke in us, being sometimes anxious about not being sure what we ought to do, and sometimes also conscious that such moments may be important, eg for our moral development. The temporalities of this process are considerably more complex than a simple model of seeing first, then evaluating second, suggest.

At stake, then, in the question of how rigidly to hold on to the dichotomy of justification and discovery is not just the status of what is placed in the discovery category, although this alone should give us cause for concern. At stake is also our account of reason and rationality, and how rich and complex we allow ourselves to see it can be. One way forward would be to work to provide richer and more complex accounts of either justification or discovery, and some legal scholars have done this.[41] Another way, this being the strategy I adopt in this book, is to construct an alternative model, one not beholden to the otherwise commonplace associations with either, eg with one being conscious and the other less than conscious, or one being deliberate and the other not. This, of course, is not easy to do, and I find myself unsure of my footing at each turn. Nevertheless, I attempt, in what follows, to provide some hopefully helpful suggestions for how we might construct a model that goes beyond, but also overlaps with, the contexts of justification and discovery. This model, as indicated already, goes under the label of 'inquiry'.[42]

II. Social: Interactive and Collective

Inquiry, as modelled here, is an activity that we engage in together, both interactively and collectively. It is the task of this section to explain, in brief compass, this social dimension of inquiry.[43] At first blush, to even mention, let alone insist on and elaborate, the social dimension of inquiry seems trivial: who would disagree? Isn't it obvious that we inquire together? And yet, when we take a look at theories of adjudication, we see that the typical unit upon which theories focus is the individual judge. Even where there are panels of judges, as in appellate courts, the focus, whether in the context of discovery

[40] See, eg, the essays collected in van der Burg and Willigenburg (1998).

[41] See, eg, Anderson (1996).

[42] I recognise that 'inquiry' is also a term with a long history. For instance, the term has been especially important in pragmatism, as in the work of Charles Sanders Peirce and John Dewey. I welcome these echoes, but as I construct my own model of inquiry, adapted in particular to the context of adjudication, I do not rehearse this history further here. For an essay comparing the exercise of 'inquiry' in the arts and sciences, see Young (1996). For an example of reference to 'inquiry' in theories of argumentation, see Walton (2013), ch 7.

[43] Many subsequent sections of this book elaborate on the social dimension of inquiry, but also of imagination and language. The aim in this section is to introduce the importance of this dimension.

or justification, is very much on individuals. There is, of course, nothing wrong with that in itself: inquiry is, in part, something that individuals engage in. However, in emphasising the social dimension of inquiry, I wish to place the accent elsewhere.

As already hinted at above, the social dimension of inquiry itself has two branches: the interactive and the communal. I insist on this for, as common as it is to see only the individual level be discussed in theories of adjudication, when there are reactions to this individualism, they often occur at the level of community or collectivity. In other words, reactions to individualism often seek to explain individual dynamics by reference to shared, communal dynamics. One can see the tendency to both emphasise the individual, or to react against that by emphasising the collective, and thereby missing out on the interactive, in the debate between Ronald Dworkin and Stanley Fish.[44] In broad terms, in this debate: where Dworkin bases his theory of law as integrity on a lone heroic and one must say male figure (none other than Judge Hercules), Fish, in his reply to Dworkin, places emphasis on the collective, ie on the community of users of a language and its styles, genres, and commonplaces. There is some truth to both, but there is also something that both miss: the importance of the interactive level, and its distinct dynamics.

Again, there is plenty of recognition within legal theory, and perhaps especially with those theories that address the common law tradition, of the communal or collective aspects of legal reasoning. Karl Llewellyn, Brian Simpson, and more recently, Gerald Postema and John Bell, have all emphasised the importance, for the common law, of the, at times remarkably small, community of like-minded legal professionals.[45] The communal or collective level is important, and I will be returning to it, but my point is that the social dimension of inquiry is not exhausted by collective dynamics. There are also interactive dynamics, ie there is something in between the individual and the collective levels.

A. Interactive

To help us redress the balance we can draw on an important book by Anthony Laden, *Reasoning: A Social Picture*.[46] Laden explains that the standard view of reasoning is that of an:

> … activity of reflectively arriving at judgement through the alignment of the progress of our thoughts with certain formal structures in order to better navigate the world, to solve

[44] Dworkin (1982); and Fish (1982). See also Schelly (1985).

[45] See Llewellyn (1960); Simpson (1973); Postema (2002) and (2003); and Bell (1986). Bell, for instance, speaks of 'the social activity of legal justification', adding 'If one is to participate in this activity, one has to work within the framework of premises and criteria of what constitute acceptable legal arguments which it defines': (1986), 50. Paying attention to the 'social activity of legal justification' is vital, as I also argue in this book. But, as this quote illustrates, and as we can also see in Llewellyn and Simpson especially, reference to the communal or collective is often understood to be a source of consensus or, more generally, a stabilising and constraining factor. That is certainly one important aspect of communal or collective dynamics, but another, which I seek to emphasise more here, is that of flexibility and change. Communal language, for example, cannot merely be a source of stability and constraint; it must also be a resource that is alive and pliable to transformation.

[46] Laden (2002).

> particular problems and, perhaps, seek out the truth or the good. I am reasoning according to this picture when I am working out the implications of a moral commitment, or figuring out whether the evidence in front of me is sufficient to justify my belief in the truth of a proposition, or figuring out how best to accomplish my aims given the obstacles I face.[47]

Laden proposes a different, social picture of reasoning. He offers it explicitly as an alternative to the individualistic or monadic standard picture. A paradigmatic analogy for him is of reasoning as a casual conversation. The analogy is significant for various reasons, eg, in conversation, unlike in one-way communication, surprise is a feature, not a bug: 'conversation thrives on a certain degree of surprise', whereas 'surprises in one-way communication are a sign of failure.'[48] Further, conversation is an open-ended activity, and does not have 'a natural end':

> … casual conversation is an activity … which is structured as on-going … [it] leaves room for playfulness, for offering new ways of seeing or occupying or shaping spaces of reasons we inhabit which can be rejected without offence or a disruption of our relationships … It affords low-cost opportunities to attempt to re-shape those spaces and low-cost opportunities for others to either accept or reject our suggested changes. At the same time, it provides us opportunity to take responsibility for our positions, and thus to fully engage in the reciprocal and open-ended offering of invitations that my alternative [social] picture says is definitive of the act of reasoning.[49]

The reference to the issuing of invitations is important. It allows Laden to characterise the following acts as typical in a social account of reasoning: 'proposing, engaging, conversing, and other activities of mutual attunement', as distinct from 'calculating, deducing, problem-solving and judging', which are typical in monadic pictures of reasoning.[50] For Laden, 'I am reasoning', on the social account, 'when I am listening to your response to what I have said and taking it seriously', or 'when I am telling a story in response to something you have said'.[51] Indeed, more strongly, reason in the social sense 'requires that we are not commanding or ordering, ignoring or manipulating, blindly obeying or deferring'.[52] When you take 'my words as potential reasons … you leave some space for them to make a difference in what you do' and, similarly, 'offering you what I take to be a reason and not a command, means that I leave space for you to rebut or criticise it'.[53] A good reasoner, on this account, is much like 'a good listener: someone who is able to hear others' words as invitations, and be affected or moved by them, and someone who is able to hear and appropriately react to the responses her own invitations prompt'.[54] Good reasoning builds, develops and shapes relationships.[55]

Foregrounding relationality, and interactive dynamics, as he does in his account of reason, Laden also manages to dislodge some of the other associations connected to

[47] Ibid, 9.
[48] Ibid, 119.
[49] Ibid, 101.
[50] Ibid, 8.
[51] Ibid, 8–9.
[52] Ibid, 13.
[53] Ibid, 28.
[54] Ibid, 46.
[55] Ibid, 101.

reason as 'cold, hard or calculating.'[56] Significantly for present purposes, this includes emotion. As he puts it himself, his account 'blurs the boundary between reason and various standard contrastive terms like emotion, feeling, sentiment, affect.'[57] A reason can have, as part of its content, an affective attitude, ie the giving of a reason can 'communicate[] something about my emotional or sentimental relationship to what I am saying or to whom I am saying it.'[58] Thinking of reasoning as relational, and of reasons as invitations, opens up a whole host of carriers of communication, including emotions, and this in a broad sense, eg encompassing cares, dispositions, moods, episodes, attitudes and experiences.

Laden's analogy with causal conversation is especially evocative. Many of us can surely relate to the qualities of a good conversation: on-going and open-ended, laden with the unpredictability and surprise that comes with responsiveness to the other, rich with modes of communication, including emotion, and with plenty of space, as Laden puts it, 'for playfulness, for offering new ways of seeing or occupying or shaping the spaces of reasons we inhabit'.[59] Reasoning together, interactively, says Laden, 'often requires … a willingness to follow a path that hasn't (yet) been fully laid down.'[60] It also often requires avoiding 'closing off criticism', leaving 'open the possibility of further challenges to what we say.'[61] A causal conversation, in other words, is like a joint exploration, ie akin to an experiment we engage in together.

I have only given the briefest of insights into Laden's complex and rich account, but already this brief glimpse of 'reasoning as the responsive engagement with others as we attune ourselves to one another'[62] offers some very helpful resources for a more socially-oriented model of inquiry.

Some readers, however, may find that this has little do with law and legal processes. Indeed, there are moments in his book when Laden himself draws on the language of law, but he associates very much with the standard picture of reason. He explains this in the following way:

> The standard picture draws a close connection between reason and the authority possessed by laws and rules, an authority that can be described as the right to rule or command or pass judgment. This connection supports a central feature of the standard picture: that reasoning is an activity aimed at reaching conclusions, and thus aspires to be decisive.[63]

Elsewhere, he also associates the standard model with 'good decision-making and effective advocacy', which he characterises as involving 'the ability to skilfully invoke the rules of reason in service of one's aims.'[64] Law here, whether under the guise of legislation or adjudication, and whether in the persona of the judge or the advocate, seems to be very much at odds with a causal conversation. It seems to be the very paradigm of

[56] Ibid, 13.
[57] Ibid.
[58] Ibid.
[59] Ibid, 109, fn 5.
[60] Ibid.
[61] Ibid,15.
[62] Ibid, 8.
[63] Ibid, 49.
[64] Ibid, 46

the assertive, decisive, will-imposing, monadic and individualistic reasoning; as Laden puts it, 'a kind of normative bulldozer that clears paths for action and belief.'[65] But is it? Even if there is some truth to the idea that reasoning in a legal context is full of decisiveness and assertiveness, does that exhaust the picture of the exercise of reason in adjudication?

My suggestion is that, in fact, Laden's social picture of reasoning, and his analogy with casual conversation, can reveal to us many of the interactive dynamics that adjudicatory practice involves. One obvious place where we can see it is in the interaction between advocates and judges in oral submissions. Naturally, advocates prepare these submissions with certain ends in mind, and there is no doubt that a large part of what advocates do is attempt to persuade judges and impose their will upon them. Nevertheless, as anyone who has observed or listened to exchanges between advocates and judges will attest, this interaction is not one that any one person, no matter how persuasive, can control. In the US context, especially, but also to a lesser degree in the UK, the relations between advocates and judges are indeed interactive. They resemble much more a dialogue than a monologue. They are much more like a conversation, even if these conversations are considerably more charged than casual conversations typically are. These interactions also often end abruptly, eg because of time limits, as in the US context, which suggests they could go on, if only time permitted. There is also room for surprise, and often humour, as judges test the arguments of counsel, and counsel improvise replies. And although advocates always keep in mind the interests of their client, both advocate and judge are also conscious of a duty to the moral and political quality of the law, as well as the legitimacy and authority of the court. At stake in many of these interactions, then, is much more than which side is to win, and it is precisely often the implications of deciding one way or the other that are being tested by the question-and-answer interaction of advocate and judge.

A brief example here will have to suffice.[66] Consider the following exchange between judge and counsel, in the case of *California v Carney*,[67] heard in the US Supreme Court, where the issue was whether a motor home fell within the definition of a vehicle (if it did, then the police did not need a warrant to search it):

> **Judge:** What would you do with a houseboat?
>
> **Lawyer:** A houseboat? I think that would be covered, and I think that the –
>
> **Judge:** It has wheels?
>
> **Lawyer:** No, it's a vessel, and it is covered by the same rule. …
>
> **Judge:** Well, I want to be more specific. There is a houseboat. It's tied up to a dock that's got no motor on it at all. It's just sitting there. And it's hooked up to the sewage, electricity, etc, and it's right beside a house. The house is covered, and the boat is not?
>
> **Lawyer:** That's correct. It's sort of like an automobile that is parked right next to the house in the driveway. The automobile might not be covered, and the house is.

[65] Ibid.

[66] In the second part of this book, and thus in the context of each of the case studies I examine, I seek to pay attention to how each of them enables the interactive aspect of the social dimension of inquiry. This sometimes involves attention to interaction between advocates and judges, as manifest by (some) reports of judgements.

[67] *California v Carney* 471 U.S. 386 (1985).

Judge: But the automobile has a motor in it –

Lawyer: That's correct.

Judge: – and the houseboat does not.

Lawyer: No. There may be oars. There may be some way to move that from one place to another.

Judge: There 'may be'. May be. I've seen houses moved, too.

[Laughter]

Lawyer: As have I. I've passed a few of them on the beltway.

Judge: You've got to get more than that.

Lawyer: Certainly. Again, the objective indicia of mobility would be what the officers are looking to. Perhaps in Your Honour's example, they would be looking to see if there's oars there. There's no motor. There's no way to move that thing.

Judge: Well, let me add one more thing. It's been tied up there for the last 36 years.

[Laughter]

Lawyer: If the officer doesn't know that, I don't see why he should be called to that particular knowledge. One thing he does know about when he is dealing with a house –

Judge: The moral is, don't live in a houseboat.[68]

There is genuine interaction in this exchange. And though it may be far from casual, there is a sense in which it involves responsiveness (the advocate's skill is, in part, an ability to respond to the worries the judge is expressing, while keeping in mind her client's interests), as well as surprise, accompanied by humour, and even a willingness to play. There is uncertainty here too, with hesitation on both sides, and thus a tentative exploration rather than the assertion of a decisive, non-revisable will.

The question-and-answer involving such hypotheticals is only one example of the interactiveness of inquiry, and we will encounter such further examples later, for instance with metaphors and figures. The general point is that there is space for interactive inquiry within adjudication. Indeed, we should go further and say that there is a need for it, for without it, it would be harder to make better judgements as to how a certain way of deciding the present case might impact on law and its relevant institutions in the future.

The interactive aspect of inquiry, however, does not stop with interactive dynamics between advocates and judges. It may also include interaction between judges, including in the course of oral argument and in written judgements. We know written judgements are sometimes circulated in draft form, and that judges respond to each other's arguments in the course of their written opinions. Judges, however, are not merely interacting with the advocates and other judges involved in the present case. They are also inviting responses from other, future addressees of their opinions, including as yet unknown addressees. I will be exploring this more in the next section, but suffice to say for now that, when looked at through the rubric of Laden's social picture of reasoning, and his analogy with casual conversation, we see that the discourse of a judgement is not a mere exercise in persuasion, but that it involves proposals for reasoning together.

[68] See the transcript of oral argument, available online: www.oyez.org/cases/1984/83-859.

This can take many forms, whether that be, for instance, by the deployment of a scenario in obiter, or by the offer of a metaphor which calls for unpacking by future audiences, or by the signalling of doubt, and therefore inviting revision, of a judge's own conclusions. There is, then, much more interaction in adjudication than first meets the eye.

All this suggests a very different approach to the use of language in legal contexts, namely: not as mere exercises in imposition of a will, and thus persuasion, assertiveness and decisiveness, but as invitations to think further together. There may be scope, in this respect, to connect the above interactive aspect of the social dimension of inquiry with attempts to articulate what has been called 'the dialogically extended mind'.[69] On this view, language is seen as enabling 'skilful intersubjective engagement'. Language is approached as 'a dynamic activity' that 'enables dialogical engagement with an interlocutor'.[70] Language is less the tool that one person uses to impose their will on another, although that can happen too, and more, or at least sometimes, that which allows for interaction, that which makes possible a conversation.[71] This interactive use of language, I would suggest, is pervasive in adjudication.

B. Collective

I have spoken so far only of interaction, and of the interactive aspect of the social dimension of inquiry. But it is not a great leap from there to the communal or collective aspect. Interaction, for all its talk of invitations and responsiveness to another, and for all its emphasis on surprise and willingness to traverse paths less well travelled, also needs anchors and hinges, and mechanisms for stabilising expectations. If, however, we take the experimental dimension of inquiry seriously, as I will be exploring in the fourth section of this chapter, then this stabilising still has to be one that is not too dogmatic, that remains revisable and resourceful, changeable and open to being made less stable. There is a need, certainly, for that which can be shared, and memorably so. But, equally, there is a need, in this case for a language, that, though shared, is also something that can be returned to and played with. Are there modes of language that balance memorability with resourcefulness? The reader will not be surprised to hear that I suggest there are, and that they include, perhaps paradigmatically, the kind of artefacts I will be exploring in Chapter 2 and, in more detail, in the second part of this book.

In characterising the social character of cognition or knowledge, scholars have pointed to a whole range of different kinds of shared or common forms or technologies that facilitate a whole range of communal or collective tasks. In terms of forms or technologies, these include, for instance, scripts, which are said to assist in de-complexifying social life, stabilising expectations and facilitating interaction in

[69] Fusaroli, Gangopadhyay and Tylen (2013).

[70] Ibid, 34.

[71] See also the emerging scholarship on 'interactive minds' and 'interactive science': eg Tylen et al (2010); the Interacting Minds Centre: http://interactingminds.au.dk/en/ and the Journal of Interactive Science: www.jois.online/index.php/jois.

certain kinds of situations.[72] They also include, for example, physical and material objects, which facilitate joint attention, and can function as scaffolds for social conversations, eg public statutes or monuments.[73] Stories and narratives, of course, are one of the major kinds of technologies that human beings have deployed, both to remember lessons learnt and to pass them on to future generations, while also serving as current resources for negotiating social change.[74] Examples of this are legion, eg think of the telling and re-telling (re-telling here being crucial) of oral epics, fables, parables and other literary forms.[75] We can thus ask, what kinds of forms and technologies, ie what forms of language, what kinds of structures and genres, visual, linguistic, gestural and others, enable which kinds of communal cognitive activities, from joint attention, through to shared intentions and dynamic coupling?

There are a number of different theoretical approaches to this question, ie how to conceptualise the social character of cognition.[76] Some theorists, for instance, speak of the 'socially extended mind',[77] 'socially extended knowledge',[78] or 'distributed cognition.'[79] Common to these approaches is an intuition that cognition, knowledge, judgement, or any number of other mental processes, are not confined to individual brains, but occur, in some sense to be specified, at the social, ie communal and collective, level.

Indeed, the point is sometimes made more strongly: that there are certain kinds of cognitive operations that are not possible for individuals. These are operations that require communal and collective patterns, supported by rituals and technologies that are shared and refined over time. Law itself sometimes features as a paradigmatic example. For instance, in Shaun Gallagher's work on the 'socially extended mind', law serves as the example of a 'large and complex institution', which makes possible and hosts a range of 'cognitive and communicative processes' that require collaboration and co-operation.[80] As Gallagher notes:

> Judgements made in such contexts, and the specific kind of judgements that are made, are forms of cognition that depend on a large and complex system without which they could not happen. Indeed, these cognitive practices are such that in principle they could not happen just in the head. Even in the case of a highly trained attorney who seemingly does her legal reasoning in her head, what she does, and what makes it the kind of cognition that it is, depends not only on the fact that she has previously engaged in the workings of the legal system (receiving

[72] On scripts, see Schank and Abelson (1977).

[73] On scaffolds, see Sterelny (2010) and Colombetti and Krueger (2015).

[74] Out of a large literature, see, eg, Koschorke (2018); Boyd; (2009); Herman (2003); Collins (2013) and (2017). Cognitive narratologists have also reflected on how narratives themselves depict social minds in actions: literature, then, is not only a tool of inquiry in its social dimension (generating and reinforcing, while also transforming, shared stories), but is also a highly reflexive tool, a mode of reflection on its status as enabling the social mind: see, eg, Palmer (2010).

[75] It is important to remember that re-telling, especially in oral cultures, is not mere repetition. A story re-told is also, often, a story transformed. For a discussion of oral legal cultures, see Vesting (2018), chs 3–5.

[76] See, eg, Carter, Clark, Kallestrup, Palermos and Pritchard (2018); Rogoff (1990); and Kaufmann (2011). A classical figure, whose importance for legal theory remains largely unexplored, is Lev Semenovich Vygotsky: see Vygotsky (1978), and for a discussion of Vygotsky and his legacy, see Wertsch (1985).

[77] Gallagher (2013).

[78] See Carter, Clark, Kallestrup, Palermos and Pritchard (2018).

[79] See Anderson, Cairns and Sprevak (2018).

[80] Gallagher (2013), 7.

> her training and tuning her cognitive abilities in law school by following specific practices of that educational institution), but on the on-going workings of the legal system.[81]

Gallagher, then, in part based on the illustration of a legal system, urges us to think of the mind 'not as a repository of propositional attitudes and information, or in terms of internal belief-desire psychology', but instead 'as a dynamic process involved in solving problems and controlling behaviour and action … in dialectical, transformative relations with the environment',[82] which is composed of 'mind-extending' shared tools and technologies, such as language itself, but also rules, eg of evidence or procedure, and rituals, and other institutional habits. Together, these tools and technologies form an institution, which, again, makes certain cognitive and communicative processes possible, ie ones that would not be possible for an individual mind. As Gallagher puts it, 'Such institutions allow us to engage in cognitive activities that we are unable to do in the head, or even in many heads.'[83]

Gallagher's approach, which remains undervalued in legal theory,[84] points towards a very different way of approaching inquiry in its social, ie communal and collective, aspect. Certainly, it, along with other approaches that stress the social dimension, reminds us that language is less, and certainly not only, something that happens in an individual mind, and more something that, to quote Daniel Dor, 'resides between speakers'.[85] Language, on this view, can only be 'properly understood as a property of the social-cultural network'; it is a 'collectively-constructed communication technology, a social communication software'.[86] This is very helpful, but to be compatible with the model of inquiry, as I am constructing it here, and especially with its experimental dimension (which I discuss in the next section), language, and other technologies, must be conceptualised not only as shared and functioning as a 'communication technology', thereby making possible certain cognitive operations on multi-mind and across-time scales, but also as something that is itself pliable and revisable, and serves as a resource for change and transformation.

We thus need to ask not only how language, and its various forms, including various genres and other literary variations, can be shared, eg be memorable, serve to capture joint attention, etc, but also how it can be both memorable *and* resourceful. Under this approach, language becomes less something operating in the background, eg like scripts which guide us less-than-consciously, and more like a technology we can actively play with and co-construct, and indeed re-construct, together. This is not to say that all of language, all the time, has to function in this way, but at least some of it, sometimes, must. What might be some examples of such linguistic forms in the legal context? Here, what I call in this book artefactual language comes to the fore: by signalling its own artifice, these linguistic forms capture our attention and call on us to participate, ie to do things with them. In particular, they call on us to do things with them interactively

[81] Ibid.

[82] Ibid.

[83] Ibid.

[84] See also De Jaegher and Di Paolo (2007) on 'participatory sense-making'.

[85] Dor (2017), 108.

[86] Ibid. For Dor, interestingly, it is also 'collectively designed for a very specific communicative function: the instruction of imagination … it allows communicators to communicate directly with their interlocutors' imaginations' (ibid.). See also Dor (2015).

and communally. In that sense, they remain alive as language forms, ie they do not allow themselves to be too ready to hand (with apologies to Heidegger).[87] I shall be saying more about this in the next chapter on 'Artefacts', but let me give two other examples, non-artefactual ones, that I do not develop in this book.

The first example of a linguistic form that is both sharable and resourceful, or that lends itself to being shared and being transformed together, is the genre of the commonplace. Commonplaces have a long history in the legal context, and of course beyond.[88] In the legal context, they have taken a variety of forms, including proverbs, sayings, formulas, maxims, rules and principles. They vary in how sharable and memorable they are: those that include repetition of sounds, eg alliteration, or some other rhythmic element are more sharable and memorable than those that do not.[89] Similarly, those that allude in some way to cultural knowledge, as sayings or maxims often do, are more easily sharable and memorable than, say, rules or principles without such allusions. A proverb like 'Birds of a feather flock together', which combines repetition of sound with allusion to cultural knowledge, is more shareable and memorable than, say, a principle like 'No one can profit from their own wrong', even though this principle, too, is quite sharable and memorable.

But how, one might ask, are these forms not only shareable and memorable but also resourceful? Here, perhaps somewhat paradoxically, one could argue that the more well-known the commonplace, the more it is capable of being made to mean different things. This is a point that was made already some centuries ago by Francis Bacon in his work on maxims.[90] Maxims, Bacon thought, and especially where not structured into a system but instead loosely held together by a community familiar with them, lent themselves to being re-made. Such forms function less like guides for individual minds to follow, eg rails upon which an individual cognition proceeds, and more like labels that can be attached to any number of attitudes or decisions. They are eminently re-usable, and because they are so familiar, and thus well-worn, they can be re-used in any number of unpredictable ways. Some of the contemporary work in legal theory on principles has recognised this, eg Dworkin's work on how differently principles apply when contrasted with rules,[91] though without explicit reference to the long history of such forms in the common law and beyond.[92]

[87] For a helpful collection of essays on Heidegger on language, see Powell (2013). Generally, we might say, the language of poetry is what allows us to not take language for granted, and not over-instrumentalise it. In this respect, and in many others, poetry is crucial epistemologically, ethically and politically.

[88] For the commonplace book in the Renaissance, see Moss (2011). See also, recently, Jefferson (2019).

[89] See also Tiersma (1999).

[90] See Bacon (1803). For a recent discussion, see Geng (2019).

[91] See Dworkin (1986). See also Stein (1966). Of relevance here too might be Viehweg's (1993) [1974] focus on topics in his theory of legal reasoning.

[92] See, eg, in law, Davis (2020); and beyond, see, eg, Jolles (2017), ch 5; Eden (2001); Grant (2016); and, recently, Hui (2019). I should clarify that although commonplaces, including maxims, can be used in many different ways, and thus can serve as flexible and transformative resources, I would not make the argument that they are especially good at enabling inquiry. This is because the language of commonplaces, precisely because it is so worn and conventional, is not usually artefactual, ie it does not signal its own artifice. In this respect, although I do think commonplaces can, somewhat paradoxically, help collective language be not only memorable but also resourceful, I would still insist on the primacy of artefactual language in enabling inquiry. Of course, the devil would be in the detail, and we would need to pay attention to the specific language in question. Here, it helps to remember the very many different forms these have taken, and including not just

Another example, and again not one that I can develop here, is the narratological structure of precedent. If we take seriously, as I think we should, the common law as, in part, a process of reasoning collectively with cases, and thus fact patterns, then we can think of the form of the case, and the patterns of facts that can be extracted from it, as precisely a tool or technology that is both shareable and resourceful. As many have recognised, what pattern of facts, ie what story or narrative, in what genre, with which archetypal characters etc, is extracted from a past case or from strings of past cases can vary, ie it is variable and subject to change by many hands. What one subsequent court treats as relevant, at a certain level of generalisation, another court might not, choosing instead to either concretise those patterns of facts or make it more abstract, thereby also changing its scope of applicability, and thus its legal significance.[93] Changing the level of generalisation is just one of many narratological tools, ie just one of the ways that we, as a community, can play with those patterns of facts, or stories/narratives. We can also, for example, introduce another character into the story, or change the relative importance, eg the level of agency, of a character already featuring in the story. Judges in the common law do this all the time, ie they play together with the patterns of facts of cases and thereby also change and transform their legal significance. This is a very dynamic practice. It is contested and argued over, and often remains un-resolved, while still serving as a resource for joint attention and joint construction.[94] Precedential language, then, can also be thought of as a mode of collectivity that balances the memorable and the resourceful.

I have barely brushed the surface of what could be said about the social aspects of inquiry. Given the overall claim of this book, namely, that artefacts and related processes of imagination are valuable insofar as they enable inquiry, these two aspects of the social dimension inform and infuse my approach to language and imagination, as well as the case studies in the second part. We will, then, have occasion to refer to the social dimension often. As we do, I will seek to pay special attention to the particular ways that distinct artefacts, and related processes of imagination, enable the interactive and collective aspects of inquiry.

III. Diachronic

So far, we have seen that inquiry is situated in a space beyond, but also overlapping to some extent with, the contexts of justification and discovery, and that it has a social dimension, including both interactive and communal aspects. I add, now, one further dimension to the model of inquiry: the diachronic dimension. By this I mean to point to the multiple temporalities within which inquiry operates, with a particular emphasis on two points: first, that inquiry occurs both in the immediate, real time of a present case as well as over extended periods of time; and second, that it involves balancing past-oriented, present-oriented and future-oriented concerns, with its future-oriented

maxims, but also 'gnome, paroimia, proverb, sententia, precept … adage, epigram, apothegm, apophthegm': see Hui (2019), 4. Some of these forms may function more artefactually than others.

[93] See Stone (1985).

[94] See, eg, Jackson (1988); Bricker (2019); and the essays in Hanne and Weisberg (2018).

aspect being particularly important and also largely neglected. Let me take each point in turn.

A. Inquiry Over Time

There is no doubt that an important aspect of inquiry, whether when conducted individually, interactively or communally, is that it occurs in the real time of a present case. There is much that we have not yet explored, perhaps especially about the interactive dynamics in a courtroom, as between advocates and judges, judges and judges in an appellate court, and between judges and advocates on one side and witnesses or members of the public and the press on the other side.[95] These might seem like trivial concerns, but they are not. Particular interactive dynamics have important, long-lasting and often unpredictable effects on the future development of law and its institutions. We know, for instance, how important the jury has been for legal development. Part of the reason why is how the jury's inclusion changed the interactive dynamics of courtrooms, with advocates and judges addressing themselves to the jury, and with the jury's black-box decisions themselves forming an engine of legal change.[96] The moment one includes another category of audience into a procedure, like the trial, is also a moment in which one introduces changes in interactional dynamics, which, again, can have all kinds of effects. And, of course, there is also the question of how those interactions are designed, including how they are facilitated by the architecture of courtrooms, with there being important differences between, say, the adversarial and inquisitive procedures, not to mention the various alternatives in Alternative Dispute Resolution mechanisms.

Important as they are, however, it is not the activities of inquiry occurring in the real time of present cases that I want to emphasise here. For the activities of inquiry occur not just in real time, but also over time, and this in various degrees of duration and intensity. Noticing this is important, for it can lead to identifying and being able to evaluate, including seeing the value of, certain forms of communication that only really become visible when one considers the over-time perspective. Perhaps under the influence of positivism, with its tendency to prioritise the identification of the content of a legal system at a particular point in time,[97] it is easy to miss the many different forms of language deployed to facilitate communication over time, and thus also the many different states of becoming or un-becoming which laws can take on. Indeed, it is arguably less the philosophers, and much the historians of legal change and development, who have given us insights into these forms and states.[98]

[95] See also the above section on the social dimension, including the possibility of connecting in this respect with interactive science.

[96] See, eg, Milsom (2003).

[97] See, eg, Raz (1980).

[98] An important contemporary scholar, working both in philosophy and history of law, who has emphasised the temporal dimension is Gerald Postema. See, eg, Postema (2004) and (2018). Despite overlap, there are some differences between his approach and the one I adopt here. For example, although Postema criticises the positivist commitment to studying 'momentary legal systems', he retains the positivist interest in 'propositions of law': see Postema (2018), 164–6. Part of my point in this section is that if we approach inquiry in adjudication diachronically, we need to pay attention to a much wider range of forms and expressions of language, many of which would not be classified under propositional language (or take the form of rules or principles).

Consider, for instance, the expressions paid attention to by the historian of Roman law and society, Clifford Ando.[99] Paying close attention to the practices of analogy by Roman jurists, Ando confesses to being 'particularly charmed by those moments when the jurists feel some anxiety about the aptness of the analogy, which they flag by the insertion of some word such as quodammodo, "somehow", as in "A should be understood somehow on analogy with B".'[100] Ando also points out the significance of the expression 'quasi', as in for instance 'quasi-contract', adding: 'all knowledge systems … rely on it: it expresses doubt about the capacity of language itself, or at the very least the capacity of the person who employs it, to give accurate and full accounting of the world with the discursive and lexical means at one's disposal.'[101]

Expressions like 'somehow' or 'quasi' seem quite superfluous, if they are visible at all, from a perspective that focuses on the propositional content of a legal system at a particular moment in time. They become, however, crucial when one extends that perspective to one stretched out over time. These terms signal something that is in the making, eventually ripening into some new category, or, alternatively, remaining but a forgotten, not-taken-up possibility, an unrealised potential. Expressions like this – perhaps one can call them 'transitional expressions' – may also be said to include, for instance, the 'not yet', or the 'almost', or 'the not quite', the 'nearly', or prefixes like neo-X, eg 'neoliberalism', or double negatives, eg 'this is not not a contract'. They can also be expanded to include other forms of signalling doubt or the prospect of change, such as confessions as to uncertainty about some principle, or statements that simply directly say that some area of the law, or again some rule or principle, requires more attention, eg from Parliament, Law Reform Commissions, scholars or indeed future courts.

I take such expressions to be part of the activity of inquiry over time. In this sense, the ontology of law under the model of inquiry is very rich: it includes not only those propositions or assertions made with confidence as to what the current state of the law is, eg taking the form of rules, principles or other grand or formulaic statements, but also extends to the signalling of attitudes, eg of doubt, difficulty, and uncertainty, and the making or un-making of possibilities and potentials, which are often characterised by different forms and expressions of language. Under the longer diachronic frame, we come to see, and possibly also see the value of (for, after all, they make change possible), transitional modes of language, ie forms and expressions of language with which we can build provisionally, incompletely, suggestively. If there is need of an analogy here, we might think of these forms as sketches, in crayon or black ink, and thus as preparatory work that may or may not find its way into more fully realised forms, eg a painting in oils with a full colour palette. That analogy, though, also has its limits, for it suggests that there are forms that are fully realised, whereas, and perhaps especially in the common law, we might think of all law as sketch-like, always to some degree unfinished, and thus all in different stages of making or un-making a work-in-progress as the saying goes.[102]

Another difference is that Postema is more concerned with the temporalities of practical reason, as this is affected by law. This is an important project, but not my focus here.

[99] See Ando (2015a).

[100] Ibid, 36.

[101] Ibid, 39.

[102] The unfinished character of these forms and expressions of legal language, which become visible under a diachronic approach to inquiry in adjudication, is different to what legal theorists refer to under 'defeasibility'.

I am hardly the first to point to the importance of seeing law as stretched out over time. Alan Hutchinson, for example, has also spoken of the common law as a work-in-progress that is never complete or finished;[103] or as a law that 'is always moving, but never arriving.'[104] Hutchinson avoids telling the story as one of inevitable development, or progressive, even if incremental, change. He emphasises, instead, that 'the common law is better understood as a rutted and rough road that has innumerable twists and turns and no particular destination', where 'any particular route taken has been chosen from among the countless and constantly proliferating possibilities for change.'[105] Hutchinson also speaks of cases as 'temporary lighthouses,'[106] and of the overall structure, or, perhaps, better atmosphere, of the common law as 'loosely assembled, creatively constructed, unpredictably changeable and ideologically loaded.'[107] Relatedly, he also characterises the common law as 'messy, episodic, and experimental effort to respond and adapt to the contingent demands that the political and social milieu places upon it.'[108] I am drawn to Hutchinson's characterisation of the common law, though I do not approach it as much as he does through the lens of ideology. As I will elaborate on more under the experimental and normative dimensions of the model of inquiry, I see these modes of experimental communication and cognition to be attempts to sense, never completely, and only ever tentatively, values, vulnerabilities and interests that might be at stake in a certain cases and in other potentially similar cases in the future.

In addition to these transitional expressions and forms of language, and accompanying attitudes, eg signalling doubt, difficulty, or uncertainty, we can also consider the presence of other kinds of normative expressions, the status of which is somewhat ambivalent. One such expression, to which I shall return to later (in the final section of this chapter), is that of 'interests'. The status of this language is not clear: compare it, for instance, to the language of rules, standards, principles or even remedies. Geoffrey Samuel, who has pointed to the use of this language, says of it that it is 'much less normative and more descriptive than a right', but 'has the ability to be wide-ranging as an analytical tool that functions both within the law and within the facts.'[109] The use of

For example, for Schauer, to speak of defeasibility is to speak of 'any common law rule [that] is tentative, remaining continuously open to defeat in a particular case or subject to modification as new situations arise', (2009), 105. This, however, already posits a finished rule, it then being said that it could be defeated by 'new situations'. My point here is that we need to pay attention to incomplete, unfinished, and potential or possible resources for future legal development, and these will not tend to be picked up on if we look solely at rules or principles, no matter how defeasible we claim they are. To model inquiry diachronically, I would suggest, is to take these modes of existence of legal phenomena seriously. It is to attempt to capture a much wider range of forms and expressions of legal language, accompanied by a wider range of epistemic attitudes, including epistemic emotions, than is arguably captured by the framework of defeasibility.

[103] Hutchinson (2005), 18. See also MacLean (2012), developing a processual theory of law, in part based on a reading of Whitehead's metaphysics. Further, as Postema points out, classical common law jurisprudence is a rich resource of insights on the diachronicity of law, eg Oliver Wendell Holmes spoke of the common law as 'a series of successive approximations', and referred to it as something that 'is always approaching and never reaching consistency': see Postema (2018), 165–6, citing Holmes (1995), 1: 213. On Holmes, see also Mendenhall (2017).

[104] Hutchinson (2005), 291.

[105] Ibid, 15.

[106] Ibid, 131.

[107] Ibid, 189.

[108] Ibid, 273.

[109] Samuel (2017), 1.

the language is loose; sometimes it is indeed used as a substitute for a right, but other times, as in the expression 'public interest', or 'interest in free competition', it seems to point to 'objectives or states of affairs which are or would be to the person's or to the public's advantage' or to 'categorise a type of harm suffered, eg financial interest, mental health interest'.[110]

Samuel's overall definition of an interest is 'some state of affairs in which a person or class of persons – or sometimes a non-personified thing, such as environment or justice – has an advantage or a concern'.[111] For Samuel, this language of 'interests' can be used to signal something requiring or deserving of some sort of legal response or legal protection, perhaps yet to be determined. Samuel is enthusiastic about the language of interests, saying that it 'can play a central role in legal thought and legal reasoning',[112] but it may be that its very point and value is in it playing precisely a less than central role, ie a more ambivalent, if not marginal, though no less important for that, function. An interest may, or may not, become a right, or it may become the object of the protection of some rule or principle. It may also continue to float in a somewhat ungainly and unstable way within legal discourse, as if waiting to see if it acquires enough momentum to achieve a more stable status.

In his analysis, Samuel also mentions the language of 'expectations', and indeed this may be another example of a floating, provisional, uncertain normative insight, something that is possibly worthy of protection, but without it being clear how. Other candidates might be 'harm', or reference to a 'good', 'value' or 'vulnerability'. As Stephen Waddams has stated:

> The perceptions that conduct is wrong, that an agreement has been broken, that reasonable expectations have been disappointed, that something belonging to another has been taken, that the defendant has done something unfair, or that a benefit has been unjustly retained, while not in themselves legally conclusive, have been highly relevant.[113]

It is not a surprise that Waddams' perspective is that of a historian, tracing the dynamics of legal change over time. His own focus on the language of 'policies' may also constitute another example of a language that does not have the assertive or propositional, or source-recognised, status of rules, but which clearly has played and continues to play vital roles in signalling and enabling legal change.[114] The very language of 'remedies', ie as something worthy of a remedy, and especially after the extinction of the writ system, might serve as yet one more example of an interstitial legal technology, a sort of temporary, floating prototype, which hovers suggestively across time. All these expressions, I suggest, are a part of the much richer legal ontology under the guise of the over-time, long-term view of inquiry.

In addition to forms of language and expression, we may also point to other kinds of practices that come into view under the guise of inquiry-over-time. We may think

[110] Ibid, 4–5.
[111] Ibid, 5.
[112] Ibid, 6.
[113] Waddams (2003), 16.
[114] In a way, part of the point here is that to speak of 'sources' is already to adopt a temporal perspective that is too backward-looking, neglecting the forward-looking aspect of legal reasoning, language and communication. An interesting temporal concept, which may better capture some of these temporal dynamics, is that of 'intimation', as deployed by Neil Walker (2014).

of these as generative legal technologies, which, in Peter Goodrich's language, are 'sites of invention, of the beginning of any given justificatory argument.'[115] Consider, for instance, citation practices. Interestingly, some of these practices have come into view not via the employment of a longer-term perspective, but when examining the dynamics of relations between two legal traditions, eg of two or more courts in dialogue.[116] Thus, for example, Nico Krisch, writing about the dialogues between European and domestic courts in the area of human rights, who noticed that courts were employing a citation practice, ie the 'but see X' or 'and see also X' citation, often employed by common law courts for commonwealth authorities.[117] Such citations do not state why it is that some cases are being cited, and sometimes not even whether they are being cited as contrasting or as not-too-far-removed alternatives to what is being treated as directly authoritative or relevant. And it is precisely this silence, or this under-determined status of what is cited, that allows it to function as a generative technology, capable of functioning as a starting point, and thus as a resource, for a future submission or judgement.

Readers will no doubt be able to point to many more examples of suggestions and hints, or other proto-like constructions or floating uncertain signals. One could take the entire body of so-called obiter dictum, all the byways and allegedly unnecessary excursions, tangents, diversions, which, full of potentiality, may, or may not, give rise to hardened conventions. For the present book, the point is that the artefacts I shall be discussing live precisely both in the real time of inquiry, but perhaps even more so in stretched out time of inquiry-over-time.

B. Projecting into the Future

I mentioned, at the outset of this section, that there was another aspect to the diachronic dimension of inquiry I wanted to emphasise. This is the idea that inquiry balances past-looking, present-looking and future-looking orientations. Scholars of legal reasoning have of course recognised this, eg Frederick Schauer, Jeremy Waldron, Neil MacCormick and Gerald Postema have theorised such balancing acts, noting also the importance of the future-looking dimension for precedential reasoning.[118] Indeed, as pointed out in the Introduction to this book, one of the roots of this project was my grappling with what MacCormick meant by 'consequential reasoning', including his shift from talking broadly about consequences to talking more narrowly about hypothetical implications.[119]

[115] Goodrich (2015), 143.

[116] See also Glenn on what he calls devices of 'cosmopolitan legal thought' (2013). In fact, legal reasoning in a global context, and especially perhaps the practice of transnational courts, such as the European Court of Human Rights, may be a rich resource for further examples of forms and expressions of language, and other devices (such as citation practices), that generate and communicate possibilities for further, future development, eg by other legal traditions or other courts. I have discussed some of the potentially relevant literature here in Del Mar (2017c).

[117] See Krisch (2010), ch 5.

[118] See Schauer (1987), 572–3; Waldron (2012); MacCormick (2005), ch 6; and Postema (2004), (2018).

[119] See Del Mar (2015c).

Let me, first, backtrack a little. One of the difficulties with developing a theoretical frame for evaluating the artefacts I discuss in this book, ie fictions, metaphors, figures, and scenarios, is that they do not fit in easily, if at all, into an approach to adjudication that focuses on decision-making in the present case. Indeed, the very dichotomy of justification and discovery makes most sense if one focuses exclusively on the making of an instant decision. The moment one opens this up to the respect a judge may have, for instance, to the law's past, and to the care and concern a judge may have for the law's future, then we begin to notice the need to move beyond that dichotomy and notice all the other processes involved in adjudication. It is especially the latter, ie the care and concern for the law's future, that looms large or that is most absent from a focus on decision-making in the instant case. For those with such a focus will typically be very interested in theorising the relationship between the past and the present, eg by deploying the language of the 'application' of laws to the present facts. Indeed, that very problem, ie the problem of how to understand the relationship of past and present, eg whether or when, if ever, the past is determinate or indeterminate of the present, has arguably been the focus of theoretical efforts.

The difficulty is that such a focus, and such a way of framing the central problem, pushes the question of the future, and thus the future-oriented aspect of inquiry, out of view, or at the very least into the shadowy margins. As noted above, I am not claiming that the future-oriented aspect of legal reasoning has gone entirely un-observed. Far from it: for instance, one can see it appearing in theoretical work under the guise of the ethics of universalisation or universalisability,[120] or the duty and value of law's generality,[121] and abstraction.[122] Nevertheless, to my reading, it remains the case that most discussions of legal reasoning, including common law reasoning, centre on the properties of the language or other features of past statutes and cases (so as to theorise how determinate or indeterminate in meaning they are), and on the activities of interpretation or application of past sources to present facts. And, again, what one risks de-emphasising, if not ignoring, in such a framing is the question of the future.[123]

How, then, does the question of the future arise? Judges, when deciding a present case, are concerned not only with whether or not they are appropriately respecting the past, and also not only on doing justice in the present case, but also on the implications

[120] See, eg, Hare (1952); and MacCormick (2009).

[121] See, eg, Schauer (2009), 24–29.

[122] See, eg, Lucy (2017); and McArthur (2014) on Hume's arguments on 'general laws'.

[123] As Postema also observes, even those theorists who have sought to address legal temporalities, such as Dworkin, have generally focused on the law's past. Dworkin, Postema says, 'directs our attention to law's temporality, but, like many who discuss the role of time in law, he calls attention only to law's apparent obsession with the past, ignoring the law's wider involvement in time's flow': (2018), 161. Interestingly, and in ways that deserve further study, Postema suggests an analogy between music and legal reasoning: 'Like grasping a melody by fitting the present tone-durations into a musical trajectory from past into an anticipated future, it [ie reasoning with law] requires fitting the present meaning of a proposition of law into a temporal trajectory from past into the future where that future involves others – official and civilian alike – who will take present actions and decisions as part of the trajectory of the propositions they seek to understand. This mode of reasoning is not, as many critics suppose, merely retrospective – fixing a future by imposing on it a rule based on inferences from a given past – but rather a matter of fitting the present proposition and its guidance for present action into a future that can and must be anticipated. It is unavoidably path-dependent, but not rigidly path-determined. Rather, law, and its mode of reasoning, is concurrently retrospective and prospective, a matter of appreciating the past and anticipating the future': ibid, 166. See also Postema (2004).

of their past-construing and present-deciding activities on the future. The future here includes both the moral and political quality of the law, as well as the legitimacy and authority of the court, eg its workability, but also in terms of its relations with other institutions and other courts, in its jurisdiction and beyond. Legal reasoning, then, involves projection into the future. Further, this projection is not an afterthought, but very much part of the reasoning process, ie it is part of the process of inquiry, as I am modelling that here.

This projection into the future takes a variety of different forms. A typical one involves judges considering the implications of the proposed justifications offered by rival counsel in the case on future similar cases. Some call this procedure 'testing', and others the process of 'universalising', but however one calls it, this is a process that involves generating hypothetical future cases, some very close but still different to the present case, and some fanciful and exaggerated, in order to tease out just how the proposed justifications would play out in such cases. This process may result in the dismissal of one or indeed both proposed justifications, with a third alternative being crafted, or in the refinement of one or another of the proposed justifications. Here, the future is as it were being put into the service of the present, deployed to improve the quality of the justification of the present decision. But sometimes, scenarios, as I call them in this book, are also offered in obiter, not in order to improve the present justification, but simply as signals to future courts that more work may need to be done on the values, vulnerabilities and interests at stake in this area of the law. This is a complex process, and I will be saying more about it when I consider the value of scenarios in Chapter 8.

There are many ways in which judges project into the future. Thus, for example, a test for whether a warrant is required will be rejected if the court thinks it might lead to the police having, or being seen to have, too great or too arbitrary a power to invade a person's privacy. Or it may be rejected because it might hamstring police work, or simply give no guidance at all, being unworkable in practice either way. Or judges may look into the future to consider the evidentiary implications of a certain decision, eg how, if a certain requirement were to be introduced, eg before breach of duty could be proved, it would be difficult, if not impossible, to prove it or indeed disprove it in practice. Similarly so for other kinds of implications: for instance, in terms of the workload for a court, or for the court's international reputation, or for the legal system's relations with other legal systems, eg indigenous communities or international legal traditions and institutions. The point is that the more one observes what courts do, the more one sees that they often have regard to the future, and in many different ways.

As a number of legal scholars have pointed out, projecting into the future is not easy; it risks being overly speculative, and it may end up losing sight of the pleas of justice in the present case, most especially pleas based on rights.[124] On the other hand, it is, to some extent, unavoidable; it simply is part of what it means to attempt to do justice in a case. The courts, and especially the appellate courts with which this book is concerned, are under a duty to care not only for the parties in the present case, and for the law's past, but also for the moral and political quality of the law in the future, and for the authority and legitimacy of the court and related institutions, again in the future. We cannot and

[124] See, eg, Levi's (1965) reply to Weschler (1959).

should not hide from view the difficulty of this task. Indeed, what I propose is that we foreground that difficulty, and examine the ways that the judges project into the future, often uncertainly and tentatively.

Further, judges do not do this alone and only in one instant case. Instead, as the other aspect of the diachronic dimension above was designed to show, judges communicate to future audiences and thus across time. Mindful of the limitations facing any one judge, eg, in terms of assessing the moral and political quality of the law after this case, a judge will often look for ways to decide the present case while keeping options open as to how best to articulate the law. It is this space of inquiry I am especially interested in, and thus in the experimental, tentative, unfinished and provisional expressions and devices that allow judges to introduce resources, as to whether a law should change, or how it should change, and thereby invite future audiences to assist them in that task. One can also see here the connections between the social and the diachronic dimensions of inquiry: interactive and collective inquiry into the future and over time. It will not surprise the reader to learn that it is there, in that space of inquiry, that the artefacts explored in this book are especially valuable. Fictions, for instance, are precisely ways of coping with the difficulties in articulating a fully principled justification in the present case, deferring that principled justification to a future case, while signalling the need for further thought, and indeed inviting others to work on it together. Similarly so, though in different ways, with respect to metaphors, figures or scenarios.

Writing, recently, about the importance of theorising the relationship between law and time, Postema laments the approach to law's temporalities in twentieth-century jurisprudence.[125] To the extent that the dominant approach to law in the last century was to think of it as a 'system of rules or norms … perhaps fitting together in some manifestly regular and rational system', it is likely that law will be conceived of 'as atemporal'.[126] Hart, for instance, was clearly interested in law's temporality, eg one of the principal reasons for which he criticised Austin's theory was that it could not explain the continuity of law-making power and the persistence of law through time.[127] However, says Postema, Hart 'did not explain how or why some events or actions in a community's past have normative relevance and force over time; rather, he presupposed such an account'.[128] Hart still located 'the normative significance of law in a "momentary legal system", a current time-slice of living law.'[129] This, says Postema, was a mistake: 'momentary legal systems are abstractions from temporally extended, enduring legal systems and get their significance from their place in the temporally extended systems'.[130] Hence, Postema concludes, 'legal theory must take as a primary task explaining the essential temporal character of law'.[131] Throughout this book, I resist talk of essences or natures, but I would agree with the general tenor of Postema's remarks: for too long in legal theory, the temporalities of law have been either ignored or marginalised. Redressing

[125] Postema (2018).
[126] Ibid, 163.
[127] Ibid.
[128] Ibid, 164.
[129] Ibid. See also Raz (1980).
[130] Postema (2018), 164.
[131] Ibid.

the balance is long overdue.[132] I have sought to contribute to that endeavour in a modest way by modelling inquiry in adjudication diachronically.

IV. Experimental

Let me summarise where we are. We have made room for a model that goes beyond, but overlaps with, the contexts of discovery and justification. This is a space for what I am calling a model of inquiry. We have also added two dimensions to the model of inquiry: namely, social and diachronic dimensions. Under the social dimension, we included two aspects: interactive and communal. Under the diachronic, we also had two aspects: inquiry not only in real time but also over time, and inquiry in the sense of balancing multiple temporal orientations, with an emphasis, given its relative neglect in the theoretical literature, on the future. I now wish to add a third dimension: the experimental. In adding this dimension, I wish to focus on the mental attitudes, and the tones and styles of expression, that enable and sustain inquiry. As with all the dimensions of inquiry sketched in this chapter, some of what I say in this section will overlap with other points I will be making on artefacts and imagination in the second and third chapters, respectively, as well as, more concretely, in the second part of the book. Nevertheless, the experimental dimension is important enough to risk repetition.

I have already had occasion to question the focus of some theorists of adjudication on the making of decisions in instant cases. Making a decision in a single case is of course important. Many theorists have stressed the 'heteronomy of law', the sense in which it impinges on our autonomy, and the sense in which it is needed sometimes to draw arbitrary lines in the shifting sands of disagreement in a community.[133] This is undoubtedly important, but it is just one of many functions of law and one of the many activities engaged in adjudication. As we saw above, when we stretch out the time of inquiry, and come to focus more on legal change, we also begin to notice forms of expression, as well as techniques and technologies, that do not fit under the rubric of decision-making in the instant case. Instead, they make sense, and can be seen as valuable, as modes of communication over time.

What are the mental attitudes, and the tones and styles, of these modes of communication? One way to get at them is to contrast them with what we expect to see under the rubric of decision-making: assertive propositions, a tone of inevitability, a style that admits of no doubt but is instead bursting with confidence and authority. If one's exclusive focus is on decision-making, one might well point precisely to such features: eg to the need for clarity, transparency, and sincerity in reason-giving, or to the virtues of articulating 'bright-line rules', precise formulas and doctrines, and expansive principles, and one might well praise visionary judges who work hard to achieve that assertive clarity, that air of inevitability, that scope and range of vision. One might, of course, just as well see the same inevitability and brashness, but approach it with scepticism: as a show

[132] See also the important recent work on legal temporalities, see, eg, Chowdhury (2017) and (Forthcoming); Grabham (2016); and the essays in Beynon-Jones and Grabham (2018).

[133] See, eg, MacCormick (1995).

or display, which either masks the real reasons or causes for decisions or hides what is an underlying and inescapable uncertainty.[134]

Sometimes, these points are made in a more conciliatory way, ie as a matter of differing styles amongst judges of different temperament, or in different ages where different styles reign supreme. Thus, famously, Benjamin Cardozo in his lecture on 'Law and Literature',[135] argued that one could find six different types or styles of judgements:

> … magisterial or imperative; laconic or sententious; conversational or homely; refined or artificial, smelling of the lamp, verging at times upon preciosity or euphuism; demonstrative or persuasive; tonsorial or agglutinative, so called from the shears and the pastepot which are its implements and emblem.[136]

Cardozo appeared to suggest that the tide, at the time of his lecture in 1925, was changing away from the magisterial or imperative, and towards something more, shall we say experimental. Indeed, this was a term that Cardozo himself used, referring both to the Constitution, and to 'all life' as 'an experiment': 'Every year', he added, 'we have to wager our salvation upon some prophecy based upon imperfect knowledge.'[137] Taking precisely the long view, ie the view of inquiry over time, Cardozo explained that 'The development of law is conceived of, more and more, as a process of adaptation and adjustment. The pronouncements of its ministers are timid and tentative approximations, to be judged through their workings, by some pragmatic test of truth.'[138] At least that is where his own preferences seemed to lie: in the 'tentative gropings towards the inductive apprehension of a truth imperfectly discerned.'[139] 'We grope and feel our way', said Cardozo; 'What we hand down in our judgements is an hypothesis.'[140] Preference though it may have been, it also read as an apology, almost a confession of failure. 'Most of us', Cardozo wrote, 'are so uncertain of our strength, so beset with doubts and difficulties, that we feel oppressed with the need of justifying every holding by analogies and precedents and an exposure of the reasons.'[141]

What if, however, we did not see these 'tentative gropings towards the inductive apprehension of a truth imperfectly discerned' as failures and vices, but instead very much as successes and virtues? To do this, we need to move away from an ideal of adjudication and reasoning that posits an all-knowing individual, a hero, with his monological confidence, his decisiveness and assertiveness. We need to replace the alpha male, Judge

[134] For an interesting discussion of inevitability, see Brooks (2003). Brooks employs the concept of 'retrospective prophecy', which he associates with the 'demonstration of inevitability: it had to be this way, and no other way': (2003), 87. Retrospective prophecy, he says, 'perfectly characterises the constitutional narratives written by the Supreme Court, and perhaps indeed most legal narrative in general. It is a prophetic narrative cast in the backward mode, implicitly arguing that the ruling in the case at hand is the fulfilment of what was called for at the beginning': (2003), 99. Brooks identifies here an important judicial style and device, and it may be that he is right to say it characterises 'most legal narratives in general'. My point is to suggest that in addition to such styles and devices of inevitability, one can also find, at least in common law judgements, evidence of experimentalism.

[135] Cardozo (1925).

[136] Ibid, 702.

[137] Ibid, 709.

[138] Ibid, 705.

[139] Ibid, 703.

[140] Ibid, 706.

[141] Ibid.

Hercules, with an ideal of an inquiry that is interactive and collective, ie a deeply social and collaborative, though also agonistic, activity, and one that is typically stretched out over time, and that thus takes time and requires time. As soon as we do this, very different mental attitudes and tones and styles of expression not only come into view but also emerge as alternative standards and ideals. Indeed, we may then begin to see 'tentative gropings' or 'timid and tentative approximations' not as failures, and not as matters to be avoided if only it were possible, but as precisely what is called for, what enables rather than obstructs inquiry.

As feminist scholars have pointed out, the very male ideal of the individual reasoner, with an untrammelled will, independent and confident, casts a long shadow over the theory of adjudication (and much else besides). For a long time, much too long a time, it has set the standards of what counts as good legal reasoning or adjudication at its best.[142] We need, then, a different language, with different tones and styles of expression, and a different set of mental attitudes, which we can hold up as a standard. 'Experiment' is one possible label for this. Experiment, of course, also has its own baggage, and may itself be associated either with a Whiggish story of incremental improvement and gradual progress, or with that of a lone scientific genius, fiddling and testing until he can run through the streets shouting 'Eureka'.[143] A different kind of 'experimentalism' needs to be resuscitated, with a different genealogy and tradition, one that is more playful, more self-reflexive, and more social. I shall not have the time and space here to develop such a different story in full, but in what follows I offer a glimpse into some places that we could look. In doing so, I hope to convey a sense of the experimental dimension of inquiry.

A. Experimental Science

In her recent book on *The Experimental Imagination*, Tito Chico says that for her, the 'term experiment draws on its two predominant meanings as connoting experience and as tentative.'[144] Drawing on a range of figures, from Samuel Johnson to Michel de Montaigne, and up to Ian Hacking, Chico emphasises experiment as an action, a kind of doing, a trial or an 'essai', a trying out.[145] The focus in Chico's book is on the positive contribution of experiment, not on its lack, or how it falls short of something. Further, for Chico, experimenting is 'likewise a discursive, rhetorical mode, an act of imaginative work tied to the protocols of genre and, more broadly, a sense of literariness.'[146] Thus, in her book, which focuses on science and scientific practice, Chico seeks to bring out the

142 See Conaghan (2003), and the feminist judgements project, eg Hunter, McGlynn, Rackley (2010).

143 There is a fascinating history of 'experiment', and associated genres, such as the *experimentum*, within the history of science: see, eg, Daston (2011). Some of this history has a great deal of overlap with legal history, see, eg, Pomata (2011). It would be exciting to inquire into this overlap further, perhaps initially via certain key figures in this story, eg Sir Francis Bacon. Some of the most relevant historical parallels here are between legal and medical cognition, expression and practice: see, eg, MacLean (2002). On the relation between medical and legal reasoning generally, see also Samuel (2015).

144 Chico (2018), 3.

145 Ibid, 3.

146 Ibid.

literariness of that practice, not as an optional add-on, and not as a failure which might bring about success, and thus not only a means to a greater end, but as the very character and animating spirit of scientific practice.

Throughout Chico's book, the focus is on the doing and experiencing of this 'literariness' as a form of action and interaction. Thus, for example, in pointing to the role and value of figurative language in scientific practice, Chico seeks to recall the etymology of 'trope' as something that 'conveys motion; it embodies a turning.'[147] In 'troping', we might say, we make 'connections and relations that may or may not be "proper" to the original object", and, in doing so, we make meaning.'[148] Experimenting, then, is itself a form of making. It is not an inadequate and unfortunately necessary means on the way to something being made, but is, in itself, a form of making, doing, acting, and interacting. 'Literariness', Chico says, 'is itself a form of making.'[149]

This literariness of experiment in science is one place to look in developing an alternative genealogy of experimentalism. Thanks to it, we can pay attention to the poetic character of inquiry, and to its character as a mode of making, especially making together. It is no surprise that, under this approach, 'tentativeness' plays such a prominent role, but not one born out of fear or inadequacy, but more so out of care and the delicacy of the task. It is out of respect for the difficulty of what is to be done, eg the difficulty of making a law with moral and political quality, and to a recognition that such difficulty may never be overcome, that it must always remain difficult, that one proceeds tentatively, trying out different possibilities, generating ever more perspectives, leaving room for and inviting others to suggest alternatives.

B. Sophistry

The other place where we might look for an alternative genealogy of experimentalism is the neglected, and often mocked and derided, tradition of sophistry. As characterised by Plato, the sophists were money-hungry opportunists, relativists with no moral compass, mere peddlers in language games, rootless, un-disciplined showmen with no epistemic credentials. On this view, they were deceitful tricksters, who amassed fortunes by exploiting young and weak audiences susceptible to their silver tongues, their flowery, mindless and irresponsible rhetoric. They needed to be replaced by those who had real insight and real knowledge, which was built on unshakeable foundations and unchanging truths. These were, of course, those schooled in the Platonic academy, the masters in Platonic metaphysics, the philosopher kings.

The sophists never really recovered from the direct attack on their character and practices by Plato. This is deeply unfortunate, for the sophists could be understood to have been precisely purveyors of the arts of experiment. This was so in ways that were thoroughly playful and social, and that were, moreover, modes of making as well as knowing. Their politics, too, deserves more attention: one has to remember, for instance, that they charged fees because they had to earn their living, and were not born, as Plato

[147] Ibid, 10.
[148] Ibid.
[149] Ibid, 5.

was born, into elite aristocratic families; and that their education of the young, including again non-aristocratic, non-elite youth, honing their abilities to argue for contrary positions, was a contribution to the vibrancy and vitality of democracy in this period of Greek history. No wonder they were seen as threats to a social order to be governed, ideally, by aristocratic philosopher kings.

As Susan Jarratt has argued – seeking, in particular, to show the relations between sophistry and contemporary feminism – the sophists practiced a form of knowing that was rhetorical, 'a mode of reasoning and decision-making which allows humans to act in the absence of certain, a priori truth.'[150] The crucial point is that sophistic practices are not an absence of knowing, or something one might learn on the way to learning to be a knower, emerging from out of the darkness, as in Plato's imagery, and ascending into the heaven of concepts. Sophistic practices *are* knowledge practices, but they rest on an understanding of 'knowledge and values as historically contingent.'[151] Where philosophy emphasised the eternal and the universal, sophistry emphasised the temporal and contingent. Various domains of sophistic practice contained their own kinds of devices, ie their own distinctive ways of doing, or we might say, experimenting.

One of Jarratt's most fascinating examples is that of sophistic historiography. Jarratt shows how the sophists, in their 'denial of progressive continuity', ie in the 'conscious attempt' they made 'to disrupt the metaphor of a complete and full chain of events with a telos', deployed the rhetorical tools of antithesis and parataxis.[152] Antithesis, which involved 'playfully pairing opposite words', created 'an openness to the multiplicity of possible causal relations';[153] while parataxis, which consisted in a 'loose association of clauses without hierarchical connectives or embedding',[154] enabled the 'employment of probable arguments in the reconstitution of provisional historical narratives'.[155] The sophists deployed these ways of making, these modes of experimentation, in their re-telling, their re-fashioning, and indeed their re-making of historical myths or events, eg as in the 'Encomium of Helen' by Gorgias. As Jarratt shows, in his speech, Gorgias 'puts into play a quartet of possible causes for the abduction [of Helen], any two of which could be set up as an antithesis'; he 'does not exclude three causes in favour of one … but focuses the discussion on the interplay among the causes.'[156]

For Jarratt, sophistic historiography was both a mode of experimenting and a way of knowing. Making and knowing are not a matter of excluding possibilities in favour of one, going on to make it seem inevitable, and establishing it as canonical or foundational. On the contrary, it is a matter of generating possibilities, of playing with options; it is an art of knowing that is deeply self-reflexive, but also social, for it invites others to engage in activities of self-reflexive evaluation, eg who is to blame for the abduction of Helen. As Jarratt puts it:

> A sophistic method works by exposing and exploring a range of possibilities for knowledge and action and implicitly theorising the process of their acceptance by the community less

[150] Jarratt (1991), 8.
[151] Ibid, xix.
[152] Ibid, 11–12.
[153] Ibid, 21.
[154] Ibid, 24.
[155] Ibid, 21.
[156] Ibid, 22.

> on the basis of logical validity and more on the force of their 'rhetorical', persuasive and aesthetic, appeal. Rearrangement is revaluation.[157]

This self-reflexive complexification of history has a deep political value. As Jarratt says: 'Laying out a number of causes for a past event in a quasi-literary form is taken as the occasion for exploring issues of vital importance for the present and future of the individual in the polis and for the state itself.'[158] Part of the point is that there is no way of overcoming this state of uncertainty, this experience of possibilities; there is no ultimate further end of enlightenment. The caves, it turns out, are inhabited not by the sophists but by the philosophers, who cannot bear the glare of reality, with all its roughness, its multiplicities, its potentials that cannot be quite controlled by some unquestionable schema. Here, in the rough ground, one must practice a different art: a more subjunctive and experimental one. If one seeks certainty, decisiveness, or assertiveness, then one must descend down into the cave, where one can isolate oneself from the activities of re-telling and re-making.

Sophistry, then, especially in the interpretation of feminist scholars like Jarratt, may be one tradition we could turn to recover an alternative, and largely lost genealogy of experimentation.

C. The Genre of Dialogue

In addition to a certain literary approach to the practice of science, and the sophists, there is another source of the experimental tradition: the theory and practice of the genre of dialogue.

As Virginia Cox has shown, in the early Italian Renaissance,[159] the dialogue was a 'means for exploring truth', designed as a self-reflexive provocation to the reader.[160] At its most experimental, the Renaissance dialogue disoriented the reader with initial positions being questioned from multiple angles, and called upon the reader to exercise active judgement. This was even more so when, as was common with Italian Renaissance dialogues, what was at stake was how one should behave as a courtier. The dialogue, in this respect, was not a set of rules about how one should behave, but instead a series of conversations which brought to light the kinds of difficulties one might experience as a courtier, again calling on the reader to exercise active judgement as to how best to behave. As Cox puts it, 'The dialogue was conceived by the humanists as a provocation to the reader: a form of argumentation which deliberately eschewed the self-sufficiency of the treatise, and actively challenged its readers and critics to pursue the quest it had begun.'[161]

As with the two other sources mentioned above, there is an intimate relation here between experimentalism and activity: experimental forms or genres are experimental in part because of how they remain unfinished, requiring the active collaboration of the

[157] Ibid, 28.
[158] Ibid, 59.
[159] Cox (1992). See also, for the English context, Wilson (1995).
[160] Cox (1992), 68.
[161] Ibid, xiii.

reader or listener. There are different traditions of dialogue, eg Lucianic, Platonic, and Ciceronian, and it is interesting that the ones that Cox identifies as most experimental, eg the most loosely conversational, are also often the ones that wear their fictionality on their sleeves. This is so, for instance, with Lucian's rather informal, fantastic dialogues, with 'speaking animals, abstractions and personifications, sea-gods, nymphs, and the dead',[162] contrasted with the more sober, formal, authoritarian dialogues of Cicero.[163] The key differences concern how the reader is positioned, which Cox explains, interestingly, by reference to an analogy with legal proceedings:[164]

> Some dialogues … like treatises, place their readers in the position of 'scolari', diligently absorbing their master's words, without making any contribution of their own. Another type of dialogue exists, however: a court case conducted in the absence of a judge, where the reader takes on a far more challenging, arbitrational role.[165]

In these latter dialogues, 'the reader is forced [I would prefer to say, 'called upon'] to weigh the speakers' opinions for himself'.[166] Again, this is very unlike a treatise: 'A treatise casts its writer and reader in the role of master and pupil. In the dialogue [or at least some forms of it], on the other hand, their relationship is more like that of a pair of hunting companions, sharing equally in the excitement, the fatigue and the glory of the chase'.[167] Of course, one might say that the treatise is a written form, and the dialogue is oral; this is true, and I shall return to this point in a moment, but one can then also contrast the experimental dialogue with, say, the much more didactic, monological oral forms of the lecture or the sermon.[168] Indeed, the dialogue form, especially in the way it invites the reader's activity, expresses 'profound unease with the epistemological assumptions which inform conventional didactic modes'.[169] Again, rather than teaching from a position of authority, the aim was to 'unfold', before the reader, 'a dialogue between conflicting perspectives, to sharpen their sense of the issues involved and open a space for the exercise of their own moral judgement'.[170] The experimental dialogue remains unfinished; there is, in it, a kind of 'calculated irresolution'; it showcases a 'shared fund of epistemological wariness'.[171]

[162] Ibid, 11.

[163] As Cox further observes: 'Where the Greek dialogue most typically takes the form of a causal conversation, struck up on a street-corner between strangers or passing acquaintances, the Roman dialogue is a far more exclusive affair, frequently set in a patrician villa' and involves 'the gathering of a chosen few': ibid, 13. In the Ciceronian dialogue, the speaker is usually someone of 'a relatively high social status', close attention is paid to 'historical accuracy', and there is 'an overwhelming concern with decorum': ibid, 14.

[164] This is perhaps not accidental because, in order to be properly understood as an epistemic genre and practice, the dialogue needs to be placed in the longer tradition of cultures of disputation, of the in utrumque partem, of agonism. As Cox observes, underlying the practice of dialogue was the humanist belief 'in the possibility of reaching truth – a human and collective truth – by means of disputation. Within the fictional exchange of the dialogue, rhetorical discussion is used as an instrument in the search for truth on moral issues and, outside this fiction, the dialogue itself is conceived of as a *provocatio*, spurring the learned reader on to join the continuing question': ibid, 62. For more on the dialogue in this vein, see Marsh (1980). For a fascinating cultural history of disputation in the Medieval period, see Novikoff (2013).

[165] Cox (1992), 3.

[166] Ibid, 4.

[167] Ibid, 44.

[168] Ibid.

[169] Ibid, 48.

[170] Ibid, 54.

[171] Ibid, 65.

For all its self-reflexivity, however, the early Italian Renaissance dialogue was still, in its own way, mimetic, imitating the dynamics of everyday, informal conversation. Cox refers to this style of dialogue as 'dramatic', and says that in these dialogues, 'Poetic elements like character and setting, rather than mere ornaments, become constitutive elements in any meanings which might be seen to emerge'.[172] Much like artefacts in general (as I will model the term in the next chapter) these kinds of dialogues mesh mimetic immersion with self-reflexivity: they contain poetic elements which both draw us in to the dialogue, as if we ourselves were participants in the conversation,[173] while also reminding us that the dialogue is being staged. Cox says that these 'dramatic' dialogues were 'self-consciously embodying a conception of the relation between language, social practice and cognition';[174] they explicitly 'staged the act of communication'.[175] At the same time, they drew their readers in, making them feel as if they were present at the scene of the conversation.

For Cox, this art of the dramatic, experimental dialogue was short-lived, indeed all too short-lived. Soon, and towards the late sixteenth century in Italy, the dialogue tended 'increasingly to portray a dialectical argument, which proceeds systematically through the stages of definition and division to an unequivocal conclusion'.[176] It began to take a much more didactic form, in which the learning process consists of a 'transfer of knowledge from a greater vessel to a lesser'.[177] It came to be associated not with 'conversation, decorum, opinion' but with 'doctrine, authority'.[178] It showed an 'increasing preoccupation with system, method, and order.'[179] Cox expresses the contrast in this way:

> An ordered argument … implies the presence of an ordering intellect: an intellect, moreover which, at the moment of writing, is in full possession of all its stages and assured of its conclusion. The impression of simultaneity essential to the workings of the open dialogue is utterly negated by a structure which refers the reader to that frozen moment … when the writer puts pen to paper. A truly open dialogue … is the product of 'diverse lingue' and 'vari intelletti', including, crucially, that of the reader, the new occupant of the vacuum created by the author's self-annihilation. In the ordered dialogue, on the other hand, the presence of a pre-ordained and immutable structure, which announces its autonomy from the contingencies of its fiction, has the effect of closing the dialogue to any intervention by its reader, and reducing their role to the passive one of the reader of a treatise.[180]

The playful epistemology of the 'open' dialogue, with its collective, interactive, and generative experience of doubt and uncertainty, comes to be replaced with a very different attitude, with an emphasis on authority and dogma, and accompanied by very different forms, eg the tone and style of the treatise, or with the 'closed' dialogue.

[172] Ibid, 3.
[173] Indeed, this was part of the politics of the early Italian Renaissance dialogue: readers of these dialogues felt they were members of a select and polite society.
[174] Cox (1992), 6.
[175] Ibid, 7.
[176] Ibid, 89.
[177] Ibid, 94.
[178] Ibid, 93.
[179] Ibid, 99.
[180] Ibid, 102.

For Cox, drawing in this respect on the scholarship of Walter Ong, part of the reason for this transformation, which shows also the fragile experimentalism of any genre, including the dialogue, was the increasing reliance on print, and the technology of writing rather than the art of orality. Where the culture of orality was stronger, one saw more rhetorical techniques like the *exemplum*[181] and analogy, and a general 'conception of intellectual activity as essentially discursive',[182] and, crucially, also as essentially social, conversational, and dialogical. Where the culture of writing, or the book, became stronger, then this 'brought with it new tendencies towards an impersonal, authoritative discourse'.[183] The book, partly 'by virtue of its physical completeness', ie something whole one could hold or see at one time, produced an 'illusion of finality', ie something with 'a fixed authorial viewpoint, which readers may accept or refuse, but whose remoteness and self-sufficiency they cannot realistically challenge'.[184] Furthermore, the book, together with other devices, eg diagrams, minimised, if it did not exclude, fictionality, ie that self-reflexive quality which was so important to the experimental, dramatic dialogue.[185] The increasing dominance of print, it seems, made it all the harder to both fictionally stage conversation, and, at the same time, maintain its life-likeness, ie, 'the inconclusiveness, the false starts, the dead ends, the sheer messiness which characterise conversation in its natural sphere'.[186] Of course, we cannot be too harsh, and too cynical about, print and the book form, for, tellingly, in this medium we also come to see the rise of experimental forms, eg the essay.[187] Nevertheless, Cox surely does have a point that something of the interactive dynamics are lost when the experimental, dramatic dialogue is replaced with genres like the treatise or the textbook. Perhaps some of that experimental quality, which is, at once, much more social, is recaptured by what I am calling the artefactual quality of language, with its related processes of imagination.

D. The Ethics of Collaborative Ambivalence

In all the above three sources of a potential alternative genealogy of experimentalism, ie the literary practice of science, sophistic historiography, and the Renaissance dialogue, experimentation is not failure or vice, or a practice lacking in some requisite status of knowledge, logic or reasoning, but is itself a rich, resourceful, mode of making, knowing and reasoning. This is a tentative mode, but not with an air of embarrassment and shame. This is not a mode that is exercised under the shadow of some fully formed belief, as if everything else that falls below it lacks maturity. Instead, it is what I have been calling inquiry: a deeply social activity, which occurs both in real time and especially over time, and which, we can now add, is experimental in its tone, style and attitude.

[181] For more on the *exemplum* as a genre, see Scanlon (2007).
[182] Cox (1992), 103.
[183] Ibid, 105.
[184] Ibid.
[185] Ibid.
[186] Ibid, 110.
[187] Ibid, 113.

What we need to be looking out for, then, under the dimension of the experimental, are modes of tentative generation of possibilities, highly self-reflexive ways of making, modes of re-telling, techniques and technologies for moving and turning, for creating alternative framings and perspectives.

An interesting list of candidates of such experimental forms and modes are the following suggestions from Amélie Rorty, who mentions them, surely not without accident, as activities that may enable an 'ethics of collaborative ambivalence', and who also uses the language of 'experiment':

> They involve routines and techniques used in exploring, extending and revising the range of possible options. A random list of such imaginative thought experiments includes varying variables to construct hypothetical or counterfactual examples, drawing on analogies and metaphors, extending possible affordances of events and situations, redescribing, enlarging or narrowing the scope or context of choice, changing distinctive agent perspectives, pretending, free associating, simulating, and role playing, projecting empathic identification, changing the criteria for relevance in decision making, applying idealised models to non-ideal conditions (or vice-versa), revising standard interpretations of polarising distinctions and categories, reifying and deconstructing reifications, etc.[188]

It will not surprise the reader to learn that I shall be suggesting that, as I model them here, artefacts and related processes of imagining feel welcome in such company, and that the four case studies developed in the second part of this book, ie fictions, metaphors, figures, and scenarios, at least when used well, are exemplars of what enable inquiry, given its experimental character. In future work, however, we may wish to cast the net much more widely, capturing more varieties of calculated irresolution in legal thought, more of the generative work of doubt and provisionality, more of the ways in which we make room for the multi-vocal, dialogical modes of cognition. We may see evidence of this in a whole range of different forms, styles and genres of thought and expression: in indirectness, hinting, suggesting, connecting tentatively with open-ended citation, and with uses of language that point to and foreground, as if celebrating, their own ambiguity.[189]

V. Normative

We have reached the final dimension of the model of inquiry. So far, the emphasis has been on the processes of inquiry, and I have emphasised its social, diachronic and experimental character. But what, one might ask, is the object of inquiry? What is it in the service of? Here, is where we need to turn to what I am calling the normative dimension of inquiry, ie that the objects of inquiry, as modelled here, are the values, vulnerabilities and interests that might be at stake in a case and in cases potentially like it in the future. One can see, already in that formulation, the link with other dimensions of inquiry, eg the 'might' is crucial, and refers to the experimental dimension, while the

[188] Rorty (2014), 400.

[189] For a recent history of ambiguity, see Ossa-Richardson (2019).

reference to 'cases potentially like it in the future' points to the diachronic dimension, and especially to its future-oriented aspect. This is to be expected, for we are touching the same elephant just in different places.

I proceed in four steps. First, I reflect on the very term 'normative', and consider how this dimension of inquiry sits with the debate over the relationship between moral and legal reasoning. Second, I turn to the three objects referred to above, namely, values, vulnerabilities and interests. Third, and related to the second step, I consider what access we have, ie how we sense or discern, these values, vulnerabilities and interests. And fourth, I return to all the dimensions of inquiry together, and articulate why inquiry is so important to adjudication. We will thereby reach one of the central questions this book is trying to both ask and answer: how can persons engage in inquiry? What enables them to do so, and how can they do it well? Or, more elaborately: what assists persons to engage, and to engage well, in socially, diachronically, experimentally sensing what values, vulnerabilities and interests might matter in a case and in cases potentially like it in the future?

A. Legal and Moral Reasoning

I choose the term 'normative', as in the normative dimension of inquiry, to signal that I see inquiry in adjudication as closely related to, but not quite the same as, moral reasoning. Of course, the character of 'moral reasoning' is itself a complex, hotly contested topic. But even taking a very broad view of moral reasoning into account, eg one that attempts to remain neutral on debates such as those between generalists and particularists, or as between those with Aristotelian, virtue- or perception-based views, and those more sympathetic to Kant and more rule-based accounts of practical reason, or any number of positions in between,[190] there still remain some important differences between moral reasoning and what I am calling inquiry in adjudication.

On the one hand, I wish to respect the idea that judges are tasked with doing justice, and this not just in the instant case, but also in relation to the law's past as well as its future. This suggests that, outside of exaggerated disagreements between positivists and natural lawyers, it is not helpful to draw rigid distinctions between moral reasoning and reasoning in legal contexts.[191] On the other hand, and as I shall elaborate on in a moment, the way I model inquiry is somewhat at odds with many of the ways that the problems and issues of moral reasoning are framed. It would be surprising if it were otherwise, ie if the institutional context of adjudication did not at all affect the character and standards of the exercise of reasoning in adjudication. It is, in part, in order to balance these considerations that I prefer to speak of the 'normative' rather than 'moral' dimension of inquiry.

[190] In terms of positions in between, see, eg, MacCormick (2009) and Herman (1993).

[191] On the exaggeration of disagreements between positivists and natural lawyers, at least in the context of the law of nations, see Waldron (2011). In general, throughout this book, I have avoided the terminology of positivism and natural law. This is not only because there are so many varieties, including different histories, of these terms, but also because reference to them carries the danger of unnecessary and unhelpful polarisation of the issues and their debate.

Without wishing to enter exegetical questions, and being especially concerned not to caricature any theoretical views, it may be possible to say that the approach I am advocating is in the vicinity of natural law and interpretivism. Like the adherents of these views, the approach I am pursuing recognises the very close relationship between moral and legal reasoning.

Nevertheless, there are also differences. One of these differences is a matter of tone: the account presented here does not claim as much moral status as natural law or interpretivist theories sometimes, at least to my ears, claim. For instance, I do not think it is helpful to approach the exercise of adjudication from the perspective of a position that allegedly has unproblematic access to the morally correct answer, or the objectively right answer. Human beings, including theorists evaluating the work of judges, are simply too limited in their knowledge and capacities to claim such access. This does not mean that there are not morally better and worse responses to particular situations, or better and worse ways to reason in such situations. My approach is not that of a sceptic, relativist or anarchist. Instead, my approach is to foreground the difficulty of doing justice, and thus to think of the process as an on-going activity, one which we engage in together, ie interactively and collectively, and over time, and one which we never be wholly satisfied with, nor ever complete or finish. Nevertheless, this is still a process that we ought to engage in, and one that we can do more or less well. We have a duty to engage in the task of doing justice, of working to improve the moral and political quality of the law, while being mindful that this is not something we can ever really claim to have achieved. Further, our task is never satisfied, not on any one occasion or at any end point, but that does not mean we can give up and not do it.[192]

There are other reasons, too, for not situating inquiry in adjudication in the same frame, within the same problem space, as moral reasoning. One important reason is that often, the problem space set up for moral reasoning is that of an individual making a decision in certain given circumstances, ie deciding how they ought to act in a particular situation before them. In addition, the situation facing the moral decision-maker is often presented as involving a choice between two options. I am not denying that individuals are sometimes faced with decisions of this kind, and it may well be that some of the qualities of moral reasoning can only be captured by setting up the problem space of moral reasoning in this way. However, there seem to me to be important differences between this way of setting up the problem space of moral reasoning and the practice of inquiry in adjudication.

[192] Partly for these reasons, and partly because I think there are distinct characteristics of, and pressures on, the operation of legal reasoning in the institutional context of adjudication (for instance, the sense in which legal reasoning needs to balance past-present-and-future-oriented considerations), I resist characterising, as Dworkin did in his later work (2011), legal reasoning as a branch of moral reasoning. Another reason for resisting the image of legal reasoning as a branch of moral reasoning is that it can hide from view the insight that moral reasoning is itself influenced by, and constrained by, law: see, eg, Honoré (1993). I recognise that the issues here are considerably more complex than I can address. My principal aim in mentioning them is to exercise caution and be mindful of the institutional particularities of the law; hence the inclination to speak of the normative, rather than moral, dimension of inquiry. None of this is meant to downplay or occlude the many rich and complex inter-relations and extensive overlap between legal and moral reasoning (see, eg, Allan (2018)); on the contrary, I hope this book contributes, however modestly, to the investigation of those inter-relations.

The process of inquiry in adjudication is much more complex than the image of an individual making a decision between two paths: it involves multiple persons, who are members of a community and an institution, ie the court, with its own network of relations with other institutions, engaged in an activity of doing justice over time, and balancing past-oriented, present-oriented and future-oriented concerns. Further, although a judge, or a panel of judges, may well be presented with two options, by counsel for the two opposing sides, they are not limited to choosing those options, but may well craft other ones, including compromises between them. And, again, although the making of decisions, and justifying them, is a very important part of adjudication, that is not all there is too it: a good deal of adjudication involves communication with future audiences, including generating potentially relevant resources for dealing with the general questions raised by a case in the future. This process of communication is simply not one that is captured by a theoretical frame that is focused on an individual making a decision in certain given circumstances.

Of course, moral theorists have themselves grappled with the limitations of a model of moral reasoning that situates a lone individual in the position of decision and choice. Iris Murdoch and Elizabeth Anscombe both spoke of the importance of not limiting our understanding of moral life to the instant of making a moral decision.[193] They spoke, and others since them, eg Lawrence Blum, some virtue theorists, some particularists and situationists, some feminist care theorists, eg Margaret Olivia Little, of the importance of our long-term cares and dispositions, as well as of an ability or capacity for situational responsiveness, which it is not quite possible to capture on the basis of a rule-governed faculty of decision-making. Blum, for instance, asks: 'How do agents come to perceive situations in the way they do? How does a situation come to have a particular character for a particular moral agent?'[194]

Questions like this point to the need for a more diachronically rich approach to moral agency. They reveal that a broader perspective is required: one that takes into account our moral life over time, including the capacity for certain languages and certain forms of life, including institutional habits, to make us blind or less sensitive to certain values, vulnerabilities and interests. Many of these theorists have also spoken of the irreducible difficulty of moral life, including the difficulty of exercising that situational responsiveness, or the ability to sense that a certain situation requires moral reflection and action, and an ability to sense which aspects of that situation are of moral significance. Little, for instance, says that 'awareness of the morally relevant features of a situation is no easy or automatic matter.'[195] Her examples of what is 'really involved in seeing what is morally relevant' also give a sense of just how difficult such awareness can be:

> Often it means noticing what is not present: noticing that a student is not in class; spotting in a busy crowd that a child, though surrounded with adults, is not accompanied by any of them. Or again, noticing subtle patterns: that a patient asks for more pain medication on the nights after she has had a visit from her husband. Or again, noticing what is so pervasive that it tends to be invisible.[196]

[193] See Murdoch (1956) and (1970); and Anscombe (1958).
[194] Blum (1991), 701.
[195] Little (1995), 121.
[196] Ibid.

These are important lessons, and hugely important correctives to approaches to moral agency that focus on the individual exercising their independent will to choose an option. I am very drawn to these theories, precisely because they do not focus solely on an individual making a decision, and because they do not hide away the difficulties of moral life. They pick up on, in much more sophisticated ways than the decision-focused theories, on the kinds of tasks and difficulties experienced by judges in adjudication. And, indeed, some legal theorists have sought to extend these moral theories to adjudication.[197] There is much to learn from them, and nothing that I say here is intended as a critique of them.

Nevertheless, there is one difference between the way I am modelling inquiry and the way even these theories tend to frame moral reasoning. Given the above section on the diachronic dimension of inquiry, the difference will by now be familiar: it refers to one of the particularities of exercising inquiry in the context of adjudication, namely its multi-temporal, and especially future-oriented, aspect. In adjudication, and keeping in mind that I am focusing on contemporary English appellate-level courts, the task of doing justice involves respecting the law's past and caring for its future, including its moral and political quality, and the authority and legitimacy of the law's institutions. Arguably, even the above moral theories to which I am deeply drawn, do not foreground this multi-temporal, and especially future-oriented aspects of adjudication. To repeat, this is not to deny the relevance of these theories of moral reasoning for anyone interested in adjudication. Quite the contrary: there is much of vital importance in these theories for any theory of adjudication. But I think there is also enough of a difference between moral reasoning, at least as framed by the above moral theories, and the practice of inquiry in adjudication, that I prefer to speak not of the 'moral' dimension of inquiry, but instead of its 'normative' dimension.

B. Values, Vulnerabilities and Interests

We have passed, even if much too quickly, the first step in this section, ie to see the overlaps, but also some of the differences, between what I am calling the 'normative' dimension of inquiry, and theories of 'moral reasoning'. But how exactly is this dimension 'normative'? What are the specific objects of inquiry, and in what sense are they 'normative' objects? That is the second step I now turn to.

The normative objects of inquiry are values, vulnerabilities and interests. I do not mean to use these terms in too technical a manner: the objects of inquiry can be multiple, and there is, in any event, considerable disagreement on how to taxonomise the normative, including whether one can or should appeal to any one foundational concept of the normative. One might, for instance, speak of the differences between norms and values, or between conventions (still conceived of as normative) and norms, and one might attempt to reduce the variety of the normative to some allegedly foundational normative phenomenon, eg harm or suffering, or one might employ a rich and fine-grained range of normative phenomena. My approach is halfway between these: I do

[197] See, eg, Michelon (2012) and (2018); van Domselaar (2020); and see also Del Mar (2014).

not think it is helpful to attempt to reduce the normative objects of inquiry to any one foundational object, but nor do I wish to introduce any rigid or extensive taxonomy for what normative objects can be discerned. The trifecta offered here of 'values, vulnerabilities and interests' introduces some distinctions, but these are meant to be rough, and again, not exhaustive of the possible normative objects of inquiry.

As I use the terms, both interests and vulnerabilities refer to individual or group level normative phenomena and are applicable not only to humans but to any form of life. Values, on the other hand, are meant to capture normative phenomena that are less anchored in an individual or group, and are often more abstract, such as solidarity, and cultural, religious or linguistic diversity, or appertaining to institutions and relations between them, eg the authority and legitimacy of a court, or concerning the quality of relations between courts and legislatures or between courts of different jurisdictions. That is the first difference: from a certain perspective, we have interests and vulnerabilities on one side, and values on the other.

What about the difference between interests and vulnerabilities? Here, it helps to see that persons can have interests, some of which may be worth protecting, while not being especially vulnerable. Thus, a company's CEO may have an interest in receiving a bonus, even if, when compared to the position of the company's shareholders or employers, she is far from being vulnerable. Interests, on the way I think of the term here, are thinner normatively than vulnerabilities. They may or may not deserve protection: they may matter to certain individuals or groups, and because of that they deserve our normative attention. But they do not prima facie call out for protection. In this respect, interests are unlike values and vulnerabilities, which I would argue do call out prima facie for our protection, and not just our normative attention. Nevertheless, interests may well, depending on the circumstances, be deserving of protection.

To repeat, when compared to interests, vulnerabilities are thicker normative phenomena. I have already given one example of an interest: a financial one, eg a CEO's interest in receiving a bonus. But we can think of many other interests that individuals or groups may have: an interest in one's reputation; an interest in one's standing to sue; an interest in the transparency of reason-giving by governance institutions, and so on. By interest, then, I mean to include almost anything that might matter to an individual or group, from their particular perspective. I am not suggesting that all these interests are on the same normative scale, and some may indeed shade into thicker normative phenomena. Normative thickness here is very much a matter of degree.

Vulnerabilities, on the other hand, are less subjective and also, as noted above, thicker. They do have a prima facie claim to be protected, subject to possible exceptions, eg when conflicting with certain values. They refer to the rich range of positions that individuals or groups, and any life forms, can find themselves in, though sometimes without being aware of it: eg the vulnerability of persons in a mental institution that is due to go into administration; or the vulnerability of a particular group of refugees in light of the incoming government's immigration policy; or the vulnerability of a certain species of animal, for example, in the face of a planned factory; or the vulnerability of a river to some new development. Some vulnerabilities may be thought of as involving states or experiences of harm and suffering by individuals, groups and life-forms, but some, as noted above, may not, in part because they are potential states of harm and suffering, and in part because individuals, groups or life-forms may never be conscious of them. In this respect, consider environmental vulnerability, but also consider the situation of persons who think it their duty to perform some action, say soldiers or carers, and who do not necessarily even consider themselves to be vulnerable. All these, I would suggest, are examples of vulnerabilities, and these not only deserve our normative attention, as with interests, but also our normative protection, though this may be subject, once more, to certain possible exceptions, eg clashes with certain values.

To summarise, the normative objects of inquiry are, roughly: values, vulnerabilities and interests. Where interests and vulnerabilities are normative phenomena appertaining individuals, groups and life-forms, values are less grounded in particular experiences or states of individuals, groups and life-forms and are more abstract and relate to qualities we might seek, as a community, in our laws, our institutions and our relations with other communities. Interests are thinner normative phenomena, and refer more to cares or concerns, wishes or desires, of particular individuals, groups and life-forms. Interests have a claim on our normative attention, but they do not have a prima facie claim to protection. Nevertheless, and depending on the circumstances, interests may well be deserving of protection. Vulnerabilities, in turn, are thicker normative phenomena, and they do have a prima facie claim to protection. Some of them may involve experiences and states of harm and suffering by individuals, groups and life-forms, but others may not, there being some other, less-phenomenologically-based, sense in which they are in danger or under threat, eg of extinction or exploitation.

To reiterate, these differences between values, vulnerabilities and interests are not designed to be either rigid distinctions. Sometimes, it will be not clear how to classify something, eg is speaking a language an interest, a vulnerability (say when the language is a minority one, and under threat of extinction), or a value (say, linguistic diversity)? For my purposes here, these questions of classification and taxonomy are not the key ones. The key questions, as will become clear in a moment, are ones of access to these normative objects, ie how we can sense them, including sense which ones might be relevant or salient. This trifecta is also not designed to be exhaustive of the range of normative phenomena that inquiry might have as objects. The reference to values, vulnerabilities and interests is, instead, meant to be indicative of the kinds of objects that inquiry might have. The point is to see there is a range, and that it comes in degrees of normative thickness: inquiry may need to sense not only those normative phenomena that have prima facie claims to protection, but may need to cast the net wide, capturing as much as it can of what is worthy of our normative attention, going on to consider and evaluate which of these are deserving of protection.

Indeed, this need to cast the net wide is one of the reasons why I have included the thin-normative notion of interests, rather than the thicker notion of rights. This is not to under-estimate the importance of rights, but it is to suggest that the language of rights is just one of the possibilities, ie one of the possible ways to capture what are the normative objects of inquiry, though of course one that may be made particularly relevant and salient by the law's past, eg in jurisdictions and traditions where there are bills of rights, or where courts use the language of rights. On the trifecta I have introduced here, rights may be found across the range of values, vulnerabilities and interests. But that trifecta also goes considerably beyond that which may be protected by rights.

Earlier in this chapter, I referenced Geoffrey Samuel's work on interests. One of his key points is that judges may often utilise the language of interests because they are as yet unsure whether, or how, to best protect something that may require protection but not have the status of a right in that tradition or jurisdiction. The protection of 'interests' in a case, or in a string of cases, might come to be recognised as especially important, and move on from the granting of a remedy to protect an interest to the more robust protection of a right, but it also may not.

Samuel provides a number of examples in which talk of 'legitimate interests' or 'sufficient interests' enabled the singling out of a claimant amongst other claimants, or enabled some damages or higher damages to be awarded in particular cases, but without engendering the kind of controversy that might accompany the characterisation of something as a right. Samuel points out how the language of interests 'provided a means of giving concrete expression to intangible goods, such as loss of an expected profit, or intangible harms, such as deprecation of a collective group of objects through the destruction of a single item'.[198] He shows how 'interests' may have 'helped transform the law of delict from a quasi-criminal law of actions'.[199] Indeed, he argues that the use of the notion of an 'interest' may have been one of the most important vehicles for 'the development of a more sophisticated private law'.[200] There may well be good reason, then, to include within the objects of inquiry a notion that is less normatively thick than other notions, such as rights, or for that matter, vulnerabilities and values. This is especially so when we remind ourselves that inquiry is something that occurs over time, and that takes time.

C. Access to Normative Objects

How can persons involved in adjudication have access to, make insight into, or sense, which values, vulnerabilities and interests might be relevant to the case before them and to cases potentially like it in the future? Here is where the other dimensions of inquiry come back into the picture: persons involved in adjudication rely on the social, diachronic and experimental dimensions of inquiry in order to gain access to, make insight into, or sense or discern, which values, vulnerabilities and interests might be relevant. Given their own limitations, epistemic and otherwise, as well as the sheer difficulty of the task of doing justice, persons involved in adjudication will engage in the processes of inquiry, inviting others to make insight, or sense, together with them, interactively and communally, in real time and over time, and employing all the resources of practices and forms of experiment.

At this point, we can also add another important feature of 'access' to values, vulnerabilities and interests, and one to which I will be returning when investigating artefacts and related processes of imagination. As individuals, persons have access to normative objects at a level of experience, ie as embodied, sensory and affective persons. In other words, access to values, vulnerabilities and interests for human beings is mediated by their experiences as embodied, sensory and affective creatures. This is especially so when making insight into which values, vulnerabilities and interests *might* be relevant, and thus ones those persons may not have considered to be relevant before. This has

[198] Samuel (2017), 22.
[199] Ibid.
[200] Ibid.

some consequences for both the process of inquiry, and for how we need to characterise the values, vulnerabilities and interests themselves.

Insofar as our access, as persons, to normative objects is via our experiences as embodied, sensory and affective creatures, then that which we have access to has to be such as to be capable of being experienced by us as creatures of that kind. In other words, we encounter phenomena that we experience as a value, vulnerability or interest in a certain way, ie precisely as embodied, sensory and affective beings. In everyday life, many of these experiences will involve direct personal involvement, as when we interact with our fellows, and experience the variety and intensity of emotions those interactions bring: from love to hate, from indignation to pride, from sadness to joy, and so on. It is, in part, through those experiences, in particular situations and scenes of life with others – as, for instance, described so beautifully in Adam Smith's *Theory of Moral Sentiments*[201] – that we acquire our knowledge of normative objects.

Nevertheless, although this direct experience in particular situations and scenes of our lives with others may be our primary means of acquiring normative knowledge, it is one of the key claims of this book that this is not our only means of access to normative objects. We can also make insight into, come to sense, and learn to see the potential relevance of, certain values, vulnerabilities and interests by processes of imagination: we do not need direct personal involvement, but we need something like it. We still need some level of experience, as embodied, sensory and affective creatures, but that is an experience that can be simulated, as precisely in processes of imagination.

I mentioned earlier that if this is the sort of access that we can have, ie an access mediated either by direct or by simulated experience as embodied, sensory and affective creatures, then certain consequences also follow for the character of the values, vulnerabilities and interests that we encounter. In direct experience, we encounter these normative objects in reflective, conscious feelings in the course of being engaged in or participating in certain situations and scenes with others. In simulated experience, as in processes of imagination, our experience is not direct, but it nevertheless still requires a similar grounding in relatively particular situations or scenes.

If we are to take seriously, as I try to in this book, that we are embodied, sensory and affective creatures, then it follows that in order to make insight into or sense the relevance or salience of a certain value, vulnerability or interest, we have to have an encounter with some situation or scene, something that is relatively particular and thus which can be experienced by us. Nevertheless, it does not follow that this encounter must always be direct: it can be simulated. This will especially be so when we are generating insight, or sensing, some value, vulnerability or interest that we may not have ourselves directly experienced before, eg a form of intense jealousy, say, which we may not have ourselves felt, or the desperate quality of the life of an asylum seeker who fears being returned home. In these cases, to have any chance of sensing the relevant values, vulnerabilities and interests, we shall have to deploy our imaginations, and not just, or even mainly on our own, but together with others.

This is equally so with the more abstract values referred to above: in order to sense that a certain value may be relevant, we need to have some kind of experience of it,

[201] See Smith (2002) [1759].

but this may be a simulated experience. For instance, with respect, say, to the value of the authority of a court, our access to this as a value that might be relevant to a certain case or potential cases like it in the future needs to be mediated by the direct or simulated experience of what it would be like for a court and those working in to lose that authority. Another way to put this point is that we encounter values, vulnerabilities and interest as evaluative-factual complexes, ie we have access to them, and can understand and have knowledge of them, always necessarily imperfectly, only as we experience them in particular situations or scenes.[202] Nevertheless, this experience need not be direct: it can, once again, be simulated. Indeed, sometimes, if not often, it will have to be simulated.

I recognise that the claims above, especially as to access to normative objects as affectively-embodied beings, require considerably more defence than I can afford here. Nevertheless, I take it to be important to make them explicit, rather than treat them as unspoken assumptions. Again, I will be returning to them to some extent in the ensuing discussion of artefacts and related processes of imagination, and of course in my discussions of the case studies in the second part of this book. As we shall see, the artefacts of inquiry I have in mind are precisely different ways of simulating experience of normative objects. The making and experiencing of these artefacts, then, through the related processes of imagination, is a way in which persons engaged in adjudication can make insight into, or sense, those values, vulnerabilities and interests that might be relevant to a case before them and to cases potentially like it in the future. We need such artefacts and related processes of imagination because our access to normative objects is necessarily mediated by our character as embodied, sensory and affective creatures. We also need them because of the limitations of our direct experiences, because of the institutional pressures in the context of adjudication, and because of the sheer difficulty of attempting to do justice in adjudication.

D. The Duty to Inquire

I turn now to the fourth and final point in this section, and thus to the overall importance of exercising inquiry in its normative dimension in adjudication. The most important point to make here is that inquiry in its normative dimension is an ongoing, open-ended and never complete process. There is no such thing as 'mastery' of normative objects; no such thing as complete normative knowledge of, say, all the possibly identifiable and potentially relevant values, vulnerabilities and interests. Given that I have insisted above on their character as evaluative-factual complexes, and that they are experienced by us in direct or simulated experiences of particular situations and scenes of life, it must be the case that they are always changing and that new values, vulnerabilities and interests are emerging. There is always normative work to be done, and there is thus always a duty to engage in inquiry in its normative dimension, ie to engage interactively and communally with others, in real time and over time, deploying the forms and techniques of experiment, in order to make insight, or sense, which

[202] I have made this argument in more detail elsewhere: see Del Mar (2016b).

values, vulnerabilities and interests might be relevant in a case and in cases potentially like it in the future. This is a task that is made a little easier by the submissions of counsels and parties in particular cases, and by the law's past. But it is not exhausted by them: judges cannot shirk from their duty to engage in inquiry by confining themselves to those submissions and pleas and to the law's past. Indeed, even if they wanted to that would be impossible, given the need for reconstructing, in light of the present, not to mention the future, the meaning of the law's past. Judges must, of course, respect the law's past, but they are also under a broader duty: the duty to exercise inquiry into vulnerabilities, values and interests that might be at stake in a certain case and in cases potentially like it in the future.

Of course, this duty to exercise inquiry has its limitations. Indeed, the necessity of there being limitations is built into the very model of inquiry, as I have been constructing it here. In saying there is a duty for judges to inquire, I do not mean to suggest that judges ought to engage in all-out moral theorising or systemisation, generating or seeking to generate all the possibly relevant normative objects in a case, or thinking of as many possible like cases in the future as they can. Not at all; on the contrary, the model of inquiry as I have constructed it recognises, indeed it begins with and foregrounds, the limitations of persons and the difficulties they face in doing justice. That is precisely the reason for emphasising the need for social, diachronic and experimental dimensions of inquiry. To engage in inquiry is not to attempt to play the role of a Hercules. The call for a duty of inquiry is not a call for heroes who will make the law morally perfect or even the best it can be. Again, I am resisting imposing such standards on the practice of adjudication. But resisting imposing such standards, and thus not expecting or requiring judges to act as grand moral theorists, does not mean that one ought to avoid the duty to do normative work, ie precisely to engage in inquiry. Again, that duty arises not solely because of the respect that needs to be paid to the submissions and pleas of counsel and parties coming before the court, and thus respecting their rights to be heard, to be listened to, to be responded to. It arises also because of the care that needs to be taken as to the law's future. In what follows in the rest of this book, we will see how artefacts, and related processes of imagination, enable, at least when used well, in ways to be clarified, this activity of inquiry, and thus enable those engaged in adjudication to balance the different temporal orientations of doing justice.

To summarise: there are two broad sources of the duty to engage in inquiry in adjudication. The first is the sheer necessary never-ending and incomplete quality of the task of inquiry, based in part on our own limitations of access to normative objects, but also on the ever-changing scope of those normative objects. The second relates to the requirement to do justice in adjudication and its different temporal orientations, ie to the law's past, to the present case, and to law's future. As embodied, sensory and affective creatures we are always coming up against our own limitations, both personal and institutional, as well as the inevitable and inescapable difficulties of doing justice. We cope with this in various ways, attempting to make our task easier by introducing certain procedures, eg having well-trained counsel make submissions, and by having institutional repositories, archives and assistance with finding materials. But we cannot hide, and nor should we hide, from the basic and never finished or complete duty to be responsive to the ever-changing normative environment. I have tried, in constructing the model of inquiry, to show both how we exercise that duty as well as to argue for it being a duty.

I realise that the issues brushed over in this chapter require considerably more detailed argument than I could muster. I hope to have at least outlined a basic case of and for inquiry. The task now, which is the primary task of this book, is to consider how it can be enabled.

2

Artefacts

This chapter focuses on what I am calling 'artefacts'.[1] In this book, I model artefacts as forms of language that: 1) signal their own artifice, thereby also capturing our attention; and 2) call upon us to participate, ie do things with and thanks to them. Artefacts play a crucial role in this book: they are the forms of language that are made by, and that also invite, processes of imagination.

Let me emphasise from the outset that separating artefacts from related processes of imagination risks being misleading. As modelled in this book, artefacts and processes of imagination are mutually dependent phenomena: processes of imagination construct artefacts, and artefacts invite, sometimes successfully, processes of imagination. They form a duo: they are each a model in their own right, but they are so closely related that one could think of them as a single model. This is important because it might otherwise be thought that a formal analysis is sufficient, ie that it would be sufficient to point to the forms of language that are then conceived of as necessarily involving the exercise of imagination. That is not my account: I think we need to have our eye in part on the form (in this case, of language) and in part on the response of persons to it (in this case, processes of imagination). Thus, there is no such thing as inherently artefactual language, in the same way that there is not, for instance, inherently vague language. Instead, language is only ever relatively artefactual (or vague), ie whether it is depends in part on the character, position and circumstances of the receiver, the reader or listener, of language. At best we can say that there are some formal properties of language that render it conventionally likely that they will be received as artefactual (or vague), and, indeed, I shall be pointing to those in the case of artefactuality. But it remains the case that any artefactuality of language is only ever relative, and thus also contingent on how it is experienced by its readers or listeners.

It is, then, only for purposes of structuring the book, and attempting to be as clear as possible, that I separate out the discussion of artefacts in this chapter, and the discussion of imagination in the next. In addition, it must be remembered that this duo of artefacts and related processes of imagination only makes sense, as important and valuable features of adjudication, within the other model constructed in the previous chapter, namely inquiry. That is because of the overall claim made in this book, namely that artefacts and related processes of imagination are valuable in adjudication insofar as and when they enable the process of inquiry.

[1] I do not mean to refer to the ontological theory of law known as 'artifact' theories of law: see, eg, Burazin, Himma and Roversi (2018). I refer, instead, to a particular quality of language.

Bearing all this in mind, this chapter focuses on articulating the important dimensions of artefacts. I engage in this task in five steps. In the first three, I situate my approach within three broadly similar, yet different, approaches to the study of language and its forms: rhetoric in section one, cognitive humanities in section two, and fictionality in section three. Having so situated my approach, I then turn to the two dimensions of artefactual language. In section four, I turn to the first dimension of artefactual language, namely its signalling of artifice, and I explain its character and also the variety of ways in which language can signal its own artifice. In the fifth section, I turn to the second dimension of artefactual language, namely how it calls upon us to participate, and here, too, I explain both the feature in general, as well as pointing to the many different ways we are called upon to do things with and thanks to artefactual language.

I. Rhetoric

I do not attempt, in this book, to offer a general theory of (legal) language.[2] Instead, I wish to point to one particular kind of way in which language may work, or to certain features that some forms of language may have. Nevertheless, my identification of these features is related, in broad terms, to other approaches to language. Without aiming to be comprehensive, in this and the next two sections, I look briefly at three traditions: rhetoric, cognitive humanities and fictionality respectively. I do so with a view to drawing upon their resources, while also pointing out some differences in approach.

In this section, I turn to the rhetorical tradition. This is in itself a daunting task, and I must repeat again that my aim is not to cover the field or even state its most important theoretical commitments. Rather, my aim is two-fold: first, to pay tribute to this tradition, from which I have learnt and continue to learn a great deal, and which is also highly under-valued in contemporary legal scholarship; and second, to clarify the similarities and differences of approach. It may be that what I am calling artefactual language can be thought of as a branch of the rhetorical approach, but I am not too concerned here with such classificatory matters. What matters is what the rhetorical tradition teaches us about language, though not, at least in some cases, with wholescale acceptance of those lessons.

Put in the broadest terms, the lessons I take from rhetorical approaches to language include: 1) that language connects to us as affective, sensory and embodied beings, ie we are capable of, and indeed enjoy, responding to the appeal that language makes to our affective, sensory and kinesic knowledge and memory; 2) that language is deeply social, ie that it is a resource for relating with others, whether in one-to-one or one-to-many interactions, or for a community and its identities and values over time; and 3) that it is something that is connected, in complex ways, to the exercise of power, ie it is both capable of creating power imbalances and enabling the powerful to exploit the vulnerable, as well as being a resource of the vulnerable against the powerful. These are just

[2] I drop the parentheses from here, but throughout, I have primarily in mind legal language, and especially the language found in common law judgements.

some of the lessons of the rhetorical tradition, but they are certainly important ones, and they are crucial also for this book.

Some treatments of rhetoric, and some rhetorical approaches to language, also adopt positions which I here resist. These include: 1) associating language too closely with persuasion, as if the paradigmatic rhetorical interaction involved one person, with knowledge of a specific end in mind, using the means of language to persuade another person or a group of persons to that end; 2) the tendency to treat the rhetorical power of language as operating solely or mainly at an unconscious or less-than-conscious level; and 3) the association of rhetoric with a small domain of language forms, ie so-called rhetorical forms, such as tropes, schemas and figures, which are then sometimes treated as merely optional or ornamental. I turn now to say a few words about each of the three positions I am resisting.

A. Persuasion, the Unconscious, and Ornament

i. Persuasion

The first is associating language too closely with persuasion. Persuasion is, of course, a vitally important aspect of language use, but it is just one aspect. The problem with associating language too closely with persuasion is that it presents it as a mere instrument, as something which the person using it can control. But language is not something we can control or master. It is too complex but also too social a phenomenon for that. Once released by someone, language takes on a life of its own, its meanings becoming dependent on how they will be received, and thereby re-made, by others. Further, treating the paradigmatic rhetorical relation as involving one person in the active and epistemically superior position not only neglects the social character of language, but it also hides from view the many occasions in which we do not have a specific end in mind or simply do not know, or are unsure, as to where we want to, or think we ought to, end up. We do not only use language for specific ends. We also use language to try things out, to cope, to experiment, to invite others to think with us, to communicate in ways that do not involve the manipulation or attempt at control of another.[3] Further, again, the very idea of the 'use' of language, of approaching language only as a means or as an instrument or tool, is too reductive an approach to the lives of language for us, especially as members of multiple communities. We can and should recognise the importance of persuasion practices, including the many ways that language is associated with power, but we need not and should not let these important insights about language dominate too much our understanding of language and our relations to it.

ii. The Unconscious

The second position I am resisting, which can sometimes be found in rhetorical approaches to language, is the tendency to treat the rhetorical power of language as

[3] For a brilliant account of rhetorical inquiry, albeit in the specific context of sixteenth century English drama, see Altman (1978).

operating solely or mainly at an unconscious or sub-conscious level. There is no doubt, of course, that one way in which language affects us is at levels below fully conscious awareness. It would be impossible for language to play the role it does, especially socially, if it did not affect us in more ways than we can possibly be aware of at any one time. Nevertheless, the cognitive power and value of language is not limited to such less-than-conscious or involuntary effects. This seems all too obvious, but it requires emphasis because some rhetorical approaches to language, including some recent cognitive approaches to rhetorical tropes, schemas and figures, treat them as having primary cognitive effects at the less-than-conscious level. It is important, certainly, to keep in mind that some forms of language may indeed exercise great power especially at the less-than-conscious level, eg proverbs and other kinds of sayings might be good examples. But this important insight should not cloud from view the possibility that the cognitive effects of language can be accompanied by conscious awareness, and that this conscious awareness can also come in many modes, eg accompanied by a whole variety of epistemic attitudes. As we shall see, this will be crucial for making room for what I call artefacts, or artefactual language.

iii. Ornament

A third and final position that I resist is an approach to rhetoric, even amongst those who are sympathetic to the rhetorical tradition, as delineating a narrow domain of so-called 'rhetorical language', eg language that is figurative rather than literal, or the language of tropes, schemas and figures as opposed to allegedly ordinary language. This position is misleading if only because so-called 'ordinary' or 'literal' language is full of such so-called 'figurative' elements. This is not to say that there might not be distinctions that could be made, at the level of language or use or in terms of our relation to language, which might relate in broad terms to the distinction between, say, figurative and literal uses of language. Indeed, what I call artefactual language does have something in common with some ways in which theorists have approached figurative language. But to do this is quite different to treating the rhetorical tradition as one merely pointing to some particular form of language use. Instead, the rhetorical tradition is an overall approach to language, rich and multi-dimensional, and not reducible in that way.

Further, to understand rhetoric in this broader way helps thwart another unhelpful position that is sometimes taken to so-called figurative language, ie that it is but optional or ornamental, that it introduces colour into a discourse, but that this is just an add-on, a mere flourish and thereby superfluous or dispensable, and thus replaceable by literal expressions, especially in the context of discourses that aim for 'clarity' and 'rigour', such as is sometimes said of philosophy and law. I do not propose to argue against this position at this point, as this entire book is an argument against this kind of approach to artefactual language, and rhetoric more broadly. As we shall see in more detail in the case studies in the second part of this book, I argue that fictions, metaphors, figures and scenarios cannot be dismissed as mere ornaments or optional flourishes of colour; rather, they contribute to inquiry in their own distinctive ways, and thus deserve to be treated seriously as distinct and irreplaceable epistemic devices.

B. Rhetoric in Legal Scholarship

i. *Rhetoric, Community, Character*

Many of the points above will be familiar to those who have engaged with the rhetorical tradition, both outside and inside legal scholarship. Although I do not wish to make any historical claims few would disagree with the idea that at least in English-speaking legal scholarship of the last half-decade, the figure most influential in the turn to rhetoric has been James Boyd White. Re-issued recently, on occasion of its 45th anniversary, White's *The Legal Imagination* was, and remains, undoubtedly a milestone in approaches to legal language, and much else besides, including legal education and law and humanities.[4] That tome, and it is, in its full edition, very much a tome, was important to me also, as signalled if only in my adoption of the very term 'imagination'. Famously, in the preface to that book, White said:

> I think the law is not merely a system of rules (or rules and principles), or reducible to policy choices or class interests, but that it is rather what I call a language, by which I do not mean just a set of terms and locutions, but habits of mind and expectations – what might also be called a culture. It is an enormously rich and complex system of thought and expression, of social definitions and practices, which can be learned and mastered, modified or preserved, by the individual mind. The law makes a world. And the law in another sense, as the profession we teach and learn and practice, is a kind of cultural competence: an art of reading the special literature of the law and an art of speaking and writing – of making compositions of one's own – in this language. It is a branch of rhetoric.[5]

There are several features of this that are important: one is the insistence on the dynamic relations between the activities of writing language and reading it; another is the reference to 'culture', and thus to the social life of language, connected to 'an enormously rich and complex system of thought and expression'; yet another is the idea that law, as a language, is involved in 'making', which brings to mind the Ancient Greek term 'poiesis', meaning 'making', and thus locating legal language not only in relation to rhetoric, but also to poetics; and, of course, the characterisation of law, in its character as an art of language, as being a 'branch of rhetoric'. Important, too, and added directly after the above quote, was White's acknowledgement of the relations between language and power, though not in a way that reduced uses of language to acts of coercion, but that recognised the role of legal language in 'structur[ing] sensibility and vision.'[6] In this way, White brought into view the diachronic character of legal language, reminding us of the importance of the work it does, in a community, over time.

For many decades now, since 1973, White has continued to develop his rich and complex approach to legal language. This has included arguing against reductive approaches to rhetoric. Thus, for instance, in his collection entitled *Heracles' Bow*,[7] White argues against a characterisation of rhetoric 'as a failed science', as 'what we do when science doesn't work.'[8] Rhetoric is not best understood, he says, by treating it 'as

[4] White (2018) [1973].
[5] Ibid, xiii.
[6] Ibid.
[7] White (1985a).
[8] Ibid, 31.

the ignoble art of persuasion.'[9] Rhetoric cannot be reduced to thinking of it 'either as a second-rate way of dealing with facts that cannot really be properly known or as a way of dealing with people instrumentally or manipulatively, in an attempt to get them to do something you want them to do.'[10] Instead, a rhetorical approach to legal language helps us see law 'as a set of resources for thought and argument',[11] but also as very much an activity, and a social activity at that.

Under this more robust and rich approach to rhetoric, we do not think of law merely as a set of words on a piece of paper, but rather, again, as an activity, as a way of making, and especially making together, ie of acting, interactively and communally, with words. In very broad terms, White said, to study law was to study 'the ways we constitute ourselves as individuals, as communities, and as cultures, whenever we speak'.[12] It was to notice the dynamics of speaking and listening, of writing and reading, and the role of language as a means of relating with others, of making and remaking a common, even if still hotly contested and diverse, culture. It is not an accident that White has used many relational terms when characterising the operation of legal language, speaking of it, for instance, as a form of 'translation', or a 'conversation', as when he asked us to 'see the statute as a way of starting a conversation'.[13]

Further, linking rhetoric with knowledge, White stressed the sense in which it was an art of 'making', which was 'tacitly creative', while also acknowledging 'both its limits and the conditions of uncertainty under which it functions'.[14] White, then, did not see legal language as closing down possibilities for meaning-making, but rather precisely as offering resources for its continual transformation. For instance, as he pointed out many times, 'reading a legal text is often not so much reading for a single meaning as reading for a range of possible meanings';[15] or, again, that 'there is in the law an openness to multiple stories, multiple languages.'[16] This was so, in many respects, because law was a social, interactive and communal, activity. As he put it:

> … the law can be seen as the culture that we remake whenever we speak as lawyers. To look at law this way is to direct one's attention to the way in which we create new meanings, new possibilities for meaning, in what we say; to the way our literature can be regarded as a literature of value and motive and sentiment; to the way in which our enterprise is a radically ethical one, by which self and community are perpetually reconstituted; and to the limits that our nature or our culture, our circumstances and our imagination, place on our powers to remake our languages and communities in new forms.[17]

As this quote reveals, for White, to think of the law under the guise of the rhetorical tradition is also to think of its ethical and, at once, political dimension. White has always asked, and urged us also to ask: 'what voices does the law allow to be heard, what

[9] Ibid.
[10] Ibid, 32.
[11] Ibid, 33.
[12] Ibid, 35.
[13] Ibid, 41.
[14] Ibid, 44.
[15] Ibid, 78.
[16] Ibid, 174.
[17] Ibid, 41.

relations does it establish among them? With what voice, or voices, does the law itself speak?'[18] The law, understood as rhetoric, with its traditional emphasis on ethos and pathos, and on the social activity of speaking and listening, is ethically and politically vital because it has the capacity to 'create new possibilities for meaning and action in life and constitute human communities in distinctive ways'.[19] It establishes 'roles and relations and voices, positions from which one may speak.'[20]

This approach had concrete consequences for how legal scholars could, and should, read judicial opinions, ie not merely as 'results', but as exercises precisely in ethos and pathos. Scholars could and ought to look at 'the character the court gives itself in the writing and the opportunities for thought and community that it creates';[21] to consider less the 'message' and more 'the language it makes as it places one item next to another, the community it makes with its several audiences'.[22] These exhortations as to how to read were accompanied by exhortations as to how to write, eg with respect to judges, for sensitivity to certain values in composing judgements, to 'many-voicedness; the integration of thought and feeling; the acknowledgement of the limits of one's own mind and language, and an openness to change them; the insistence upon the reality of the experience of other people, and upon the importance of their stories, told in their words'.[23] These values, White said, were 'essential to our own best ideas of justice'; they were 'political as well as intellectual and aesthetic virtues'.[24]

ii. Rhetoric, Power, Violence

White influenced, and continues to influence, multiple generations of legal scholars.[25] These scholars have themselves built their own rich and complex pictures of law-as-rhetoric, with their own distinctive influences.[26] The work of Peter Goodrich is exemplary in this respect. Like White, Goodrich has for many decades engaged with rescuing the continued relevance of the rhetorical tradition for understanding legal language and legal practice in general. He has spoken, for instance, of 'the great merits and the obvious attractions of rhetoric', including:

> … its ability to study the determination of human behaviour and speech in terms of the contingent and topical, the social and historical, facets of public dialogue, as well as its conception of language as communication within a context and by means of the inherently figurative and ambiguous semantics of actual usage.[27]

[18] Ibid, 42.

[19] Ibid, 107.

[20] Ibid, 98. Elsewhere, White said: 'Every time one speaks as a lawyer, one establishes for the moment a character – an ethical identity, or what the Greeks called an ethos – for oneself, for one's audience, and for those one talks about, and in addition one proposes a relation among the characters one defines': (1985b), 690.

[21] White (1985a), 118.

[22] Ibid, 118.

[23] Ibid, 132.

[24] Ibid.

[25] See Etxabe and Watt (2014); and Sarat and Kearns (1994).

[26] For example, see Mootz (2006) and (2010); and Constable (2014).

[27] Goodrich (1984), 176.

Like White, too, Goodrich is especially sensitive to the politics of legal language, and foregrounds the following questions: 'Who is speaking? Who has the right to speak? Who is qualified to do so? Who derives from it their own special quality, their prestige, and from whom, in return, do they receive if not the assurance, at least the presumption that what they say is true?'.[28] These are certainly vital questions, and Goodrich is also right to remind us to always keep looking for how legal language 'must also exclude and stigmatise – define out',[29] making so many voices, and so many experiences, inferior or invisible. And he is right, too, to say that it is a language 'of elite or professionalised power … the language of authority'.[30] Sometimes, for Goodrich, law being a language of authority goes along with seeing it as taking 'the discursive form of monologue, distance … and specialisation'.[31] He says:

> Law, as a linguistic register or as a literary genre, can be described linguistically or discursively in terms of its systematic appropriation and privileging of legally recognised meanings, accents and connotations (modes of inclusion), and its simultaneous rejection of alternative and competing meanings and accents, forms of utterance and discourse generally, as extrinsic, unauthorised or threatening (modes of exclusion). … characteristic modes of legal utterance as social discourse – as a hierarchical (stratified), authoritarian (distanced), monologic (uniaccentual), and alien (reified) use of language.[32]

Without doubt, this captures well some of the ways that legal language works. But it is a major argument of this book that it is not the only way. There are, if you like, more enchanted and enchanting uses of legal language; we need not despair; there is also hope and possibility in legal language.

And, in fact, Goodrich has recognised this too. There are times in his scholarship when he has come closer to the emphasis that White placed on the generative character of legal language. For example, in a paper on 'Antirrhesis: Polemical Structures of Common Law Thought', Goodrich criticised the approach taken to rhetoric, and rhetorical analyses of legal language, by the great Belgian legal philosopher, Chaim Perelman, which Goodrich characterised as focusing on the capacity of law 'to produce agreement. For Chaim Perelman', Goodrich said, 'the function of the revival of the study of oratory was to facilitate communication, to identify specific messages, and to align legal orator and legal audience.'[33] Resisting this approach, Goodrich instead emphasised, at least as I read him, the contestable and contested character of legal language. The 'practice of legal oratory', Goodrich reminds us, recalling also the sophists,[34] was 'adversarial',[35] 'associated not so much with the felicitous use of speech as with disputation, casuistry, apologetic, proof and polemic.'[36]

[28] Ibid, 185.
[29] Ibid, 189.
[30] Ibid, 187.
[31] Ibid, 187.
[32] Ibid, 175.
[33] Goodrich (1994), 57.
[34] Ibid, 60.
[35] Ibid, 59.
[36] Ibid, 60.

Although Goodrich does not dwell on this, the reference to the sophists might indeed be helpful, reminding us of the experimental character of language, of how it can be used to argue for either side of an issue or question, this being the great sophistic, and later rhetorical, art of *in utrumque partem* in Latin, or the *dissoi logoi* in Greek. For legal language to be capable of being used in this way suggests its pliability, its resourcefulness, the sense in which it not only closes off options, ie wreaking epistemic violence on other ways of speaking, and on the normative worlds of persons and communities without voice, but also retains a certain potentiality and possibility for the creation of new paths and new voices. There is both violence and redemption, both destruction and hope, in the language of the law.

iii. The New Rhetoric

The reference to Perelman cannot go without comment, for his attempt to bring new life to the rhetorical study of legal language was also highly influential, including on some contemporary analytical legal philosophers of legal reasoning.[37] Originally published in French in 1958, and in English translation in 1969, Perelman and Olbrechts-Tyteca's *The New Rhetoric: A Treatise in Argumentation*, brought rhetoric into the mainstream of theories of argumentation and reasoning, perhaps especially within the civil law tradition.[38] This book, like White's, is also a heavy tome, and there is great deal to learn from it. Nevertheless, some of the positions it takes up vis-à-vis rhetoric, and as applied to argumentation, mark differences between it and the approach I take here. These differences are visible already in how Perelman and Olbrechts-Tyteca characterise 'the object of the theory of argumentation', which they say is 'the study of the discursive techniques allowing us to induce or to increase the mind's adherence to the theses presented for its assent.'[39] This orients their account, as Goodrich also observed, into focusing on language that successfully persuades, ie that results in acceptance, by the audience, of the position intended by the speaker or author. As they say in another formulation, their interest is in 'the discursive means of obtaining the adherence of minds',[40] and this leaves little scope for what I am calling in this book inquiry, especially its experimental dimension. Perelman and Olbrechts-Tyteca are not bashful in their selection of object; indeed, they are explicit about how this focus has the effect of putting beyond their scope other kinds of uses of language. The way they characterise these other uses, however, is also at odds with the approach taken in this book. Thus, they say:

> We consider a figure to be argumentative, if it brings about a change of perspective, and its use seems normal in relation to this situation. If, on the other hand, the speech does not bring about the adherence of the hearer to this argumentative form, the figure will be considered an embellishment, a figure of style. It can excite admiration, but this will be on the aesthetic plane, or in recognition of the speaker's originality.[41]

[37] Most obviously, Neil MacCormick, see, eg, MacCormick (2005).
[38] Perelman and Olbrechts-Tyteca (1969).
[39] Ibid, 4.
[40] Ibid, 8.
[41] Ibid, 169. The idea of a change of perspective is an excellent one, but it is, at least to my mind, severable from the idea of adherence.

The moves made in this passage, ie opposing argument and aesthetics, or argument and style, and banishing all 'figures' of language that are not argumentative to the status of 'embellishments', which may 'excite admiration' but are otherwise seemingly superfluous, are at odds with the approach I take in this book. Having said that, it is important to observe that Perelman and Olbrechts-Tyteca are very much conscious of and explicit about these choices, and admit that their approach means that 'we shall never deal with what some would deem essential aspects of the study of figures.'[42] They deliberately confine their analysis of the rhetoricity of language, and in particular figures, to 'the connection existing between their effects and factors of a general kind that enter into persuasion'.[43] As I have suggested above, although persuasion is an important element of rhetoric, it is not its only element. To approach language rhetorically need not mean that one must confine oneself to the persuasive uses that language may be put to, and nor does it mean that one must accept a division between figurative and non-figurative language, or between language that is argumentative and language that is ornamental.

In saying all this, I do not intend by any means to detract from the extraordinary achievement of Perelman and Olbrechts-Tyteca's *New Rhetoric*. Much of their conception of argumentation was and remains rich. It also challenged many orthodox views prevailing at the time, some of which are still very much alive today. For instance, Perelman and Olbrechts-Tyteca articulated part of the point of what they tried to achieve in the following way:

> We combat uncompromising and irreducible philosophical oppositions presented by all kinds of absolutism: dualisms of reason and imagination, of knowledge and opinion, of irrefutable self-evidence and deceptive will, of a universally accepted objectivity and an incommunicable subjectivity, of a reality binding on everybody and values that are purely individual.[44]

In combating these oppositions, they sought to find the rough, complex, rich middle ground, where one did not seek 'perfect thought imitating divine thought',[45] or where one did not exclude from knowledge all that which did not 'conform to this ideal of clarity and distinction.'[46] Perelman and Olbrechts-Tyteca fought hard to carve out a space that did not accept a dichotomy between the 'objectively and indisputably valid' on the one hand, and 'the realm of the arbitrary and subjective' on the other hand. Their equal sympathy for the rough, pragmatic reasonableness of everyday language as well as technical argumentation was, and remains, important, and deserves further attention by anyone interested in the life of legal language and legal thought.

I have not sought above to offer any overview of the rhetorical tradition in legal scholarship. Far from it. My aim has been to situate my own approach as closely related to the rhetorical tradition in general, but also in some ways slightly different from at least certain strands within that tradition. As will become evident, I will also be referring to and drawing on the rhetorical tradition extensively in the rest of this book.

[42] Ibid, 179.
[43] Ibid, 1.
[44] Ibid, 510.
[45] Ibid.
[46] Ibid, 511.

It is probably still the case that scholarship of all kinds, legal scholarship included, remains traumatised by, and has as yet to recover from, the treatment of rhetoric by philosophy, eg by the classical philosophy of Plato. We still struggle to find ways of articulating knowledge, and its standards, in ways that makes room for what the old traditions of rhetoric did make room for: practices of invention, contingent interventions on particular occasions, interaction and communal life, the craft of thought, and the arts of making.[47] A great deal of work remains to be done to recall, and bring to bear on our understandings of law, that great tradition of rhetoric, sophistry, and its predecessors, and to rescue it from relative obscurity, from being confined, at the best of times, and mostly not even, to a platonic footnote. It is time to flip the coin and consider what matters might look like if all was but a footnote not to Plato, but to Gorgias.

II. Cognitive Humanities

Recent decades have seen the rise of a vital new area of inter-disciplinary research: cognitive humanities. Many of the leading proponents of this approach come from literature departments,[48] and have thereby developed innovative new approaches to language and other features of literary practice, including reading practices.[49] Some of these scholars have also turned their mind to legal language, and that in turn has also influenced a number of legal scholars. The approach is important because, somewhat like the rhetorical tradition, but without its heavy historical baggage, the cognitive humanities have sought to go beyond certain otherwise-well entrenched dichotomies, such as those between mind and body, or reason and emotion, or the individual and society.

A. 4E Approaches to Cognition

A broad way into this approach is to recall a cluster of related claims about human cognition, made across a range of disciplines, which collectively have come to be known as '4E approaches to cognition'. The '4E' refers to four terms all beginning with E, each of which has challenged certain traditional views about cognition, and all of which can be combined together into a new overall approach: embodied, embedded, extended and enactive cognition. 4E approaches include and relate, rather than distinguish and separate out, 'mind, thought, reasoning, perception, imagination, intelligence, emotion and experience', and they combine 'conscious, unconscious-but-potentially-conscious and strictly non-conscious states and processes.'[50] Let us briefly turn to each of the four Es.

[47] This is so, of course, not only in the context of legal scholarship: see, eg, Carruthers (1998). It is also important to underscore that there are exceptions in legal scholarship. In addition to those mentioned above, see also, eg, Scharffs (2001); Shaw (2012) and (2017); Watt (2009); Berger and Stanchi (2017); and, recently, Gaakeer (2019).

[48] See, generally, Zunshine (2014); Garratt (2016); and Burke and Troscianko (2017).

[49] See, eg, Palmer (2004) and (2010).

[50] Anderson, Wheeler and Sprevak (2018b), 2.

i. *Embodied*

On the *embodied* view, 'psychological states and processes' are characterised as 'routinely shaped, in fundamental ways, by non-neural bodily factors.'[51] Amongst the leading exponents here are: George Lakoff and Mark Johnson, who have argued for the dependence of our concepts on embodiment, ie on body schemas, and our memories of them;[52] Andy Clark, who has developed accounts of the integral role of the body in intelligent action;[53] and Alva Noë and Shaun Gallagher, both of whom have developed embodied theories of perceptual experience.[54] Many of these approaches to embodied cognition, Lakoff and Johnson included, place the emphasis on the unconscious or less-than-conscious role of embodiment, with the role of the body, and our experience of it, being determinative of many mental processes, including the emergence of concepts and the uses we make of them. For example, on the Lakoff and Johnson view, one way we may 'experience our bodies' is 'as containers into which we put things and out of which things come'; this experience generates the 'metaphor of containment', which becomes 'a preconceptual cognitive schema',[55] which then structures and determines our cognition in various ways. As we shall see in a moment, the embodied approach has been especially influential in what we might call 'cognitive legal scholarship'.[56]

ii. *Embedded*

The *embedded* view also stresses the importance of the body, but places that body within a particular environment, the overall picture being one of cognition as a body adapting to and within a certain environment. Theorists within this approach typically seek to identify 'certain environmental props, niches or scaffolds' that adaptive intelligent action draws upon as it navigates its way through the world.[57] Known as 'cognitive niche construction', this practice consists of persons building 'external structures that, often in combination with culturally transmitted practices, transform problem spaces in ways that promote, or sometimes obstruct, thinking and reasoning.'[58] For instance, 'a bartender may achieve the successful delivery of a large and complex order of cocktails … by exploiting the fact that different kinds of cocktail often come in differently shaped glasses',[59] with those differently shaped glasses serving as a kind of external mnemonic, or cognitive niche, that allows the bartender to manage the complexity of the task. On this view, humans are sometimes characterised as 'natural born cyborgs',[60] ie 'creatures who are naturally evolved to seek out intimate unions with non-biological resources'.[61] The point for present purposes is that language itself

[51] Ibid, 3.
[52] See Lakoff and Johnson (1980); and Johnson (2018).
[53] See, eg, Clark (1997).
[54] See Gallagher (2005); and Noë (2004). See also Tschacher and Bergomi (2011).
[55] Anderson, Wheeler and Sprevak (2018b), 3.
[56] I also return to this approach in more detail when discussing metaphor in ch 6.
[57] Anderson, Wheeler and Sprevak (2018b), 4.
[58] Ibid.
[59] Ibid.
[60] See Clark (2003).
[61] Anderson, Wheeler and Sprevak (2018b), 4.

can be understood to be one such, quite specific, cognitive niche. I will be returning to this point, as it has influenced certain approaches to legal language.

iii. Extended

Embedded cognition is quite close to the third E, namely *extended* cognition. This latter approach also foregrounds the relationship between body and environment, or put another way, situates the operation of cognition within an environment. But it goes further than the embedded approach and sees cognition as something that can extend beyond the skull and skin. In other words, on this view:

> … there are actual cases of intelligent thought and action, in which the material vehicles that realise the thinking and thoughts concerned are spatially distributed over brain, body and world, in such a way that certain external factors are rightly accorded fundamentally the same cognitive status as would ordinarily be accorded to a subset of your neurons.[62]

A typical example is a phone, which can be conceptualised to be a 'part of your mnemonic machinery, alongside some of your neurons'.[63] This approach has not been as influential in legal scholarship, but one can see how it might be, eg how the importance of archives to legal thought might be captured by this model of extended cognition.[64]

iv. Enactive

Finally, there is the *enactive* approach. Like all three of the above approaches, this one also seeks close relations between mind, body and environment. What it adds is the diachronic dynamics, for it foregrounds the unfolding of cognition 'in looping sensorimotor interactions between an active embodied organism and its environment'.[65] The emphasis here is on 'lived experience', and thus on how 'cognition depends on a tight and dynamic relationship between perception and action.'[66] What becomes especially important on this view is our sensorimotor knowledge, eg knowledge of 'what something would be like if I walked around it'.[67] Like the extended view, the enactive view has also not been as influential in legal scholarship as the embodied and embedded approaches. I shall, however, be returning to the importance of 'sensorimotor knowledge' when I discuss the kinesic mode of participation of the imagination in the next chapter.

To this briefest of possible descriptions of 4E cognition one should also add that there have also been important attempts to explore and emphasise the 'social dimensions of the 4E mind', eg scholars have spoken of 'socially distributed cognition', where, for instance, groups are conceived of as having minds, or where 'I think some of the

[62] Ibid.

[63] Ibid, 4.

[64] Although it may not have been explicitly drawn upon, one can see how compatible this view is with some historical and theoretical approaches to legal knowledge, eg on archives see Halliday (2014); and the emerging literature on 'legal materiality', see Kang and Kendall (2020).

[65] Anderson, Wheeler and Sprevak (2018b), 6.

[66] Ibid.

[67] Ibid.

thoughts I think because, or perhaps only because, I am part of a particular social group', or where my mind is extended by others in the same or a similar way to which it would be extended by technology.[68] As far as I am aware, these approaches have yet to find their way into legal scholarship.[69]

B. Cave's Cognitive Approach to Literature

It is in this context, and as against this background, that we witness the emergence of the cognitive humanities, with humanists, especially literary scholars, seeking to combine these new approaches to cognition with humanistic methods. A leading exponent of this approach is Terence Cave, who in his own work, eg in his excellent *Thinking with Literature*,[70] or by way of editorial efforts as part of his Balzan prize on 'Cognitive Approaches to Literature',[71] has paved the way for what unique insights are on offer when one combines cognition and literature together. For Cave, it is clear that (here writing with Deirdre Wilson):

> … cognition can no longer be conceived as primarily geared to rational thought rather than to action, or as ontologically and functionally distinct from emotion, imagination and motor response. Nor can it be regarded as separate from that environment in which it operates, the total human ecology.[72]

For Cave, this reconceptualisation of cognition has consequences for one's approach to the use of language, both generally and in literature. For instance, we begin to see language as itself a communicative resource and a feature of the environment, thanks to which we can, interactively and communally, think together. Thus, on this view, 'language is radically under-specified because it is radically mobile, subject to the constraints of time', as is to be expected in interaction between persons in particular situations.[73] This is a language that is 'on the wing, on the hoof, on the run', and which, as such, is accompanied by certain 'strange cognitive pyrotechnics'.[74]

The kind of 'strange cognitive pyrotechnics' that Cave has been especially sensitive to are the mutual relations between bodily movement and gesture, on the one hand, and language and literature on the other. Thus, Cave has pointed to numerous examples of how 'language (whether oral or written) can successfully mediate motor resonance, even enhance it, while inserting it into the whole network of cultural and conceptual resources that individual humans have at their disposal'.[75] The point is to show how, in reading, we depend on our sensorimotor memory and knowledge, and how certain forms of language bring 'to the reflective surface traces of the reader's pre-reflective

[68] Ibid, 7–8. See, eg, Kaufmann (2011); and on 'participatory sense-making', de Jaegher and di Paolo (2007).
[69] See section II of ch 1 for more discussion.
[70] Cave (2016).
[71] See, eg, Cave and Wilson (2018a).
[72] Cave and Wilson (2018b), 18.
[73] Cave (2018a), 167.
[74] Ibid.
[75] Cave (2018b), 14.

sensorimotor response'.[76] The elements of language that this approach points to are not only the obvious candidates of 'verbs and adverbs', but include a wide range of linguistic features; indeed, as Cave argues, 'in fact any element of language, including the movement of a sentence, can give rise to kinesis effects'.[77] Perhaps more radically, on this view, one might not even pay as much attention to the traditional categories of language, such as verbs, adverbs, nouns, sentences, and so on, but to sounds embedded across such forms. For instance, the 'sh' sound, as in 'swishing, shifting', says Cave, 'is a salient, audible feature of the overall kinesic effect',[78] where 'kinesic effect' is understood as the experience of an echo of an embodied action.[79]

This is a complex theory to which I cannot do justice; my aim is merely to mention it as an example of how cognitive literary studies has drawn on the above different approach to cognition to study language and, more broadly, meaning-generating practices via language, in a different way. I shall, in any event, be returning to this approach, and especially to kinesic intelligence, in the next chapter.

C. Spolsky's Fictions

Readers might well ask what relevance this has to law and legal scholarship. A number of scholars have sought to answer that question, each in distinctive and original ways. I shall here briefly mention only two: Ellen Spolsky and Steven Winter.[80] In doing so, I aim not to summarise their views, but simply to point to them as resources akin to what I am trying to develop in this book, though sometimes with some differences in approach.

Ellen Spolsky is one of the pioneers of what may be called 'cognitive legal humanities'. Her work connects with many of this book's claims and attitudes. Drawing sometimes on the rhetorical tradition,[81] and at ease with both the latest developments in philosophy of mind and cognitive science as well as in literary theory and history, Spolsky's work captures the sense, important also for this book, in which persons, interactively and communally, often experiment together in order to cope with the limitations of their own knowledge and with the fact that they find themselves, inevitably and inescapably, in conditions of uncertainty. As Spolsky has said, she is interested in exploring 'the systematic uncertainty of our ways of knowing, and the importance of the interpersonal.'[82] This includes an interest in the importance of 'misunderstanding'.[83]

In a variety of papers and books, Spolsky has urged us to 're-think the interchange among acting bodies, rhetorical forms and emergent meaning',[84] and to do that with

[76] Ibid.

[77] Ibid, 16.

[78] Ibid, 18.

[79] Ibid, 13–14.

[80] See also Johnson (2018). Johnson, although not as extensively as Spolsky and Winter, nevertheless does pay attention to law.

[81] For instance, Spolsky has argued, in a paper on embodied cognition, that 'Classical rhetoric was … about producing motor resonance: (2018), 225.

[82] Ibid, 227.

[83] Ibid.

[84] Ibid, 226.

particular attention to the social dynamics of cognition.[85] In keeping with the above turns to embodiment in 4E cognition, Spolsky has often emphasised the vital significance of 'kinesic intelligence', tying not only mind, body and world together, but also bringing those into play with literature and its many forms. Thus, for example, Spolsky has said that she is interested in 'how the forms of fiction appeal to what human bodies know about action, how words pull readers into their imagined worlds by engaging audiences' kinesic intelligence'.[86]

I shall be returning, in the next chapter, to Spolsky's work on fictional forms and kinesic intelligence, but for now I would like to emphasise another of her contributions, which deserves much more attention than it has received amongst legal scholars. This can be found in her book, *Contracts of Fiction: Cognition, Culture and Community*.[87] Here, Spolsky brings to bear her approach, rooted in the cognitive humanities, on fictional forms, arguing overall that 'our human systems of knowing not only tolerate fictions but actually depend on knowing how to make use of them'.[88] Spolsky's category of fiction is very broad: she includes, for instance, 'poems, an entire genre, or even a library, or a museum'.[89] What interests Spolsky is how such fictions both hold and yield social knowledge. In this respect, Spolsky uses the language of 'niches', saying of the poem, genre, library or museum that it 'is just such a niche in which the poet, the novelist, the reader, the painter, or the audience for any of these, finds shelter when reflection is needed, and where the possibilities for reconstruction and change can be considered and enacted'.[90]

Spolsky's sense of forms, including forms of language, that offer 'shelter when reflection is needed', including 'possibilities for reconstruction and change', is important for this book. What I am calling artefacts can be thought of precisely in this way: as niche constructions, which are the result of interactions and communal activities, and which generate space and time for persons to engage together in making, and, at the same time, also reconstructing and transforming, knowledge. Different contexts of practice will involve different forms of making, eg in the context of inquiry in adjudication, this involves the making of insights into potentially relevant values, vulnerabilities and interests, but the general dynamics of making, and what enables such making practices, may well be similar across different contexts.

Spolsky is further interested, as I am in this book, with what features of language enable us to treat them in this way, ie as niche constructions that generate shelters for reflection. In broad terms, she argues that this has to be a language that somehow stands out from the ordinary run of linguistic communication. 'Language forms not found in everyday speech', she says, 'advertise themselves as a different kind of object, and ask readers to grant them distance and refrain from speedy response'.[91] In so doing,

[85] Spolsky draws, for instance, on Shilbach et al (2013), and endorses the view that knowledge is understood as situated in the embodied interactions among people.
[86] Spolsky (2018), 226.
[87] Spolsky (2015).
[88] Ibid, xxiv.
[89] Ibid, 7.
[90] Ibid.
[91] Ibid, 53.

they 'allow audiences to detach it from the demands, including, importantly, the time demands of ordinary communication'.[92]

Understandably, one of Spolsky's examples is poetic language. The genre of lyric, for example, 'is often hyperbolic', and this has the effect of 'removing its audiences from their routines of ordinary communicative discourse to a place where new ideas and new connections can emerge'.[93] One can read Spolsky's book as a kind of defence of poetry and the cognitive work it enables. On the back of her work, we can look to identify other features of poetic language and consider how they are related to possibilities for cognitive play. For example, we might look to the surprising juxtapositions set up by poetic language, or to its unfinished sentences, its ellipses, its ironies, its allusions, its repetitions of sounds, and its impossible perspectives, and we can understand that these offer particular kinds of shelters for reflection, or, as I would prefer to say, space and time for inquiry.

A fascinating example that Spolsky engages with in her book is that of the genre of the grotesque. This genre, which advertised its own 'foreignness', its own 'outlandishness',[94] did so through 'confusing' combinations of seemingly opposing objects and imaginary figures, 'in which things that should be kept apart are fused together'.[95] This, in turn, has the effect of slowing us down and capturing our attention, as if the form was standing on the banks of a river in which we were swimming obliviously, and picked us up and placed us beside it, giving us time and space for thought. The genre of the grotesque did this quite dramatically, again 'outlandishly'. Works in this genre, says Spolsky (drawing here on the work of Geoffrey Harpham),[96] 'stand at a margin of consciousness between the known and the unknown, the perceived and the unperceived, calling question the adequacy of our ways of organising the world, of dividing the continuum of experience into knowable particles'.[97] Here, Spolsky emphasises an aspect of the genre that points to it being more than just something that captures our attention by its own strangeness. The genre of the grotesque goes further, and actually confuses us, helps create a certain imbalance or disorder in us. This, she says, is part of what makes works in the genre of the grotesque popular:

> Their popularity is evidence that their cognitively destabilising forms feed some hunger in us: they stimulate, encourage, or strengthen our easily overwhelmed abilities to remain open-minded. We need them to keep us alive to the possibilities of reframing settled understandings, of renegotiating social contracts.[98]

Spolsky's point is that the 'disorder' one encounters in works of the grotesque, and the resulting confusion and imbalance it creates, 'incubates the emergence of new understanding'.[99] Our social work together, ie our generation of meaning or the making

[92] Ibid.
[93] Ibid, 36.
[94] Ibid, 199.
[95] Ibid, 201 (quoting Geoffrey Harpham).
[96] See Harpham (1982).
[97] Spolsky (2015), 201.
[98] Ibid, 205.
[99] Ibid, 221.

of insights together, interactively and communally, in real time and over time, depends on us artificially creating pockets of imbalance, confusion and disorder. In creating these environments or niches, we give ourselves the opportunity, precisely by having to cope with the imbalance, of generating new resources, new paths, new alternatives and new possibilities that we might not have been able to generate otherwise.

This perspective, on the work that fiction can enable, is vital for this book. We shall see shortly how I have tried to incorporate it into the very structure of the model of artefacts, which, in part, signal their own artifice, thereby capturing our attention, and at the same time, call on us to participate, and thus to do things with and thanks to them, eg often precisely by unbalancing or disorienting us, or by giving us unfinished sentences to complete.

For me, however, and this may well mark a difference between this book and Spolsky's, niche constructions need not result in, and are not only or even especially valuable because they enable, co-operation and agreement. For Spolsky, it seems, the 'contracts of fiction' she speaks of, and here, her very terminology of 'contract' suggests this too, are valuable because they 'accommodate agreement among people who, sharing a habitat, necessarily share an interest in cooperating'.[100] Co-operation and agreement is important, but the work of fictions, in Spolsky's sense, is by no means confined to that: it can also generate, and also be valuable in generating, contestation and disagreement; it can open up and reveal conflicting associations or value orientations. Even though legal practice certainly needs shared resources, rituals and cognitive habits, it requires less agreement than we often think. In fact, in many ways, legal practice thrives on disagreement.

D. Winter on Legal Cognition

A second figure whose work may be positioned within the 'cognitive legal humanities' is Steven Winter. Like Spolsky, Winter is well informed by recent work on cognition. Furthermore, like I do in this book, he emphasises the importance of 'imagination'. He says:

> By far the most important conclusions to emerge from this recent work on cognition are two: first, that imagination is central to the cognitive process; and, second, that imagination is embodied. The workings of the mind simply cannot be understood without appreciating the pivotal role of embodied imagination in all aspects of cognition, language and thought.[101]

The embodied dimension of cognition is certainly crucial to Winter, and it is important, also, for this book, eg as one of the modes of participation of the imagination, discussed in the next chapter. However, an emphasis on embodiment, as important as it is, can carry the danger of focusing too much, or placing too much explanatory pressure, on unconscious or less-than-conscious processes. This has repercussions for how richly one can model the work of the imagination, as well as the forms of language

[100] Ibid, 198.
[101] Winter (2001), xi.

that are both constructed by the imagination and invite it to be exercised. This is not to critique the embodied perspective offered by Winter: I take it to be an important contribution to our understanding of legal cognition. But it is to say that although there are overlaps between Winter's approach and that which I take in this book, there are also some differences, especially in understanding the relation between language and imagination.

For Winter, 'meaning arises in the imaginative interactions of the human organism with its world, and these embodied experiences provide both the grounding and structure for human thought and rationality'.[102] What 'cognitive theory' can do, he says, is 'make explicit the unconscious criteria and cognitive operations that structure and constitute our judgment',[103] ie precisely its grounding in embodied experiences. In developing this approach, Winter also seeks to re-orient the way we think about reason and rationality in adjudication, and this in ways that are very congenial to this book. Thus, for example, he speaks of cognition having to 'be dynamic and adaptive', ie 'enabling successful application and adjustment to contingent and changing situations', and this means that 'it cannot consist solely or even primarily of passive operations that depend upon content and correspondence'.[104] He continues:

> It follows that cognition is not principally representational, propositional or computational, but rather involves processes that are imaginative, associative and analogical. A growing body of empirical and theoretical work demonstrates that human brain processes are imagistic and cross-modal. They are imagistic in that they involve highly schematic images that are not dependent on any particular sensory modality such as the visual, the kinaesthetic, or the spatiotemporal. They are cross-modal in that the different sensory modalities do not operate as discrete systems. Rather, they combine to form global mappings.[105]

The references here to the cross-modal character of cognition, and thus the importance of relations between 'the visual, the kinaesthetic, or the spatiotemporal', resonate with the approach I take in this book, and which I elaborate on more in the next chapter. Furthermore, the idea that legal thought can be approached as primarily imagistic, including experiencing particular images but also working on the various ways they can be related in patterns, eg analogical or associative ones, is also a direction I am most sympathetic to, and which enters into the discussion of some of the case studies in the second part of the book.

Where our approaches begin to differ is in the role one gives to such images. For Winter, it seems, such images, which he theorises as 'image-schemas', grounded in embodied experiences, both determine and explain our thought. Winter quotes Richard Rorty: 'It is pictures rather than propositions, metaphors rather than statements, which determine most of our philosophical convictions'.[106] Winter is interested in identifying conditions of possibility of 'comprehension', or 'patterns of inference' or 'semantic productivity'; he wants to identity the 'unconscious rules of our language games'.[107]

[102] Ibid, xii.
[103] Ibid, xiii.
[104] Ibid, 5–6.
[105] Ibid.
[106] Ibid, 56.
[107] Ibid, 2.

The order of explanation, if I have understood his account, is often from an initial identification of, say, a metaphor deployed in legal reasoning, thereafter moving toward its grounding in particular embodied experiences, with the idea being that those embodied experiences explain and determine the operation of the cognition guided by that metaphor. These embodied experiences to which particular acts of cognition, and relatedly particular forms of language, such as metaphors and metonymies, can be traced, are basic and foundational. Examples of such basic or foundational embodied experiences include 'balance, part-whole, object, source-path-goal, force-barrier, and container'.[108] These 'image-schemas', as he also calls them, following Lakoff and Johnson, 'provide structure to human thought and a measure of apparent unity and determinacy in our interaction with the world.'[109]

Winter is fighting a particular battle: in particular, against criticisms that might be levelled at such forms of language, and their related processes of cognition, and accusations of them as arbitrary, ornamental, ad hoc and isolated, and by implication superfluous or not especially important, or irregular and un-systematic. As he puts it:

> [First] … where one might have assumed that such a cliché ['forest of constraint'] is arbitrary in meaning, it turns out to be grounded in basic embodied experience. Second, where one might have assumed that an idiom of this sort is merely a matter of colourful expression, it turns out to be rich in conceptual and semantic content. Third, where one might have assumed that such a colloquialism is just an isolated trope, it turns out to be a product of underlying conceptual metaphors that constitute a quite significant part of our conceptual system. Fourth, where one might have assumed that a figurative expression of this sort is subjective and quixotic, it turns out to be highly conventional and quite regular and orderly in its use. In short, we have seen that imaginative rationality is embodied, grounded, and systematic in operation.[110]

It is for this reason, in order to combat these criticisms, that Winter emphasises the structure, order and systematicity of the relations between cognition, or rationality understood broadly, and embodied experiences or image-schemas.

These are important points, but the danger with setting up the theory in this way is that it can result in neglecting the more dynamic relation between language and cognition, and to downplaying what Winter in fact also wants to emphasise: namely, the sense in which reason is 'flexible and adaptive',[111] or 'imaginative, creative and fecund'.[112] The more, it seems, we explain the operation of cognition by reference to it being grounded in certain basic embodied experiences, and the more systematic we make these relations to be, the less room we have for what I have called, under the model of inquiry, 'experiment'. The more regular, orderly, structured and systematic we make cognition out to be, the less space we create for what Spolsky has called 'imbalance', disorientation or confusion, and the manners with which we cope with them. And the more unconscious or less-than-conscious we characterise those processes to be, the more we miss of the more, though not wholly, deliberate, voluntary and self-reflexive modes of cognition.

[108] Ibid, 15.
[109] Ibid.
[110] Ibid, 18.
[111] Ibid, xiv.
[112] Ibid, 21.

Put more generally: at stake is precisely how we model the relationship between language and cognition; whether we position it primarily at the level of something that tacitly guides us, mostly without our awareness, or whether we balance out its tacit qualities with its more reflexive ones. In this book, I point more to the reflexive qualities of the relations between language and cognition, though not in a way that subscribes to a rigid dichotomy between tacit and reflexive, or between sub- or un-conscious and conscious experiences. Tacitness and reflexivity are matters of degree, but I attempt here to articulate a kind of relation between language and cognition that picks up more on the resources of reflexivity.

There are more recent theories that have continued Winter's call for more work at the intersection of cognitive science and humanities. For example, there is the important scholarship of Linda Berger, who has, in a series of papers as well as most recently in her book on *Legal Persuasion* with Kathryn Stanchi,[113] made significant contributions to our understanding of the role and value of a range of cognitive operations and their linguistic analogues, including metaphor and metonymy.[114] Indeed, Berger and Stanchi's work reveals also the insights to be gained by placing into dialogue the cognitive sciences together with feminist legal theory as well as critical race theory, for instance in relation to metaphor, or stories and narratives.[115]

This is all company that this book humbly seeks, even if, in some of the strands of this literature, there is still more emphasis on quick, less-than-conscious fast cognitive processing, or an endorsement of splits between fast and slow thinking. As important as these insights are, I suggest in this book that there is much to be gained in going beyond such divides, eg between thinking fast and slow, and in placing more emphasis on the resourcefulness of reflexivity, mixed in with elements that are less-than-conscious. All that being said, there is no doubt that cognitive legal humanities is one of the most vibrant of all current inter-disciplinary domains of legal scholarship, and deserves more attention from the legal academy. I hope that this book, with its account of artefacts and related processes of imagination, makes a contribution, however small, to this literature.

III. Fictionality

The third and final theoretical tradition and literature that I wish to identify as broadly overlapping with the approach I take to language in this book is that of the study of fictionality. As with rhetoric and the cognitive humanities, this field of study is much too rich and complex to attempt either a map or a summary of it. Instead, I pick up on some of the moves made and draw on them to carve out the approach I take.

To avoid confusion, I should at the outset mention that one of the case studies in the second part of this book involves examining 'fictions' (in Chapter 5). I define these, however, in a particular way, and although I draw on some of the literature on

[113] Berger and Stanchi (2017). This impressive book is also significant in how it tries to combine insights from both the rhetorical tradition and the cognitive science.

[114] See, eg, Berger (2004), (2007) and (2013). I return to some of Berger's work on metaphor in ch 6.

[115] See, eg, Berger and Stanchi (2018); see also Stanchi (2002); Delgado (1989); and Matsuda (1989).

fictionality in that context, my focus there is on the role and value of fictions specifically in enabling inquiry in adjudication. By contrast, in this section, I am concerned with how we can draw on the literature on fictionality to help inform and illuminate the general way I approach language, and in particular artefactual language. As we shall see, this means that I will give particular attention to so-called 'markers' or 'signals' of fictionality. These, in turn, will bear on both dimensions of artefactual language examined in the final two sections of this chapter.

A. The Rise of Fictionality

Recent years have witnessed a burst of scholarship, including much debate, on the history of fictionality. Within the English-speaking academy, one of the key pieces to have sparked the debate was Catherine Gallagher's 'The Rise of Fictionality'.[116] For Gallagher, fiction begins in the eighteenth century, when 'readers developed the ability to tell it apart from both fact and (this is the key) deception'.[117] Gallagher carves out a space between, or beyond, the more usual divide that is drawn between truth and falsity, ie precisely the space of and for fictionality.

If, for Gallagher, fictionality begins in the eighteenth century, the natural question becomes: what was missing in the earlier periods? Gallagher is of course not denying that there were literary forms that, in some ways, resemble the ones that emerge in the eighteenth century. However, she argues that those earlier forms were 'blatantly fictional', ie they 'did not really test fictional cognition, for they so very clearly required suspension of disbelief'.[118] They did this through what Gallagher calls 'very ostensible signs of artifice', such as 'fantastic beasts'.[119] What was lacking, in summary, in the earlier period were two things: '1) a conceptual category of fiction, and 2) believable stories that did not solicit belief'.[120] What one sees in the eighteenth century, with the rise of the novel, is precisely those two things combined: the novel is 'something that is experimenting with this line between fiction that deceives (pretends to be real) and fiction that does not deceive'.[121] 'The idea', as Gallagher says, 'is that fictionality in the sense of something that does not deceive but is also not fantastic comes into the picture with novels at a certain point'.[122]

If the 'very ostensible signs of artifice' relate to the older, too 'blatantly fictional' literary forms, what were the presumably less ostensible signs that pertained to fictionality, and especially the novel? Here, Gallagher emphasises one particular sign: the creation of particular, but still non-referential personal names. Both of these elements are important, ie the non-referentiality, ie the fact that no person is picked out by the name created, as well as the particularity of the person that is created in the fictional

[116] Gallagher (2007).
[117] Ibid, 338.
[118] Ibid, 340.
[119] Ibid.
[120] Ibid.
[121] Ibid.
[122] Ibid.

world. For Gallagher, the fictionality of the novel in the eighteenth century 'inhered in the creation of instances' that were non-verifiable or non-falsifiable.[123] Historically, the crucial period, at least in the English context, appears in the shift from the novels of Defoe to that of Fielding:

> In England, between the time when Defoe insisted that Robinson Crusoe was a real individual (1720) and the time when Henry Fielding urged just as strenuously that his characters were not representations of actual specific people (1742), a discourse of fictionality appeared in and around the novel, specifying new rules for its identification and new modes of nonreference. And it is on the basis of this overt and articulated understanding that the novel may be said to have discovered fiction. What Fielding had that Defoe lacked was not an excuse for fictionality but a use for it as a special way of shaping knowledge through the fabrication of particulars.[124]

It would be a fascinating question for historical investigation to inquire whether the origins of the 'fabrication of particulars', as Gallagher puts it, and especially by way of the invention of personal names, could be traced back to the use of imaginary personal names in legal proceedings. After all, the history of fictional personal names, at least in English common law,[125] is a rich one (not only for persons, but also for places or events, eg 'Blackacre'), and we know from other studies just how close, for instance in the early modern period, the activities of law and literature were.[126] Be that as it may, the crucial point for present purposes is more that Gallagher associates the emergence of fictionality with less 'ostensible signs of artifice', ie a particular class of linguistic markers, in this case, fictional proper names, and, one might add, the accompanying formal or material feature of them, ie capitalisation, as in 'John Dee'. Indeed, the formal or material aspect is vital here: the use of the proper name 'Tom Jones' is a 'convention alerting the reader to the fact that the name refers to nobody in particular, to a fictional entity, for individual reference at the time was normally signalled either through initials and blanks … or by pseudonyms that often referred to the moral qualities of persons'.[127]

What is also crucial is what Gallagher suggests is made possible by this new space of fictionality, ie the readerly experience of it. For it is by no means the case that this fictionality functions as an obstacle to deep and resonant, including affectively resonant, experiences of literature. Indeed, quite the opposite:

> … the characters' very fictiveness had a strong emotional appeal. That apparent paradox – that readers attach themselves to characters because of, not despite, their fictionality – was acknowledged and discussed by 18th century writers. … they noticed that the fictional framework established a protected affective enclosure that encouraged risk-free emotional investment. Fictional characters, moreover, were thought to be easier to sympathise or identify with than most real people.[128]

[123] Ibid, 341–2.
[124] Ibid, 344.
[125] See, eg, Sparkes (2015) re the fictional names used in the history of the fiction of ejectment.
[126] See, eg, Hutson (2017); Altman (1978); Eden (1986); and Trimpi (1983). It is impossible to resist quoting from Sidney's *Apology* (1868) [1595]: 'And doth the Lawyer lye then, when under the names of John a stile and John a noakes hee puts his case? But that is easily answered. Theyr naming of men is but to make theyr picture the more lively, and not to builde any historie; paynting men, they cannot leave men nameless': (1868), 53.
[127] Gallagher (2007), 352.
[128] Ibid, 351.

For the present book, the idea that fictionality does not pose an obstacle to, but in fact enhances, affective involvement is crucial, and I will be saying more about affective involvement as a mode of participation of the imagination in the next chapter. Also important is the range of epistemic attitudes and activities that Gallagher says was made possible, and again encouraged and enhanced, by fictionality:

> The readers of these early novels were encouraged to anticipate problems, make suppositional predictions, and see possible outcomes and alternative interpretations. In short, the reader, unlike the character, occupies the lofty position of one who speculates on the action, entertaining various hypotheses about it. These thematically triggered reactions coincide with and magnify the more abstract formal demand that early fiction writers placed on their readers: asking them to take the reality of the story itself as a kind of suppositional speculation.[129]

Supposition, but also other modes of speculation, involving for instance the generation of hypotheticals, are, on the approach I take in this book, very much part of the activity of imagination. Indeed, Gallagher's approach is strongly akin to the one taken here: on the one hand, we have artefacts which capture our attention by signalling their own artifice (for Gallagher, signal their fictionality), and call on us to participate, eg precisely to suppose, speculate or hypothesise, and, on the other hand, we have the processes of imagination, ie entering a distinctive epistemic frame (for Gallagher, the space of the fictional), where we suspend or transform certain epistemic norms and commitments, while at the same time participating along a spectrum of affective, sensory and kinesic involvement.

Gallagher claims quite a lot, historically speaking, for fictionality, speaking not only of the relations between fictionality and, say, 'affective speculation in courtship' or 'merchant and insurers calculating risks', but also as a necessary condition for 'modern subjectivity' in general.[130] Religion, science, and law too, all make an appearance in this story:

> … almost all of the developments we associate with modernity – from greater religious toleration to scientific discovery – required the kind of cognitive provisionality one practices in reading fiction, a competence in investing contingent and temporary credit. One telling acknowledgement of the benefits of such mental states was the increasing use of the word fiction to mean "a supposition known to be at variance with fat, but conventionally accepted for some reason of practical convenience, conformity with traditional usage, decorum, or the like," as in 'legal fiction'.[131]

However cautiously we may wish to take these historical claims, surely Gallagher is right to point to the enormous contribution that fictionality, or the fabrication of particulars, makes to enabling what she calls above 'cognitive provisionality'. Indeed, it is precisely these practices of cognitive provisionality, which both make and rely on artefacts, that this book defends under the canopy of the value of imagination in adjudication.

There is one more feature of Gallagher's account that I wish point to. For in addition to her discussion of the signs of artifice, or the markers of fictionality,

[129] Gallagher (2007), 346.
[130] Ibid.
[131] Ibid, 347.

Gallagher also observes that devices of fictionality are also marked by what she calls 'incompleteness'.[132] Devices like fictional proper names, for instance 'Anna Karenina', are 'necessarily incomplete'; 'The proper name "Anna Karenina" is made up of a finite set of sentences.'[133] This incompleteness, or one might say under-specification, is important, for it allows not only for cognitive provisionality, but also for an active kind of participation on behalf of the reader, including an affective one: 'Whether foregrounded or backgrounded … incompleteness, like uncanny accessibility and finish, invites the reader's emotional investment in the lack itself'.[134] Indeed, if the device 'actually created an impression of totality so strong that the incompleteness and disjunctions disappeared, there would be no inviting gaps for the reader to slip through, no subjective blanks to be overcome by her own idealised ego'.[135] Devices of fictionality, or artefacts, contain certain formal features that at least enable, if not make more likely, the reader's or listener's active participation. Artefacts, in short, not only signal their own artifice, but they also call upon us to participate, and they do so in a variety of ways, eg through being incomplete, under-specified, or discontinuous.

B. Relative Signposts of Fictionality

Gallagher's claims have not gone unchallenged, perhaps especially her historical claims. I cannot examine these fascinating historical disagreements in detail, though I wish to emphasise that they are also of theoretical significance, as historical disagreements often are. They also deserve further attention, especially by legal historians, given the close links between legality and fictionality. What I would like to do is to briefly consider some of the replies to Gallagher's claims.

i. The Long History of Fictionality and Self-Referentiality

Thus, Monika Fludernik, in her recent 'The Fiction of the Rise of Fictionality',[136] encourages us to work with a much larger historical canvas when addressing the history of fictionality. 'Fictionality', Fludernik says, 'is not a simple object of analysis but a concept with its own history, diverse instrumentalisation, and complex conceptual range'.[137] For example, the invention of non-referential proper names, so important to Gallagher's account, is said by Fludernik to have a long history: 'Onomata (names) not attested in history or myth' were employed in ancient comic genres, as well as to the Greek novel; they also appear in 'most stories in *The Canterbury Tales*'.[138]

Fludernik's examples are multiple and go considerably beyond the deployment of nomina, or fictional proper names. They include, for instance, the medieval genre of the

[132] Ibid, 359.
[133] Ibid, 358.
[134] Ibid, 359.
[135] Ibid, 360.
[136] Fludernik (2018).
[137] Ibid, 70.
[138] Ibid, 80.

exemplum, which is a genre that brings to mind the long history of using supposed cases or hypothetical scenarios in the history of argumentation.[139] The history of allegory, too, might be mentioned, especially when it is seen as a move to 'rescue culturally important texts from being downgraded to the status of fables'.[140] Perhaps most obviously, there is the history of poetic genres, eg lyric, with its 'address to non-existent or absent personae, abstract entities, or mythological and even non-human beings', or its creation of 'virtual scenarios not linked to definite time and space co-ordinates'; or its 'expressive non-communicational utterances that are not meant to provoke a direct response on the part of recipients'.[141] Indeed, for Fludernik, fictionality may be most broadly associated with practices of self-referentiality, at least those which result in some sort of aesthetic appreciation by the reader, viewer or listener:

> Fictionality thus largely overlaps with the practice of the arts but includes stories told with the purpose of illustration and instruction. Fictionality, like storytelling, emphasises self-referentiality to the extent that fictional speech acts or artifacts claim attention for themselves, thus often involving aesthetic appreciation .... Since the recipients bracket real-world truth claims as the primary meaning of such artifacts (for example, a painting of a French landscape is not taken as a kind of map that would help visitors to that part of France orient themselves), fictionality – unless explicitly marked by general labels (novel, play, etc.) – to some extent lies in the eyes of the beholder.[142]

Fludernik here refers to the relativity of fictionality (which is also important to this book, in the form of the relativity of artefactuality), ie the sense in which markers or signposts of fictionality depend on their being taken up as such by their beholders.[143] And this is also something that has come to be emphasised in other responses to Gallagher's claims, or in other contributions to the debate over fictionality.

ii. *Fictionality as a Communicative Act*

For instance, Simona Zetterberg Gjerlevsen, who draws on the brilliant analysis offered by Richard Walsh in his *Rhetoric of Fictionality*,[144] treats fictionality as a 'communicative act'. For Walsh, as Gjerlevsen notes, 'fictionality depends on the way it is signalled by the author and interpreted by the reader'; and thus it follows that 'fictionality should not be regarded as a property within the text'.[145] This then becomes historically quite complex, for what might tend to succeed in communicating fictionality will vary in different

[139] Ibid, 72. See also Scanlon (2007).
[140] Fludernik (2018), 79.
[141] Ibid, 81.
[142] Ibid, 78.
[143] Though it is not entirely clear, at least to me, just how much of a relativist Fludernik is in this respect, eg she says: 'The phrase "to some extent" expresses the line between artifacts that have explicit markers and frames of factuality or fictionality (which clinch the matter) and those that are open to interpretation due to a lack of contextual or internal determination': ibid, 78, fn 9. The idea that some markers may 'clinch the matter' does seem to indicate commitment to there being some markers that are unconventionally fictional, ie that guarantee a reader will take them to be fictional. Insofar as this does signal an unconventionalist or non-relativist position with respect to fictionality or factuality, I would resist it.
[144] Walsh (2007).
[145] Zetterberg Gjerlevsen (2016a), 178.

times and places. Indeed, the shifts here will be not only as to markers of fictionality, but also as to markers of factuality, with no doubt all kinds of play at the seams between the fictional and the factual. What may strike some readers, viewers or listeners, in particular times and places, as a signal of realism or factuality, eg the omniscient narrator or the flashback, may be experienced by others, in other times and places, as signals of fictionality.

What is also important in this context, and as emphasised by Zetterberg Gjerlevsen, is that treating fictionality broadly as a mode of communication employing contingently successful markers of fictionality renders it possible to look for evidence of fictionality not only in works of literature, but also in nonfiction. Indeed, Zetterberg Gjerlevsen herself points to the use of thought experiments in philosophy as an example of fictionality in nonfiction.[146] It is precisely such islands, so to speak, of fictionality in the nonfictional discourse of the law that I pay attention to in this book.

iii. Signposts of Fictionality

In her entry on 'Fictionality in the Living Handbook of Narratology',[147] Zetterberg Gjerlevsen discusses some of the scholars who have provided further examples of (relative, and at best robustly conventional) signposts of fictionality, including Gerard Genette, Kate Hamburger, Dorrit Cohn, Michel Riffaterre, Jean-Marie Schaeffer, Monika Fludernik and Wolf Schmid. Again, these are important for my purposes, for their character as markers of fictionality overlaps with, even if it does not always map perfectly onto, what I am calling artefacts. I will therefore be returning to them in the next two sections, and especially section IV of this chapter. For now, by way of illustration, let me mention just a few more examples of these. Riffaterre offers a long, and helpful list of them:

> Signs pointing to the fictionality of fiction are many and well known. The list is extensive: authors' intrusions; narrators' intrusions; multiple narrators; humorous narrative that acts as a representation of the author or of a narrator or that suggests an outsider's viewpoint without fully intruding; meta-language glossing narrative language; generic markers in the titles and subtitles, in prefaces, and in postfaces; emblematic names for characters and places; incompatibilities between narrative voice and viewpoint and characters' voices and viewpoints; incompatibilities between viewpoint and verisimilitude, especially omniscient narrative; signs modifying the narrative's pace and altering the sequence of events (backtracking and anticipation, significant gaps, prolepsis, and analepsis); mimetic excesses, such as unlikely recordings of unimportant speech or thought … and, finally, diegetic overkill, such as the representation of ostensibly insignificant details, the very insignificance of which is significant in a story as a feature of realism … the farcical exaggeration, the biblical reference, and the narrator's stated viewpoint bespeak artifice and focus on the presence … of that narrator in the scene. These are signs of fictionality.[148]

Riffaterre speaks of these examples as signs of 'the fictionality of fiction', but as the reference above to Zetterberg Gjerlevsen indicates, this does not mean we need to confine

[146] Ibid, 176.
[147] Zetterberg Gjerlevsen (2016b).
[148] Riffaterre (1990), 30–1.

them to marking the distinction between fictional and non-fictional genres. Instead, we can see them as pointing to fictional devices that may be found equally in fictional and non-fictional genres. Furthermore, some of these may well function more as signals of artifice, and some more as calls for participation, and some as both simultaneously. Again, I shall return to this issue in the next two sections of this chapter.

C. Fictionality: Immersion and Reflexivity

Above, when discussing Gallagher, I mentioned her important point that fictionality is not an obstacle to, but indeed enhances, immersion or participation, including embodied, affective and sensory participation. Fictionality, in this sense, is not the same as the illusion of reality; it is not the same, for instance, as complete suspension of disbelief. Instead, fictionality refers to something that invites a dual and simultaneous awareness, resembling precisely the account of the imagination in this book: namely, immersion combined with reflexive awareness of artifice. In closing out this section on fictionality, I wish to return to this point, for it is vital to my account. In doing so, let me mention two theorists that have made this point, ie as to the compatibility between fictionality and immersion, very persuasively: first, Jean-Marie Schaeffer, and secondly, Richard Moran.[149]

i. The Ludic Feint

In what is a veritable tour de force, *Why Fiction?*,[150] Schaeffer offers a comprehensive account of fictionality, including tracing it back to its development from childhood games, especially role-playing, linking it to pretend play fights of animals, and cataloguing the various differences between different fictional art forms, from literature to digital games. Common to all this great variety is the 'pragmatic frame', the signalling of fictionality that allows us to immerse ourselves, without the risks and burdens of the ordinary stream of action and interaction. Indeed, as Schaeffer points out early in his book, 'one cannot understand what fiction is if one does not take as a starting point the fundamental mechanisms of "doing-as-if" – of ludic feint'.[151] Also important are what he calls 'blockages', ie reminders of fictionality: these 'prevent the immersion extending itself up to the global pragmatic frame that establishes the work as a fiction'.[152] Both the initial frame, as well as the blockages, serve to distinguish fictionality from the 'lure', ie from a practice that involves deceiving another into something, examples of which

[149] On this mix of reflexivity and immersion, see also Polvinen (2016) and (2017). For instance, Polvinen argues that 'the role of the clearly signalled fictionality of the literary work in the reading process, and in how readers' minds are able to assume a perspective that is simultaneously aware of the fictionality of the events it follows and yet fully cognitively and emotionally engaged with them': (2017), 140. Stephen Halliwell's work on mimesis (2002) deserves special attention here, recovering a much richer meaning of 'mimesis' for Aristotle than has often been ascribed to it, and one that arguably allows for precisely this simultaneity of reflexivity and immersion.

[150] Schaeffer (1999).

[151] Ibid, xii.

[152] Ibid, 39.

range from the 'behavioural lure', as when an 'animal selectively imitates the specific behaviour of another animal, in general with the end of inducing an error in its potential predator or prey'[153] to lies, and importantly also to failed fictions.

This last category is interesting, for it serves as a reminder of the relativity of fictionality. Schaeffer's example is the infamous fictional biography of Sir Andrew Marbot by Wolfgang Hildesheimer.[154] Marbot never existed, and although Hildesheimer did include some hints of fictionality, they were so subtle that even expert reviewers were deceived into taking it as a real biography. What the book revealed was how powerful were the conventional signs of factuality, in this case linked to the genre of biography. The example is important for it also helps Schaeffer to counter a certain objection to immersion in fictionality, ie concerning 'the dangers of immersion'. This is a complaint that has a long history, stretching back at least to Plato, as to how the mimetic arts are sources of falsity, duping us into believing the reality of what is but necessarily an inadequate copy. Schaeffer argues that Marbot is not 'an experimental proof of the dangers of immersion'; on the contrary, it throws light on the constitutive rule of all fiction: 'the institution of a pragmatic frame appropriate to fictional immersion'.[155] That frame, to recall, is what Schaeffer calls the 'ludic feint' or the 'shared feint'.[156] The further twist in this example is that Hildesheimer actually intended a 'ludic feint', and this despite including, as it turned out, too powerful, signals of factuality or markers of realism. What this shows is that fictionality cannot be secured by 'the intention of the creator', and that fictionality is a 'communicative' phenomenon.[157] Indeed, we may add, sometimes what may be intended as a 'lure', employing signals of factuality or markers of reality, may be taken by a certain audience as a 'ludic feint'. There are no guarantees here: fictionality is relative, and dependent to a degree on the contingency of social conventions, though this is of course not to deny that new forms of signalling fictionality can also be invented.

The example of the Marbot 'biography' is important, too, because for Schaeffer immersion in a fictional world does not involve the treatment of 'the imaginary universe' as a 'real universe'. Again, this would be to collapse the category of fictionality into the lure or the lie. Our immersion in fictional worlds is gated, as it were, by a pragmatic frame, and is also accompanied by reminders of its own fictionality:

> The function of the ludic feint is to create an imaginary universe and to lead [I would say invite] the receiver to immerse himself in this universe. It is not to induce him to believe that this imaginary universe is the real universe. The situation of ludic feint thus distinguishes itself profoundly from that of the serious feint. In this last case the function of mimemes is to deceive the beliefs, that is, the conscious instant that regulates our direct interactions with reality; in the fictional device their function is to engage the representational attitude (perceptive or linguistic-semantic), it being understood that a shared feint implies that we know it is a matter of mimemes, a knowledge that stimulates the specific usage that is advisable to make of the universe generated by this representational attitude.[158]

[153] Ibid, 45.
[154] Hildesheimer (1984).
[155] Schaeffer (1999), 122.
[156] Ibid.
[157] Ibid.
[158] Ibid, 131.

A fiction, as Schaeffer adds, 'is not obliged to denounce itself as fiction', as if it was but a cheap trick, really a lure, but, 'it should be announced as fiction'.[159] This announcement, which comes in various forms, ie tacit or explicit, helps to 'limit[] the space of the game at the interior of which the semblance can operate without the representations induced by the mimemes being treated in the same manner as would be the "real" representations mimed by the fictional device'.[160] A nice analogy offered by Schaeffer is that of a perceptive illusion: 'The situation of fictional immersion could in fact be compared to the one in which we find ourselves when we are victims of a perceptive illusion all the while knowing that it is a matter of an illusion.'[161] There is, further, a certain pleasure – a complex one, with its mixed character of self-reflexivity and immersion – associated both with voluntarily experiencing the illusion and voluntarily enjoying fiction.[162]

ii. *Artifice and Emotional Involvement*

As for Schaeffer, for Richard Moran, whose essays were recently collected into a volume entitled *The Philosophical Imagination*,[163] awareness of fictionality is by no means an obstacle, but instead enhances immersion. One of Moran's critical targets is Kendall Walton's suggestion, in his *Mimesis as Make-Believe*,[164] that the emotions we experience in fictional worlds, whether in works of literature or cinema, are not real emotions, but fake ones.[165] This is sometimes known as the 'problem' or even 'paradox' of 'fictional emotions', the question being how it is that we can experience, sometimes very intensively, fictional works emotionally when we know we are in a fictional world.

Helpfully, Moran places this problem or paradox on its head, and in so doing, deflates it. He points out that, in fact, 'Much of our emotional life is directed at various modal facts: things that might have happened to us but didn't, things we might have done, how things could have turned out differently'.[166] It turns out that, if we reflect on it even briefly, 'comparatively little of one's emotional attention concerns objects in the actual here and now'.[167] The problem or paradox only works as such when so-called fictional emotions are placed up against a very limited background of emotions, eg rage directed at someone before us or fear experienced when walking the street at night. This framing of the problem or paradox, makes us think that fictionality is an obstacle, as Moran explains in the following quote:

> In framing the philosophical problem [of fictional emotions], the implied contrast is always with the real thing, because the very thing to be explained is how (awareness of) fictionality is compatible with the appearance of genuine emotional attitudes. This naturally encourages the idea that it is the sense of fictionality that needs to be overcome, or diminished, or distracted

[159] Ibid, 137.
[160] Ibid.
[161] Ibid, 166.
[162] Ibid, 292. Schaeffer only briefly mentions the theme of pleasure, but he also recognises that it is an important one.
[163] Moran (2017).
[164] Walton (1990).
[165] See also Simpson (2015).
[166] Moran (2017), 5.
[167] Ibid.

> from, if we are to make sense of such responses. And this, in turn, encourages the idea that artificiality, the assertion of the status of the work as artefact, or the elaboration of conspicuous features that play no role in the construction of any fictional truths, must detract from emotional engagement in thus detracting from the coherence of the fictional world depicted. It is, I believe, the framing of the original problem itself that leads the mind in this direction.[168]

It is while in the grip of this framing that Walton identifies certain features of fictional works as 'inhibiting psychological participation', eg 'the "conspicuous brush strokes on the surface of van Gogh's Starry Night"'.[169] This, however, argues Moran, is a mistake. The presence of artifice is not an obstacle; in fact, it makes immersion, in the sense of 'emotional involvement', easier:

> … for it would appear to be the very features of the work that do indeed detract from the realistic presentation of the fictional world that actually enhance, and don't inhibit, the intensity and richness of one's emotional involvement with it. We know that Starry Night would not really be more emotionally engaging if Van Gogh had calmed down and left out all that overwrought brushwork. And the highly artificial, figurative, self-conscious language spoken, for example, by Macbeth does not interfere with our ability to gripped by the play and his situation.[170]

Part of the point here is that trying to capture what is going on in the fictional world by reference to belief, or, its fictional cousin, make-believe, is too strong or too crude. In fictional worlds we are neither believing nor make-believing, but we are still participating, eg we are still involved emotionally. We do not need believe, or fake-believe, to participate in fictional worlds. As Moran says, here referring specifically to the effects of rhetorical features of language, such as 'figuration, allusion, rhythm, repetition, assonance, and dissonance': 'the way such rhetorical features work on the emotions does not seem to rely on either believing or make-believe something to be the case'.[171] In describing how fiction works, or can work, we need not apologise for the presence of artifice. Instead, we should see artifice as 'directly responsible for the ability of these lines [containing rhythm and figuration] to elicit any feeling'.[172]

For Moran, noticing that our experience of fictional worlds need not be burdened by belief or make-belief, and, thus that there is no problem or paradox of fictional emotions, also opens up the way to a different way of approaching the activity of the imagination. Although I cannot enter into details here, for I shall be discussing imagination in the next chapter, let me just note that for Moran, we need to think of the activity of imagination as involving change or transformation, for instance in attitude or perspective, but not, and this is crucial, at the level of belief:

> Although this may be most easily seen in the case of rhetoric, it is quite generally true for both philosophy and literature that much of what they aim at is not on the level of specifically

[168] Ibid, 8.

[169] See Walton (1990), 277. In this context, consider also Richard Wollheim's concept of 'twofoldness': see Wollheim (1987). For Wollheim, when we experience visual art, we experience both its recognitional and its configurational aspects, ie we apprehend both what it is depicting and how it is doing so. The general point is that awareness of the configurational is not an obstacle to the recognitional aspects of experiencing visual art. For an application of Wollheim's concept to literary character, see Smith (2011).

[170] Moran (2017), 9.

[171] Ibid, 9–10.

[172] Ibid, 10.

> altered beliefs but, rather, such things as changes in the associations and comparisons one makes, differences in the vivid or 'felt' appreciation of something already known, or changes in one's habits of attention and sense of the important and the trifling. And although such changes of mind are something different from the acceptance or rejection of certain beliefs, there is nothing to be gained by assimilating them all to the category of the non-cognitive.[173]

Thus, for Moran, the fact that imagining, and its modes of involvement, for instance emotional involvement, do not connect to the structure of belief does not render them cognitively un-important. There is no reason, he reminds us, why we must characterise the domain of the cognitive so narrowly as to confine it to belief or make-belief. The kind of immersion, participation or involvement in fictional worlds is cognitively rich, including, potentially, emotionally so, and it is all the more so for not being burdened by belief, while being enhanced by awareness of fictionality. To understand this better, however, what we need is a richer, more distinctive picture of imagination. I will turn to that task in the next chapter.

I have focused, in the above account, on fictionality largely in literary theory and history, and to a more limited extent in philosophy. Fictionality has, of course, also received some attention in legal theory and legal history.[174] My point here, again, is not to summarise the relevant literatures, but to draw on them, briefly and selectively, to inform the model I am constructing. What we can take, in broad terms, from the above discussion of fictionality is that it helps us understand how certain forms of language can signal such fictionality, though only ever conventionally, and thus relatively and contingently, so, and, at once, invite a particular kind of self-reflexive immersion, namely one that does not reduce it to the experience of the illusion of reality or some sort of make-belief, but that combines reflexivity with immersion. As we shall see, it is precisely this mix that makes imagination so unique and valuable.

IV. Signalling Artifice

I have now proceeded through three rich and complex traditions and literatures: rhetoric, cognitive humanities and fictionality. Each of these contributes significantly to this book's general approach to language, including its artefactuality. In this and the next section, I articulate more fully my own approach, though this continues to be informed and inspired by the above.

In what follows, I seek to outline, as clearly as I can, what I mean by the two dimensions of artefacts, and also to give some examples of their variety. In this section, I turn to the 'signalling of artifice', its function and its varieties. In the next section, I focus on how artefactual language calls on us to participate, and again the various ways it can do that. Of course, it must be remembered that these are two sides of the same coin: they point to two dimensions that must be present for there to be artifactuality, all the while

[173] Ibid, 37–8.

[174] See, eg, Eden (1986); Barfield (1947); and, more recently, Petroski (2018). I address the topic of legal fictions in ch 5.

keeping in mind the important proviso that there is no language that is inherently artefactual, but is only ever relatively, and thus contingently, so.

Further, and at the risk of testing the patience of the reader, let me also recall that to separate out what I am calling artefacts with imagination risks being misleading: they form a duo, with artefacts being both constructed by imagination, but also inviting exercises of imagining. With those provisos in mind, let us turn to this first dimension of artefacts.

A. Exclusions

When forms of language signal their own artifice, they attract attention to themselves. To signal artifice is to bring to our attention the very means of language, ie to its character as a form or a means of communication, such that it puts us on epistemic alert. To experience language in this way, in turn, is also to be invited to enter a distinctive epistemic frame and to participate, ie precisely, to imagine. To get a handle on this, we can begin with some exclusions, ie what signalling artifice does not include. I shall here mention four categories of exclusion, though there may well be others.

i. Material Presence

First, there may be ways of inviting attention to the material presence of language that need not involve signalling its artifice. Thus, for example, one could create a very large sign, with each letter as large as a house (think of the Hollywood sign on the hills in California), or one could make some lettering very bright and shiny, or some words could be underlined or made bold, or one could shout out a word very loudly, and all this could bring the attention of its readers or listeners to its material presence. This would not, however, tend to bring that language to our attention in the specific sense in which I mean, ie it would not be signalling its own artifice: it would not be bringing attention to language as a form or a means of communication, with the effect of placing us on epistemic alert.

ii. Falsity and Nonsense

Second, to signal artifice is not necessarily to flout one's own falsity. Thus, for instance, consider the sentence 'This sentence is not true', or other paradoxical statements of this kind. Or a statement that 'It is raining outside', when we can all perfectly well see that it is sunny. We may be puzzled about such statements, but they need not attract attention to themselves as a form or a means of communication. Puzzlement can be important to the experience of language as signalling its own artifice, but it is neither necessary, nor sufficient.

Similarly so with language that presents itself as nonsense, or one that is garbled in some way that strikes us incoherent, or one that we experience as a mistake, eg a misspelling, or some formatting error. All this may puzzle us, or, in certain circumstances, annoy or worry us, but it need not amount, and would not ordinarily amount, to an experience of language signalling its own artifice. There has to be some sense in which we experience the language as still working, or as being constructed with the intention to work, ie to communicate in a specific way.

iii. The Usable

Third, and more controversially, to signal artifice is not, at least not paradigmatically, to signal one's status as an instrument, tool or device. This is more controversial, and more difficult to articulate, because a pragmatic mode does generally infuse the model of artefacts I am constructing. Further, the second dimension of artefacts does pick up on some of the ways that pragmatists have spoken about devices of thought, eg idealised or approximated models, ie precisely as things we can do things with. Within this first dimension of artefacts, however, we can say that something can present itself as usable, as affording some further action with it, but nevertheless not signal its own artifice. A visual diagram, for example, to take a case from visual rather than linguistic forms, may present itself as usable, but it may not signal artifice: it does not bring attention to itself as a means of communication; rather, it directs our attention in particular ways, or invites us to make certain inferences. It may happen, of course, that many of the devices that do present themselves as tools or instruments for further action also signal their own artifice. That may be the case, but it does not seem to me to be necessarily so.

To signal artifice, then, requires something more than merely presenting oneself as usable, or as an instrument or device to think with. There must be something that, in bringing attention to itself as a means of communication, puts us on epistemic alert, and, in doing so, invites us to enter into a distinctive epistemic frame.

iv. The Impossible, Improbable or Unrealistic

Fourth, and finally, some of what has been included as signals of fictionality has been designed to mark a distinction between the fictional and realistic, or the fictional and the plausible or probable. Dorrit Cohn, for example, in her *The Distinction of Fiction*,[175] has provided a number of such allegedly distinguishing marks of fiction. One example is the splitting between narrator and implied author.[176] Other related examples pointed out also by other scholars, include the use of free indirect discourse and interior monologue, which grants us, as readers, access to the inner worlds of others that we would not ordinarily, in everyday life, have access to; or the extensive use of dialogues, which, again, strike as unrealistic or unlikely to occur in reality.

I do not mean to include these as signals of artifice. What I mean by the signalling of artifice is not the signalling of something that is ordinarily impossible, implausible or improbable, though, as we shall see, some artefacts may include such impossibility, implausibility or improbability within them, eg certain hypothetical scenarios or thought experiments. The line to be drawn is not between that which is fictional on the one hand, and realistic on the other. Rather, the line is between those forms of language

[175] Cohn (1999).
[176] Ibid, 124.

that, always relatively and contingently, strike us as pointing to themselves as forms or means of communication, with the effect of putting us on epistemic alert. Signalling artifice does not necessarily mean presenting oneself as impossible, or as highly improbable, or otherwise unrealistic.

B. Varieties

Although I have pointed to a few exclusions above, I generally mean the category of signalling artifice to be large and expansive, and inclusive of many different ways in which such artifice may be signalled. There are, in other words, many different ways in which we may be brought on epistemic alert, and in which some aspect of our epistemic reflexivity is triggered.

i. Explicit/Implicit

One way to taxonomise these different possibilities is to divide them into explicit and implicit signals of artifice. In the section on 'Fictionality' above, I discussed briefly the work of Jean-Marie Schaeffer. At one point in his account, Schaeffer speaks of the different ways that fictionality may be 'announced': 'According to the cultural context and the type of fiction', he says, 'this announcement is more or less explicit.'[177] In terms of less explicit announcements, this will rely on certain conventions, on 'tacit' or 'implicit knowledge':

> For example, our implicit knowledge of the outstanding traits of cinematographic fiction means that when we turn on the television in middle of a program we know right away if the images that succeed one another are part of a documentary or part of a fictional film – except in the case of a fiction film founded on the formal mimesis of the documentary genre (such as certain passages of Zelig by Woody Allen) or a documentary that borrows its construct from fiction (like Nanook of the North by Robert Flaherty).[178]

Maintaining his focus on multiple fictional forms, Schaeffer also gives a variety of examples of the more explicit announcements of fictionality:

> The forms that this announcement takes, when it is explicit, are in addition very diverse according to the types of fiction. In the case of oral literature, the role is generally filled by conventional introductory formulas. For verbal fiction in the regime of writing, it is usually the paratext that takes the responsibility for it, whether it is by explicit generic indications or in a more tacit manner by the type of title retained … in other forms of fiction the pragmatic contract materialises itself in the form of a veritable physical frame. This is the case of the theatrical scene – to measure its efficacity as a frame of fictionalisation, it is enough to think in contrast of street theatre and of the difficulties that can happen there to trace the limits between the game and the reality.[179]

[177] Schaeffer (1999), 137.
[178] Ibid.
[179] Ibid.

Schaeffer's division and examples are helpful, but I want to cut across them. Thus, what I propose as the distinction between explicit and implicit forms of signalling artifice both includes, but does not quite map onto, his division into explicit and tacit announcements of fictionality.

By explicit, I mean statements of the form 'Let us suppose' or 'Let us take', or 'Let us treat it as if', or 'What if we said …'. I take these to be explicit forms of signalling artifice because they bring our attention to language as a form or means of communication; we are put on epistemic alert, and thereby invited to enter a distinctive epistemic frame. Within this frame, and as we shall see when we consider imagination in the next chapter, we selectively suspend otherwise habitually relied on epistemic norms or commitments. By implicit signalling of artifice, in turn, I mean both the kind of very convention-reliant forms that Schaeffer has in mind with 'implicit' or 'tacit' announcements, as well as those that are less convention-reliant, but still, of course, convention-infused, such as paratextual or generic indicators, eg labelling something as a 'novel' or as a 'thought experiment'. Both implicit and explicit signals of artifice invite us into a state of epistemic reflexivity, where we ready ourselves, as it were, for participation, immersion or involvement, but where such participation is accompanied by awareness of being in a distinctive epistemic state.

Later, in this book, I will be looking at examples of signalling artifice in legal language, which includes plenty of explicit signalling (as we find with 'Let us suppose such and such', or 'What if so and so'), as well as implicit signalling (as we find, for instance, in some legal fictions or in some metaphorical language). For now, I propose collecting as many examples as possible, with a view to clarifying more what is involved in this experience of reading or listening to language that signals its own artifice.

ii. *Estrangement, Epistemic Alertness and the Space of Artifice*

The question we can ask ourselves is: what highlights the artificiality of language? What brings into view its own status as something made, constructed? What brings into view the seams of language, as if we were revealing the inner workings of a clock? One possibility here is to consider when we have an experience of language as somehow interrupting us, as somehow estranging us from the ordinary flow of reading or listening.

To speak of 'estrangement' is of course immediately to bring to mind the work of the Russian literary theorist, Victor Shklovsky. In his 'Art as Device', Shklovsky calls on the experience of 'estrangement' to mark a difference between prosaic and poetic language.[180] He characterises prose, and its rhythms, as an 'automatising factor', as making reading accessible, easy, as if to lull us into forgetting that we are reading or listening at all.[181] The language of poetry, however, he characterises as 'disrupting the rhythm, of disrupting it unpredictably.'[182] Shklovsky also speaks of poetry as

[180] Shklovsky (2015).
[181] Ibid, 173.
[182] Ibid.

'decelerated, distorted speech',[183] and of 'poetic language' as 'being foreign, surprising, difficult'; 'The language of poetry', he says, 'is difficult, laborious language which puts the brakes on perception.'[184]

Shklovsky's perspective is helpful for present purposes, as long as we generalise it, and thus not confine it to any specific literary genres. What forms of language stop us, as it were, in our tracks, and yet still engage us epistemically? One might think here of forms of language that strike us as overtly patterned, for instance because they repeat a sound over and over, eg as in alliteration, or where something is overtly symmetrical, eg as when we employ a trope of reversal, saying for example: 'X came to conquer Y; but instead Y conquered X', or where something strikes us as a jarring juxtaposition, eg as we have in metaphorical language, for instance, equating Richard with a lion, or humans with wolves.[185] In all these cases, something strikes us out of the ordinary, but still as a form or means of communication. Something, in short, surprises us, though this is a very epistemic, or reflexive, kind of surprise. Something may be exaggerated, eg as above, too patterned, or perhaps overtly stylised, and this triggers us (again, contingently, for we may be so used to it that we no longer notice it or are immune from it) into an awareness of it as a form or means of communication. We enter into a state where we become conscious of that form of language as an artefact, ie, as something made or constructed, announcing itself as a means of communication, but still engaging us epistemically.

An interesting example, which Dorrit Cohn and others speak of, and which I would be minded to include as a signal of artifice, is the introduction of an imaginary character, for instance, through a capitalised proper name. For Cohn, for instance, this is 'a decisive signal for the reader's recognition of … novelistic status', ie a 'status that is determined by the presence of an imaginary speaker incarnated as a character within the fictional world.'[186] And we can recall here, too, the emphasis placed on non-referential, and yet particular, proper names by Gallagher.[187] The capitalisation of a non-referential name can, indeed, stop us in our tracks, at least when we are not used to it, and even then it can retain a glimmer of this effect. Thus, for example, referring to 'John Dee', or 'Mr Shamtitle', or even 'Blackacre' as a place, can have the effect of putting us on epistemic alert, mindful that we are being invited to engage in a process of imagining. Indeed, the invention of imaginary figures will be one of the case studies I will look at more closely in the second part of this book, examining the 'Officious Bystander' in Chapter 7. Notice, though, that the Officious Bystander is not a proper name. It does use the formal device of capitalisation, which in this case strikes us as somewhat artificial, as if giving embodied status to something that does not deserve it, and it does thereby point to the making of a character. In this respect, the invention of an imaginary character can, when accompanied by, say, capitalisation, signal artifice.

[183] Ibid, 172.

[184] Ibid, 171.

[185] Much more could be said here about the phonetic dimension of artefacts. On this, see Forrest-Thomson (2016), who speaks of 'all the rhythmic, phonetic, verbal and logical devices' of poetic artifice, which result in the production of 'alternative imaginary orders'.

[186] Cohn (1999), 125.

[187] See Gallagher (2007); see also Gallagher (1995).

Although, as noted above, signs of fictionality that rely on our sense of what is possible, probable or plausible in reality are not what I have in mind in terms of signals of artifice, there are some closely related forms that may be included. Thus, for instance, examples of absurdity or the grotesque, and perhaps in general many comic forms, including irony and satire, may have the effect of putting us on epistemic alert, and inviting us to enter a distinctive epistemic frame. Put another way, as already noted above, the key question is not impossibility, improbability or implausibility. Those features may or may not be present. The key is whether the language points to itself as a means of communication, and this can happen, whether or not the content of what is being communicated strikes us as impossible, improbable or implausible. The distinction can be a fine one, eg consider the distinction between saying 'the belt spoke' and saying 'Along came a Speaking Belt'.[188] I am minded to say that although both would strike us as impossible, improbable or implausible, only the second also alerts us to its status as a language, as a form or means of communication, doing so, in this case, through the device of capitalisation.

Finally, it is worth mentioning that, in future work, we may also draw on the rhetorical tradition in carving out a space for the signalling of artifice, and thus point to language we experience, again contingently, as tropic, as somehow twisted or turned, as with metaphors, metonyms, or the whole range of tropes and figures celebrated in the history of rhetoric. In doing so, however, we would have to be careful not to slip into the endorsement of some division between figurative and literal language. The point is not to bring to bear some theory as to the referential or non-referential theory of meaning, or some division between what strikes as true and what strikes as false. Again, what I am trying to do, along with other theorists who have spoken of the category of the fictional, is to make space for a third mode of cognition: not truth/falsity, or realistic/unrealistic, but precisely a distinctive epistemic frame, akin to the category of the fictional. The question is what triggers us to enter into it. And here, the point to make is that some language, which the rhetorical tradition has sometimes identified as tropic or figurative, can do the trick. When it does do the trick, it does so because it signals its own artifice, and not because we evaluate its content as not corresponding to the world as we know it. In a sense, the experience is a thinner one than the experience of something as false, impossible, improbable, or unrealistic; it points to a state of epistemic bracketing, but one nevertheless that calls upon us as active epistemic agents, as agents that do things with and thanks to those artefacts.

It is time, now, to turn to the second dimension of artefacts, and precisely the sense in which they call upon us to participate in different ways.

V. Calling on us to Participate

On the one hand, artefacts put us on epistemic alert, or give us epistemic relief from the otherwise-relied-upon epistemic norms and commitments, and in this sense they are active vis-à-vis us as subjects who experience them; but on the other hand, artefacts

[188] On speaking belts, see Fludernik (2018), 82.

also call upon us as active epistemic agents, and thus present themselves as needing and requiring further work by us. In this section, I address this second dimension of artefacts, the other side of the coin to signalling artifice, and thus I turn my attention to the sense in which artefacts call upon us to participate. This is the sense in which they treat us as beings who construct, build, make, and who do so in a variety of ways, drawing upon our character as embodied, sensory and affective animals. Perhaps in the broadest sense, this second dimension of artefacts attempts to capture the way they enable and invite us to play: to play with them and thanks to them, and thereby transform and change both them and us in the process.

A. Playing-in-General and Playing-a-Game

i. Playing as an Analogy for Participating

Play is indeed a useful concept to work with in this context, and this is all the more so given that it has been deployed in related treatments of fictionality and fictional experience.[189] An important distinction in this context is that between playing-in-general and playing-a-game. In Schaeffer's discussion of fictionality, which was discussed in the third section above, I mentioned that Schaeffer linked his notion of the ludic feint or the shared feint, which he conceived to be crucial to fictionality, to the role-playing of children and to the play-fighting of animals. Both of these can be taken as good examples of playing-in-general. A game like chess, which, for the purposes of this argument, we can conceive of as being constituted by its rules, can serve as an example of playing a game. It may be that this is best seen not as a distinction in kind, but as one of degree. Where role-playing and play-fighting is less governed by rules, a game like chess is more so. Thus, for example, what constitutes a move at all, ie what counts as a permissible or relevant action in the context, or what constitutes a move likely to be seen as appropriate, eg fun, is, in the case of role-playing or play-fighting, less closely regulated than in chess. Indeed, the stronger normative language of permission, appropriateness or correctness feels more natural in chess than it does in role-playing or play-fighting or, to give one more example, building LEGO together, where one is more comfortable with a language of fun, pleasure and beauty.

Playing-a-game, then, though this of course depends on the game, is typically more governed or regulated (it is striking that we are drawn to the language of law and politics here) and controls more tightly what is permissible, appropriate, correct or even relevant. Playing-in-general, by comparison, although any process of it may involve certain normative commitments, which are either conventional in that culture, or a private convention between the two or more players, is less governed or regulated, and thus less structured, less controlled and more open. What constitutes playing-in-general, in short, is much more susceptible to improvisational negotiation between the players involved. In that respect, it may be said to carry more risks, eg of disagreement and even conflict, which, at least at the level of constitutive rules, is virtually excluded in games like chess.

[189] Eg, Iser (1993) [1991]. I return to Iser briefly below.

What does this distinction between playing-in-general and playing-a-game have to do with fictional worlds, or indeed with artefacts? The distinction is relevant because on one view, what fictional language does is to give instructions, for example in the form of permissions and prohibitions, for certain mental and/or physical actions. Thus, one might view fictional language, eg the language of a novel, as a set of instructions, or, if you like, rules for how to play that particular fictional game. For those who do not accept the distinction between playing-in-general and playing-a-game, such a view can be extended also to role-playing, eg claiming that it too is structured like a game, and that, for instance, the props used in such games are instructions, eg instructions to use this stick as a sword, or this hat as a helmet.

The view I am describing, crudely and incompletely, resembles the view argued for by Kendall Walton in his *Mimesis as Make-Believe*.[190] We have already seen, in the third section above, Moran suggesting that we can understand fictionality, or fictional experience, in ways other than through the rubric of belief or make-belief, and as we shall see also in the next chapter, to enter into a distinctive epistemic frame is not necessarily to make-believe, or even to suspend disbelief. We can extend the critique further and suggest that insofar as the above view of our participation in fictional worlds resembles that of Walton's, it is not the approach taken in this book. Instead, in this book, I approach the playing that is engaged in as a result of and thanks to artefacts as much more like playing-in-general than playing-a-game.

As we shall see, taking this approach is important, for it helps us see how certain artefacts, eg fictions, metaphors, figures, and scenarios, can enable inquiry. It would be difficult, for instance, to see how artefacts and related processes of imagination could enable inquiry in all its dimensions, especially social, diachronic and experimental, if those artefacts functioned more like the constitutive rules of a game. If they did so, it would be hard to see, for example, how a metaphor could enable interactive and communal experimentation in real time and over time. It would, instead, be an instruction for others to perform certain kinds of mental actions, which could then be evaluated to be appropriate, correct, relevant, or as permissible or prohibited. Metaphors, however, and other artefacts, do not function like that. They are not analogous to the constitutive rules of games. They are much more analogous to the kinds of invitations one can be the addressee of in role-play or play-fighting, ie the addressee of actions that call upon some response, but do not determine what that response ought to be.

The analogy with role-play or play-fighting only goes so far, however, for if we were to stick to it too rigidly it would confine us too much to anchoring the evaluation of the response to the intentionality of the original invitation, as is reasonable in the case of role-playing and play-fighting. In the case of artefacts, however, especially if we are to take seriously, as I seek to do in this book, their capacity to enable inquiry over time, then the invitations issued by artefacts cannot be controlled by the intentions with which they are constructed. It makes little sense, and would simply be too reductive, to think of metaphorical cognition, or to characterise what persons some time later do with and thanks to metaphor, as limited by the original intention with which they are

[190] See Walton (1990).

uttered or composed. This is not to say that intention may not be relevant; just that it is not determinative, ie in the terms above, it does not set up a game, but it does invite play, and play that may even at times be more open than that of role-play or play-fighting.

ii. Play and Fictionality

Artefacts, then, in this second dimension, call upon us to participate, ie to do things with and thanks to them. This kind of participation is more akin to playing-in-general than it is to playing-a-game. Some theorists have arguably characterised the experience of fiction in similar ways. Thus, for instance, Eileen John in her 'Reading Fiction', emphasises the active and generative role of the reader, loosening the relation between what we can or ought to do with a fiction from the intention of the author.[191] As John puts it, 'I see the reader as generating the interesting conceptual results, whereas in other accounts the author or text generally receives the credit for presenting the reader with a new conception.[192] John also speaks of how 'fictions are indirectly suggestive about a concept',[193] and adds:

> … works of fiction, rather than providing new ways of thinking [prescribed by an author], sometimes lead us to places of obscurity or untested areas in entrenched ways of thinking. In getting us there, the work provides a context in which we can think fruitfully about the conceptual issues raised, where the line of inquiry we pursue is integrated into our efforts to judge the characters and events.[194]

It is perhaps no accident that John uses the language of inquiry. The point is that what artefacts do, in this sense of them calling upon us to participate, is to open up a space in which the possibilities are under-determined, though also not wholly indeterminate; a space precisely for trying things out. There is still room for the exercise of normative judgement, just as there is in playing-in-general, where we may experience some improvisation as appropriate or inappropriate, or fun or boring, but it is certainly not as tightly regulated, and thus also not determined by pre-existing rules, as in the case of playing-a-game.

It may be that it is also something like this view that Wolfgang Iser endorsed in his rich and complex book on *The Fictive and the Imaginary*.[195] Iser's conception of the fictive has much in common with the approach taken to fictionality, and to artefacts, in this book. For instance, Iser also rejects dependence on 'the old fiction/reality dichotomy', adding:

> I propose at the outset to conceive of the fictive as an operational mode of consciousness that makes inroads into existing versions of world. In this way, the fictive becomes an act of boundary-crossing, which, nonetheless, keeps in view what has been over-stepped. As a result, the fictive simultaneously disrupts and doubles the referential world.[196]

[191] John (1998).
[192] Ibid, 333.
[193] Ibid.
[194] Ibid, 340.
[195] Iser (1993) [1991].
[196] Ibid, xiv–v.

An actor playing Hamlet, for instance, cannot wholly identify himself with Hamlet; he always remains partly himself, 'which means that his body, his feelings, and his mind function as an analogue, enabling him to represent what he is not'.[197] There is, here, as is also mirrored in the two dimensions of both artefacts and imagination as I model them, a dual structure. Artefacts signal artifice and, at the same time, call upon us to participate. When we imagine, as we shall see in more detail in the next chapter, we enter a distinctive epistemic state and, at the same time, participate.

Also significant is that Iser insists that 'fictions in general elude clear-cut definitions, let alone ontological grounding', and thus 'can be grasped only in terms of use'.[198] Further, and now directly relevant to the points made above, Iser also insists that this use 'is potentially manifold'.[199] Thus, it comes as no surprise to see Iser drawing on the language of play. He says, for instance: 'By opening spaces of play, the fictive compels the imaginary to take on a form at the same time that it acts as a medium for its manifestation'.[200] The 'compels' in this sentence may sit slightly at odds, at least to my ears, with the idea of 'opening spaces of play'. Hence, I prefer the language of enabling and inviting, or a little more strongly, calling upon our participation. But there is still considerable overlap. For instance, like Iser, I am more interested in 'what the text does, rather than what the text is meant to mean',[201] though I see 'what it does' as being closely linked with what we do with it or thanks to it. And when Iser says that 'Instead of seeking to pin down a single meaning [of a fictive text], we may be better advised to recognise the multiplicity of possible interpretations as a sign of the multiplicitous availability of the imaginary',[202] our views come to be very close indeed.

B. Varieties of Inviting Participation

What are, then, some of these invitations? How do artefacts call upon us to do something with them or thanks to them? Artefacts may, for instance, call upon us to relate two images to each other, potentially resolving a semantic clash or some other surprising juxtaposition, as happens often in metaphor. Artefacts can also call on us to complete something: they can do so by being under-specified, as in leaving blanks to be filled in by the reader, as in ellipsis, or in alluding to something. This does not mean they prescribe exactly what needs to be completed and how. The openness of any one call to completion can vary in degree. Even where there is a high degree of prescriptiveness in, say, an ellipsis or an allusion, there is still considerable room for the reader or listener to construct their own possibilities.

In addition to offering themselves up as strange juxtapositions or as under-specified, and thus calling upon us to do things like relate images or fill in the blanks, artefacts can also invite us to go elsewhere, to travel around as it were, or to digress

[197] Ibid, 17.
[198] Ibid, xv.
[199] Ibid.
[200] Ibid, xvii.
[201] Ibid, 6.
[202] Ibid, 19.

with a view to returning, as with allegory or irony, or with other invitations to take on certain perspectives and imagine what they are like. Artefacts can also present themselves as incongruous in some way, or dislocated, again calling upon us to put things together, or to make something out of what might first strike us as a disjointed set of fragments. Again, the idea is not that there is necessarily a prescribed, and therefore appropriate or correct or even relevant, way of putting them together or making something whole. Rather, the idea is that the form of the artefacts gives us the task, and sometimes some of the resources for, and the pleasure, even if also difficulty, of making sense ourselves.

We might say, in a broad sense, that certain language forms, eg to recall, those that are under-specified, invite us to be active in different ways. Although some may prescribe what is to be made more than others, the kind of participation they invite is, again, much more akin to playing-in-general than to playing-a-game. There are very many acts of making, including mental acts of making. One can speak, as above, of relating, of putting together, including putting in an order, of making whole, of associating, of substituting, of condensing or extending, of varying, and of reversing. All these, and no doubt many others, can be thought of as different kinds of participation that artefacts call upon us to perform.

Characterising participation in this way may seem rather abstract, almost as if these are analytical operations of a disembodied mind. But I do not think they need to be, or indeed can be, understood in this way. In fact, my approach to participation is to see these as abstractions from what are affective, sensory and embodied experiences. Thus, all these forms of making are also, even when they are so-called 'mental acts', often accompanied by, or dependent on the memories of, our emotions, our senses and our bodies. Others have recognised this too. For instance, Terence Cave in his work on *Thinking with Literature*,[203] speaks of the importance of under-specification in literary works as a kind of 'animated affordance', for it 'invites the spectator's cognitive faculties to supply what it takes to make the storyworld come alive.'[204] I will be returning to the issue of how to bring out the kinesic, sensory and affective modes of participation in the next chapter. For now, what is crucial is to see that this is what artefacts invite, and that they do so in different ways.

It is crucial to insist on the variability with which artefacts call upon us to participate, and thus on the many different things that they can call on us to do. I do not, for example, want to limit the operations invited by artefacts to mere associations, as important as such associating is. Similarly, although artefacts can certainly present themselves as fragmented or disjointed, as a wilderness of instances so to speak, and thus call upon us to synthesise them, to use a very loaded Kantian term, this is only one of the ways in which artefacts can be, and only one of the things they can call upon us to do. This is important for, as we shall see, on some views of imagination, it is limited to precisely such associating and synthesising. On the view I adopt here, artefacts can call upon a whole range of other kinds of cognitive operations. Again, the better term is 'playing' or 'making'. Both these terms have their advantages: 'playing' helps us keep in mind that

[203] Cave (2016).
[204] Ibid, 9.

artefacts often invite interactive and collective forms of making. And 'making' helps us keep in mind the active character of this process, and how it is not reducible to simply holding things together, eg over time, as with cognitions of identity, or making them whole, or relating and associating them. Soon, in the second part of this book, we shall see also how the various artefacts of legal language call upon us to participate, ie to play, to make, in a whole range of distinctive ways.

C. Poetic Language, Rhetorical Language and Pragmatic Devices

There are three domains in which we might look further to capture some of the variety of different ways of calling upon us to participate: studies of poetic language; studies of rhetorical language; and studies of pragmatic devices. Needless to say, I cannot do justice to them here. Instead, I shall simply mention a few possibilities.

i. Poetic Language

In his book on *Poetic Argument*,[205] Jonathan Kertzer gives examples of a wide range of 'conceptual operations' that one may engage in as a result of, and with the assistance of, poetic language, eg 'substitution, conflation, variation, reversal, and even contradiction'.[206] Poetic language is difficult to fit into a mould that insists on communication as a means of acquiring agreement, or the assent of another to what one is already committed to as a truth. That does not mean, however, that poetic language is bereft of argumentative, or argument-like, resources. Very much to the contrary: poetic language selects, makes salient, emphasises or highlights, hides or occludes, and much else besides. Through its 'rhythms, correspondences, analogies … flow of images'[207] it can, for example, create opportunities to take up perspectives, and from there, make insights, eg, into what, from that perspective, might matter. Kertzer points to a number of interesting poetic devices, eg 'the uses of silence in poetry', or 'suppressing causal or other links', thereby 'inviting readers to supplement them, to explore which ones' might be most relevant.[208]

Some genres of poetry may reveal the role and value of certain artefacts better than others. For instance, lyric has often been associated with playing, in all kinds of ways with address. As Jonathan Culler has observed, lyric has addressed 'time, winds, urns, trees, or the dead' and has asked 'them to do something or to stop what they are doing'.[209] Employing the figure of apostrophe, as when one addresses non-existent persons, things or events, as if they were real and capable of understanding one's plea, lyric thus can be seen as allowing us, both as authors and readers of lyric, to make

[205] Kertzer (1988).
[206] Ibid, 52.
[207] Ibid, 7.
[208] Ibid, 41.
[209] Culler (2015), vii.

insight with perspective. Further, genres like lyric are by no means so rule-governed as to make surprise impossible. Quite the contrary, as Culler once again observes, genres are more like prototypes, which are 'not just a historical evolution but a historically evolving set of possibilities with potential to surprise'.[210] Perhaps it can help to think of poetic language as akin to sculptures, which transform a certain space, create it as a space, and also make available certain perspectives from which we, as readers, can go on playing with and making.

ii. Rhetorical Language

As with poetic language, so with rhetoric. I have already had occasion to refer to how this book is informed by rhetorical approaches to language. Here, I want simply to point to rhetorical tropes, schemas and figures as candidates for artefacts that call upon us to participate, thereby at least potentially enabling inquiry. I do so while keeping in mind the qualification referred to in the first section of this chapter, namely that the rhetorical approach to language cannot be and should not be reduced to identifying only certain particular features of language.

One interesting place to look for rhetorical tropes, schemas and figures working in this way is in the practice of science. I mentioned, in the section on rhetoric above, the work of Tito Chico.[211] But there are also others who have contributed importantly to the study of the role and value of rhetorical language in scientific practice.

An outstanding example is Jeanne Fahnestock, whose brilliant book on *Rhetorical Figures in Science*[212] was one of my inspirations for this project. Fahnestock makes a number of moves which are important: she resists the dominance of metaphor, pointing to a wide range of rhetorical tropes, schemas and figures; she resists the distinction between the figural and the literal, and thus argues against the possibility of translating or paraphrasing the figural into the literal; and she argues especially forcefully against the idea of treating tropes, schemas and figures as mere optional ornaments.[213]

In place of a distinction between the literal and figurative, Fahnestock proposes continua, for instance, of iconicity. On this view, a 'figure is a condensed or even diagram-like rendering of the relationship among a set of terms, a relationship that constitutes the argument and that could be expressed at greater length',[214] and that, one might add, thereby invites readers to further extend them. Figures, like metaphor, but also like antimetabole, or antitheses, 'express a particular line of argument and simultaneously … induce [I would say invite] an audience to participate in that argument simply by virtue

[210] Ibid, 90.
[211] See Chico (2018).
[212] Fahnestock (1999).
[213] Incidentally, as Fahnestock observes, there is an old tradition of understanding the figures as ornaments (eg in Cicero), but 'several historians of rhetoric have pointed out that the traditional conception of ornament as embellishment, or quite literally as embroidery, probably misses an essential meaning in the original term. The Latin ornamentum also means furniture, apparatus, and equipment, so that ornament may be more closely related to the notion of essential fear or 'armament' than it is to adornment': ibid, 18.
[214] Ibid, 24.

of their form'.[215] Drawing on Kenneth Burke, Fahnestock says that figures may be thought of as offering:

> … formal patterns that invite the audience's participation because they awaken an attitude of collaborative expectancy in us. For instance, imagine a passage built about a set of oppositions (we do this, but they on the other hand do that; we stay here, but they go there …). Once you grasp the trend of the form, it invites anticipation regardless of the subject matter. Formally, you find yourself swinging along with the succession of antitheses.[216]

Sometimes this 'swinging along' may indeed function as a mode of persuasion, prompting the audience to come to see the same view as that espoused by the speaker or author. But sometimes, such formal patterns may invite more robust, more open-ended participation from the audience. Figures put things together in all kinds of ways, but they can do so in ways that leave much to be done, and where what is left to be done is not predicted, for not predictable. Figures can also place things out of order, eg antimetabole, 'in which two key terms switch places',[217] can serve to undo certain habitual associations, and show a possibility we had not yet until that moment even conceived as possible.

Rhetorical tropes, schemas and figures, then, especially in all their variety, might also be mined for further examples of artefacts that call upon us to participate in a variety of ways.

iii. Pragmatic Devices

Finally, we might here mention the very many different kinds of pragmatic devices, also often deployed in scientific practice. As Catherine Elgin, Anthony Appiah,[218] and others have pointed out,[219] the practice of the sciences, including not only the hard sciences, but also economics, and the social sciences, 'unabashedly relies on models, idealisations, and thought experiments'.[220] Elgin for instance positions these devices as ones that 'are known not to be true',[221] but we can resist this characterisation of them, dependent as it is on the distinction between truth and falsity that I am not relying on, and place them instead on the plane of fictionality.

Idealisations, eg in the form of imaginary perspectives, give us plenty to do, for we might need to take up that perspective and play it out, as we do, for instance, with the *Homo Economicus* idealisation in economics. Similarly so with thought experiments, which are often highly under-specified, and thus call upon further imaginings in our processing of them. The frequency with which we find such devices in scientific practices, and in both the natural and social sciences, should surely suggest to legal scholars that it would be surprising indeed if we also did not find them in legal practice. And, indeed, it is the argument of this book that we certainly do also find them in legal

[215] Ibid, 34.
[216] Ibid. For an interesting recent argument as to the importance of antithesis, see Harris (2019).
[217] Fahnestock (1999), 41.
[218] See Appiah (2017).
[219] See, eg, the essays in Levy and Godfrey-Smith (Forthcoming).
[220] Elgin (2017), 1
[221] Ibid.

practice, and that, on the whole, the quality of legal practice is better with it than it would be, if it would at all be possible, without it.

In closing this section, and this chapter, I need to reiterate a point I have made a number of times already, and one that is also linked to the above domain of pragmatic devices. To say that one can find artefacts amongst the pragmatic devices employed in science is not to say that we can think of them as mere tools or instruments, or as mere toys or props. This is important because we risk otherwise taking an approach to language which makes us think it is possible for us to master it, as if language was something we could use in any manner we like, for whatever ends we wish. But language is not like that. Its complexity and its social character require that we respect its relative autonomy. Perhaps we can even say that language is much more our master than we are masters of it, though it is best to avoid the terminology of 'mastery' altogether. The relationship between language and thought is much more dynamic than the terminology of 'mastery' asserts, in whichever direction. Language is looser, and less predictable, with more scope for pleasure and surprise, though also difficulty and misunderstanding. That, however, is not only a sober reminder, but also a cause for celebration.

3

Imagination

There is one more key model that this book needs to articulate: imagination. This term, which has received so much renewed attention of late, especially within philosophy, but also extending out to histories of science, political theory, psychology, and, to a limited extent, in legal scholarship, is used in a bewildering array of ways. In this book, I model it in a very particular way. Imagination, as modelled here, is a combination of two processes: first, it involves entering a distinctive epistemic frame, which is an active and deliberative process of constructing a certain epistemic attitude, including selectively suspending certain epistemic norms and commitments while retaining others; and second, it involves participating along a spectrum of different degrees of affective, sensory and kinesic involvement. It is the duality and combination, ie the fact that both processes are occurring simultaneously, that is key. Imagination, in this sense, is not an escape from the world. On the contrary, it is a particular kind of engagement with the world. It is not a passive withdrawal, but a mode of active involvement. Also crucial is that it is not necessarily or even paradigmatically a solitary activity, or one that is best approached as occurring in a single mind. Rather, as approached in this book, processes of imagination are often, if not typically, social, ie both interactive and collective, and occurring in real time and over time.

Before going any further, it is important to re-emphasise that separating imagination from artefacts, and thus from certain forms and uses of language, risks being misleading. The two form a duo. Processes of imagination construct artefacts, and processes of imagination are invited to be exercised by artefacts. Nevertheless, as with artefacts, it is possible, though solely for the purposes of presentation, to separate out processes of imagination and articulate their various dimensions. It is the daunting task of this chapter to do just that.

I develop and elucidate dimensions of imagination in five parts. In the first, I draw on some of the literatures on imagination to help craft and carve out the model of imagination I construct. As always, the aim is not to be comprehensive. The literature on imagination is simply too large, the uses of the term too multiple, to do that. Instead, the aim is to help steer the course by avoiding certain shoals, and thus showing how the model of imagination constructed does not approach imagination in certain ways, eg it does not treat it as a rare exercise of genius, and it does not seek to burden imagination with the demands of creativity.

The second to fifth parts of this chapter then focus on elucidating and elaborating the various dimensions of the model of imagination. In the second, I turn to the process of entering a distinctive epistemic frame, which is the first of the two processes that are combined in exercises of imagination. Here, I discuss the different ways in which one may enter that distinctive epistemic frame, and thus also the different epistemic norms and commitments that one may suspend, and the different kinds of epistemic attitudes and modes of expression that one may deploy. Then, in the third to fifth parts I discuss the three different, though also often inter-related, ways in which one may participate when one imagines. Thus, in the third part, I look at affective modes of participation, and thereby consider the relations between imagination and emotion. In the fourth part, I look at the sensory mode of participation, and especially at the role and character of mental imagery. And finally, in the fifth part, I consider the kinesic mode of participation, and thus the role of the simulation of movement, gesture and posture, and more broadly the role of the body in processes of imagination.[1]

I. Approaching Imagination

Attempting to understand the workings of imagination is an intimidating task. This is not only because the term itself has been used in many ways – as many, for instance, as mind, thought or reason – but also because of what has often been at stake when it has been used, eg the status of aesthetics, rhetoric, emotion, and much else besides. An added difficulty is that it is not just a matter of delineating imagination, eg by distinguishing it from other mental processes and actions, such as memory, but also a matter of understanding how it relates to those mental processes and actions, eg belief, knowledge, perception, and so on. Further, theorists who have reflected on imagination have covered the full sweep of extremes, from those who take imagination to be in some sense fundamental, a sine qua non of the mind, to those who think it is at best a superfluous and dangerous pass-time.[2] The literature is pretty much impossible to grasp as a whole.

The literature is also very much alive and kicking. In recent decades, and in keeping with a general trend of philosophy, including analytical philosophy, which has extended the scope of its investigations to topics it has neglected or derided, such as emotion and imagination, there has been a burst of scholarship on imagination.[3] Reflecting on this renewed attention, Amy Kind has pointed to four recent debates as especially consequential in triggering philosophical interest in imagination.[4] The first was the debate in metaphysics, in part in relation to meaning (sparked, for instance, by Saul Kripke), and especially by reference to issues in the epistemology of modality.[5] The second was that of philosophical treatments of aesthetics and the arts. The work of Kendall Walton and Gregory Currie in the 1990s are good examples in this respect.[6] A third source was the

[1] There is an important difference between the terms 'kinesic' and 'kinetic'. The first refers to our processes of apprehending or simulating movement, whereas the second refers to the movement itself (eg the movements, gestures or postures themselves). See eg Banks and Chesters 2018b, fn 11. Thus, whenever referring to a mental process, I use the term 'kinesic', and whenever referring to the description of actions in language, I refer to the term 'kinetic'. In doubt, I use 'kinesic'.

[2] For overviews, many stressing the variability of imagining, see, eg, Strawson (170); Salis (2014); Kind (2013); Jorgensen (2018); Brann (2017) [1991]; Kearney (1988); Gosetti-Ferencei (2018); Cocking (1984); Pettersson (2016); White (1990); Ferraris (1996); Van Leeuwen (2013); and Dorsch (2014).

[3] See, eg, the essays collected in Kind and Kung (2016); and in Kind (2016).

[4] Kind (2018).

[5] See Kripke (1980).

[6] See Walton (1990) and Currie (1990).

debate over our understanding of other minds, and thus including both sociological theory as well as psychology, especially via the development of the simulation view.[7] And the fourth was the debate over mental imagery, engaged in by both philosophers and psychologists.[8] Imagination was appealed to in all these debates, but with different matters being at stake in each of them.[9]

This already gives a sense of the complexity of this topic. It has been nestled in amongst, and is inextricable from, both intra- and inter-disciplinary quarrels. But to this can be added much else: debates between classicists and historians of Ancient philosophy over Aristotle's pronouncements on *phantasia* and thinking in images;[10] debates in classical pragmatism, and especially via the scholarship of John Dewey and his concept of 'dramatic rehearsal', over the role of imagination in deliberation and decision-making;[11] the debate, within literary historians and theorists, over the meaning of imagination in Romanticism, especially in Samuel Coleridge;[12] debates within Kantian philosophy over the third *Critique*, and the role it gives to imagination;[13] debates over the moral imagination in general, for instance distinctions drawn by Iris Murdoch between the ego-infested practices of fantasy and the moral quality of imagination,[14] or debates over Martha Nussbaum's characterisation and defence of the moral imagination;[15] debates within the philosophy and psychology of emotion, especially with respect to empathy, over the role of imagination; debates over the social imagination or the social imaginary, as in the work, for instance, of Benedict Anderson, Charles Taylor or Cornelius Castoriadis;[16] and debates in the philosophy and psychology of education and development over the role of imagination, eg as pioneered by Paul Harris.[17] No doubt, even this extended list of argumentative contexts in which imagination has been appealed to is far from exhaustive.

It is important to recall these many different debates and argumentative contexts because it should help us realise that no one model of imagination can somehow rise above or resolve all these many different disagreements. Equally important is the context, and thus also the limited scope, of the present book: practices of adjudication, and especially the contemporary common law. Further, as I have been emphasising throughout, the model of imagination provided here is designed so as to dovetail with the account of artefacts, and the artefactuality of language, provided in the previous chapter. Accordingly, it is not the aim of this book to provide a general model of imagination. Instead, what I offer is one possible model, and one that seems to me well suited to the adjudicatory context. Having said that, it is a model that seeks to be relatively inclusive of a whole variety of different, and otherwise often opposed, positions on the distinctiveness

[7] See Gordon (1986); and Heal (1998); and see also Goldman (2006); and Nichols and Stich (2003).

[8] The leading figures here were Stephen Kosslyn, Zenon Pylyshyn, Jerry Fodor and Daniel Dennett. For an overview of the debate, see Tye (1991).

[9] Possibly coming later, but still influential, was the reflection on philosophical methodology, and the role of imagination in the practice of philosophy: see, eg, Gendler (2010).

[10] See, eg, Nussbaum (1986).

[11] See, eg, Fesmire (2003).

[12] See, eg, Bruhn (2009).

[13] For a discussion, see, eg, Arendt (1982); and Kneller (2007).

[14] See, eg, Murdoch (1970); and see also Broackes (2011).

[15] See, eg, Nussbaum (1995).

[16] For a discussion, see, eg, Bottici (2014).

[17] See Harris (2000).

as well as the value of imagination, its relations with other mental processes and actions, and its internal taxonomy.

A. Exclusions and Focus

i. Genius, Creativity and Dreaming

As inclusive as the model is, there are also some important ways in which it seeks to avoid certain characterisations of imagination. For instance, in general terms, I avoid thinking of imagination as the rare exercise of genius, and see it, instead, as an ordinary, everyday capacity, which we exercise often, though always keeping in mind that it may be exercised in particular ways in particular contexts, such as the adjudicatory one. For similar reasons, I also seek to avoid burdening the model of imagination with that of creativity: whatever one's model of creativity, exercises of imagination need not be creative, though they may be.

Relatedly to this, the model developed here is not one that presents imagination as a withdrawal from reality, or as a passive experience we undergo when we switch off, eg close our eyes and daydream. On the contrary, the model is one of imagination as a mode of engagement with the world and others, and as very much an activity, engaged in with others, and both in real time and over time. Connected directly to this is that imagination is not approached as something that occurs solely or even predominantly in an individual mind, but more so as something that we do together. Imagination, in this book, is approached as an active, social, ie both interactive and collective, process, and one which can be spread out over time.

Further, the model developed focuses on the more conscious and deliberate processes of imagination, though this must be placed against the background that this book seeks to question rigid divisions between conscious and less-than-conscious processes. Thus, although the model seeks to make room for how processes of imagination may be a mixture of conscious and less-than-conscious processes, its paradigmatic examples are not, for instance, of dreams, day-dreams or hallucinations. The paradigmatic examples, instead, that I have in mind are: supposing together that something is so and so (when we do not know whether it is, or when we know it is not), constructing and playing together with a metaphor, taking up together an imaginary perspective and simulating what happens as it unfolds, and constructing and playing together with a hypothetical scenario.

ii. Imagination, Experience and Perception

These exclusions and orientations, however, still leave many questions unanswered. Some of these relate to what is said to be included and what is excluded from processes of imagination. One of the most pressing of these, at least one of the most debated in recent years, is whether imagination is necessarily something that has a certain experiential phenomenology, eg affective, sensorial, and/or kinesic, and, if so, whether that means that certain kinds of mental processes, which one might otherwise be tempted to characterise as imagination, ought to be excluded because, arguably, they lack such experiential phenomenology. The typical candidates for such exclusion have been supposing or assuming, or in other cases of what has been also called 'propositional imagination' or 'imagining that'. This is a complex debate, which I will be alluding to throughout this chapter, but in general my approach is this: the model of imagination proposed does posit that imagination has a distinct phenomenology, ie there is a specific experiential quality to imagining. Nevertheless, the exact content of that experiential quality can take on a variety of different forms and degrees of involvement, including paradigmatically affective, sensorial and/or kinesic involvement.

To put this another way: to imagine is to experience, and it is often to experience affectively, sensorially and kinesically, but the exact manner and degree of this experience can vary widely. Thus, on the lower scale of experiential involvement, I include practices of supposition, which, like Margherita Arcangeli,[18] I take to have a distinct phenomenology. The scale can range, from supposition all the way to such intensively affective, sensorial and kinesic experiences as role-playing together, where we imagine ourselves to be certain imaginary characters and play out the scenes and narratives of their interactions. In general, and as I shall discuss further below, especially under the section on entering a distinctive epistemic frame (section II), I try to encompass a wide range of epistemic attitudes and mental processes and combine this with and link it to an equally wide understanding of experience, including emotional experience (as per section III). My aim is to capture some of the richness and variety of processes of imagination, and to avoid rigid splits and divisions between propositional and non-propositional imagination, or imagining-that and imagining-how, or sensorial imagination and supposition.

The question of the relations between imagination and perception, or experience more broadly, is of course much knottier than the above might suggest. One of the ways that imagination has been defended as fundamental to the human mind, indeed sometimes as a faculty of it, has been via its role in making perception, and, more broadly, experience, possible. Thus philosophers from Aristotle to Wittgenstein, and perhaps especially, though in different ways, Kant and the Scots, including David Hume and Adam Smith, have stressed the fundamental importance of our ability to see-as, and thus to experience others and the world meaningfully, eg as persons and objects with identities over time, rather than a random flux of unrelated sensations. These scholars have disagreed over the provenance of such an ability. Kant, for instance, thought we had to be born with it, whereas Hume and Smith thought we acquired it empirically, by making habitual associations. Despite the disagreements, many theorists have agreed as to its importance. I do not have a horse in this race. In this book, my focus is on largely conscious and deliberate processes of imagining. Thus, although I certainly recognise the importance of such less-than-conscious or less-than-deliberate processes of seeing-as or treating-as, as in the ordinary run of perception and experience, they are not my focus. Nevertheless, this does not mean that I am un-interested in the general ability to see-as, or indeed in any one experience of seeing-as. In this respect, I acknowledge that we can engage in conscious and deliberate acts of seeing-as, eg as famously discussed by Wittgenstein, I can will myself to see a duck, and I can will myself to see a rabbit,

[18] Arcangeli (2018).

but not both at once. Thus, in the model of imagination developed here, I include such experiences of seeing-as, but I limit these to largely conscious and deliberate acts, even if, importantly, they also contain some less-than-conscious and less-than-deliberate elements.

To say this is important because it is common to define imagination as somehow necessarily involving a withdrawal from experience, or at least from immediate sensory stimulus. Thus, to pick out an example almost at random, Alan Richardson, in a rich and stimulating discussion of imagination in cognitive literary studies, defines imagination in the following way:

> Imagination names a mental faculty or (perhaps better) an interrelated set of mental capacities and activities concerned with modelling entities and events that are not immediately present to perception and that may or may not have counterparts in the lived world. I can close my eyes right now and imagine a red, ripe apple, even if none is present. Or I can blend stored images of apples with those of gold statutes and jewellery and imagine a gold apple, even if I've never seen one. Further, I can imagine something physically impossible.[19]

Richardson points to some important examples of imagining, including imagining non-present objects, blending them with others, or imagining things, objects or events that are 'physically impossible'. However, it is not necessary to limit imagination in this way, and thus to require imagining to be divorced from things 'immediately present to perception' or from 'counterparts in the lived world'. We can imagine with eyes wide open, so to speak, and in the course of engaging with the world and others. What matters is less whether we are experiencing the real world, and more how we do so, ie with what epistemic attitude, in what epistemic frame. I can be perceiving an apple before me, but treating it, eg affectively, sensorially, and kinesically, as say, a really heavy cannon ball or as a grenade, and I do this, say, in the course of a pretend game with others. When I hear someone speaking, I can hear them as, or I can will myself into hearing them as, an old man, even if they are a young child. Thus, although many acts of imagining may well involve simulating some experience, whether affective, sensory and/or kinesic, in a way that disengages us from others and the immediate world around us, processes of imagination need not do so.

Does this mean that all mental acts and processes of projection, eg anticipation, predicting, planning, and others, are also acts and processes of imagination? My answer is, once again, that this depends on the epistemic attitude with which or epistemic frame in which one engages in such mental acts or processes. Some, perhaps most, acts and processes of anticipating, predicting, and planning are done without entering a distinctive epistemic frame, or without the conscious and deliberate construction of an epistemic attitude that, say, suspends certain otherwise relied on epistemic norms and commitments. When, for instance, to draw on an example provided by Timothy Williamson,[20] I plan my crossing of a river by planning where, eg on which rocks, in what order, I will place my foot, I am not entering a distinctive epistemic frame or suspending any epistemic norms and commitments; quite the contrary, I am very

[19] Richardson (2014), 225.
[20] Williamson (2016).

much relying on them. Contrast this with my standing on the bank of a river and consciously and deliberately seeing the rocks as accumulated, frozen tears of the river. In the latter, I do not have my eyes closed, ie I am engaging with and relating to the world, but I am doing so in a distinctive epistemic frame, and with a particular epistemic attitude. It is, thus, this second kind of act or process that I include in the model of imagination, and not the first (of planning to cross the river), even if they possibly rely on some similar cognitive capacities.

iii. Learning from Imagination

At this point, however, an important objection might be raised. This is the famous objection made, in different ways, by Jean-Paul Sartre and Wittgenstein, namely, roughly, that if, or to the extent that, imagination is something that I engage in consciously and deliberately, so I control what goes into the content of any act or process of imagining, and thus – this is the alleged killer blow – I cannot be surprised by anything I imagine.[21] It follows, for Sartre and Wittgenstein, that I cannot learn anything from imagination. For example, on their view, I can will myself to imagine the Eiffel Tower, but any act or process of such imagining, insofar as it is conscious and deliberate, will only contain that which I myself have put there. Therefore, they say, I cannot be surprised by anything I find, and, therefore, I cannot learn anything from the content of what I imagine.

The problem with this objection is one I have already alluded to: it depends on a rigid distinction or divide between conscious and less-than-conscious, or deliberate and less-than-deliberate processes. Put another way, it does not consider the possibility that imagination combines two processes: one in which we enter a distinctive epistemic frame, doing so consciously and deliberately, and one in which we participate, doing so along a spectrum of affective, sensorial and kinesic involvement. Crucially, this second limb of the dual process of imagining does have the capacity to surprise us, and it is one from which we can learn. Thus, I can will myself into imagining the Eiffel Tower, but in the process of doing so, eg in the process of constructing mental imagery of it, or simulating moving around it or looking up at it or climbing it, I can be surprised by and learn from what I imagine. There are less-than-conscious and less-than-deliberate aspects to this second limb of imagining. Further, there can be a complex process of to-and-fro, between consciously and deliberating controlling what I imagine and between the mix of conscious and less-than-conscious, deliberate and less-than-deliberate elements in participating, eg I will myself into imagining the Eiffel Tower, but I find as I do so, eg when I construct mental imagery, that I am imagining the surrounding Parisian landmarks, and so I will myself to separate out the Eiffel Tower and focus, say, solely on its structure, but then, as I do that, I find myself adding, say, birds of all kinds squatting on different parts of the structure, and so I will myself into deleting them, and so on. The point is: I can indeed be surprised

[21] See Sartre (1972); and Wittgenstein (1980). For a discussion of this objection, see McGinn (2004); and Stock (2007).

by and learn from what I imagine, even if, or to the extent that, my acts and processes of imagining are conscious and deliberate.

iv. Duality and the Recreative View of Imagination

I have emphasised, in the above, the duality of the process of imagining, namely, that 1) on the one hand, we consciously and deliberately enter a distinctive epistemic frame, where we take up or construct some particular epistemic attitude, one of particular epistemic interestedness and not general epistemic indifference, which typically involves selective suspension of certain epistemic norms and commitments; and, 2) on the other hand, we participate, along a spectrum of affective, sensory and kinesic involvement, this being an experience that has a mix of conscious and deliberate as well as less-than-conscious and less-than-deliberate elements. It may be easier to enter that distinctive epistemic frame with the help of artefacts. These do, after all, as I have modelled them in the previous chapter, invite processes of imagination. However, we can also enter a distinctive epistemic frame without them; indeed, we can create artefacts by imagining, thereby also inviting others to imagine with us.

The duality of imagining, ie this simultaneous combination of two processes, is crucial to the model of imagination I offer in this book. One might think of this duality as a kind of structure or architecture of imagination, and certainly some scholars have drawn on this language of 'structure' or 'architecture' when speaking about imagination.[22] Some have of course offered very different structures or architectures. One popular approach, which also has many attractions, is to avoid positing a distinct structure or architecture of imagination, and instead to say that imagining processes are simply recreations of other mental states, actions and processes. The recreative view, as it has been called, has been championed by Greg Currie and Ian Ravenscroft.[23] One reason why this approach is attractive is that it builds in lots of variability: after all, on this view, there are as many processes of imagination as there are mental states, acts or processes to recreate. I do not wish to argue directly against this view – again, it has many attractions – but I construct an alternative model. I do so because I have found the model I offer here more helpful in trying to capture the distinctive epistemic character of imagination, especially within the context of adjudication, where I argue that it can enable processes of inquiry. Splitting the process of imagination into two, then, provides the opportunity, within both limbs, to articulate the distinctive epistemic contribution of imagination, which may not be visible if we simply treat processes of imagination as recreations of other mental states, acts or processes.

B. Imagination and Memory

I mentioned earlier that one of the difficulties with theorising imagination is not only that it is difficult to delineate its boundaries, distinguishing it from other mental acts

[22] See, eg, Nichols (2006).
[23] Currie and Ravenscroft (2002).

and processes, but that even when one has done that, the question of how imagination relates to other mental acts and processes remains. One of the key mental acts and process, which has sometimes been treated in the same breath as imagination, but which has also often been related to it in complex ways, is memory. After all, if one defines imagination as being about making present, eg to one's 'mind's eye', objects or events that are not present, then the overlap with memory, which one could conceive of as doing precisely that, is very considerable.

Indeed, the issue of just what difference there is between memory and imagination has loomed large: for example, if one thinks that all that one can imagine must be based on what one has experienced, with it being possible to blend and mix those experiences but not create new imaginary objects or events that one has not experienced, then the difference between memory and imagination virtually dissipates. Indeed, if one has, as was arguably the case in ancient thought, a robust account of memory, where it is not just a passive recipient of sensations, but very much an active, ordering, synthesising, meaning-making capacity, or even faculty, then one leaves little room for imagination to add.[24] Alternatively, if one's account of memory is not so robust, as is more common in modern and contemporary scholarship, but one nevertheless thinks that imagination can only work with elements of past experience, then imagination is left a minor, even if still important role, of linking and associating past experiences. The stakes, then, in distinguishing and relating memory and imagination are high.

There are at least two possible consequences of a close association of, if not identity between, memory and imagination. One is that it can tend to limit imagination to the processes of linking and associating past experiences, as well as blending elements of existing ones. Another is that it can characterise anything reproduced in imagination, precisely because of its reliance on memory, as but a pale copy of the original experience. Let me say a word about each, for I resist both of these moves in the model of imagination I propose.

i. Association, Combination and Synthesis

The characterisation of imagination as an art of linking, associating and blending the images of past experiences has a long history. As Iser points out, imagination has long been theorised as a 'means of combination'.[25] However, as Iser perceptively adds, we cannot isolate this account of imagination from the context in which it was articulated, namely as part of a defence of empiricism: 'As a means of combining, the imagination is identified with its function, but this results less from the imagination itself than from the need to give plausibility to the acquisition of knowledge from experience'.[26] The history is a complex one in another way, for although this view of the role of imagination was championed by associational psychology, there were also important internal debates

[24] There is a rich history of the arts of memory, see, eg, Carruthers (2008).
[25] Iser (1993), 174.
[26] Ibid.

and disagreements within associational psychology about just how to characterise the workings of imagination. As Iser explains:

> So long as the eighteenth century view of the imagination prevailed that it acted as a means of combining – and this applies particularly to the first generation of association psychologists – it was characterised mainly in accordance with the guidelines of empirical cognition; it was conceived of as a mechanistic operation linking together existing data. As such, it was used as a foundation for cognition without any satisfactory account of how it could achieve such a status. This lack, however, preoccupied the second generation of association psychologists, who revealed the imagination as a synthetic power by describing it as a process of dynamic flow that fuses heterogeneous elements into a unity.[27]

In general, imagination was seen as a means of combining experiences, but there was much disagreement as to 'how the combination was guided, and how it was possible to join disparate data'.[28]

This debate found its way beyond philosophy and associational psychology, to literature and culture more generally, especially within the Romantic movement. The Romantics, and most emblematically Samuel Coleridge, wrestled with this view of imagination. In one sense, seeing imagination as a means of combining past and present experiences gave it a fundamental role in cognition: what would cognition be without its ability to link objects across time, thus constituting identity, or to associate one event as occurring after another, or to synthesise disparate sensations into meaningful wholes? On the other hand, however, thinking of imagination in this way also made it difficult to present it as especially creative: many of the processes of association could be characterised as less-than-conscious, and they could be presented in a deflationary way, as but cutting and pasting rather than achieving the status of the creations of an artistic genius. As Richardson has put it, 'Coleridge seeks to liberate imagination, from the empiricist senseless and passive memory, and substitute a more dynamically creative imaginative faculty', one precisely not confined to 'cut and paste from dreary images stored by memory, but instead something genuinely creative'.[29]

Coleridge was notoriously unclear, however, as to what this alternative account might be. Bruhn, who has published a series of papers to attempt to resuscitate the importance of the Romantic understanding of imagination, and connect it to recent work in the cognitive sciences, reminds us of the distinction Coleridge drew between the primary and the secondary imagination.[30] Where the primary imagination is akin to the less-than-conscious unifiying or blending that makes everyday life possible, the secondary imagination is different:

> It [the secondary imagination] dissolves, diffuses, dissipates, in order to recreate; or where this process is rendered impossible, yet still at all events it struggles to idealise and unify … in conditions of deviant or limit-case conceptualisation … the imagination hovers restlessly between uncertain and conflicting image-options, which appear spontaneously to generate and degenerate.[31]

[27] Ibid, 175.
[28] Ibid, 176.
[29] Richardson (2011), 674.
[30] Bruhn (2009).
[31] Ibid, 551.

There is no doubt a great deal to recover from these struggles with trying to articulate the more generative and experimental side of imagination, and one not too burdened by the traditional view of imagination as a means of combination of past and present experiences. The struggles, though, do suggest that it is important to find a way not to limit imagination from the beginning by conceptualising it as a means of combination. It is not enough, in other words, to simply add an extra layer, or a twist, to imagination conceived primarily or fundamentally as a combinatory craft. None of this is to ignore or under-estimate the importance of processes of association, combination, synthesis and other related processes, whether conscious and deliberate, or less-than-conscious and less-than-deliberate, or, as I prefer to think of it, some mixture of both. It is, however, to seek to make room for a more active, more epistemically involved, model of imagination from the outset, one that maintains a link to memory, but also one that is not confined to either making sense of what one experiences or recreating those experiences and combining them in various ways. This is important, for if we limit imagination in this way, we occlude from view the richness and variety of processes of imagining.

The art of combination may be one kind of operation imagination can engage in, but it is just one of many other modes. Further, some of the artefacts that are created by processes of imagination, and that invite it, are not necessarily best understood through the filter of combination: our construction and experience of fictions, scenarios and figures could be good examples, but even metaphor, which may seem like a good candidate for an art of combination, can be greatly misunderstood if it is confined, as it might easily be under the associational approach, to something like an implicit simile or a camouflaged comparison. I should add that we ought not to assume that the above approach to imagination, ie as a means of combination, is but of historical interest. There are many contemporary examples of philosophers and psychologists who continue to think of it in this way.[32] Again, to be clear, I have not, in the above, presented arguments directly against this view: my plea is simply not to confine imagination to these important combinatory operations.

ii. Pale Copies of the Original

The second aspect of a close, or complete, identification of imagination with memory is that it can bring along with it a particular approach to the sensory character of imagination, and especially with respect to mental imagery. One need only recall the famous, and highly influential, image of the wax and seal, deployed by both Plato in the *Theaetetus*[33] and by Aristotle. In *De Memoria et reminiscientia*, for example, Aristotle characterised images, or *phantasmata*, as impressions, 'just as persons do who make an impression with a seal'.[34] However, if images are impressed originally in this way, any subsequent recall of them, any later recreation of them in imagination, in the mind's eye, so to speak, is likely to be understood as a pale copy of the original. For Hume, too, where our initial experiences are striking and vivid, any subsequent recall of them,

[32] See, eg, Novitz, who defines the 'fanciful imagination' as 'the ability which people have to fabricate or invent by combining ideas, images, belies, words, or physical objects howsoever they choose': (1987), 2.

[33] See Plato (1875), 103D.

[34] See Aristotle (1908), 450a–b. See also Bloch (2007).

in the mental imagery of our imaginations, is bound to be less so, and perhaps increasingly less so the greater the time difference between the original experience and the recall.[35]

I shall be returning to mental imagery later in this chapter, but the general point is this: if we adopt this view of imagination as working with but pale remnants of originally vivid experiences, we risk confining ourselves, from the outset, to a very narrow account of the sensory character of imaginings. There is no compelling reason to stack the cards from the beginning like this, ie to relate imagination to memory in this way. It is at least possible, if not likely, that processes of imagination have their own distinctive character. This includes mental imagery, which we may more carefully approach as having its own distinct phenomenology, and not one appropriately characterised as but a weakened version of allegedly more intense original experiences. Put another way: mental images can be intense experiences in their own way; perhaps, in some ways, they can be even more intense than run-of-the-mill ordinary experiences, eg our entire attention can be focused on some mental image, deeply involving us affectively and kinesically, and to a greater extent than when we are acting and interacting in the course of ordinary experience.

There is undoubtedly a complex and rich relationship between memory and imagination, but it is best to avoid theorising imagination on the back of memory, as if it were just memory-plus. Our understanding of imagination, not only, but certainly also, in our understanding of its sensory dimension, risks being highly impoverished otherwise.

C. Perspectival Imagining

How might we, then, begin to move away from this habit of linking imagination to memory, and confining it to a means of combining past and present experiences, including seeing mental imagery as but a pale copy of the original? One way is to consider the importance of perspective, ie of initial framing, but also of the construction and enactment of imaginary perspectives, in processes of imagination. I return to the importance of perspective at various points in this book, eg in Chapter 6 on metaphor and in Chapter 7 on figural imagining. For now, let me but mention that this aspect of imagining has not gone unnoticed in the history of scholarship about imagination.

i. *French and Scottish Perspectives*

In her work on imagination in the Enlightenment, Genevieve Lloyd stresses precisely this role of the construction of perspectives and, equally importantly, of their multiplicity and the insights generated by moving between them.[36] Lloyd shows, for instance, how both Montesquieu and Voltaire take 'the strategy of multiple voices well beyond the limits of a two-sided debate, offering a plurality of epistemological and moral perspectives.'[37]

[35] See Hume (1978) [1739], 1.1.1.
[36] Lloyd (2013).
[37] Ibid, 26.

Thus, in Montesquieu's *Persian Letters*, for example, in which 'no one perspective is presumed to be an exclusive point of access to truth', the 'shifts between perspectives introduce an intellectual flexibility which allows judgement to occur'.[38] Similarly, in Voltaire's *Philosophical Dictionary*, the 'interplay of voices plays out in conjunction with irony in such a way that within any one voice we cannot be sure whether anything is being advanced for serious consideration'.[39] Voltaire's emphasis, says Lloyd, is 'on the movement of thought in the search for truth, rather than the stasis of belief'.[40]

The work of the Scots, Hume and Smith especially, can also be understood in this way, ie as conceiving of imagination not only, or even mainly, as an associational art, but also, or even more so, as a perspectival one. This is of course especially clear in Smith, who bases his entire moral theory, in *The Theory of Moral Sentiments*, on the construction of, and reflection on, 'different perspectives on an action', including the imaginary perspective of the impartial spectator.[41] Also importantly, in Smith, we see the close connection between emotion and imagination at the level of perspective: sympathy, which plays such a central role in Smith, both in our acquisition of moral knowledge and in any one process of moral deliberation, is perspectival, if not multi-perspectival. Indeed, an important interpretation of Smith draws on the dynamics of theatre to explain his moral theory.[42] 'Spectatorial sympathy', as it has also been called, is, as Lloyd explains, an 'active imaginative response, changing of places, imagining oneself into another's situation'.[43] The process of moral judgement, for Smith, is a multi-perspectival art, involving the affective simulation of multiple perspectives and moving between them.

ii. Dramatic Imagining

The relations between perspective and imagination have been observed and emphasised by many philosophers: Martha Nussbaum, Elisabeth Camp and Richard Moran are just three prominent examples, and this list could be significantly extended if one also included scholars of what we may call the perspectival moral emotions, ie sympathy, compassion and empathy. I will be returning to these views, for instance in Chapter 6 on metaphor. For now, let me briefly point to Moran's view by way of illustration of the distinctive importance of perspectival imagining, which will thereby also helps us to distance ourselves from a view of imagining as solely or even mainly an art of combination and synthesis.

For Moran, what he calls 'dramatic imagining' is a specific kind of imagining, which demands its own account that is not reducible to other kinds, eg cognitive or propositional imagining, or what he also calls hypothetical or counter-factual imagining. As Moran says: 'What we do when we imagine the propositions concerning Macbeth's accession to the throne seems to be a very different sort of thing from what we do when we imaginatively enter into such events and respond with either horror or anger,

[38] Ibid, 41.
[39] Ibid, 47.
[40] Ibid, 58.
[41] Ibid, 104. And see Smith (1759).
[42] See, eg, Marshall (1984); and Brown (1992–3).
[43] Lloyd (2013), 105.

and our stake in our imaginings is different.'[44] Constructing and enacting a perspective has a particularly pronounced affective intensity. The following passage by Moran, though long, is worth quoting in full:

> Imaginatively adopting a perspective on something involves something different from the sort of imagination involved in ordinary counterfactual reasoning. Hypothetical reasoning involves seeing what would follow from the truth of some proposition. It does not involve either feigning belief in that proposition or determining what would follow from the fact of one's believing it. There need be no reference to oneself, either as believer or as any sort of psychological subject, and one does not determine the truth of a counterfactual by imagining 'what it would be like' to believe the antecedent. By contrast, imagination with respect to emotional attitudes may require such things as dramatic rehearsal, the right mood, the right experiences, a sympathetic nature. It thus says more about a person that he is either able or unable to imagine something in this way, and he bears a different responsibility for it. More is revealed and given of oneself than in the case of ordinary counterfactual reasoning, where one only needs to be provided with the proposition in order to reason from the assumption of its truth. By contrast, imagination with respect to the cruel, the embarrassing, or the arousing involves something more like a point of view, a total perspective on the situation, rather than just the truth of a specifiable proposition. And imagining along these lines involves something more like genuine rehearsal, 'trying on' the point of view, trying to determine what it is like to inhabit it. It is something I may not be able to do if my heart is not it.[45]

Moran is surely on to something important when he tries to delineate the specific relations between imagination and emotion that are at play when we 'try on' a point of view and attempt to 'determine what it is like to inhabit it'. The heightened presence of emotion, it should be added, is not the only way to bring out the distinctive importance of perspectival imagining: one might also draw on the role of the body. Arguably, our kinesic intelligence is also triggered and heightened by the adoption of a perspective. Similarly so with the sensory aspect of imagining: in enacting a perspective, in trying to 'determine what it is like to inhabit it' in Moran's terms, we may well find ourselves constructing mental imagery. Further, we may want to think carefully about the difference between the adoption of a point of view on the one hand, and that of a perspective on the other: the former may well be a thin version, involving less affective, sensory and kinesic involvement, while the latter may involve a much thicker degree of involvement, eg consider the difference between imagining the point of view of a camera, and the perspective of a person.

There might be further refinements we might want to make about the importance of perspectival imagining and, again, I will be returning to this topic later in the book. Nevertheless, the general point holds: that there is something distinctively important about constructing and enacting perspectives, and, crucially, this aspect of imagining is not something that can be captured if we confine ourselves to a view of imagining as a means of combining or blending pale copies of original sensory experiences.

[44] Moran (2017), 17.
[45] Ibid, 25.

D. The Social Dimension of Imagination

There is one final point to make in this all-too-brief discussion of different approaches to imagination. In fact, we can relate this final point to the discussion above concerning perspective. The rehearsal of perspectives, especially in the plural, and thus movement between perspectives, can help us bring into view the social character of imagining. This is all the more so if we draw, as scholars above have when discussing perspectival imagining, on analogies with drama and theatre. Whether it be playing roles together with others on the stage, or experiencing a performance as a spectator, in both cases, what emerges into view is the sociality of imagining. In this book, I seek wherever possible to emphasise the importance of that sociality.

But emphasis is one thing; and articulating the ways imagining is social is another. And this is not easy, at least because it carries along with it all the complex problems of what it is to think about the social. In the chapter on inquiry, I sought to bring out two aspects of the social dimension: its interactive and its collective character. And both are, indeed, also important when thinking about the social dimension of imagining. This is perhaps especially so with respect to imagining, as when compared to inquiry, for the tendency here is to shift between the first-person view where imagining is what occurs inside an individual's head and the third-person view where imagining takes on the form of a collective imaginary that is then said to determine individual consciousness. It is thus especially important to keep in mind the interactive aspect, and to make room for imagining as something that we can do together, but interactively, and thus without necessarily sharing the same content or even experience of imaginings.

i. Imagination between the Individual and the Collective

One scholar who has confronted the difficulties of articulating the social dimension of imagining is Chiari Bottici. In her *Imaginal Politics*,[46] Bottici argues specifically against the reduction of imagination either into a first-person or a third-person account. Bottici's argument is, in part, historical. For Bottici, whereas imagination, in the form of *phantasia*, is taken so seriously by the Ancient philosophers – especially, of course, Aristotle, for whom imagination is necessary for thought, action, knowledge and deliberation, and thus for engagement with and participation in reality – in the modern epoch, it comes to be associated with unreality, and from there with an individual subjectivity. This is especially so 'for those philosophers engaged in defining the new scientific method'; for them, imagination, 'far from being a source of light, as in Aristotle, becomes a source of darkness and a potential perturbation of the methodical work of reason'.[47] Thus, in the seventeenth century, 'the great century of rationalism, the critique of imagination became commonplace'; imagination becomes, as it does for example for Pascal, 'a mistress of errors and falsity … a powerful enemy of reason that can control and, at times, even entirely dominate it'.[48] Following on from the seventeenth century's

[46] Bottici (2014).
[47] Ibid, 21–22.
[48] Ibid, 22–23.

critiques, amidst the rise of scientific method and the tributes paid to reason, imagination is relegated 'to the sphere of the unreal', and comes, in the eighteenth century, to be associated with 'the newly constituted sphere of aesthetics'.[49] For imagination, this is more bad news, because the approach to aesthetics in this period is one of increasing 'subjectification', which, says Bottici, 'culminates in the modern concept of art':

> If science is the domain of reason and understanding – where an objective knowledge of the world can be attained – imagination has a function in the sphere of aesthetics precisely because of its capricious, unpredictable, and above all subjective character.[50]

I have not preserved the careful details of Bottici's account, for instance her analysis of the incorporation, but also sidelining, of imagination in Kant's defence of the autonomy of reason.[51] But in general terms, the story is one of the ever further distancing of imagination from what are thought to be standards of objectivity, rationality and scientific method, and the ever more commonplace positioning of imagination as but a pleasurable and dangerous pass-time of a capricious individual, precisely that realm of the unreal, of withdrawal from reality, of the indulgence of fantasy, of wistful and disinterested play in the realm of art.

The history of imagination does not, of course, stand still, and Bottici shows how there is a pushback against this positioning of imagination at the level of the individual subject. However, the pushback takes imagination to the other extreme: to a kind of technology of socialisation, a collective opium in which all individuals are seen to be immersed and determined by. This is the passage from the individual imagination to 'the imaginary', as for instance pioneered by psychoanalysis and structuralism. There is a move here away from the individual faculty, and towards the allegedly shared social products of the collective imaginary, eg 'myths, fables, fairy tales, rituals and totemic practices';[52] and also 'novels, melodrama, dress, codes, eating habits, as well as social and political symbols'.[53] For Lacan, for instance, or for Levi-Strauss:

> … the Imaginary becomes a structure constitutive of our being, the context we are immersed in: far from being the autonomous subjects that are presupposed by modern theories of imagination posited as an individual faculty, the underlying idea is that we are captivated and thus constituted by the imaginary in which we live.[54]

The move towards the collective imaginary, made initially in the twentieth century by psychoanalysis and structuralism, continues in the contemporary scholarship of, for instance, Charles Taylor, and his account of the 'social imaginary'.[55] For Taylor, according to Bottici, this social imaginary consists of:

> … the ways people imagine their social existence, how they fit together with others, how things go on between them and their fellows, the expectations that are normally met, and the deeper normative notions and images that underlie those expectations … the way in which

[49] Ibid, 23.
[50] Ibid, 24.
[51] Ibid, 24–26.
[52] Ibid, 33.
[53] Ibid, 37.
[54] Ibid.
[55] See Taylor (2003).

> ordinary people imagine their social surroundings as they are conveyed by images, stories and legends.[56]

This is important work, but as Bottici argues, the problem with this pushback against the positioning of imagination at the individual level is that it makes it difficult to see the connection between imagination and agency, or what role there might be for our capacity to imagine. As Bottici puts it, 'If we are born within social imaginaries that cultivate us as social beings, how we can escape from them?'[57] Or, we could add: how can we transform them, work with them in more conscious, more deliberate, and less determined ways? It seems we are trapped in a dilemma:

> If we begin with the imagination as an individual faculty, the problem is how to explain the influence, at times overwhelming (because it is constitutive), of social contexts. If we begin with the imaginary understood as a social context, the problem is how to account for the emergence of the free imagination of individuals.[58]

ii. The Imaginal

The point of Bottici's account, and the reason she speaks not of imagination or the imaginary, but instead of the imaginal, is to offer a way out of this seemingly intractable choice. In doing so, Bottici draws on a number of figures, for instance Cornelius Castoriadis and especially Hannah Arendt. Castoriadis, for example, in his *Imaginary Institution of Society*,[59] is painfully aware of this split and tension between an individual imagination and a social imaginary. Nevertheless, although he helpfully points to the tension, according to Bottici, he does not quite 'overcome the dichotomy'.[60] What is needed is a focus on something in between the individual and the collective, ie something that is 'both the product of an individual faculty and of a social context as well as the result of a complex yet-to-be-determined interaction between the two.'[61] This complex interaction must not be held hostage to a rigid division between conscious processes and unconscious dynamics: what is 'unconscious and conscious can co-exist'.[62] The 'imaginal', then, is 'both conscious and unconscious, individual and social'.[63]

It is at this point that Bottici seeks to build on some of the late, and lesser known, work of Arendt in her *Lectures on Kant's Political Philosophy*.[64] Here, says Bottici, Arendt develops 'a theory of judgement based on the concept of imagination'.[65] For Arendt, 'imagination is the faculty that mediates between the universal and the particular by providing both schemata for cognition and exemplars for action',[66] but the

[56] Ibid, 38.
[57] Ibid, 39.
[58] Ibid, 41.
[59] Castoriadis (1987).
[60] Ibid, 53.
[61] Ibid, 54.
[62] Ibid, 62–3.
[63] Ibid, 66.
[64] See Arendt (1982).
[65] Bottici (2014), 97.
[66] Ibid, 98.

forms that imagination works with are not determinative of processes of judgement. These forms are 'examples', and the 'example is the particular that contains in itself or is supposed to contain, a concept or a general rule',[67] but this being a concept or rule that it itself does not articulate, that it withholds, or defers; that is precisely its character as an example. That promise, but at the same time deferral of generality or universality, is precisely what characterises the normativity of exemplarity and leaves room for judgement, which was also conceptualised by Arendt as a kind of thoughtfulness, infamously missing from Eichmann.[68] The exercise of judgement, in turn, leaves open the possibility of changing and transforming the collective resources of the imaginary, eg adding or subtracting, or performing other kinds of operations on the examples, and thus creating further opportunities for judgement by others in the future.

Bottici's account, as well as Arendt's, deserves more careful reflection than I can bestow upon it here.[69] The point, for present purposes, is to stress, along with Bottici, the importance of not neglecting the social character of imagination, and thus not examining imagination solely at the level of the individual. However, this has to be done in a way that avoids slipping into the other extreme, whereupon we would offer an overly deterministic picture of a social imaginary in which we are inescapably held captive. This balancing act is not easy to pull off, but one way to do so is precisely to keep in mind, on the one hand, the exemplary character of the forms of the imaginary, and, on the other hand, the operations of judgement. In this book, I do not deploy the language of exemplarity and judgement, but the dynamic relation I seek to set up between artefacts and processes of imagination is similar.

Artefacts are shared resources: within the context of adjudication, they are part of the collective, communal technologies we draw on. Artefacts, however, are not best conceived of as determining the operation of individual persons. Instead, they are constructs of processes of imagination, and in turn invite other processes of imagination in the future. Those processes of imagination, in turn, are not merely, and even not dominantly, occurrences in an individual head: they are typically activities that we perform together, interactively. We invite others to suppose, we communicate metaphors which we play with together, we enact fictional perspectives doing so in different ways, and we construct and offer variations on or counter-examples to fictional scenarios. These are activities that occur in a social context, both interactive and collective, and they cannot be understood if we focus too much on the level of the individual. But neither do they determine individual action: there is still much scope here, and much value in, individual subjectivity operating in and adapting to particular circumstances.

The above account of approaches to imagination has not aimed to be comprehensive. Further, I have ranged across many different approaches, often with rather large brushstrokes. I recognise the danger of this, and I want to reiterate that none of what I argue above is meant to be a direct critique of other models of imagination. My aim has been to draw on these past important accounts to situate the model I here propose. It is time, now, to articulate that model in more detail.

[67] Ibid.
[68] See Arendt (1963).
[69] See also Stonebridge (2011).

II. Entering a Distinctive Epistemic Frame

The first limb of the model of imagination I here propose consists in entering a distinctive epistemic frame. In broad terms, to enter a distinctive epistemic frame is an active and deliberative process of constructing a certain epistemic attitude, including regulating the epistemic distance we take and selectively suspending certain epistemic norms and commitments, while retaining others.

To understand what I mean by this notion, we need to proceed in two steps: first, to consider its threshold characteristics, ie what is included and what is excluded from this activity of entering a distinctive epistemic frame; and second, to examine its variability characteristics, ie the different ways we can enter this distinctive epistemic frame. Of course, it must always be remembered that this is just the first limb of the process of imagination, which, as above, is a combination of two mental processes: entering a distinctive epistemic frame *and* participating along a spectrum of affective, sensory and kinesic involvement. It must also be remembered that, in this book, I seek to connect closely processes of imagination to artefacts of language, and thus that what I say here about imagination needs to be read with one eye on how it both constructs, and is invited by, artefacts of language. To be clear, I am not claiming that processes of imagination must always be related either to artefacts in general, or to artefacts of language. Nevertheless, for the purposes of examining adjudication, given especially the importance that language plays in that context, it is helpful to relate artefacts and processes of imagination to each other.

A. Threshold Characteristics

Although an important aspect of the model of imagination I am proposing is that it seeks to be inclusive of a wide variety of ways in which we might imagine, and seeks then to build in as much variability as possible, nevertheless it is also the case that I aim to carve out a possible way of distinguishing processes of imagining from other kinds of cognitive or epistemic experience or activity. Within this first limb of imagining, then, before we can confront the internal variability of ways of entering a distinctive epistemic frame, we must consider what are its threshold characteristics.

i. Largely Conscious and Deliberate

A good way into this is to compare imagining to other paradigmatic mental states and processes, eg belief. Plausibly, we can take belief as a process that aims at truth. Put another way, we can say that belief is governed by the norm of truth.[70] When

[70] I have always been puzzled by the use of legal and political terminology in analytical philosophy, as for instance here in the expression that belief is 'governed' or 'regulated' by a norm of truth. For theories of belief along these lines, see, eg, Shah (2003); Railton (1994) and the essays collected in Chan (2014). I should make clear that I am not necessarily endorsing this view: just using it as an illustration of why we need to be careful about either associating imagination too closely with belief or contrasting it too much with belief.

we believe something, we might say, we are committed to certain epistemic norms and commitments, which we take to help secure our beliefs as true. We take care, for instance, that what we believe is supported and justified by the evidence available to us, and we take care that our beliefs are coherent. Believing includes being sensitive to the possibility of being proven otherwise, and therefore entails certain standards of sensitivity to evidence, as well as reflection on whether, or how, prone to bias we may be, eg having a tendency, with respect to certain sources of evidence or certain topics, to ignore counter-examples. Arguably, this view is compatible with the idea that we can believe in degrees, and this suggests that believing can be accompanied by a variety of epistemic attitudes, eg conviction in our beliefs, or a moderate degree of confidence in, say, the testimony of others. In this sense, it is important to see that belief is strongly connected to affects, including most obviously epistemic emotions.

When we compare imagining to belief, we see both some similarities and some differences. It is better to speak here of 'comparison' rather than 'contrast', for if we seek to distinguish imagination and belief too strongly, we may also miss the many ways in which imagination can overlap with certain aspects of belief.

One crucial difference is that whereas we might plausibly think that we do not quite choose what we believe, we do (largely) choose when, what and how we imagine. This suggests that an important threshold characteristic of entering a distinctive epistemic frame is that it is 'will-dependent'.[71] This is not to deny that some of what we imagine, on other ways of understanding imagination, may be called less-than-conscious and less-than-deliberate imaginings, eg dreams, day-dreams, hallucinations, etc. Very importantly for my purposes, it is also not to deny that there are ways in which processes of imagining are mixtures of conscious and deliberate, and less-than-conscious and less-than-deliberate, processes. Nevertheless, it is to insist that, for the purposes of the model of imagination in this book, entering a distinctive epistemic frame is a largely conscious and deliberate process. When, then, compared to belief, entering a distinctive epistemic frame is a process more conscious, and more deliberate, than belief.

The same might be said if we were to compare imagining to experiencing in general, for instance to perceiving, hearing, tasting or other aspects of experience: we do not ordinarily think of those processes as ones accompanied by awareness that we are undergoing them. They are paradigmatically less deliberate and less reflexive processes. We do not ordinarily think of them as ones we choose to engage in, ie we simply perceive, hear, taste, and so on, as we experience the world, though we may of course reflect on those experiences either during or after undergoing them. Certainly, we can choose to close and open our eyes, or to focus on experiencing a certain taste, eg a meal at a good restaurant, but even then, arguably, we let ourselves experience something rather than actively and deliberately engaging in a particular kind of epistemic process. We could say, drawing on the previous chapter, that when we enter a distinctive epistemic frame, our consciousness takes on a particular quality, ie we become aware of artifice; we are put on epistemic alert.

[71] For the use of this language, see also Arcangeli (2018), eg 75.

ii. An Active Process

If we begin, as I have just done in the above paragraph, to think about differences between imagining and experiencing, eg perceiving, then we also begin to get at another threshold characteristic of imagining, and one which is closely linked to the idea of it being largely conscious and deliberate or will-dependent. This is the idea that it is an activity; that it is an active process; something we do rather than something we undergo. Belief is not quite the best comparator to this threshold characteristic because there is a sense in which we can think of belief as an activity, or at least as a combination of passivity and activity. Consider, though, a paradigmatically less active mental state or process, eg apprehending or understanding something, or merely 'grasping a content'.[72] When compared with these states, entering a distinctive epistemic frame is considerably more active; it involves doing something.

There are different ways of understanding this, eg that we actively construct a certain epistemic attitude, or that we actively regulate our epistemic distance to the content of our attitude, or that we selectively suspend certain epistemic norms or commitments, while retaining others. All these ways of speaking are circling around the same idea, namely that there is something active in the process of imagining. When we merely apprehend or understand something, we are not, at least not paradigmatically, doing something active; we are not, for example, doing something active with some proposition, and we are also not doing things with others, eg interacting with them. Perhaps, similarly, at least in some cases when we are experiencing, eg when we are undergoing an experience of perception or some other sensory stimulus: in those cases, too, we speak more readily of something happening to us rather than us doing something. This sense, then, of actively doing something, as well as doing it largely consciously and deliberately, is an important threshold characteristic of imagination as I model it in this book.

iii. Regulation of Epistemic Distance

We can do more with the comparison of imagination with belief. I mentioned earlier that, plausibly, belief is governed by the norm of truth, however this is understood. When we believe, we are sensitive to what the evidence tells us is true, eg to what we can safely or reliably take to be true or justify as true. This seems not to be the case when we are imagining. Some philosophers call this aspect of imagination its 'truth-independence'.[73] This gets at the idea, but may be too strong, especially when we recall that imagining, or at least many kinds of imagining, is constrained by our background knowledge and is a mode of engaging with the world rather than withdrawing from it. I prefer to think of this in a different way, ie as a matter of regulating our epistemic distance, including constructing an epistemic attitude in which we suspend certain epistemic norms and commitments while retaining others. Thus, there may still be senses in which, in the course of imagining, we seek to imagine what we take to be plausible, and even in some ways probable or likely, but we do so within a certain epistemic frame.

[72] The language here is Gottlob Frege's: see Arcangeli (2018), 57.
[73] See, again, Arcangeli (2018), eg 98–9.

The delicate task here is articulating a threshold characteristic, but not doing this so rigidly as to exclude what we may want to include, and thus not reducing too much the variability of different ways of imagining. Again, when imagining, we may want to retain a whole range of epistemic norms and commitments that overlap with those we ordinarily do rely on when, say, believing or perceiving. We do not need any strict divide between imagining on the one hand and believing or perceiving on the other. Ideally, the model of imagining should be compatible with a whole host of specific epistemic attitudes and ways of regulating epistemic distance.

iv. Epistemic Engagement

There is also another related point. Although we may, in broad terms, say that imagining is 'will-dependent' and 'truth-independent', and this makes it broadly different to believing and perceiving, we would not want to push this so far as to think that imagining is epistemically disinterested. In other words, we would not want to push the contrast with belief and perception to such a degree that imagining becomes a withdrawal from the world, ie a process of cutting ourselves off entirely or bracketing off the world and others around us. Instead, and this returns us to the emphasis on activity, imagining is better modelled as a mode of epistemic engagement. Imagining is a way in which we engage with the world, and not a way in which we disengage with it.

Thus, for example, it is not the case that when we imagine we necessarily suspend all disbelief, or that we allow ourselves to act in epistemic abandon, without taking any epistemic responsibility. We do not, in imagining, suspend *all* epistemic norms and commitments. We do not, as it were, take our hands off the wheel and put our foot blindly down. Instead, we actively regulate the epistemic distance we take, and we actively construct an epistemic attitude, selectively suspending certain epistemic norms and commitments, while retaining others. To enter a distinctive epistemic frame, then, is more like a carefully modulated, selective form of epistemic participation, a special kind of involvement and engagement with the world and others. Truth-independence, then, does not mean epistemic disinterest or epistemic irresponsibility; it means, instead, a specific kind of epistemic interest or epistemic responsibility. It is not a matter of giving up epistemic ambitions, but instead pursuing them in a distinctive way.[74]

v. Purpose-Built and Time-Bound

There is another threshold characteristic that is related to the emphasis I have been placing on imagination being largely conscious and deliberate, involving regulation of epistemic distance, and being a mode of active epistemic engagement. This is the sense of pragmatism involved in entering a distinctive epistemic frame, ie the sense in which that epistemic frame is purpose-built and thus has a temporary status. To say this is not to say that when we enter a distinctive epistemic frame, we need to have in mind the aim or purpose with which we build it. It is instead to say that, in entering a distinctive

[74] For more on relations between belief and imagination, including knowledge, see van Leeuwen (2013), and Kind and Kung (2016).

epistemic frame, we are aware that we are engaging in a time-bound activity, in which we will be participating in certain ways, and for a certain period of time, in order to enable something, eg some form of interaction with others, or to generate something, eg an experience or some insight, which we may go on to use. We can see this as another way of cashing out the idea that when we imagine, we are aware of artifice, ie precisely something being built as an artefact, and thus for a certain, perhaps yet to be determined, purpose.

The activity we engage in, then, when we enter a distinctive epistemic frame is an activity accompanied by a sense of the pragmatic, ie of doing something with something, for a certain, perhaps yet to be determined, purpose. It is not something entirely open-ended and on-going. It is not, for instance, as open-ended and on-going as believing or perceiving. This does not mean, once again, that it entails going completely off-line and withdrawing from epistemic interest. It is more like going on-line in a particular way: a particular way of engaging in epistemic activity. If we need an image, we could say that imagining is not a matter of closing one's eyes, but instead a matter of looking out of the corner of one's eye.

vi. Further Threshold Questions I: Acceptance

We have now accumulated a raft of threshold characteristics of this first limb of imagining, ie entering a distinctive epistemic frame. I have argued that it is: 1) largely conscious and deliberate or 'will-dependent'; 2) an active process, ie it involves doing something, often with others; 3) a matter of regulating epistemic distance, including constructing a specific epistemic attitude in which we selectively suspend some epistemic norms and commitments while retaining others (one could call this 'truth-independence', as long as one keeps in mind the qualifications I have made above); 4) a matter of being epistemically interested and engaged in particular ways; and 5) accompanied by a sense of the purpose-built and time-bound.

We have seen, albeit very briefly of course, how these characteristics can help us see both the differences, as well as some similarities, with other mental processes, such as belief, perception, and apprehension or understanding, or merely grasping a content. We have also seen how the epistemic attitude in question that we construct when entering a distinctive epistemic frame is something different from the one that typically accompanies belief, ie conviction, or full confidence and trust in the evidence, which also correlates to certain kinds of epistemic acts, eg the making of assertions or claims.

Of course, this still leaves open plenty of difficult threshold questions, concerning what is to be included and what excluded. Consider, for instance, the mental process or epistemic attitude of acceptance.[75] Acceptance is unlike belief in a variety of ways. Thus, where to believe that *p* is to be committed to the truth of *p* (while remaining sensitive to evidence otherwise), to accept that *p* is not necessarily to be committed to its truth. It may be a more pragmatic matter of adopting a policy of deeming, positing or postulating that *p*. We might also think that whereas we can believe in degrees

[75] On acceptance, see Cohen (1992).

(again, we can have strong or weak beliefs), acceptance does not come in degrees; instead, we either accept *p* or do not accept *p*.[76]

Could we say acceptance is included within the first limb of imagining, that of entering a distinctive epistemic frame? The answer has to be that 'it depends'; the activities that acceptance as an epistemic attitude picks out, eg deeming, positing or postulating, or, for some, supposing, as when we accept something for the sake of argument, could certainly serve as examples of the kinds of activities we engage in when we enter a distinctive epistemic frame. We can accept, then, in ways that are largely conscious and deliberate, and involve being active, regulating epistemic distance, engaging epistemically, and doing so in a manner that is purpose-built and time-bound. There could be ways in which to accept, eg to accept something for the sake of an argument, or to suppose that something is so, or to treat something as if it were true, is to enter a distinctive epistemic frame.

Nevertheless, acceptance is also very close to being an attitude and an activity that involves no real sense of regulating epistemic distance, including selectively suspending any epistemic norms or commitments. Perhaps when we are conscious of accepting-rather-than-believing, then we are suspending, say, the epistemic norm of truth or aiming-at-truth. But some acts of acceptance, or some of what we may do when we adopt the epistemic attitude of acceptance, may not involve, say, any conscious awareness of artifice and its purpose-built and time-bound character; it may be business as usual, and acceptance then may signal something more like tentative believing than imagining. I acknowledge that the matter is delicate and complicated. There is more work to be done on acceptance and its relation to imagination. My point here is to say that some kinds of activities and attitudes that acceptance may pick out could be included, while others may not.

vii. Further Threshold Questions II: Entertaining, Conceiving, Hypothesising

More difficult questions arise as to a whole host of other epistemic attitudes or activities, eg assuming, presuming, hypothesising, considering, conceiving, and entertaining. My approach, once again, is to be as inclusive as possible, ie to look, first, for ways of accommodating such epistemic attitudes and activities into the realm of imagination. Nevertheless, it is also important to stick to certain threshold characteristics. Thus, as above, where some epistemic process is more passive, such as was the case above with apprehending or understanding, or merely grasping a content, then I would be inclined to exclude it.

Similarly, on some ways of understanding 'entertaining', as when we entertain a proposition, this is very close precisely to merely apprehending. To that extent, entertaining would be excluded. According to Arcangeli, entertaining is different to supposing, for when we suppose, unlike when we entertain, we are committed to exploring at least the direct consequence of what we suppose; in that sense, supposing is more active than entertaining.[77]

[76] See the discussion in Arcangeli (2018), 96–102.
[77] See Arcangeli (2018), 94.

Similar points might be made about conceiving or considering: these are typically thought of as quite passive, and closer to mere apprehending, and insofar as that is so, they would fail to meet the threshold characteristic of epistemic activity. Similarly, some acts of conceiving or considering, as with some acts of assuming or presuming, may again be close to belief, and be modes of more tentative commitments to truth.

Cases of hypothesising, too, are in the same category: some of what we may hypothesise may be in the course of ordinary action, in which we are not suspending any epistemic norms or commitments: we may, for instance, be generating candidates for belief, or we may be engaged in activities of prediction or anticipation. In such cases, we may be both generating and evaluating hypotheses by reference to the usual epistemic norms and commitments. Other cases of what we might loosely call 'hypothesising', as when, for instance, we imagine hypothetical scenarios, would be included.

One would have to look at each case in its particular context. One would have to examine each attitude or mental act or process in question and consider how it fares against the threshold characteristics. I would not be so bold as to wish to exclude, say, assuming, presuming, hypothesising, conceiving, considering, or entertaining on principle, even if, on balance, the case for including them is weak, for they tend not to be ways of entering a distinctive epistemic frame.

As we might recall from the previous section, the above way of articulating the threshold characteristics of imagining are quite different to some of the other ways that philosophers have sought to distinguish imagining from other mental states, acts and processes. For instance, I have not sought here to make constructing mental imagery, or 'imagining from the inside',[78] or imagining from a perspective, as core features or criteria for what counts and what does not as imagining. Again, wherever possible, I have sought to incorporate what has been excluded by some philosophers as not part of imagination, and thus to construct a model of imagination in which we can see the richness and variability of imagining.

Modelling this first limb of imagining as a process that is largely conscious and deliberate, active, and involving regulation of epistemic distance, epistemic engagement and a sense of the purpose-built and time-bound, does I hope strike a balance between being inclusive, and thus enabling us to capture some of the variability of imagining, while at the same time being sufficiently precise to enable the identification of an object of study.

B. Richness and Variety

Let me turn now to how we might taxonomise this richness and variability. Part of what I shall say here will overlap with the second limb of imagining, which precisely tries to capture some of the variability of ways in which we are active when we imagine. Nevertheless, there are some points to be made here that refer specifically to the first limb of imagining.

When we enter a distinctive epistemic frame, we actively construct an epistemic attitude, and we selectively suspend certain epistemic norms or commitments while

[78] On 'imagining from the inside' as a necessary element of imagination, see Peacocke (1985).

retaining others. What might some of these epistemic attitudes be? Which epistemic norms or commitments might we suspend, and which ones might we retain? That is one set of questions we can ask. When we ask them, we can pay attention to four different issues: first, the quality of the epistemic attitude, ie varying degrees of confidence or tentativeness; second, the modality of the epistemic attitude, eg whether it pursues something consciously false, or merely implausible or unlikely, or something else entirely; third, the kind of epistemic norm or commitment that is suspended; and fourth, the relation of these three issues to the kind of epistemic act exercised. I will explore these briefly in a moment.

Another set of questions concerns how these various ways of entering a distinctive epistemic frame might relate to a whole host of other operations or mechanisms. These may include, for example, relations with affective, sensory or kinesic modes of participation. These will be the focus of the second limb of imagining, which is designed precisely to capture the different ways in which we participate when we imagine. Linked also closely to the affective mode, and thus discussed in that section below, is the question of the proneness of different kinds of imagining to what has been called 'imaginative resistance' or 'imaginative blockage'.[79] But there are also other operations or mechanisms we might bring into the picture, eg the relation to intentionality (or the degree of deliberative control over mental content), action, desire, knowledge or inferentiality. I shall not attempt to be comprehensive here, but merely give a sense of the richness on offer, and thus consider the further research that can be done.

i. Epistemic Attitudes, Norms, Commitments and Acts

Turning to the first set of questions, there are, to repeat, four different issues we can consider: 1) the quality of the epistemic attitude; 2) the modality of the epistemic attitude; 3) the kind of epistemic norm or commitment suspended; and 4) the relation of these three to the kind of epistemic act exercised. Let me address each in turn.

By the quality of the epistemic attitude I mean to refer to the degree of confidence or tentativeness with which we can enter a distinctive epistemic frame. Though I ruled out conviction, and thus a quality of an attitude that relates closely to belief, from the realm of the imaginative, this still leaves a lot of room for qualities of epistemic attitudes that are less-than-certain. We may enter a distinctive epistemic frame with a very heightened sense of uncertainty, with little to go on, or a poor sense of what may be relevant or what could serve as a guide to orient ourselves. Faced, for example, with a decision for the first time (or indeed, any subsequent time!) as to whether to marry, we may enter a distinctive epistemic frame where we dramatically rehearse possibilities, eg possible futures, with a sense of almost dizzy uncertainty, lacking any confidence about our ability to make a good decision, or even to simulate possible futures. One could contrast that heightened sense of tentativeness and disorientation with a case where we have a relatively familiar problem that has arisen once again, and where we have a better grasp of the possibilities and their likely consequences.

[79] See, eg, Gendler (2000). The literature on 'imaginative resistance' is now large and growing. For a recent discussion, also relating to imagination and emotion, see Shanto (2019).

In general, the quality of the epistemic attitude will be one of uncertainty and tentativeness. It will be marked by a certain degree of hesitation. One might speak here, for instance, of a subjunctive mood, marked by a sense that we could go this way, or perhaps that way. Again, however, this still leaves a good deal of room for different degrees of uncertainty, eg varying strengths of determination to engage in a more or less elaborate process of experiment and exploration. Sometimes, for instance, we sense the importance of deferring a decision on a matter, being mindful of how little we know; sometimes, we sense that we have accumulated almost sufficient resources in order to articulate the principle of our decision. Entering a distinctive epistemic frame can thus vary along the dimension of the quality of our epistemic attitude.

The modality of our epistemic attitudes can vary too. By this I mean that the content of our epistemic attitudes can vary on a degree of possibility or connection to reality.[80] For instance, we can be aware we are pursuing, eg, supposing as being so, something that we know is otherwise. We can thus be supposing something as true that we know to be false. Or we may be supposing something to be so when we are unsure whether it is true or false. Or, we may be imagining, eg constructing mental imagery of, something that we know is impossible, or merely implausible or unlikely. I may be imagining a world in which all trees are inverted, with their roots above the ground and their branches and leaves underground; or I may imagine persons with impermeable skins, never liable to be broken; or I may imagine a world without scarce resources. I can also imagine worlds that are not so far removed from what I take to be real or possible, that involve just a relatively minor variation, eg a world in which the leaves of all trees are a certain shade of green.

It is important, for the workings of imagination, that we can deliberately will ourselves to imagine things that we are aware are hyperbolically or fantastically impossible, but also, that we can equally deliberately will ourselves to imagine just minor variations of what we take to be real. We are even able to suppose things that we could not construct mental imagery of, eg in Descartes' famous example, a chiliagon, ie a thousand-sided figure. Put another way: when we imagine, we can take as much epistemic distance to what we know, or take ourselves to know, as we like. This is both a value as well as a danger of imagining. In any event, the modality of our epistemic attitudes is rich in variability.

The above two issues bear a close relation to the third, ie which epistemic norms or commitments we selectively suspend and which we maintain. I am not suggesting that we must always select which epistemic norms or commitments to maintain, though occasionally we may do that. Perhaps we may also not be quite so conscious, at least not in a way that we articulate to ourselves every time we imagine, as to which epistemic norms or commitments we are suspending. Nevertheless, when we enter a distinctive epistemic frame, we often do selectively suspend certain epistemic norms or

[80] To be clear: to speak of the modality of the epistemic attitude is different from considering the threshold question of when we imagine. As indicated earlier, I do not think we need to be pursuing something consciously false in order to imagine. Prima facie, to enter into a distinctive epistemic frame is not dependent on us experiencing something as false or unrealistic in some way. Nevertheless, it can be that, once we are in the distinctive epistemic frame, we pursue something that we are aware is false or unrealistic, eg as when we construct an entirely unrealistic utopia.

commitments. A common one is truth: we free ourselves to construct mental imagery, or participate in some other way, with respect to matters that, as above, we know to be false, or when we do not care whether they are true or false, eg correspond to what we take to be real states of affairs.

But we can also be unsure whether something is so or not, and so we suspend not so much the epistemic norm or commitment of truth, as, say, one of subjecting the content of our epistemic processes to requirements of justification by available evidence. Or we may, when for instance setting out to explore a metaphor, suspend the epistemic norm or commitment of relevance, or reference, or coherence. We may want, in exploring a metaphor, to allow ourselves to generate as many possible imagistic or affective associations as we can with the source of a metaphor, eg as many associations as we can with the sun, in the metaphor 'Juliet is the sun', and we may find it useful in that endeavour to suspend the epistemic norm of looking only for possibly relevant comparisons. Similarly so with the epistemic norm or commitment of coherence: we may seek to maintain other epistemic norms or commitments, but not that of coherence, and thus seek to generate incoherent propositions or images; there may well be circumstances in which we think that pursuing incoherence, at least as an exercise of imagination, is an epistemically promising strategy, ie it assists in what I have called inquiry.

Another way to think about the variability on this third issue is to consider the range of epistemic virtues and epistemic vices, and consider how we might transform some of them, ie switch what we consider otherwise to be a virtue into a vice, and vice versa. Thus, we typically consider superstition, gullibility or naivete to be epistemic vices, but we may deliberately adopt them, for instance constructing an imaginary figure that is superstitious, gullible or naïve, and imagine what we see or feel from that perspective in a certain context. Similarly, we may suspend the epistemic virtue of humility, discernment or parsimony, and, again, adopt the identity of a fictional perspective of someone with great hubris, who has no sensitivity to subtle distinctions, and is highly repetitive, and consider how this informs some domain of inquiry.

The point for now is not to consider what may be useful as an exercise. It is just to give a sense of the possibilities. Others have made cases for the epistemic virtue, or epistemic utility, of what we otherwise consider to be epistemic vices, eg Adam Morton has written in defence of nosiness, obsessiveness, wishful thinking, denial and partisanship,[81] and elsewhere, of 'the virtue of ignoring evidence and the virtue of not thinking too hard'.[82] Again, I neither endorse nor criticise such defences here; my point is that the options we have, when crafting the epistemic attitude we adopt in the distinctive epistemic frame of the first limb of imagining, are vast. We have a whole range of epistemic norms and commitments we can suspend, and others that we can transform from negative to positive valence, or vice versa.

Finally, we can relate these three issues to the kind of epistemic act exercised. Thus, for example, if we are adopting an epistemic attitude of consciousness of falsity (this being at once the modality of the epistemic attitude, as well as corresponding to the suspension of the epistemic norm of truth), we may, for instance exhibit that attitude

[81] Morton (2014).
[82] Morton (2012).

in the epistemic act of supposing something is so when it is not so, and doing so with a high degree of tentativeness (this being the quality of the epistemic attitude); or we may exhibit it by engaging, with a high degree of confidence (the quality of epistemic attitude), in counterfactual construction of mental imagery or perspective, as in counterfactual imagination (a kind of epistemic act). Or I may, with a high degree of tentativeness (the quality of epistemic attitude), construct mental imagery (this being a kind of epistemic act) of a perspective that I take to be plausible or at least possible (the modality of epistemic attitude). Or, to give one more example, I may relate two images to each other (this is the epistemic act, as with metaphorical imagining), with a low degree of uncertainty (say because it is a familiar metaphor), pursuing highly implausible correlations between the source of the metaphor (this being both the modality of the epistemic attitude, as well as suspension of the epistemic norm or commitment of relevance or coherence).

There may be a whole range of other epistemic acts, or other modes of participating in imagination, or, to think of it yet another way, other ways of constructing artefacts, eg one could allude, or allegorise, or one could speak ironically or sarcastically. We could no doubt relate all these to the quality and modality of epistemic attitudes, and to different epistemic norms or commitments that are suspended. There is richness and variability, in the first limb of imagining, in the epistemic acts which we can engage in, from supposing to pretending, and from constructing mental imagery to adopting a fictional perspective. These different epistemic acts will map onto, as we shall see in a moment, the different modes of participating in the second limb of imagining.

ii. Other Operations and Mechanisms

The second set of questions mentioned above relate to how we might taxonomise the variety of ways in which we enter into distinct epistemic frames by considering how they relate to other operations or mechanisms, eg intentionality (or the degree of deliberative control over mental content), action, desire, knowledge or inferentiality. Rather than attempting to address these in any consistent way, which would be outside the scope of this book, let me illustrate how this might be done with one kind of imagining, namely supposition.

In her recent and important book, *Supposition and the Imaginative Realm*,[83] Margherita Arcangeli argues for the inclusion of supposition in the imaginative realm.[84] In doing so, she combats a long list of philosophers who argue otherwise,[85] some because they think imagination has a phenomenology that supposition does not; some because they argue that imagination is connected to the affect system and supposition is not; and others because they claim that imagination involves some kind of participation, eg construction of mental imagery, which, they argue, supposition does not involve.

[83] Arcangeli (2018).

[84] Others who, on different grounds, argue for the inclusion of supposition include: Meinong, Flew, Hannay, Mulligan, Currie and Ravenscroft, Nichols and Stich, Goldman, Weinberg and Meskin: see Arcangeli (2018) for references.

[85] Eg, Peacocke, White, Gendler, Kind, and Balcerak-Johnson: see, again, Arcangeli (2018) for references.

An important part of the background to Arcangeli's argument is that she endorses one of the dominant approaches to imagination in contemporary philosophy, namely the 'recreative view': that imagination is 'the capacity to mimic or recreate non-imaginative kinds of states'.[86] Accordingly, Arcangeli notes that there are two principal types of imagination recognised in the literature: 'sensory imagination, which has sensory perception as its non-imaginative counterpart; and cognitive imagination, which has belief as its counterpart.'[87] Where sensory imagination involves the capacity to simulate sensory experience, cognitive imagination is the 'capacity to consider propositional representations without commitment to their truth'.[88] The purpose of Arcangeli's book is to argue that there is a third type of imagination, not reducible to either sensory or cognitive imagination, namely supposition.

Given her recreative view, Arcangeli ends up arguing that supposition can be understood to be the imaginative counterpart, or recreation in imagination, of a type of acceptance. I agree with Arcangeli that there is a strong case to make for the inclusion of supposition into the imaginative realm. I do not think, however, that it is necessary to endorse the recreative view in order to do that. Indeed, Arcangeli herself suggests, though only in one off-hand remark, that whereas supposition can be understood as the recreation of doxastic acceptance, another type of acceptance, ie pragmatic acceptance, may be 'supposition itself'.[89] What interests me here, however, are less the merits of her proposal, and more the operations and mechanisms that Arcangeli relates to her account of supposition.

Part of the case for the inclusion of supposition for Arcangeli is that it shares certain features of both sensory and cognitive imagination, and these include most prominently will-dependence and truth-independence. Where matters get trickier is with other features attributed to sensory and cognitive imagination, including phenomenology, emotionality, or what kind of participation supposition involves, including how much it connects to action, desire and our background knowledge. I shall be returning to issues of phenomenology and affect, so for now let me simply signal that for Arcangeli, phenomenology includes more than imagining 'from the inside' or involving the experience, eg perspectival experience, of mental imagery, and extends to what has been called in the literature 'cognitive phenomenology'.[90] As we shall see, this is a move I endorse, for it also helps us to notice a greater range of emotional experiences that relate to the less sensory modes of imagining, eg precisely supposition, but others too.

Let us, then, focus on how supposition is active, or involves some kind of participation. For Arcangeli, this is important, for it distinguishes, as I have done above, following her lead, supposition from mere apprehension, exactly on the basis that the latter lacks the kind of activity that I associate with imagination. As Arcangeli puts it, 'in supposing that *p* we are doing something with *p*'.[91] The question is: what are we doing when we suppose, and how is what we are doing similar and different to what we do when engage in sensory or cognitive imagination?

[86] Arcangeli (2018), 3.
[87] Ibid, 4.
[88] Ibid.
[89] Ibid, 133.
[90] See, eg, Bayne and Montague (2011).
[91] Arcangeli (2018), 56.

According to Arcangeli, when we suppose *p* we isolate or quarantine *p* in ways that we do not when we sensory imagine *p* or cognitively imagine that *p*. Supposition, she says:

> … shows a much more 'channelled', non-holistic dynamics. A particular supposition seems to come in isolation. Supposing does not involve any aptness to make up a story which integrates a given content as a proper part, but it simply requires us to take the content for granted … in supposing that *p*, one sticks only to *p* and its logical consequences.[92]

When we sensorially imagine or cognitively imagine something, our imaginative processes are so strongly connected to various operations and mechanisms, eg affect and inferentiality, that we find ourselves 'exploring' the content of what we are imagining. If, in Arcangeli's example, Mary sensorially or cognitively imagines that the Earth has become a desert, this process connects to 1) her background knowledge, eg to her knowledge as an adventurer, and 2) her affect system, eg given her background knowledge as an adventurer, she experiences excitement rather than dread. Both of these connections spur her on to imagine further, eg she might 'imagine that there is a way to clean herself in some way, say by exploiting whirls of sand'.[93] These imaginings, informed by her background knowledge, 'are guided and shaped by her affective response',[94] and importantly, they thereby connect to her dispositions to act and desire, eg her desire to survive, spurring her on to imagine further.

All this is in keeping with much of what scholars have said about imagination, eg that 'imaginings to a large extent bring our background knowledge and personal attitudes into play'.[95] But is supposing like this? And if it is not, does that mean it cannot be included in the imaginative realm? Arcangeli acknowledges that in supposing, 'there is no call for such an exploration', for when we suppose 'the only focus is the given content and its direct implications'.[96] Notice, though, that this is already some form of activity: even if we are not so active as to explore widely, ie with an inferentiality that connects to operations and mechanisms of action, affect, and desire, we still do something with what we suppose, ie we 'draw what is directly inferable from it'.[97] On the example above, when Mary supposes, rather than sensorially or cognitively imagines, that the Earth has become a desert, she must 'stick to this proposition', inferring only, for instance, that 'water is a rare and precious resource'.[98]

Supposition here 'emerges as a highly controlled process that only takes as inputs states that can be regimented in this sequential functioning'.[99] That is significant: it shows that different types of imagining can be connected to the making of inferences

[92] Ibid, 42.
[93] Ibid.
[94] Ibid.
[95] See Walton (1990); Harris (2000); and Goldman (2006). Paraphrasing, Goldman (2006), Arcangeli says: 'to imagine that I am living in ancient Troy and observing Helen, is quite different from supposing that I am living in ancient Troy and observing Helen. It seems that in the latter case I simply have to put forward the hypothesis, to stipulate that I am living in ancient Troy and observing Helen. In the former case I am engaged in something more complex: I have to open the doors of imagination in order to really envision what it would be like to live in ancient Troy and to observe Helen': (2018), 58.
[96] Arcangeli (2018), 43.
[97] Ibid.
[98] Ibid.
[99] Ibid.

in different ways, eg they can be more or less direct, or more or less exploratory, and they can draw on our background knowledge in a more or less extensive manner, eg we need some knowledge still to directly infer that water is a rare and precious resource in a desert.

When we sensorially or cognitively imagine, then, we do much more than treat some state of affairs as if it were true, or with conscious knowledge that it is false. For instance, we may construct a perspective, enacting a particular fictive identity, experiencing emotionally and in different sensory modalities, and go on to explore, in ways that we may be surprised by, and learn from, including by triggering aspects of our personal and background knowledge that we had not drawn on before. When we suppose, and, on Arcangeli's view, treat some proposition as if it were true, we may not have as intense an experience, eg in terms of affect. Nevertheless, Arcangeli insists, and I agree, we are still doing something active, we are still participating, and doing so in ways that still connects to certain operations and mechanisms, including background knowledge and the making of inferences.

Furthermore, as Arcangeli observes, supposition can often trigger further acts or processes of imagining, including sensory or cognitive imagining, and in that sense, we can say it is indirectly connected to affect, action, desire, and the other operations and mechanisms that sensory and cognitive imagining are more tightly and directly connected to.[100] None of this is to apologise for supposition, as if it were an inferior form or mode of imagining. In fact, there may be distinct advantages to being less directly and more loosely connected to these various operations and mechanisms. For instance, we can argue that supposition is 'freer' than sensory or cognitive imagination, for there 'is almost no limitation on what can be supposed, whereas there are limitations on what can be imagined'.[101] Precisely because sensory or cognitive imagining is more self-involving, ie it connects more strongly to our personal and background knowledge, and to our sensory, affective and kinesic experiences, it is also more prone to 'blockage' or 'resistance', ie we may resist imagining some content at all, or, even if we manage to force ourselves to imagine, we will experience blockage and be unable to continue. Typical examples that are provided here involve some morally repugnant content, eg killing babies for fun. The point is that whereas we may be unable or unwilling to sensorily or cognitively imagine killing babies for fun, we may be able or willing to suppose it. As Arcangeli puts it, 'not only morally repulsive contents or plain contradictions can be supposed, but even impossibilities'.[102] And that, in turn, can have benefits, eg for inquiry or decision-making.

This does not mean, as above, that supposing is entirely disconnected from various operations and mechanisms. Unlike with mere apprehension, we are still doing something when we suppose, and thus there may be occasions when we resist even supposing something. Further, like sensory or cognitive imagining, supposing may also involve, even if in a lesser intensity, pleasure.[103] The point is that these are matters of degree,

[100] Ibid, 37–9.

[101] Ibid, 51.

[102] Ibid, 52.

[103] Elizabeth Picciuto argues that 'we enjoy supposing'. Further, she says, 'Someone who enjoys supposing is apt to solve problems creatively, to consider several possible courses of action and choose what seems best, to empathise and become a more efficient social actor, to innovate and to discover': (2009), 488.

and that there is great richness and variety in our modes of imagining, ie in different ways of entering a distinctive epistemic frame, and the different epistemic attitudes and epistemic acts and processes we can perform, with all of these connecting in different ways to various operations and mechanisms. Supposition, with its relatively high degree of isolation or quarantining of the content of what is being supposed from affect, action, desire, sensory experience, or proneness to exploration, gives us 'a high degree of freedom about the contents that can be supposed',[104] and this can play a crucially important role when we are confronting content that we may otherwise find difficult to imagine.

In this section, on the first limb of imagining, that of entering a distinctive epistemic frame, we have already begun to cast an eye on the second limb, ie on the different modes of participation involved when we imagine. It is time that we turn to that second limb and articulate in more detail the richness and variety of modes of participation. Conveying that sense of richness and variety has also been one of the major aims of this section. Although I have insisted on certain threshold characteristics imagining, ie a) being largely conscious and deliberate; 2) being an active process; 3) involving regulation of epistemic distance; 4) being epistemically engaged; and 5) being accompanied by a sense of the purpose-built and time-bound, the emphasis has been on showing: 1) just how many different epistemic attitudes we can construct and take up when we imagine; 2) the different epistemic norms and commitments we can suspend or transform; and 3) also the different ways, involving their own benefits and dangers, of entering a distinctive epistemic frame. My point, to reiterate, is less to insist on certain divisions, eg between sensory and cognitive imagining, or those two and supposing, and more to invite us to explore the richness and variety of the imaginative realm.

III. Varieties of Participation I: Affective

On the model of imagination I propose in this book, when we imagine we combine two processes: first, we enter a distinctive epistemic frame (as explored in the previous section), and second, we participate along a spectrum of affective, sensory and kinesic involvement. It is crucial for my account that we combine both processes, and that entering a distinctive epistemic frame is not an obstacle to participation, but is both compatible with it as well as often enhancing it. But what is it to participate? What kinds of participating does imagining involve?

This is not an easy question, but it is the question I seek to confront in the three sections that complete this chapter. The choice of the three kinds of participation, ie affective, sensory and kinesic, is not meant to be exhaustive. There may be other kinds of participation involved in imagining, and other scholars may find it more useful to draw on other kinds of languages or philosophical traditions, eg phenomenology.[105] For present purposes, however, these three modes are the most important: they connect, as I shall be demonstrating later in this book, with the practice of inquiry in

[104] Arcangeli (2018), 67.
[105] See, eg, Casey (2000).

adjudication. Put another way, it is crucial that imagining involves affective, sensory and kinesic participation, for these modes of participating are crucial ways in which inquiry is enabled, ie without experiencing emotions, or engaging in sensory or kinesic simulation,[106] we would not be able to make insights into potentially relevant values, vulnerabilities and interests.

Having said that, my point here is not that all acts of imagining are intensively affective, sensory and kinesic; instead, my point, in keeping with the spirit of the previous section, is to convey something of the richness and variety of modes of participating when we imagine, some of which may be very low on the scale of affective, sensory or kinesic involvement. Further, my claim here is not that all processes of imagining must include all three, ie that they all involve some level of affective, sensory and kinesic involvement. In fact, some processes of imagining may only involve affective involvement, and even then, on a very low scale or only indirectly, eg precisely as with supposition. Once again, imagination is simply too large, too complex, too capacious, a domain of activity to make any sweeping claims. We do better to approach it as flexibly and delicately as we can.

With all that in mind, I turn in this section to the first mode of participating: the affective mode. To do this is to seek to bring into view the relations between imagination and emotion. Needless to say, this deserves considerably more attention than a single section like this can devote to it. Many scholars have noticed the tight and complex relations there are between imagination and emotion. As Hume, for instance, pointed out in his *Treatise of Human Nature*: 'It is remarkable, that the imagination and affections have a close union together, and that nothing, which affects the former, can be entirely indifferent to the latter'.[107] For some theorists, the two are so closely intertwined that they argue it is difficult to think of acts or processes of imagining that do not involve some emotion, and equally, difficult to think of acts or processes of emotion that do not involve some imagination.[108]

While I acknowledge the closeness and complexity of the relations between imagination and emotion, I do not seek to make any claims here about their mutual inextricability. I also do not seek to develop anything as grand as a theory of emotion, and therefore hope that much of what I say will be compatible with a range of views one may hold about emotion. Having said that, as shall become clear in a moment, I fully endorse a view of the emotions that recognises their cognitive importance, and thus also the unique epistemic access that emotions provide us with in terms of our relations with the world and others. My aim, instead, is more modest: it is to explore some of the ways, most pertinent to this book, that imagining may involve and connect to the emotions, and thereby to give a sense of the rich and various ways that we draw on emotions when we imagine.

[106] Throughout these three sections I sometimes use the language of 'simulation': by this I mean nothing more than a shorthand way of referring to participation in the second limb of imagining, as long as this is accompanied by the first limb, ie entering a distinctive epistemic frame. Thus, I can experience emotion without entering a distinct epistemic frame, as in the ordinary run of experience; when, however, I do experience emotion – or participate affectively – when accompanied by entering a distinctive epistemic frame, then I am, in my terminology, 'simulating' affectively.

[107] Hume (1739) [1978], 2.3.6.

[108] See Morton (2013).

A. The Epistemic Importance of the Emotions

The first task is to recognise the epistemic importance of the emotions: how they provide us with unique epistemic access, including access to the world, to understanding others, and to matters of value. We know, of course, that the power of emotions, including the relations between emotion and language, or emotions and rhetoric, has long been recognised. We would need only to cast our minds back to the practices of rhetoric and rhetorical training, including theories and manuals of rhetoric – most obviously in Aristotle, but also, later, in Quintilian, Cicero, Agricola and others – to find not only acknowledgements of the importance of the emotions, but also complex accounts of how emotions relate to memory, to the processing and relative vividness of mental imagery, to voice and gesture, to particular genres, tropes and figures of speech, to the presentation of self, and to the dynamics of relations between speakers and an audience.[109] I shall be returning to some of these insights in the next two sections. For now, the point is simply to recall that theorising about the emotions and their role and value is a long one, and indeed, that at least some of the contemporary turn to affect, including amongst analytical philosophers, has arguably occurred via sophisticated treatments of Ancient, and especially Aristotelian, thought.[110]

Even the most superficial awareness of Ancient approaches to emotion shows us that they recognised that emotions were not optional add-ons to the practice of rhetoric. Instead, for the Ancients, emotions were integral both to the practice and the education of rhetoric. Further, although the Ancients recognised the power of the emotions, they did not conclude from this that emotions were somehow entirely outside the operation of our will, or entirely irrational processes that overcame us spontaneously and made us blind to others and the world around us. Indeed, to the contrary: the Ancients recognised that an orator could deliberately work up an emotion in himself, and draw on that experience to learn something, eg to engage better with the world and others, and that an orator could also strategically induce an audience into particular kinds of emotions, thereby again helping them see or understand something they might not otherwise see or understand.

i. Salience, Relevance, Attention

Contemporary theorists, too, have sought to combine recognition of the power of the emotions, involving, for example, bodily experiences, with accounts of how emotions are related to access to the world and others, including values and other normative phenomena, as well as to knowledge, reason and deliberation. One way that theorists have done this is via the concepts of salience, relevance-making and attention. Catherine Elgin, for instance, has argued that 'emotions are sources of salience'; we can think of

[109] See, eg, Mack (2011); Vickers (1988); and Hawhee (2004).
[110] See, eg, Nussbaum (2001).

them as 'patterns of attention, highlighting certain features of a domain and obscuring others'.[111] Elgin continues:

> By rendering previously ignored features and previously unknown patterns salient, emotions provide new insights into a domain. They enrich our cognitive capacities by sensitising us to likenesses and differences, patterns and discrepancies that we would otherwise overlook.[112]

Elgin also shows why reflection on our emotions, including reflection on differences between emotions, may have epistemic significance. 'When I learn', she says, 'to distinguish between regret and remorse, my emotions better track my sense of responsibility'.[113] For Elgin, the refinement of one's knowledge of the world and oneself depends in part on our emotions, as well as on reflections on our emotions. 'To some extent', she says, 'refinement of the sensibilities is a matter of learning to tell different feelings apart'.[114]

Other theorists, too, have emphasised this sense in which emotions are means of drawing attention, ie making salient, and further enabling the exploration, of aspects of the world and others, including normative aspects, which we otherwise would not notice or be in a position to deliberate about. Sabine Roeser, for example, says that we need to conceive of the 'emotions as a form of practical rationality and a potential source of moral wisdom'.[115] Emotions here include emotional dispositions, such as caring, as well as particular emotional episodes, eg of compassion: without these, we would simply fail to notice, let alone be responsive to, morally relevant features of situations and the experiences of others. The key point is that emotions are not an optional add-on, which could somehow be replaced by more complex emotion-less cognitive states or by more fine-grained knowledge. Emotions have their own distinctive epistemic importance:

> The affective phenomenology of emotions is not a trivial add-on to a cognitive state that could be equally informative by itself. The affective phenomenology of emotions provides a richness of experience that cannot be substituted by a purely cognitive state.[116]

One can draw here an analogy with sensory experience: we could not simply reproduce or supplement what we can experience with our senses by some highly complex propositional structure. 'Sense perception', as Roeser says, 'is infinitely richer than purely propositional evidence'; 'Experiencing with one's sense cannot be replaced by reading up on propositional evidence'; and so, 'analogously, we can argue that someone who has purely cognitive moral beliefs but does not experience any affective states misses an important aspect of what it means to have moral knowledge'.[117] For Roeser, the key emotions in question, ie those that provide us with attentional and access capacities to 'ethical aspects of risk such as autonomy, justice, fairness, and equity', are those of 'sympathy, empathy, compassion, enthusiasm, and indignation'.[118] I will be returning to

[111] Elgin (2008), 43. On emotion and attention in the legal context, see White (2020); and van Domselaar (2020).
[112] Elgin (2008), 45.
[113] Ibid, 47.
[114] Ibid.
[115] Roeser (2018), 159.
[116] Ibid, 160.
[117] Ibid.
[118] Ibid, 161.

Roeser, as she is also one of the few philosophers who have spoken about how emotion enables interactive and collective moral deliberation. For now, the crucial point here is the epistemic irreplaceability of emotions.

ii. Understanding, Knowledge, Judgement

A similar case for the epistemic irreplaceability of emotions has recently been made by Rick Furtak. In his *Knowing Emotions*,[119] Furtak also argues that emotions are 'experiences through which we can apprehend important truths about ourselves and about the world'.[120] For Furtak, emotions give us 'a kind of understanding that is accessible to us only by means of our affective experience'.[121] Indeed, his claim is even stronger than that: he argues that it is 'only by feeling emotions that we are capable of recognising the value or significance of anything whatsoever'.[122] Whether or not one accepts that without emotions we would have no access to value, one can still agree, and I do agree, with Furtak that emotions provide us with unique access, ie that the kind of access emotions give us could not be given to us by any other mode of knowing, including knowing value.

The key point, once again, is that emotions are not 'mere feelings' that 'are just unintelligent disruptions: pangs, tremors, and meaningless bodily sensations, which bear no inherent relation to the surrounding world'.[123] This is not to say that emotions are not connected to our bodies. Indeed, for Furtak, emotions 'involve a distinctive variety of embodied cognition';[124] he speaks throughout his book of 'embodied affective recognitions'.[125] It is simply to recognise the irreplaceable, cognitive and epistemic importance of the emotions, and thus the 'highly specific' access that our emotions give us, in part precisely because of the way they involve our bodies and our senses.

Not everyone agrees that our bodies are a necessary dimension of affective experience. Furtak, for instance, cites Solomon and Nussbaum as examples of influential philosophers of emotion who 'claim that embodied feelings are inessential factors that cannot reveal the identity of an emotion',[126] and he accordingly criticises them for 'overstating the case for cognitivism'.[127] For Furtak, our bodies are a necessary part of emotional experience, and they help us identify different emotions. Emotions not only activate 'a set of intelligent attitudes and beliefs', but also involve 'a felt sense of bodily agitation.'[128] 'It is', he says, 'through our living, feeling bodies that we emotionally recognise significant aspects of the situations in which we find ourselves'.[129]

I want to leave open the possibility that there are some emotional experiences which do not involve felt senses of bodily agitation, while nevertheless agreeing in broad terms

[119] Furtak (2018).
[120] Ibid, 3.
[121] Ibid.
[122] Ibid.
[123] Ibid, 6.
[124] Ibid, 4.
[125] Ibid, 14.
[126] Ibid, 45.
[127] Ibid.
[128] Ibid, 33.
[129] Ibid, 46.

with Furtak that no account of emotion can afford to ignore the role of the body in affective experience. As he puts it at another point in his book, emotion 'should not be regarded as a mindless bodily state or a disembodied mental state'.[130] Instead, we need to be mindful of the complex relations between emotions and embodied cognition. Furtak is surely right that our view of the cognitive importance of emotions should not be restricted to a narrow view of cognition, ie one bereft of the body, as if we were discussing minds in vats. We ought not to be afraid of acknowledging the role of the body, as if this would somehow cheapen or thin-out the cognitive importance of the emotions. Without involving the body, and thus without broadening an account of cognition to include embodied cognition, we make it harder to understand how emotions 'alert[] us what has meaning or value, as far as we are concerned, and which brings to light matters of significance that we care about'.[131] For example:

> We are physically moved when we recognise an apparent danger and appreciate its significance, and the turbulent feeling of being shaken by fear is our way of recognising a looming threat. … our embodied affective feelings are about features of the surrounding world, and they can reveal these features to us in their significance.[132]

We ignore, then, the body in any account of the emotions, at our peril.[133] Still, while recognising the relations between embodied cognition and affect, we might nevertheless want to be a little careful about linking emotions too closely to embodiment, or at least careful about how we do so. Given the ways that embodied cognition is tied to action in an environment, if we link emotions too closely to embodied action, we may miss the possibility of certain emotional experiences that are loosely tied to action. We may thereby miss the sense in which emotions provide us with ways of exploring or rehearsing possibilities, rather than just 'being receptive to significant features of the world, which already matter to us'.[134] In other words, if we focus our account of the emotions by looking only or mainly at examples of emotions-in-action, or at the role and value of emotions in orienting ourselves as embodied beings in certain environments, we may lose from sight the way in which emotions can also operate off-line, as it were, or at least with less direct connections to action, desire and ecological adaptation.

Furtak's general point, however, holds: emotions provide us with unique access to features of the world, others and values. Emotions are distinct modes of knowing, without which we would struggle to make meaning, relate with others, and generally orient ourselves in the world. Of course, although there are some theorists who would not accept this broad approach to the emotions, most of the action in the scholarship on emotions treats this as the starting point, rather than the end point, of controversy. Even once one moves, for example, beyond disagreements between those who associate emotions with conative states, ie with desires and action-states, and those who approach them cognitively, there is no end to different views about how to articulate this.

For instance, as Christine Tappolet has pointed out, cognitive approaches to emotions differ amongst themselves as to whether emotions are kinds of judgements

[130] Ibid, 53.
[131] Ibid, 76.
[132] Ibid, 72.
[133] See also Colombetti (2017).
[134] Furtak (2018), 83.

(eg Solomon, Nussbaum), or thoughts (eg Greenspan), or construals (eg Roberts).[135] Part of what is at issue in these debate is just how conceptual the cognitive character of emotions is: if emotions are judgements, for instance, and if one needs conceptual skills to make judgements, then are we to say that children do not experience emotions, or experience them in a way that is not cognitively important for them?[136] What this shows is the difficulty in characterising the importance of emotions, ie to not push this so far as to make it so conceptually complex that it restricts the account too far, either by reference to the class of persons, not to mention other living creatures, who can experience emotions, or by reference to the pervasiveness, variety and regularity of emotional experience.

Tappolet's own preferred approach to the cognitive importance of the emotion, ie the perceptual theory, aims precisely to avoid these shoals, and especially the dangers of injecting too much reliance on conceptual skills into emotions. On this account, as she puts it, 'the representational content of the emotion is non-conceptual', ie 'emotions need not have conceptually articulated, propositional concepts', and thus, for example, it is 'not necessary to possess the relevant evaluative concept, such as the concept of the fearsome, in the case of fear,' to experience fear.[137] This is certainly a promising view, especially insofar as it can inform us, as Tappolet does, how emotions can provide us with unique access to both thin and thick values, including both the thin values of goodness and badness, as well as the thick values of kindness, courage and cruelty, or Tappolet's own examples of being admirable, pride-worthy, shameful and fearsome. Nevertheless, for my present purposes, I do not intend my recognition of the importance of the emotions to be incompatible with disagreements at the level of how to articulate the cognitive importance of the emotions, or at the level of the range of values that emotions give us access to. For present purposes what matters most is recognition of the irreplaceability of emotions, and their status as unique modes of knowing, including knowing value.

B. Emotion and Imagination

Armed with this recognition, we need to proceed to think more about the variety of emotional experiences, and how they might relate to imagining. One matter that immediately arises is the importance of seeing that emotions can come in a variety of diachronic forms, eg they can be short-term experiences, as in emotional episodes or reactions, as well as long-term ones, eg moods or dispositions lasting days, months or years. This is important because it already gives us a glimpse into the complexity of any attempt to theorise the emotions. If we take just episodes as our focus, for example, we will see that, as Tappolet observes, any 'typical episode of emotion, say fear, involves [or may involve] a number of different components':

> a) a sensory experience or more generally an informational component; b) a kind of appraisal; c) physiological changes; d) facial expressions; e) characteristic feelings; f) cognitive and attentional processes; and g) an action-tendency or some other kind of motivational component.[138]

[135] Tappolet (2016), 9. See also Helm (2007).
[136] Tappolet (2016), 13.
[137] Ibid, 16.
[138] Ibid, 8.

As soon as we notice this internal complexity of just one diachronic form of emotional experience, in this case, episodes, and we recall the very many different diachronic forms of emotions, we become all too dizzy with the possibilities and complexities. Further, again, even if we restrict ourselves to episodes of emotions, we soon begin to realise that we restrict our accounts of emotions too much if we focus only on certain alleged paradigmatic emotions, such as fear, and that we need to encompass a wide range of emotions, including what I shall call in a moment 'epistemic emotions', such as surprise, wonder, curiosity, and doubt. Again, my point here is not to rescue us from such complexity. On the contrary, I seek to embrace it, and to draw on it to help us see the many different relations between emotion and imagination.

i. Perspective

Perhaps the most obvious of these relations, and the one that has arguably received most attention in the literature on how emotions and imagination interact, is that of perspective. There is no shortage of accounts, including in legal scholarship, on the affective qualities of perspectival imagination, most emblematically, empathy, sympathy and compassion. I have on other occasions engaged with these issues, and do not propose to rehearse the same moves here.[139] I will also be returning to the specific dynamics of perspectival imagining when discussing the case study of metaphors and figures in the second part of this book (in Chapters 6 and 7, respectively). In general terms, however, it is important to underscore that there is a close relation between imagining from a perspective, whether a fictional one, or the perspective of another person, and emotion. Part of the challenge is to have a sufficiently subtle account of what perspective amounts to, eg how it is more than simply a point of view. To imagine the perspective of another person is very different from imagining the point of view of a camera angle. Consider, for instance, the following helpful passage from a paper by Karen Simecek:

> A perspective captures a particular complex orientation (a general evaluative attitude) towards experience, which acts as a 'tool for thinking', since such an orientation will govern how we go about making sense of our experience as well as directing the thoughts and feelings we have in response to what we experience. Such a perspective will be shaped by 1) our location in space and time (and the information we have access to); 2) what we believe the world is like; 3) what we (personally) value; and 4) what we take to be significant (in terms of what we are disposed to take as significant given our values and beliefs). Perspective affects what we will attend to, the connections we will make and how we will organise our thoughts in order to make sense of our experience. We should therefore think of a person's perspective as a set of implicit beliefs, commitments and values.[140]

Here, to adopt a perspective is also to adopt certain evaluative attitudes, where such evaluative attitudes may well take the form of affective dispositions and related emotional episodes, eg caring for a person and experiencing love or compassion for them. To imagine perspectivally, then, whether this be imagining oneself in the shoes of another or imagining how another would experience such-and-such a situation,[141] will often,

[139] Del Mar (2017a); and see the essays in Amaya and Del Mar (2020).
[140] Simecek (2015), 501. See also Camp (2009) and (2013).
[141] On this distinction, see Goldie (2000) and Coplan (2011).

if not necessarily, involve the emotions. One might even have the view that emotions are necessarily perspectival: they bring to our attention, and give us access to, values from a particular perspective. Certainly, we might say, emotions are modes of relevance or salience-making, and such modes of selectivity are necessarily perspectival. I leave that issue aside, but surely Simecek and others are right to correlate emotion, value and perspective so closely to each other.

Simecek also points to the importance, both for moral agency and the acquisition of moral knowledge, of switching between perspectives. Speaking in particular of poetry, Simecek stresses the way that 'poetry can shift perspective'.[142] Reading a poem, and engaging with its language, 'helps to shift our perspective because it reprioritises certain thoughts, feelings, memories, associations and emotions in our experience'.[143] When reading a poem, we are invited by the poem's language or structure, 'to go on' in various ways, including affective ways of going on.

Put another way, to experience a poem is not just to experience some pleasure in the sounds of the words, and neither is it merely to construct some mental imagery by reference to the words, but it is also often to adopt the perspective, or perspectives, embodied in the poem, and thereby to go on to experience ourselves and the world around us from that perspective or those perspectives. The poem lives on in us, as it were, and this is in part because of how it is perspectival, or multi-perspectival, and because part of the power of it being perspectival is the constitutive role of emotions in any perspective. In experiencing a poem, 'we can see how different emotional responses can pull us in different directions and how this triggers a process of re-evaluation'.[144] Further, this perspectival mode of imagining is also deeply self-involving: 'The poem's perspective', says Simecek, 'shapes the reader's experience, which brings the reader's own perspectives to bear'.[145] One crucial way, then, in which emotion relates to imagination is via perspectival imagining.

ii. Epistemic Emotions

There are, however, also less obvious relations between emotion and imagination. Here, we can begin to draw on what some theorists have called 'epistemic emotions', or what Hume called the 'calm passions',[146] and we can thus see how even quite seemingly highly cognitive imaginings, as well as suppositions, but also other kinds of epistemic attitudes and acts, can include affective involvement. Some of the work in this domain has been done by psychologists: Paul Thagard, for instance, has written of the vital importance for science of emotions such as curiosity, interest, wonder, and the avoidance of boredom.[147] One of the roles for such emotions, according to Thagard, is that they are 'key inputs to the process of selecting questions'.[148]

[142] Simecek (2015), 508.
[143] Ibid.
[144] Ibid.
[145] Ibid, 509.
[146] See Hume (1739), 2.3.3.
[147] Thagard (2002).
[148] Ibid, 241.

Perhaps the most important contribution, however, in respect of the epistemic emotions, has been made by certain pragmatist-oriented epistemologists. Earlier, I mentioned Elgin, who either alone or in collaboration with Nelson Goodman, has done a great deal to enrich approaches to knowledge, including by reference to the role and value of the emotions.[149] Another contemporary theorist, also in the pragmatic tradition, who has likewise found an important role for epistemic emotions, is Christopher Hookway. In a number of papers, Hookway has argued that 'affective states', including both 'sentiments and emotional responses', 'have an essential role in our practice of epistemic evaluation'.[150] Indeed, Hookway has gone so far as to say that 'the rationality of our beliefs … depends upon the rationality of (some of) our affective responses',[151] and insofar as that is so, the 'regulation of our affective responses forms an important part of the regulation of our beliefs and inquiries'.[152] Drawing in part on Charles Peirce's theorising of doubt, Hookway argues that the emotion of doubt, as well anxiety, play vital and positive roles in inquiry, eg the emotion of doubt will help us determine what counts as an important question or what part of our inquiry requires 'our attention or consideration';[153] our 'epistemic anxieties', in turn, 'suggest to us when doubts need to be taken seriously'.[154] Some of Hookway's remarks are devoted to showing the less-than-conscious role of these epistemic emotions, operating as it were beyond 'reflective rational control':

> … evaluations which are manifested in our emotional and affective responses can reflect unarticulated standards of evaluation, can explain how our evaluations lead us to act in accordance with them, and can explain how the influence of our evaluations can spread through our systems of beliefs and attitudes in appropriate ways, in spite of the fact that their influence is not subject to reflective rational control.[155]

That may well be so for some epistemic emotions, but this does not exclude the possibility of more conscious and more deliberate uses of emotions, precisely as part of practical or theoretical rationality, or more broadly, as part of inquiry. Indeed, one of the ways in which we can break our patterns of salience and relevance is by deliberate resort to certain emotions,[156] and here, too, we begin to see the correlation between epistemic emotions and imagination. We can, for instance, fabricate doubt, eg we can construct an imaginary tribunal of respected scholars, and look upon our work from their perspective, generating questions and most probably considerable doubts and anxieties!

[149] See, eg, Elgin (1996).
[150] Hookway (2008), 51.
[151] Ibid.
[152] Ibid.
[153] Ibid, 61.
[154] Ibid, 64. See also Hookway (1998), where Hookway focuses on the epistemic qualities of the emotion of doubt, eg he says: 'To doubt a proposition is to take an evaluative stance towards it. In ordinary English, this may involve thinking that it is probably false: if I doubt that the mechanic has finished servicing my car, then I tentatively anticipate that he has not. But, especially in philosophy, it also covers cases where we find that the available evidence is insufficient to warrant either acceptance or rejection of a proposition – or hold that it is unclear whether the evidence is sufficient for that purpose': (1998), 204–5. I would add that the emotion of doubt, as well as of course the emotion of confidence, is also something that can be signalled to readers and listeners in a variety of ways, including often very subtle ways, and that this is something that is common in common law judgements.
[155] Hookway (2008), 59.
[156] See also White (2020).

Further, if we do reflect upon our epistemic practices, we will probably see that they are very often accompanied by, if not driven by, epistemic emotions, such as 'feelings of knowing, of doubt, of certainty, and of familiarity.'[157]

It is true that some of our epistemic emotions, eg wonder or curiosity, tend to arrive unannounced, felt without deliberate effort; they can also surprise us in their strength and motivational energy. Nevertheless, there are also ways in which we can generate wonder and curiosity in ourselves, eg precisely by making something we once thought familiar much less familiar. The use of metaphor is a good example, which sometimes does the job of turning the less familiar into the more familiar, eg we think of the, at one time, unfamiliar internet as the more familiar bulletin board, but equally sometimes it does the opposite, eg thinking of the familiar constitution in an unfamiliar way by equating it to a 'living tree'. Strangeness, itself, then, or estrangement, and thus the experience of a certain kind of emotional detachment, or emotional disorientation, can have important epistemic functions, and, again, this may sometimes be generated consciously and deliberately. Certainly, epistemic emotions can be reinforcing: as Ronald de Sousa points out, 'feelings of certainty or rightness' play important, often less-than-conscious roles in epistemic inquiry, bearing for example 'on specific beliefs or on the validity of inferences'.[158] But epistemic emotions can also be means of triggering, or be essential parts of the experience of, more experimental processes, and various kinds of speculating.

One example, to which I will be returning in the second half of the book, is the role of emotions in the processing of scenarios or thought experiments (in Chapter 8). Elsewhere, I have gone as far as to refer to these, at least in the context of legal education and adjudication, as 'emotion experiments'.[159] The idea is that part of the value of such short, pithy, and also often humorous or hyperbolic narratives, is that they allow us to simulate our emotional responses to those narratives. Typically, then, in experiencing such narratives, eg constructing mental imagery, or enacting a perspective, our emotions are also involved. Thought experiments, eg those in moral philosophy, including the famous trolley cases, also depend on emotional responses.[160] One first feels a certain gut reaction to a certain scenario, and one then goes on to examine, still guided by what those emotions have made salient, what might be the reason one felt a certain way. Often, the emotions in question may have to do with whether one sympathises with one or another character in the scenario, or how strongly one does so. Further, this kind of emotional simulation can also be generated deliberately in order to cast doubt on something one thought, or which was presented to one, as unquestionably correct. In other words, emotional simulation of this kind is an active means of inquiry. Here, then, there is an obvious and close link between imagination and emotion.

iii. Emotion and Supposition

Emotion and imagination can also be correlated in less obvious ways, including in the context of imaginings that seem to have little to do with emotion, such as for example

[157] De Sousa (2008), 186.
[158] Ibid, 191.
[159] See Del Mar (2018b).
[160] See, eg, Prinz (2007).

supposition. Here, we can return briefly to Arcangeli's account of the emotionality of supposition. For Arcangeli, to recall, it is important that supposition does not involve the emotions directly: the very point, and value to inquiry, of supposition is that it allows us to isolate and quarantine some proposition from our personal and background knowledge, allowing us the freedom to suppose something that it may be difficult for us to imagine in a more affective or sensory way.

Nevertheless, this does not mean that supposition is bereft of emotionality; nor does it mean that it is entirely protected from resistance. Arcangeli, for example, argues that there is something like 'suppositional refusal' or 'suppositional resistance'. Although, in general, 'supposition is considerably free and almost any proposition can be the object of a supposition', nevertheless 'we might find ourselves refusing to supposing some propositions that are hard and require effort to suppose'.[161] Arcangeli's example is that 'I might refuse to suppose that my cat has an incurable disease'.[162] The refusal here is based not an incapacity to suppose, but 'because I very much want it to be false that my cat has an incurable disease'.[163] Arcangeli contrasts supposition in this respect with merely entertaining or apprehending 'that my cat has an incurable disease'. Unlike supposition, entertaining or apprehending have what she calls 'neutral intentionality'; they are entirely effortless, not connected to inferentiality (even the direct inferentiality of supposition); and they are unconnected to desire. For Arcangeli, supposition is connected to the affect system, but only indirectly and unidirectionally: it does not take emotional outputs as its input, but it can lead, for instance by triggering further imagining, to emotional outputs. Perhaps, though, her very example of suppositional refusal suggests that supposition too, though relatively distant from direct and intense emotional experiences, nevertheless has some direct emotionality to it.

The relations, then, between emotions and imagination are complex. There are more obvious examples of those relations, eg as when we imagine perspectivally, and experience the emotions of compassion or indignation, or when we simulate emotional responses to hypothetical scenarios. But the relation of emotions to imagination goes considerably beyond such cases, and includes epistemic emotions, such as doubt, wonder, curiosity, annoyance, fear of boredom, which can be generated through processes of imagination, or emotions that accompany more paradigmatically cognitive or epistemic acts, such as precisely supposing that something is so. Either way, in all these cases, emotions have a unique epistemic standing: they provide us with attentional capacities, marking the salience or relevance of something, and they provide us with access to features of the world, ourselves and a whole variety of normative phenomena that we would otherwise not have access to.

C. The Social Dimension of Emotion

There is one final point that I need to make in this section on the relations between emotion and imagination. Throughout this book, I have been emphasising the importance of the social dimension, eg of inquiry. This extends, of course, to emotion.

[161] Arcangeli (2018), 89.
[162] Ibid.
[163] Ibid.

Although I cannot review this entire literature here, there have been important recognitions of the social character of emotion. Damien Boquet and Piroska Nagy, for instance, in their history of medieval emotions, point to work by Gustave Le Bon and Gabriel Tarde around the turn of the twentieth century, on communal emotions and the emotions of crowds.[164] Later, other historians, such as Johan Huizinga[165] and Norbert Elias,[166] also contributed to the power of emotions to both hold together customs and normative sensibilities, while sometimes also being the means via which they change. Sociologists of religion, too, most famously Emile Durkheim, noted the vital role of collective emotion in the attractions of and maintenance of religion and religious rituals.[167] More recently, other scholars have recognised the capacity of emotion, at a social level, to be a vehicle of moral change, eg consider the work of Anthony Appiah on honour, or Julien Deonna and Raffaele Rodogno on shame.[168] This is important work, and shows us both how the experience of emotion has social dynamics, as well as how morally important emotions experienced collectively and communally can be.

The social dimension of emotions can also be important epistemically. Epistemic emotions, such as doubt or curiosity, or even the pleasure that accompanies confronting some tricky puzzle, is not only experienced at an individual level, but is often communicated to others and felt by others too. When a judge, for instance, confesses to difficulty in a certain case, that judge is not only, or perhaps even not mainly, communicating some propositional content, but also communicating, and signalling to others, an affective attitude, eg precisely doubt as to the tenability or coherence of some area of the law or some rule or principle. Similarly so the other way round: when a judge expresses great confidence in some principle, this signals to others that no further critical attention is needed on that principle, and the collective attention of the community is diverted elsewhere.

If, as Lorraine Code insists, 'a viable epistemology' must 'take adequate and realistic account of the extent to which cognitive activity is a communal process',[169] and we recognise the role of epistemic emotions, then it follows that we must take seriously the role of emotions in epistemic communities. Code herself mentions one such emotion: 'trust', as in 'learning who is to be trusted',[170] is surely one such hugely important communal epistemic emotion. Indeed, it may be that much of what is theorised under the language of 'authority', eg the authority of certain sources, including the differing degrees of authority, ranging from binding to merely persuasive, may be correlated to the experience of certain emotions, such as feelings of rightness, certainty or correctness, or trust, for instance. There is certainly room for an approach to standard topics in legal theory, such as authority and validity, through the frame of collective, epistemic emotions.[171]

[164] Boquet and Nagy (2018), 191.
[165] Huizinga (1996) [1919].
[166] Elias (1994) [1939].
[167] Durkheim (1995) [1912].
[168] Appiah (2010); and Deonna and Rodogno (2011).
[169] Code (1984), 48.
[170] Ibid.
[171] This is not a new suggestion: the work of certain legal realists already points in this direction, especially that of Leon Petrażycki (2011).

Further, emotions are not only part of the collective dynamics of a group but are also part of the interactive dynamics of any particular sequence of deliberation or indeed imagining together. Roeser, mentioned earlier, has called for more work on the role of emotions in 'collective moral deliberation':

> In collective moral deliberation about risks, people can critically scrutinise each other's emotions and the moral values the emotions might point to. Moderators of collective moral deliberation about potentially risky technologies should explicitly encourage people to reflect on their emotions, and they should not shy away from asking questions about emotions, examining them and letting people appeal to each others' emotions. This can contribute to critical emotional-moral reflection in a collective, socially extended setting.[172]

Roeser's argument is partly normative: she is advocating for the benefits of greater reflexivity about the role of emotions in collective moral deliberation. But these arguments are of course reliant on there being such an emotional dimension to collective moral deliberation in the first place. Some of Roeser's examples of socially extended knowledge, ie where knowledge is the result of a collective effort, or where 'knowledge is distributed over a group or constituted by a collective', as when 'a team of scientists who together contribute to new knowledge',[173] are ones that call upon the emotions in experience of them, eg images and narratives. Roeser says:

> Images and narratives provided by artists and writers can have a strong impact on people's emotions and risk perceptions, thereby shaping public discourse … works of techno art can be seen as examples of extended knowledge, by being external 'tools' or artefacts that can aid reflection, cognition, and knowledge acquisition, providing input into emotions, and they can play a role in societal debates about technological risks.[174]

From the perspective of this book, it is no accident that Roeser speaks of 'images and narratives', or indeed of 'artefacts'. Roeser stresses the emotional dimension of these, but one can equally see them as exercises of imagination. Indeed, part of their value may be that they allow for affectively-charged interactive and collective imaginings. And, in what follows in part two of this book, I shall be pointing precisely to how the case studies examined there, ie fictions, metaphors, figures and scenarios, enable varying degrees of emotionally-involving processes of interactive and collective imagination. Emotion, then, is not only epistemically significant in its own right; it is also vital to the operation of imagination, both individually and socially.

IV. Varieties of Participation II: Sensory

One of the key ways in which we may participate when we imagine involves our senses. To speak of the senses is, of course, to speak also of the body, but I shall defer speaking of the body, and what I shall kinesic simulation, to the next section. In this section, my focus is on sensory forms of involvement in the second limb of imagination, and

[172] Roeser (2018), 161.
[173] Ibid.
[174] Ibid, 164.

especially on the construction of mental imagery. I acknowledge this focus on mental imagery to be a drawback. Perception has been by far the most popular filter through which sensory participation has been examined. One could argue that 'visual perception dominates our sensory experience', and so it is natural that 'visualising has dominated the study of sensory images, scientific and literary alike'.[175] Even if that is so, and even if to some extent it is justifiable to focus on the construction of mental imagery, it is important we keep in mind that what is said here about visualising may not hold for other kinds of sensory modality. As Richardson has said:

> Other sensory modalities engender their own kinds of imagery, however: auditory (that song running in your head), haptic (imagine the heft of a granite paperweight in your upturned palm and the feel of its smooth, cold surface), motoric (now imagine hurling that granite chunk against a wall and notice how you subtly 'feel' the appropriate bodily movements).[176]

I will be returning to what Richardson here calls the 'motoric' modality in the next section (I call it kinesic). But otherwise, I shall be focusing on the construction of mental imagery. I shall not enter into the complex debate as to whether mental imagery exists, a debate that has been as passionate in philosophy as in psychology.[177] Rather, I am more interested in the qualities of sensory modes of imagining, and thus especially in the unique characteristics of mental imagery, as compared to other kinds of experience, eg, perception.

One final preliminary point needs to be made: it is not my claim in this book that imagining always includes sensory participation, even when we take into account there can be varying degrees of it, eg degrees of vividness in one's mental images, or duration of sensory participation. When we suppose for example, or in other kinds of imagining 'that x', both of which may be so fast as not to allow, for instance, for the construction of mental imagery, we may not participate in a sensory way, eg simulating instead, say, our emotions or kinesically. Nevertheless, sensory participation is an important mode of imagining, and one with a long history.

A. Aristotle on *Phantasia*

Indeed, it is useful to begin in the distant past, with the Ancients, because the debate amongst them, and for a long time after by reference to them, has a great deal to teach us about sensory participation. We have already seen how one approach to imagination, popular amongst the Ancients, was to think of imagination as a reproductive faculty, recalling, though less vividly, the images impressed, like seals on wax, in one's memory. Although I resist this way of approaching imagination, one can nevertheless separate out the claim as to the character of imagination from these accounts, and focus instead on what they said about the character of mental imagery.

The key figure, unsurprisingly, is Aristotle, who referred to imagination, or *phantasia*, across a whole range of works, including examining *phantasia* not only in human beings

[175] Richardson (2014), 227.
[176] Ibid, 227–8.
[177] For an overview, see Tye (1991).

but also in animals. For some scholars, it is clear that Aristotle insists that *phantasia* is impossible without images or *phantasmata*. In *De Anima* (*On the Soul*), for instance, it is said that Aristotle defends a view of *phantasia* that sees it as a kind of 'movement (kinesis) produced by a sensation actively operating'.[178] For Aristotle, on this view, no one could learn anything, or generally think, or perhaps even be conscious, without an actively operating sensation, which continues to be active even when we are not actually perceiving. According to Bottici, 'Aristotle can say that, whenever the mind is actively aware of something, this awareness is always accompanied by an image'.[179] *Phantasia*, as the faculty of actively producing *phantasmata*, becomes fundamental to just about everything: consciousness, thought, deliberation, action, appetite, and desire.

With respect to action, developed most clearly in Aristotle's *De Motu Animalium*,[180] *phantasia* is necessary in part because the *phantasmata* it produces and puts in motion are laden with emotion, and thereby lead to action. This is also why the inducement of *phantasia* plays such an important role in Aristotle's *Rhetoric*,[181] but also in the rhetorical tradition in general (I will come back to this point). Further, *phantasia* is also important to deliberation: one of the powers of *phantasia* is what Aristotle calls *phantasia bouleutike*, or 'deliberate imagination'. According to Bottici:

> The expression designates the capacity to produce and compare the various images (*phantasmata*) with one another. The general idea is that, in order to deliberate upon our actions, we need to calculate future things and compare them with present ones and that we do this precisely through images and thoughts of them … [through] operations of breaking down and combining images … … deliberative *phantasia* is a prerogative of beings endowed with reason (*logos*) because deciding what to do is the task of reasoning. Therefore, not only is *phantasia* a crucial ingredient of our mental life, but it is also something that, insofar as it enables us to deliberate, is a specifically human faculty associated with reason.[182]

One can already get a sense here of the many different and complex roles that Aristotle found for mental imagery. Not everyone, however, agrees that mental imagery was so crucial an ingredient for Aristotle's conception of *phantasia*. Perhaps most influentially, Martha Nussbaum argued, in her close reading of Aristotle's *De Motu Animalium*, that it is false to think that for Aristotle imagining had to involve the generation of images.[183]

For a start, even when Aristotle might be interpreted to be referring to images, we should not think of these on analogy with pictures, eg paintings, or generally representations, but something much more dynamic and sketchier, more diagrammatic than pictorial.[184] In fact, says Nussbaum, it is more accurate to think of *phantasmata* for Aristotle not as images, but as appearances. The terms '*phantasma*' and '*phantasmata*', says Nussbaum, serve 'to indicate Aristotle's interest in the way a scene looks to the living creature, what his awareness of it is, what he perceives it as'.[185] For Nussbaum,

[178] Bottici (2014), 17. See Aristotle (1987).
[179] Bottici (2014), 18.
[180] See Nussbaum (1986).
[181] See Aristotle (2018).
[182] Bottici (2014), 19.
[183] Nussbaum (1986).
[184] Ibid, 229–230.
[185] Ibid, 244–5.

Aristotle's *phantasia* is closer to Wittgenstein's seeing-as, than it is some internal mental cinema, to the mind's eye, as the saying goes, which is also why Aristotle connects it so strongly to action, and indeed to both human and animal action. For Aristotle, 'the animal who phantasises will not just perceive an object, but perceive it as a thing of a certain sort, a thing that could become for him an object either of pursuit or of avoidance'.[186] According to Nussbaum:

> *Phantasia*, then, is the animal's awareness of some object or state of affairs, which may well prove to be an object of desire. It can serve both to present the object of desire initially, and, later, to specify the object at hand as what is desired … I am thirsty; I have (in the absence of the object) a *phantasia* of drink. I think see a water fountain and direct my attention to it as drink.[187]

Nussbaum's interpretation suggests that even when Aristotle refers to the mind's capacity to see when the object in question is not directly before one, what is meant by seeing is not the generation of an image in one's mind's eye, but something more like the simulation of the appearance of an object. It is a kind of simulation of seeing-as.

This sounds very plausible for an account of *phantasia*-in-action, but what about deliberative *phantasia*? Does the character of visualising here change? Recall, that in deliberative *phantasia* for Aristotle we look 'to the future, weighing one possible course of action against another.'[188] Aristotle is very explicit that this process involves choosing 'one *phantasmata* out of many'.[189]

Nussbaum's interpretation of this passage begins with acknowledgement of the importance of projection into the future: unlike animals, Aristotle seems to be saying, which 'act only according to the awareness of the moment', human beings can 'look to the future and to past experience, deliberating and weighing one "this" against another'.[190] In so doing, they can: 'see the consequences of an action as following from that action – the two "appearings" being thought by reason as a unity';[191] and they can 'measure one set of consequences against another in terms of some criterion whose maximisation is desired – thus relating the two sets of consequences and making a unified appearing'.[192] There is, then, a role for seeing here, and Aristotle clearly refers to the use of *phantasmata* in reasoning, eg in *De Anima*, he says that 'When one calculates, using the *phantasmata* or *noemata* in the soul, as if one saw the things, and plans for the future in view of the present'.[193] But even here, it seems, Aristotle closely links what one sees to the process of seeing, and thus, one might say, more to appearances as they appear in the course of action, ie sketchy and ephemeral, than to images, at least if our analogue for that are pictures, eg paintings or photographs.

[186] Ibid, 246.
[187] Ibid, 261.
[188] Ibid, 263.
[189] Ibid.
[190] Ibid.
[191] Ibid.
[192] Ibid.
[193] Aristotle, quoted at Ibid. See Aristotle (1987), III.7.

On the back of Aristotle's work, then, we might say, along with Jennifer Gosetti-Ferencei, the following:

> … visual images are in many ways unlike pictures or photographs – they are ephemeral, they may be more indeterminate, they can be manipulated by will alone as photographs cannot. Imagining may enact thinking in visual form, about possible or absent objects, but there is not a 'picture', as it were, in the mind.[194]

Thinking carefully, then, and, as far as possible, not anachronistically, about what Aristotle may have meant, suggests that for Aristotle *phantasia* deals less in images than in appearances. Further, if we take this interpretation of *phantasmata* as appearances seriously, and we thus reflect on the phenomenology of appearances-in-action, we will come to see the importance of Nussbaum's plea that we think less of pictures and more of sketches or diagrams; or of Gosetti-Ferencei's point that we see these images as indeterminate and ephemeral.

This interpretation chimes well with a view of *phantasia* as activity: just like perceiving, which is also an activity, to imagine, for Aristotle, is to do and act. Thus, to understand *phantasia*, we must place it in the context of action and its phenomenology. Simulating seeing, on this view, is also a form of doing, of acting in the world.

It is clear, even from this briefest of engagements with Aristotle and mental imagery that some kind of activity of visualising is, for Aristotle, crucial for practically all of our mental life, including the most complex deliberative problems. As Nussbaum puts it, for Aristotle:

> There is nothing (whether practical or theoretical) that is simply abstract; I cannot think of a pure proposition. For every thought there is some episode of symbolising or envisaging that … provides a concrete vehicle for the thought. I do not simply think of the Principle of Non-Contradiction, in all its abstract purity. At the same time, I am also somehow symbolising it to myself, whether by imagining an example of it, or a logical formalisation, or even by saying some words.[195]

For Aristotle, then, 'all our thinking, theoretical as well as practical, is necessarily accompanied by some activity of *phantasia*'.[196] As Ned O'Gorman, who has also urged against a reading of *phantasmata* as pictures, has said:

> *Phantasia* [for Aristotle] is a distinct part of the psyche, essential to all animal action and all human thought, including deliberation, contemplation, and creativity … Judgement (*krisis*), whether private and mental or public and deliberative, entails deliberation about appearances, and more basically, psychic and epistemic processes that depend on *phantasia*.[197]

The question remains just how exactly to conceive of this sensory, symbolic, concrete, or non-propositional content. The hint we have from Aristotle is that it is somehow closely connected to action, analogous to the dynamics of seeing and the sketchiness, ephemerality and indeterminacy of appearances. To think of appearances, then, is quite different to thinking of pictures. In the case of the latter, our attention is on the status

[194] Gosetti-Ferencei (2018), 188.
[195] Nussbaum (1986), 266.
[196] Ibid.
[197] O'Gorman (2005), 23.

of the picture as a representation, eg the sense in which it corresponds to, or resembles, as if a mirror, the world. In the sense of the former, that of appearances, we are less reproducing a picture than recreating the experience of seeing, and thus emphasising the selectivity of what we see, that we see from a viewpoint, and that we see in the course of action, and thus, precisely, ephemerally, sketchily, and indeterminately. To think of sensory participation in this way is also to think of it as an activity, ie as something active we are doing, as a participant, and not as a passive observer or viewer of pictures playing out in our inner mind's theatre.[198]

B. The Rhetorical Tradition

I referred earlier to the importance of Aristotle's concept of *phantasia* for the rhetorical tradition. An interesting question may arise here: is there a tension between the emphasis placed on imagery in the rhetorical tradition, and in particular on vivid imagery, including accounts of its power over audiences, and what Aristotle says about *phantasia* as the simulation of appearances? After all, it might seem that what is being called for in the elevation of vividness is something like the crafting of pictures, which are then thought to sway audiences in much the same way as paintings or the moving images of cinema do.

i. Energeia and Enargeia

In fact, there are a number of scholars of the rhetorical tradition that have been resisting that view, and urging us to see that at least some, if not many, rhetorical practices appealing to sensory participation, including deploying imagery and inviting audiences to construct it, have more in common with Aristotle's view of *phantasia* as the simulation of appearances. For example, Luuk Huitink, in his account of 'Enargeia, Enactivism, and the Ancient Readerly Imagination', draws on enactive theories of cognition to show that what was being reproduced in rhetorical speeches, and thus also what audiences were being invited to imagine, were enactive experiences.[199] Huitink explicitly positions his account against 'pictorialist' accounts of seeing with the mind's eye.[200] The first step here is to give a sense of how different an enactivist account is:

> The enactivist account understands vision in terms of an ongoing, attentive interaction between an embodied observer and the environment, mediated by the observer's mastery of the laws of sensorimotor contingencies, defined as the regularities in how sensory stimulation depends on the movements of the perceiver or the percept. Our bodies … relate to interaction potentials ('affordances') of the environment.[201]

[198] It may be that this more active interpretation, less focused on static representation, and more on the simulation of action, should also apply to the understanding of *mimesis* in Aristotle and the Aristotelian tradition, but I leave this question for another day: see Halliwell (2002).

[199] Huitink (2018).

[200] Ibid, 169.

[201] Ibid, 176–7.

We see, here, how potentially misleading it is to separate out the three modes of participating being articulated in this chapter, ie affective, sensory, and kinesic, for they often intertwine and work together in complex ways. In particular, in Huitink's account, we see the importance of understanding seeing as part of kinesic dynamics. Seeing, Huitink argues, is a form of acting or doing in a specific environment. If one adopts this view of seeing, then crucial consequences follow for sensory participating, or the simulation of visualising. What we do when we imagine is 'to simulate an embodied exploration':

> It is like 'going through the motions' of actual visual perception, but in the frame of 'as if' and with sensorimotor feedback (often called 'resonances' in this context) provided from memory rather than the environment. It is by definition multimodal, involving … the whole sensorimotor array, including the exteroceptive modalities, dominated by vision, and proprioceptive and kinaesthetic modalities (a sensory awareness of bodily postures, movements, and embodied aspects of emotions).[202]

How, one might ask, does this relate to the rhetorical tradition? Huitink's point is that what rhetorical speeches often describe, and what they thus invite audiences to imagine, is precisely the experience of seeing-as-action-in-an-environment. Crucially, what 'vividness' amounts to is less the detail of a picture, eg, again, a painting or a photograph, and more the life-like recreation of a scene of action. On this view, what rhetorical speeches or texts try to do is to compose passages that 'enable readers to undergo an enactive visual exploration of the represented space'.[203] Thus, 'examples of visually vivid writing … often contain an internal point of view, tied to a character, [with] explicit indications of bodily movement or travel'.[204] Huitink provides several examples, for instance from Demosthenes and Cicero. Here is a passage from a speech by Demosthenes:

> So when we were now travelling to Delphi, necessity compelled us to look upon that scene – homesteads levelled with the ground, cities stripped of their defensive walls, a countryside all emptied of its young men; only women, a few little children, and old men stricken with misery.[205]

And here is an excerpt from a speech by Cicero:

> I seemed to see some coming in, some going out, some reeling with drink, some dozing after yesterday's potations. The floor was filthy, swimming with wine, littered with wilting garlands and fishbones. What more could anyone have seen who had entered the room?[206]

As Huitink observes, what made these passages 'vivid' for the Ancients, was not their detailed descriptions. In fact, the detail here is scant. What is crucial is how the passage recreates the experience of seeing, precisely from a perspective, with selective attention, and a kind of kinesic impressionism. In both, there is an emphasis on movement and action, and the verbs used are awash with bodily actions and gestures, eg in the Cicero passage, 'reeling', 'swimming'. Thus, rather than having 'a detailed description of … furnishings', such as walls and doors, Cicero's passage instead describes the actions

[202] Ibid, 178.
[203] Ibid, 179.
[204] Ibid, 182.
[205] Ibid.
[206] Ibid, 172.

of entering or exiting a room. This, says Huitink, 'evokes a sense of three-dimensional space more effectively than a disembodied description of the room's dimensions would'.[207] It invites persons to imagine by re-enacting a scene. I will be coming back to the importance of simulating movement, gesture and/or posture in the next section; for now, the important point is that what counts as vivid imagery in rhetorical speeches and texts are not more and more descriptive details, as one might imagine if one's analogue was pictures like paintings or photographs, but instead life-like, dynamic simulations of enactive experience, ie of selective, adaptive visual engagement with and in an environment.

Is Huitink's view too one-sided? Is this really the way that the rhetorical tradition understands the 'vividness' of mental imagery? The matter is complex and contested, as one would expect. Difficulties arise, for instance, as to what Aristotle meant in his *Rhetoric* and *Poetics*[208] when he enjoined orators to 'bring images before the eyes' of the audience. For Debra Hawhee, for instance, in her account of what she calls 'rhetorical vision',[209] there is a close correlation between what Aristotle thinks makes a good metaphor, and for the more enactive, kinesic or animated way of understanding *phantasia*, or, we might say, using another important term in the Ancient context, '*energeia*', which, unlike '*enargeia*', is precisely more concerned with movement.[210] Thus, for example, for Aristotle, 'a good man is foursquare is a metaphor but does not signify *energeia*'; however, the phrase 'having his prime of life in full bloom' is not only a metaphor, but one that is full of *energeia*, via the dynamic concept of being in 'full bloom'.[211]

What is meant by vividness in rhetoric and poetics, then, for Aristotle has a lot to do with this sense of animation, of movement, of kinesis: 'The distinction between metaphor sans *energeia* and metaphor partnered to *energeia* makes all the difference for stimulating the eyes of hearers'.[212] That attention to *energeia* is what Aristotle praises in Homer, for instance.[213] Aristotle praises Homer for how 'he makes everything move and live'; for Aristotle, says Hawhee, 'movement and life, *kinesis* and *zoos*, are what confer rhetorical presence'.[214] A good example, quoted by Aristotle, is the following passage from Homer: 'Then to the plain rolled the ruthless stone, and the arrow flew … and of spears: they stood in the ground longing to take their full of flesh … the point sped eagerly through his breast'.[215] As Hawhee says, 'in all of these something seems

[207] Ibid, 183.

[208] See Halliwell (1987).

[209] Hawhee (2011).

[210] For more on relations between these terms, see O'Connell (2017a) and (2017b); and see also Plett (2012). Although they ought to be distinguished, they can also be combined. Thus, eg Jonathan Bate recently points out: that whereas *enargeia* 'suggests the poet's ability to create visual images in the imagination of the reader or listener', and *energeia* 'is associated more with dynamism and motion', they can be combined to powerful effect: (2019), 31. According to Bate 'Shakespeare's engagement with the classical tradition was at its most characteristic in the fusion of *enargeia* and *energeia*. He conjures images everywhere (*enargeia*), but he is at his most vital when he creates motion (*energeia*)': Ibid. Anticipating the discussion below concerning *ekphrasis*, we can add another observation from Bate, namely that it is via '*ekphrastic* moments in motion' that Shakespeare combines *enargeia* and *energeia*, thereby 'conjuring the illusion of movement in a still image': Ibid, 31–2.

[211] Hawhee (2011), 153.

[212] Ibid, 154.

[213] For more on Homer along these lines, see Grethlein and Huitink (2017).

[214] Hawhee (2011), 154.

[215] Ibid.

living through being actualised'; everything is brought to life by being animated, either moving or wanting to move. It is this, according to Hawhee, that Aristotle, and others in the rhetorical tradition working in this vein, train rhetoricians to be able to do, ie to make lively images so as to engage audiences in 'deliberative phantasia, leading to belief formation and decision making'.[216] As Hawhee puts it, in this tradition:

> ... words facilitate vision. They have the capacity, in bringing energetic images before the eyes, to compete with, or perhaps even overtake, what is already before the eyes of the audience, to lift them out of the present by flooding their eyes with active images from the past or projected into the future.[217]

And, crucially, on this view, the kinds of images rhetorical speeches and texts do, or at least ought to, evoke, in order precisely to have this effect on audiences, are ones that re-create the active, enactive character of experience, including, especially, seeing.

And yet, it seems, not all of rhetorical imagery is evocative because it is animated or animating. Hawhee, for instance, also mentions that for Aristotle some metaphors work because they are 'beautiful either in sound or in meaning or in visualisation or in some other form of sense perception.'[218] Thus, it 'makes a difference whether the dawn is called "rosy-fingered" or "purple-fingered" or worse still, "red-fingered"';[219] here, we might well ask: what makes the difference? It does not seem to be a sense of animation or movement; perhaps there is an affective element, with red being associated too much with negative affect, eg of warning, of war, or of violence, to resonate with most readers' or listeners' experience of dawn; or, is there some element here that is more centrally sensory, visual, relatively independent of action and movement? The debate continues.

ii. Ekphrasis

One other ancient term one might be inclined to mention here is that of '*ekphrasis*', which, in contemporary treatments, tends to be associated with the painting of pictures in words, and sometimes even more narrowly as that of the description of a painting in a text. According to Ruth Webb, however, to think of *ekphrasis* in these ways is to misunderstand the way it was deployed in ancient rhetorical practice and theory.[220] *Ekphrasis* was understood more broadly as 'the use of language to try to make an audience imagine a scene'.[221] In Ancient Greek education, emphasis was placed, eg in the *progymnasmata* exercises, on the ability of students 'to think themselves into the scenes and to feel as if they were present' eg 'at the death of Patroklos, the making of the Shield of Achilles'.[222] *Ekphrasis* here is the much broader technique of making present or creating presence, whether oneself or the audience one is addressing. In rhetorical manuals, for instance in Hermogenes' *On Invention*, what is meant by the 'ekphrastic' mode of presentation is 'attention to the appearance of persons (the look in Ajax's eyes, the quality of his

[216] Ibid, 159.
[217] Ibid.
[218] Ibid, 152.
[219] Ibid.
[220] Webb (2009).
[221] Ibid, 3.
[222] Ibid, 19.

movements) and things (his sword glinting in the darkness) and to the details of his actions (Ajax's movements, his violent attack)'.[223] Here, again, we see the correlation between 'bringing before the eyes', 'making present', and '*energeia*', including the vital role of recreating, or enabling the simulation of, experience, ie of appearances in action. Further, in this tradition, emotion matters enormously: a description is all the more ekphrastic if it is affective. As Webb puts it: 'Ekphrasis is therefore part of an intimate communication between speaker and addressee which has an impact on the recipient which is always imaginative, and often emotional'.[224]

Even as treated by Quintilian, who speaks explicitly of 'painting images', and certainly ones that are affectively-laden, or which will be associated in the experience of an audience with certain kinds of emotions, *ekphrasis*, says, Webb, is more akin to re-enactment, to the simulation of an experience and not to the reproduction of a static representation. What the rhetor imitates is 'not the object itself', but instead 'the act of seeing':

> Quintilian is not primarily attempting to convey information about a specific reality, but rather to prompt his audience to re-enact internally the act of seeing such a sight, and therefore to achieve an approximation of what an actual witness might have felt.[225]

Part of the point is the emphasis on the activity of the audience: that, once invited in by ekphrastic techniques, they will go on to generate further images, to simulate experience autonomously. The rhetor does not describe all that the audience is being invited to imagine: the relationship between the text or speech and the audience is considerably more dynamic. The idea is that, if the rhetor is especially skilled, only a few phrases will be necessary to transport the audience into a certain perspective, laden with affective associations, which they will go on to enact themselves. It is a matter of activating the imaginations, including the sensory participation, of the audience, not feeding them pictures. As Webb says:

> When integrated into a full-scale speech, *ekphrasis* served to involve the listener imaginatively and emotionally in the events at issue, making them share the speaker's indignation at a crime or, in the more complex examples, altering their perception of a fact by placing them in the situation of an eyewitness and making them share that viewer's experience.[226]

We have here a specific use of *ekphrasis* as a means of persuasion, ie of an audience being manipulated to share the views being advocated by the rhetor, but this need not be the only use available of ekphrastic techniques. Indeed, throughout this book, I emphasise a different use: one that enables inquiry. For now, the key point is that sensory participation can be invited by the use of particular kinds of language, and that this language need not be one that describes what is to be visualised, but instead prompts sensory participation in the audience by inviting them to re-enact the experience of a scene. The seeing in question, then, the character of the mental imagery, is not one of generating pictures as if they were paintings, but instead involves something much more active: a simulating of appearances, the character of which may well be sketchy, ephemeral,

[223] Ibid, 66.
[224] Ibid, 85.
[225] Ibid, 128.
[226] Ibid, 193.

and indeterminate, and tied closely to affect and kinesis. Even if there is a relatively independent sensory element, as we saw with Aristotle's examples of a rosy-coloured dawn, it is artificial, surely, to separate those out entirely from the overall experience of simulating appearances.

It is difficult, in this context, to resist quoting a little from Quintilian's manual of rhetoric, which also conveys the intertwinement of affective, sensory and kinesic modes of participation. Noting that the prime duty of the rhetor is 'stirring the emotions of others', Quintilian says that before that can be done, the rhetor himself must be moved by the emotions he seeks to stir in others. But how can this be done? Quintilian answers:

> But how are we to generate these emotions in ourselves, since emotion is not in our own power? I will try to explain as best I may. There are certain experiences which the Greeks call φαντασίαι [*phantasmata*], and the Romans *visiones*, whereby things absent are presented to our imagination with such extreme vividness that they seem actually to be before our very eyes. It is the man who is really sensitive to such impressions who will have the greatest power over the emotions. Some writers describe the possessor of this power of vivid imagination, whereby things, words and actions are presented in the most realistic manner, by the Greek word εὐφαντασίωτος [*effantasiotos*, or possessor of *phantasia*, a vivid imagination]; and it is a power which all may readily acquire if they will. When the mind is unoccupied or is absorbed by fantastic hopes or day-dreams, we are haunted by these visions of which I am speaking to such an extent that we imagine that we are travelling abroad, crossing the sea, fighting, addressing the people, or enjoying the use of wealth that we do not actually possess, and seem to ourselves not to be dreaming but acting. Surely, then, it may be possible to turn this form of hallucination to some profit. I am complaining that a man has been murdered. Shall I not bring before my eyes all the circumstances which it is reasonable to imagine must have occurred in such a connexion? Shall I not see the assassin burst suddenly from his hiding-place, the victim tremble, cry for help, beg for mercy, or turn to run? Shall I not see the fatal blow delivered and the stricken body fall? Will not the blood, the deathly pallor, the groan of agony, the death-rattle, be indelibly impressed upon my mind?[227]

Quintilian's reference to hallucination, and the sheer power of imagery, brings to mind all the great fears associated with imagination: of irrational, uncontrollable, flights of fancy. But it must be remembered that he is here giving advice to orators on how to deliberately generate certain emotions in themselves, in order that they may stir the emotions of others. The process is very much a deliberate, rational and controlled one. Also of note is the strong relation noted in this passage between mental imagery and emotion, as well as the very clearly kinetic language of the imagery evoked by Quintilian, eg the assassin bursting suddenly, trembling, begging, turning to run, blows being delivered, bodies falling, and so on. There may well be a relatively independent quality of sensory vividness, but we divorce it at our peril from affect and kinesis.

C. The Contemporary Literature

How do these insights of the Ancients and the rhetorical tradition figure in contemporary debates? What one notices when looking at the contemporary literature through the

[227] Quintilian (2002), 6.2.

filter of the Ancient one, and especially the rhetorical tradition, is that contemporary treatments of mental imagery often focus on imagining isolated images or propositions, which are divorced from the narratological or communicative context that is placed so front and centre by rhetorical practice and theory. The examples invoked are ones that ask how we imagine, say, a purple dragon, or the Eiffel Tower.[228] Consider the following examples of sensory imagination:

> I can close my eyes right now and imagine a red, ripe apple, even if none is present. Or I can blend stored images of apples with those of gold statutes and jewellery and imagine a gold apple, even if I've never seen one.[229]

I do not mean to deny that we have this capacity, and that it is an important one. But there is a sense when one compares such examples to those above of Demosthenes, Cicero or Quintilian, that the examples contemporary scholars often work with are restricted, or again, ripped out of the communicative context in which they often occur.

There are a number of contemporary philosophers for whom imagination is not possible without mental imagery. Amy Kind is a prominent example.[230] For Kind, without making mental imagery necessary for imagination, it is difficult to account for what she calls 'the directness' of imagining, ie the intentionality or aboutness of imagination, and the 'active nature of imagining', ie the fact that it is something we do rather than something that happens to us, as well 'imagining's phenomenology', ie that there is something it is like to imagine.[231] Where we cannot construct mental imagery of something, eg as with Descartes' famous example, the chiliagon, or thousand-sided figure, then, according to Kind, this is not imagination. For Kind, this image-less cognition may be, for instance, conceiving something or supposing something. Imagination, on this view, has to be made closely analogous to perception: like perception, imagination has to have some of its qualities of directness, activity and phenomenology.

In emphasising mental imagery, Kind is fighting a particular fight: arguably against the dominance of propositional imagination in the contemporary philosophical literature, and thus seeking to bring back in the more experiential aspects of imagining. I am sympathetic to this, but my approach, as already signalled, is to seek instead a more inclusive model of imagination, and to try to capture its variability and richness. This includes making room for processes of imagination that both involve and do not involve sensory participation, or the construction of mental imagery. Nevertheless, I take on board the spirit of the message that Kind and others who defend the constitutive role of mental imagery convey, namely that sensory participation, including the construction of mental imagery, is very important. I very much agree that we should not focus too much on propositional imagination in our attempts to understand processes of imagination. If sensory participation was not one of the modes of participation available to us when we imagine, then imagination would be all the poorer, and no doubt considerably less useful to us than it is. It therefore matters that we take sensory participation seriously, and it matters how we characterise what is going on when we construct mental imagery or participate in a sensory mode.

[228] See, eg, McGinn (2004).
[229] Richardson (2014), 225.
[230] See also Kind (2017).
[231] See Kind (2001). For a recent discussion of some of Kind's claims, see Stokes (2019).

Part of what is at stake here, and as we have already seen above, is just how to conceive of perception, seeing and visualising. If we are to analogise sensory participation in imagining to perception, then it obviously matters what our account of perception is. It also matters of course whether we are pointing to similarities or to differences between perceiving and imagining. One interesting recent account, which does seek to emphasise similarities, and one that arguably echoes the insights of the Ancients as I have discussed them above, is that provided by Renate Brosch.[232] Brosch argues that that we should drop the 'pictorial idea of perception, conceiving of it' instead as 'processual', ie 'as an incomplete visual field that can always potentially be supplemented'.[233] Just like imagining, says Brosch, 'real perception is an action controlled, ongoing form of exploration'; 'the retinal image' in real perception 'is full of imperfections and blind spots'.[234]

This matters, too, for how we model the relation between language and imagination, and it may also matter to the capacity of the sensory mode of participation in imagination playing a role in inquiry, perhaps especially in its experimental dimension. The point is that it matters whether one views mental imagery, including the mental imagery that we sometimes construct when invited to do so by language, as determinate or as indeterminate. Further, indeterminacy in mental imagery stimulated by language need not be a disadvantage; on the contrary, it can be an important and beneficial part of engaging with language. As Brosch observes by reference to the experience of reading fiction:

> … an optical poverty of visualisation [in reading fiction] is not a lack but an advantage for the reader: it means that mental images during reading remain polyvalent to an extent real ones [ie real pictures, such as paintings] are not. Their indeterminacy allows for constant transformation. Because visual indeterminacy ensures the adaptability of images to information received at a later stage, it is an enabling capacity, not a constraint.[235]

The emphasis here is on the relationship between the character of mental imagery, or what we imagine as we read, and the activity, including pleasure, of the reader. As Brosch puts it: 'readers often relish the suggestiveness of visual blanks left by a text. It may even be this fragmentary suggestion of a larger whole that makes the experience of reading fiction so compelling'.[236] Once again, for Brosch, this does not mark a difference, but rather a similarity with ordinary perception: 'indeterminacy, uncertainty, blanks and gaps are an ordinary feature of default visualisation and do not so much challenge readers to continuous filling-in as leave them leeway to establish good continuation'.[237]

[232] Brosch (2018).

[233] Ibid, 3.

[234] Ibid, See also Troscianko (2013); Caracciolo (2013); and Scarry (1999). For instance, Caracciolo says: 'the dynamics of our imaginative engagement with narrative texts are, to a great extent, experiential, because of the way they involve the reader's virtual movements': (2013), 90. According to him, readers, 'in their imaginative engagement with narrative texts … do not need to construct a picture-like mental image': (2013), 91. Reading is much more 'tailored to the body and sensory systems': (2013), 92. For Scarry, too, reading is much more a process of the recreation or simulation of the active, embodied process of perceiving. Accordingly, Scarry pays special attention to 'the techniques used by writers to provoke more robust imagining', as when shadows are described as 'crossing a wall': see (1999), 200.

[235] Brosch (2018), 3.

[236] Ibid, 4.

[237] Ibid.

Like perhaps the rhetorical practitioners and theorists, what Brosch is noticing is the significance of the character of sensory participation as incomplete, uncertain, inviting, indeed requiring, further unspooling by the reader. It is perhaps no accident that she too emphasises movement and animation:

> It stands to reason that in experiencing oneself as part of a story world, movement is primary, as it is in everyday actual perception, where it is the proof of animation, an essential part of survival, and the most basic reassurance of being alive and connected.[238]

Although some kinds of description in language may evoke sensory participation, and the construction of mental imagery, that is not kinesic, this will be relatively rare, or at least much less intense and less vivid, than it is when connected to movement and animation. As Brosch puts it: 'descriptive passages alone do not suffice to produce intensified visualisation'.[239] What is generally needed, for a more 'intensified experientiality' to emerge is the simulation of an experienced space.[240] In fiction, this is often achieved perspectivally, ie by the creation of a 'subjective, emotional filter of a perceiving fictional character'.[241] 'Readerly imagining', says Brosch, 'is highlighted when fictional characters are especially mentioned as seeing something',[242] and this is often made possible precisely through references to movement and kinesis.

I have strayed, already, into the next section. For this, however, I do not apologise. As I have suggested, sensory participation, or treatments of mental imagery, are often too isolated from discussions of both affective and kinesic modes of participation. Even when we construct mental imagery that is not laden with affect or kinesis, mental imagery retains this element of appearance from a perspective, and in a way that often invites us, if not requires us, to generate further imagery, eg precisely by changing perspective, either kinesically or affectively. When I close my eyes and imagine an apple (to recall the kind of example favoured by contemporary philosophers), and even if I, with some deliberative effort, isolate that apple from everything else around it, eg the scene or situation in which it might be found, I still construct the image of the apple from a particular angle, ie it is still the appearance of an apple that I simulate. Further, even this appearance is likely to be somewhat fuzzy and blurry,[243] or indeterminate, which is handy, for it allows me to deliberately enhance or it transform it if I wish.

None of this means that I cannot be surprised by the imagery I construct, and this is so even in these examples of highly deliberate sensory participation. I may find myself imagining a green apple at first, which surprises me, and then deliberately force myself to imagine it as red. Even, then, in cases of highly deliberate sensory imagining, there are elements of it that are not entirely within our control. Again, what is key, apart from the mixture of the conscious and less-than-conscious, or deliberate and less-than-deliberate elements, of sensory participation, is that I am active, for what I simulate sensorially is always limited, always pregnant with possibilities for further simulation.

[238] Brosch (2018), 5.
[239] Ibid. 7.
[240] Ibid.
[241] Ibid.
[242] Ibid.
[243] See McGinn (2014).

My aim in this section has not been to do justice to the debates over mental imagery, or what has also been called, recently, 'imagistic cognition'.[244] Instead, I have sought to point to some neglected resources, especially from the Ancient sources, and the rhetorical tradition, to give a sense of the dynamism of sensory participation, including how connected it can be to affect and kinesis. We shall see that this matters when we confront some of the examples to be examined in the second part of this book, and especially with respect to metaphors, figures and scenarios. For all of those, to different degrees, involve sensory participation, and, in so doing, as I shall be claiming, often enable inquiry in the context of adjudication.

V. Varieties of Participation III: Kinesic

The importance of the body, and its own distinctive intelligence, what we may call 'kinesic intelligence', has now been mentioned a number of times in this book. We saw, for instance, in Chapter 2, the significance that has been given to embodied cognition in the second-generation cognitive sciences under the section on cognitive humanities. We also saw it clearly in the preceding section, where appeal to the body, movement, animation and kinesis played such a key role for the Ancients, and in the theory and practice of rhetoric. Indeed, the rhetorical tradition is worth engaging in further with respect to the topic of the kinesic mode of participation in imagination.

A. Kinesis in the Rhetorical Tradition

Recall the passages from Homer, Demosthenes, Cicero and Quintilian in the previous section. In all of them, making present via the creation of vivid imagery was closely associated with the use of kinetic language, which invited audiences to simulate movements, and re-enact certain perspectives, often with accompanying emotions. Huitink, who referred in particular to the Demosthenes and Cicero passages, emphasised the pervasiveness in these excerpts of reference to bodies and actions, and to the perspectival and enactive descriptions of scenes. In the course of this, Huitink also pointed to the importance of certain 'bodily-action verbs', and to certain studies done by neuroscientists which show how readers' exposure to those verbs when reading fiction 'activates regions of the brain associated with perception and kinaesthesia'.[245]

These studies show that 'readers simulate vertical and horizontal movements as expressed or implied by verb phrases, as well as the orientation of objects as implied by the use to which they are said to be put'.[246] Indeed, the closer one looks at rhetorical passages, the more 'details of human action' one sees.[247] In further examples, eg by Orestes and Quintilian, Huitink shows how rhetorical devices, including direct quotation of

[244] See, eg, Gauker (2018).
[245] Huitink (2018), 184.
[246] Ibid.
[247] Ibid.

'characters' verbalisations of perceptual-enactive experiences', invite readers to re-enact, by simulating, movement, precisely from particular perspectives in particular narrative scenes.[248] These texts also invite affective simulation of often quite 'visceral emotions',[249] or at the very least a 'felt sense of bodily involvement'.[250]

Like Huitink, Caroline van Eck, in her work on *Classical Rhetoric and the Visual Arts in Early Modern Europe*,[251] emphasises the importance of kinesic simulation in crafting the experiences of readers and viewers. This kinesic simulation relates not only to movement in narrative sequences, but also to gesture and posture. The point is that references to movement, gesture and posture are meaning-makers: they are modes of communicating meaning and inviting others to make it. Gesture, for instance, including 'the eyes and the expressions of the face', was taken to 'externalise thought, emotion or memory'.[252] In a sense, gesture itself was thought to be a language, which 'everyone acquired while growing up', and one which was 'felt to be closer to the emotions, less prone to misunderstanding than words, and hence more powerful in swaying the emotions'.[253] Hence, many rhetorical texts and speeches appeal to gesture, and invite audiences to simulate gesture, and, equally, simultaneously, emotion.[254]

Further, we can characterise the devices of those rhetorical texts and speeches as themselves being forms of movement. Thus, not only is gesture or posture a kind of language that is closer to the emotions than words themselves, but certain devices of language are themselves modes of movement. As van Eck says, one way to think of figures of speech is to see them as involving 'a departure from the straight line',[255] as diversions or tangents; tropes, too, are precisely twists, ie they twist language, and they invite us to twist with them; figures of style, in turn, are 'connected to the gestures of human body', while also being thought of as 'shapes' or 'aspects';[256] *schemata*, as Quintilian calls figures of speech, also refer, in the original Greek sense, to 'attitudes or movements of the body, such as reclining, sitting or turning around', and Quintilian refers specifically[257] to 'attitudes and gestures', 'those features whereby a text deviates from the normal and straightforward', and which 'are crucial for persuasion', for 'they animate speech' and they 'make it human'.[258]

There is, then, a very close connection, already recognised by the Ancient theorists and practitioners of rhetoric, between words, their capacity to generate meaning, and kinesis or movement. To recall, this is especially the case for passages that have *energeia*, and thus make something present before the eyes of the audience by using 'words that signify motion', often animating the inanimate.[259] Rhetoric, it turns out, moves us by itself deploying the arts and techniques of movement, including precisely figures,

[248] Ibid, 187.
[249] Ibid.
[250] Ibid, 189.
[251] van Eck (2017).
[252] Ibid. 4.
[253] Ibid, 4.
[254] See also Kendon (2004).
[255] van Eck (2017), 6.
[256] Ibid, 6.
[257] Quintilian (2002), Book 9.
[258] van Eck (2007), 161–2.
[259] Ibid, 7.

schemas and tropes of language, as well as bodily-action verbs. In doing so, it generates meaning, not merely reproducing what is known, but also, eg by twisting words, opening possibilities for new concepts, new patterns, and new kinds of abstraction. It is as if reasoning itself, including the conceptual work of abstraction, is rooted in movement, in contortion, in twisting, in changing familiar gestures, postures or bodily habits.[260]

B. Kinesic Intelligence: Conventional and Generative

Recent generations of scholars have been re-discovering these ancient insights, sometimes with but often without recourse to this tradition. Two of the standout theorists in this respect are Ellen Spolsky and Guillemette Bolens.

i. Ellen Spolsky

I have already had occasion to refer to Spolsky's work a number of times in this book. In this context, too, Spolsky has made important contributions. Drawing on the rhetorical tradition, Spolsky has said explicitly that 'classical rhetoric was … about producing motor resonance',[261] and that we should take our cue from this to recognise just how important 'kinesic intelligence' is to the experience and processing of reading, including reading fiction. Forms of fiction, says Spolsky, rely on and 'appeal to what human bodies know about action, how words pull readers into their imagined worlds by engaging audiences' kinesic intelligence'.[262] This goes not only for first-person kinesic intelligence, and the experience one has of orienting oneself in an environment, but also for second-personal and third-personal kinesic intelligence, as when we have experiences of interacting with other bodies or acting collectively with them.[263]

In her earlier, important paper, 'Elaborated Knowledge: Reading Kinesis in Pictures',[264] Spolsky defined kinesic intelligence broadly as 'our sense of the relationship of parts of the human body to the whole, and of the patterns of bodily tension and relaxation as they are related to movement'.[265] Here were some of her examples of what we know when we know kinesically:

> Kinesic knowing is knowing that you lean toward a heavy trunk to push it, and that you swing your arm backward to throw a ball forward. Kinesic sense is also a spatial understanding of the relation of limbs to torso – their relative lengths and bulk and their relative extension and natural orientation.[266]

Kinesic knowledge is knowledge of 'one's own body poise and control, or lack thereof'.[267] For instance, 'part of our bodily intelligence to be able to distinguish between stable and unstable positions', eg 'between postures which … can be maintained indefinitely and

[260] See also Sheets-Johnstone (2011).
[261] Spolsky (2018), 225.
[262] Ibid, 226.
[263] See Shilbach et al (2013); Gallese (2014); and Duff (2014).
[264] Spolsky (1996).
[265] Ibid, 159.
[266] Ibid.
[267] Ibid, 160.

those which cannot'.[268] And, importantly, we draw on this knowledge when we engage with both linguistic and visual forms: for instance, 'our kinesic intelligence is called upon to help us understand two-dimensional pictures or icons, from Rembrandt's sad prophet to the international traffic sign for a school children's crossing'.[269] That we draw on kinesic or embodied knowledge to make sense of linguistic or visual forms is important. Others, too, such as Lakoff and Johnson, Raymond Gibbs,[270] Shaun Gallagher,[271] as well as Arthur Glenberg and Michael Kaschak, have pointed to how 'linguistic meaning is grounded in bodily activity',[272] or to how 'language is made meaningful by cognitively simulating the actions implied by sentences'.[273] Further, these theorists also recognise, as Spolsky would too, that language can grow through the introduction of novel or unfamiliar bodily actions; in other words, new possibilities of meaning can be generating by 'highlighting new affordances for action'.[274]

Spolsky recognises all this, but she is also after something more radical. Glenberg and Kaschak, for example, argue that a sentence may be judged 'nonsensical' if it does not make kinesic sense, ie if it does 'not mesh in a way that can guide action'.[275] Spolsky thinks this is taking the conventional approach to kinesic intelligence too far. For Spolsky, we can deliberately produce tensions between kinesic simulations, and this can be highly generative: the kind of 'epistemological conflict' that kinesic techniques can generate, eg giving us mixed kinesic signals, or incommensurable invitations to simulate kinesically, is 'good for us'.[276] In the same way that we learn to walk by managing imbalance, so there is generative potential in incommensurable or incoherent kinesic simulation. By trying to cope with such kinesic discordance, as when, for instance, a text invites us to both pull and push at the same time, or when we are asked to both exit and enter simultaneously, we generate meaning, or at least resources that might later come in handy. Such kinesic discordance, Spolsky appears to be saying, 'provides openings for imaginative leaps on which initially survival, and eventually complex thinking, depend'.[277]

Spolsky's insight here is an important one and may also echo what the classical rhetoricians meant when they appealed to distortion or twisting in the making of meaning. On the one hand, there is no doubt that the communication and generation of meaning is dependent on and appeals to conventional knowledge of movement, gesture and posture. However, there are limits to this conventional approach to kinesis. Kinesic techniques can also be used in more radical ways: as when we push to extremes what is kinesically comprehensible, distorting or twisting, or indeed inviting incompatible kinesic invitations, so as to prompt the activity of making meaning. Kinesic intelligence is crucial to both sides of the coin of meaning: its conventional and its generative side.

[268] Ibid, 162.
[269] Ibid, 160.
[270] Gibbs (2005).
[271] Gallagher (2005).
[272] Glenberg and Kaschak (2002), 558.
[273] Ibid, 559.
[274] Ibid, 563.
[275] Ibid, 559.
[276] Spolsky (1996), 174.
[277] Ibid, 178.

ii. Guillemette Bolens

Another scholar who has also theorised this more radical potential of kinesis, and who has contributed greatly to our understanding of kinesic simulation as part of the experience of reading literature, is Guillemette Bolens. In the second chapter of her *The Style of Gestures*,[278] Bolens provides two examples of what she calls 'kinesic tropes', both of which function to generate kinesic simulation. The first of these examples comes to us courtesy of Maurice Merleau-Ponty, himself of course a pioneer of the central role of the body in human perception and cognition. At one point in the *Phenomenology of Perception*, Merleau-Ponty says:

> If I stand in front of my desk and lean on it with both hands, only my hands are stressed and the whole of my body trails behind them like the tail of a comet. It is not that I am unaware of the whereabouts of my shoulders or back, but these are simply swallowed up in the position of my hands, and my whole body posture can be read so to speak in the pressure they exert on the table.[279]

In this passage, Merleau-Ponty directs us specifically to simulate kinesically: he is, after all, inviting us to reflect on how his body feels to him in a particular posture. But what is striking, and what Bolens picks out, is the use of the image of a 'tail of a comet'. As Bolens observes, the 'comet simile adds information whose expressive force complexifies, for kinesic reasons, the philosophical elucidation'.[280] Indeed, much like Spolsky suggested, what is happening here is the deliberate setting up of a kinesic discordance: we have, on the one hand, the fixity and stability of the hands on the table, and, on the other hand, the whizz and bang, or 'extreme speed'[281] of a comet tail. Bolens elaborates on this as follows:

> While analysing an aspect of the lived body, Merleau-Ponty opts for a simile that generates a semantic tension with respect to kinesic intelligence: the majority of the body is experienced as recessive and fleeting because the hands are motionless and exert a fixed and stable pressure that concentrates all sensorial and perceptual attention to them. The interest of this philosophico-literary style resides in the way it induces a focus on the trope, as the reader's kinaesthetic and kinesic intelligence prompts her to seek a semantic balance between a strong logical pressure and a fast and fuzzy motion. It is precisely this semantic and sensorimotor tension that is at the core of Merleau-Ponty's explanatory analysis.[282]

Similes and metaphors, then, but other tropes too, rely on our abilities to simulate, both sensorially as well as kinesically, but often especially the latter. They draw on our kinesic knowledge and intelligence to convey meaning, but they also invite us – they are, after all, artefacts of language – to explore further. By setting up something that does not quite make kinesic sense, that is somewhat kinesically discordant or incoherent, they give us something to do, here precisely to try to balance out, to smooth out, the kinesic disturbance.

[278] Bolens (2012) [2008].
[279] Quoted at ibid, 66. See Merleau-Ponty (2002), 115.
[280] Bolens (2012), 66.
[281] Ibid, 67.
[282] Ibid.

The second example is less obviously about the body, but also depends on our kinesic knowledge and our ability to simulate kinesically in order to make kinesic sense out of something that does not. It comes from Augustine's *Confessions*, with Augustine here addressing God as in the second-person:

> Then do the heaven and the earth contain you, since you fill them up? Or do you fill them up and yet keep some of you uncontained, since they cannot confine you? And where do you pour out whatever is left of you after the heaven and earth are filled up? Or do you not need to be contained by anything, you who contains all, since what you fill up you fill up by containing it? For it is not the vessels, full of you, that give you stability, because were they to be broken, you would not spill out. And if you were to spill over us, you would not splash on the ground but would uplift us, you would not disperse but gather us.[283]

The kinetic language in this passage is quite incredible. Augustine himself is theorising by simulating kinesically, and he is inviting readers to simulate with him as they read him. As Bolens notes, 'divine transcendence' in this passage is 'conceptualised by means of action verbs associated with the physics of liquids: filling up, containing, spilling over, splashing down'.[284] Augustine plays with, and frustrates, some of our kinesic expectations, eg that when something fills up, it spills over. He 'first triggers the physical kinetic simulation of liquid spilling over and splashing down … in order then to deny the inferences elicited by this induced perceptual [and kinesic] simulation'.[285] Here, then, the kinesic discordance, tension or disturbance is produced by resisting certain otherwise expected kinesic inferences. Augustine portrays the divine as something that both fills and contains, 'since it fills by containing', such that 'when its container breaks, it uplifts and gathers rather than falls and splashes'.[286] The point is that simulating kinesically in this way, and relying not only on our conventional expectations of what ought to happen kinesically, but also on the generative potential of kinesic tension if not kinesic incoherence, has an 'epistemological and affective impact' on the reader.[287] In this case, it is a way of theorising the divine, but also inviting readers to reflect on it themselves, precisely by participating in the kinetic world of the text.

C. Kinesic Approaches to Literature and Beyond

I chose the above two excerpts, from Merleau-Ponty and Augustine, because they are both from texts that do not present themselves as primarily literary or fictional. Kinesic theorising, or kinesic reading, are common to all kinds of texts. Much of the work though, like Bolens' own, on kinesic writing and reading has been devoted to literary and fictional texts, which often display the most complex and most playful examples. Other scholars, in addition to Spolsky and Bolens, who have made important contributions in this respect, ie on kinesic simulation, broadly under the canopy of cognitive literary

[283] Quoted at ibid, 68. See Augustine (1925), 1.3.3.
[284] Bolens (2012), 68.
[285] Ibid.
[286] Ibid, 69.
[287] Ibid.

studies, include Terence Cave, Elaine Scarry, Karin Kukkonen, Marco Caracciolo, Kathryn Banks, Timothy Chesters, and Teenie Matlock, to mention but a few.[288]

What many of these approaches have in common, is what Brosch, who I referred to in the previous section, describes as insights into the role of 'bodily movement in the reading imagination', including recognition that readers' experiences tend to be more intense (affectively, for example) and more meaningful overall when 'certain forms of human bodily movement are rendered in the narrative',[289] as well as recognition that reading often affords precisely an 'opportunity for an active exploration of a non-existent environment by simulating (or enacting) a hypothetical perceptual experience on the basis of one's experiential background.'[290]

There is room here, in other words, both for communicating content in kinetically-rich language, as well as for setting up kinetically-rich textual environments in which readers can explore and experiment. As Brosch puts it, drawing on Caracciolo's work, the 'reader's imagination works like a blind person's cane or a flashlight in a dark room, helping to explore the story world, but leaving gaps that lie outside the relevant and remain unfilled'.[291] Fictional forms are thus often able to do both at once: give enough content to help orient the reader, while also leaving the reader to explore and experiment. They do this in part narratologically, eg by playing with perspective, or as between different layers of narrative, and in part through the use of language, eg through the deployment of tropes. As Bolens put it: 'Literature is powerful because, more than any other type of discourse, it triggers the activation of unpredicted sensorimotor configurations and surprises the mind with its own imaginative and cognitive potentialities'.[292] The point is that kinesic participation in literary texts plays an important role in this balancing of orientation and experimentation.

i. 'Kinesic Style'

I will not be able to do justice to this growing literature on the kinesic dimensions of literature, but there are a few especially pertinent insights that are important to mention. One comes from Bolens herself, namely her idea of a 'kinesic style'. A person can have 'kinesic style' but so can a text, a character in a text, or an author. Broadly speaking, 'kinesic style' is something that ties together 'strands of personal expression, corporeal and mental, gestural and verbal':[293]

> The kinesic style concerns the particular manner of all movements performed by a person in events that are liable to make sense to her (perception, sensation, and embodied cognition) and to others (presence, expression, and communication), including the slightest nuances, perceived or not, intentional or not.[294]

[288] See, eg, Caracciolo (2014); Barsalou (2008); Matlock (2004); Kukkonen (2014) and (2018); Banks and Chesters (2018); Gallagher (2005); Gibbs (2005); Jeannerod (2006); Berthoz (2000); and Cave and Wilson (2018).

[289] Brosch (2018), 5.

[290] Ibid.

[291] Ibid, 6. See also Caracciolo (2014).

[292] Bolens (2012), 17.

[293] Ibid, 21.

[294] Ibid.

'Kinesic style', adds Bolens, 'manifests itself at this specific level of a corporeal organisation of meaning'; it is 'an omnipresent perceptible parameter'.[295] The reference to 'kinesic style' is helpful, for it offers another filter, in addition for instance to the affective and sensory, with which we can approach texts, like legal judgements, or the literary qualities of particular judicial voices. Reflecting on my own kinesic tendencies, I have, for instance, throughout this chapter spoken of the two 'limbs' of imagination, which are exercised simultaneously. Or, in terms of certain grammatical turns of phrase, I am aware that I often speak of what might be so 'on the one hand', and 'on the other hand'. When I was still a student, I recall my teachers telling me that I was too fond of parentheses: there were too many digressions in my writing; it was not disciplined enough!

One could see the use of parentheses, as well as, say, the use of dashes or commas, as part of a 'kinesic style', and one which has consequences for how one communicates and generates meaning. Certain kinds of movements, gestures or postures can come to dominate particular texts or domains, eg certain areas of the law, and for that reason too it is important not to entirely subjectivise the concept of 'kinesic style'. Indeed, if we take the above generative potential of kinesic simulation seriously, we might say that one of the ways that legal change can occur is by changing a 'kinesic style', eg initially perhaps by creating kinesic disturbance, and thereby necessitating a search for a different kind of kinesic balance or kinesic coherence. If, as Karin Kukkonen says, 'The literary text conjures a richly inhabited lifeworld that is thick with embodied experiences',[296] so can legal texts, even if they may use different techniques or with different intensities and frequencies.[297]

ii. Kinesic Literary History

The question of style also brings into view the importance of historical contexts when addressing questions of kinesis. Movement, gesture and posture all have histories. How persons experience their bodies is dependent on all kinds of cultural, ecological, political and technological factors. Bolens herself is acutely aware of this, and thus says explicitly that 'Kinesic analysis takes place within a semiotic frame that is necessarily defined historically and anthropologically by the affects and beliefs associated with the human social body'.[298] And cognitive literary scholars are beginning to explore the unique dynamics of movement, gesture and posture within particular historical contexts.

A recent example is Kathryn Banks and Timothy Chesters' collection on *Movement in Renaissance Literature: Exploring Kinesic Intelligence*.[299] It is fascinating, for instance, to think of the relation between particular genres, as well as literary forms, and kinesis. Comedy, for example, has arguably especially strong links with kinesis, and it may be that certain genres draw on kinesic simulation more than others. As Banks observes in her chapter on Rabelais, comedy often involves 'modality switches',[300] perspectival shifts,

[295] Ibid, 22.

[296] Kukkonen (2018), 6.

[297] A wonderful example is the way the reader was invited to simulate movements in medieval Welsh law texts, eg moving within the court from room to room, or moving from court to country, and back again: see Stacey (2018), chs 1 and 2.

[298] Bolens (2012), 49.

[299] Banks and Chesters (2018a).

[300] Banks (2016), 96.

or other kinds of movements. Some of the incongruity we find in certain sorts of humour relies heavily on embodied incongruity or incompatibility, eg think of Laurel and Hardy, or other pairings of the thin guy with the fat guy, the short man with the tall man.

Banks and Chesters certainly point to comedy, but also mention, for instance, the proverb or adage: the popularity of Erasmus' adages, for instance, which he argued had to be 'charming riddles', with 'apt and absolute brevity', act often 'as a complex injunction to bodies called upon to perform an impossible movement'.[301] Some proverbs, and perhaps some legal maxims or principles too, may work especially because they offer opportunities for kinesic simulation, including kinesic discordance. A striking example, which I recall vividly courtesy of my father, is 'Festina lente' or 'hurry slowly'.

Further, particular historical contexts may have especially strong affective associations with certain gestures or sequences of gestures: think, for instance, of Orpheus turning back to look at Eurydice, who reaches out to him. As Ullrich Langer in the above collection points out, these kinds of gestures, in turn, may resonate ethically or politically in certain cultures. Langer himself draws a tantalising connection between the gesture of 'turning toward the beloved' and acts of pardon or mercy.[302]

As these historical studies have also shown, part of the power of the kinesic is its relation to the affective. Indeed, certain movements, gestures or postures are inseparable from certain affective associations. Timothy Chesters, for example, points to the verb 'to peacock' as a piece of language that both provokes movement and affective association; we simulate 'a peacock's strutting and spreading his feathers', and we associate this, in particular times and places, and in particular cultures, with the emotion of pride.[303] Indeed, sometimes, rather than explicitly articulating a certain emotion, we may signal or communicate our affective attitudes through kinetic language, eg by appealing precisely to certain movements, gestures or postures.

Further, we should not think that kinesic participation is somehow an add-on to what can be a kinesically-free abstract or conceptual thinking or writing. In fact, as we saw with Merleau-Ponty and Augustine above, where matters get especially abstract, as they of course also do in legal thought, we often find ourselves reaching for and drawing on our kinesic knowledge. The kinesic techniques here may involve not only reference to specific movements, gestures or postures; it may be that other kinds of expressions, such as subjunctive language, as in 'almost' or 'perhaps', also work because they work kinesically. As Kirsti Sellevold has observed, such 'scalar expressions' 'trigger implications (intended inferences) which may be set aside if they prove to be irrelevant', and they work because they enable a kind of 'cognitive gap', which we might think of as a bodily pause or a breath, of a step aside or a matter of being still.[304]

iii. Kinesic Communication

But for all the possible kinesic pyrotechnics, we should not think that kinesic participation only occurs in the rarefied domains of literature or in highly abstract thought.

[301] Banks and Chesters (2018b), 8.
[302] See Langer (2018).
[303] Chesters (2018), 67–8.
[304] See Sellevold (2018); and Carston (1998).

Making and inviting kinesic inferences, deploying and relying on kinesic expectations, is a basic way in which we communicate and deliberate, by ourselves and with others. As Teenie Matlock has argued:

> In everyday thought, people mentally simulate all sorts of actions. They imagine themselves and others running on trails, driving cards, and jumping out of planes. They imagine nonvolitional agents in action, such as leaves falling from trees and waves crashing on the shore. People also imagine actions they have never witnessed, such as King Kong climbing a skyscraper or a flying saucer zipping across the sky. They even imagine abstract geometrical shapes rotating in space.[305]

Kinesic simulation is all pervasive. There are many ways to investigate this further: Terence Cave and Deirdre Wilson, for instance, have looked for relations between embodied cognition and relevance theory, claiming that their collective project has yielded consensus on the importance of the kinesic to communication:

> What has emerged is a consensus that relevance theory recognises the role of the body in cognition and communication; that it is concerned with the cognitive and communicative effects of both verbal and non-verbal acts; and that it accepts that communicative acts are often laden with features which trigger sensorimotor or affective responses (or both) in the hearer.[306]

And Cave himself has done pioneering and brilliant work on the kinesic work of language in literature but also beyond.[307] Indeed, it was through Cave's work that I first encountered the possibilities, both conventional and generative, that kinesic participation offered. This was in part because, unlike some other theorists of embodiment, Cave did not push all his explanations of kinesic participation to the level of the unconscious. Instead, he has shown how certain forms of language can 'bring to the reflective surface traces of the reader's pre-reflective sensorimotor response'.[308] This is important for my purposes, because my focus throughout this book, whether it be with respect to artefactuality or imagination, is on the strange mix of conscious and less-than-conscious processes. Further, Cave has also shown that 'kinesis is delivered' not only by 'verbs and adverbs', but that 'in fact any element of language, including the movement of a sentence, can give rise to kinesic effects'.[309] This also includes the sounds of a text, eg Cave has written of the kinesic effects of the 'ch' and 'sh' sounds, as in swishing, switching.[310] And, perhaps most importantly, Cave has always had an eye on the sheer playfulness of human cognition, and on how the kinesic contributes to 'inventiveness, flexibility, [and] adaptation'.[311]

iv. The Kinesic Activity of the Imagination

Keeping in mind the kinesic mode of participation should also help us not to forget the activity of imagination. Throughout this chapter, I have been emphasising that

305 Matlock (2004), 1389.
306 Cave and Wilson (2018b), 19.
307 See Cave (2016), (2018a), and (2018b).
308 Cave (2018b), 14.
309 Ibid, 16.
310 Ibid, 18.
311 Ibid, 24.

imagination is not something that happens to us, but something we do: that it is an active process, and one that is largely deliberate and conscious, though it also contains less-than-deliberate and less-than-conscious dimensions. Whether we are speaking, along with Dewey and others, of dramatic rehearsal,[312] or of perspectival imagination, we must remember that, as José Medina has put it, drawing also on Wittgenstein, 'imagining is a doing'.[313] Sensory imagination, or the construction of mental imagery, can be, as I argued in the previous section, an important aspect of imagining, but it itself is not disconnected from acting and doing. Again, as Medina has put it:

> Imagining is not something that simply happens to us, as if we were mere passive spectators of the theatre of the imagination. Rather, it is something that we do, something that requires active participation, a form of action and interaction.[314]

My point in this section has been that acknowledging the presence of kinesic participation in imagining can help us see that. What we often do when we imagine is a kind of 'rehearsal of embodied and interactive exploration of the world'.[315] This makes it especially important that we do not reduce imagination to the construction of images, or 'sequence of images or propositions'.[316] We both 'learn to imagine with and through others in basic and direct bodily interactions',[317] and we continue to imagine by and through our bodies. The 'embodied and action-based, kinematic and re-enactive'[318] aspects of imagination are crucial to how we acquire it and how we exercise it; so much of our imagination is, as Medina says, 'tied to the activation and combination of memories of sensorimotor patterns'.[319] Further, by reflecting on imagination, we can bring to bear 'a critical tool for interrogating our sensibilities – our embodied cognitive and affective attitudes, and our propensities for action'.[320] We cannot, then, afford to ignore the kinesic mode of participation in imagination.

[312] See, eg, Fesmire (2003).
[313] Medina (2013), 318.
[314] Ibid, 319.
[315] Ibid, 320.
[316] Ibid.
[317] Ibid, 322.
[318] Ibid, 323.
[319] Ibid.
[320] Ibid, 333.

4

Enabling Inquiry

In the above three chapters, and perhaps especially in the last two, I have often been quite abstract and deliberately at a distance from the details of legal thought. With this chapter, serving as it does as a bridge between the first and second halves of this book, I begin to tilt the balance in the other direction: towards the details of legal thought, and in particular, towards the details of the four case studies that I explore in the second part of the book, namely fictions, metaphors, figures and scenarios. The broad aim of this chapter, then, is to relate the three models explored in the previous three chapters to each other, and to show, in summary form, how artefacts and related processes of imagination, and especially the four cases studies I explore in the second part, can enable inquiry in adjudication.

I pursue this broad aim in three sections. First, I offer an account of how the four case studies explored in the second half of this book are examples of artefacts, and how they invite certain processes of imagination. In the second and third sections, I then proceed to show how they can be valuable in adjudication, ie how they can enable inquiry. In the second section, I focus on the individual level; in the third section, on the social level, including both interactively and collectively.

Before I go on, let me recall the overall argument of this book. It is that artefacts and related processes of imagination are of value to adjudication insofar as they enable inquiry. It may also help at this point to recall the three models elaborated on in the past three chapters:

1. Activities of inquiry (Chapter 1) are social, ie both interactive and collective, processes that: are not reducible to, but overlap with, the contexts of discovery and justification; occur in real time and over time; are experimental in their cognitive and expressive character; and the object of which is the making of insight into what values, vulnerabilities and interests might be at stake in a case and in cases potentially like it in the future.
2. Artefacts (Chapter 2) are forms of language that: first, signal their own artifice, thereby capturing our attention; and second, call upon us to participate, ie to do things with them.
3. Imagination (Chapter 3) is a combination of two simultaneously exercised and active processes: first, we enter a distinctive epistemic frame, which is an active and deliberative process of constructing a certain epistemic attitude, including selectively suspending certain epistemic norms and commitments, while retaining others; and second, we participate within that epistemic frame along a spectrum of affective, sensory and kinesic involvement.

Artefacts and processes of imagination are closely connected to each other. In this book, they form a dynamic duo: we cannot study imagination in adjudication solely by reference to mental processes, and we also cannot study artefacts of language in adjudication without paying attention to how they are made and how they invite certain kinds of mental processes. Language and mind, as I analyse them in this book, are coupled together, even if, in general, I make no claims about the reliance of imagination on language. The claims made in this book are deliberately limited: I have not developed a general theory of language, but instead have merely pointed to one aspect or use of it, namely its artefactuality. The same goes for 'mind': I have sought to understand one aspect of the mental activities and processes that go on in adjudication, namely the activity and process of imagination. Thus, I readily acknowledge that there are aspects of language in adjudication that are not constructed and do not invite processes of imagination, just as I am happy to say that there are mental activities and processes in adjudication, including possibly some exercises of imagination, that are not illuminated by studying the artefactuality of language. Nevertheless, again, in this book, artefacts of language and processes of imagination are related closely together: one cannot really understand one without the other.

As much as they form a duo, however, artefacts and imagination are also related in this book to a third model: inquiry. The three models, then, form a trio. This triadic relationship is, as above, a contingent one: namely, I argue that artefacts and imagination can enable the activities of inquiry in adjudication. Nevertheless, they do not always and do not necessarily do so: it depends on the artefact in question, and especially on whether it on the whole does successfully invite imagination; it may also depend on how well we imagine with and thanks to the artefact. With those provisos, this book argues that artefacts and related processes of imagination are one of the best ways we have for making normative insight, including individually, interactively, and collectively, and in real time and over time. What are the normative insights in question? They are insights as to the potentially relevant values, vulnerabilities and interests at stake in a case and in other cases that may be like it in the future. By constructing fictions, metaphors, figures and scenarios, and by inviting others to imagine by reference to them, judges and advocates, as well as others who may be involved in the adjudicative process in various ways, eg scholars and citizens, can make normative insights together. This is the basic argument, but of course it requires much unpacking. I turn now to offering a summary of it, with one eye on what follows in the second part of this book.

I. The Four Case Studies

A. The Variability of Artefacts and Processes of Imagination

Fictions, metaphors, figures and scenarios: these are the four artefacts that I shall be exploring in the second part of this book. These artefacts are constructed by, and in turn invite, processes of imagination. They are artefacts in different ways: they signal their own artifice in particular ways, and they call upon us to do things with them in particular ways. Similarly, they involve different processes of imagination: we enter distinctive epistemic frames when we imagine them, and we participate thanks to them and with them in distinctive combinations and degrees of affective, sensory and kinesic involvement.

The four case studies I have chosen provide a flavour of the range of different kinds of artefacts and processes of imagination one can find in adjudication. With respect, for instance, to imagination: where fictions (the first case study) involve a low degree of affective, sensory or kinesic participation, and are akin more to supposition, scenarios (the final case study examined) involve a high degree of participation, with persons simulating their emotional reactions to the actions and events in the scenario, constructing mental imagery of what is done or what occurs, and what might be done or what might occur, and sometimes simulating the movements, gestures and postures of characters in the scenarios kinesically. The different degrees of participation each have their own benefits and drawbacks. With fictions, for example, given their low degree of participation, we can enjoy a great deal of freedom, for we are much less constrained in what we can suppose than what we can imagine when participating at a high degree of affective, sensorial and kinesic involvement. On the other hand, fictions do not generate as many resources for future audiences, and certainly not as many as, for instance, metaphors, figures or scenarios. These latter artefacts generate those resources in part because of the high degree of participation they call upon from their recipients.

The case studies focused on have been selected not only because they are fascinating and difficult cases in their own right (at least to me!), but also because they convey something of the richness and variability of both artefacts and processes of imagination. Nevertheless, as I hope Chapters 2 and 3 have shown, there is a great deal more richness and variability to be had. Indeed, a major aim of the book has been to offer a series of general models, as developed in the first part, which others may find helpful in both locating and investigating the many other kinds of artefacts, and related processes of imagining, that one can find in adjudication.

Where, for instance, I focus on fictions, studies might be done on other related but distinct artefacts, such as deemings, references to quasi- language, eg as in this is a 'quasi-contract', or the use of 'almost' or 'perhaps', eg 'this is almost a contract', or 'perhaps this is a constitutional issue', or subjunctive language, eg 'this could be of interest to a public lawyer as much a private one'. Similarly, where I focus on metaphors, studies could be done, as some have of course been done, on simile, metonymy, synecdoche, and catachresis, but also other kinds of relating one or more things to each other, eg allusion, allegory, parody, or irony. Where, in the chapter on figures, I focus only on the invention of imaginary characters in tests of liability, eg the Officious Bystander, others might like to look more broadly at the play of perspective in legal thought, for instance through the creation of archetypal characters in the construction of legal knowledge, through the attribution of personhood to non-persons, or through the use of imaginary names for imaginary legal actors, such as Shamtitle, or John Doe and Jane Doe. Finally, with respect to scenarios, one could look at a whole range of other literary forms that invite related, but still different, processes of imagination, such as proverbs, riddles, parables, and other appeals to the genres of comedy, tragedy, epic and lyric.

To say this is by no means to claim that these four case studies are examples of four broad categories. I make no such taxonomic claims about artefacts or related processes of imagining. It may be that one could say, for instance, that one could divide them into

1) playing propositionally (fictions); 2) playing with relations (metaphors); 3) playing perspectivally (figures); and 4) playing narratively (scenarios). Again, however, I do not attempt such classification here. I do not do so because I think the possibilities are too rich, too varied, and I do not wish to close them off. The models of artefacts and imagination that I offer are meant to be capacious: difficult to pin down, leaking, overflowing with remainders that do not fit. My examples are just that: examples, mere drops in an ocean. Having said that, I try to be as clear as I can about each of them, and thus also about the various differences between them.

B. Artefacts

In what sense, then, are the four case studies examples of artefacts? Let us take each in turn:

1. *Fictions*: I understand a fiction to be a temporary suspension of an operative fact while allowing for the imposition of the same normative consequence. Thus, for example, although a successful negligence claim ordinarily requires proof of causation, and although that proof ordinarily means that the breach in question must materially contribute to the injury, in the case of *McGhee v National Coal Board*,[1] the court temporarily suspended the operative fact of the causation requirement in its material contribution interpretation, allowing Mr McGhee to recover, ie obtain the same normative consequence. The court treated it as if Mr McGhee had proved causation, whereas the evidence showed only that the breach materially increased the risk of the injury and did not materially contribute to it. A fiction like this one is an artefact: it says, either explicitly or implicitly, that we are to treat such-and-such an operative fact as having been proven when we know it has not been, ie we are to treat something *as if* it was so, when we know that it is not so. A fiction is a form of language that captures our attention by signalling its own artifice, eg explicitly through its 'as if' formulation, and it also calls upon us to do something with it. It does the latter because it creates a temporary contradiction, ie a discordance between what we know to have been proven and what, by contrast, we are being called upon to suppose was proven. We are thus called upon to do something with the artefact, eg to de-fictionalise it, to render smooth the discrepancy it creates.
2. *Metaphors*: metaphors are artefacts because they involve more or less explicit signalling of artifice, putting us on epistemic alert either by employing strange identity statements, eg explicitly stating that a constitution is a living tree, or by implicitly juxtaposing images, eg placing the image of a colony's jurisdiction alongside the image of a mistress in her own house.[2] In employing such strange identity statements or by juxtaposing images, metaphors also call upon us to do something with them, ie to explore and possibly resolve the tension or incongruity created between the identity statements or the juxtaposed images.

[1] *McGhee v National Coal Board* [1972] 1 All ER 2008. Subsequent references are to *McGhee* (1972).
[2] *Edwards v The Attorney General of Canada* [1930] AC 124. Subsequent references are to *Edwards* (1930).

3. *Figures*: although there are many ways in which imaginary figures can feature in legal thought, I focus here on the construction of imaginary characters deployed in legal tests, eg the Officious Bystander as a test for the implication of terms in contract law. These figures are artefacts because they capture our attention by signalling artifice, eg we capitalise the Officious Bystander, also employing a comic term, ie officiousness, in a non-comic context. At the same time, the artefact calls upon us to do something with it, ie it is highly under-specified for it only explicitly refers to two characteristics (being officious and being a bystander), leaving other characteristics to be added or these to be interpreted, and with its actions and interactions with others being under-determined, ie it is up to us to provide them when we apply the figure to the case before us.
4. *Scenarios*: scenarios, as I use the term, refer to the use of short, fictional narratives, which are crafted, eg by advocates, in order to show the absurdity of a rival argument, or by judges to test the implications of a certain proposed ruling. These short, fictional narratives are artefacts because they involve the implicit or explicit signalling of artifice, eg implicit when they are caricatures or involve hyperbole or exaggerated facts, and they call upon us to do something with them. They do the latter precisely by being short and under-specified, thereby requiring us to fill in the details, as well as react to them, possibly going on to offer variations on them or counter-scenarios to them.

Each of the four case studies offered in this book, then, are artefacts, though each in distinctive ways.

C. Processes of Imagination

How are the case studies processes of imagination? Let us, again, take each in turn:

1. *Fictions*: when we confront fictions, we enter a distinctive epistemic frame, where we construct a specific epistemic attitude, selectively suspending certain epistemic norms or commitments, eg we suppose something is so when we know it is not, thereby suspending the usual intolerance of contradiction or inconsistency in our belief set, or the usual insistence on evidence-based justification on what we believe. At the same time as we enter a distinctive epistemic frame, we also actively participate: to suppose is to do something active, and in ways that connects, even if indirectly and thinly, to our affects. Further, in a later case, the fiction invites us to consider whether we would like to continue supposing, by extending the temporary suspension of the operative fact, or to cease doing so, for instance by introducing a new rule or exception, or by reducing the past case 'to its facts'. Fictions are a very thin form of imagining, in the sense of having a low degree of participation, but they are still included in the imaginative realm in this book because they involve doing something active with a proposition, ie precisely supposing it to be so, in a distinctive epistemic frame, ie when we know it is not so.
2. *Metaphors*: metaphors involve entering a distinctive epistemic frame, and constructing an epistemic attitude, where we suspend, for instance, the otherwise-relied-on norms of referentiality or identity, and/or loosen our usual commitment

to relevance. At the same time, we also actively participate, eg we simulate affects in relation to a certain image, carrying them over to the other side of the metaphor, and/or we construct mental imagery by exploring our knowledge of a certain image, and/or we simulate kinesically, as when a metaphor sets up a kinesic tension or kinesic discordance. For instance, in the case of a constitution being said to be a living tree, we simulate affects we have with trees, eg as positive oxygen-contributing, shade-providing, aesthetically-pleasing parts of nature; we simulate mental imagery we have of trees, eg we construct mental imagery of trees with leaves, or their roots, or the shadows they cast; and we simulate kinesically, eg we imagine them growing, or we imagine sitting under them and protecting ourselves from the sun or the rain. In so participating, and then carrying over to the other side of the metaphor, ie here, a constitution, we generate possibilities for how to approach constitutional interpretation, eg more adaptive and thus progressive, or perhaps root-based and thus more conservative.[3]

3. *Figures*: in constructing, or in working with, an imaginary character like the Officious Bystander, we enter a distinctive epistemic frame, where we construct a specific epistemic attitude, suspending, for instance, our usual reliance on treating proper names as referring to real individuals, or our usual commitment to thinking of persons as more than just functions of one or two characteristics. At the same time, we also participate actively, eg we simulate an imaginary perspective, drawing on our affective, sensory and kinesic knowledge to simulate the actions and interactions of such an imaginary character with the relevant persons in the case, as the test calls for.
4. *Scenarios*: when we process scenarios, we enter a distinctive epistemic frame, where, depending on the character of the scenario, we suspend certain epistemic norms, eg the probability of something occurring, as when the hypothetical facts are hyperbolic or exaggerated, or referentiality, as when the scenario includes characters who we either know not to exist or know not whether they do exist. At the same time, we participate actively, eg by simulating our emotional reactions to what is done or what occurs in the scenario, as when sympathising with one or another character or being indignant at another, and we construct mental imagery or simulate certain movements, gestures or postures kinesically.

Each of the four examples to be explored in the second part of this book are artefacts and are constructed by, and invite, processes of imagination. Of course, there is only so much that can be said about them in the above summary way, but I hope that even these short observations give a sense of their artefactuality and how they differently involve processes of imagination.

It can be further observed here that although I present the four case studies as examples of the general framework, ie the three models and their relations between them,

[3] As we shall see in ch 6, the matter, with respect to this metaphor, is more complicated. The metaphor, as originally introduced, was by no means straightforwardly equating constitutions with living trees, but it has, since then, gone on to be used as if it did.

I am also mindful that no general framework can ever contain any one specific case study. Not only is the work of fictions, metaphors, figures and scenarios too rich for any one framework to explain; but so is the work of any one particular example we call a fiction, metaphor, figure or scenario: particularity always leaks beyond theoretical models; it can never be wholly tamed.

D. The Contingency of Artefactuality

At this point, I must recall an important qualification to the general conclusion that the above four cases studies are all examples of artefacts and their related processes of imagination. It must be remembered that there is nothing inherently artefactual about these or any forms of language. This is because, as mentioned throughout this book, there is a dynamic relationship between artefacts and imagination. One cannot just look at a certain form of language and claim that it is artefactual. This is because any form of language is only ever relatively, and at best conventionally likely to function as, artefactual. We cannot completely divorce the form and experience of language from each other. Another way to put this is that nothing guarantees a form of language that it will be artefactual: its artefactuality depends, in part, on whether it can capture our attention, call upon us to do something with it, and, in the terminology of imagination, invite us to enter a distinctive epistemic frame where we participate in certain ways.

All of the above artefacts, then, can lose their artefactuality. This is perhaps most obvious with metaphors. Indeed, a good example is the very language we use to signal the time-bound character of metaphorical language: we refer to dead and alive metaphors. But this language of death and life as applied to metaphors no longer really signals its own artifice, and it no longer really calls upon us to do anything. It thus no longer invites processes of imagination. In reading the phrase 'this is a dead metaphor', we are no longer stopped in our tracks; the language has lost its capacity to surprise us and to prompt us into imagining.

Is it only particular examples of metaphors that can lose their artefactuality, or can the entire form, eg metaphorical language as such, lose its character as being artefactual? That is a difficult question: when I say that artefactuality is relative, I refer mainly to specific examples, ie to specific uses of language, such as referring to metaphors as dead or alive, and not to general forms, such as metaphorical language. Nevertheless, I would be inclined to answer 'yes' to the bigger question too: the artefactuality of any form is contingent, and dependent on the mental habits and capacities of persons in particular communities at particular times and places. Perhaps some forms of language are more artefactually robust than others, but none have their artefactuality guaranteed. Language and, equally, cognition, are simply too socially- and culturally-situated for it to be otherwise.

This contingency and relativity of artefactuality already points to the next section: where language loses its artefactuality, and no longer invites imagination, it does not contribute to inquiry. It then ceases to be valuable, at least in terms of this book, ie it ceases to enable inquiry in adjudication. Let us now examine this argument more closely.

II. Enabling Inquiry I: Individual

Artefacts and related processes of imagination can enable inquiry; when they do, they are valuable. The devil here is in the detail, as part two of this book will go on to demonstrate, but there are still some observations we can make in general terms. To do so, it will be convenient to organise the basic case for the value of artefacts and related processes of imagination by reference to three levels: the level of the individual judge; and the two social levels: the level of interaction, especially in the courtroom, and the level of the community. In this section, I focus on the individual level; in the next on the social. It is, of course, somewhat misleading to separate them; indeed, as we shall soon see, discussion of the individual level will inevitably encroach upon the two social levels.

With respect to each level, I will also be paying attention to the multiple diachronicities at play, ie how the judge needs to decide the case but is also involved in signalling to future readers, or how interaction on some issue can, through artefacts, be deferred to a later point, or what resources artefactual language generates for a community over time. Further, in each case, I will seek to connect artefacts and related processes of imagination to the other two dimensions of inquiry: its experimental dimension, and its normative dimension, ie the sense in which the object of inquiry is the making of insights into what values, vulnerabilities and interests might be at stake in the case at hand and in cases potentially like it in the future. And, I shall wherever possible, seek to relate the general discussion to the four case studies examined in the second part.

Although throughout this book I emphasise the social dimensions of adjudication, as well as that of inquiry, language, emotion, and imagination, there is no doubt that artefacts and related processes of imagination are also important at the level of the individual. By 'individual', I have in mind especially judges, though one could no doubt also make a similar, though of course also different, case for advocates or other individuals involved in the adjudicatory process.

A. The Difficulties of Judging

A good place to begin here is to recall what was said in Chapter 1 about the difficulties of judging. Judging is difficult for many reasons. One is that judges themselves are epistemically limited, as we all are: they do not have the foresight of an omniscient being, and they have their own personal mix of their own background and experience, which is both a resource for them as well as a possible cause of bias. Further, judging is difficult because judges are also institutionally constrained: judges have only so much time to hear arguments in a case, being to some extent dependent here on the quality of counsel submissions, and only so much time to reflect on it, with only so many resources available to them, eg clerks, libraries, etc. Finally, judging is difficult because of the heavy duty to do justice, and this in many different ways: judges must decide the case, and offer a plausible and attractive justification for it; but also, and in doing so, they must be respectful of the law's past and they must care for its future, including the future of its related institutions, especially the authority and workability of the court.

In the first chapter, I offered inquiry as a model that tries to both capture the difficulties of judging, ie foregrounding them rather than ignoring or side-lining them, while at the same time trying to give a sense of how those difficulties are confronted and coped with. Because of the difficulties of judging, judges often employ a more experimental attitude and more experimental epistemic practices, eg being less assertive, and embracing uncertainty rather than pretending it is not there, for instance by confessing to the difficulty of a case or by signalling some rule, principle or area of the law that needs revision. Further, judges also often call for immediate assistance, both from other judges if on a multi-bench case, as is common in the appellate jurisdiction, and from advocates in the instant case; and they often call for deferred assistance, as when they communicate to future readers, including future judges, advocates, but also a much broader range of persons, including scholars and citizens. To do all this is precisely to engage in activities of inquiry. Inquiry, one might say, is the default mode of judging under conditions of both considerable epistemic and institutional limitation and equally considerable uncertainty.

All this might make inquiry sound like an apology, as if it is the best we can do under difficult circumstances. But it is not a note of apology I want to sound here: inquiry is not something we could replace if only we could improve, eg our institutional conditions, or the character of legal resources. It is important to see inquiry more positively: as the way in which creatures like us, not only with epistemic limitations, but also as affectively-embodied and social creatures, engage interactively and collectively, in the never-complete and always-difficult task of making normative insights. Inquiry is not something to be embarrassed about. Rather, in order to make normative insights, ie in order to sense what values, vulnerabilities and interests might be at stake in a case and in others potentially like it in the future, we need to engage in inquiry, precisely that experimental and social process, which occurs both in the real time of a case as well as being stretched out over time.

The argument of this book is that artefacts and related processes of imagination can enable inquiry. Put another way, at the level of the individual judge, constructing artefacts with one's imagination and being invited by artefacts to imagine can enable an individual to engage in inquiry. Artefacts and related processes of imagination are well suited to this task. In the context of artefacts, one reason for that is that artefacts help capture attention: they are ways of generating the valuable and scarce resource of cognitive attention on a particular issue. Further, in calling upon us to do something with them, artefacts also stimulate and animate us, ie artefacts thus not only help us to attend to some particular issue, but they also help us to maintain our focus and mental energy, precisely by involving us in some task, eg as above, de-fictionalising a legal fiction, or smoothing out the discordance of a metaphor.

There are further benefits for the individual in the context of related processes of imagination: to begin with, in imagining, when we enter a distinctive epistemic frame, we buy ourselves space and time for reflection and deliberation. Having our attention captured through the signalling of artifice, and being called upon to do something active, we engage in the process of actively constructing an epistemic attitude. In this frame, we are still epistemically interested, but without the burden of all of our epistemic norms and commitments. This is not a case of 'letting it all hang out', suspending all disbelief, indulging in fantasy, and being epistemically irresponsible; quite the contrary: it is a specific way of being epistemically responsible, a distinct, and rich, way of reasoning, reflecting or deliberating about some issue.

Furthermore, and perhaps most importantly of all, when we imagine, we connect, by participating along a spectrum of affective, sensory and kinesic involvement, to our character as affectively-embodied and social beings. The process of making normative insight is dependent on embodied and affective experience: we cannot make normative insight, and thus sense what values, vulnerabilities and interests might be at stake, without engaging our emotions and our bodies. Imagining helps us do precisely that: to engage our emotions and bodies, doing so in the relatively safe space of a distinctive epistemic frame.

In addition, and I will be returning to this in more detail in the next section of this chapter, we must remember that we, as individuals, are social beings: more than we often realise, we interact with others and are engaged in joint activities with them. Thus, it is also of value to us, as individuals, that artefacts and related processes of imagination enable and enhance our sociality: artefacts are joint resources, and processes of imagination are typically interactive and communal, and they thereby connect to our irreducible sociality as individuals. Without artefacts and related processes of imagination it would be much more difficult for us, as individuals, to engage in inquiry with others.

When an individual judge is confronted, as she must always be, with the difficulties of judging, she will find herself needing to 1) create time and space for inquiry, and 2) have resources with which to inquire, these being resources that allow her to make normative insights, and thus connect to her as an affective and embodied creature. Similarly, such a judge will need ways to 1) invite others to inquire with her about a common issue, ie to attend to it, and to maintain focus and energy on it; and 2) to invite not only those immediate others in the instant case, but a wide range of persons, including those that may inquire in the future, when they have more resources than the judge has at this point in time. The argument being made in this book is that artefacts and related processes of imagination help the individual judge precisely with these tasks. To repeat, they help an individual judge to create space and time for inquiry. They help the judge to construct, as it were, a relatively safe, but still epistemically interested and responsible, shelter for thought and experience, both for her individually, and for her as a social being.

Putting matters this way might sound to some as if artefacts and related processes of imagination were just modes of discovery. This, however, would be a mistake: inquiry, as argued in the first chapter, overlaps with but does not reduce to either discovery or justification. Artefacts and related processes of imagination are not just valuable as processes of discovery. They also contribute to the justification of those decisions. At the same time, however, artefacts and related processes of imagination are also not reducible to the context of justification, and this is because they are also modes of communication: they are ways of signalling attitudes, eg about the need for legal change, to future audiences and users of the law, as well as ways of generating resources for those future audiences and users to change, if they so decide, the law. How do artefacts and related processes of imagination do all that? How do they, in other words, overlap with but also go beyond the contexts of discovery and justification? How do artefacts and related processes of imagination enable judges to decide, justify their decisions, but also, to bring in the future-oriented dimension of inquiry, signal attitudes and generate resources for future audiences?

B. The Four Case Studies

At this point, it will help to bring back into view the four case studies to be examined in the second part of this book:

1. *Fictions*: fictions invite relatively thin processes of imagining, but these are nevertheless active epistemic acts. When we deploy a fiction, we treat something as proven when we know it has not been or we are unsure whether it has. Further, fictions are artefacts: as above, fictions signal their own artifice and call upon us to do something with them. In both these ways, fictions help us to attend to an issue, and to maintain focus and energy on it. They also help us to invite others, both immediate others and especially others in the future, to inquire. Fictions also help us decide a case: in suspending the operative fact of proof of causation, but retaining the normative consequence, the court in *McGhee* (1972) decides to allow Mr McGhee to recover, imposing negligent liability on his employers. Further, the court draws on the same rule to justify their decision: precisely by treating causation as if it had been proven, the court justifies its decision by the requirements of negligence, including the requirement to prove causation. Mr McGhee can recover because he has proved all the elements of negligence, including, fictionally, causation. Of course, if we only focus on the work of a legal fiction at the level of justification offered by a judge, then we might well criticise it: for is it not really disapplying one of the requirements of the rule? In a sense it is, although it is still drawing on the language of the rule. But to think of fictions in this narrow way is to miss their value, which goes precisely beyond both discovery and justification. Fictions are temporary suspensions of operative facts: they are communicative devices, signalling attitudes to future audiences and users. In employing a fiction, a judge decides the instant case, justifies her decision, and at the same time signals to future audiences and users that the rule in question needs attending to in the future; indeed, that the rule may need to be changed. The court in the case of *McGhee* (1972) suggests that perhaps (note the experimental tone) the material contribution interpretation of the proof of causation needs to be changed, eg in the context of the disease of dermatitis, or diseases like it, thereby also raising the question: which are or might be like it? Further, in the context of that case, the court also provides some resources for those future audiences and users, including judges, advocates and scholars, because it suggests that the language of material increase in risk, rather than material contribution, might be the better language to use (again, in circumstances of dermatitis, or injuries that are or might be like it). The artefact of the fiction, through its signalling of artifice, eg its use of 'as if' language, invites future readers to imagine: to continue to suppose, thus continuing the fiction, or to find ways of de-fictionalising, eg introducing a new rule or a new exception. What are the values, vulnerabilities and interests that this artefact, and its related processes of imagination, helps judges detect? To answer this properly, we would need to delve

into the details of the *McGhee* (1972) case, which I will do in Chapter 5. For the moment, we can say that the fiction here is helping judges identify the vulnerability of employees to the actions of (one or more) employers, where the injuries in question (one of the issues is just what is the relevant category of injuries) occur over longer periods of time and where the science still struggles to identify how exactly those injuries come about.

2. *Metaphors*: as artefacts, signalling as they do their artifice and calling on us to do things with them, eg explore and potentially resolve their sensory or kinesic discordance, metaphors help us attend to certain issues, and to maintain focus and energy on them. When we process a metaphor, we enter a distinctive epistemic state, and thus metaphors help us create time and space for inquiry. Further, as more extensive exercises of imagination, involving a higher degree of involvement (than fictions, for instance) affectively, sensorially and kinesically, metaphors connect to us as affective and embodied beings. Metaphors are also very well suited to inviting others, eg to explore a metaphor together in an instance case, or to extend the process of inquiry over time, at least as long as a metaphor remains alive. In all this, metaphors can help us make insights into what values, vulnerabilities and interests might be at stake in a case and in others potentially like it, eg in the case of the metaphor of the constitution as a living tree, we can experimentally probe the sense in which it might be appropriate to interpret a constitution, especially in light of changing social norms and conditions, or we might tentatively explore the level of constitutional autonomy that a colony has to its imperial centre, for instance, whether, or to what extent, it is bound by the empire's constitutional precedents. A metaphor can certainly feature in the justification for an instant decision. In the *Edwards* (1930) case, where the living tree metaphor was deployed, the metaphor features in the Privy Council's justification of its interpretation of a provision of the *British North America Act*, and one which excluded the relevance of the English constitutional precedents relating to whether 'persons' was or was not inclusive of women. As originally deployed, its most immediate use was to help legitimise the authority of the Privy Council as an imperial court. But the value of the metaphor was not confined to that decision alone: some time later it was picked up as a signal of the need for further inquiry as to methods of constitutional interpretation. Further, metaphors, as with this metaphor, do not just signal the need for further inquiry, but also generate resources: in this case, for example, affective, sensory and kinesic associations with living trees, including variable and sometimes contradictory associations, eg one can associate living trees more with sturdy roots or more with leaves in changing seasons. Indeed, although quite worn, the metaphor continues to work as an artefact, still inviting audiences and users to imagine. In this respect, metaphors play a part enabling inquiry: they contribute to both discovery and justification, but they also go beyond that, signalling attitudes and generating resources across time.
3. *Figures*: like metaphors, figures also invite relatively extensive exercises of imagination, with a high degree of involvement along the affective, sensory and kinesic spectrum. In that respect, they too connect to individuals as affective and embodied beings: they typically involve persons constructing mental imagery, from a perspective, and kinesically simulating movements, gestures and postures of

imaginary persons. They also typically involve persons simulating the emotions of not only the imaginary character in question, but also the either real or imaginary characters it interacts with. When a judge employs the Officious Bystander test in contract law, the judge constructs an imaginary figure with limited characteristics, ie a) officiousness and b) being a bystander, and constructs actions and interactions in a scene that involves the Officious Bystander observing and asking questions to the parties at the time of their negotiating the contract. The Officious Bystander test is also clearly an artefact: it signals its own artifice, eg by capitalisation of O and B, and bringing to mind a person with no referent in the real world, and calls upon us to do something active, ie precisely to construct such an imaginary figure and its actions and interactions. In this respect, it captures our attention, and allows us to maintain focus and energy on the issue in question, ie whether or not to imply such-and-such a term into this particular contract. What values, vulnerabilities and interests does the employment of the Officious Bystander test allow us to sense? Again, the devil here is in the detail, but generally, one could argue that, depending on the particular case, the Officious Bystander test allows us to probe, experimentally, how far the freedom of contract can be pursued, and when it must be curtailed in the name, for instance, of not allowing the exploitation of vulnerability. One could argue, more controversially, that the Officious Bystander test is a way of tentatively exploring whether, and to what extent, the duty of good faith ought to be incorporated into English contract law. The Officious Bystander test allows a judge to make a decision in a particular case, on the basis of whether to imply a term or not, and to justify that decision, precisely by asserting that a term ought to implied or not. But, although it is part of the justification of a case, the value of the Officious Bystander device goes considerably beyond any instant case: it signals the need for further work, eg on the tensions between freedom and equality in contract law, and it generates resources, doing so typically via the characteristics attributed to the imaginary person: officiousness and being a bystander, with subsequent judges and advocates exploring, for instance, what 'officiousness' entails. The use of the Officious Bystander withholds articulation of abstract principle, eg the introduction of a principle of good faith, while nevertheless allowing judges to explore a range of related values, vulnerabilities and interests in particular circumstances. Figures also lend themselves to being imagined interactively and collectively, in real time, as when advocates exchange different versions of what the Officious Bystander asks and/or how the parties answer, and over time, eg by collecting examples of how the Officious Bystander has acted and interacted in past cases, we can begin to see patterns we might not otherwise see. Figures, then, are powerful means of enabling inquiry, perhaps especially so because they connect so strongly with the perspectival aspects of imagining, which greatly heightens affective, sensory and kinesic involvement.

4. *Scenarios*: finally, as with metaphors and figures, scenarios are also high on the spectrum of affective, sensory and kinesic involvement of imagination. They are also artefacts, sometimes signalling their own artifice with explicit language, eg 'what if so-and-so', and sometimes implicitly, eg through the use of imaginary characters or hyperbolic hypothetical facts. In that sense, like the other examples above, they help capture and hold attention. Like them, too, they enable individuals

to connect to their character as affectively-embodied beings: processing a scenario, a judge is likely to simulate her affective reaction to the actions and events in the scenario, perhaps sympathising with one of the characters in the scenario or perhaps feeling indignant at another character. This is very much an active process, not only because of the affective, sensory and kinesic participation, ie simulating emotion, constructing mental imagery from a variety of perspectives, and simulating movements, postures and gestures, but also because scenarios lend themselves to being played with, including played with together. Typically, scenarios, precisely because they are pithy, short, under-specified narratives, call upon us not only to fill gaps, but also to revise them, eg construct variations of them or construct counter-scenarios to them. In all this, scenarios help individuals to make insight into the values, vulnerabilities and interests that may be at stake in a case and others like it. Indeed, scenarios are an especially good means of looking into the future, rehearsing possible circumstances so as to consider the implications and consequences of deciding and justifying one way or another. When, for instance, a judge, in dealing with a case involving potential limits on the choice of an innocent party to accept or reject a repudiation in contract law, as in the case of *White & Carter v McGregor*,[4] explored in detail in Chapter 8, processes a scenario that asks her to simulate her affective reactions to an expert going abroad and writing a report against the wishes of the original offeror, then that judge is experimentally probing the circumstances in which the law can legitimately curtail freedom of contract and require the party faced with the repudiation to accept it and to sue for damages. Might, for instance, the value of economic efficacy be at stake, or some other values for the parties, eg damage to reputation in the continuance of a contract, or the legitimacy of the law or the authority of the court in forcing a party into an unwanted contract or in intervening between the private affairs of persons? Constructing a scenario and inviting others to imagine, who then also construct variations on the scenario, or offer counter-scenarios to it, enables inquiry: it assists in the difficult process of making normative insights. Some scenarios feature as part of the decision and its justification in a case, eg by conveying some unwanted implications or consequences of one side's proposed ruling, they are a way of preferring the other side's ruling. Other scenarios, in turn, are articulated in obiter dicta, only tangentially relevant to the justification, but generating resources for future courts when confronted with what they take to be a similar issue.

Fictions, metaphors, figures and scenarios: all of them are valuable at the level of the individual, connecting to us as affectively-embodied creatures, and being valuable for the making of decisions, justifications of them, signalling attitudes and generating resources, both in the real time of a case and with respect to the future, though all in different ways, and with varying degrees of involvement in imagination. Faced with the difficulties of judging, and keeping in mind the limitations they operate within, including both epistemic and institutional, individual judges have a need for experimental means of creating space and time for thought, and especially for making normative insights. These experimental means must be such that they allow for more tentative exploration,

[4] *White & Carter v McGregor* (1962) SC (HL) 1.

and they must connect to the affective and embodied character of individuals. Without the relative epistemic safety of experiment, and without access to affects and the body, normative insights could not be made, or at least be much harder to make. The argument here is that, at the level of the individual, artefacts and imagination enable precisely that making, doing so by allowing us and giving us resources with which to experiment and connecting to our affects and our bodies.

C. Virtue Theory

There are a number of ways of further spelling out the value of artefacts and imagination for individuals in adjudication. I shall not develop them in detail here, but it may be helpful to list them briefly, including indicating where future work may be especially promising. In what follows, then, I take a glance at virtue theory, pragmatist epistemology, and work on the value of imagination in the history and philosophy of science.

One very promising way to argue for the value of artefacts and imagination is to draw on virtue theory. If one thinks of virtues as acquired character traits, and one further extends virtue theory to the domain of epistemology, one then opens up the prospect of epistemic virtues, ie virtues that are beneficial for epistemic inquiry. Of course, there is considerable disagreement in the literature on just what ought to count as a virtue, eg some theorists think of mental faculties as virtues. If one is sympathetic to the idea of imagination as a faculty, one might indeed be tempted to draw on the theories supporting 'faculty virtues'.[5] Throughout this book, however, I have not taken that view, preferring instead to speak of imagination as a specific kind of epistemic activity. This does not mean that one must then, in order to make a link with virtue theory, try to translate imagination itself into a virtue, eg imaginativeness. The danger I see in doing that is that it will push one's account of imagination into the realm of a rarefied exercise of genius, dependent on some account of what it means to be creative. I have resisted that too, preferring to see imagination as an ordinary, everyday process, which we exercise often, and often without creativity, though also one that takes on specific qualities in particular contexts.

There remains one further option, however, for connecting to virtue theory. And that is to think of epistemic virtues as character traits, and to consider the links between artefacts and imagination on the one hand, and the development and flourishing of certain character traits on the other hand. Some of the character traits that scholars have defended as beneficial for inquiry have included: open-mindedness, intellectual courage, intellectual caution, intellectual humility, intellectual generosity, epistemic temperance, intellectual perseverance, inquisitiveness and curiosity.[6] Some of these virtues, as well as others, have also been applied to the adjudicatory context.[7]

[5] See, eg, Greco (2010); and Goldman (1992).

[6] The literature is large: see, eg, Zagzebski (1996); Baehr (2011); Roberts and Wood (2007); and the essays collected in DePaul and Zagzebski (2003). For a recent overview with references, see Turri, Alfano and Greco (2017).

[7] See, eg, the essays collected in Amaya and Ho (2012); and in Amaya and Del Mar (2020).

Further, in some accounts of these virtues, perhaps most obviously open-mindedness, inquisitiveness and curiosity, appeals are made to the value of imagination. For instance, Jason Baehr, in his account of open-mindedness,[8] speaks of the importance of detaching oneself from one's commitments, considering alternatives to one's view, and imagining or conceiving ways of thinking where no data is available. This connects very closely to the way I have modelled imagination, and also to how I have sought to relate it, at the individual level, to the practice of inquiry. I have emphasised, for example, that imagination involves entering a distinct epistemic frame, where we selectively suspend certain epistemic norms or commitments, while retaining others. Entering a distinctive epistemic frame can also include bracketing some of our personal knowledge or value orientations. Where, for instance, we imagine figurally, and thereby participate affectively, sensorially and kinesically from an imaginary perspective, then we are indeed detaching ourselves from some of our personal knowledge and value orientations. For example, if we are imagining well, we imagine not what we ourselves would have asked the negotiating parties, but what an Officious Bystander in the circumstances would have asked. One might, then, be able to link this process to the development and flourishing of the character trait of open-mindedness, thereby benefiting inquiry.

Even, however, where imagination is not appealed to directly, we may nevertheless want to claim that artefacts and imagination contribute to the development and flourishing of a whole variety of epistemic virtues. Constructing and processing a metaphor, for instance, takes time: we attend to a piece of language that signals its own artifice to us, and we do something with it, eg entering a distinctive epistemic frame in which we suspend, say, the epistemic norms of reference or coherence, we explore and seek to resolve the kinesic discordance set up by a metaphorical relation. Insofar as this is a process that takes time, as well as effort, it can contribute, for example, to the epistemic virtues of caution and perseverance. Where, as with all of the case studies, but perhaps especially with metaphors, figures and scenarios, to construct and process artefacts is very much a social process, then this may well contribute to the epistemic virtues of intellectual humility and intellectual generosity. Imagining a metaphor together, and seeing how differently others do so, or being witness to the many different ways that others construct imaginary perspectives, or observing the manifold variations others can invent for scenarios, we come to 1) attend to the limits and finitude of our own cognitive dispositions or affective associations, and 2) appreciate the benefits of inviting and including the views of others. Further, constructing fictions, metaphors, figures and scenarios is often motivated precisely by an individual, faced with the difficulties of judging and thus under conditions of uncertainty, calling on others to assist the task of inquiry by participating in an interactive or collective effort of imagination, not only in the real time of a case, but also over time. This could, in itself, be seen to be an exercise of intellectual humility and generosity: mindful of one's own limitations, aware that we are unlikely to be able to articulate a well worked-out theory or grand principle, we postpone and defer, inviting others into a dialogue with us, as well as beyond us.

[8] Baehr (2011), ch 8. In his taxonomy of 'inquiry-relevant challenges and corresponding groups of intellectual virtues', Baehr groups 'open-mindedness' together with other virtues contributing to 'mental flexibility', including 'imaginativeness', 'creativity', intellectual flexibility', 'agility', and 'adaptability': (2011), 21.

One of the ways, then, in which we can see that artefactual language and related processes of imagination, have a vital role to play in enabling inquiry, is by noticing how they help develop and nourish a whole range of epistemic virtues. I have here barely brushed the surface of possible links, eg in his taxonomy of 'inquiry-relevant challenges', Jason Baehr lists the following as important challenges: 'initial motivation', 'sufficient and proper focusing', 'consistency in evaluation', 'intellectual "wholeness" or integrity', and 'endurance'.[9] I have referred, in this section, but also throughout the book, to the ways in which artefacts and imagination contribute to, perhaps especially, 'initial motivation', and 'sufficient and proper focusing'. Artefacts capture our attention by signaling artifice, and they call on us to participate, ie do things with them: in so doing, arguably, they not only get inquiry going, but also help maintain it.

D. Pragmatist Epistemology

In addition to virtue theory, one could also draw, as I have already a number of times in this book, on pragmatist epistemology. A number of pragmatist-oriented epistemologists have made explicit reference to the value of what I would call artefacts and related processes of imagination in epistemic inquiry.

A stand-out example is Catherine Elgin. In her chapter on 'Shifting Focus' in her *Considered Judgement*,[10] Elgin engages in an extended defence of 'devices that can enhance understanding even when they do not augment our stock of literal truths'.[11] Elgin arguably casts the net more widely than I do in this book, eg her 'devices' include, with particular reference to the practice of science, 'approximations, idealisations, simplifying assumptions, and other falsifications that contribute to our understanding of phenomena',[12] and, although one would need to look at specific case in detail, it is likely that not all of these would count, in my language, as artefacts, eg not all would signal their own artifice, and they would still operate within the ordinary epistemic frame of inquiry in which no epistemic norms or commitments are suspended.

But Elgin has also plenty of examples of other devices that resonate with the case studies I explore, eg she refers to thought experiments as 'vehicles for exploration and discovery, providing contexts in which features may be demarcated, their interplay examined, their implications drawn out'.[13] Emphasising, as I have done in the chapter on inquiry, the experimental dimension, and thus the importance of taking more tentative attitudes, and engaging in more exploratory epistemic tasks, Elgin defends the capacity of such devices, eg thought experiments, to 'transform our understanding'.[14]

Some of Elgin's examples also point to some of the features, and their functions, that I have pointed to with respect to artefacts: eg artefacts can exaggerate or be highly under-specified, and in so doing, not only do they signal artifice but they also invite us

[9] Ibid.
[10] Elgin (1996).
[11] Ibid, 170.
[12] Ibid.
[13] Ibid, 181.
[14] Ibid.

to do things with them. Elgin's point is that we should see this signalling and experience of artifice as an epistemic process, ie a process of transforming and enhancing understanding. Thus, for instance, 'When we realise the moral absolutes exemplified in cowboy films do not extend beyond the fictive realm, we learn something about the moral ambiguities and complexities of human life and about the simplifying assumptions of the genre'.[15] Cowboy films are exaggerated, in their own generic way, such that their imaginary characters strike us as caricatures, but it is precisely this artificiality and simplification that contributes to their epistemic value for inquiry. As Elgin points out, where such devices do not directly contribute to the growth of factual knowledge, they 'display relevance, sensitivity, fecundity',[16] which can be highly valuable to epistemic inquiry. Some fictions, for instance, can provide attention: 'the fiction of gas', for example, says Elgin, 'provides focus'.[17]

Importantly, Elgin's examples also point to the affective dimension of inquiry. Her suggestion, in this respect, is that some 'fictional devices', as she calls them, can help un-block the emotions that frustrate understanding, while releasing others that assist understanding. For example, Elgin claims that 'By transposing events into an alien medium or milieu, fictions can distance us, disengaging emotions that block understanding', and, equally, she observes that 'fictions sometimes activate emotions that advance understanding'.[18] Where we are 'caught up', for instance, 'in the fervor of a political movement or moment', a fiction like *The Crucible* can help us 'discover the dangers of enthusiasm'.[19] Other fictions, eg ones that make us laugh, for instance *Don Quixote*, can also have an effect of creating emotional distance between us and some of our ideas, and this too can be beneficial for inquiry. But fictions, to stick with Elgin's terminology, as noted above, can also trigger emotions directly helpful for inquiry, eg epistemic emotions, like surprise, doubt, trust, puzzlement, confusion, and wonder. Consider, for instance, the confusion and puzzlement caused by some metaphors, eg as a result of setting up kinesic discordance or kinesic disorientation.

Part of the value of such artefacts, as I would call them, is not only their connection to epistemic virtues, but also precisely their capacity for engaging our emotions, some of which may connect more or less directly to the practice of inquiry. We might say that experiencing bewilderment, if not frustration, when confronted with some beguiling metaphor, is a way of creating epistemic energy: it triggers the kind of sensation of imbalance that we need in order to get our techniques of balancing, or of smoothing out and resolving, to work, and sometimes to work hard. Some metaphors may hurtle us into a perspective that is entirely unfamiliar, and that raises questions we had not previously asked. Speaking, for instance, of the metaphor of 'philosophy as a boot camp', Elgin observes that this metaphor 'effects a realignment'; as soon as we are invited to think of philosophers as 'warriors', for example, we begin to ask different sorts of questions about what might be 'the virtues and values' that 'we think philosophers need'.[20]

[15] Ibid, 182.
[16] Ibid, 183.
[17] Ibid, 184.
[18] Ibid, 186.
[19] Ibid.
[20] Ibid, 200.

This kind of 'realignment' can be vital for inquiry: we are jolted out of our habits, we can no longer associate automatically and effortlessly. We confront a metaphor, we experience disorientation and re-alignment, and we generate new questions, thereby advancing understanding. Thought experiments, metaphors and other 'devices', then, 'affect the constitution and adoption of orientations, the construction and application of category schemes, the generation and extinction of saliences, the fixing and blurring of focus'; in doing so, argues Elgin, 'they therefore function cognitively' and 'frequently advance understanding considerably'.[21]

Elgin's account is one of a number of pragmatist-oriented epistemologies, sensitive also to affect and aesthetics, that we could draw on to further enrich our understanding of the connections between artefacts and imagination on the one hand, and the practice of inquiry on the other. In future work, for instance, one could attempt to identify inquiry-blocking instruments, and then try to show how artefacts and imagination can help un-block them. Drawing on CS Peirce, Susan Haack for instance has shown how 'absolute assertions', ie claims 'that this or that conclusion is absolutely certain, absolutely exact, or absolutely universal' can block inquiry.[22] We might see artefacts and imagination as ways of dissolving such 'absolute assertions', often precisely by allowing us to take distance to certain epistemic emotions, eg over-confidence in or over-enthusiasm about some assertion.

E. The History and Philosophy of Science

It is perhaps no accident that pragmatist epistemologists, including those who make explicit reference to artefacts and imagination, like Elgin above, have often focused on the practice of science. Although, as Lorraine Daston has pointed out, the Enlightenment brought with it a 'fear and loathing of the imagination in science', polarising the personae of the artist and scientist, and thus excluding aesthetics from the alleged rigour and objectivity of science, this began to change in the twentieth century, with recent decades of scholarship engaging precisely with the aesthetics of scientific inquiry.[23]

Daston offers some fascinating historical arguments for how this fear and loathing of imagination came about. One is the above-mentioned polarisation of the personae of artists and scientists: the nineteenth century, for instance, saw a 'confrontation of individualistic, brashly subjective art with collective, staunchly objective science',[24] and this had very consequential ramifications for attitudes to imagination, which was placed very much on the individualistic, subjective side. Another related historical argument concerns what Daston calls the 'history of facts'. In the early modern period, facts were understood to be 'historical particulars about an observation or an experiment performed at a specific time and place by named persons'.[25] By the seventeenth century, however, facts came to be associated with 'alleged detachment from inference

[21] Ibid, 204.
[22] Haack (2014), 322.
[23] See Daston (1998). Daston herself is a pioneer in the historical aesthetics of science.
[24] Ibid, 75.
[25] Ibid.

and conjecture', as if they were 'nuggets of pure experience, strictly segregated from any interpretation or hypothesis that might enlist them as evidence'.[26] Facts were no longer something one made or fabricated, as in the original etymology of the term 'fact', which derives from the verb 'to do' or 'to make',[27] but instead became 'a particular truth known by actual observation or authentic testimony as opposed to what is merely inferred, or to a conjecture or fiction'.[28] Changing the meaning of 'facts' in this way, as Daston observes, 'snapped the philological bonds that had tied words like "factitious" and "manufacture"',[29] and coloured negatively 'once-neutral words like "fabricate" (originally to form or construct anything requiring skill) or "fabulist" (teller of legends or fables)', which now 'acquired an evil odor of forgery and deception in addition to their root sense of construction'.[30] As Daston adds, '"Facts" and "artifacts" had become antonyms, in defiance of their common etymology'.[31]

In all of this, imagination did not fare well. As Daston puts it: 'In keeping with the opposition of natural facts to human artifacts, the errors that most terrified Enlightenment savants in theory and practice were the errors of construction, of a world not reflected in sensation but made up by the imagination'.[32] It was thought that scientists had to be protected from the illness or madness of imagination: 'Scientists were as much at risk as poets form diseases of the imagination.'[33] In the Enlightenment, especially, imagination was associated with the 'marvellous', the 'monstrous', the 'fantastic', which led, for instance in the arts, to 'the debauchery of genius.'[34] In this period, the opposition of 'the faculties of reason and imagination' was 'banal and enduring'.[35] Again, the nineteenth century, and the rise of Romanticism in the arts, did not help, for imagination was often related to the 'cult of individual subjectivity', to being 'the wellspring of genial creativity', a kind of 'unbidden, darkling force'.[36] Part of the problem here, in terms of the recognition of the value of imagination in science, was that the 'artistic imagination' was seen as 'freed from all constraints of reason and nature', and therefore as 'wild, ineffable',[37] unpredictable, epistemically un-interested and epistemically irresponsible. Again, the 'wild imagination potentially contaminated the purity of facts, and this is why it came not only to be feared but also loathed'.[38]

The ghosts of these changes and shifts in meaning still remain with us, though, as suggested above, the tide is turning. Partly this is because of the work of historians of science, such as Daston herself.[39] But it is also because of the scholarship of

[26] Ibid.
[27] Ibid.
[28] Ibid, 75–6.
[29] Ibid, 76.
[30] Ibid.
[31] Ibid.
[32] Ibid.
[33] Ibid, 77.
[34] Ibid, 79.
[35] Ibid, 78.
[36] Ibid, 83.
[37] Ibid, 88.
[38] Ibid, 91.
[39] The historical-aesthetic work on mathematics is important here, see, eg, Netz (2009); and Gamwell (2016).

aesthetically and affectively oriented philosophers of science or epistemologists, such as Peter Godfrey-Smith and Elisabeth Camp.[40] These scholars turn precisely to the epistemic value of artefacts, ie to how the making and processing of artefacts plays an important and beneficial role for the practice of inquiry, and not only in science, but, eg in philosophy too.

Godfrey-Smith, for instance, discusses 'models' and 'fictions' in science, whether these be physical (eg wind tunnels), computer simulations, or pictorial or narrative-based thought experiments.[41] Godfrey-Smith speaks of a certain 'style, mode, or element of theoretical science, a style characterised by indirect representation of natural affairs', which he explicitly connects to the 'imagination and hypothesis'.[42] These models or fictions, then, involve 'a deliberate detour',[43] without which the practice of science would find it difficult to make epistemic progress.

Acknowledging the work of scholars on models, or 'intermediate constructions', in science,[44] Elisabeth Camp, in turn, has also argued for 'an essential role for imagination within a paradigm case of rational inquiry', ie the practice of science.[45] For instance, Camp has done some wonderful work on what she calls 'frames', which she says 'guide our overall interpretation of a subject by providing a perspective, or an intuitive principle for noticing, explaining and responding to that subject.'[46] Importantly, Camp does not locate the generation of frames to some rare flashes of genius, but instead sees them as 'ubiquitous in ordinary life', observing them 'in political discourse, in intimate interpersonal agreements, in informal commentaries on movies'[47] and in technical discourses such as philosophy and science.

The concept of a 'frame' here is broad, and is inclusive of a whole range of ways in which we can be encouraged to change frames, at once changing what we notice or take to be salient, including how we affectively or evaluatively load or label certain actions, objects of events. Frame-shifting devices might include jokes, slurs, irony, as well as metaphor. As Camp puts it, 'metaphors often play a theoretically and empirically fruitful role in scientific inquiry because they stand in need of clarification: because they are inchoate, intuitive, and only partly consistent.'[48] As I have suggested for artefacts, metaphors call upon us to do something with them. In Camp's terminology, the 'greater permissiveness' of metaphors 'engages imagination in a richer, more intuitive, and flexible way'.[49] For Camp, all this means that metaphors 'can guide attention and suggest hypotheses in epistemic circumstances where a more precise structural analogy would be stymied'.[50]

[40] See the essays collected in Levy and Godfrey-Smith (Forthcoming).

[41] Godfrey-Smith (2009), 103–4.

[42] Ibid, 103.

[43] Ibid.

[44] Including Godfrey-Smith, but also Ronald Giere and Michael Weisberg. To this list one could add Mary Hesse and Max Black. See, eg, Giere (1999); Weisberg (2013); Hesse (1963); and Black (1962).

[45] Camp (Forthcoming), 1.

[46] Ibid, 2.

[47] Ibid, 4.

[48] Ibid, 24.

[49] Ibid.

[50] Ibid.

Recent scholarship in the philosophy of science, but also in the methodology of philosophy, has also been more sympathetic to the epistemic value of artefacts, eg the value of thought experiments.[51] In a similar vein is the work, led by Amy Kind and Peter Kung, on the relations between imagination and knowledge, which, in direct contrast to the nineteenth century association of imagination with the wild and free, sees imagination instead as a constrained process, often only departing minimally from reality.[52] This work could connect to perhaps the more long-standing recognition of the value of imagination in moral philosophy, inspired, once again, by pragmatist epistemology, and especially John Dewey.[53] I have referred to some of these approaches already in this book. My point in referring to some of them again here is to point to the possibility for further inter-disciplinary collaboration as to the value of artefacts and related processes of imagination, encompassing science, philosophy, morality and law.

F. Dangers and Risks

Given the weight of the history against recognition of the value of imagination, these more positive accounts and defences are surely welcome. Nevertheless, the need for such accounts and defences should not blind us to some of the dangers of artefacts and related processes of imagination. As noted above, artefacts can fail to signal their own artifice, and thus fail to capture our attention and call on us to do something with them. Equally, we can fail to actually imagine, ie no longer actually entering a distinctive epistemic frame, or participating affectively, sensorially or kinesically, but instead, for instance, treating what once were artefacts as but shorthand for more automatic, thoughtless mental operations. With respect to figural imagining, for instance, individuals can imagine in ways that enhance their already-biased views, eg not really inhabiting the imaginary perspective of another, but instead using it as a vehicle for their own views, and worse, hiding that they are theirs. Similarly with scenarios: these can affect judges so much that they do not enter a distinctive epistemic frame: they simply react emotionally to the scenario, and decide accordingly. In these examples, individuals are not really imagining: they are not making the effort to imagine, whether that be constructing the imaginary perspective of another, or constructing variations of or alternatives to a scenario. They are no longer active, but instead passive, and they thus no longer contribute to, but in fact obstruct, the practice of inquiry. These dangers, however, are arguably best illustrated in more detailed engagement with particular examples. I will thus be returning to them in the second part of the book.

Artefacts and imagination are certainly valuable at the level of individuals. We have seen how they can enable inquiry by individuals, doing so in a range of ways. I have also referred briefly to some other literatures, namely virtue theory, pragmatist epistemology, and the history and philosophy of science, to show that there may be further

[51] See, eg, Stuart, Fehige, Brown (2017); and Stuart (2019). Recently, the Junkyard Blog, established by Amy Kind, has facilitated cross-disciplinary conversations on the value of thought experiments in different contexts of inquiry, see, eg, Miscevic (2019).

[52] Kind and Kung (2016).

[53] See, eg, Johnson (2018); Fesmire (2013); and Nanay (2016).

resources there for articulating the links between artefacts and imagination on the one hand, and inquiry on the other hand. All this is important, but it is also very limited by remaining tethered to the level of the individual. I turn now to another dimension of the value of artefacts and imagination: namely, how they enable inquiry socially, including both interactively and collectively.

III. Enabling Inquiry II: Social

Despite attempting to focus, in the section above, on the level of the individual, I have often strayed into the interactive and collective levels. This is both appropriate and inevitable: it can be misleading to separate out these levels: individuals are social beings, and inquiry, as I have modelled it here, is deeply social. It is social in two respects: first, it is interactive, and here I have primarily in mind interaction between persons directly involved in a particular case, especially the judges and the advocates; and second, it is collective, involving, especially when we combine this with a longer diachronic perspective, a much wider range of persons, including not only judges and advocates, but also scholars and citizens. Chapter 1 of this book offered more details on both of these aspects.

With respect to interaction, in that first chapter, I discussed the view of Anthony Laden in his social picture of reasoning, who offers a way of de-individualising our understanding of reasoning and understanding it instead as akin to a casual conversation in which dialogical responsiveness to the views of others matters more than the monological imposition of a decisive will, and I offered an example[54] of the interactive dynamics between judges and advocates in courtrooms (in that case, by reference to scenarios). This suggested that we approach language differently: not as the instrument of an individual, trying to persuade others to think alike, but instead as the resource of a casual conversation, and thus as something enabling skilful, intersubjective and dialogical engagement.

The role of language, then, in the interactive aspect of the social dimension of inquiry is to make such dialogue possible and allow it to flourish. This means we must ask: what forms of language enable interactive inquiry in this way? For instance, what forms of language allow for the play of multiple voices, not shutting down difference and disagreement, but instead enabling the exchange of views, hopefully in ways that are not so confrontational as to be obstacles to dialogue? Recalling the importance of the experimental and normative dimensions of inquiry, we can add: what forms of language enable interactive exploration of values, vulnerabilities and interests that might matter in a case and in other cases potentially like it in the future? Of course, language is only one side of the picture, and so should also ask: what are the mental processes and activities that enable and contribute to interactive inquiry? For instance, daydreaming is something we tend to do alone, and it does not lend itself to being done interactively. Are there other kinds of mental processes and activities that do lend themselves to be done interactively? I will return to these questions in a moment.

[54] From *California v Carney* 471 U.S. 386 (1985). Subsequent references are to *California v Carney* (1985).

The first chapter also referred to the collective aspect of inquiry. Here, by reference to work on the 'socially extended mind', 'socially extended knowledge' and 'distributed cognition', I noted the importance, to inquiry, of shared or common forms or technologies that facilitate collective tasks, including jointly attending to a problem, as well as collectively amassing resources with which to tackle it. Language also mattered on this view, and was conceived as a 'communication technology', making possible certain cognitive operations on multi-mind, across-time scales. For collective inquiry to be possible, and for multiple parties to be able to be involved over time, there is a need for forms of language that are both memorable and resourceful, which can last over time but still remain pliable and revisable. There is, in other words, a need for language that sticks, so to speak, and thus survives long stretches of time, but that simultaneously serves as a mechanism for change and transformation. In that chapter, I mentioned commonplaces, and related linguistic forms, such as maxims and proverbs, as well as the narratological structure of precedent as examples of such language, but are there others? Again, what forms of language enable collective inquiry, especially over time? What kinds of mental processes and activities do such forms of language make possible, such that they enable and enhance the quality of collective inquiry? I will be returning to these questions, too, in a moment.

It will not surprise the reader to learn that, in broad brushstrokes, the answer to both sets of questions, ie as to what forms of language and what mental processes and activities enable and enhance the quality of interactive and collective inquiry, is that this is precisely what artefacts and related processes of imagination do. What both interactive and collective inquiry need is artefactual language, and the processes of imagination that both construct artefacts and are invited by them. It is by no means the only thing that interactive and collective inquiry need. Much more is needed, eg a certain institutional infrastructure; certain other technologies and resources, eg knowledge-storing and knowledge-collecting technologies, devices and strategies; an education system, and more. But artefacts and related processes of imagination are one important ingredient.

A. The Four Case Studies

Serving as this chapter does as a bridge between the first and the second parts, let me, before confronting the above questions head on, consider the four case studies, and show how, in general terms, they contribute to interactive and collective inquiry:

1. *Fictions*: fictions are a good example of an artefact the value of which is almost entirely invisible without reference to the interactive and collective aspects of inquiry. Although fictions are valuable to an individual judge, enabling her to make a decision and justify it, the real value of fictions emerges when it is seen as a communication device, ie as something that signals the need for further attention and reflection on some particular rule by future readers. Fictions can be understood to be modes of delay or deferral: they buy time for others to amass further resources, eg further cases, that can then be considered with a view to seeing whether the time has come to de-fictionalise, and introduce either a change

to the rule, a new rule, or an exception to the rule. Fictions enable and enhance both interactive and collective inquiry, for they preserve the possibility for variety and disagreement. Indeed, fictions are quintessential dialogical invitations to others, and not monological impositions of will. Fictions leave it up to others to decide whether to maintain the fiction or to de-fictionalise, and also how to de-fictionalise. Some fictions may introduce some resources, eg as we shall see in Chapter 5, the fiction in *McGhee* (1972) does suggest that, within the proof of causation requirement, the language of material increase in risk may, in these kinds of cases (which kind is one thing that remains to be determined by future readers), be more appropriate, ie protect the relevant values, vulnerabilities and interests better, than material contribution. Nevertheless, generally, fictions either generate few resources or thin ones: again, in that sense they leave a great deal up to others to decide. In doing so, they do not enable interactive dynamics quite as well as do the three remaining case studies. Fictions are, as it were, almost too dialogically generous, leaving so much for others to do that there is little interaction with the original author of the fiction. Nevertheless, they contribute to enabling interactive and collective inquiry, for they do not shut down interactive or collective effort: instead, they invite it and they require it. Fictions, one might say, create time and space for others to contribute to the inquiry: in the case of *McGhee* (1972), this was an inquiry into what interpretation of the causation requirement is most appropriate within a certain range of injuries. It is only with the passage of time, in and beyond the *Fairchild* case,[55] and with the contributions within this period from a wide range of persons, including judges, advocates, scholars and citizens, that an arguably better answer than could have been provided in *McGhee* (1972) becomes possible.

2. *Metaphors*: like fictions, but in a more extensive way, for they also involve more intense participation in the second limb of imagining, metaphors lend themselves to interactive and collective inquiry. One way in which metaphors have been understood is that they are instruments or means of persuasion: ways of monologically imposing one's will on another. This recipient or addressee of the metaphor is seen as being duped into a particular view, so overcome and blinded by the power of metaphor that they cannot but help to agree with the view of the author of the metaphor. I do not deny that this is possible: metaphors can have powerful effects, and sometimes persons do use them in this highly strategic and forceful manner. If that was all there is to metaphor, then it clearly would not contribute to interactive and collective inquiry. However, there are at least some uses of metaphor, and some receptions of it, that are not like this. Recalling and foregrounding the difficulties of judging, metaphors are at least sometimes, if not often, used by judges under conditions of uncertainty, and as a way of groping towards the interpretation or articulation of a principle, or to some other form of legal change. Further, and most importantly, they are not just the means by which individuals experiment: they are also invitations to others to do so. When a metaphor enters a conversation, it functions to signal a relatively safe epistemic space, though still one that is epistemically

[55] *Fairchild v Glenhaven Funeral Services Ltd* (2003) 1 AC 32.

interested and responsible, in which others can participate. Indeed, metaphorical language is such that it leaves open differences with how the tension it creates, eg the semantic discord or kinesic disorientation it sets up, can be explored and possibly resolved. When a judge says, for example, that a constitution is a living tree,[56] this leaves open more possibilities than a statement that, for instance, a constitution is to be interpreted liberally or in keeping with changes in social norms. This is the case both within the courtroom, where the injection of a metaphor can lead to interaction between advocates and judges who play interactively with the metaphor, or do so collectively and over time. In the case of collective inquiry, a wider range of persons can participate in the joint exploration of the metaphor, as has indeed been the case, and very intensively so, with respect to the living tree metaphor. Further, the living tree metaphor is both memorable and resourceful: its popularity in the literature, and its broader cultural resonance, is testament to its memorability, and the many different and often contrasting ways in which it has been understood show that it is clearly resourceful, ie that it is very much pliable and revisable. Further, the way the metaphor has gone on to be explored is not explicable by reference to the intention with which it was first used. The metaphor was certainly useful to the individual judge (Lord Sankey), but its value is not confined to its use by an individual judge in an instant case. One must consider the career of a metaphor over time: how it lends itself to being played with by multiple voices in more or less extended bursts of dialogical and joint imagination.

3. *Figures*: when an individual judge employs a figure, eg the Officious Bystander test in the law of implied terms in contract, they are deciding, and justifying their decision, in an instant case, but they are also, as with fictions and metaphors, postponing the task of articulating a non-figural, and more abstract principle. In that sense, to employ a figure is an invitational act, enjoining others to participate collectively in working on this particular problem, namely in what circumstances courts ought to intervene in the freedom to contract, and for what reasons. In this respect, the Officious Bystander lends itself to collective inquiry over time: should the principle of good faith be incorporated into English law? If so, how should it be understood? What is its scope, how far does it reach? The Officious Bystander test allows for a joint exploration of this issue casuistically, amassing case examples, working out particular answers to particular questions, while keeping one eye on the overall shape of the case law. Something similar may be said for other figures, eg the right-thinking member of society test in defamation law, or of course the famous and growing family of reasonable persons in a whole range of areas of the law. They are means of withholding statements of grand principle, postponing the articulation of a general theory, and instead involving a whole range of persons solving problems in particular instances, but still grouping them together, all being precisely applications of the figural test in question. Further, the Officious Bystander, and other figures, are arguably more understandable, more accessible, to non-legally trained persons: in that respect, they also invite

[56] As the *Edwards* (1930) case has often been interpreted to have said. As we shall see, in ch 6, the picture is more complicated.

the participation of citizens in the adjudicatory process, and call upon broader cultural resources, eg as to what being officious or being a bystander might entail. The use of figures, though, is not only valuable to collective inquiry over time. It also invites interaction: in the course of a particular case, advocates will exchange different, and typically contrasting, versions of the Officious Bystander. The test is precisely flexible enough to enable the submission of contrasting exercises in imagination, with the two sides constructing different accounts of what the Officious Bystander asks and how the parties in the negotiations respond. As we shall see in Chapter 7, the Officious Bystander test has been applied in a bewildering array of ways, and some of those ways may be at odds with its value as enabling inquiry. The point, for now, is that it precisely allows for this multiplicity, and it does so by inviting persons to imagine. And persons do precisely that: both imagining interactively in the courtroom, ie exchanging contrasting accounts of the narrative, and imagining collectively over time in a wide range of venues, including both later courtrooms, law school classrooms, and scholarly publications.

4. *Scenarios*: scenarios are in many ways paradigmatic examples of interactive and collective inquiry. In the courtroom, they are often introduced by advocates, who sometimes use them as an especially persuasive mode of *reductio ad absurdum*, showing how their rival advocate's proposed ruling leads to absurd implications or consequences. In this, they sometimes succeed, with judges being swayed uncritically by certain powerful, sometimes because they are humorous or otherwise memorable, scenarios. But scenarios are not only instruments of destruction or persuasion. Sometimes, judges confronted by a scenario offered by an advocate go on to play with it: as indicated by the example from *California v Carney* (1985) quoted in Chapter 1, judges will sometimes, if not often, introduce variations or propose counter-scenarios, probing and testing the advocates before them. In this respect, scenarios very much lend themselves to interactive inquiry in the courtroom, as, indeed, they also often do in the law school classroom. The interactive play with scenarios is by no means epistemically disinterested or irresponsible. On the contrary, the interactive exchange that scenarios enable and enhance allow those involved in them to experiment, and to make normative insight, eg to consider the scope of a particular principle, or whether a certain constitutional interpretation may have unintended consequences on certain other constitutional principles or other areas of the law, or, more broadly, for instance on the authority of the court. The value of scenarios, however, is by no means limited to interactive inquiry in a courtroom. Scenarios are often articulated by judges in judgements in the form of obiter: not strictly speaking necessary to the instant justification, they are offered by judges as resources for future readers, signalling that some rule or principle may require further attention. As we shall see in Chapter 8, some of the scenarios that begin their life in this way, ie in the margins of obiter, come to eventually take centre stage, and lead to changes in the law. They do so over time, and after a string of cases in which persons are collectively engaged in imagining together: all processing the scenario, simulating their affective reactions to it, and considering what import this has for the values, vulnerabilities and interests that might be at stake in cases of that kind. Scenarios contribute to interactive and collective inquiry precisely because they are artefacts, ie by capturing attention,

calling upon others to do things with them, and thereby engaging imaginations of persons.

The four case studies explored in the second part of this book, then, are precisely the forms of language and related processes of imagination that lend themselves to enabling and enhancing the quality of interactive and collective inquiry. How can we further articulate these links, ie between artefacts and imagination on the one hand, and interactive and collective inquiry, on the other hand? By reference to what literatures? Let me turn to each, respectively, and offer some suggestions. Again, I shall be doing so only briefly, in some cases referring back to literature already discussed, and in other cases proposing some ways forward for future work. I shall look first at interactive inquiry, and then second at collective inquiry.

B. Interactive Inquiry

There are a number of literatures that we could look to in order to get a better understanding of what makes for good interaction for the purposes of inquiry, and what could enable and enhance the quality of that interaction. The theory and history of the genre of dialogue, might be one;[57] another would be the work on the second-person, and this in developmental psychology, neuroscience, and philosophy (including ethics, as in the work of Martin Buber and Emmanuel Levinas);[58] yet a third could be to look at what has been called in recent decades 'interaction science'.[59] In all of these, there is an interest in what makes for good interaction.

Despite the many different contexts in which interaction occurs, there are arguably some common points: that good interaction is not the monological imposition of one will on another, but that it involves responsiveness to otherness; that it is often marked by a mixture of imitation and asymmetry, the important point being that good interaction cannot be wholly synchronised, but must instead leave room for difference, disagreement and the relatively autonomous exercise of the will by all persons involved; and that good interaction needs tools: some that enable the relatively smooth running of the interaction, eg common rules, scripts, and habits, and some that leave room for misunderstanding, imbalance, discordance, tension, suspense and unpredictability. These points are important, for without them, interaction dissolves either into the first-person exercise of the will, eg using language as a means of persuading others, or third-person collective or joint action, where there is no or little room for difference, disagreement and asymmetry between persons involved.

If we put this view of interaction into the context of inquiry, we can come to appreciate why interaction is valuable for inquiry. Put another way, if we understand interaction in this way, we can come to see why it is an important dimension of inquiry,

[57] See the references to dialogue in the experimental dimension of inquiry in ch 1. See also Markova (2017).

[58] See Buber (1958) [1923]; Levinas (1991); and see the essays on the second person collected in Eilan (2016).

[59] See the references given in ch 1.

and why it is not reducible to the role played by individuals or collective dynamics. Without the space for interaction, ie without its mix of predictability and unpredictability, and the space it creates for difference and disagreement, as well as its oscillation between stability and imbalance, inquiry would be all the poorer: it would lose a lot of the dynamics needed to explore and experiment, risking dogmatism, lack of critical reflexivity, and a loss of the ability to generate alternatives and possibilities.

In the context of common law adjudication, interaction is encouraged by the adversarial structure: set up like a debate or a contest, with two sides pitched against each other, and both with opportunities to respond to, and potentially rebut, each other. Further, interaction in the courtroom occurs not only as between the advocates, but also between the judges on a multi-panel bench and between the judges and the advocates. Indeed, the interactive dynamics are often very complex: the advocates, for example, may not address each other directly, interacting instead via their submissions to the judges; and the judges, in a multi-panel bench, also interact indirectly, eg addressing the advocates with questions or remarks that shed, either critical or positive, light on their fellow judges' remarks or questioning. Interaction in the courtroom, then, given how it is set up institutionally, needs tools that allow that interaction to occur, and ideally also enhance it, eg avoiding making it either too predictable or too unpredictable, or too smooth or too discordant.

The most obvious and important tool developed for this purpose is language, together with the mental processes and activities that it facilitates and encourages. Within the third literature mentioned above, ie interactive science, there has been extensive attention paid to 'language as a tool for interacting minds'.[60] Language is not the only relevant tool, and some fascinating work has been done, though a great deal remains to be done, especially in the legal context, on visual tools, eg calendars, diagrams, or other elements of design,[61] but language is an especially important tool.

The approach that interactive science takes to language is to resist the hitherto dominant focus on how language augments individual cognition, and instead to consider how it augments interaction. For instance, interactive scientists have looked at: 1) how 'language extends the "interaction space" in space and time, liberating interaction from the immediate context, and stretching it over distance and time; 2) how language enables 'joint attentional scenes (past, present, or fictional)'; 3) how 'language enables interacting people to align and share higher-order situation models and action plans'; and 4) how 'language guides our attunement at a cultural level to certain aspects of visual, auditory and spatial perception'.[62]

The point here is, once again, not merely to show how language allows us to act jointly or do things together, but how it also allows for interaction. For example, certain forms and expressions of language, including the manners in which it is used, allow specifically for interaction: eg the very form of a question calls for and invites an

[60] Tylen et al (2010).

[61] See, eg, Bender and Marrinan (2010); and Stjernfelt (2007). There are fascinating links to explore further here between, on the one hand, enabling interactive inquiry in legal contexts and, on the other hand, visual, material and book history.

[62] Tylen et al (2010), 4–5.

answer, and the practice of not finishing sentences also invites another to complete it. As Kristian Tylen et al put it:

> … turn taking patterns and rhythms, along with a number of language internal and external semiotic resources such as prosody, intonation, stress patterns, gesture, facial expressions, gaze direction and bodily posture … all … contribute to the unfolding meaning of the discourse.[63]

Some of these dynamics are so prevalent, so familiar, to us that we do not notice them. Arguably, we only notice them when they are absent, eg when one person dominates, never letting others speak.

The reader will have noticed the overlaps here with what I have called in this book artefacts: these are precisely forms of language that call upon us to do things with them, eg by being incomplete, or by requiring some other mental process or activity from us. Artefacts, one might say, are built for turn-taking: someone proposes an artefact, and another is, or multiple others are, invited to do something with it. Someone formulates a question, inviting another to answer it. Someone leaves a sentence incomplete, ending say in an ellipsis, and this invites someone to complete it. Importantly, what persons are invited to do is not, or at least need not be, pre-determined: invitees of artefacts can be enabled to carry on in their own way. I have already given examples above: fictions, metaphors, figures and scenarios. They all, in different ways, enable and enhance the quality of interaction. Artefactual language, then, works in part because it works interactively: it calls upon others to get involved, and to offer their own extrapolations, explorations, versions and variations, eg of metaphors, or of scenarios, or of the actions of a figure. Artefacts lend themselves precisely to this form of interactive exchange, and in so doing, they contribute to inquiry, which, again, needs precisely these kinds of interactive dynamics.

None of this is to romanticise the practice of inquiry in the context of adjudication. It may, at one level, seem strange to speak of turn-taking, responsiveness to otherness, leaving space for multiple voices, and so on, in the cut-and-thrust of the courtroom. But the points made above about interactive dynamics are broad enough to encompass both competition and co-operation: the image here is not that of a dialogue in which everyone helps each other out. Indeed, the point is that artefacts allow for both difference and disagreement, for variation and for contestation, although one could argue that they do so in less confrontational ways, eg to swap rival extrapolations of a metaphor or rival enactments of a figural test is arguably less confrontational than to make directly contradictory assertive statements to each other. When we exchange our interpretations of a metaphor we are somehow co-operating: after all, we are both focusing on the same metaphor, and we are both engaged in the same kind of mental process or activity, and we are doing that together in the relatively safe space of a distinctive epistemic frame. Nevertheless, at the same time, metaphor makes possible and encourages us to exercise that imagination differently, sometimes starkly differently. Metaphor, and other artefacts, we might say, spark and maintain interaction: they enable joint attention, but they also leave it under-determined.

Further, the interactive processing of artefacts is sometimes accompanied by surprise and humour, eg by way of a strange twist offered on a scenario, and may be experienced

[63] Tylen et al (2010), 5. See also Goodwin (2000).

as pleasurable, even under conditions of great tension and competition as in adjudication. To introduce an artefact is often to jolt the conversation, ie to unbalancing it, creating perhaps some friction or at least the danger of misunderstanding, but at the same time enlivening it, infusing it with possibility.

C. Collective Inquiry

Artefacts and related processes of imagination are of value to inquiry in its interactive aspect. They also contribute to enabling and enhancing the quality of collective inquiry. Here, as above, we ask related but distinct questions: what forms of language are such as to survive over time, and thus be memorable, while at the same time being pliable and revisable? What forms of language keep collective inquiry alive? Which forms lend themselves to involving the participation of a wide range of people? Which forms do so over longer periods of time? Again, my answer here is that artefactual language is precisely a source of such forms. Artefacts foster collective inquiry over time because they involve a wide range of people imagining together. What literatures might we look to in order to develop that connection further? What literatures can help us consider what forms of language, related to which kinds of mental processes and activities, are valuable for communities over time?

i. Collective Epistemic Virtues

One candidate literature is the emerging discussion of collective epistemic virtues, ie attempts to relate virtue theory to social epistemology. There is plenty of disagreement within this literature on how to connect collectivity to virtue, eg whether to think of social groups as themselves somehow acquiring and possessing virtues in ways that are not reducible to the sum of all the individual virtues, or whether to think of how certain collective arrangements, eg institutions, with their rules, habits, and rituals, enable the fostering and flourishing of virtues that could not be pursued either by individuals on their own or by individuals acting independently. As Miranda Fricker, one of the key voices in this debate, has pointed out, we do colloquially often refer to a jury as being 'fair-minded', or a research team as being 'tenacious', or an appointments committee as being 'scrupulous', and so on.[64] Is this just loose talk which ought not to be taken too seriously,[65] or is there more to it: again, might there be either collective virtues or collective arrangements that enable particular kinds of virtues? And how might such virtues be related to epistemic activity?[66] Recalling some of the virtues mentioned at the individual level in the preceding section: can we, and how can we, speak of, say, open-minded, humble, courageous, generous or inquisitive collectives, eg courts, or communities of legally-trained persons, or the broader polity with respect to say criminal matters?

[64] Fricker (2010), 235.
[65] See, eg, Cordell (2017).
[66] See also Lahroodi (2007); and Brady and Fricker (2016).

The first step, which might seem small but is still an important one, is to acknowledge that community matters for the production of knowledge and the process of investigating it. As Lorraine Code has put it, 'as human beings, we are cognitively interdependent'.[67] To find our way towards collective epistemic virtues, we must first acknowledge the irreducible and vital role of epistemic communities, and in doing so resist a long-standing philosophical tradition 'that construes the knowledge-seeking enterprise as essentially solipsistic, urging that only what has been discovered by the enquirer's independent efforts is worthy of being called knowledge'.[68] Code herself says that any 'viable epistemology' must 'take adequate and realistic account of the extent to which cognitive activity is a communal process', eg as members of an epistemic community, we learn 'who is to be trusted', with whom and how we can co-operate and collaborate:

> The success of the entire cognitive enterprise is dependent upon something like an honourable and cooperative, if tacit, agreement between information purveyors and knowledge seekers, where participants in the agreements sometimes are in the role of giving, sometimes of seeking. On both sides, epistemic responsibility is of the essence.[69]

This 'epistemic responsibility', which Code appears to organise around certain specific kinds of epistemic roles, is not a romantic view of an idyllic community which never has disagreements; quite the contrary, it requires the acceptance by members of the community 'of the need constantly to scrutinise the method [eg of science] itself, as well as the procedures within it', including 'loosening the demands of its orthodoxy'.[70] In other words, once we begin to see that, even as individuals, we play different roles in an overall epistemic community, relying on each other in various ways, including being dependent on others to criticise us, to help us out of pictures that may grip us, and blind us to alternatives and possibilities, then we get closer to seeing and capturing the importance of collective epistemic dynamics, and, at once, collective epistemic virtues. On Code's approach, it matters whether an epistemic community is organised in such a way as to enable persons within it both to collaborate together, each performing a different task within a joint epistemic project, as well as to step back or the side, and to scrutinise and potentially criticise others and their claims and methods.

Notice that to argue in this way is not necessarily to posit any collective agency or group mind. It is not directly to say that, for instance, a court is open-minded. But it is to pay attention to dynamics that are only possible to instantiate collectively, eg at a certain scale, over a certain period of time, and with the participation of a wide range of people, who inhabit, for instance, different roles and responsibilities. This might involve paying attention, as Fricker does, to the institutional rules, norms and or procedures that allow groups to develop such that, even if the individuals in question are not, for example, fair-minded, the group as a whole is. One can imagine, for instance, how requiring a unanimous decision, and thus not allowing for dissent, might produce a collective dynamic in a jury that is fair-minded, and this in a way that would not be so if each

[67] Code (1984), 45.
[68] Ibid.
[69] Ibid, 48.
[70] Ibid, 49.

person, individually, had to form their own individual view. One can also imagine what difference it would make if the deliberations of the jury were not secret, eg they were recorded and would be capable of being scrutinised by lawyers later. The point here is not to endorse any one particular rule, norm or procedure, but simply to say that these devices and designs of collective dynamics matter enormously for the emergence of epistemic virtues, or vices, at a collective level. Some of these rules, norms or procedures may be such as to be almost invisible to the persons participating in the collective: they might come to be aware of them, were they to reflect on them, but awareness or knowledge of them does not feature as part of their collective dynamics. Others, by contrast, might be very much reflexive: their value might be such that they require all the members of the epistemic community to keep them in mind, eg jury members might need to keep in mind, and be reminded to keep in mind, the requirement of proof beyond reasonable doubt.

Could we draw on this literature on collective epistemic virtues to further develop the connections between artefacts and imagination and the activities of inquiry? Surely we could, although not much attention, within this literature, appears to have been paid to the qualities of language that an epistemic community might need. For instance, in order for an epistemic community to enable and enhance the flourishing of collective open-mindedness and inquisitiveness, which would be of value to collective inquiry, such an epistemic community might need an appropriate language. This would need to be a language that would allow the community as a whole to detach itself from its commitments and consider alternatives to its views (to recall Baehr's interpretation of open-mindedness). A language like this would need to have the capacity to surprise, to pull members of the community out of their ordinary run of communication with each other, and to enable them to pause and hesitate together. This would need to be a language that makes the use of it less automatic, less ready to hand, and thus something in itself strange or requiring attention and care.

Arguably, artefactual language does precisely that: when an epistemic community includes within its collective resources, eg written judgements available on accessible databases, language that is, say, metaphorical, or language that involves the construction of imaginary figures or hyperbolic hypothetical scenarios, then this is a language that maintains the capacity to surprise, allowing members to detach themselves from otherwise automatic uses of language, and to generate alternatives and possibilities, eg through different extrapolations of a metaphor, or through different enactments of an imaginary figure, or different affective reactions to a hypothetical scenario. The point is that artefactual language may create conditions for the emergence of particular kinds of collective dynamics, ie ones in which we imagine together, collectively, over a period of time. Further, artefactual language, and perhaps especially metaphors, figures and scenarios, which connect so readily to us as affectively-embodied creatures, is highly accessible to a wide range of participants, including not only lawyers, but also scholars and citizens.[71] In that respect, too, artefactual language, and its related processes of imagination, can contribute to the democratic quality of an epistemic community.

[71] On the participation of the citizenry in adjudication, see also Levenbook (2000). For Levenbook, this participation is enabled via certain characteristics of common law precedent, namely its exemplarity. See also Petroski (2018).

ii. Cognitive Humanities

In addition to work on collective epistemic virtues, we might also draw on other literatures, eg scholarship in the tradition of the cognitive humanities or in the rhetorical tradition, eg work on collective or social imaginaries.

Drawing on the first of those strands, we could ask: what makes certain communities more open to experiment? What was it, for instance, about the practice of Ancient Greek mathematics that made it such a robustly experimental epistemic community? According to Reviel Netz, part of the story is how accepting and responsive the community was to the practice of hypothesis. Reviel emphasises the many ways in which practitioners of Ancient Greek mathematics were invited to look beyond, eg 'looking at a point and imagining it as a balance; looking at the blank space defined by five points and imagining there is a pentagon'.[72] In the case of Ancient Greek mathematics, this collective work of hypothesis was enabled by specific kinds of diagrams, which called precisely for such hypothetical engagement.[73] And no doubt there were also other kinds of enabling conditions, eg in the fourth to fifth centuries BCE, the political conditions were such that experiment, including 'political experiment' was very much in the air.[74] Nevertheless, the point remains: there were certain kinds of technologies, in this case, visual technologies, that prompted and encouraged experimentation, eg by requiring extended hypothetical reasoning. One can point to other examples: for instance, the extensive reliance on the genre of allegory or pre-figural interpretation in Christian communities. Indeed, allegory might be seen to be precisely a form of language that fosters and facilitates certain kinds of communal epistemic dynamics.[75]

Hypothesis, or allegory, in turn, might be related more generally to what opportunities for abstraction, and especially changes in abstraction, including shifts of perspective, communities allow, eg through their visual or linguistic technologies. Ellen Spolsky, whose work we have already encountered before in this book, has pointed to the relations between a community's responsiveness to poetry, eg lyric poetry, and its epistemic capacities. As Spolsky notes, drawing on Culler,[76] lyric is 'often hyperbolic, thus turning the poem from a reflection or report into the performance of a revelation', and this element of performativity can have the effect of 'removing its audiences from their routines of ordinary communicative discourse to a place where new ideas and new connections can emerge'.[77] More generally, Spolsky argues that poetry 'both depends on our ability to perform the gradiant, bidirectional, fictional, and generative work of abstraction, from words to images and from specific images to more and newer ideas, and also strengthens that ability through practice.'[78] Where, then, a community

[72] Retz (2009), 28.
[73] See Netz (1999).
[74] Netz (2009), 49; see also Lloyd (1979).
[75] See, eg, Fletcher (1964).
[76] Culler (2015).
[77] Spolsky (2015), 36.
[78] Ibid, 46.

allows for the flourishing of poetry, or poetic language in general, then it can enhance its capacities for abstraction. We might ask: what is it about poetry that can have this effect? Spolsky's answer resonates with the account I have offered of artefacts:

> Language forms not found in everyday speech advertise themselves as a different kind of object, and ask readers to grant them distance and refrain from speedy response … [they] allow audiences to detach it from the demands, including, importantly, the time demands of ordinary communication.[79]

This kind of language, then, can 'spark revisionary thinking in communities in need of it'.[80] Precisely by inviting imagination, artefacts of language can 'contribute to the sustainability of communities by encouraging adaptation to change'.[81] On the one hand, they can foster joint attention, including over time, but they can also, at the same time, call for many different members of the epistemic community to participate in the re-making of them, eg as with metaphor, working jointly on it, elaborating it in different ways, by reference to different kinds of affective, sensory or kinesic associations. Again, this language need not be language with a big 'P', as in grand Poetry. Instead, we can point to the poetics of ordinary language, with its stops and starts, its unfinished sentences, its allusions and witticisms, its rhythms and repetitions, its sometimes discordant juxtapositions, its detours and roundabouts: all this, arguably, contributes to keeping a language, and at once an epistemic community, alive.

It is important to note that the relevant technology need not be language. Spolsky, for instance, speaks of the visual genre of the grotesque, and how its 'very foreignness … outlandishness … invited audiences to enjoy the recession of their rational selves in favour of sensory understanding',[82] disengaging them from ordinary routine, causing 'confusion' and disorientation,[83] and engaging imaginations of persons. As Spolsky says further about the visual grotesque: these are forms that encourage 'scepticism', eg being in two minds, and they are also 'subversive'.[84] More broadly, the visual grotesque is an example of 'how disorder incubates the emergence of new understanding':[85]

> Their popularity is evidence that their cognitively destabilising forms feed some hunger in us: they stimulate, encourage, or strengthen our easily overwhelmed abilities to remain open-minded. We need them to keep us alive to the possibilities of reframing settled understandings, of renegotiating social contracts.[86]

Spolsky's framework, with the positive epistemic valence it gives to dislocation, imbalance, disorder, disorientation, and confusion, is certainly one we could surely draw on in connecting artefacts, and related processes of imagining, to the practice of collective inquiry.

[79] Ibid, 53.
[80] Ibid, 198.
[81] Ibid, 24.
[82] Ibid, 199.
[83] Ibid, 201.
[84] Ibid, 204.
[85] Ibid, 210.
[86] Ibid, 205

iii. The Rhetorical Tradition

Finally, we could also draw on the rhetorical tradition. For example, as James Boyd White has shown, we could look at the community-making as well as community-transforming character of certain kinds of language. An interesting resource here might be work on the imaginaries of philosophical language, as highlighted and analysed by feminist scholars, such as Michèle Le Doeuff and Marguerite La Caze.

Some of this work has emphasised more the disciplining of certain kinds of forms of language, including the way they exclude certain voices and experiences. Thus, in her *The Analytical Imaginary*, for example, La Caze examines the epistemic work of certain 'metaphors … analogies, thought experiments, myths, and models', showing how they structure debates, establish certain shared assumptions, and 'also work to persuade and to provide support for a particular view and to exclude alternate views and methods'.[87] This is an important point, and I do not deny that some forms of language that I have identified under artefactual language can function in this way. From my perspective, though, when language functions in this way, it loses its artefactuality, functioning no longer to signal artifice and invite imagination, and instead reinforcing habits and ways of seeing, feeling and understanding.

Further, as noted above, there is a delicate balancing act in any artefact: it must to some extent discipline, for it enables joint attention, which is of course always selective, and can therefore constitute epistemic injustice. But, when an artefact functions as an artefact, it balances this disciplining with opening and generating, ie allowing for alternatives and possibilities to multiply. La Caze is sensitive to this also, pointing out for example that it is a mistake to think that 'images can be entirely removed from philosophy', or that 'language can be purified of ambiguity'.[88] The two points are connected, for, as La Caze notes, the 'openness of images is consonant with the unfinished nature of philosophy'; further, the lack of 'precision' in philosophical language is not a bug, but instead a feature, for it 'is related to its [ie philosophy's] potential for opening up new possibilities'.[89] Indeed, what La Caze calls 'images', or what we might also call artefacts, can be signs, as Le Doeuff has also pointed out, of difficulties or contradictions in a particular philosophical system.[90] These 'images' can thereby also be moments or spaces in which a certain philosophy can be especially generative. As La Caze puts it, although some of the work of 'images', eg as in metaphors, can be disciplining and structural, some of it can also be generative: 'Images', she says, 'can start off debate, open philosophy up to new ideas, and connect a text to previous philosophical work'; they can constitute 'a shift of thought or progress in a debate'.[91] La Caze offers a vital reminder of the danger of certain forms of language, which, in my terminology, lose their artefactuality, and which can beguile us and blind us to certain assumptions. These forms of language are, in some respects, relevance-makers, and thus also irrelevance-makers, excluding certain voices and experiences, Nevertheless, they also, as La Caze observes, have a generative capacity.

[87] La Caze (2002), 1.
[88] Ibid, 7.
[89] Ibid.
[90] See Le Doeuff (1989).
[91] La Caze (2002), 14.

The question, from the perspective of this book, is how a community can enhance the generative capacity of certain forms of language, while keeping a critical eye on its disciplining and structural functions. Part of the answer is artefactuality, which, as I have been emphasising, is only ever a contingent and relative feature of language. The other side of the coin is imagining, ie we must actually make the effort to imagine. To put it another way: an epistemic community that is dominated by a language that is no longer artefactual, or only weakly so, is also a community where its members fail to imagine or do so very rarely. Such a community, I would argue, also weakens itself as an epistemic community, ie it endangers its capacity for collective inquiry. Part of what it means to be a responsible epistemic community is to keep caring for its language, ie to keep reviving it, and keep re-making it by protecting its artefactuality and its capacity to invite the members of that community to imagine. Where this is lost, eg when the taste for irony or allegory or fables and parables is lost, communities become arguably less democratic and more thoughtless, and this, as Hannah Arendt amongst others have shown, is not only epistemically dangerous, but also morally and politically so.[92]

[92] See Arendt (1963).

PART II

Case Studies

5

Fictions

With this chapter, we begin part two of this book. As we shall see, each of the four case studies explored in this second part have at times been offered as foundational to legal thought, ie as the genera of which other devices are mere species. I seek instead to model them much more narrowly, ie as specific sorts of artefacts, with related specific processes of imagination. I acknowledge, however, that these terms have been used much more broadly, and although I cannot do justice to that in what follows, I do attempt to engage with some of the literature on each of these four. Even in the limited way in which I model them, they each deserve much more attention. Again, to be clear: I do not attempt in this part to offer fully-worked out theories of fiction, metaphor, figure and scenario. I also do not aim to survey the enormous literatures on these devices. Instead, my overall aim is to show this book's framework, with its three models, at work in legal practice, and thereby to give some more concrete sense to the value of artefacts and imagination for inquiry in adjudication.

Fiction in adjudication is a notoriously knotty and difficult subject. As I mentioned in the introduction, grappling with these difficulties was where this book began. Part of what makes it difficult is that there is very little consensus in the literature on what to count as a fiction. Indeed, much of the controversy around this topic is disagreement on whether there are fictions at all in law, and if so, whether they are all pervasive or mere antiquated curiosities.

Often, in addition, the claims made as to the existence and extent of legal fictions are made in very different contexts: across systems and traditions of law, and at very different times and places. To give just one sense of this: Peter Birks, in his well-known article on fictions in Ancient Rome and the English common law,[1] argued that whereas there were no fictions, properly speaking, in Ancient Rome, there were fictions in the English common law. In the case of Roman law, there were no fictions because, essentially, they involved no false ontological statements, but were instead openly and explicitly convenient short-hand transfers of normative consequences, eg applying, in certain circumstances, the same consequences to non-citizens as to citizens. By contrast, in England, argued Birks, the devices deployed did involve making false ontological claims, often duplicitously, eg that some X happened when it did not, as in the fictions that there had been a promise when there had not. For Birks, this was so much the worse

[1] Birks (1986).

for English law: in utilising fictions, they obscured and retarded the principled growth of the law.

Of course, this way of characterising fictions already associates them with something dishonest and deceitful, changing the law while pretending no change had been made. And this is, indeed, the other complicating factor: many ways of defining fictions already incorporate negative valences, eg speaking of fictions not only as duplicitous ways of concealing legal change, but also as ways of obfuscating the law (this being said to be in the financial interests of the lawyers), or as irrational and outmoded means of legal development.[2]

Finally, fictions are a topic that sit uneasily between highly abstract, philosophical treatments,[3] and deeply contextual, historical ones. Philosophically, definitions of fictions are often entangled with a philosopher's broader metaphysical and epistemological views, which then make some of the definitions of fictions incommensurable. And, historically, fictions have been studied in a wide range of different contexts, again making them difficult to compare with each other. These contexts have included Ancient Rome,[4] Rabbinic jurisprudence,[5] the medieval and Renaissance periods in both civil law[6] and the common law,[7] and beyond, eg in Chinese law.[8] Further, the topic of fictions cuts across both legal and literary history and theory, and is thus often treated as part of a broader investigation of fictions and fictionality.[9]

In what follows, and partly as a result of fictions being nestled amongst these very different literatures and debates, I do not offer anywhere near a full survey of the range of available definitions and taxonomies, or the many different examples given of fictions,[10] or the many arguments for and against fictions. My focus, instead, is on: 1) articulating my own approach to fictions, set against the backdrop of part one of this book, and thus as an artefact with related processes of imagination; and 2) giving a sense of how fictions can be valuable to inquiry.

I pursue these aims in two sections. In the first section, and by way of introducing as well as situating my own model, I engage with Lon Fuller's famous three articles on legal fictions.[11] These articles were the impetus not only for my reflections on fictions, but also for this book as a whole, and so it is only fitting that I pay them tribute. In the

[2] The attack on fictions as a means of obfuscation in the interests of lawyers was made most powerfully by Jeremy Bentham: see Ogden (1932). The characterisations of fiction as irrational and outmoded means of legal development was made most famously by Sir Henry Maine: see Maine (1861).

[3] See, eg, Kelsen (2015); and Ross (1969). For a recent overview of the philosophical debates, see Chiassoni (2019), chapter on 'Judicial Fictions'.

[4] See Ando (2015); and Thomas (2011), ch 6.

[5] See Moscovitz (2015).

[6] See Olivier (1975); and MacLean (1999).

[7] See Milsom (2003); Baker (2001); and Shmilovits (2019).

[8] See Ruskola (2013).

[9] See, eg, Eden (1986); Barfield (1947); Stern (2017a); Higgins and Leps (1998); Morgan (2004); Kayman (1997); Waithe (2012); Korda (2013); and Temple (2010); and Stone (1985). Sometimes, the term 'legal fiction' is used by literary historians to denote a work of literary fiction that also deals with legal issues, as in, eg 'the legal fictions of Charles Dickens', but this is not the way I use the term here. I refer to the specific device of a fiction deployed by judges in the course of adjudication.

[10] See the examples collected in Del Mar and Twining (2015).

[11] Fuller (1930–31).

second section, I shall illustrate the more abstract claims made in the first section with the specific example of the use of fiction of causation in *McGhee v National Coal Board*,[12] and some cases both before and after that case. Thus, my own discussion will focus, as throughout this book, on contemporary English common law.

The argument, in brief, is that fictions are artefacts because they involve a more or less explicit signalling of artifice in judgements, either through the explicit 'as if' form, or by way of implication given what is known to have been proven or not proven. Further, as artefacts, fictions call upon us to do things with them, eg either to keep supposing or to de-fictionalise them. Fictions invite exercises of imagination because, in processing a fiction, we enter a distinctive epistemic frame where we tolerate contradiction, eg between what we suppose to have been proven and what we know has been or has not been, and we participate, ie precisely supposing, which is a thin way of participating in imagination.

As I model fictions in this book, they are closely related to practices of proof. The positioning of legal fictions at the level of proof is significant, because it no longer requires us to think of fictions as somehow contradictions with reality; they are not contradictions with what we take to be real, but with what we know to have been proven or not proven. This is a decidedly pragmatic, and not a metaphysical, approach to fictions.

The effect of a fiction in adjudication is the temporary suspension of an operative fact, ie a proof requirement, in a rule, while retaining its normative consequences. This can be beneficial for inquiry because it enables the judge to make a decision in a case while not changing the law, and at the same time signal to future readers that the law may need to be changed, eg that an exception may need to be introduced to the new rule, or a new rule may need to be crafted, which changes the proof requirements for the related normative consequences. The idea of fictions not being changes in the law is also significant, and at odds with many views of fictions, eg as hidden or duplicitous modes of legal change.[13]

The account I offer is also at odds with the usual and dominant negative evaluation of fictions in the literature. One exception is Fuller: his is the most prominent overall sympathetic account of fictions in modern times. Hence also the extensive engagement with Fuller's view in this chapter. Nevertheless, although I seek on the whole to defend the value of fictions in adjudication, insofar as they enable inquiry, I do not defend the idea that fictions are always valuable. As with the other case studies explored in this book, I argue that fictions are valuable insofar as they enable inquiry. Where a fiction becomes automatic, ie no longer signalling artifice, and no longer involving exercises of imagination, then it arguably no longer serves to communicate the need for a change in the law, and thus does not any longer contribute to inquiry.

Fictions can be powerful ways of enabling the interactive and communal making of insight, in an instant case and especially over time, into what values, vulnerabilities and interests may be at stake in a case and in cases of a similar kind in the future. But they also need not have that effect, working instead to stultify and obstruct inquiry. Their value, like all the case studies explored in this book, is contingent.

[12] *McGhee v National Coal Board* [1972] 3 All ER 1008.

[13] See, again, Birks (1986), Maine (1861), and many others.

I. Approaching Fictions

This book began when I read, and then re-read, on multiple occasions, Fuller's three articles on fictions.[14] The articles have both inspired and baffled many,[15] and they remain the anchor for any contemporary treatment of legal fictions, at least in the Anglo-American literature. They have also often been read very selectively: the focus has tended to fall on the first two articles, which deal with defining fictions and identifying the motives in their uses. The third article, which engages more closely with the views of Vaihinger, has mostly been characterised as a flamboyant and wild frivolity, and has often been ignored. Indeed, as has been common with treatments of Fuller in general,[16] his work on fictions too has been generally characterised as interesting but un-disciplined.

Although I shall be disagreeing with Fuller on some points, I do not think the above is a fair assessment: all three articles have a great deal to offer any serious student of fictions, eg on fictions as a linguistic phenomenon; on the relationship between fictions, presumptions and estoppel; on fictions and legal change; on fictions and the psychology of judging; and on similarities and differences between fiction in law and fiction in other domains of practice, especially science. Further, Fuller's discussion is wonderfully rich and stimulating, and prepared to admit to uncertainty and engage in speculation. And, it is also a discussion that swims against the tide, offering a number of distinct arguments for the importance of fictions in law.

In what follows, I engage with the three articles, though slightly out of order. I begin with the first article, then turn to the third, before finishing with the second. I do this because both the first and third article deal with issues of definition and identification of fictions, but also more broadly with respect to the deployment of fictions in other disciplines, especially science. The second article concerns motivations for the use of fictions and will thus allow for a discussion of the value of fictions in adjudication.

A. Defining and Identifying Fictions

In general, for Fuller, a fiction is 'either 1) a statement propounded with a complete or partial consciousness of its falsity, or 2) a false statement recognised as having utility'.[17] As the prominent reference to 'statement' makes clear, Fuller associates fiction with a particular use of language. In fact, one could read all three of his essays as an experiment with thinking about legal language through fictions. And yet, the above definition also suggests that fictions are not only a linguistic phenomenon: they involve mental processes too, eg 'complete or partial consciousness of falsity' or 'recognition of utility'. Further, when we add what Fuller covers in his second article, ie the various motives

[14] Fuller (1930–31). The three articles were also published as a book, but all references here are to the articles.

[15] For other engagements, see the essays collected in Del Mar and Twining (2015); Petroski (2018); Soifer (1986); Campbell (1983); and Knauer (2010).

[16] For a critical discussion of this tendency, see Rundle (2012).

[17] Fuller (1930–31), 369. The first article appears at pages 363–399.

behind the use of fictions, some conscious and some less-than-conscious, then we see again that although Fuller emphasises the linguistic character of fictions, he also sees that they cannot be understood without reference to the mental processes that accompany their creation and subsequent life. Indeed, as the above definition also reveals, Fuller is nuanced about mental life, eg his category of 'partial consciousness' is an interesting one, and one I shall return to. Fuller thus recognises that there are relations between fictions as a linguistic phenomenon and as a mental one, and this in complex and rich ways.

i. Fictions and Language

On the linguistic side, Fuller's enthusiasm about fictions comes at times very close to thinking of them as characteristic of almost all of legal language, though again, in nuanced ways. Thus, Fuller asserts that: 'Fictions are, to a certain extent simply the growing pains of the language of the law', and that 'the evolution of our legal language has, for the most part, proceeded' through and thanks to fictions.[18] Here, Fuller sometimes appears to speak of fiction and metaphor in the same breath, eg 'A fiction is frequently a metaphorical way of expressing a truth'.[19] For example:

> In the law we speak of the *merger* of estates, of the *breaking* of contracts, of the *ripening* of obligations … In the action of trover, the defendant is alleged to have *found* a chattel he may really have taken by force. In actions arising under 'the attractive nuisance doctrine' the defendant is alleged to have *invited* children (of whose very existence he may have been ignorant) to visit his premises.[20]

In keeping with this blurring of any distinction between fictions and metaphors, Fuller also speaks of fictions as either 'live or dead'. Thus, Fuller says:

> There are live and dead fictions. A fiction dies when a compensatory change takes place in meaning of the words or phrases involved, which operates to bridge the gap which previously existed between the fiction and reality.[21]

In the above examples, 'merger', 'breaking' and 'ripening' are no longer alive, ie they are 'not felt as metaphors', having 'become naturalised in the language of the law' and 'acquired a special legal significance which comes to the mind of the lawyer when they are used'; by contrast, the language of 'finding' in trover or 'inviting' in attractive nuisance are still alive, ie they are still 'felt as fictions'.[22] The point here is not that 'finding' or 'inviting' are inherently different from 'merging', 'breaking' or 'ripening', but simply that whereas the latter have undergone the process of change in meaning, becoming technical uses of what were once fictions, the latter have not: their 'possible changes in meaning have not occurred. Since they have not, the statements remain fictions'.[23]

[18] Ibid, 379.
[19] Ibid, 370.
[20] Ibid, 371–2; original emphasis.
[21] Ibid, 373.
[22] Ibid, 371–2.
[23] Ibid, 372.

Fuller's first article gives many examples of this process in both Roman law and English common law, eg Fuller speaks of 'delivery', 'conversion' and 'estate' as at one time being 'felt as fictional',[24] but then undergoing a process of 'inevitable compensatory change in word meaning' during which 'the expressions acquired a new, non-fictional meaning.'[25]

Fuller's diachronic approach to fictions is important; we need to pay attention to the life of fictions over time, including both how certain forms of language can come, in the terminology of this book, to cease to signal artifice, as well as how fictions can contribute to legal change. However, Fuller's very broad approach to fictions, identifying them with metaphors and metaphorical change of meaning in legal language is, for my purposes, too broad. I shall be discussing metaphors in the next chapter; for now, it can simply be stated that the important difference between fictions and metaphors in this book is that the former is connected to practices of proof in ways the latter is not. To employ a fiction, on the approach taken here, is to suppose that an operative fact of a rule has been proven, when it is known that it has not been, or it is uncertain whether it has been. Further, the legal change that fictions *may* contribute to is not dependent on shifts in the meaning of words, but instead on shifts in the requirements of proof, eg in the form of an exception to a rule, or with the introduction of a new rule with different proof requirements.

This seems straightforward enough, but it is not. This is because, although some fictions involve explicit signalling of artifice, eg 'let us treat this requirement as having been proven when we know it has not been', some of the signalling of artifice by fictions is more implicit, and relies precisely on a sense that the language we are using jars against our knowledge or judgements about reality. Thus, for instance, when we speak, in the attractive nuisance doctrine, of a defendant 'inviting' children to visit his premises, we signal artifice by the tension between the conventional meaning of 'invitation' and the knowledge, or likelihood, that the defendant was ignorant of the very existence of the children on his premises.

What is significant about this signalling, from the perspective of how I approach fictions, is not so much the strained meaning of 'inviting', but instead the temporary suspension of the requirement to prove that the children were not trespassers, ie that they were on the defendant's land with the landlord's consent. The normative consequence, ie that the defendant owes a duty of care, obtains despite the usual requirement that no duty of care is owed by defendants to those who trespass on their land. It obtains, for now, in the specific case of children. Normally, one has to prove that the landowner invited the relevant persons onto his land. One has to prove this in order to show that they were not trespassers. In the case of children, however, we suppose that they have been invited, even when we either 1) know they have not been, eg because the landowner could prove he was not aware of them, or 2) are unsure whether they were, eg because the evidence is unclear, or because it would be difficult to obtain any such evidence.

On the way I view fictions, when a judge first uses the language of 'inviting' in this context, she is not changing the law, but deciding the case, ie imposing a duty of care

[24] Ibid, 374.
[25] Ibid.

despite the absence of proof that the children were not trespassing, and signalling to future readers that the law here may need to change, ie that in cases, say, involving children, an exception to the rule that the defendant does not owe a duty of care to trespassers may need to be introduced. The strained character of 'inviting' is, on the view I embrace here, a means of signalling artifice, inviting others to imagine; it is not itself a means of changing the law.

There is, then, an important sense in which fictions are a linguistic phenomenon, and an important sense in which, in signalling artifice implicitly, the artefactuality of fictions relies on our experience of the strained character of certain uses of language. However, it is not the strained character of certain uses of language that is key to the role that fictions play in contingently facilitating legal change. The key, instead, is how the use of a fiction communicates to future readers the potential need for new or different proof requirements in a certain class of cases.

Fuller himself makes reference to the distinction between explicit and implicit fictionalising, or, in my terminology, explicit or implicit signalling of artifice. He introduces a distinction between what he calls 'assumptive' and 'assertive' fictions, where the former takes an explicit 'as if' form, and the latter an 'is' form.[26] Thus, for example, the following fiction found in Roman law is an assumptive fiction: 'If, in case Aulus had been a Roman citizen, such a judgement ought to have been rendered, then render such a judgment'.[27] In this example, the language of 'if', and 'had been' makes it clear that one is assuming something known to be false. The assertive version of this fiction would be: 'Aulus is a Roman citizen', which can also be conceived of as a way of straining the meaning of 'citizen'.

The important point for present purposes is that either way, one is supposing something has been proven, namely that Aulus is a citizen, and thus has standing to sue or be sued in a Roman court, whereas one knows that has not been proven, or one is uncertain about whether it has been. The effect of the fiction is to temporarily suspend the requirement to prove citizenship in Aulus's case, while signalling to future courts that others in Aulus's position might also not need to prove they are citizens. In this case, the implicit signalling of artifice in the 'assertive' fiction, 'Aulus is a Roman citizen', comes from the straining, in the circumstances of the case, of the meaning of the term 'citizen'. The signalling of artifice, in this sense, can be circumstantial or situational: it is experienced as artifice within what is known in the context of the case.

ii. Knowledge in a Loose Sense

I have been speaking here of 'what is known' in a loose way, and Fuller too deliberately speaks loosely: sometimes referring to what is known, and at other times to what one is 'conscious' of or what one 'recognises', eg as being false and as having utility. The looseness here is not a vice, but a virtue of the explanation. Fuller approaches this characteristically broadly: he speaks of 'the line between belief and disbelief' being 'frequently blurred', and of how sometimes we are 'aware' of a statement's 'inadequacy or

[26] Ibid, 390.
[27] Ibid.

partial untruth', although we 'may have believed it in the sense that [we] could think of no better way of expressing the idea [we] had in mind'.[28] Fuller is grappling with something important, and it is because of this blurring of the line between belief and disbelief that he says, as per his definition, that 'we have a fiction … when the author of the statement positively disbelieves it, or is partially conscious of its untruth or inadequacy'.[29]

For my purposes, we can draw on Fuller's insight in a particular way. Keeping in mind the link I am drawing between fictions and proof, we can say that we employ a fiction when we suppose something has been proven and, at the same time, we either 1) know it has not been proven, because there is positive evidence to the contrary, eg evidence of Aulus being a 'barbarian', or 2) when we are uncertain about what has been proven or whether any proof could be obtained. Building in uncertainty is important, and when, in the above shorthand, I refer to 'what is known to have been proven', I mean that to be inclusive of uncertainty, ie about what has been proven, or what could have been.

iii. Fictions, Presumptions, Deemings

As important as it is, for Fuller, to allow for degrees of consciousness of falsity, ie to speak of 'complete or partial consciousness', nevertheless some level of consciousness of falsity is, for him, necessary for a fiction. This is important because it allows Fuller to distinguish fictions from lies: after all, as long as there is some consciousness of falsity, there can be no deception. It also allows him to distinguish fictions from other devices that may be placed in the vicinity of fictions, especially presumptions. For Fuller, whether it is conclusive or rebuttable, a presumption 'assumes something which may possibly be true', where as a 'fiction assumes something which is known [at different degrees of belief] to be false'.[30] Some of what Fuller includes as examples of presumptions others may be tempted to call 'deemings'. Thus, Fuller speaks of the 'presumption' of death, where someone is 'unheard of for 7 years'.[31] This, says, Fuller, is not a fiction, even if it is cast as a conclusive, and thus irrebuttable, presumption, for it is 'usually true' or could at least be true. There is, agrees Fuller, something 'formal' and 'arbitrary',[32] about the presumption: why choose, after all, 7, rather than say 6 or 8, or 7.5? But, despite the formality or arbitrariness, or even the sense in which we may speak of some presumptions as 'distortions of reality', the key point is that they are not fictions, for fictions, for Fuller, require some consciousness of falsity, which is missing from presumptions.

If one approaches fictions by relating them not so strongly to 'consciousness of falsity', but to knowledge, loosely speaking, of what has been proven, then the difficulties as to where to draw the line between fictions, presumptions and deemings,[33] are more easily resolved. Presumptions are not temporary suspensions of operative facts: instead, presumptions, like deemings, are simply rules, but ones that are arguably more

[28] Ibid, 368.
[29] Ibid.
[30] Ibid, 393.
[31] Ibid, 398.
[32] Ibid.
[33] See also Fuller's discussion, at ibid, 393–399.

formal and arbitrary. They too are closely connected to proof, but, again, they are not temporary like fictions are, but standing rules of proof, albeit of a distinct kind. They are rules that already build in certain approaches to what has to be proved: for instance, a presumption shifts the burden, from the person relying on the rule to the person defending it, eg if I can show that a person has been unheard of for seven years, I do not need to show that he has died; the person on the other side, contesting my claim, can, if the presumption is rebuttable, defeat my claim if he can show that the person is not dead.

The line between presumptions and deemings can then perhaps be drawn in this way: first, where presumptions can typically be rebuttable, deemings cannot; and second, often presumptions are indeed employed, as Fuller points out, when we think that what is presumed is also likely, eg that someone unheard of for seven years is indeed dead. That example is perhaps not the clearest example of a presumption, for it is so arbitrary that it feels more like a deeming: deemings, one might say, revel more in arbitrariness than presumptions do. Further, deemings are also more likely to be employed by legislatures than by courts;[34] presumptions are, after all, softer, less assertive than deemings, even conclusive and irrebuttable ones. But neither presumptions nor deemings are fictions: again, this is because fictions are temporary in ways that deemings or presumptions are not.[35]

To employ a fiction, as I approach it, and thus to suppose that something has been proven when we know, loosely speaking, that it has not been, is not to create a rule: it is to decide the case by allowing the normative consequences of an existing rule to obtain even though the operative fact(s) of the rule have not all been met, and, at the same time, to communicate to future readers the potential need for a new rule, or a new exception to the rule.

B. Vaihinger and Imagination

We have now effectively worked our way through the first of Fuller's articles. In doing so, I sought to show how Fuller's approach to fictions bears some similarity, but is also different, to the way fictions are approached in this book, perhaps especially by reference to how they are artefacts. The second article, as mentioned above, refers to the motives behind the use of fiction, but because this goes more clearly to the evaluation of fictions, I shall discuss it last. Before turning to it, let me turn to the third of Fuller's essays on fiction, and for many the most enigmatic. It will allow us to say a little more about the

[34] A great deal more could be said about deeming here. Deemings certainly deserve their own theory and history. On the idea that deemings are used more in legislation, consider the following from Lord Radcliffe: 'The word "deemed" is used a great deal in modern legislation. Sometimes it is used to impose for the purposes of a statute an artificial construction of a word or phrase that would not otherwise prevail. Sometimes it is used to put beyond doubt a particular construction that might otherwise be uncertain. Sometimes it is used to give a comprehensive description which includes what is obvious, what is uncertain, and what is, in the ordinary sense, impossible' Lord Radcliffe, *St Aubyn v Attorney-General* [1952] AC 15, 53. This passage is quoted in Lord Walker's (2016) lecture on 'The Wonderland of Statutory Hypotheses'. Lord Walker examines further examples of statutory 'fictions', eg hypothetical tenants.

[35] For more on the distinction between presumptions and fictions, see De Gama (2015).

similarities and differences between Fuller's view and the one taken here, especially with respect to fiction as a process of imagination.

i. *The Activity of the Mind – and the Body*

With the third essay,[36] Fuller expands the scope of his investigations, and magnifies the significance of fictions, considerably. Having written the first two articles, Fuller is adamant that fiction is not simply an optional ornament, and it is also not of 'antiquarian interest merely'.[37] Indeed, he says, with respect to fictions: 'we are in contact with a fundamental trait of human reason.'[38] Accordingly, Fuller insists that 'to understand the function of the legal fiction, we must undertake an examination of the processes of human thought generally',[39] and this he duly does, with Hans Vaihinger as his primary guide.[40]

Together with Vaihinger, Fuller's scope in this article is truly impressive: it encompasses law, economics, mathematics and physics. Fuller's examples, drawing on Vaihinger, include the social contract, *homo economicus*, atmospheric pressure, gravitational pull, and free will. Where in the first article, fictions were a looking-glass through which to understand the growth of legal language, fictions in the third article become the key that will unlock the mysteries of the mind. Following Vaihinger, who in turn was himself inspired by Kant, Fuller implores us to recognise the active nature of the human mind:

> Our minds are not mere passive reflectors of the external world; they are instruments for enabling us to deal with that world. As instruments is it any wonder that they alter reality? The whole human body is an elaborate machine for altering the environment in which we are placed.[41]

There are several ideas in this passage: one is the activity of the mind, a feature that I have also stressed in my characterisation of imagination. Another is the idea that our minds are 'instruments' that enable us to deal with the world by altering reality. 'Altering reality' is a broad concept, certainly, but Fuller has some specific ideas about what this might entail, drawing on Vaihinger's focus on 'contradictions', but going, as we shall see in a moment, considerably beyond.

A third idea, which appears in the above passage, but which unfortunately Fuller does not develop, is the role of 'the whole human body'. Fuller characterises our bodies as 'machines', which would be a metaphor I would resist, but his general point, that our bodies are ways of engaging-by-altering the environment is an important and stimulating one. Also important is that Fuller offers no apologies for this alteration: 'this alteration of reality', he says, 'is not a sign of the weakness of the human intellect, but

[36] Fuller (1930–31), 877. The third article appears on pages 877–910.
[37] Ibid, 878.
[38] Ibid.
[39] Ibid, 879.
[40] See Vaihinger (1968) [1911].
[41] Fuller (1930–31), 885.

rather of its strength'.[42] Alteration, to introduce yet another metaphor (the third article is packed to the brim with metaphors), is 'the sign of good mental digestion; it indicates the vigor and capacity of our minds'.[43] For Fuller, in this third article, it seems that our minds are stomachs, while our bodies are machines. Metaphors aside, Fuller's overall emphasis on activity, on the importance of our bodies, and of the benefits of engaging with reality by altering it, chime well with the approach taken to imagination in this book.

ii. Altering Reality: Two Operations

Fuller has two specific operations in mind for how we engage with reality by altering it: first, processes of simplification and organisation; and second, processes of 'converting new experiences into familiar terms'.[44] With respect to simplification and organisation, he has in mind 'artificial abstractions', like the *homo economicus*.[45] These fictions are useful, but they are also purpose-built: so, for instance, 'The fiction that man is an "economic animal" has great utility when one's problem is to develop laws of economic behaviour; taken as a foundation for ethics it would be disastrous.'[46] Another example of a device that not only simplifies but also organises is that of the distinction between a 'Thing and its Properties';[47] yet another is our 'instinctive tendency to conceive of classifications in geometric terms'.[48] Fuller's sense of simplification and organisation is a rich one, and ranges from simplifying models through to metaphysical concepts and even visual aesthetics. He also makes it clear that these operations of simplification and organisation often happen without persons being aware of them.[49]

I cannot do justice to Fuller's rich speculations as to the operations of simplification and organisation: they provide some fascinating clues as to how one might go about writing a rich history of the dynamics of abstraction, not only in law but across the social and natural sciences. In that respect, they go considerably beyond what I attempt in this book. There is also another difference: insofar as Fuller characterises these operations as less-than-conscious, then they differ markedly from the focus in this book on largely conscious and deliberate processes, though ones that are often a mixture of conscious and less-than-conscious elements.

Fuller's second class of operations involve converting new experiences into familiar terms. Here, again, he casts his net widely, speaking for instance of analogy as well as 'metaphorical contamination', ie roughly, the idea that once a metaphor is in place, it tends to be drawn upon and extended often in unpredictable and sometimes unhelpful ways, eg 'The lawyer, after calling the corporation a person, may assume that the corporation, like the human being, must die, all at once'.[50] Here, Fuller appears to see both

[42] Ibid, 886.
[43] Ibid.
[44] Ibid, 887.
[45] Ibid.
[46] Ibid, 888.
[47] Ibid, 889.
[48] Ibid, 891.
[49] Ibid, 889.
[50] Ibid, 894.

inescapability, asserting that 'our thinking proceeds through analogy and comparison',[51] and danger, as with 'metaphorical contamination', or in the capacity of concepts to 'induce reification'[52] and to 'exert a kind of centripetal force by which it seeks to clear the field of anomalies and exceptions'.[53] Insofar as that is where Fuller takes the distinction, this marks a difference in our approaches: I would resist the idea, for instance, that all our thinking is reducible to analogy and comparison. I would also resist speaking of metaphors as something that is 'contaminating'.

There are, however, other connections between this second operation and some of what I have argued in this book: for instance, although Fuller does not think of them in this way, some of his examples of processes of converting new experiences into familiar terms are full of kinesis, eg 'affinity of chemicals', 'flow of electricity', 'pull of gravity'.[54] Further, and in this respect echoed much later by Spolsky,[55] Fuller speaks of the processes of the mind as involving controlled falling, as exercises in coping with imbalance. He says, by reference to Vaihinger:

> Vaihinger points out that much of our thinking consists in the process of opposing mistakes which are mutually compensatory. If the mathematician supposes a curve to be made of straight lines, he makes his mistake harmless by supposing in turn that the straight lines are infinitely short. Vaihinger likens thought to the process of walking. Walking consists of a series of falls, each arresting and compensating the other just in time. So thinking consists in a series of mutually opposed mistakes.[56]

In his final words of the three articles, he extends Vaihinger's strongly kinesic characterisation of thought to legal reasoning:

> The ultimate problem of the law is balance. Nothing will take the place, in a student of the law, of a sense of tact and balance – not even a burning desire to 'get the facts' or to know 'the societal background' … Is it mere accident that it is a law word, the word 'judgment', which has come in common speech to express precisely this sense of tact and balance, so indispensable in any abstract sense?[57]

Tact and balance are wonderfully suggestive ways to think of the activity of imagination: engaging in reality by altering it, learning precisely from those deliberate acts of imbalance, and doing so with our whole bodies. Certainly, throughout this book, I have sought to emphasise the role of the body: as affectively-embodied animals, we learn and think via our bodies. Our experience of language, and processes of imagination, are, like other aspects of our experience and mental life, deeply infused and imbued with embodiment and kinesis. Fuller's wonderfully stimulating exploration provides some further examples and ideas with which to explore those connections between kinesis, embodiment and legal language and thought.

[51] Ibid, 898.
[52] Ibid, 900.
[53] Ibid, 899.
[54] Ibid, 893.
[55] See Spolsky (2015).
[56] Fuller (1930–31), 896.
[57] Ibid, 910.

C. Motives and Value

We have now seen how Fuller engages with fictions as windows onto language and mind, often going considerably beyond the legal context. In the second of his articles, Fuller fastens much more directly onto law, with a focus on the motivations behind the uses of fiction in adjudication. Fuller thus asks: 'What motives lead courts and legal writers to employ the fiction?'[58] In some ways, given that he also thinks a lot of the work of fictions, both at the level of language and mind, is less-than-conscious, the question is a surprising one. Indeed, I think it is also a restrictive one. It is one thing to argue, as I do here, that the construction of fictions and the subsequent processes of imagination they invite, is a largely deliberate and reflexive process, and it is another to narrow down the evaluation of fictions to the motivations with which they are issued. The latter approach does not necessarily follow from the first.

The value of fictions can be related to, but does not depend on, the motivations with which they are issued. Indeed, we shall see this with all the four case studies in this book: they all, to some extent, take on a life of their own after their initial creation, and generate resources in ways that could not be predicted by their authors. In that respect, one can miss a great deal of their value if one anchors the analysis too closely to the motivations of their authors. Let us, however, stick for now with Fuller, as he squeezes a great deal out of what is a narrow approach to the evaluation of fictions. Fuller's 'ultimate end', as he puts it, in this second article, is 'to make possible an intelligent criticism of the worth of the fiction as a device of legal thought and expression',[59] and in my judgement he certainly does that.

i. A Taxonomy of Motives

Fuller's answer to the question of what motivates the use of fictions is to offer no less than nine categories of fictions, though some of these are more clearly related to motivations behind them than others. They are: 1) expository fictions; 2) emotive fictions; 3) historical fictions (which will be my focus below); 4) abbreviatory fictions;[60] 5) apologetic or merciful fictions;[61] 6) fanciful and habitual fictions (which we use to 'amuse ourselves');[62] 7) general and special fictions; 8) procedural fictions; and 9) statutory fictions.

By expository fictions, Fuller has in mind 'a means for conveying' what the judge 'had in mind'.[63] There is overlap between the expository fiction and the abbreviatory one. The point that Fuller is making by referring to 'expository', is that the motivation is to avoid extensive 'circumlocution which would otherwise be necessary', eg rather than repeating the rules that apply to corporations, one simply says that we treat corporations as persons,

[58] Ibid, 513. The second article appears on pages 513–546.

[59] Ibid, 513.

[60] These Fuller refers to as 'mere convenient shorthand, which avoids length repetition, such as can be found in the German Civil Code where it is said that A is to be treated as if it were B': see ibid, 537.

[61] Eg, the fiction that 'everyone is presumed to know the law' is an apology 'for the necessity in which the law finds itself': see ibid, 539.

[62] Ibid, 540.

[63] Ibid, 516.

thereby transferring to them the rules that apply to persons. Expository fictions are ways of presenting the material in a conveniently abbreviated manner. Emotive fictions, on the other hand, 'induce conviction that a given legal result is just and proper',[64] eg 'The persuasive fiction of the "acceptance" of a gift delivered out of the presence of the donee operates to keep intact the notion that no one can secure a title without an expression of his will'.[65] In many respects, in almost all the non-historical fictions, the motivations appear to be either convenience or inducement. It may be that Fuller is right that some fictions are used in this manner, but even if he is, such uses would clearly not be especially helpful to inquiry in adjudication; I therefore leave them aside.

ii. Historical Fictions: General Observations

The most interesting of the various motivations behind fictions is that which Fuller captures under the label of 'historical fictions'. This is the category that Fuller discusses in most detail, and which relates most closely to his earlier statements that fictions are 1) the 'growing pains' of the growth of legal language, or 2) 'the cement which is always at hand to plaster together the weak spots in our intellectual culture',[66] or 3) that which is used 'to escape the consequences of an existing, specific rule of law', as where 'the fiction of "inviting" in the attractive nuisance cases is intended to escape the rule that there is no duty of care toward trespassers'.[67]

In general, for Fuller, a historical fiction is a way of deciding a case and introducing 'new law in the guise of the old'.[68] As noted above, this marks a very important difference between his approach and mine: I do not conceive of a fiction as introducing a change in the law, at least not while a fiction functions as an artefact and invites processes of imagination. The effect of a fiction, on the approach taken here, is not a change in the law but instead the temporary suspension of an operative fact, ie a proof requirement, of a rule, while retaining the normative consequences of that rule. It allows a judge to decide a case, while communicating the need for a potential change. The judge communicates this by deploying an artefact, and thereby signalling artifice and inviting others to do something with it, eg either continue to suppose or de-fictionalise it. Where a fiction becomes entrenched, and no longer serves to signal artifice, it may come to be treated effectively as a new rule, though not an explicit one: but then it has become a rule, and it also no longer enables inquiry. Of course, it is also possible for later courts to quarantine the case on its facts, and treat it as an anomalous decision, and go back to insisting on proof for all the operative facts in the rule. Again, this is the value of a fiction for inquiry: it gives members of the legal community time to consider whether to introduce a change, eg by creating an exception or a new rule, with different operative facts relating to that normative consequence.

Despite this difference, it is useful to follow Fuller in his enumerations of the different motivations behind the 'historical fiction'. Ostensibly, Fuller mentions four such

[64] Ibid, 517.
[65] Ibid, 518.
[66] Ibid, 513.
[67] Ibid, 516.
[68] Ibid, 518.

motivations: 1) motives of policy; 2) emotional conservatism; 3) conservatism of convenience; and 4) intellectual conservatism. However, in addition to these, Fuller also discusses, as we shall see, what he calls 'peculiar advantages of fiction', and compares the utility of fictions to that of estoppel and presumptions.

iii. Historical Fictions: Motives of Policy, Emotion and Convenience

Motives of policy involve a judge, who is 'fully conscious that he is changing the law', to 'deceive others into believing that he is merely applying existing law', doing so for 'reasons of policy'.[69] Fuller thinks that to ascribe this motive to judges is to be 'uncharitable to the courts', for, given the distinction he has already introduced between fictions and lies, fictions do not really involve any deceit.[70] Nevertheless, Fuller acknowledges that fictions 'may obscure the process of legislating', and that they 'may serve to create the impression that the change is no greater than that involved in the ordinary case where legal principles are extended by way of analogy'.[71] Again, from my perspective, none of these problems arise, for fictions are not ways of introducing change into the law. Therefore, they are neither deceptive, nor do they obscure changes being made.

The next three motives all relate to some form of 'conservativism', the idea in broad terms that fictions are used to preserve existing language. Thus, 'emotional conservativism' is the motivation behind the use of a fiction that 'satisfies' a judge's 'own longing for a feeling of conservatism and certainty', a 'feeling that the law is the same and that existing law determines the case at hand is a comforting one'.[72] It is not a deception of others, as the motive of policy suggests, but instead a form of 'self-deception'.[73]

The motivation of 'emotional conservatism' is a dark way of characterising what may be better thought of as an exercise of humility and caution. It is also at odds with the way in which I have characterised the practice of inquiry, especially in its experimental dimension: judges experiment, but they do so, when they do it well, carefully, and mindful of their own epistemic limitations to foresee the future. Fictions are ways of balancing the respect for the law's past, doing justice in the instant case, and caring for the quality of the law in the future, and this balancing is something that requires some 'conservativism', in Fuller's language, but also some willingness to experiment, eg signal and communicate the need for change.

The third motivation, 'conservativism of convenience', refers to 'a judge or legislator who wishes to change the law and who knows exactly why he wishes to change it and precisely what reform he desires to achieve', and who could if he wanted to 'state the new rule accurately and completely in non-fictitious language', but who decides instead to 'employ a fiction … because this will avoid discommoding current notions'.[74] The motivation here sounds like laziness, ie avoidance of 'troublesome adjustments',[75] but

[69] Ibid, 519.
[70] Ibid.
[71] Ibid, 520.
[72] Ibid.
[73] Ibid.
[74] Ibid, 523.
[75] Ibid.

what I want to emphasise is the idea that the picture with respect to this motivation is of a judge who knows what the rule ought to be. This can be contrasted with the fourth motivation of 'intellectual conservatism'.

iv. Historical Fictions: Intellectual Conservatism

In the fourth motivation, the 'judge may adopt a fiction … because he does not know how else to state and explain the new principle he is applying'.[76] Here, by recognising the judge's uncertainty, and considering fictions as a way of coping with it, Fuller comes closer to the position that I am adopting in this book. To recall, this is the claim that fictions are ways of enabling inquiry, for they allow a judge, mindful of her own limitations, both epistemic and institutional, to call on others to help. Fuller does emphasise limitations: he says, for instance, that 'the human mind is a machine subject to certain limitations' in the sense that 'human reasons must always proceed by assimilating that which is unfamiliar to that which is already known'.[77] But he remains very much at the level of the individual judge, not taking into account the social and diachronic dimensions of inquiry.

Indeed, the narrow focus on motivations, and talk of what 'a judge' is seeking to achieve in employing a fiction, restricts Fuller's evaluation of fictions dramatically. Nevertheless, Fuller's idea that judges may employ fictions precisely when they are unsure how to articulate the relevant principle is very helpful for present purposes: it points precisely to the value of fictions as enabling inquiry over time, in company with others, as to what that principle ought to be. We can see fictions, then, more positively, as processes, as Fuller also calls them at one point, of 'intellectual adaptation'.[78]

Fuller's discussion in this context of the example of the fiction of attractive nuisance is an instructive one. The example is as follows:

> A young girl, living in an industrial district, is injured while playing with other children on a turntable maintained by a railway on an unfenced lot. A suit is brought on her behalf against the railway. Is the railway responsible for the injury?[79]

Fuller's discussion begins by urging us to 'attempt to follow the mental processes of the judge deciding this case'.[80] The judge will know that no landowner will owe a duty of care to trespassers on his land. Thus, if the girl is a trespasser, then the railway will not be liable. In order for there to be a duty of care, the person on the land must be an 'invitee', ie they must have been invited onto the land by the landowner in the sense of the landowner having 'permitted [them], expressly or impliedly, to come on his land'.[81]

The judge may well be unsure as to how to proceed. The judge wants to do justice in the instant case and to care about the quality of the law in the future, ie all the potential cases in the future involving other children who get hurt on private property. At the

[76] Ibid, 524.
[77] Ibid, 525.
[78] Ibid.
[79] Ibid, 526.
[80] Ibid.
[81] Ibid.

same time, the judge wants to respect the law's past, ie precisely its existing rules and principles of liability. Further, the judge is also mindful of her own limitations, both epistemic and institutional, in being able to articulate a new principle. It is instructive to see how Fuller explores the ways that the judge may cope with these difficulties and limitations.

The judge, says Fuller, may 'for some reason or another … feel[] that the case is more like that of the "invitee" than that of the ordinary trespasser'.[82] Ought that, then, to be the ground of the decision? Fuller answers: 'That would hardly do, because after all the child was a trespasser'.[83] Fuller goes on:

> Shall the judge say that the rule is different as to children? That would be establishing a rather broad proposition. Who would be 'children' within the meaning of the suggested rule? And would the landowner be responsible in a case where the child was aware of the danger? Perhaps another tack would be better. Can we say that the distinguishing feature is the fact that the child was attracted to the land by the structure which resulted in her injury. But again, where is the line to be drawn? People generally, and children in particular, may be 'attracted' by any number of things … Should we strike out boldly and say that the landowner owes a duty of care toward all trespassers when he knows, or ought to know, of the likelihood of their presence on his land? That, too, seems a rather broad doctrine. In a sense every landowner who has not securely fenced his property knows that trespassers may be on his land.[84]

We see here Fuller simulating a judge's generation of possibilities, ie possible justifications for the case, with implications for the future, combined with awareness of her own limitations in being able to foresee the proper scope of a potential new principle. Clearly the judge must decide, but, as this passage makes clear, it is not simply a matter of deciding in the instant case and offering a justification for it, but also a matter of respecting the law's past and caring for the quality of the law in the future, eg avoiding principles that are likely to be over-broad or lead to impractical and unjust implications, whether for plaintiffs or defendants, or the legitimacy, authority and workability of the legal system.

What might a judge do in these circumstances, ie in which 1) she wants and needs to decide; 2) is unsure of the principle to be articulated; and 3) also wants and needs to communicate to others that some change may be needed in the law, calling on them in the future to help to articulate a careful, appropriately-scoped principle? One possibility is precisely to employ a fiction:

> Is it not possible that the judge in this dilemma may go back to the point from which he started, namely, the feeling that, in some way or other, this case is more like the case of an invitee then that of the ordinary trespasser? Why not say that the defendant must be 'deemed to have invited' the child on to the land? This brings the case within the cover of existing doctrine and puts an end to these troublesome attempts to state a new principle.[85]

Putting aside the language of 'deeming', Fuller offers a most instructive example of a judge finding their way towards a fiction. Fuller still reads the employment of a fiction as

[82] Ibid.
[83] Ibid.
[84] Ibid.
[85] Ibid, 527.

being motivated by conservatism, but one can see it in another way: precisely as supposing something has been proven, ie that the child was an invitee and not a trespasser, when it is known that there was no such proof or even proof to the contrary.

Further, by straining the meaning of 'invitee', the fiction here is also an artefact, ie in context of this case, it signals its own artifice. It allows a judge to decide the case, and offer a justification, but it also calls upon the help of others, inviting them to consider, in the future, just how to articulate an appropriate principle. This may be an exception to the general rule for children, or it may be some new principle involving some requirement to prove 'attraction'. The point here is that the judge is unsure, and the fiction assists in the making of normative insights, ie insights about which values, vulnerabilities and interests might matter, eg the value of private property, the vulnerability of the children, and the interests of the landowner.

Fuller's notion of 'intellectual conservatism' captures the respect for the law's past, together with humility and caution in the face of a future difficult to foresee. What it arguably does not capture is the capacity of fictions to enable inquiry. Fuller appears, at least to me, to be struggling precisely with the sufficiency of the motivations of conservatism in this case in the following passage:

> The judge, whose mental operations have been outlined, was not thinking of fooling others, nor was he carried away by an emotional desire to preserve existing doctrine. Neither was he considering the 'convenience' of preserving current notions. Indeed, he may have been acutely aware that his own fiction would introduce inconvenience and obscurity into the law. He was simply seeking a solution for the case, which was intellectually satisfying to himself. And that solution turned out to involve a forcing of the case into existing categories, instead of the creation of a new doctrine.[86]

Fuller is surely right to think that the above categories of expository or emotive fictions, or the motivations of policy, emotional conservatism or convenience do not quite fit. But neither is the 'mental process' of the judge really explicable on the basis of 'intellectual conservatism', though that may be part of it. Fuller himself in this passage says that another part of it is 'seeking a solution for the case', but this too, on Fuller's own simulation of the judge's mental process, is not all. For, as above, the judge is clearly projecting into the future, considering potential principles and investigating their scope.

Further, the judge in Fuller's account is weighing and balancing different values, vulnerabilities and interests that may be at stake in future similar cases. In the language of this book, the judge is engaging in inquiry. Mindful of her own limitations in being able to make normative insight, the judge employs a fiction, deciding the case but also signalling and communicating to others that there is more inquiring to be done. The social and diachronic dimensions of inquiry are crucial to understanding what is going on in Fuller's own example, and likewise they are crucial to seeing the value of fictions in adjudication.

Indeed, Fuller comes close to the position being advocated in this book when he mentions, albeit very briefly, that perhaps some fictions can be thought of as 'exploratory fictions'.[87] 'Fictions of this variety', he says, are 'constructions "feeling the way" toward

[86] Ibid.
[87] Ibid, 528.

some principle', which may, he adds, be especially important in 'developing fields of the law, fields where new social and business practices are necessitating a reconstruction of legal doctrine'.[88] Here, Fuller alludes to the diachronic, as well as the experimental, dimensions of inquiry. What he could have added, which I am stressing, is the collaborative character of this process: the way in which fictions invite others to join in the interactive and collective effort of 'feeling the way' toward some principle.

v. Fictions as Scaffolding: Temporary, Provisional Irritants

As noted above, having discussed motivations behind the employment of 'historical fictions', Fuller also proposes that fictions have some 'peculiar advantages.' One of them makes reference to a metaphor sometimes deployed when talking about fictions, namely 'scaffolding':

> The fiction is often likened to a scaffolding. This is usually with the implication that the fiction should be discarded as soon as possible ... But the figure is apt in another sense. The fiction is like a scaffolding in that it can be removed with ease. The fiction seldom becomes a 'vested interest', it does not gather about it a group of partisan defenders. No one will mourn its functions.[89]

This is an important observation: perhaps unlike presumptions and deemings, fictions are less likely to have committed adherents. Put another way: fictions are not meant to survive; again, they are temporary suspensions of operative facts. They are a kind of provisional irritant, which brings attention to itself, through its artifice, in part in order to signal that something that needs to be done with it, ie precisely that it ought not to remain forever but needs at some point to be resolved, eg either by being quarantined to the facts of the case or by introducing a new exception or a new rule. As Fuller puts it, 'the fiction is always ready to give way to a more "adequate" explanation'.[90] Similarly so for the example above: 'The courts which have decided the "attractive nuisance" cases on the basis of a pretense may not have discovered the correct principle, but at least they have not obstructed its later discovery'.[91] Thus, it is an advantage of the fiction not only that no-one will mourn its own passing, but also that it itself calls for more work. In a sense, the fiction calls for more work by calling for its own extinguishment as a fiction.

vi. Fictions and Proof: Fiction, Presumption and Estoppel

There is one final helpful observation Fuller makes in this second article, and in this he also comes closer to the account offered here. Fuller compares fictions to two other devices, and in doing so, puts all three in relation to practices of proof. The way he phrases this, ie saying fictions are 'but one of a large class of devices, all of which may serve, intentionally or otherwise, to obscure the growth of the law',[92] sounds negative,

[88] Ibid, 527–8.
[89] Ibid, 529.
[90] Ibid.
[91] Ibid.
[92] Ibid, 531.

but we can rephrase it along the lines above, ie not as obscuring the growth of law, but instead as signalling the need for it to be changed. This is, in fact, in line with Fuller's own remarks as to the non-deceptive qualities of fiction, and the way we experience the language of fiction as strained, and therefore as something requiring attention and resolution.

What Fuller helpfully adds here is reference to the 'operative facts' of rules. Let us consider a rule that says that 'where operative facts A and B are present, then normative consequence X ought to obtain'. Now consider that a situation arises in which we are unsure whether A or B – let us say, B – ought, in a certain class of cases, to remain an operative fact. Moreover, there is a possible further operative fact, C, which we may want to replace B with, but we are as yet unsure whether that is indeed the right way forward. In other words, we do not yet want to commit to creating an exception ('usually A and B, but in such and such circumstances, not B but C'), nor a new rule ('if A and C, then X'). What options are available to us? Fuller lists three:

1. Fiction ('When Facts A and C are present, permit an allegation that B is present even though it is known that B is actually absent from the case').
2. Presumption ('Say that Facts A and C raise a presumption that B is present').
3. Estoppel ('State that the existence of Facts A and C "estops" the party to deny that fact B is present').[93]

Fuller says that it may be attractive to use the presumption 'when Facts A and C can be said to have any tendency at all to prove Fact B',[94] and to use estoppel 'If there is any conduct of the party which can form the basis for denying to him the privilege of disproving B'.[95] Then Fuller adds: 'If all else fails, there is left only the bald pretense of the fiction'.[96]

Fuller's insights here are important, though, in my judgement, he unnecessarily casts them in a negative light. From the perspective of this book, the point, ie the value of all three of these devices, including the fiction, is not 'to obscure the reform which has taken place, because each device serves to preserve in form the notion that Facts A and B remain the foundations of the liability in question'.[97] Instead, the point is to be careful about introducing a new rule or a new exception to a rule. From this perspective, the fiction is the most humble and cautious of all three.

In fact, one could argue that fiction is the only one out of these three that does not introduce a change in the law. Presumptions and estoppel are, after all, rules: they announce that parties can, in the future, rely on them in presenting their submissions and organising what they need to prove. Fictions do not do that: for the moment, no change has been made, and the rule continues as before. What has been introduced is a signal that something is possibly not quite right with the law, and that it demands further attention and reflection. The fiction does this precisely at the level of proof: it

[93] Ibid, 531–2.
[94] Ibid, 532.
[95] Ibid.
[96] Ibid, 533.
[97] Ibid, 532.

temporarily suspends, in the instant case, the need for proving some operative fact, B in the above example, leaving it open to whether A and C ought to form the foundation of a new exception or a new rule. This does introduce some uncertainty, but there is no hiding from this; in fact, to the contrary, attention is brought to it via the signalling of artifice. Further, what can be viewed as uncertainty from one perspective, is also cautious, humble and enabling of inquiry from another perspective. Uncertainty here is not something to apologise for: it is an inevitable and unavoidable result, not only of our epistemic and institutional limitations, but also very much part of our on-going and never complete task of doing justice.

D. Fuller and Beyond

We have now found our way through Fuller's three articles. Of course, I have done so only selectively, and without coming even close to exhausting its riches. I hope it is clear to any reader who has not yet read Fuller's articles, how any student of legal reasoning stumbling upon them for the first time would find them so deeply stimulating and rich. I would not have written this book without them. This is not to say there are no disagreements in our approaches; indeed, I have sought to identify them clearly above. Nevertheless, Fuller's articles remain an inspiration, and all the more so on every subsequent re-reading.

In order to be as clear as possible, let me reiterate the approach I am taking to fictions. I am characterising fictions, insofar as they are artefacts, as language-based modes of signalling artifice, calling for further work, eg potentially de-fictionalisation, and doing so by explicitly or implicitly presenting a tension, if not a contradiction, between what is being supposed to have been proven on the one hand, and what is known, in a loose sense, to have been proven on the other. As processes of imagination, fictions involve entering a distinctive epistemic frame where such tension or contradiction is tolerated. They also involve participating in the form of supposition, namely supposing a certain operative fact, ie a proof requirement of an existing rule, has been proven, when it is known that it has not been, or it is uncertain whether it has.

Although fictions do not involve high degrees of affective, sensory or kinesic participation, processing them nevertheless still involves participation: as argued for in the chapter on imagination, supposition is a variety of imagination and connects, even if indirectly, to our affects.[98] To say that fiction, as a process of imagination, involves a low degree of participation is not to offer an apology; on the contrary, this kind of imagination is beneficial precisely because it involves a low degree of participation. It can be a benefit not to have to construct mental imagery, or simulate our emotional reactions, or perform kinesic simulations.

[98] See Arcangeli (2018). Fictions certainly give rise to highly affectively charged language, not only in scholarship but also sometimes by judges, see, eg, the reference by Justice Lush to the 'revolting fiction' of the lost modern grant: *Angus v Dalton* (1877) 3 QBD 83, 94. For a discussion of the fiction of the lost modern grant, see Dowling (2003).

Nevertheless, even if it does not involve a high degree of participation, to construct or confront fictions is still to engage in imagining. Indeed, as long as we imagine, and thus also as long as fictions still function as artefacts, fictions can be valuable to inquiry. They are helpful not in the sense that they create changes in the law, but rather because they enable the making and justifying of a decision in the case precisely without changing the law, while signalling to future readers the potential need for a change. Fictions are ways of creating space and time for interactive and communal inquiry over time.

i. Arguments for and against Fictions

This approach to fictions is at odds with a wide range of other approaches, including other arguments for and against fictions.[99] Amongst arguments against fictions, which dominate the literature, it has been said:

- that they are lies and/or encourage forms of deception;[100]
- that they deliberately sow confusion, making law and its language and procedures incomprehensible to ordinary citizens, and thus keeping it the monopoly of the limited class of lawyers, who accordingly profit;[101]
- that they involve deciding a case on grounds that are not articulated, thereby exhibiting a lack of principled justification and stifling the principled development of the law;[102]
- that they are, at best, necessary in 'immature' or 'under-developed' legal systems, eg ones without established legal academies or with poor judges, and that they are therefore an 'immature' means of legal change, which, if the development is as it should be, will be replaced first by equity and then by rational legislation;[103]
- that they are illegitimate exercises of power by judges, involving attempts by judges to deceptively usurp legislative power;[104] and
- that they are instruments of injustice, eg ways of ignoring important limits on certain powers, or other inconvenient rules, to achieve outcomes that are in the interests of the powerful.[105]

[99] For an overview of the literature on legal fictions, see Del Mar (2015b).

[100] Bentham was the most vociferous advocate of this argument.

[101] Once again, the most passionate exponent of this criticism was Bentham. For a recent discussion, see Tusseau (2019).

[102] See Birks (1986); Olivier (1975); Maine (1861); Demos (1923). Baker called this 'the main objection to fiction'; it was 'not so much that it is untrue – after all, it deceives nobody, and has no dishonest purpose – but that it works off the record, without overt legal reasoning, and therefore suppresses principle': (2001), 55. To give one more example: 'fictions tend to prevent investigation as to the fundamental principle underlying a rule of law, and to retard the framing of a statement of the rule in strictly accurate terms. By giving an erroneous reason for the rule, they make it difficult thoroughly to understand and apply the rule. Indeed, the adoption of an erroneous reason for a doctrine inevitably leads to misapplication of the doctrine': Smith (1917), 153. See also Smith (1918).

[103] See Maine (1861); and Birks (1986). This was a popular view amongst American legal theorists in the early twentieth century, eg Roscoe Pound: see Pound (1959) and (1999) [1963].

[104] Again, Bentham is the principal source for this argument.

[105] See, eg, Lind (2015) who gave the example of the fiction of *terra nullius*; see also Motha (2018). I by no means deny that fictions can be used for such purposes: as with all the artefacts examined in this book, they can all be studied as acts of epistemic violence.

Amongst the arguments for fictions, though it must be said that most of these read like apologies rather than defences, it has been claimed:

- that fictions are necessary and inevitable, eg as above, in certain systems that are not developed enough;[106]
- that they are modes of incremental legal change, typical of the common law, and that thus employment of them may be motivated by characteristic common law judicial caution;[107]
- that they are the products of human and institutional imperfection, and therefore, as realists, we should tolerate them;[108]
- that they sometimes enable more just decisions, precisely because they allow for the circumvention of otherwise harsh or unjust rules, or harsh and unjust results of the application of certain rules in certain cases;[109] and
- that they are useful in all kinds of ways, eg as shorthand, and thus as convenient abbreviations, or because they hardly, if at all, disturb the current state of legal language.[110]

ii. The Argument in this Book

In this book, I argue for the value of fictions in ways that cut across, but largely differ, from these arguments, whether for or against fictions. My argument is that fictions are valuable insofar as they enable inquiry. Many of the above arguments, either for or against fictions, rely on seeing them as instruments of legal change, some more duplicitous, and some less so. In other words, common to almost all of them is the idea that fictions are ways of introducing a change into the law. On the account I provide, fictions are instead ways of deciding an instant case, justifying that decision, and, at the same time, signalling the potential need for a change. They are not themselves a direct means of legal change.

Further, the defence of fictions offered here makes no apologies for them: they are not necessary evils. Instead, being mindful of the limitations, both epistemic and

[106] The most famous exponent of this view is Vaihinger (1925) and, given the influence of Vaihinger on him, Fuller (1930–31). Vaihinger remains highly, and I would argue unduly, neglected in legal scholarship and the social sciences generally: for discussions, see Fine (1993); and Kobow (2014).

[107] See Moglen (1998). Notice that this is different to what I am arguing here: I am not arguing that fictions are a mode of incremental legal change; I am arguing that they are ways of deciding and justifying the instant case, while signalling the need for potential change.

[108] Fuller (1930–31) can, at times, be understood in this way.

[109] See Lind (2015), who in addition to offering examples of 'nasty and pernicious fictions', also discusses beneficial fictions, eg the fiction of the personality of the ship helped avoid the evasion of responsibility by ship-owners. This argument can be found in numerous discussions of fictions, perhaps most prominently in pre-Benthamite literature, eg in Blackstone. In vol 3 of his *Commentaries on the Laws of England*, Blackstone says that 'fictions of law, though at first they may startle the student, he will find upon farther consideration to be highly beneficial and useful: especially as this maxim is ever invariably observed, that no fiction shall extend to work any injury; its proper operation being to prevent a mischief, or remedy an inconvenience, that might result from the general rule of law. So true it is that 'in legal fiction justice ever abides': (1829), 42.

[110] This is a popular argument, present for example also in Fuller (1930–31), though also one that sometimes leads its adherent to argue that there are no such things as legal fictions: see, eg, Kelsen (2015). See also Olivier (1975).

institutional, of individual judges, fictions are ways of enabling the social and diachronic dimensions of inquiry: they involve more persons, over longer periods of time, working together to improve the quality of the law. A subsequent court, when faced with the prior court's temporary suspension of an operative fact, has a choice between three options: 1) to quarantine the prior court's decision on its facts, and re-assert the rule and apply it with its usual operative facts; 2) to continue the fiction, and thus extend its temporary suspension; or 3) to de-fictionalise it, introducing either a new exception to the rule or a new rule. The point is that a fiction allows the choice: it creates time and space for later courts to consider, for instance, whether they have accumulated a sufficient number of cases, to make a more confident and careful assessment of the appropriate scope of any new exception or rule. In so doing, a fiction enables persons in the future to generate insight as to what values, vulnerabilities and interests are at stake in some area of the law.

In that sense, fictions are not tied to any assessment of the maturity or level of development of a legal system: they are one of the instruments by which inquiry can be enabled in adjudication. Their key aspect is not so much the avoidance of some unjust consequences of the application of a rule, though this may often be part of it, but more the concern with the quality of the law in the future. In other words, the defence of fictions here is not based primarily on the idea that they are necessary to avoid injustice in a particular case. It is, instead, that they are one of the available means of engaging in inquiry in adjudication, and thus balancing respect for the law's past, doing justice in the instant case and caring for the law in the future.

All this remains highly abstract, however. To give some more concrete sense to how fictions, as artefacts, with related processes of imagination, can enable inquiry, I turn to a contemporary example from negligence law.

II. Fictions of Causation

In 1972, the House of Lords delivered judgement in the case of *McGhee v National Coal Board*.[111] The case has become famous, but its beginnings were modest, with the initial decisions in the Scottish courts, both of which Mr McGhee lost, not being reported until after the House of Lords decision, where he won. Lord Justice Hope, writing extra-judicially, and comparing the stature of the *McGhee* case with that of *Donoghue v Stevenson*,[112] said of it that 'It has turned out to be a case of the greatest importance for the humane development of our law relating to liability for personal injury'.[113] As Lord Hope also observed, whereas *Donoghue* was decided entirely on the pleadings, with the case never going to proof, the role of evidence, what was proved, and what was required or not to be proved, was of utmost importance in *McGhee*.

[111] *McGhee v National Coal Board* [1972] 3 All ER 1008. All subsequent references to this judgement are *McGhee* (1972).

[112] *Donoghue v Stevenson* [1932] AC 562.

[113] Hope (2003), 588.

In what follows, I first look in detail at *McGhee* itself, with special focus on the House of Lords judgement, but also with some attention to the judgements in the Scottish courts. As with all the artefacts examined in this book, their value is often not discernible on the basis of an instant case. Therefore, I turn, in the second and third sections, to some of the cases that preceded *McGhee*, as well as some of the cases after *McGhee*. Throughout, my overall aim is to articulate, as clearly as I can by reference to a concrete example, the value of fictions in enabling inquiry.

A. Mr McGhee's Dermatitis

James McGhee was a labourer, who worked in the Prestongrange brickworks, near Edinburgh in Scotland. For fifteen years, his job was to empty pipe kilns. This was a job he took immediately after school. In 1967, when he was 31 years old, he was transferred to work in different kilns. These kilns were used not for making pipes, but instead for making bricks. This was hardly a promotion, as the 'working conditions there were much hotter and dustier than in the pipe kilns'.[114] Mr McGhee was part of the 'burnt team', whose job was to 'remove the bricks from the burning zones inside the kiln when the baking process was over'.[115] As Lord Hope described it: 'The floor of the kiln was covered in ashes from the coal burnt in the fires at the rear of each burning zone, and the men spent much of their time covered in ashes and brick dust'.[116] It did not take long for the hotter and dustier conditions to have their effect on Mr McGhee: five days after he began, he 'felt extensive irritation on his skin', and he was soon diagnosed with dermatitis.[117]

We need to know a little more about the working conditions, and in particular, what the National Coal Board did, or rather, did not do, to alleviate the effects of the hot and dusty atmosphere in which Mr McGhee and others worked. One of the things the Board could have done was to allow the pipe kilns to cool before sending in the 'burnt team' to remove the bricks from them. The pipe kilns would then have been less hot, and thus possibly less likely to cause harm. And Mr McGhee did indeed initially plead that because the Board did not do this, they breached a duty of care to him. In this contention, he failed in the Scottish courts and did not pursue this claim in the House of Lords.

But there was another precaution that the Board could have taken, and this was to provide adequate washing facilities, and in particular showers, for Mr McGhee and his co-workers. Without such washing facilities, the workers had no easy or quick way to get the dust off their bodies. For Mr McGhee, this was a serious problem: he lived some four kilometres away, and without washing facilities at work, his home was the closest place he could take a shower and properly clean away the dust. Further, Mr McGhee was in the habit of cycling to work: the way to work was easy, as it was largely downhill, but

[114] *McGhee* (1972), 1009, per Reid LJ.
[115] Hope (2013), 589.
[116] Ibid, 589.
[117] *McGhee* (1972), 1009, per Reid LJ.

the way back home required considerable effort, involving a long climb uphill, which must have been difficult after hours of cleaning out pipe kilns. Some years previously, the Board had provided washing facilities for workers, but the baths that were part of the premises had closed in 1963, and now, apart from some washbasins and towels, and occasionally soap, no adequate washing facilities were available. At least this is what Mr McGhee argued, both in the Scottish courts and in the House of Lords. On this ground, both sets of courts agreed: in failing to provide adequate washing facilities, the Board had breached its duty of care to Mr McGhee.

i. The Scottish Courts

So far so good. But it is not enough for a plaintiff to succeed in a negligence suit to show that the defendant owed and breached a duty of care to him. He also needs to show that the injury he sustained, the dermatitis, was caused by the breach. This turned out to be quite some stumbling block. In fact, it was the reason why Mr McGhee's case failed in the Scottish courts.

At first instance, Lord Justice Kissen found that Mr McGhee did not discharge his burden of proof, which required him to 'show on a balance of probabilities that the employer's breach of duty caused or materially contributed to his injury'.[118] The evidence from the medical experts at the first instance trial was that the 'lack of shower baths' 'increased the possibility but not made it a probability' that he would contract the disease.[119] Though pressed, the 'furthest the medical witnesses were willing to go was to say that the provision of showers would have materially reduced the risk of contracting the disease'.[120] This, said Lord Kissen, was not good enough: material increase in risk was not the same thing as material contribution; after all, this was what the evidence showed explicitly, with the medical witnesses refusing precisely to go so far as to say that the lack of washing facilities materially contributed to the contraction of the disease. It is worth setting out Lord Kissen's statement on the evidence in full:

> As I have maintained earlier, the pursuer, in order to succeed, must also establish, on a balance of probabilities, that this fault on the part of the defenders 'caused or materially contributed to his injury', that is, to his contracting dermatitis. Dr Hannay's evidence was that he could not say that the provision of the showers would probably have prevented the disease. He said that it would have reduced the risk materially but he would not go further than that. Dr Ferguson said that washing reduces the risk. Pursuer's counsel maintained that a material increase in the risk of contracting a disease was the same as a material contribution to contracting the disease and that Dr Hannay established this by his evidence. I think that defenders' counsel was correct when he said that the distinction drawn by Dr Hannay was correct and that an increase in risk did not necessarily mean a material contribution to the contracting of the disease. The two concepts are entirely different. A material increase in risk may refer only to possibilities and may not make a possibility into a probability. It may strengthen the possibility but that cannot mean that in all such cases the possibility has become a probability. What the pursuer has to show is that, as he avers, he would not have contracted the disease but for

[118] Hope (2013), 592.
[119] Ibid.
[120] Ibid.

> the defenders' breach of duty. He has to show that this was probable and the degrees of risk have no relevance unless they make the contraction of the disease more probable than not contracting the disease. He cannot succeed if the only inference from the evidence is that lack of shower baths is a possibility as a cause of his having contracted the disease and that the provision of shower baths would have increased the possibility of his not contracting it but not made it a probability. That is the only inference which I can draw from Dr Hannay's evidence and that was the best evidence for the pursuer. Causal connection between fault and the contraction of the disease has not been established.[121]

When Mr McGhee appealed from this first instance decision of the Lord Ordinary, the judges in the Inner House agreed with Lord Kissen. Lord President Clyde said explicitly: 'the risk of dermatitis and causation of dermatitis are two quite separate matters'.[122] Therefore, causation had not been proved, and therefore Mr McGhee's case failed.

ii. The Appeal to the House of Lords

But Mr McGhee did not give up. Like Mrs Donoghue, who had also failed in the Scottish courts, Mr McGhee turned to the House of Lords. And here, as noted above, he succeeded. The discussion focused on the proof of causation, and, unlike the Scottish courts, the House of Lords decided that Mr McGhee had indeed proved the requisite causal link between the lack of washing facilities and the dermatitis that he contracted. That a duty of care had been owed and that it was breached was all admitted before the House of Lords. Proof of causation was the sole issue.

Counsel for Mr McGhee had only one argument: they contended 'that it was enough for McGhee to have proved that the Board's failure to provide shower baths "materially increased the risk" of his contracting dermatitis'.[123] Counsel for the other side, which included Lord Hope as junior counsel, had, it appeared, a simple riposte: material contribution is what had to be proved, and it was not. The evidence could not be clearer: the experts had been pressed, and they consistently refused to say that the lack of washing facilities had materially contributed to the disease. And yet, the House of Lords found for Mr McGhee. How did they do so?

Here, we need to proceed slowly and consider the judgements of each of the Lords, each of whom offered a separate opinion. To recall, this is one of the features of contemporary common law reasoning, namely: that it does not discourage, but on the contrary facilitates the writing of separate opinions, each with their own descriptions of the evidence and each with their own arguments, tone and style. Further, each opinion is in the first person, thereby exhibiting the individuality of common law reasoning: the judges sharing not only their arguments for deciding one way or the other, but also their uncertainties and difficulties. The opinions are highly discursive: they are not structured as logical maps, with one observation leading inexorably to another. Rather, they meander, moving from a discussion of the facts, to possibly relevant past cases,

[121] Lord Kissen quoted in *McGhee v National Coal Board* (1972) SLT (Notes) 61.
[122] *McGhee v National Coal Board* (1972) SLT (Notes) 61, per Clyde LP.
[123] Hope (2013), 592.

and to possibly relevant values, vulnerabilities and interests in this case and future cases. And, although the decision in favour of Mr McGhee is a unanimous one, they also disagree as amongst each other as to the grounds upon which to justify that decision, as well as what are the relevant values, vulnerabilities and interests to take into account when balancing respect for the law's past, justice in the instant case, and caring for the quality of the law in the future. Again, these are not superfluous or marginal features of contemporary common law reasoning: they are a crucial part of how it operates. This is also why it is important we look at each opinion, and at the relations between them.

iii. Lord Reid

Throughout his judgement, Lord Justice Reid stressed the uncertainty of medical knowledge in this area. The evidence in this case did not show, 'perhaps no one knows' he added, 'just how dermatitis of this type begins'.[124] The medical knowledge was uncertain, yes, but the medical evidence was not: as Lord Reid repeated, 'The medical evidence is to the effect that the fact that the man had to cycle home caked with grime and sweat added materially to the risk that this disease might develop'.[125] But, Lord Reid said, 'in cases like this we must take a broader view of causation'.[126] The 'legal concept of causation', he added, 'is not based on logic or philosophy. It is based on the practical way in which ordinary man's mind works in the every-day affairs of life.'[127] He then added a crucial sentence:

> From a broad and practical viewpoint I can see no substantial difference between saying that what the respondents did materially increased the risk of injury to the appellant and saying that what the respondents did made a material contribution to his injury.[128]

Having said this, Lord Reid directly concluded that the appeal should be allowed. The sentence is, therefore, crucial. However, it also remains open to different interpretations. One could read it as saying that, in this case, for the purpose of deciding it, material increase in risk is to be treated as if it proved material contribution. Or, one could read it to mean that, in this case and in all future cases (of a certain class, it not being quite clear what class), material increase in risk was sufficient proof of material contribution. Or, more strongly even, one could read it to mean that one no longer needed to prove material contribution, but only material increase in risk, with that now being the relevant terminology for proving causation.

That Lord Reid's statement is open to these interpretations is important. But it is also the case that the second and third interpretations would be quite bold: after all, either one would constitute quite a dramatic change in the law. Surely, if Lord Reid had wanted to make it clear that the House was changing the law in this way, then this

[124] *McGhee* (1972), 1010, per Reid LJ.
[125] Ibid, 1011.
[126] Ibid.
[127] Ibid.
[128] Ibid.

necessitated not only a more explicit statement to that effect, but also some consideration of the factors by which it was limited, eg the class of cases to which it might apply. But Lord Reid does neither of these things. Instead, he remains largely at the level of the facts of the case, refusing to generalise, and restraining his comments to the evidence. It is, then, the first of the interpretations that is the more plausible interpretation, ie that in this case, for the purpose of deciding it, proof of material increase in risk is to be treated as if it was proof of material contribution. Again, it is important that all these are available as interpretations, but it remains the case that the first is more plausible.

It is also this first interpretation that constitutes a fiction. To make this clear: Lord Reid's statement, especially in the context of the circumstances of the case, signals artifice, doing so by creating a tension between what is being taken to have been proven (material contribution) and what is known to have been proven (material increase in risk). For those who come to read Lord Reid's judgement later, they will be confronted with this artifice, and in so being, their attention will be captured, and they will be called upon to do something active, ie to either continue the fiction or to de-fictionalise. Put another way: later readers, by considering Lord Reid's judgement, are invited to imagine, ie they are invited to enter a distinctive epistemic frame where they tolerate the contradiction or tension between what is taken to be proven and what is known to have been proven, and they participate, doing so by supposing that something has been proven when it is known that it has not been.

What is known to have been proven in this case is that the lack of washing facilities materially increased the risk of the disease: the experts explicitly refused to go further, and thus refused to say that the lack of washing facilities materially contributed to the disease. To say that there is no difference, in this case, between material increase in risk and material contribution is, effectively, to employ a fiction: it is to temporarily suspend the operative fact of material contribution, allowing, in this case, material increase in risk to be sufficient. Crucially, for my view, this is not to change the law: it is to decide the case, justify that decision, and still leave open the possibility that later courts will introduce either an exception or a new rule, simultaneously making clearer in what class of cases the exception or rule is to apply. Of course, a later court could say – in part to justify their introduction of an exception or rule – that what *McGhee* did was to change the law, ie that the second or third of the above interpretations of Lord Reid's statement is the correct one. But *McGhee* itself, at least in Lord Reid's judgement, does not determine the matter one way or another. It leaves open possibilities for the later court. In fact, it leaves open three such possibilities:

1. that *McGhee* was decided solely on its peculiar facts, and should be quarantined from any further legal significance, with material contribution, and not material increase in risk, being the relevant proof requirement for all cases;
2. that the fiction in *McGhee* should be continued, and that, for now, we should continue to temporarily suspend the operative fact of material contribution, allowing, perhaps, for material increase in risk to be sufficient proof in the next case; and
3. that *McGhee* in fact changed the law, or that now a change in the law should be made explicit, namely, that in a certain class of cases, it now being said in which, material increase in risk is sufficient for proof of causation.

We shall see in a moment how subsequent courts entertained these possibilities, with the case of *Fairchild*[129] on the whole opting for option 3, most obviously in Lord Justice Hoffmann's judgement.

iv. Lord Wilberforce

Let us, however, return to the other judgements in *McGhee*. Lord Justice Wilberforce's opinion was next. The judgement is interesting for our purposes because Lord Wilberforce explicitly refers to there being fiction at work in this case. Like Lord Reid, Lord Wilberforce reiterates what needs to be proved: 'that the breach of duty caused or materially contributed to the injury'.[130] And Lord Wilberforce also reiterates what the expert evidence showed, ie what was proved: Mr McGhee's own expert 'could not say that if the appellant had been able to wash off the dust by showers he would not have contracted the disease. He could not do more than say that the failure to provide showers materially increased the chance, or risk, that dermatitis might set in'.[131]

How did Lord Wilberforce deal with this tension between what had to be proved and what was proved? He did so in two, related, ways: first, to suggest that once material increase in risk was proved by the plaintiff, that the onus could then be switched to the defendant, allowing the defendant to show that although some risk may have increased, the cause of the disease should really be attributed to something other than the risk, eg another cause; and second, to suggest an analogy between this case and two other earlier cases (to which I shall return below), the effect of which was that, in certain cases, material increase in risk could be enough to show that 'on a balance of probabilities', the breach of duty 'caused or materially contributed to his injury'.[132] Lord Wilberforce then said this:

> … the default [ie the breach of duty] here consisted not in adding a material quantity to the accumulation of injurious particles [as in the allegedly analogous previous two cases] but by failure to take a step which materially increased the risk that the dust already present would cause injury. And I must say that, at least in the present case, to bridge the evidential gap by inference seems to me something of a fiction, since it was precisely this inference which the medical expert declined to make. But I find in the cases quoted an analogy which suggests the conclusion that, in the absence of proof that the culpable condition had, in the result, no effect, the employers should be liable for an injury, squarely within the risk which they created and that they, not the pursuer, should suffer the consequence of the impossibility, foreseeably inherent in the nature of his injury, of segregating the precise consequence of their default.[133]

The language here is somewhat tortured: it twists and turns under the pressure of what Lord Wilberforce refers to as 'the evidential gap'. It is as if the language is gasping for air, trying to find some way, as again Lord Wilberforce says, to 'bridge' that 'gap'. Lord Wilberforce admits that to bridge that gap, to make the inference, is 'something

[129] *Fairchild v Glenhaven Funeral Services Ltd* [2003] 1 AC 32. All subsequent references to this judgement are *Fairchild* (2003).
[130] *McGhee* (1972), 1011, per Wilberforce LJ.
[131] Ibid, 1012.
[132] Ibid, 1013.
[133] Ibid.

of a fiction'. But he also seems to step away from adopting a fiction, though the way he does so, by reference to the analogy with the two previous cases (which he himself distinguishes in the first sentence of the above quote) is hardly persuasive. Neither is it especially persuasive to refer to an onus of proof not having been met by the defendant, ie the defendant not having shown that the breach had no effect, as if they could, even if they had been asked, which they had not. Although, again, like Lord Reid, Lord Wilberforce's judgement allows for multiple interpretations of it, its primary effect is similar: to temporarily suspend the operative fact of material contribution, while signalling to future courts that the law may here be changed, and possibly by reference to the two previous decisions, which also deal with 'industrial diseases'.[134]

v. *Lord Simon*

Lord Wilberforce may have been the only one of the judges to explicitly refer to 'fiction', but he was certainly not the only one to notice, and to state, that there was a tension in the case between what ought to be proved, ie material contribution, and what was known to have been proven, ie material increase in risk. Lord Justice Simon, whose judgement followed Lord Wilberforce's, repeated what the medical evidence showed: that 'Neither consultant would … go so far as to say that washing after work would have made it more probable than not that the appellant would have escaped dermatitis'.[135] Like Lord Wilberforce, Lord Simon sought help from the two previous decisions relating to injuries 'caused by two (or more) factors operating cumulatively', saying of them that they showed that 'the law does not require a pursuer or plaintiff to prove the impossible', instead allowing a successful suit 'if he proves on a balance of probabilities that the breach or breaches of duty contributed substantially to causing the injury'.[136] This was to introduce yet another expression into the mix: not 'material contribution', and not 'material increase in risk', but instead 'substantial contribution'. Once more we see how loose discursively the common law can be. Lord Simon thus says, relating this back to the case:

> In my view, a failure to take steps which would bring about a material reduction of the risk involves, in this type of case, a substantial contribution to the injury. In this type of case a stark distinction between breach of duty and causation is unreal. If the provision of shower baths was (as the evidence showed) a precaution which any reasonable employer in the respondents' position would take, it means that such employer should have foreseen that failure to take the precaution would, more probably than not, substantially contribute towards injury; this is sufficient prima facie evidence.[137]

'In this type of case': a phrase repeated twice in the above passage. But which type is that? Lord Simon does not say. Without more, to say 'in this type of case', and not specifying what type, is, pragmatically, like saying 'in this case'. But the passage above also reveals another aspect of this case: that the judges all placed great weight on the fact of the

[134] Ibid, 1012.
[135] Ibid, 1013–14, per Simon LJ.
[136] Ibid, 1014.
[137] Ibid.

admission of both a duty of care having been owed, and the duty having been breached. That Lord Simon placed great weight on this is clear from his penultimate sentence: 'To hold otherwise [and say that causation had not been proved in this case] would mean that the respondents were under a legal duty which they could, in the present state of medical knowledge, with impunity ignore'.[138] Here, too, Lord Simon points to one of the undeniable factors in this case, and possibly, in the future, other like cases: that the medical knowledge was uncertain.

For our purposes, however, what is crucial is less that the knowledge was uncertain, and more that it was known that what was proven, ie material increase in risk, was not what needed to be, ie material contribution. Lord Simon's way of bridging the evidential gap – to use Lord Wilberforce's language – was to suggest a middle term, in part based on the analogy with the previous cases, namely 'substantial contribution', which hid from view, as it were, the tension between material increase in risk and material contribution. To do this, arguably, is also to use a fiction: it is effectively to temporarily suspend the operative fact of material contribution, though it is perhaps more assertive than a judgement that does not offer an alternative, neutral language. Be that as it may, without specifying, at least to some degree, in what type of case 'substantial contribution' would be sufficient, it is difficult to attribute to Lord Simon the introduction of a new exception or a new rule.

vi. Lord Kilbrandon

There were two further judgements: Lord Justice Kilbrandon's and Lord Justice Salmon's.

Like the other judges, Lord Kilbrandon noted the uncertainty of medical knowledge: 'It is, in the present state of medical knowledge, impossible to say that if the appellant had taken a shower he would certainly not have got the disease, and it is equally impossible to say that another man, in exactly the same case as the appellant, would have on the contrary certain got it'.[139] He also noted that whereas Mr McGhee had proved that the breach reduced the risk of injury, he had not proved that 'he would more probably not have contracted the disease had the bath been provided'.[140] Again, like Lord Simon, Lord Kilbrandon was impressed with the admission of both duty and breach of that duty, and he noted that once this 'has been accepted', the argument that causation had not been proven here became 'untenable'.[141] To make the argument, one would have to insist on 'drawing a distinction between the possibility and the probability of the efficacy of the precautions', but again, depending 'on the nature of the case' it may be untenable to insist on such a distinction.[142]

At this point, Lord Kilbrandon introduced more terms into the fray: 'When you find it proved', he said, 'that the defendants knew that to take the precaution reduces the risk, chance, possibility or probability of the contracting of the disease', and when they failed to do so, and the disease occurred, 'it is difficult to see how those defenders can demand

[138] Ibid, 1015.
[139] Ibid, 1015, per Kilbrandon LJ.
[140] Ibid.
[141] Ibid, 1016.
[142] Ibid.

more by way of proof'.[143] Interestingly, from the perspective of the fourth case study to be discussed later in this book, ie scenarios, Lord Kilbrandon here engages in some scenario-imagining of his own:

> Suppose it to be the duty of employers in certain circumstances to supply safety belts. They do not do so, and an employee is injured in a way which would not have happened if the belt had been provided. But he cannot prove that the failure to provide it contributed to the accident, because it is certain that if it had been provided he would not have used it. In the present case, the appellant's body was vulnerable, while he was bicycling home, to the dirt which had been deposited on it during his working hours. It would not have been if he had had a shower. If showers had been provided he would have used them.[144]

Here, Lord Kilbrandon in fact opens up a possible defence for a future defendant: proof that, even if the precaution were available, the plaintiff would not have used it, though he also asserts, perhaps with more confidence than the evidence allowed, that in this case Mr McGhee would have used the washing facilities, had they been provided. This latter claim is questionable, for is it not more likely that, given his habit of going straight home, Mr McGhee would not have used the shower facilities, even if they had been there? Presumably he would then have needed to wash himself again, following his arduous cycle up the hill? The scenario also does some further work, pressing upon us similarities between the arguably clearer danger of not providing seat-belts and the arguably less clear one of not providing showers.

Lord Kilbrandon's judgement then ends abruptly: he simply concludes that 'in my opinion he [Mr McGhee] has succeeded in showing that his injury was, more probably than not, caused by or contributed to by the respondents' failure to provide a shower bath'.[145] This, in effect, is to create a fiction: it is to ignore the contradiction or tension between what was proved and what needed to be proved, thereby temporarily suspending the operative fact, ie proof of material contribution, while retaining the normative consequence, ie allowing a successful suit in negligence.

vii. Lord Salmon

We come, finally, to Lord Salmon's judgement. By now, the moves to be made are familiar. Lord Salmon also notes that 'it was impossible in the present state of medical knowledge to say that they [the shower facilities] would probably have prevented the appellant from contracting dermatitis'.[146] But he also notes that 'the medical witness could not say that it was more likely than not that these precautions … would have prevented injury, but only that such precautions would have materially reduced the risk of injury'.[147]

How does Lord Salmon deal with the tension between what was proved and what needed to be proved? He switches the plane of discussion to situations where more than one factor can be a cause (as in the other two previous decisions, to which

[143] Ibid.
[144] Ibid.
[145] Ibid.
[146] Ibid, 1017, per Simon LJ.
[147] Ibid.

I shall return), saying: 'It is not necessary … to prove that the respondents' negligence was the only cause of injury'.[148] Strictly speaking, this is of course not the issue in this case: it is not a situation where multiple causes exist, but where the question is the causal link between one breach of duty and the injury. By taking us, however, to a context in which that is what matters, we come arguably to loosen our otherwise-steadfast insistence on what constitutes a cause: for if there are multiple causes, they each can be quite weak ones; the accumulation of possibilities, as it were, appears like a holistic probability, and then all that remains is that one prove one possibility. And, indeed, Lord Salmon enjoins us to not be 'unrealistic' and to exercise 'common sense':

> In the circumstances of the present case it seems to me unrealistic and contrary to ordinary common sense to hold that the negligence which materially increased the risk of injury did not materially contribute to causing the injury.[149]

This statement is a good example of what we might call implicit signalling of artifice: in the circumstances of the case, our attention is captured by the contradiction or tension between what has been proven, ie material increase in risk, and what needs to be, ie material contribution. We are invited to suppose that something has been proven when it is known it has not been. A fiction is at work. Like Lord Kilbrandon, Lord Salmon too proposes a scenario, and one which seemed designed to further encourage us to take a 'common sense' approach:

> Suppose … it could be proved that men engaged in a particular industrial process would be exposed to a 52 percent risk of contracting dermatitis even when washing facilities provided. Suppose it could also be proved that the risk would be increased to, say 90, per cent when such facilities were not provided. It would follow that if the decision appealed from is right, an employer who negligently failed to provide the proper facilities would escape from any liability to an employee who contracted dermatitis notwithstanding that the employers had increased the risk from 52 percent to 90 per cent. The negligence would not be a cause of the dermatitis because even with proper washing facilities, ie without the negligence, it would still have been more likely than not that the employee would have contracted the disease – the risk of injury then being 52 per cent. If, however, you substitute 48 per cent for 52 per cent the employer could not escape liability, not even if he had increased the risk to, say, only 60 per cent. Clearly such results would not make sense; nor would they, in my view, accord with the common law.[150]

This is a complex scenario, and I do not propose to analyse it here: what is interesting for present purposes, is some of the language used by Lord Salmon, eg we have before us a negligent employer, who is seeking to 'escape from any liability'. To allow them to do so 'would not make sense'. It would be to let them get away with something that common law cannot stand for. The common sense of the common law is at stake. Indeed, Lord Salmon goes on immediately after this passage to reiterate the importance he ascribes to not allowing the Board to escape with impunity: to allow the defendant to succeed here, would mean that 'an employer would be permitted by the law to disregard with impunity his duty to take reasonable care for the safety of his employees'.[151] Clearly, then, part of what is at stake in this case is the vulnerability of workers to employers – powerful

[148] Ibid.
[149] Ibid.
[150] Ibid, 1018.
[151] Ibid.

employers who sometimes, if not often, may seek to escape from their responsibilities. At stake, too, is the legitimacy of the common law and the authority of the court: after all, would the law and the court not be failing to do justice if it enabled powerful employers to evade responsibility in this way?

Lord Salmon's judgment overlaps in many respects with that of his fellow judges. But in one respect it also differs. For Lord Salmon, unlike his fellow judges, does attempt to articulate what he calls a 'rule':

> My Lords, I would suggest that the true view is that, as a rule, when it is proved, on a balance of probabilities, that an employer has been negligent and that his negligence has materially increased the risk of his employee contracting an industrial disease, then he is liable in damages to that employee if he contracts the disease notwithstanding that the employer is not responsible for other factors which have materially contributed to the disease.[152]

Here, Lord Salmon does further specify the category of case that limits the scope of the proposed rule: namely cases involving 'industrial disease'. He also states the rule in a way that incorporates the two previous cases mentioned earlier, for he explicitly states that the situation he has in mind may involve numerous multiple causes.

Lord Salmon, therefore, may be said to do at least two things in his judgement: one, to employ a fiction by stating, as above, that we are, in this case, to treat material increase in risk as equivalent to material contribution, ie we are to suppose something has been proven when we know it has not been; and two, to propose a rule that materially increasing risk is sufficient for proof of causation in cases of industrial diseases. Which is it to be? Like the other judgements, Lord Salmon's judgement also leaves this open.

We have now traversed the five judgements in the *McGhee* case. I have argued that at least some of them employ a fiction. However, if we limit ourselves to this case alone, there is not much that can be said in favour of the use of a fiction. After all, one could argue, it obscures the justification of the decision: just what is the law after this case? Put another way: what is the legal significance of this decision? Is it not made murkier, rather than clearer, by the fiction? Does it not obstruct the principled development of the law? Is it not, in reality, that the judges are legislating, ie changing the law, but hiding that they do so? Or, worse, are they not ignoring the law's past, and the operative facts of its rules, and simply deciding what they think is most fair and just overall?

My argument here is that we can, and ought to, look at the judgements in this case in a different way. The employment of a fiction can be valuable, and that is because it can enable inquiry. The use of a fiction here helps the judges to balance respect for the law's past, doing justice in the instant case, and caring for the quality of the law in the future. To see how, though, we need to expand the diachronic scope of our analysis: both by looking back, but especially by looking ahead. Given that I cannot here delve into all possible cases either side of *McGhee*, I shall restrict myself to some brief remarks on the two previous cases referred to above (*Bonnington*; and *Nicholson*),[153] and two cases following *McGhee* (*Wilsher*; and *Fairchild*).[154]

[152] Ibid.

[153] *Bonnington Castings Ltd v Wardlaw* [1956] AC 613; and *Nicholson v Atlas Steel Foundry and Engineering Co Ltd* [1957] 1 WLR 613. All subsequent references to these judgements are *Bonnington* (1956), and *Nicholson* (1957), respectively.

[154] *Wilsher v Essex Area Health Authority* [1988] 1 AC 1074 and *Fairchild* (2003). All subsequent references to the first case are *Wilsher* (1988).

B. Before *McGhee*

The two pre-*McGhee* cases of *Bonnington v Wardlaw* and *Nicholson v Atlas Steel Foundry* both played an important role in *McGhee*. They were part of the law's past, decided approximately 15 years before *McGhee*, and were presented as relevant to the dispute in *McGhee* by the advocates for both sides. The judges were both influenced by these cases and sought to show them respect. Both cases were appeals to the House of Lords from Scotland, and, still more significantly, they both involved labourers working for employers who had breached duties of care, under both common law and statute, and where the workmen faced difficulties of proof of causation. In both cases, also, the labourer plaintiff had contracted pneumoconiosis, and the relevant medical science was, if anything, more uncertain than in the case of dermatitis.

Despite the similarities, there were also differences, and one potentially very significant difference at the level of causation: namely, in both of these cases, there was more than one source of the dust particles, with the relevant breach of duty relating to a relatively minor source (no breach of duty was found for the major sources of the dust).

In both cases, the plaintiff succeeded in the House of Lords, and it is interesting for our purposes to consider briefly how they did so.

i. Bonnington

In *Bonnington*, in the First Division in Scotland, on appeal from a decision of the Lord Ordinary, the Lord President dissented from the majority's view that causation had been proved. Impressed clearly by how minor the relevant source was (in that case, the swing grinders rather than the pneumatic hammer, for only the former involved a breach of duty), Lord President Clyde stated that 'the mere fact that a breach of duty could cause the injury does not amount to proof in law that it did, and leaves the onus of proof … undischarged'.[155] On the evidence, he said, it has not been 'established that any material contribution to the atmosphere from dangerous dust emanated from the swing grinders'; 'All the evidence points to the pneumatic hammer (the innocent cause) as the most probable one'.[156]

For Lord President Clyde, what was most at stake in this case was the danger, in loosening the causal requirements, of 'so extensive an obligation on employers, which would amount to little short of a guarantee that in such shops no silica dust will be allowed to escape into the atmosphere of the shop'.[157] 'In that setting', he continued, 'a workman who gets pneumoconiosis need only find some fault which might have started his disease in that factory, then an altogether novel obligation will be possible on employers'.[158] The requirement of material contribution, then, served as a limit on just how extensive employers' obligations could be said to be.

[155] *Wardlaw v Bonnington Castings* (1955) SLT 320, 338, per Clyde LP.
[156] Ibid, 339.
[157] Ibid.
[158] Ibid.

The majority in the First Division, however, found a way to overlook the fact that the plaintiff had not proved material contribution: they said that the plaintiff had at least shown that 'failure to deal with the dangerous silica dust at the swing grinders' was an 'addition of … danger', and with the plaintiff having done so, the onus then shifted to the defendants 'to show that this addition to the danger from silica dust did not, and, indeed, could not, have been a contributing cause of the pursuer's disease'.[159] Lord Justice Russell, also shifting the onus in this way, qualified the decision in various ways, saying 'This issue is narrow', and confessing to 'Having anxiously considered the relevant evidence'.[160] In a sense, then, the device of shifting the onus of proof allowed the majority to overlook the lack of proof of causation, in the form of material contribution, by the plaintiff.

When *Bonnington* came to the House of Lords,[161] which affirmed the First Division decision in favour of the plaintiff, Lord Reid was uncomfortable with the device of shifting the onus of proof. But this of course left the very considerable obstacle of the plaintiff having to show 'that on a balance of probabilities the breach of duty caused or materially contributed to his injury'. Lord Reid's solution was to call upon the assistance of the *de minimis* principle, and in doing so, making material contribution a question of degree:

> It appears to me that the source of his disease was the dust from both sources, and the real question is whether the dust from the swing grinders materially contributed to the disease. What is a material contribution must be a question of degree. A contribution which comes within the exception of the *de minimis non curat lex* is not material, but I think that any contribution which does not fall within that exception must be material.[162]

This was a very significant move. It was the first step in loosening the causal requirements, though it remained unclear in what kind of case the requirements were being loosened. Once a degree-based approach was made possible, new language also emerged: thus, Lord Reid spoke of how he thought 'it was sufficiently proved that the dust from the grinders made a substantial contribution.'[163] Although 'much the greater proportion of the noxious dust' came from the pneumatic hammer, and thus the innocent source, 'some certainly came from the swing grinders … the proportion was not negligible'.[164] 'Substantial contribution' and a 'proportion' that 'was not negligible' introduces new language in an overall approach that is sympathetic to loosening causal requirements, treating them as matters of degree.

ii. Nicholson

A year later, in 1957, similar facts arose for consideration in the House of Lords in the case of *Nicholson*. Armed, now, with the decision in *Bonnington*, the House was

[159] Ibid, 342, per Carmont LJ.
[160] Ibid, 347, per Russell LJ.
[161] *Bonnington* (1956).
[162] Ibid, 621, per Reid LJ.
[163] Ibid, 622.
[164] Ibid.

arguably more confident and more assertive. They referred to 'the test recently laid down' in *Bonnington*, which was 'that a contribution is material unless the maxim *de minimis* can be applied to it'.[165]

It is also in this decision that we see the language of risk enter the picture, though still in the context of multiple sources, some of which were innocent: if 'the workman is in certain circumstances forced to inhale noxious particles of dust without having any legal ground of complaint' (because the source of those particles is an innocent one, not involving a breach of duty by the employer), then 'it must be doubly incumbent on the employer to safeguard him against any additional risk'.[166] In this case, said Viscount Simonds: 'owing to the default of the respondents, the deceased was exposed to a greater degree of risk than he should have been'.[167] Lord Justice Cohen, too, said that 'the respondents' failure to provide adequate ventilation must increase the risk to which the workmen are exposed', such that, when 'reading the evidence as a whole, I think it establishes that, to use the language of Lord Reid in *Bonnington*, "on a balance of probabilities the breach of duty caused, or material contributed to" the injury'.[168] *Bonnington* was applied in *Nicholson*, but in ways that already pointed to the potential emergence of a new language: an increase in risk.

iii. The Significance of Bonnington and Nicholson for McGhee

In *McGhee*, then, when the House was confronted with these two cases as possibly relevant, they could find in them some support for a decision in favour of Mr McGhee. The causal requirements had been loosened, eg a degree-based approached had been taken by Lord Reid, and new language had been proposed: 'substantial contribution', 'not negligible', 'addition to danger', 'increase in risk'. Nevertheless, there were also difficulties in relying too much on these cases, which the above judgements from *McGhee* reveal (speaking of 'analogies' with these cases, but not going further than that): for those cases involved multiple causal sources, and they also revealed some 'anxiety' in the possibly too extensive scope of a new obligation placed on employers.

Having had the benefit of these two prior decisions, the judges in *McGhee* arguably did have room to offer, more assertively than those two decisions had, a new rule or a new exception to the rule that material contribution was required to be proved. If they wanted to find in favour of Mr McGhee, then they had several choices:

1. To say that in the case before them material increase in risk was to be taken as equivalent to material contribution, ie to employ a fiction.
2. To replace the language of material contribution with material increase in risk in a certain kind of case, but then they would have to specify which kind of case.
3. To allow the plaintiff to prove only material increase in risk, and then shift the onus to the defendant to show absence of material contribution.

[165] *Nicholson* (1957), 778, per Simonds V.
[166] Ibid, 778, per Simonds V.
[167] Ibid, 781, per Simonds V.
[168] Ibid, 782, per Cohen LJ.

The House in *McGhee* did not take options two and three: again, as above, although the characterisation of the legal significance of the judgements is arguable (which is part of the point), they came closest to the first of the above options, ie employing a fiction. In doing so, the Lords contributed to the growing momentum of a group of cases which were inquiring into the values, vulnerabilities and interests at stake in this area, including the vulnerabilities of workers in industrial conditions to long-term diseases, and the interests of employers in not having placed on them too-extensive obligations. The Lords contributed to the momentum, thereby also respecting the law's past, but not so assertively as to create a new rule or a new exception. Instead, they deployed a fiction, and they communicated to future courts that change might be required.

C. After *McGhee*

i. Wilsher

Change, however, took some time. When *McGhee* next came up for extensive consideration by the House, in *Wilsher v Essex Area Health Authority*,[169] the opinion about *McGhee* that seemed to have prevailed, was the following:

> The conclusion I draw … is that *McGhee* laid down no new principle of law whatever. On the contrary, it affirmed the principle that the onus of proving causation lies on the pursuer or plaintiff. Adopting a robust and pragmatic approach to the undisputed primary facts of the case, the majority concluded that it was a legitimate inference of fact that the defenders' negligence had materially contributed to the pursuer's injury. The decision, in my opinion, is of no greater significance than that and to attempt to extract from it some esoteric principle which in some way modifies, as a matter of law, the nature of the burden of proof of causation which a plaintiff or pursuer must discharged once he has established a relevant breach of duty is a fruitless one.[170]

This statement by Lord Justice Bridge has often been repeated, in both judgements and in scholarship. It is perhaps sometimes overlooked that the specific and immediate context in which Lord Bridge referred to *McGhee* not laying down a new principle was that of shifting the onus: one could thus rephrase the above statement to say that '*McGhee* laid down no new principle as to the shift of onus'. Even, however, if one argued for such an interpretation, the passage is an extraordinarily confident one: it certainly seeks to minimise, if not pull the rug entirely underneath, the legal significance of *McGhee*.

My point here is to not argue whether this was the best interpretation of *McGhee* or not: the point, instead, is that it was an available one, ie an option precisely made possible by the House in *McGhee* having adopted a fiction. Disagreement about the legal significance of *McGhee* was possible, and that alone is a matter of considerable interest for any student of common law reasoning: its significance was not static, but subject to re-evaluation, including even complete quarantining of it as having any legal significance whatever. Although such re-evaluation is always possible to a degree, the use of a

[169] *Wilsher* (1988).
[170] Ibid, 1090, per Bridge LJ.

fiction arguably increases the scope of possible re-interpretations: one can, once again, treat the case as having been decided solely on its facts, or one can treat it as having established, but not fully articulated, a new rule or a new exception to a rule.

ii. Fairchild

That it was possible to treat *McGhee* as having established a new rule or a new exception to a rule came into view most clearly in the case of *Fairchild v Glenhaven Funeral Services Ltd*,[171] decided just over 30 years after *McGhee*. In *Fairchild*, the issue once again was proof of causation. As with *McGhee*, the case involved industrial employment and the suffering of a disease (this time, mesothelioma, caused by inhaling asbestos dust) over a long period of time. The potentially very considerable difference with *McGhee*, however, was that there was more than one employer, it being uncertain in which course of employment Mr Fairchild inhaled the asbestos dust that caused him to suffer mesothelioma. What significance, then, should *McGhee* have for Mr Fairchild's case, and, given the concern for the quality of the law in the future, for cases potentially like Mr Fairchild's?

Here, the House once more disagreed, though it is plausible to argue that the majority view was that *McGhee* did establish a new rule or a new exception to a rule, which now, in *Fairchild*, could be made explicit. In other words, now, with the benefit of time, and not only the accumulation of the cases, stretching at least from *Bonnington*, but also including jurisprudence from other legal systems, as well as the now-quite large scholarship, the case could be de-fictionalised, its tentative gropings replaced with a more assertively articulated rule. Over time, we had become wiser as to the possible sets of facts, and also with the values, vulnerabilities and interests that were at stake. We were now, collectively, in a much better position than before to articulate a better principle, eg one that we could limit more accurately than we could before.

That the House in *Fairchild* did seek to articulate, with more confidence, a new rule was clear from a number of the judgements. Lord Justice Bingham, for instance, opened in a style that could itself be subject to literary analysis and historicisation:

> The essential question underlying the appeals [in *Fairchild*] may be accurately expressed in this way. If (1) C was employed at different times and for differing periods by both A and B, and (2) A and B were both subject to a duty to take reasonable care or to take all practicable measures to prevent C inhaling asbestos dust because of the known risk that asbestos dust (if inhaled) might cause a mesothelioma, and (3) both A and B were in breach of that duty in relation to C during the periods of C's employment by each of them with the result that during both periods C inhaled excessive quantities of asbestos dust, and (4) C is found to be suffering from a mesothelioma, and (5) any cause of C's mesothelioma other than the inhalation of asbestos dust at work can be effectively discounted, but (6) C cannot (because of the current limits of human science) prove, on the balance of probabilities, that his mesothelioma was the result of his inhaling asbestos dust during his employment by A or by B or during his employment by A and B taken together, is C entitled to recover damages against either A or B or against both A and B?[172]

[171] *Fairchild* (2003).
[172] Ibid, 40, per Bingham LJ.

The use of multiple numbering and capitalised letters (A, B, C), is a style that presents itself as scientific, having stripped itself of any reference to facts that tie it too closely to the facts. No such style is visible in *McGhee*. It is a style that bespeaks confidence and a determination to offer more determinative guidance for future courts. And, accordingly, Lord Bingham was quick to say, with respect to *McGhee*, that it was 'preferable', when characterising the legal significance of *McGhee*, not to 'resort to fictions', but instead, 'in the interests of transparency', to state 'the courts' response to the special problem presented by cases such as these … explicitly'.[173] What were the 'cases such as these'? They were precisely cases that had the six conditions identified in the passage above. Where a case had such six conditions satisfied, 'it seems to me just and in accordance with common sense to treat the conduct of A and B in exposing C to a risk to which he should not have been exposed as making a material contribution to the contracting by C of a condition against which it was the duty of A and B to protect him'.[174] What was the legal significance of *McGhee* in this account? For Lord Bingham, it seems, what was decided in *McGhee* was that, as a matter of law, 'in the circumstances no distinction was to be drawn between making a material contribution to causing the disease and materially increasing the risk of the pursuer contracting it'; this, his Lordship said, was 'the ratio of the decision, closely tied though it was to the special facts on which it was based'.[175]

One can see in Lord Bingham's judgement still some hesitation about just how strongly to characterise what was decided in *McGhee*: although it decided a question of law, it was 'in the circumstances' and 'closely tied' to its 'special facts'. Nevertheless, despite the hesitation with respect to *McGhee*, Lord Bingham does not hesitate to articulate a general rule.

Lord Justices Hoffmann, Nichols and Rodger also agreed with Lord Bingham that *McGhee* changed the law. Lord Hoffmann was perhaps the most forthright of all the Lords in this respect: 'the House [in *McGhee*] decided that materially increasing the risk that the disease would occur was sufficient to satisfy the causal requirements for liability'.[176] Like Lord Bingham, Lord Hoffmann appeared to suggest that it was possible that *McGhee* had employed a fiction, but in any event, even if that were so, it should now be taken to have changed the law:

> There are … passages in the speeches which suggest that materially increasing the risk of disease is being treated as equivalent to materially contributing to the injury – making the illness worse than it would otherwise have been. But this, as Lord Wilberforce pointed out … is precisely what the doctors did not say. They refused to say that it was more likely than not that the absence of washing facilities had had any effect at all. So when some members of the House said that in the circumstances there was no distinction between materially increasing the risk of disease and materially contributing to the disease, what I think they meant was that, in the particular circumstances, a breach of duty which materially increased the risk should be treated *as if* it had materially contributed to the disease. I would respectfully prefer not to resort to legal fictions and to say that the House treated a material increase in risk as

[173] Ibid, 68.
[174] Ibid.
[175] Ibid, 55.
[176] Ibid, 75, per Hoffmann LJ.

> sufficient in the circumstances to satisfy the causal requirements for liability. That this was the effect of the decision seems to me inescapable.[177]

We see here what the fiction in *McGhee* enables: with the passage of time, a later court can de-fictionalise the case, characterising it now as having decided, even if not as explicitly as it might have, a new rule, ie that for a certain type of case material contribution is no longer required to be proved, and that it is now sufficient to prove material increase in risk. But what 'type of case'? After all, this question needs to be answered if one is providing a rule. Here, Lord Hoffmann, like Lord Bingham, though possibly even more explicitly, sought to give guidance, and thus also set some limitations on the rule:

> What are the significant features of the present case? First, we are dealing with a duty specifically to protect employees against being unnecessarily exposed to the risk of (among other things) a particular disease. Secondly, the duty is one intended to create a civil right to compensation for injury relevantly connected with its breach. Thirdly, it is established that the greater the exposure to asbestos, the greater the risk of contracting that disease. Fourthly, except in the case in which there has been only one significant exposure to asbestos, medical science cannot prove whose asbestos is more likely than not to have produced the cell mutation which caused the disease. Fifthly, the employee has contracted the disease against which he should have been protected.[178]

When these five features are present, said Lord Hoffmann, the 'rule' that 'would be more in accord with justice and the policy of common law and statute to protect employees against the risk of contracting asbestos-related diseases' would be 'one which makes an employer in breach of his duty liable for the employees injury because he created a significant risk to his health, despite the fact that the physical cause of the injury may have been created by someone else'.[179] With the passage of time, arguably, the judges are now in a better position to see what values, vulnerabilities and interests are at stake. The fiction, in short, enables the judges to inquire, and in doing so, it helps them better to balance respect for the law's past, doing justice in the instance case, and caring for the quality of the law in the future.

Of course, for all the confidence I have suggested characterises *Fairchild*, at least in comparison with, say, *McGhee*, the case still limits itself in all kinds of ways. Thus, for instance, the five features set out by Lord Hoffmann, or even, though perhaps to a lesser extent, the six conditions articulated by Lord Bingham, are still relatively close to the facts in *Fairchild*: they still hesitate to go too far beyond the circumstances, both for example referring to diseases caused by exposure to asbestos. Much is still left possible. Although it does seek to introduce a new rule (replacing the language of material contribution with material increase in risk in a certain type of case), it also limits the scope of the applicability of any such rule, anchoring it still at least relatively close to the facts of the case. It still allows, even if less openly than *McGhee*, for its legal significance to be re-interpreted in subsequent cases.

[177] Ibid, 75; original emphasis.
[178] Ibid, 74.
[179] Ibid, 74–5.

iii. Beyond Fairchild

Post *Fairchild*, the inquiry continued and continues still: cases such as *Baker v Corus*, *Sienkiewicz v Grief*, *BAI v Durham*, and *Zurich*[180] have returned again and again to *McGhee* and to *Fairchild*, and to *Fairchild's* re-characterisation of *McGhee*.[181] The common law churns over its cases over and over. The repetition is important, as is the constant re-characterisation, including to some extent re-description of the facts of the past cases in light of the present facts and, also, in light of now further possibly similar cases in the future.

What I have sought to show is that what counts in this story is not just attempts to articulate a new rule or a new exception to a rule, though that can happen, and does in *Fairchild*, but that there are other ways in which certain attitudes are communicated, certain new terms of phrase proposed, and in general ways in which time and space is created for further inquiry. This is so not only as between the judges, but also scholars and, in this context, experts from medical science and the industrial employment context. One of those ways is through the use of a fiction, and the ways in which it, as an artefact, signals artifice, inviting others to do things with it, ie to imagine, supposing something has been proven when it has not been, and considering whether to extend the fiction or to end it.

In this string of cases, the fiction in *McGhee* is, over time, extinguished: the case is said, in *Fairchild*, to have changed the law. This is as it should be: it shows the fiction working well. The judges, and scholars, after *McGhee* were irritated by the fiction: that is the fiction doing its job, ie precisely signalling artifice by displaying a contradiction or tension between what was taken to be proved and what was known to have been proven. It triggered the imaginations of those who came after, and, in so doing, enabled interactive and collective inquiry over time into what values, vulnerabilities and interests were at stake in this area. Were the fiction to become entrenched, it would no longer signal artifice, no longer irritate, no longer invite others to imagine, and thus no longer enable inquiry. It would then cease to be valuable. But the fiction in *McGhee* is not like that: it remained an irritant and a trigger for imagining, and it was thus of value to adjudication.

[180] See, eg, *Baker v Corus* [2006] 2 AC 572; *Sienkiewicz v Greif* [2011] 2 WLR 523; *BAI (Run Off) Ltd v Durham* [2012] 1 WLR 867; and *Zurich Insurance Plc UK Branch v International Energy Group Ltd* [2016] AC 509.

[181] See also, eg, Steel (2015).

6

Metaphors

Like fictions, though perhaps to an even greater extent, metaphors have sometimes been proposed as foundational for human cognition. As we saw in the last chapter, when Lon Fuller turned to consider fictions as a 'linguistic phenomenon', he quickly began to speak of metaphors, and the role of metaphorical language in legal change. The history of theorising about rhetoric and figurative language has also often been dominated by metaphor. It has, for example, often been called the 'master trope'. Of late, under the influence especially of the work of George Lakoff and Mark Johnson,[1] as well as others theorising language from the perspective of second-generation cognitive science, metaphor has become the *sine qua non* of thought. Both in our less-than-conscious, habitual action, but also as the engine of creativity, metaphor is said by many to be indispensable and even inevitable. As Raymond Gibbs observes in his recent *Metaphor Wars*, which looks at the heated debates in scholarship on metaphor: 'Metaphor scholars are often fanatical in their pursuit of metaphoricity in language and life'.[2] All this has resulted in a mushrooming of the literature on metaphor, and this from many disciplinary perspectives, including philosophy, psychology, neuroscience, the social sciences and of course linguistics. Legal scholars, too, have paid attention to metaphor – again, arguably more than to any other feature of language – often in ways that are inspired mainly by Lakoff and Johnson.[3]

This increased attention, as welcome as it is, makes it very difficult to theorise metaphor. We come precisely to see it everywhere, in almost any use of language, and in almost any mental operation. Within 'Conceptual Metaphor Theory' (CMT), metaphors have come to be characterised as 'fundamental tools that structure how people ordinarily think about abstract ideas and events', such that 'people's understanding of many aspects of everyday reality is constituted by enduring metaphorical schemes of thought'.[4] They are all pervasive and inescapable: they 'arise whenever we try to understand difficult, complex, or less delineated concepts'.[5] CMT has generated many profound and important insights about metaphor, but also beyond: for example, CMT has greatly encouraged exploration of the relations between embodiment, language and thought, and this has been hugely significant. However, because of the expansive, if not

[1] Lakoff and Johnson (1980). Their approach has come to be called 'Conceptual Metaphor Theory'.
[2] Gibbs (2017), 1.
[3] See, eg, through the work of Steven Winter and Linda Berger. I will be returning to this scholarship below.
[4] Gibbs (2017), 3.
[5] Ibid, 4.

'fanatical', scope of its theorising, it has also made it more difficult to see some of the specific work that metaphor does.

In this chapter, I seek to learn from CMT, but at the same time resist its stretching, or over-estimation, of metaphor. For instance, I agree with CMT that metaphor is no mere ornament or mere instrument of persuasion, and that it plays a very significant role in our experience of language and in making certain kinds of mental operations possible. However, rather than focusing on it as all-pervasive, and as structuring so much of our mental life, often less-than-consciously, I attempt instead to articulate it as a specific kind of artefact, with related specific processes of imagination.

Within the context of this book, this also means distinguishing metaphor from the three other case studies being considered in this second part, namely fictions, figures and scenarios:

1. A metaphor is not a fiction, for metaphors signal artifice differently to fictions, ie they do not involve setting up tensions or contradictions between what is supposed to have been proven and what is known to have been proven. They are also different kinds of processes of imagination: whereas fictions involve supposition, which are a weak mode of participation in imagination, processing metaphors involves much higher degrees of participation in imagination, ie much more involvement along the scale of affective, sensory and kinesic participation.
2. Metaphors are also not figures: the latter involve specific uses of the figure of the human person, including selective attribution of certain features of personhood, and they also involve specific kinds of processes of imagination, eg enactment of simulated movement from the perspective of an imaginary figure. Further, figures and metaphors tend to be expressed via different typical linguistic forms, eg whereas figures might employ capitalisation, as in the 'Officious Bystander', they do not ordinarily employ identity statements in the way metaphors do, eg 'Juliet is the sun'.
3. And metaphors are not scenarios, for the latter are at least more explicitly narrative-based than metaphors, even if it is true that some metaphors may also involve some narrative-based cognition, eg one could speak of allegory as a narrative-based metaphorical process.

My argument is not that there is no overlap between metaphor on the one side, and fictions, figures and scenarios on the other. It would be surprising indeed if there were not some overlap. Rather, the argument is that it is beneficial to seek out what is unique and specific about each of them as artefacts and related processes of imagination. If we do that, we may then be better able to see how they can contribute, in unique ways, to enabling inquiry.

To recall: the aim of these four chapters in this second part of this book is not to offer comprehensive theories of fictions, metaphors, figures and scenarios. It is to present them as case studies of the overall framework developed in part one of this book. Thus, in what follows, I examine metaphors in relation to the three models of part one, ie considering metaphors as artefacts and related processes of imagination, with the focus on trying to show how they can enable inquiry.

Metaphors are specific kinds of artefacts: they signal artifice in specific ways, ie either by employing identity statements, eg 'Juliet is the sun', 'sorrow is a cloak', or by juxtaposing one context of meaning to another, eg inviting a reader to relate a government and its subjects to the Queen Bee and worker bees. These identity statements or juxtapositions of contexts surprise us and put us on epistemic alert; they disorient us and interrupt us; they create tension, discordance or incongruity; and they imbalance our usual associations or what we ordinarily take to be meaningful. In doing so, they call upon us to do something with them, ie to explore how one might resolve the tension, discordance or incongruity between the different parts of the metaphor or the juxtaposed contexts.

As processes of imagination, metaphors involve entering a distinctive epistemic frame, and constructing an epistemic attitude where we suspend, the otherwise-relied-on norms of, say, referentiality or identity, and/or loosen our usual commitment to relevance. At the same time as entering a distinctive epistemic frame, we also participate, and we do so at a high level along the spectrum of affective, sensory and kinesic involvement.

Articulating the mode of participation in metaphorical imagining is the most difficult but also the most important part of understanding the value of metaphor. In brief, for I shall be returning to this in more detail, the process is a multi-stage one, involving iterative feedback amongst the various stages: 1) we experience surprise, as well as some pleasure and delight in the surprise, of the relations between parts of the metaphor or the juxtaposed contexts; 2) we dwell, though already to some extent guided by the 'target', eg 'Juliet', in the 'source', eg 'the sun', simulating affectively, eg our emotional associations with the sun, eg happiness and joy, constructing mental imagery, eg brightness/light, and simulating kinesically, eg experience of warmth; and 3) we return to the target, superimposing the results of our participation onto the target, enriching and re-orienting our understanding of the target accordingly. Even to separate out these stages, and to refer to 'sources' and 'targets', risks being misleading, for, to repeat, there is typically considerable feedback between them: we often move back and forth, for instance, between the second and third stage, all the while experiencing the strange pleasure and delight of the incongruity, and its momentary resolutions. Furthermore, this multi-stage process is often not one we engage in individually, but which we often do in the company of others, either in the real time of a conversation or over time in discourse.

This last point concerning the diachronicity of metaphors is important. As with all the case studies being considered in this book, metaphors cannot be understood as having the same, static effect over time: the way they work, and what effects they have, changes over time. Put another way, the artefactual character of metaphors, ie their capacity to capture our attention by signalling their own artifice, is relative and contingent: for instance, it is in part based on what we conventionally take to be a different context of meaning. This matters a great deal for any argument that can be made on behalf of metaphors as enabling inquiry. To the extent that metaphors work as artefacts, and thus invite us successfully to imagine, ie entering distinctive epistemic frames and participating, they can be valuable for inquiry. They can do so because, at the individual level, they connect to us as affective and embodied creatures, who rely on our affects and our bodies to make normative insights. At the two social levels of inquiry, namely the interactive and collective levels, they are ways of involving other affective and embodied creatures, facilitating interactive and collective explorations of resolving the tension, discordance or incongruity set up by different parts of a metaphor or the juxtaposed contexts.

Precisely because, and to the extent that, they put us on epistemic alert, metaphors can signal the need for further inquiry. Not only can they signal the need for further inquiry, but they also generate resources, and more so than fictions: to speak of Juliet as the sun, for instance, is to guide our explorations in particular ways, eg it makes it less salient to think of Juliet as the moon. Metaphors do guide inquiry, but they do so gently, precisely because they allow for multiple, even contradictory, explorations of possible resolutions, and they are thereby also of considerable political value. They may be of particular value with respect to especially sensitive and controversial issues, for they give some guidance on how to approach the issue, while allowing for considerable disagreement, indeed calling for on-going, interactive and collective, discussion.

Metaphors, then, when they work as artefacts, successfully inviting us to imagine, are ways of signalling attitudes and generating resources over time. They help us as individuals, as interacting persons, and as communities, to make insight into what values, vulnerabilities and interests may be at stake in a certain case and others potentially like it in the future. They help us balance respect for the law's past, doing justice in the instant case, and caring for the quality of the law in the future.

That is, in broad brushstrokes, the argument of this chapter. I develop it in two sections: first, a general section that situates, though very selectively and necessarily briefly, my own approach to metaphor amongst other approaches in the literature; and second, a more concrete section, involving the discussion of the metaphors employed in *Edwards v Attorney-General of Canada*,[6] including attention to their work over time.

I. Approaching Metaphors

It can often be easier to show how one is not approaching a certain phenomenon, than to articulate exactly how one is. Being as slippery as it is, metaphor is a good example of this. I shall therefore begin with how I am not inclined to think of metaphor. I resist attempts to: 1) characterise metaphor as mere optional ornament, or present it as a mere exercise of persuasion; 2) explain metaphorical uses of language as less-than-conscious influences of certain allegedly basic embodied experiences or orientations; and 3) reduce metaphor to a condensed simile, with related views that characterise it as a kind of analogical process, or one principally concerned with comparison of similarities and differences between the two sides of a metaphor. Having done so, we shall be in a better position to carve out a different approach, one that takes its cue from those theorists, eg IA Richards and Max Black, and more recently, Ted Cohen, David Hills, Elisabeth Camp and Richard Moran, many of whom seek to move beyond a comparison view of metaphor, and emphasise the multi-stage, iterative feedback and communicative aspects of metaphor and our experience of it.

[6] *Edwards v The Attorney General of Canada* [1930] AC 124. Subsequent references to this case are in the form of *Edwards* (1930).

A. Conceptual Metaphor Theory

As mentioned above, the dominant approach to metaphor in contemporary scholarship is the CMT. First articulated by George Lakoff and Mark Johnson in the early 1980s, CMT has gone on to influence scholarship in metaphor in just about every discipline and by reference to just about every area of discourse. As Gibbs has recently summarised it, an important motivation for CMT from the outset was the questioning of the status of metaphor as mere optional ornament, as nothing but a superfluous 'rhetorical device'.[7] CMT does acknowledge that some persons may use metaphor 'to express ideas that are difficult to convey using literal language, to state something in a compact manner, to memorably capture the vividness of our phenomenological experience, and, at times, to be polite'.[8] However, CMT insists that, in fact, metaphors are much more ingrained in our language and our thought than such limited purposes suggest. As I do in this book, and as many other theorists have in the revival of contemporary interest of metaphor, CMT resists the characterisation of metaphor as optional and superfluous. However, the way in which it resists this, pays a high price. I would argue too high a price: by articulating metaphor as fundamental, inescapable, inevitable and all-pervasive to human language and thought, it makes it more difficult to see some of the specific work that metaphor can do, especially insofar as it can enable inquiry.

Before going on to briefly explain CMT's approach, I want to emphasise that I share with it another motivation that was also present clearly from the outset amongst pioneers of CMT. CMT was developed against the background of second-generation cognitive science. As described in Chapter 2, a key aspect of this second-generation approach is emphasis on embodiment, including the role of the body in the process of making, communicating and understanding meaning in language. For CMT, to speak of metaphor is to look for ways in which meaning-making, including in the most complex and abstract of discourses, always involves the body. As Gibbs puts it, for CMT adherents, 'to maintain that metaphors are constitutive of the way people think offers a radical departure from long-standing beliefs in the literal, purely computational, highly disembodied ways people understand themselves and the world around them'.[9] From the outset, CMT theorists sought to articulate the relations between 'recurring patterns of bodily activity' and 'metaphorical understandings of many abstract concepts'.[10]

Bridging the gap between the body on the one hand, and language and thought on the other, is a motivation that I share, as I hope has been clear throughout this book. However, CMT, in its eagerness to depart from the 'traditional' view, may have tied the connection too tightly, at least with respect to some metaphors, and some processing of them. Thus, in this book, I approach metaphor with a view to acknowledging how the

[7] Gibbs (2017), 3.
[8] Ibid.
[9] Ibid, 16.
[10] Ibid, 7.

use and processing of metaphor appeals to the body, eg signalling artifice by creating kinesic discordance, and by involving us in simulating kinesically as we explore different ways of resolving the discordance. But I resist CMT's specific way of tying the connection between the body and metaphor, at least with respect to metaphors that we can characterise as artefacts, with related processes of imagination.

i. Image-Schemas

CMT's approach to metaphor is to argue that 'the source domains in conceptual metaphors are often tied to people's bodily actions and experiences'.[11] These source domains refer to a wide range of 'bodily behaviours and experiences, such as body parts, the physical condition of the body, animals we physically interact with, physically growing things in nature, building things, game-playing activities, cooking, physical sensations, physical forces, and various bodily movements'.[12] Despite this variety, what these source domains all have in common is that they revert back to, and rely on, certain allegedly basic recurring patterns of bodily actions and experiences. CMT theorists speak of these basic recurring patterns as 'image schemas', ie 'dynamic analog representations of spatial relations and movements in space', which 'have internal logic or structure that determines their roles in structuring various abstract concepts and in patterns of reasoning'.[13] These image-schemas are said to be constitutive of our language and thought, for it is by reference to them that we generate the metaphors that structure our language and thought. It is thus an important part of the theory that 'source to target domain mappings in conceptual metaphors generally preserve the image-schematic structure of the source domain'.[14]

Take any metaphor, argue CMT advocates, and you can trace it back to one or more image-schemas that determine it, and that structure our language and thought accordingly. This is best illustrated with examples. Take the following expressions:

- 'Greta is making good progress toward her PhD degree'.
- 'John has already reached several career goals'.
- 'David ran into a rough patch trying to solve the difficult math problem'.
- 'Sandra was completely stuck figuring out what to do after her divorce'.[15]

These are expressions we may encounter in everyday life. Indeed, one of the characteristics of CMT has been that it has looked for, and found, metaphors in all domains of language use, including both technical uses in specific contexts, as well as everyday uses. This has been crucial to CMT's strategy to show that metaphor is fundamental, inescapable, inevitable and all-pervasive.

To return to these examples, a CMT approach would argue 'that these expressions are conventional manifestations of an underlying metaphor in thought, namely

[11] Ibid, 23.
[12] Ibid.
[13] Ibid.
[14] Ibid, 25.
[15] Ibid, 17.

the LIFE IS A JOURNEY conceptual metaphor'.[16] This conceptual metaphor is based on a basic, recurring bodily action and experience, the image-schema of SOURCE-PATH-GOAL. This image-schema 'emerges from a variety of bodily experiences, such as when a person starts moving from one point toward another along some path with the intention of reaching a specific destination'.[17] This image-schema, as with all image-schemas, can be extended in all kinds of ways, eg as we can see in the metaphor of LIFE IS A JOURNEY. As Gibbs explains:

> … certain conventional statements about life are motivated by the LIFE IS A JOURNEY conceptual metaphor in which JOURNEY is structured by the SOURCE-PATH-GOAL schema. This image-schema is mapped onto the target domain such that … we find the correspondences that people leading a life are travellers, leading a life is motion along the path, purposes in life are destinations, progress in life is distance covered along the path, and so on. In this manner, the target domain (eg LIFE) is more specifically conceptualised via the coherent image-schematic structure of the source domain (eg JOURNEY).[18]

It is important to see that for CMT, these 'source-to-target domain correspondences … are not simply a list of features in common between LIFE and JOURNEY', and this 'is precisely because conceptual metaphors help establish a more structured conceptualisation of the target domain.'[19] Thus, the point here is not that LIFE and JOURNEYS 'share the same exact features regarding travellers, paths, destinations, and so on'.[20] Rather, 'the mapping of JOURNEY experiences onto the idea of LIFE creates the specific inferences', as in the above correspondences, eg that 'people leading a life are travellers', etc.[21] Notice that this 'mapping', or this 'drawing of inferences', is 'generally, but not always, unidirectional. We can understand LIFE in terms of JOURNEYS, but the mapping of LIFE onto JOURNEYS makes less sense.'[22]

Apart from its 'general' unidirectionality, what is also significant about this approach is that the above 'structured conceptualisation of the target domain' manifests itself in 'mostly conventional words and phrases',[23] like those in the examples above. 'Conventional metaphorical statements', on this view 'are concrete, linguistic manifestations of these different inferences',[24] made possible by the relevant image-schema. CMT's explanatory strategy is clear: look at the most conventional uses of language, ie often those that we do not give one moment's attention to as language, and look beneath them, to the underlying image-schemas that structure them. A CMT theorist then asserts a very tight link between basic, recurring bodily actions and experiences and even, or especially, the most conventional of all language uses. One can see how this can quickly take on 'fanatical' proportions, in which almost any language use can be traced back to some basic, recurring bodily action and experience.

[16] Ibid.
[17] Ibid, 24.
[18] Ibid, 25.
[19] Ibid, 18.
[20] Ibid.
[21] Ibid.
[22] Ibid.
[23] Ibid.
[24] Ibid.

ii. Deliberate Metaphors

I want to emphasise that there is much to learn from this approach, not only about metaphor, but, more fittingly, about language and thought as a whole. And, as we shall see in a moment, it is an approach that quite a few legal scholars have also found attractive. However, from my perspective, there is one basic difficulty with this approach: it focuses precisely on conventional uses of language. It thereby misses, or at least does not emphasise the importance of, what I have been calling artefacts, ie modes of language use that signal their own artifice, attracting our attention to themselves as means of communication. Signalling artifice, as I have argued, calls upon us to do something with the artefact, and this is a process that is at least sometimes, if not often, difficult, requiring some effort, though also not one without its own pleasures and delights. The related process of imagining a metaphor involves entering a distinctive epistemic frame where we selectively suspend certain epistemic norms and commitments (which ones may depend on the metaphor), and we actively participate, simulating affectively, sensorially and kinesically. Although this process is not exclusively conscious and deliberate, for it is likely to involve elements that are less-than-conscious, nevertheless it is on the whole much more conscious and deliberate than the kind of processing and experience that accompanies the use of conventional terms and phrases.

Of course, debates over CMT have included their fair share of criticisms and defences roughly along these lines, namely that CMT ignores or downplays metaphors that are not, or are less, conventional, or so-called deliberate or purposeful metaphors. CMT has dealt with this in various ways, eg by suggesting that, in fact, most 'novel' or a-typical, non-conventional, metaphors 'often are crafted extensions or elaborations of conceptual metaphors',[25] or, more interestingly, by introducing a different category of metaphors, namely 'image metaphors', which are said to 'express the mapping of mental images but not concepts'.[26] Thus, for instance, the statement 'My wife whose hair is brush fire' (André Breton) is said to involve 'mapping our mental image of a brush fire onto the domain of Breton's wife's hair, which gives rise to various concrete images in regard to the colour, texture and shape of her hair'.[27] This is interesting, and I shall be proposing something related with respect to certain metaphors as artefacts, but it is also telling that CMT presents this as a different category of metaphor, and one placed in opposition to concepts, ie as an image, not a conceptual metaphor.

The case for the uniqueness of deliberate or purposeful metaphors has been articulated perhaps most prominently by Gerard Steen:

> I propose that a metaphor is deliberately used when it is expressly meant to change the addressee's perspective on the referent or topic that is the target of the metaphor, by making the addressee look at it from a different conceptual domain or space, which functions as a conceptual source. In such cases as 'Juliet is the sun', this is precisely what is being asked of the addressee. The utterance expresses a blatant falsehood, while drawing attention to the new information presented at the end of the sentence that causes the falsehood, 'sun'. It cannot be anything but a deliberate invitation for the addressee to adopt a different perspective of

[25] Ibid, 44.
[26] Ibid, 46.
[27] Ibid. See Lakoff and Turner (1989) for details and discussion.

> Juliet from a truly alien domain that is consciously introduced as a source for reviewing the target.[28]

For Steen, there is a distinct class of metaphors that are 'deliberately, consciously produced for their special communicative possibilities'.[29] This is argued to be a class different from that of conventional metaphors. In conventional metaphors, 'it is quite dubious whether the addressee is in fact being asked to actually change their perspective on the topic of the sentence'.[30] By contrast, in the case of deliberate metaphors, this is 'a relatively conscious discourse strategy that aims to elicit particular rhetorical effects'.[31]

Not everyone agrees. Gibbs, for instance, is quite sceptical of drawing the line, as Steen does, between deliberate and non-deliberate metaphors. As he puts it, 'there are significant problems with interpreting certain textual signals as necessarily reflecting particular states of mind (ie deliberate consciousness), especially when these signals are used with other aspects of language'.[32] For Gibbs, further, 'people do not first recognise anomalies', as with, arguably, deliberate metaphors, 'and only then derive appropriate metaphorical meanings'.[33]

These points all have their merits. Thus, I share some of Gibbs' scepticism as to how much we can rely on certain states of mind being present when certain metaphors are articulated. And I understand Gibbs' reluctance to ascribe some necessary first stage of recognising anomalies for many, if not most, metaphors. Nevertheless, there is room for something like Steen's category of deliberate metaphors. Even if they may have some less-than-conscious elements, some metaphors are surely proposed as communicative devices, signalling certain kinds of attitudes, and generating certain kinds of resources.

It may, however, be too strong to say, as Steen does, that these deliberate metaphors 'aim to elicit particular rhetorical effects'. Partly, this depends of course on what one means by 'particular rhetorical effects', and I would insist that even if some aspect of certain uses of metaphor have intentions to persuade, that need not be their only or even most important purpose, let alone effect. The general point is that we need not place so much explanatory pressure on the intention behind the use of the metaphor: when a metaphor functions as an artefact, as it may contingently do, those on the receiving end of the metaphor, ie its readers or listeners, can experience it as signalling artifice, namely as attracting their attention to its use as a means of communication, inviting them to do something with it. We need not overlay the experience of encountering a metaphor with any intention with which it may be articulated: a metaphor can signal artifice, and be experienced as an artefact, even without an intention that it be experienced as one, and, relatedly, it may not be experienced as an artefact even if it is intended as one.

Further, the effect of a metaphor, ie how it may lead others to imagine in the future, will not be controlled by any intention with which it may be made. That is, indeed, part of its value, especially for interactive dynamics and for a community over time. Again,

[28] Steen (2008), 222; quoted in Gibbs (2017), 84.
[29] Gibbs (2017), 83.
[30] Steen (2008), 222; quoted in Gibbs (2017), 84.
[31] Steen (2008), 223; quoted in Gibbs (2017), 85. See also Krenmayr (2011).
[32] Gibbs (2017), 89.
[33] Ibid, 84.

even if the processing of some metaphors may involve making inferences as to what might have been the intentions of those who expressed it, it would be a mistake to pin down the effect of a metaphor to those intentions. The effect of metaphors leaks considerably beyond any intentions with which they may have been expressed. Importantly, for present purposes, to recognise that any intention with which a metaphor may have been expressed need not dominate or exhaust our understanding of how metaphors are encountered and experienced, or our understanding of their effects over time, is perfectly compatible with recognising a distinct category of non-conventional metaphors, ie metaphors precisely that we experience, contingently, as artefacts with related processes of imagination. Put another way, Steen and others are right that CMT has tended to focus too much, if not exclusively, on conventional metaphors, but we need not push this legitimate critique so far as to make our theories of the processing and effects of metaphor dependent on the role of any intentions with which metaphors may be expressed.

iii. CMT in Legal Scholarship

CMT is a powerful theory and has much to offer any student of language and thought. I share its motivation to take metaphor seriously, and thus not to treat it as but an optional, superfluous ornament. I also share its motivation to theorise metaphor by paying closing attention to how it involves the body, and thus to the relations between embodiment, language and thought. What I resist is an explanatory strategy that seeks to explain, almost as if explaining away, the generative and indeed rhetorical effects of metaphor by tracing it back to allegedly basic image-schemas. By 'rhetorical effects', however, I do not mean the persuasive intention with which a speaker or author of a metaphor may utter it. As much as that may sometimes be so, not all metaphors are uttered with the intention to persuade, and even those that are, their use may have other motivations and will, in any event, have unpredictable, unintentional effects on its listeners or readers.

Metaphor is undoubtedly important for thought, but it may be too strong to say it is 'constitutive' of it or 'determines' or even 'structures' it. Metaphor is one of a number of artefacts, with related processes of imagination: it is important for language and thought, but other artefacts, eg fictions, figures and scenarios, are also equally important. Further, if we focus on what we do with metaphor – when, at least, it functions as an artefact for us – then we can also see how it generates resources, guiding a discourse or discussion gently, but not going so far as to determine it or structure it.

As noted above, a number of legal scholars have found CMT to be an attractive theory. We have encountered some of these theorists already in this book, eg Mark Johnson, Steven Winter, and Linda Berger. This is important work. It has helped us to raise vital questions and better understand relations between embodiment, emotion, aesthetics and legal language and legal thought.

For instance, in his recent book, *The Aesthetics of Meaning and Thought*,[34] Johnson, drawing in part on Winter[35] and others, argues for the pervasive and inescapable role of

[34] Johnson (2018).
[35] Winter (2001).

metaphor in structuring certain legal concepts, and therefore also guiding the development of a certain area of the law. Johnson, like Winter, has sought to show how 'legal reasoning' is 'based on the assumption of particular metaphors that supported the inferences made by the justices.'[36] Johnson observes, for instance, that the concept of property 'is rooted in certain image schemas', which is both manifested and 'extended through metaphor', or, he adds, metonymy.[37] CMT, then, advocates for a particular kind of approach to legal concepts, and one that goes against the grain of many, still dominant approaches:

> The concept 'property' is not a classical category defined by a set of necessary and sufficient conditions. Instead, the concept is a vast radially structured category with a small number of central members or prototypical cases surrounded at various distances by noncentral members, according to principles of extension such as conceptual metaphor and metonymy.[38]

The facts of certain cases are already presented to judges by reference to certain 'frames', 'within which image-schemas, radial categories, and metaphors play a central role',[39] and judges rely on these frames, but also evaluate them and extend them, in making their judgements.

Once again, this is important work, and I have no doubt that it has much to teach us about the dynamics of legal reasoning.[40] Nevertheless, my approach is a different one: it does not seek to emphasise the determining or structuring effects of certain basic image-schemas, with extensions made by way of inferences that are allowed by the 'logic' of those schemas. The approach I take seeks to pay more attention to the generative effects of certain metaphors, especially over time, and thus by way of interactive and collective inquiry.

If we take metaphor as an artefact seriously, we also need to take seriously how it signals artifice to its readers, and how it calls upon them to do things with it. We then also need to take seriously what goes on when we imagine metaphorically, including not only how we do so as individuals, but how we do so interactively and collectively. What we do with metaphor, and how we imagine when we imagine metaphorically, is not something that can be wholly explained by tracing it back to being determined or structured by certain image-schemas. At least some metaphors are not susceptible to this approach, which works arguably better with conventional metaphors that work their influence on us without us noticing it much, if at all. Adding reflexivity matters a great deal, even if we must be careful not to push this so much as to anchor it in some fully-in-control directive consciousness.

B. Metaphor and Analogy

I have so far argued, together with the CMT approach, against a view of metaphor as mere ornament, and also argued, this time contra the CMT approach, against a view

[36] Johnson (2018), 194.
[37] Ibid, 195.
[38] Ibid.
[39] Ibid, 196.
[40] See also Bjerre (1999).

of metaphor as explicable on the basis of less-than-conscious processing. There is one more approach to metaphor that I mentioned I am resisting, namely an approach that presents metaphor as a kind of analogical process, concerned essentially with comparison of similarities and differences, and, in its most blatant form, identifying metaphor as but a condensed simile, ie 'condensed' because it does not explicitly refer to something being 'like' something else, but works nevertheless in the same way as something that does, ie a simile.

This is a tempting view, and, given the complexity of metaphor, and the many different kinds of examples of its use and experience, it is likely that it too, like CMT, has some important insights to offer a student of metaphor. It has also attracted its fair share of adherents amongst legal scholars. For instance, despite recognising the value of the work of IA Richards (to whom I shall return), including his criticism of the comparison view of metaphor, Perelman and Olbrechts-Tyteca focus in their discussion on metaphor on its role as analogy: 'In the context of argumentation', they say, 'we cannot better describe a metaphor than by conceiving it as a condensed analogy'.[41]

i. Novel/Conventional Metaphors Over Time

The analogical approach to metaphor has sometimes been presented as a distinct alternative to the CMT approach. In other words, scholars developing the analogical model have argued explicitly against the CMT model, and in ways that are not dissimilar to some of the points I have made above. For example, Dedre Gentner, Brian Bowdle, Phillip Wolff and Consuelo Boronat argued that whereas the CMT model may offer valuable insights on the role of conventional metaphors, it does less well with 'novel' metaphors, which are typically processed much more slowly and reflexively.[42] The idea is that what underlies metaphorical processing, including, if not especially, in the case of novel metaphors, are the mental operations of analogy: 'structural alignment, inference projection, progressive abstraction, and re-representation'.[43]

Significantly, too, this approach is sensitive to the diachronic dimensions of metaphor, ie how we process it, and also its effects, change over time. As explained by Linda Berger, who has drawn on this approach:

> In other words, when a reader encounters a novel metaphor, the reader recognises parallel features and structures shared by the target and the source, and then the reader creates new understanding by projecting inferences from the source to the target .... as metaphors move from being novel to becoming conventional, the reader switches her mental processing of the metaphor from making a comparison to fitting an unknown experience into a prior categorisation. As a result, according to these researchers, when the reader is interpreting a novel metaphor, she is engaged in creating meaning, but when the reader is interpreting a conventional metaphor, she is retrieving meaning from a mental storeroom.[44]

These are important insights, and I share with the analogical approach the attention paid to the differences between the processing of novel and conventional metaphors,

[41] Perelman and Olbrechts-Tyteca (1969), 399.
[42] See Gentner, Bowdle, Wolff, and Boronat (2001).
[43] Ibid, 243.
[44] Berger (2013), 170.

as well as to the shifts over time in how metaphors are experienced and what they generate.

Also important is that the advocates of the analogical approach criticise the largely unidirectional focus of CMT's analysis of metaphor. To recall, the CMT approach analysed the mapping between source and target in one direction: from the source to the target. For advocates of the analogical approach, this is a mistake, as Berger once again explains (also, helpfully, by reference to shifts in this dynamic over time):

> … rather than alignment and projection moving solely from the source to the target, Gentner and her colleagues found that understanding a metaphor begins with a symmetrical alignment process. Once an alignment is found, then further inferences are directionally projected from source to target. That is, directional inference building – from source to target – arises after the initial stage, but the initial stage is side-by-side. When we try to understand a novel metaphor, we structurally align concrete or literal representations of the source or target. As we repeat these comparisons over time, we can abstract a more general metaphorical meaning, and we begin to associate the abstract meaning with the source term. Through repeated instances of structural alignment, we inductively create metaphoric categories.[45]

For instance, when first faced with the (then) novel metaphor of 'the mind is a computer', 'the reader had to try to align the characteristics and relationships existing within a computer with those existing within a mind: for example, both appear to take in data and to process it before producing some kind of report.'[46] Later, however, when the metaphor became conventional, it was processed as one referring to a category ie 'the mind fits into the category of an information-processing mechanism'.[47] Again, the attention being paid here to the differences between processing novel and conventional metaphors, given their shifts from one to the other over time, is important, including the different speeds at which they are processed, and the different degrees of reflexivity and difficulty involved.

ii. The Poetic Power of Metaphor

However, questions remain: is the processing of metaphor, ie in my terminology, one that still functions, to some degree, as an artefact, and thus one that successfully invites imagination, explained adequately by seeing it as an analogical process? If we return to the example of 'the mind is a computer', is the processing of this metaphor explained adequately by the idea that what the reader does is look for similarities between the two? Despite its emphasis on the bi-directional character, at least in the initial stages, how well is this shown in the above example, where the reader is said to think that 'both [the mind and the computer] appear to take in data and to process it before producing some kind of report'? Rather than being bi-directional, this thought process suggests a unidirectional ascription of a certain feature of computers to that of the mind, ie precisely the inputting of data and the issuing of a report. Of course, it is hardly fair to take this briefest of examples as a critical target. Furthermore, Berger herself, though attracted to the

[45] Ibid, 173.
[46] Ibid, 171.
[47] Ibid.

analogical approach, also recognises that there may be important differences between metaphor and analogy. Metaphor, says Berger, 'appears more varied, more ambiguous and thus more flexible, and more tied to emotion than analogy'.[48] These are important qualifications.

Berger notes, for instance, that whereas many analogies focus on similar features, between the source and target of an analogy, metaphors focus more on 'relationships'.[49] 'Relationships' refers not to static properties, as in features, but to certain structural dynamics. This is important to some analogies, but it is arguably especially important to many metaphors. 'The hydrogen atom is like our solar system' is an example of an analogy that 'depends mostly on similarities in the structure of the relationships in the target and the source: an electron revolves around the nucleus like the planets revolve around the sun'.[50] Similarly, the metaphor 'My job is a jail', 'is an example of a metaphor that appears to be based on an analogical comparison of relationships rather than of surface features'.[51] In addition to emphasising relationships more than features, metaphors are also 'more ambiguous and flexible', for 'the author of a metaphor is able to advance positions without being held to them'.[52] And, finally, metaphors are 'more associated with emotion', for metaphors have 'poetic power.'[53] Berger continues:

> This power is thought to arise from metaphor's invitation to see one thing 'as another', providing us with a novel perspective and generating new information in the process. In other words, we don't see Juliet 'as' the sun. But something happens to our view of Juliet that is similar to our viewing the classical Gestalt figure in which, depending on your perspective, one of two different women seems to appear. The Gestalt figure always contains the elements of both a young woman and an old woman, and the elements themselves do not change. Instead, they slip and slide before our eyes until they click into place. Although we now see something we did not see before, it is not because we have received new information: "Rather, the difference is experiential, intuitive, and holistic".[54]

I think Berger is grappling with something important here, eg the reference to perspective is important, and I shall come back to it. But what exactly does 'poetic power' mean? And what might we mean by referring to it as 'experiential, intuitive, and holistic'? Further, how else might we bring out the 'ambiguity' or 'flexibility' of metaphor? And how might the alleged greater emphasis in metaphor on 'relationships' rather than 'features' give us a clue about how to articulate further the unique processing of metaphor?

It is in this difficult space that I seek to think further: to see what the model of artefacts and related processes of imagination can add that is not quite captured by either the CMT or the analogical models of metaphor. Again, as with CMT, so with the analogical approach: there is much to learn from it, and it probably captures well some of our experience and processing of some metaphors. Further, as noted above,

[48] Ibid, 174.
[49] Ibid, 175.
[50] Ibid, 165–6.
[51] Ibid, 175.
[52] Ibid.
[53] Ibid, 176.
[54] Ibid. The internal quote is from Elisabeth Camp, to whom I return below.

there are some aspects of the analogical approach to which I am very sympathetic: in particular, the greater emphasis on novel metaphors, and the recognition of the differences in experiencing, processing, and effects of metaphor over time. Nevertheless, I am sceptical that the model of analogy can exhaust the complexities of metaphor: advocates of analogy, too, and perhaps especially in the legal context, can be somewhat 'fanatical', seeing analogical processes everywhere, whereas, at least sometimes, something more distinct may be going on.

C. Beyond Comparison

Let us go back, then, to the problems with accounting for metaphor as a process of analogy, or as I shall call it from here: the comparison view. Doing this may help us get closer to what happens when we imagine metaphorically. Many of the theorists on metaphor that I have found most stimulating, eg IA Richards, Max Black, David Hills, Ted Cohen, Richard Moran, and Elisabeth Camp, amongst others, have wrestled with the inadequacies of the comparison view. How they have done so is significant. Equally, if not more significant is just what they have proposed as an alternative to the comparison view. I shall not be able to do these thinkers justice. My aim, instead, is to draw on their work in fashioning the approach taken to metaphor in this book, ie metaphor as an artefact, with related processes of imagination.

i. IA Richards

In his short but path-breaking book, *The Philosophy of Rhetoric*,[55] IA Richards published two important chapters on metaphor. In them, he emphasised that metaphor could not be thought to be mere embellishment or decoration of discourse, but that it was a mode of thought: thought itself, he said, was 'metaphoric'.[56] Within English-language traditions of both philosophy and literary theory, Richards trailblazed a different attitude to metaphor: he re-introduced metaphor as a serious topic for theoretical attention. Richards also conveyed respect for the difficulty of the topic: 'our skill with metaphor', he said, 'is one thing – prodigious and inexplicable; our reflective awareness of that skill is quite another thing – very incomplete, distorted, fallacious, over-simplifying.'[57] Nevertheless, Richards contributed a good deal to our reflective awareness of the skill of using and encountering metaphor.

Although Richards at times spoke of 'comparison', it was clear that his understanding of that term was rich. Furthermore, he criticised a view that approached the understanding of metaphor as a search for 'resemblances', and he used language (which others, especially Max Black, were to pick up later), that conveyed the importance of the dynamic relations between different parts of a metaphor. Thus, although Richards said that thought, insofar as it is metaphoric, 'proceeds by comparison', he also, in the

[55] Richards (1936).
[56] Ibid, 94.
[57] Ibid, 116.

same breath, spoke of how metaphor involved 'a transaction between contexts'.[58] He asked us to look beyond resemblances, to 'other relations between' the different parts of a metaphor, encouraging us to resist 'our most prevalent, over-simple, ruling assumptions about metaphors as comparisons'.[59] Richards spoke, for instance, of 'interactions' between the different parts of a metaphor,[60] of the 'exchanges between the meanings of words', and how our metaphors 'are superimposed upon a perceived world'.[61] On comparison itself he helpfully said the following:

> What is a comparison? It may be several different things: it may be just a putting together of two things to let them work together; it may be a study of both to see how they are like and how unlike one another; or it may be a process of calling attention to their likenesses or a method of drawing attention to certain aspects of the one through the co-presence of the other.[62]

Clearly, even though Richards at times used the language of comparison, he was pointing to something beyond it, especially if it is understood narrowly, as but a search for resemblances or likenesses. At a crucial moment in his reflections of metaphor, Richards began to replace talk of comparison with 'connection':

> Let us consider more closely what happens in the mind when we put together – in a sudden and striking fashion – two things belonging to very different orders of experience. The most important happenings – in addition to general confused reverberation and strain – are the mind's efforts to connect them. The mind is a connecting organ, it works only by connecting and it can connect any two things in an indefinitely large number of different ways. Which of these it chooses is settled by reference to some larger whole or aim, and, though we may not discover its aim, the mind is never aimless. In all interpretation we are filling in connections, and for poetry, of course, our freedom to fill in – in the absence of explicitly stated intermediate steps – is a main source of its powers. As Mr Empson well says: "Statements are made as if they were connected, and the reader is forced to consider their relations for himself. The reason why these statements should have been selected is left for him to invent; he will invent a variety of reasons and order them in his own mind. This is the essential fact about the poetical use of language". The reader, I would say, will try out various connections, and this experimentation – with the simplest and most complex, the most obvious and the most recondite collocations alike – is the movement which gives its meaning to all fluid language.[63]

I have quoted this passage in full, as it striking and important. Notice, for instance, the recognition of the importance of the absence of stating things explicitly, and the consequent emphasis this passage places on the activity of the reader or listener of metaphor. Poetic power, here, lies less in the intentions of the author, and more in the 'experimentation', in the trying out of different connections, by the reader. Also important is that a metaphor puts together 'very different orders of experience': the idea this points to is that we cannot understand metaphor as entirely unidirectional, with one side making

[58] Ibid, 94.
[59] Ibid, 108.
[60] Ibid, 107.
[61] Ibid, 109.
[62] Ibid, 120.
[63] Ibid, 125, internal references omitted.

us see the other in some different way, but that something more richly relational is at work, ie two orders of experience, or two meaning contexts, are being related together, interacting in our minds, 'reverberating' in them, as we 'strain' to connect them.

Richards recognises that metaphors can come in many forms, and some indeed may call attention to likenesses, but on the whole, it is dangerous and much too reductive to approach metaphor as a search for likeness. 'If we call someone a pig or a duck', he said, 'it is little use looking for some actual resemblance to a pig or a duck as the ground' of the metaphorical relation.[64] The 'ground of the shift is much more recondite', eg 'an extremely simplified account of the ground here would make it something like this: that some feeling, of "tender and amused regard", say, that it is possible to have towards ducks, is being felt towards a person'.[65] Even in this allegedly 'extremely simplified account', Richards shows his great sensitivity as a reader, open precisely to that sort of richly relational experimentation, to reverberation, to the straining involved in collocating the juxtaposition of different orders of experience. What I take Richards to be moving us towards is a view where the different parts of a metaphor work together in the active mind of a reader to generate something relationally distinctive, ie not something reducible to the transfer of one property in one part of the metaphor to another, and thus not a property which is said to be a resemblance or likeness between the two parts.

ii. Max Black

In his famous paper on 'Metaphor' before the Aristotelian Society in 1955, Max Black picked up on Richards' deeply relational language, proposing, in place of what he called the 'substitution' and 'comparison' views of metaphor, an 'interactive view'.[66] On the substitution view, a metaphor is treated as 'used in place of some equivalent literal expression'.[67] The speaker already knows what they want to say, and the metaphor is but an instrument – a more or less persuasive or pleasing or surprising one – for achieving the same end as the literal expression. Thus, on the substitution view, to say 'Richard is a lion' is simply to say, in a more colourful way, that 'Richard is brave'.[68] The comparison view, according to Black, is but a version of the substitution view – for, on this view, metaphor is just a particular mode of presentation of some literal content, this mode being one of 'condensed or elliptical simile'.[69] Thus, on the comparison view, to say 'Richard is a lion' is to say 'Richard is like a lion (in being brave)', with 'the added words in brackets being understood but not explicitly stated'.[70]

What was Black's criticism of the comparison view? Black argued as follows:

> There is some temptation to think of similarities as 'objectively given', so that a question of the form, 'Is A like B in respect of P?' has a definite and pre-determined answer. If this were so,

[64] Ibid, 117.
[65] Ibid, 117–8.
[66] Black (1955).
[67] Ibid, 279.
[68] Ibid, 281.
[69] Ibid, 283.
[70] Ibid, 283.

> similes might be governed by rules as strict as those controlling the statements of physics. But likeness always admits of degrees, so that a truly 'objective' question would need to take some such form as 'Is A more like B than like C in respect of P?'. Yet, in a proportion as we approach some forms, metaphorical statements lose their effectiveness and their point.[71]

If we must speak of similarities, Black said, it 'would be more illuminating … to say that the metaphor creates the similarities than to say that it formulates some similarity antecedently existing'.[72] Black, then, is seeking to convey something of the generative power of metaphor, something that cannot be explained away by saying it but presents a pre-existing similarity. As I read him, he is also grasping for something that emerges as a result of the two parts of a metaphor being connected in the mind of a reader, and thus in ways that are not reducible to the properties of either considered separately. That this is so appears also from Black's choice of language: like Richards, Black spoke for instance of the 'interplay' between the different parts of a metaphor.[73]

Further, Black insisted that metaphor had 'its own *distinctive* capacities and achievements',[74] and, again inspired by Richards, he spoke of 'the dynamic aspects of a good reader's response' to a metaphor,[75] emphasising precisely the activity of a reader. Significantly, for my purposes, Black also argued that we often employ metaphors 'in just the cases where there can be no question as yet of the precision of scientific statement'.[76] In that sense, for Black, as for me, both the creation and the processing of metaphor involves the mind at work, groping experimentally for resources, generating 'insight'[77] and greatly enhancing 'our powers of inquiry'.[78]

Just how, then, did Black's interactive view of metaphor work? When we examine it closely, we see that there are occasions in Black's analysis where he appears to recede somewhat from a more thoroughly 'interactive view' of metaphor. Thus, for instance, he asks us to think of the source of the metaphor as a 'filter', also referring to this filter as the 'subsidiary' part of a metaphor, with the target being the 'principal' part.[79] Thus, in the metaphor 'Richard is a lion', Richard is the 'principal' part of the metaphor, and lion is the 'subsidiary' part and also the 'filter'. According to Black, what happens when we process metaphor is that we draw on 'a system of commonplaces' associated with the 'subsidiary' part of a metaphor and use it as a 'filter' via which to see the 'principal' part. Black then arguably gave a filter of his own for understanding this process of metaphorical thought:

> Suppose I look at the night sky through a piece of heavily smoked glass on which certain lines have been left clear. Then I shall see only the stars that can be made to lie on the lines previously prepared upon the screen, and the stars I do so see will be seen as organised by the screen's structure. We can think of metaphor as such a screen, and the system of 'associated

[71] Ibid, 284.
[72] Ibid, 284–5.
[73] Ibid, 276.
[74] Ibid, 284; original emphasis.
[75] Ibid, 286.
[76] Ibid, 284.
[77] Ibid, 293.
[78] Ibid, 294.
[79] Ibid, 286.

> commonplaces' of the focal word as the network of lines upon the screen. We can say that the principal subject is 'seen through' the metaphorical expression – or, if we prefer, that the principal subject is 'projected upon' the field of the subsidiary subject.[80]

It is an arresting image, but talk of 'filters', of 'seeing through', of 'screens', and of 'projection', does appear to be at odds with talk of 'interaction' or 'interplay'. The process, it appears, is largely a uni-directional one. In fact, Black himself clearly felt uncomfortable with how he characterised this process: he said, reflecting on it towards the end of his paper, 'it was a simplification … to speak as if the implication-system of the metaphorical expression remains unaltered by the metaphorical statement'.[81] For instance, in the metaphor 'Man is wolf', it is not just that this puts man 'in a special light', ie the light of the system of commonplaces associated with wolves; in addition, 'we must not forget that the metaphor makes the wolf seem more human than he otherwise would'.[82]

Black is charmingly and disarmingly open about the difficulties of articulating the processing of metaphor. I think we can learn from him, and from Richards (who spoke, incidentally, not of 'sources' and 'targets', but of 'vehicles' and 'tenors' of metaphor, respectively), and recognise that two things are important here: first, we must make room when approaching the processing of metaphor for 'interaction' or 'interplay' between the two parts of a metaphor, recognising that the way the active mind of the reader may connect the two will, at least often, not be reducible to any properties that the two may be said to share or any properties in each that may be said to resemble each other; but that second, although both parts of a metaphor may be transformed in this process, it can remain the case, and perhaps typically will be the case, that one part of the metaphor is nevertheless more the focus than the other, ie that it is the 'target' or the 'tenor' or the 'principal' subject of a metaphor. These two are not necessarily incompatible. The danger to be avoided is not to allow the second to crowd out the first, but equally, not to let the first obscure the second. In the first, we recognise that some distinctive insight is generated by a reader who combines the two parts of a metaphor, and in the second we recognise that although that is so, the overall direction of focus in metaphorical imagining may nevertheless be on one part of the metaphor, ie the target.[83]

iii. The Multi-Stage Process of Metaphorical Imagining

The approach I favour, then, taking my cue from the ways that Richards and Black sought to move beyond the comparison view, is to argue for the process of metaphorical imagining being a multi-stage one, involving iterative feedback between the different

[80] Ibid, 288.
[81] Ibid, 290.
[82] Ibid, 291.
[83] These points may well constitute a difference between this approach and that of the blending approach of Faucionnier and Turner, which otherwise strikes me as a very promising approach: see Faucionnier and Turner (2003).

stages, but still retaining an overall direction to one part of the metaphor. We may sketch this multi-stage process as follows:

1. we experience surprise, as well as a mix of perplexity, pleasure and delight in the surprise, of the relations between parts of the metaphor, eg 'Juliet is the sun', or the juxtaposed contexts of meaning, eg in the metaphor of relating the government and its citizens to that of the Queen Bee and the worker bees;
2. we dwell, though crucially already to some extent guided by the 'target', eg 'Juliet', in the 'source', eg 'the sun', simulating affectively, eg our emotional associations with the sun, such as happiness or joy, constructing mental imagery, eg brightness or illumination, and simulating kinesically, eg experience of warmth, with all these being associations that may well be largely, though not necessarily exclusively, cultural commonplaces; and
3. we return to the target, infusing the target with the results of our participation, ie our dwelling, and simulating, in the source, thereby enriching and re-orienting our understanding of the target accordingly, eg we return to Juliet, experiencing her as a source of happiness, joy, brightness, illumination, and warmth (having also, to an extent, transformed our understanding of the source, ie the sun, as something relatable to affection).

In all of this we must acknowledge that to separate out these stages, and to speak of 'sources' and 'targets', risks being misleading. This is because, to repeat, there will typically be considerable iterative feedback between these stages: we often move back and forth, for instance, between the second and third stage (in the above example, transforming our understanding of both Juliet and the sun), all the while experiencing the strange perplexity, pleasure and delight of the initial incongruity, and its momentary resolutions. Important, too, is that we generate multiple possibilities in this process. Indeed, arguably, just as important as any 'resolutions' that we may adopt are the ones that we do not: what counts, in other words, is the search, the hunt, the 'experimentation' or 'reverberation' involved in this multi-stage process. Again, to emphasise what is crucial in this multi-stage process is how the two parts of a metaphor reverberate jointly, each guided by and transformed by each other, in the affective, sensory and kinesic experience of the reader or listener, even if at distinct moments one part or another of the metaphor may be the focus of attention.

Of course, to say all this is still to leave open further elaboration of just how we participate when we imagine metaphorically, ie when we imagine as a result of encountering a form of language that functions as a specific kind of artefact. This is important because delving into the details of how we participate affectively, sensorially and kinesically can help us avoid collapsing back into the comparison view and explaining the processes of metaphor as a matter of transfer of one set of properties from the source to that of the target. In what follows then, I will continue to draw on some of the thinkers that I have found most helpful in theorising metaphor, many of whom, as above, have resisted the comparison view. I will turn first to the affective, sensory and kinesic modes of involvement in imagining metaphorically. I will then consider, for this is an equally important part of the way I am approaching metaphor, its social dimensions, ie on how we imagine metaphorically interactively and collectively.

D. Affective, Sensory and Kinesic Participation

i. Affective

It is surprising that more has not been written about the relations between metaphorical imagining and emotion. The emphasis has tended to be on the 'cognitive' aspects of metaphorical processing, where cognitive is understood narrowly, and thus at a distance from affective involvement. And yet emotions are surely crucial to understanding the process of metaphorical imagining.

Perhaps one of the obstacles to greater attention being paid to the role of emotion has been that, for some, metaphor, as an artefact, takes us into a realm where we do not feel 'real' emotions. To recall the discussion in Chapter 2, for some theorists, whatever it is that we experience when we experience fictions (understood in the broad sense, eg novels and films), that experience does not involve real, online emotions.[84] Some have referred to this as 'the paradox of fictional emotions', ie it being said to be a pressing question how we can experience real emotions when we also realise that we are in the realm of fiction.[85]

However, as Richard Moran has argued, there is no paradox here: in fact, our experience of emotion occurs much more frequently in the realm of the fictional than in the ordinary run of everyday action. Indeed, not only is artifice not an obstacle, it is often precisely a trigger of emotion. Moran has argued that it is often the techniques of artifice, eg 'rhythm and figuration', that are 'directly responsible for the ability of' some work of fiction, eg a poem, 'to elicit any feeling'.[86] It is as if part of the effect of artifice is to give us permission to experience emotion.

Within the framework of the model of artefacts I have proposed, artefacts not only signal artifice, but also call upon us to do things with them. In doing so, they may call upon us precisely to do something affective with them. This is so often with metaphor: when, thanks to the artefactual functioning of a metaphorical form of language, we enter a distinctive epistemic frame (the first limb of imagining), we also, simultaneously (in the second limb) participate actively, which may include, and in the case of metaphor will arguably often include, participating affectively.

Like Richards and Black, Moran has also criticised the comparison view of metaphor, and, in doing so, he has pointed, in this respect unlike Richards and Black, to the role of felt transformations as part of metaphorical imagining. Moran insists on the 'experiential aspect to understanding metaphor', noting in this respect how experientially thin comparison views tend to be. For instance, 'To call someone a tail-wagging lapdog of privilege is not simply to be make an assertion of his enthusiastic submissiveness'.[87] The analysis is 'not improved by taking on an open-ended list of further dog-predicates that may possible be part of the metaphor's meaning'.[88] Rather,

[84] See, eg, Walton (1990).
[85] See, eg, Yanal (1994).
[86] Moran (2017), 10.
[87] Ibid, 29.
[88] Ibid.

if we want to capture metaphorical processing, we need to get closer to what it might mean to 'experience' that person's 'dogginess'.[89]

Moran also speaks of 'the image-making quality'[90] of metaphor, and I shall return to this in a moment (as it is part of the sensory mode of involvement in imagining metaphors). For the moment, the point is that the way in which Moran approaches metaphor, namely as an experience, involves attention to its affectivity. Again, for Moran, as above, this experience is a transformative one: it involves change of some kind. But how to conceive of this change? Should we, for instance, focus, as philosophers tend to do, on changes in belief? Moran says the following:

> There are many more ways of changing someone's mind than changing his or her beliefs. Although this may be most easily seen in the case of rhetoric, it is quite generally true for both philosophy and literature that much of what they aim at is not on the level of specifically altered beliefs but, rather, such things as changes in the associations and comparisons one makes, differences in the vivid or 'felt' appreciation of something already known, or changes in one's habits of attention and sense of the important and the trifling. And although such changes of mind are something different from the acceptance or rejection of certain beliefs, there is nothing to be gained by assimilating them all to the category of the 'non-cognitive'. Appreciation of this will have literary, politics and philosophical consequences for the criticism of metaphor.[91]

As I read him, Moran is pointing to the importance of non-belief like transformative experiences, some of which at least may involve changes in 'felt' appreciations. Imagining metaphorically, then, is entangled with the active, and potentially transformative, experience of emotion.

Let us turn to an example: 'sorrow is a cloak'.[92] Of course, in this instance, we also have explicit reference to an emotion, ie 'sorrow'. But I do not think this is what plays a crucial role; we could arguably do something similar with 'Man is wolf', 'Juliet is the sun' or 'Richard is a lion'. The idea is that, as soon as we enter a distinctive epistemic frame, suspending for instance certain epistemic norms of identity and referentiality, and loosening the epistemic commitment to relevance, and thereby begin to relate the two parts of the metaphor together, ie sorrow and a cloak, we also simulate affectively. Guided in part by our affective associations with 'sorrow', we dwell in the source of 'a cloak', simulating also what a cloak provides, eg a feeling of warmth, or protection against say some wind or rain. Importantly, dwelling in the source, ie a cloak, and simulating affectively, is not the same as picking out particular properties of cloaks and transferring them over to sorrow: our affective simulation of cloaks, already guided to some extent by our past affective experiences of sorrow, is much too rich phenomenologically – it immerses and involves us in our past experiences, both personal and cultural, in ways not capturable by some property or set of properties.

It is potentially misleading to separate out the different aspects of our participation in metaphorical imagining, ie the affective, sensory and kinesic, and I shall be returning

[89] Ibid.
[90] Ibid.
[91] Ibid, 38.
[92] The example comes from a paraphrase of Keats by Ricoeur (1978), 149. The original phrase, in Keats, is: 'When by my solitary hearth I sit / And hateful thoughts enwrap my soul in gloom'.

to the others, but surely there is an especially important role for affective simulation. Part of what it means to involve ourselves in imagining this metaphor is that we simulate affectively, ie we draw on our affective experience of cloaks, and, having done so, we infuse our now-transformed experience of sorrow via that affective experience of cloaks (with our experience of cloaks also having now been transformed in this process). For example, we may now affectively experience sorrow as something comforting, ie as something protecting us against, eg anger, frustration, boredom, numbness, or anxiety. In fact, having 'sorrow' as part of the example helps prove the point: for by relating sorrow to a cloak we transform our affective experience of sorrow, not as something necessarily affectively negative, but as also potentially affectively positive, eg a source of comfort or protection. Further, although it may be less prominent in our attention, we may also transform our experience of cloaks, experiencing them now, say, more nostalgically or sentimentally than we had before.

The above affective participation is not the only affective part of the processing of a metaphor: the initial encounter with a metaphor is also affective. Thus, part of what it may mean for an artefact to function as an artefact is that, in signalling artifice for us, it also strikes us as in some way surprising or striking. We may, then, experience certain emotions, which I have earlier called 'epistemic emotions', such as surprise, doubt, and wonder, in the very initial encounter with a metaphorical form of language. Taking us out of the stream of reading or listening, the metaphor jolts us, ie we experience it as surprising or as wonderful or as perplexing. Further, in doing things with the metaphor, we also experience epistemic emotions in the search for a resolution, eg in the straining or difficulty, but also pleasure, of looking for such a resolution: is it even possible, and how might one, relate sorrow to a cloak? We may also find pleasure in eventually settling, if we do, on some resolution, ie some connection that, for now, makes sense to us, momentarily resolving the incongruity or discordance created by the metaphor. Emotion, then, plays a role both in the experience of the artefact and in the process of imagining.

ii. Sensory

We can also draw on Moran's work to articulate the sensory aspect of metaphorical imagining. As noted above, Moran stresses the 'image-making quality' of metaphor, but he approaches this in a particular way.

Drawing on Aristotle's reading of metaphor in his *Rhetoric*, Moran pays attention to the metaphors that Aristotle is drawn to, these being ones that have '*energeia*', or in Moran's language, 'that project a sense of activity'.[93] For Moran, this is a vital part of understanding metaphor, namely, that, by itself exhibiting *energeia*, it calls upon us also to be active. A metaphor works, in other words, when 'the mind of the hearer is provoked, set into motion, and engaged imaginatively with the metaphor'.[94]

[93] Moran (2017), 56.
[94] Ibid, 59.

Moran emphasises, as I have been throughout with respect to artefacts generally, that what matters is what we do with a metaphor:

> *Energeia* is thus not only on the side of what is depicted, but what is depicted is specifically figured as a living thing demanding some set of responses from the audience, some mental activity of its own. The specifically imagistic quality of live metaphor only is so because of the responsive activity of the mind. (Here as elsewhere it is a mistake to think of mental imagery as the passive perception of an internal object, rather than as a particular imaginative activity). The aim of *pro ommaton poiein* ['setting before the eyes'] is to get one's audience to *do* various things, to imagine in a lively fashion that involves much associating, connecting, and emotional responding. By contrast, a frigid style is both lifeless in itself and fails to move us.[95]

What is meant by 'imagistic' is something much more dynamic than some static account of pictures might suggest: it is something much more like the experience of adopting a certain perspective, one in which we move, and are moved, and in which, if we do construct imagery, it is from the perspective we have adopted. And, indeed, the role of perspective is one of the crucial concepts for Moran in theorising metaphor. Put another way, for Moran, the key to the relations between images and metaphor is their perspectival character. For instance, when we say of someone that he is a wolf, we also 'take up the perspective of wolfishness'.[96] This is a perspective adopted by both the composer of the metaphor, and the audience of it: 'We [including composer and audience] have taken up this particular … perspective, and now we pursue what can be noticed from it'.[97] This is less a matter of asserting something or accepting that assertion, than it is a matter of the 'adoption of a perspective'.[98]

When, then, we speak of the 'image-making quality' of metaphor, we must guard against the temptation to think of a picture with properties, as if we are but transferring, via images, properties from the source of a metaphor to its target. Something much richer is going on; something that perhaps can be captured better by understanding the transformative experience of adopting a perspective. What we also see here is the interrelation between different modes of involvement in metaphorical imagining: affective, sensory and kinesic often work together. Indeed, one way of showing that, and how, they work together is precisely by reference to the idea of perspective.

In addition to Moran, another theorist who has also emphasised the role of perspective in metaphorical processing is Elisabeth Camp. Camp is attracted to at least some version of the analogical approach to metaphor, but many of her observations also suggest that hers is far from any simple comparison view. For over a decade, Camp has been defending the cognitive and communicative importance of metaphor, claiming, for instance, that 'metaphors can sometimes provide us with our only cognitive access to certain properties'.[99] Somewhat like Black, who spoke of associated commonplaces with

[95] Ibid. Original emphasis.
[96] Ibid, 45.
[97] Ibid.
[98] Ibid.
[99] Camp (2006), 1.

a source, Camp speaks of holistic characterisations, ie a bundling together into single chunks of the complex content of the source of a metaphor.[100] As Camp put it later:

> Characterisations attribute *clusters* of features, often highly specific, experientially-represented features, to some individual or type of object or event. Rather than straightforwardly predicating those features of that subject, though, characterisation present them as fitting for it, where a feature may be fitting even if it's not actually possessed.[101]

This is important, for it helps resist a view in which, when we process metaphor, we simply transfer some defined set of properties from the source to the target: a characterisation is something richer, and not reducible to a set of properties. Further, Camp combines this notion of characterisation with the notion of a perspective. What it is to present one characterisation as fitting for another is to employ something like a perspective: it is not to assert a proposition about that something, but instead to adopt a stance from which we make certain aspects of it more central and prominent. Also importantly, for my purposes, Camp emphasises the relationship between the speaker and hearer of a metaphor: 'merely understanding the utterance [which employs metaphor] requires a hearer to mold his mind in the speaker's image' and this 'in a way that goes significantly beyond the hypothetical contemplation of a proposition'.[102] This kind of characterising, from a perspective, 'often involves attributing experientially- and affectively-loaded features'.[103] For Camp, characterising from a perspective is also part of what makes metaphor so powerful, sometimes even irresistible.

There are aspects of Camp's view where I think she puts matters too strongly: although some metaphors may be powerful in the way she proposes, no intention with which a metaphor is uttered can control the possible ways in which a reader may respond to it. It is true that when a metaphor works, it involves the listener or reader, ie it makes them part of the joint effort, sometimes together with the author, in imagining a metaphor (an important point, going to the social dimension of metaphor, and one to which I shall return). But this involvement of the reader or listener is not always best captured by speaking of the 'irresistibility' or 'anti-deniability' of metaphor.[104] To my ears, this makes the relation between the author of a metaphor and its readers or listeners too one-sided, not leaving enough room for the activity of readers or listeners.

Camp's notion, though, of metaphor as characterisation-from-a-perspective is a helpful one. Both her concepts of characterisation and perspective call for a content that is, as she put it above, experientially- and affectively-loaded. As Camp has put it elsewhere, perspectives are 'dispositions to organise one's attention, thinking and feeling in certain ways'.[105] They are more complex and richer ways of relating to something than just asserting propositions about it. They require more investment from us, including more affective investment. Further, the idea of adopting a perspective, or characterising from a perspective, also suggests something more active and more embodied: to the extent we construct images, we do so via a perspective, or we do so perspectivally.

[100] Ibid, 4.
[101] Camp (2017), 50. Original emphasis.
[102] Ibid, 51.
[103] Ibid.
[104] Ibid, 49.
[105] Camp (2015), 340.

Let us return, again, to the example of 'sorrow is a cloak', with a focus on sensory participation. Following Moran, and to some extent also Camp, any such construction of mental imagery cannot be thought of as a comparison between two static pictures, eg of some properties of a cloak, being transferred to some properties of sorrow. Insofar as we construct mental imagery, something much more dynamic occurs here: something richer, more holistic, more active and involving our bodies. For instance, when we imagine 'sorrow is a cloak' we may construct mental imagery of a particular cloak, eg perhaps our grandfather's cloak. The cloak in question is characterised from our perspective, as already meaning something to us (it also being the case that any such images are saturated with emotion). The process is not one of, say, constructing images of a cloak that is 1) large, 2) thick, 3) water-proof. We do not proceed in such a mechanical way, enumerating properties and then transferring them over. Instead, any mental imagery we construct is, as Camp puts it, experientially- and affectively-loaded: it is a cloak, from a perspective, and thus one that echoes in our experience in some way. To say this is not to posit any realm of exclusively private experience: our personal experience will undoubtedly be filtered and mediated by culture, and thus overlap, to some extent, with the experience of others. The point is that any sensory participation is perspectival: it is thick with experience from a perspective, in ways that matter us to personally, though also often in ways that resonate culturally.[106]

iii. Kinesic

The above approach, ie an affectively-rich perspectivalism about metaphor, connects also to the third kind of participation (in the second limb of imagining), namely kinesic simulation. Although there has been a considerable amount of discussion on the role of mental imagery in metaphorical processing, and some attention to emotion, there has been much less attention paid to the role of kinesis. Certainly, as above, there has been a great deal of focus on relations between embodiment and metaphor, but most of this has looked at how certain metaphors rely, mostly less-than-consciously, on certain allegedly basic bodily actions and experiences. Not much has been said about the largely conscious and deliberate process of simulating kinesically when processing metaphor. And yet, this is surely a crucial part of much metaphorical processing.

When approaching metaphorical processing, and especially metaphors that function as artefacts, we do well to think of this process as involving the simulation of sensorimotor experiences. Gibbs, whose work we encountered earlier, has recently argued that 'embodied simulation' plays a crucial role in the processing not only of metaphor, but also a whole range of other figurative language, including proverbs and parables.[107] On parables, for instance, which he sees as narrative-like metaphors, Gibbs has said:

> … people understand parables as metaphoric mappings between concrete events and more abstract principles, through embodied simulation processes. This hypothesis asserts that people ordinarily attempt to construct imaginative, embodied re-enactments of what some specific discourse must be like to participate in given their own bodily capacities and

[106] See also Ricoeur, who says: to imagine, in the sense of 'imaging' 'is not to have a mental picture of something but to display relations in a depicting mode': (1978), 150.

[107] See Gibbs (2018).

> experiences. For example, people are likely creating coherent metaphorical messages by imagining themselves performing the actions mentioned in a narrative, both when these actions refer to possible and impossible human events.[108]

Many proverbs, too, also call on and typically involve some embodied simulation: 'don't put all your eggs in one basket', or 'hasten slowly', are examples, but there are countless others. Indeed, once one turns one's mind to the kinetic dimensions of language, it is difficult not to see just how pervasive kinetically-rich language is.

Gibbs is still primarily interested in largely fast, less-than-conscious, non-effortful embodied simulations, but the point can be extended to slow, conscious and difficult processing too.[109] Gibbs points to studies on everyday language processing, showing how much people rely on kinesic simulation for comprehension. For instance, studies have shown that when faced with the expression 'to grasp a concept', 'people first make, or even imagine making, a hand movement, such as reaching out to grasp something'.[110] However, just because this process is involved in everyday language processing, and is in that context fast and less-than-conscious, does not mean that kinesic simulation cannot play a role also in the more specific cases of processing of artefactual language.

Guillemette Bolens, whose important work on embodiment we encountered earlier in this book, has also emphasised the importance of kinesic simulation in the processing of metaphor, as well as other 'figurative' forms of language. Bolens has argued, for instance, that 'figurality often entails fictive motion'.[111] We may here recall Moran's reminder above of the classic concept of *energeia*: metaphors often work insofar as they trigger us into kinesic simulation. Of course, we may well simulate kinesically anyway, even if not triggered, but some metaphors may work better, eg generate more resources, to the extent that they more readily call upon kinesic simulation, ie to the extent they invite us to move, in our imaginations, enacting some embodied action or experience.

The example we have been considering, 'sorrow is a cloak', may not obviously call upon our kinesic simulation, but any imagining of it is likely to involve some simulation of bodily action and experience. Indeed, it is difficult to see how a reader or listener of this metaphor could get to the characterisation of sorrow as, say, protective, without simulating kinesically the bodily action of putting on a cloak and feeling it around one's shoulders. We can, of course, imagine this metaphor more or less richly: we could, say, imagine ourselves about to exit our home (perhaps to get some extra wood for the fire), seeing the snow falling, and taking and placing a cloak around ourselves to protect us and keep us warm when we go outside. Or we could imagine draping a cloak around our body as we go to sit down by the fire in our home, settling in with a cup of coffee or a whisky to read some great book. How richly we imagine can certainly vary, but the point is that any process of imagining this metaphor is likely to involve some kinesic simulation, though one that is related to, in combination with, affective and sensory imagining. And, to repeat, to simulate kinesically in this way – say, experiencing the act of putting on a cloak and draping it around our shoulders – is not something reducible to picking

[108] Ibid, 100.
[109] On the variable speeds of metaphorical processing, see also Carston (2010).
[110] Gibbs (2018), 101; and see also Glenberg and Kaschak (2002); and Matlock (2004).
[111] Bolens (2012), 17.

out a property of cloaks and transferring it over, in this case to sorrow. The kinesic simulation of putting on a cloak, which, as above, may be experienced by us as the cloak of our grandfather, reverberates in our thereby-transformed experience of sorrow, with cloaks too, even if less obviously, being transformed in this process.

If one puts together the various dimensions of this metaphorical imagining – the affective, sensory and kinesic – one has a sense of how rich the quality of experience is in the processing of this metaphor of sorrow being a cloak. It is incredibly difficult to articulate this quality, and to show how it cannot be reduced to the identification and transfer of properties. I have tried to do that here by giving a sense of how such a metaphor may involve us affectively, sensorially (especially perspectivally) and kinesically. In the processing of this metaphor, we experience sorrow as a layer of protection, akin to the action of putting on a cloak, and perhaps not just any cloak, but the cloak of our grandfather, who also protected us from the elements when we were small. This transformation of our understanding – of both sorrow and cloaks, even if mainly the former – is more generative and long-lasting, perhaps precisely because it is so self-involving, than any transfer of properties could be.

E. The Social Dimension of Metaphorical Participation

I have focused, so far, largely on the process of imagining a metaphor in real time, and by an individual. But it is an essential element of the approach I take to metaphor, and to artefacts of language generally, that they are social activities, and ones that occur not only in real time, but also over time. To recall, the social and diachronic dimensions of inquiry are vital elements of it. Metaphor is no exception. In fact, metaphor is in many respects an inherently social phenomenon. I have already had occasion to stress the invitational character of metaphor, ie the sense in which to understand metaphorical processing we cannot rely merely on any intentions with which a metaphor is uttered. Although I do not wish to deny that intentions are important, I do think we must look also at the readers and listeners of a metaphor, and the active ways in which they process it. Although intentions matter, they do not control the life of metaphor: metaphor can, via readers and listeners of it, generate all kinds of resources that the author of a metaphor never predicted, and perhaps could never predict.

i. The Intimacy of Metaphor

One could bring out this social character of metaphor in different ways. Ted Cohen, for instance, has famously spoken of the intimacy-cultivating character of metaphor:

> There is a unique way in which the maker and the appreciator of a metaphor are drawn closer to one another. Three aspects are involved: 1) the speaker issues a kind of concealed invitation; 2) the hearer expends a special effort to accept the invitation; and 3) this transaction constitutes the acknowledgement of a community. All three are involved in any communication, but in ordinary literal discourse their involvement is so pervasive and routine that they go unremarked. The use of metaphor throws them into relief, and there is a point in that.[112]

[112] Cohen (1978), 8. And see also Cohen (2012).

The point is that there is a sense in which metaphor is interaction-making, if not also community-making: it helps establish, or facilitates, an interaction, eg a conversation, involving some complicity, between persons. As Cohen puts it, 'a transaction is precipitated' in which persons 'actively engage one another in coping with a piece of language'.[113] A metaphor can 'initiate explicitly the cooperative act of comprehension which is … something more than a routine act of understanding'.[114] Cohen's concept of 'intimacy', though, suggests something even stronger than an interaction or transaction: it suggests an interaction that perhaps not everyone can get involved in. As he puts it:

> The sense of close community results not only from the shared awareness that a special invitation has been given and accepted, but also from the awareness that not everyone could make that offer or take it up …. A figurative use [of language] can be inaccessible to all but those who share information about one another's knowledge, beliefs, intentions, and attitudes.[115]

For Cohen, the relevant 'community' can be small, 'even a solitary pair'.[116] In this respect, metaphor for Cohen functions in a similar way to jokes, which also involve a 'cultivation of intimacy', constituting a kind of possibly exclusive invitation to share in the complicity of getting a joke.[117] No doubt just how exclusive a joke or metaphor is, will depend on the exact joke or metaphor; there are no easy generalities here. For my purposes, the important point is that metaphors can contribute to the very creation of an interactive dynamic, and one which is more or less inclusive. Metaphors can create interaction, with persons then imagining a metaphor together, and they can facilitate on-going interaction, with persons potentially exchanging different interpretations of it as time goes on.

ii. Dialogue and Play

There have been other approaches to the interactive-making and interaction-affecting qualities of metaphor. Analysts of dialogue, in both everyday contexts as well as specific contexts, eg as in 'reconciliation talk' between offenders and victims, have shown how metaphor can help overcome certain obstacles to dialogue, as well as how metaphor shifts and develops in the course of a conversation.[118] Metaphor can be powerful, not only in the sense of being a unidirectional persuasive tool, but also in an interactive, bi-directional way, enabling persons to interact with and relate to each other, often in emotionally-taxing or politically-loaded circumstances. As much as a metaphor can sometimes 'structure' a conversation, it is also sufficiently pliable, leaving enough wriggle room, for the participants to express and signal, within the common space of a metaphor, their own distinctive experiences and attitudes.

An interesting way of thinking about the interaction-making and interaction-facilitating dynamics of metaphor may be via the notion of playing. David Hills has

[113] Cohen (1978), 9.
[114] Ibid.
[115] Ibid.
[116] Ibid.
[117] Ibid, 10–11.
[118] Gibbs (2017), 95–96; and see, eg, Cameron (2011); and Charteris-Black (2012).

argued along these lines, speaking of metaphor as a process of 'Making Things Up by Acting Things Out', and thus involving interactive improvisation:

> Hearing 'Juliet is the sun' in its concrete conversational setting, we come to suspect that Romeo imagines his newfound love to just plan be exactly that, the sun. We come to suspect that he is inspired to imagine this and in his own opinion called on to image it by the rules of a game of make-believe he spontaneously finds himself playing, a game we try to join him in playing as we struggle to make appropriate sense of his words, a game in which, as Romeo sees things, the role of the sun falls to Juliet as a matter of course … We listeners undertake … to paraphrase Romeo's metaphor, by responding to his utterance as a make-believe signal, doing our best to enter into the spirit of a game already in progress, and reflecting on the rules we find ourselves playing by if and when we succeed.[119]

Even if we discount the equation here between playing and playing a game in accordance with certain rules, we can still draw on this account to point to the interactive dynamics of imagining metaphor.

Hills' account, of course, is considerably richer, and part of its point is that this reference to make-believe pretence in games, and thus seeing metaphorical communication as a kind of game-like competence, allows us to counter other approaches to metaphor, including analogical ones. I am mentioning it here for a very selective purpose: to try to convey the interactive quality of metaphorical communication, ie how it involves signalling, in my terminology, the artifice of a form of language, and thereby how it is an invitation to others to do something with it. I do not think this must mean the readers or listeners must conform to the 'rules of a game' that they think an author of a metaphor is playing, though some reference to the possible intentions of an author is likely to be part of any metaphorical comprehension. If we think of playing more broadly,[120] however, then this could be an illuminating way to approach the study of the social character of metaphor: its invitational character, how it can involve a range of persons in a conversation, each exploring, to some extent in their own way, different possible ways of resolving the tension set up by a metaphor.

iii. Metaphor and Community

There is one final observation to make: namely, that metaphor does not only help establish and facilitate interaction in real time, thereby assisting in the interactive dimension of inquiry; it also plays a role in the discourse of a community over time. Here, too, there is scholarship we can draw on, from work on the so-called 'career of metaphor',[121] to research by communication scholars on the different ways in which change in the meaning or choice of metaphors can also result in changes in the conceptualisation of certain social topics over time.[122]

In his helpful summary of some of this literature, Christian Burgers has referred to the different dimensions of change over time, namely the different pace and type

[119] Hills (2017), 24–25.
[120] See the discussion on the difference between playing-in-general and playing-a-game in ch 2.
[121] See Bowdle and Gentner (2005).
[122] See Burgers (2016).

of change. With respect to pace, Burgers notes that 'change can occur in two temporal paces: evolutionary (slowly, continuous) and revolutionary (swiftly, discontinuous)'.[123] Evolutionary change 'occurs when metaphors are used over longer time spans during which their meaning is adjusted and negotiated, leading to slow change'.[124] Revolutionary change, on the other hand, 'occurs when new metaphors or alternative interpretations of extant metaphor are introduced at once to deal with sudden rapid developments'.[125] With respect to the type of change, Burgers here refers to change that is either incremental or fundamental:

> Incremental change implies that the meaning of an extant metaphor changes, in that it is renegotiated (interpretation of extant metaphor changes) and/or extended (new interpretation is added to extant interpretation). In the example of the EU is a building metaphor, an incremental change was when perspectives on the EU shifted from a building under construction (eg laying the foundations for the EU) to a completed building with structured deficiencies (eg closed exits). Fundamental change, in contrast, suggests differences between metaphors, in that old metaphors are replaced by new metaphors. In the example of the EU is a building metaphor, a fundamental change would be if this metaphor is actively replaced with a different metaphor, such as the EU is a family.[126]

This is not the movement to review this literature in detail.[127] The point is simply that metaphor cannot be studied by looking at one isolated use of it: as important as any initial introduction of a metaphor may be, also important is just how differently it generates resources over time. It is difficult to establish general patterns. Much depends on the metaphor in question, and what is done with it at different times. From the perspective of this book, part of the point is that metaphor can contribute to inquiry over time: it does so because, as a form of language that functions as an artefact (at least to the extent that it does that, which, again, can change over time), it keeps inviting its readers over time to engage with it, ie to imagine it. A metaphor may be a good way of involving multiple persons over time: once introduced into a discourse, and if it works to signal artifice and invite imagination, a metaphor can continue to generate insight about some domain, precisely by allowing different persons at different times to elaborate it in different ways.

Of course, a metaphor can also congeal over time, ie it can become conventional, turning into some particular reference, taking on some more fixed meaning. Insofar as that occurs, such a metaphor no longer enables inquiry; indeed, it may be an obstacle to it. As obvious as this may seem, however, it is not always easy to tell when a metaphor has become congealed, no longer functioning to signal artifice and invite imagination. Often, all it takes is one intervention, offering an alternative interpretation, which brings out the artefactual potential of the metaphor again.

If we pay attention to the social and diachronic dimensions of metaphor, we see that we must be careful about how we articulate the power of metaphor. It may be true that

[123] Ibid, 251.
[124] Ibid.
[125] Ibid.
[126] Ibid, internal references omitted.
[127] It is interesting to see Burgers referring to large-scale political metaphors. See also Walzer (1967); Musolff (2000) and (2006).

metaphor offers a way of organising a discourse, eg a certain area of the law: it can make certain things salient, and it can emphasise some matters rather than others. There is an important sense in which metaphor guides. For instance, metaphors arguably offer thicker resources to the future than fictions. In this respect, it matters what specific metaphors we have in discourse: one can and should speak, for instance, of the ethics and politics of metaphor.[128]

Nevertheless, if we keep in mind the social and diachronic dimensions of metaphor, as well as the above points about the complexity and richness of metaphorical processing, then we do well to avoid claiming too much for any one metaphor, namely that it 'structures' or 'determines' the way that something is perceived or understood. Part of the value of metaphor, then, is how it gently and delicately balances guidance with openness, or stability with change: it may nudge imagination in certain directions, but imagination remains somewhat unpredictable, open to exploration by a range of persons interacting with each other, in real time and over time.

F. Examples of Metaphors in Legal Discourse

I will, in a moment, be turning to a specific example of metaphor in adjudication. It is important to note, though, that legal discourse is awash with metaphors.[129] Some of the metaphors that legal scholars have worked on include:

- Slippery slope arguments
- Floodgate arguments
- Chains of causation
- Proportionality
- Balancing
- Narrow/broad construction
- Chilling effect doctrine
- The presumption of innocence is the golden thread of the criminal law
- Estoppel is a shield, not a sword
- Marketplace of ideas
- Wall of separation
- Human shields
- The corporate veil and its piercing
- Fruit of the poisonous tree
- Long arm statutes

[128] See Fraser (2018); and Musolff (2014).

[129] I am not suggesting that all of the examples below are metaphors; just that these are some of the metaphors that legal scholars have worked on. Whether these are metaphors, in the sense in which I model them in this book, will depend on whether they are still functioning as artefacts, and thus successfully inviting their recipients to imagine.

- Meeting of the minds
- Law is a network/law is a pyramid
- The body of the law/the anatomy of the law
- The letter/spirit of the law
- Dead letter
- Bindingness
- The parts/elements of a rule
- The common law is a river
- Crystallisation of customary law norms
- Soft/hard law
- Family of nations
- Veils of sovereignty
- Fragmentation
- Forum shopping[130]

These are just some of the metaphors that legal scholars have analysed. Future work may wish to consider whether it makes a difference whether the metaphors are substantive or procedural. It is interesting, for instance, that many metaphors in law relate to the practices of interpretation (as indeed are those I will be considering in a moment). It may well be the case that certain areas of the law attract metaphors more than others. Greta Olson has suggested that 'Metaphors function most resonantly in Constitutional discourse'.[131] Future work may wish to consider which areas, and why, and when, attract more metaphors than others.[132] Comparative work, too, in what we might call 'comparative legal poetics', would be fascinating here, eg to consider what institutional factors affect the introduction of and then reliance on metaphors in different legal traditions. And, although some work has already been done on the relations between metaphor and other artefacts in adjudication, more certainly could be done, eg on relations between metaphor and narrative (including allegory, parable, and other narrative forms), metaphor and metonymy, metaphor and irony, and much else besides.

An outstanding recent contribution to the literature is the collection on *Narrative and Metaphor in the Law*.[133] In it, for example, is Olson's chapter 'On Narrating and

[130] See, eg, Milner (1985); Hibbits (1994); Thornburg (1995); Henkin (2005); Jackson (2006); Ritchie (2010); Binnie (2007); Fludernik (2019); Berger (2002); Golder (2019); Del Mar (2017b); Wheatley (2017); Hasmujin (2007); Winter (2001); Bosmajian (1992); Larsson (2013); Anker (2015); Berger (2004); Edwards (2010); Richard (2014); Conrad (1988); Cavanagh (2019); Makela (2011); Johnson (2007); Spaulding (2012); Perelman and Young (2010); and the essays collected in the Gurnham (2016) special issue on 'Law's Metaphors'.

[131] Olson (2018), 33.

[132] See also Smith (2007), who has helpfully identified various levels of legal discourse where metaphors operate. Smith argues that there are 'four basic types or levels of metaphor operating in persuasive legal discourse. These four levels of metaphor correspond with the four basic components of any legal argument: (1) the legal principles governing an issue; (2) the tools of analysis applied to the governing principles; (3) the writing style of an advocate who is presenting the legal argument; and (4) the inherent nature of language itself, which serves as the foundation of any written legal argument': (2007), 920.

[133] Hanne and Weisberg (2018).

Troping the Law' in which Olson calls for more work on narrative and metaphor in legal discourse by way of 'recent discussions of fictionality':

> Fictionality allows for a kind of imagining of as-if possibilities that non-fictionality does not. These are more generally true propositions rather than ones that are specifically true. Law makes recourse to both narrative means, in this case discourse level variations, to describe the 'facts' at hand, as well as to metaphors in cases where matters are legally inchoate. In such moments when law resorts to the rhetoric of fictionality to explain something coherently – for instance to invent a legal fiction – law is in a moment of transformation. As-if counterfactuals to the current reality are supplied, for instance, by the metaphors that Cardozo uses in his judgements, and the narratives that are built around his metaphorisations.[134]

Olson's call is very appealing, and I have indeed sought to draw on, inter alia, rhetorical approaches to fictionality in this book. Like Olson, I too think that 'Through rhetorical fictionalisation, legal discourse can generate general solutions for conflicts for which law does not yet have a name'.[135] Rather than engage in more theoretical discussion, however, it will be best to now turn to the specific example.

II. Of Trees and Mistresses

The first section of this chapter has sought to offer an approach to metaphor, modelled as an artefact, with a related process of imagination, and capable of contributing to inquiry. As all this has been quite abstract, it is time now to explore how this approach might inform analysis of a particular example from adjudication. I shall be drawing on the metaphors that can be found in the famous case of *Edwards v Attorney-General of Canada*,[136] also known as the Five Persons case. Given what was said above about the importance of the social and diachronic dimensions of metaphor, I will, in addition to examining the case itself, consider, though necessarily briefly and inadequately, some of the ways that the metaphors from *Edwards* have continued to generate resources over time.

A. Are Women 'Persons'?

Just ten years short of a century ago, Lord Sankey, in his very first judgment as Lord Chancellor, delivered the opinion in *Edwards*. This was the only opinion in the case, with Lord Sankey speaking on behalf of all five judges, for the Privy Council at that point in time did not allow for dissenting opinions. I will shortly examine this opinion in detail. First, however, we hack to backtrack a little, and understand how the case came to the Privy Council.

[134] Olson (2018), 36.
[135] Ibid.
[136] *Edwards* (1930).

i. Arriving in the Privy Council

The *Edwards* case arrived at the Privy Council after having been decided, in favour of the government, at the Supreme Court of Canada. It had reached the Supreme Court after the Governor General of Canada had referred the following question to the Court: 'Does the word "persons" in s. 24 of the British North America Act 1967 include female persons?'. Section 24, it should be added, enabled the Governor General to 'summon qualified persons to the Senate'. In effect, the question was whether this section could be interpreted in such a way as to allow the Governor General to summon women to the Canadian Senate. As above, the Canadian Supreme Court had answered unanimously 'no' to that question, though on different grounds: whereas the majority did so in large part because of the common law disability of women to hold public office, Justice Duff had reached the same conclusion after a closer examination of the language of the *British North America Act* 1867 ('the *BNA Act*').

Although it reached the same conclusion, Justice Duff's separate opinion was nevertheless an important precursor to Lord Sankey's judgement in the Privy Council. As Robert Sharpe and Patricia McMahon have observed, in their book-length treatment of the history and legacy of *The Persons Case*,[137] some of Justice Duff's extra-judicial statements had suggested that he may approach the task of constitutional interpretation 'in grand, liberal terms'.[138] Significantly for my purposes, examining the metaphors in this case, Justice Duff had said, in a speech in 1915, that the law was 'a living organism, possessing like every living organism, within limits of course, the power to adapt itself to changing circumstances'.[139] He repeated this metaphor in a one-off reference to 'an organic rule' in his judgement,[140] though apart from this, there was no further mention of organic metaphors in his opinion.

Importantly, too, Justice Duff resisted the relevance of the common law disability for the question before the Supreme Court. He did so by stressing that the authority of the Canadian Parliament was such that there could not be a presumption, taken from the common law, in favour of excluding women from public office in Canada. 'It would, I think, hardly be disputed', said Justice Duff, 'that as general rule the legislative authority of [the Canadian] Parliament and of legislatures enables them each in their several fields to deal fully with this subject of the incapacity of women'.[141] Justice Duff therefore sought to push aside those 'extraneous facts' that might be said to limit the authority of the Canadian Parliament, including the common law disability, saying that:

> … their value becomes inconsiderable when compared with reasons deriving their force from the presumption that the Constitution in its executive branch was intended to be capable of adaptation to whatever changes permissible under the Act in the law and practice relating to the election branch might be progressively required by changes in public opinion.[142]

[137] Sharpe and McMahon (2007).

[138] Ibid, 134.

[139] Justice Duff, quoted at Ibid.

[140] *Edwards v Attorney-General of Canada* (1928) SCR 291, 301, per Duff J. Subsequent references to this judgement are *Edwards* (1928).

[141] Ibid, 294.

[142] Ibid, 299.

As Sharpe and McMahon note, having read thus far, 'the reader could be forgiven for anticipating a strong and courageous dissent, endorsing the right of women to take their place in the Senate'.[143] Instead, however, Justice Duff analysed section 24 in the context of the *BNA Act*, and placed special emphasis on the 'earlier statutes':

> It seems to me to be a legitimate inference that the 1928 British North America Act contemplated a second Chamber, the constitution of which should, in all respects, be fixed and determined by the Act itself, a constitution which was to be in principle the same, though, necessarily, in detail, not identical, with that of the second Chamber established by the earlier statutes. That under those statutes, women were not eligible for appointment, is hardly susceptible of controversy.[144]

Justice Duff, then, despite being in other respects open to a more progressive interpretation, 'could not escape the historical legal subjugation of women'.[145] Further, he had referred, in the above passage, to language that was decidedly un-organic: 'fixed' and 'determined'. Justice Duff had, nevertheless, arguably opened a door, having done so by resisting the relevance of the common law disability and emphasising the relative autonomy of the Canadian Parliament. As we shall see in a moment, this was to play an important role in Lord Sankey's opinion.

One more precursor to Lord Sankey's opinion ought to be mentioned, namely the prior jurisprudence of the Privy Council vis-à-vis Canada. By the time of the *Edwards* case, the Privy Council had already acquired a reputation as a court that was willing to resist the will of the Canadian government. Sharpe and McMahon note that, in 1929, the Privy Council 'was the source of growing frustration among most English Canadian constitutional scholars'.[146] The Privy Council had acquired this reputation through a series of cases that limited the power of the central, federal government vis-à-vis the provinces, primarily by interpreting narrowly the power of the central, federal government to legislate in relation to 'trade and commerce' and 'peace, order and good government'. In cases from 1921, and just prior to *Edwards* in the case of *Nadan v The King*,[147] the Privy Council had not pulled its punches. Indeed, so much was this so, that there were calls for abolishing appeals from Canada to the Privy Council, and these were especially vocal following the latest decision in 1926. In the end, appeals to the Privy Council from Canada were not abolished till 1949, but in the late 1920s, just as the *Edwards* case came to the Privy Council, tensions were high. A lot, it seemed, was at stake, especially in terms of the quality of relations between the British Empire and its Canadian Dominion, and thus including the very authority and legitimacy of the Privy Council itself.[148]

ii. Lord Sankey's Judgement

Lord Sankey did not keep his audience in suspense: early on in the judgement, he made it clear that 'Their Lordships are of the opinion that the word "persons" in s. 24 does

[143] Sharpe and McMahon (2007), 135.
[144] *Edwards* (1928), 301.
[145] Sharpe and McMahon (2007), 135.
[146] Ibid, 142.
[147] *Nadan v The King* (1926) AC 482.
[148] On this history, see, eg, MacDonald (1951); Herman (1976); and Roland (2007).

include women, and that women are eligible to be summoned to and become members of the Senate of Canada'.[149] His reasoning was set out in two parts (to some extent, mirroring Justice Duff's), the first dealing with 'external evidence', such as previous legislation and cases, and the second with the 'internal evidence derived from the Act itself'.[150] It was in introducing the second part, on internal evidence, that we encounter the metaphors that are of most direct interest, but the first part, too, is not without metaphorical language.

In the first part of his judgement, Lord Sankey examined examples of the exclusion of women from public office, ranging from old Germanic customary laws, Roman law, and through to the common law cases, which, as above, loomed so large for the majority in the Supreme Court. In remarking on the common law cases in particular, Lord Sankey referred with approval to Justice Duff's treatment of them, agreeing with him that one cannot separate section 24 from the 'Act as a whole', including being mindful of 'the special history of the development of Canadian legislature'.[151] In light of that history, and grouping together all these 'extraneous' examples, Lord Sankey said:

> … their Lordships do not think it right to apply rigidly to Canada of to-day the decisions and the reasons therefor which commended themselves, probably rightly, to those who had to apply the law in different circumstances, in different centuries, to countries in different stages of development. … their Lordships think that the appeal to Roman law and to early English decisions is not of itself a secure foundation on which to build the interpretation of the British North America Act of 1867.[152]

We see in this passage reference being made to a metaphor that has largely become dormant, or in my terminology, no longer functioning to signal artifice, namely that of the 'secure foundations' of constitutional interpretation.[153] It was, however, very soon after this passage, and by way of what he characterised as an introduction to the second part of his judgement, on internal evidence, that Lord Sankey began to bring in metaphors that were less dormant. Referring to 'the circumstances which led up to the passing of the Act', Lord Sankey said:

> The communities included within the Brittanic system embrace countries and peoples in every stage of social, political, and economic development and undergoing a continuous process of evolution. His Majesty the King in Council is the final Court of Appeal from all these communities, and this Board must take great care therefore not to interpret legislation meant to apply to one community by a rigid adherence to the customs and traditions of another.[154]

It is clear that what Lord Sankey realised was at stake was not only the relationship between the British Empire and Canada, and, indeed, the other communities in

[149] *Edwards* (1930), 127.
[150] Ibid.
[151] Ibid, 131.
[152] Ibid, 134–5.
[153] The most famous and most influential metaphor of foundations is of course that of St Paul's in 1 *Corinthians* 3:10: 'According to the grace of God which is given unto me, as a wise master-builder, I have laid the foundation, and another buildeth thereon'. It is interesting that part of the metaphor here is St Paul's self-character as a 'wise master-builder'. For a discussion, see Carruthers (1998), 17.
[154] *Edwards* (1930), 135.

the Empire, but more specifically the authority and legitimacy of the Privy Council. The above passage refers to two metaphors: the idea of each community being in a 'process of evolution', and the notion of 'rigid adherence to the customs and traditions' of a certain community. We also see processes of evolution being valanced as something positive, and rigidity, which is extended to rigid adherence to customs, especially in this case, English customs, as something negative. The tension between these two metaphors is parallel to another tension: between, as Lord Sankey expressed it, 'the mother country', namely England, and 'the political genius of Canadian statesmen'.[155]

As set up by Lord Sankey, the task here is a difficult balancing act, involving the protection of a number of potentially antithetical values, vulnerabilities and interests: the authority and legitimacy of the Privy Council (which, as above, was vulnerable at the time), the interests and (to Lord Sankey) the value of Empire (its benevolent paternalism, as per the 'mother country' metaphor), and the value of the recognition of Canada and its peoples as a distinct political community of its own.

It is against this background that Lord Sankey introduced the passage for which the case is famous:

> The British North America Act planted in Canada a living tree capable of growth and expansion within its natural limits. The object of the Act was to grant a Constitution to Canada … Their Lordships do not conceive it to be the duty of this Board – it is certainly not their desire – to cut down the provisions of the Act by a narrow and technical construction, but rather to give it a large and liberal interpretation so that the Dominion to a great extent, but within certain fixed limits, may be mistress in her own house, as the Provinces to a great extent, but within certain fixed limits, are mistresses in theirs.[156]

This is a remarkable passage, not least because of its multiple metaphors. There are at least three metaphors: first, there is the metaphor of the *BNA Act* planting in Canada 'a living tree capable of growth and expansion with its natural limits'; second, there is the metaphor of the exercise of interpretation by the Privy Council as being, potentially, and avoidably, one of cutting down the provisions of the Act; and third, there is the metaphor that relations between the British Empire, and especially the Privy Council, through its exercises of interpretation, and Canada can be juxtaposed with a) relations between persons (presumably husbands) on the one hand, and being a mistress in one's own house on the other hand, and b) relations between the Dominion, ie the central, federal government, on the one hand, and the Provinces on the other hand. This third metaphor is especially complex in structure, with three relations being juxtaposed: 1) being a mistress in one's own house vis-à-vis others, including, presumably, one's husband; 2) relations between the British Empire and Canada; and 3) relations between the Dominion and Provincial governments in Canada.

As Lord Sankey would have been deeply aware – again, freshly so, given this was his first judgement as Lord Chancellor presiding over the Privy Council – all the issues that this passage alluded to were hot political potatoes and bursting with controversy. The multiple metaphors in this passage not only address multiple issues, but they arguably

[155] Ibid, 135–6.

[156] Ibid, 136. In addition to the points made below, it is also interesting to observe – as one of my students pointed out – that what is planted here is an already grown tree and not, for instance, a seed.

do so in a way that seeks to create a positively-valanced balance between the various values, vulnerabilities and interests at stake.

The first and second metaphors are clearly related. They work together, as metaphors often do (it is often said, for instance, that metaphors hunt in packs). They also combine two issues into one: the question of the relations between the British Empire (and its precedents, in this case the common law disability) and the 'communities' in its 'system'; and the question of the authority and legitimacy of the Privy Council, especially in its exercise of its power to interpret the constitutions of those communities. Note, though, that the question of the method of constitutional interpretation is very much nestled in the broader and more directly pertinent issue of relations between the British Empire and its 'communities': what is at stake is not constitutional interpretation as such, or in some general way, but the interpretation of the constitutional documents of other communities by the Privy Council.

The first and second metaphors above tackle the issue with great sensitivity: they ask, the listeners to or readers of this opinion – and it is noteworthy that Lord Sankey insisted on reading out aloud this entire opinion in Court, which was unusual[157] – to see the Act in question, the *BNA Act*, as planting a tree, and to see, relatedly, the Court as a gardener. This gardener, in turn, could be either a destructive one, ie cutting down by employing narrow and technical constructions ('narrow' too here being a metaphor, though a largely dormant one) or a caring one, this being one which employs 'large and liberal interpretation' (again, 'large' is also a metaphor here, even if once more a predominantly dormant one). Large and liberal interpretation is to be preferred to narrow and technical construction; equally, the caring actions of a gardener are to be preferred to actions, eg cutting down, that show no respect for a living tree.

In this respect, these two metaphors seek to convey respect for Canada and its peoples as a political community while at the same time seeking to inject authority and legitimacy to powers exercised by the Privy Council. Indeed, the metaphors suggest that the Privy Council may need to act robustly to protect the Canadian Constitution. Showing considerable political subtlety, the metaphors present the potentially robust exercise of power by the Privy Council, at times going against the power of the local court (in this case, the allegedly narrow and technical construction by the Supreme Court), as an act of protection (benevolent paternalism again), ie as an act of care rather than destruction.

The metaphor of the living tree, then, is arguably less about progressive interpretation, than it is about the legitimacy and authority of the Privy Council to take a robust stance, potentially against the wishes of the Canadian government. Part of its political subtlety as a metaphor is that it presents this robust exercise of power as an action of caring for a living tree. Of course, one should not to be too cynical. Lord Sankey is confronted with a difficult task, and one that, as above, requires a number of values, vulnerabilities and interests to be kept in mind and balanced. The metaphor of the living tree does, in part, express respect for the autonomy of the political community that is Canada, and this is certainly a metaphor that recognises that Canada, like the other 'communities included within the Brittanic system', is 'undergoing a continuous

[157] Sharpe and McMahon (2007), 181.

process of evolution', which also means recognition that its customs and conventions will change over time. But the metaphor is seeking to do more than that: it also, if not primarily, protects the authority and legitimacy of the Privy Council in taking a robust stance vis-à-vis Canada and other communities. Indeed, the reference to 'limits' of any political autonomy is strong in the above passage: not only directly in the metaphor of the living tree, which, it is said, is 'capable of growth and expansion within its natural limits', but also with the repetition of 'certain fixed limits' enjoyed by mistresses in their own houses, communities within the Britannic system, and Dominions and Provinces vis-à-vis each other.

In fact, when looked at closely, the metaphor does not claim that the *BNA Act* is a living tree, but that it *plants* a living tree: in short, the living tree in this metaphor may not be the constitution, but instead the political community of Canada, with the Privy Council as its (ideally) caring and benevolent gardener. As conceived by the metaphor, Canada is a political community in own right, and this must be recognised and protected, but it is only relatively autonomous, ie its autonomy operates within certain natural or fixed limits. As a political community, it grows and expands, and this is a good thing, just as living trees are a good thing, but sometimes, this political community must be protected against itself, eg as when its own court (the Supreme Court) seeks to cut down the growth of its own political community (here, the capacity of women to be summoned to the Senate) by a narrow and technical construction of its constitutional provisions.

The paternalism and, at the same time, the defence of imperial power, is reinforced by the third metaphor, in which the following three are juxtaposed: mistresses in their own houses, relations between British Empire and Canada, and relations between the Dominion and the Provinces. In this obviously intensely gendered metaphor, Canada is a mistress in her own house vis-à-vis the British Empire, and the Provinces too are mistresses in their own houses vis-à-vis the Dominion government. Against the background of the controversy surrounding the Privy Council's interpretation of the central, federal government's powers as related to the provinces, the metaphor is once again remarkably politically astute: if the central, federal government wishes to keep the provinces in line, as it was clear that it wanted to, then they themselves must be kept in line by the British Empire, and its agent, the Privy Council. Thus, the authority and legitimacy of the central, federal government vis-à-vis its provinces is being equated with the authority and legitimacy of the British Empire, and especially the Privy Council, vis-à-vis the central, federal government in Canada. And both, in a clearly gendered way, are being related to the practice of good husbandry, which grants to women the relative autonomy of being 'mistresses in their own houses', but still within 'natural limits'. This is indeed a metaphorically thorough paternalism.

Lord Sankey's metaphors in this case are all the more powerful, though also strange, for how little they feature in the subsequent analysis of the 'internal evidence' of the Act. In other words, the above metaphors are not directly involved, as metaphors certainly can be, in the process of constitutional interpretation. Here, the metaphors are preparatory, and concerned more, at least as presented by Lord Sankey, with the authority and legitimacy of the Privy Council than with any particular substance or method of constitutional interpretation.

What Lord Sankey went on to do is offer in many respects a quite conventional analysis of section 24 in the context of other provisions of the Act. Lord Sankey's first move in this respect was to say that, given that in general, the word 'person' 'may include members of both sexes … the burden is upon those who deny that the word includes women to make out their case'.[158] Can those who deny this make out the case? No, they cannot, answers Lord Sankey, but not because of the importance of constitutional interpretation being progressive and keeping up with changing social conditions, but because there is simply not enough evidence in the language of the Act to discharge the burden, and there is evidence to suggest otherwise. Thus, for instance, certain provisions in the Act refer explicitly to males, with the implication being that if females were intended to be excluded by section 24, then all that was needed was for the word 'males' rather than 'persons' to be used.[159]

In terms of potentially contrary 'internal evidence', Lord Sankey went through the possible arguments one-by-one, showing why they do not work, eg by 'qualified persons' in section 24, what is meant is not that this excludes all those 'who become subjects by marriage', but rather, because of the *Aliens Act 1844*, extends to all subjects, including married women.[160] Similar kinds of arguments were countered by reference to related sections, such as section 23, again often by reference to surrounding statutes, eg by virtue of the *Women's Property Acts*, married women can possess the property qualification required by section 23.[161]

There was no reference throughout these arguments to the importance of a progressive interpretation, especially one that could be at odds with the intentions of the legislature. In fact, the analysis throughout was made on the basis of what the 'internal evidence' reveals about the intentions of the legislature. In concluding, Lord Sankey summarised the argument as follows:

> A heavy burden lies on an appellant who seeks to set aside a unanimous judgement of the Supreme Court, and this Board will only set aside such a decision after convincing argument and anxious consideration, but having regard: 1) To the object of the Act – namely, to provide a constitution for Canada, a responsible and developing State; 2) that the word "person" is ambiguous, and may include members of either sex; 3) that there are sections in the Act above referred to which show that in some cases the word "person" must include females; 4) that in some sections the words "male persons" are expressly used when it is desire to confine the matter in issue to males; and 5) to the provisions of the Interpretation Act; their Lordships have come to the conclusion that the word "persons" in s. 24 includes members both of the male and female sex, and that, therefore, the question propounded by the Governor General should be an answered in the affirmative, and that women are eligible to be summoned to and become members of the Senate of Canada, and they will humbly advise His Majesty accordingly.[162]

Note, again, the paternalism in this passage: Canada is a 'responsible and developing State'. Note, further, the self-characterisations of the Board, ie the Privy Council, as

[158] *Edwards* (1930), 138.
[159] Ibid, 141.
[160] Ibid, 139.
[161] Ibid, 140.
[162] Ibid, 143.

having exercised 'anxious consideration', mindful of the 'heavy burden' that rests upon it in disagreeing with the Supreme Court, and doing nothing but 'humbly advising' the King. Once more, what is at stake here is the authority and legitimacy of the Privy Council in caring for the communities in its system, as well as the various values, vulnerabilities and interests at play in relations between the British Empire and those communities.

iii. Imperial Metaphors

The metaphors in *Edwards*, then, especially when read in the context of the politics of the time, and also when read in the context of the judgement as a whole, including by way of attention to the multiple metaphors in the text, may be best characterised as (highly-gendered) imperial metaphors, and ones especially designed to deflect critical attention away from the exercise of power by the Privy Council. They are not, at least not directly, concerned with the proper method of constitutional interpretation in general; they are concerned with the authority and legitimacy of the Privy Council, as an agent of British Empire, and as the interpreter of the constitutions of communities within the Empire. The metaphors do play a part in the justification of the decision, but more so by way of setting the ground for the general exercise of power by the Privy Council, and less so in terms of direct involvement in the substance or method of the interpretation. They certainly play an important part in the exercise of inquiry, ie even if just confined to this one case, in the making of normative insight as to what values, vulnerabilities and interests are at stake in exercises of power by the Privy Council.

How do these metaphors achieve all this? They do so by first of all functioning as artefacts: as we saw above, not all the metaphors in the opinion were equally artefactual – in fact, many were dormant – but some certainly signalled their own artifice, bringing attention to themselves as a means of communication. This was so in particular for the living tree metaphor, and the metaphor of mistresses in their own houses. In doing so, these metaphors also invite us to do something with them: they call upon the activity of the audience, ie they involve the audience, requiring them to engage in the process of metaphorical imagining. That process is two-fold. First, we enter a distinctive epistemic frame, where we selectively suspend certain epistemic norms and commitments: here, for instance, we selectively suspend the epistemic norms of reference or direct relevance, eg we suspend epistemic norms that would otherwise force us to treat as nonsense the identity equation or juxtaposition of a political community with a living tree or a mistress in her own house. Secondly, we participate, simulating affectively, sensorially and kinesically, eg we may associate living trees with something of value, something which has its own life that is worth protecting, and indeed requires protection, and we may thus experience emotions of both respect and care, simultaneously constructing mental imagery, eg of trees bursting with life, in full bloom, green in the sunshine. Similarly with mistresses in their own houses: we may experience emotions of feeling safe and protected, as well as being proud and in control, in one's own house, while nevertheless somewhat anxious about anything outside it, and thus in need of protection so that we keep our security, with these emotions also potentially being accompanied by certain images from the perspective of the mistress in her house, eg seeing a particular house, kept neat, tidy and ordered, and one in which we know where everything is, with everything being in its proper place. We may well also simulate kinesically, eg as we encounter the metaphor of cutting down provisions, we may experience a kinesic reaction: an almost physical reaction against the idea of cutting down a living tree (the 'living' acts to reinforce the kinesic reluctance to 'cut down').

Our affective, sensory and kinesic participation in the sources, eg living tree, of these metaphors is likely to be guided, to some extent by the relevant targets, eg the political community of Canada, as well as being transformative of both sources and targets. For instance, we may now well experience the Privy Council as a caring gardener who is protective of living trees, ie the political communities planted by the imperial constitutions, or as a benevolent husband who allows us, as the mistress, to keep operating as a mistress in our own house. We may also experience narrow and technical constructions of constitutions, as arguably engaged in by the majority of the Canadian Supreme Court, as something to be avoided, now overlaid with the negative kinesic experience of cutting down living trees. And, although our understanding of trees may not be at the forefront of our attention – with our focus, on the whole, being on the target rather than the source of the metaphor – our understanding of trees may still have been transformed by our now associating them with the growth and development of political communities.

Part of the point here is that as an audience we are active: the audience participates in the process of metaphorical imagining. As we do so, we may well come under the persuasive effects of these metaphors, and all the more so because we are actively imagining. Nevertheless, the value of these metaphors, and our activities of imagining them, as readers, are not confined to their immediate power as means of persuasion. Even if we just confine ourselves to this instant case, we can see how the process of metaphorical imagining helps us to generate insight as to what values, vulnerabilities and interests are at stake in exercises of power by the Privy Council. We come, if nothing else, to appreciate the complexity of the task involved, and the multiple values, vulnerabilities and interests that need to be kept in mind. These include, as above, the value of the autonomy of political communities, the interests (and, to some, the value) of Empire, and the vulnerability of persons vis-a-vis the interests of government (in this case, this includes not only Canadian women, but also the peoples in the provinces of Canada).

B. The Life of the Metaphor After *Edwards*

We should not, however, confine our engagement and evaluation of the above metaphors to the case itself. Just as with fictions, if we confine ourselves to the one case, and do not trace the life of this metaphor over time, seeing how it generates resources across time, then we will miss its value, or confine it too narrowly, eg to mere persuasion or deft political manoeuvring. To do this in any amount of detail falls outside the scope of this chapter: all I can do is point to some examples and show how the metaphor enables inquiry over time. This is all the more so with respect to this case: perhaps no one, not even Lord Sankey, could have predicted at the time *Edwards* was decided, that it would go on to become one of the most iconic constitutional cases of the modern age, debated endlessly both by judges and scholars, and also reaching beyond into the general culture, eg being celebrated nationally in Canada in the form of an annual Persons Day.

i. Canadian Constitutional Law

A flavour for the legacy of the *Edwards* case, and, at once, the career of its metaphors, can be gleaned from even a cursory glance at another landmark Canadian constitutional decision, this time from the Supreme Court of Canada: *Reference re Same-Sex Marriage*.[163] There are no less than 75 years between the two cases, and we shall see just how influential *Edwards* had by that time become, but also how its significance had been transformed.

As in *Edwards*, the *Same-Sex Marriage* case involved a reference from the Governor in Council, with four questions being asked:

1. Was the proposed Act within the exclusive legislative authority of the Parliament of Canada?
2. Was s. 1 of the proposed Act, which extended capacity to marry two persons of the same sex, consistent with the *Canadian Charter of Rights and Freedoms* 1982?
3. Did the freedom of religion guaranteed by s. 2 (freedom of conscience and religion) of the charter protect religious officials from being compelled to perform same-sex marriages contrary to their religious beliefs?
4. Was the opposite-sex requirement for marriage for civil purposes consistent with the charter?

The 'proposed Act' referred to in the question concerned a proposal by the federal government 'for an Act respecting certain aspects of legal capacity for marriage for civil purposes'.[164] The relevant sections of the proposed Act were as follows:

1. Marriage, for civil purposes, is the lawful union of two persons to the exclusion of all others.
2. Nothing in this Act affects the freedom of officials of religious groups to refuse to perform marriages that are not in accordance with their religious beliefs.

The unanimous judgement and opinion of the Supreme Court was delivered by Chief Justice McLachlin. For present purposes, the key question is the first. To this, the Court answered in the affirmative: 'the proposed Act is within the exclusive legislative competence of Parliament, while s. 2 is not'.[165] Of the two sections, it is section 1 that is most relevant, and of the various issues surrounding legislative competence with respect to section 1, what is most significant is the Court's reasoning on the scope of section 91(26) of the *BNA Act*, which 'confers on Parliament competence in respect of "Marriage and Divorce"'.[166] At stake, then, is the interpretation of section 91(26), and in particular, whether it could be interpreted in such a way as to enable Parliament to legislate with respect to same-sex marriage, as in the Proposed Act.

Interveners in the case raised a number of objections against the government's claim that the section 91(26) did give them the requisite legislative competence. Of these, the pertinent one for our purposes was that 'the meaning of "marriage" is

[163] *Reference re Same-Sex Marriage* (2004) 19 BHRC 658.
[164] Ibid, 661, per McLachlin CJ.
[165] Ibid, 662.
[166] Ibid, 664.

constitutionally fixed, necessarily incorporating an opposite-sex requirement'.[167] The Court rejected this intervention, and it did so largely on the basis of the *Edwards* case. Indeed, the intervention, as articulated above, already contained a familiar metaphor: the idea of 'fixed' meanings. It did not take Justice McLachlin long to engage with the interveners' argument by way of a war of two metaphors:

> The 'frozen concepts' reasoning runs contrary to one of the most fundamental principles of Canadian constitutional interpretation: that our constitution is a living tree which, by way of progressive interpretation, accommodates and addresses the realities of modern life.[168]

This passage already gives us a sense of just how *Edwards* had, by this time, been transformed. By now, the living tree metaphor has metamorphosed from being, as above, an imperial metaphor, concerned with the authority and legitimacy of the Privy Council to robustly interpret the constitutions of communities within the British Empire, and where the living tree referred to the political community that was planted by the *BNA Act*, to a metaphor of general constitutional interpretation, ie as above, a 'progressive' one, which 'accommodates and addresses the realities of modern life', where the constitution itself is equated with a living tree.

Further, the transformed meaning of the metaphor is also affected by the metaphor with which it is so starkly opposed, namely the idea of 'frozen concepts' or 'fixed meanings'. Arguably, here, the living tree metaphor is more artefactual – it signals more effectively its own artifice – than the two metaphors it is opposed to (frozen, fixed), with perhaps 'frozen' being more artefactual than 'fixed'. Nevertheless, it is also clear that by this time, the metaphors on both sides had already taken on certain conventional meanings: ie that 'the constitution is a living tree' means the adoption of a certain method of constitutional interpretation, ie as above, a progressive one, and that this was in opposition to a 'frozen concepts' approach, which characterised the meanings of constitutional terms as fixed at the time of their enactment, and was more conservative in political orientation.

Even if they have become somewhat conventional, the opposition of the metaphors is significant, given the very different processes of imagination that they invite. Whereas 'the living tree' metaphor is positively valanced, with our participation involving, as above, positive affective, sensory and kinesic simulation, eg of respect, care, protection, growth, feeling alive, the 'frozen concepts' metaphor is clearly negatively valanced, inviting emotional, sensory and kinesic simulation of feeling cold, anxious, vulnerable, exposed, un-protected, trapped and stunted. Again, this effect is generated not only by the processing of the 'living tree' metaphor itself, but also by the opposition of that metaphor with the 'frozen concepts' one. Metaphors, it seems, not only hunt in packs, but in opposing gangs.

Justice McLachlin went on, immediately after the above passage, to quote Lord Sankey, referring to the metaphors of 'cutting down' the provisions of the *BNA Act* by a narrow and technical construction, and to the metaphor of being a mistress in one's

[167] Ibid.
[168] Ibid.

own house. What is emphasised, however, in the relevant quote is the more abstract idea of giving the *BNA Act* a 'large and liberal interpretation'.[169] Justice McLachlin continued:

> A large and liberal or progressive interpretation ensures the continued relevance and, indeed, legitimacy of Canada's constituting document. By way of progressive interpretation our constitution succeeds in this ambitious enterprise, that of structuring the exercise of power by the organs of the state in times vastly different from those in which it was crafted.[170]

Lost from view is the specific work that the metaphors of cutting down and being a mistress in one's own house performed in Lord Sankey's judgement. Instead, the emphasis is placed on associating the metaphor of the living tree with 'large and liberal interpretation'. This is further buttressed by reference to yet another metaphor in Lord Sankey's opinion, namely his argument that 'early English decisions are not a "secure foundation on which to build the interpretation" of our constitution'.[171] Again, one metaphor – of the living tree – has now been transformed into one advocating 'large and liberal interpretation', with all others subordinated to it, including the architectural metaphor of history as an unsecure foundation. Where, however, Lord Sankey's architectural metaphor referred specifically to the unsecure foundations of 'early English decisions', with the emphasis on 'English', the metaphor has now been transformed into one which generally casts doubt on the relevance of precedents in the distant past.

The metaphor of the living tree features in one more argument addressed by the Court. This argument, by the interveners, itself relies on a transformed meaning of Lord Sankey's metaphor. To recall, Lord Sankey had said that although the *BNA Act* planted a living tree, including a tree that was 'capable of growth and expansion', it did so 'within its natural limits'. As above, the work of the metaphor in Lord Sankey's judgement referred to the control by the British Empire, including by its agent, the Privy Council, of the autonomy of the political community planted by the *BNA Act*: the political community could grow and expand, but not too far; it had to still be kept in check by the Empire. This included being kept in check via robust exercises of interpretation by the Privy Council, all in the name of protecting the political community of Canada. By now, however, the metaphor had undergone transformation: indeed, in a sense, this limb of the metaphor had been, so to speak, de-metaphorised, with 'natural limits' taken to mean what was arguably, on some interpretation, natural to human life or within human nature, ie in this case, that same-sex marriage was unnatural, for what was natural to human life was procreation. The Court dealt with this argument in the following manner:

> The natural limits argument can succeed only if its proponents can identify an objective core of meaning which defines what is 'natural' in relation to marriage. Absent this the argument is merely tautological. The only objective core which the interveners before us agree is 'natural' to marriage is that it is the voluntary union of two people to the exclusion of all others. Beyond this, views diverge. We are faced with competing opinions on what the natural limits of marriage may be. Lord Sankey's reference to "natural limits" did not impose an obligation to determine, in the abstract and absolutely, the core meaning of constitutional terms.

[169] Ibid, 665.
[170] Ibid.
[171] Ibid.

> Consequently, it is not for the court to determine, in the abstract, what the natural limits of marriage must be. Rather, the court's role is to determine whether marriage is defined in the proposed Act falls within the subject matter of s. 91(26). In determining whether legislation falls within a particular heard of power, a progressive interpretation of the head of power must be adopted.[172]

'Natural limits' has, in this passage, been transformed once more, not now, as in the interveners' argument, referring to what is natural to human life, but instead requiring identification of a 'core meaning' (a metaphor in its own right), and one that was agreed to by all concerned. The living tree, it seems, has dropped out of the picture: where, arguably, the interveners' argument could still be related to the metaphor – with the idea of unnatural growth or expansion, and thus the equation being made between same-sex marriage and a tree growing unnaturally – the Court's interpretation of 'natural limits' has separated it out of the metaphor, now referring to an unanimously agreed meaning of a certain term. Either way, the distance to Lord Sankey could hardly be greater: what was an imperial metaphor, referring to the authority and legitimacy of the British Empire, and especially the Privy Council itself, to keep in check, caringly and benevolently, the autonomy of the political community of Canada, has become the site of debate as to the meanings of constitutional terms.

ii. The Metaphor Debated

To be clear: the point of the above analysis is not to criticise the treatment of *Edwards* by the *Same-Sex Marriage* case. I am not arguing that the Court in the later case misreads or misuses the metaphors in *Edwards*. What interests me is the transformation of the metaphor, ie how, over time, it has come to generate other kinds of resources, and, also, how it has served as a place of debate and disagreement. The transformation of the metaphor is certainly a striking one: it has come, over time, to function less as an artefact, and to take on a certain conventional meaning, one in which the metaphor functions as a signpost for a certain method of constitutional interpretation, or, sometimes, a broader theory of the meaning of constitutional terms.

And yet, the metaphor has not become entirely conventionalised. It has clearly offered guidance, perhaps especially when contrasted with the 'frozen concepts' approach, but it has also remained hotly contested. Indeed, subsequent generations of both judges and scholars have returned again and again to the metaphor, imagining it in different ways, and sometimes, significantly for my purposes, in ways that are in tension with each other. The liveliness of this debate is testament to the continued artefactuality of the metaphor, which may be diminished at certain times, as when it takes on a more conventional meaning, but which is revived again when it is imagined, as it always can be, in some less conventional manner.

One scholar who has noticed tensions and divergences in subsequent imaginings of the metaphor, while at the same time contributing herself to the revival of the artefactuality of it, is Vicki Jackson.[173] Speaking generally of different metaphors of constitutional

[172] Ibid, 666.
[173] Jackson (2006).

interpretation, Jackson has argued that the Canadian 'living tree' metaphor 'may better embrace the multiple modalities – text, original intentions, structure and purpose, precedent and doctrine, values and ethos, prudential or consequentialist concerns – of contemporary constitutional interpretation' than the metaphor (more common in the US) of the 'living constitution'.[174] Jackson goes on:

> Unlike the less tethered 'living constitution', it [the 'living tree' metaphor] captures the idea of constraint, the role of text and original understanding in the roots of the constitutional tree and the role of precedent and new developments in its growth.[175]

Here, Jackson participates in the imagining of the metaphor by constructing alternative imagery of it, associated with different emotions: the roots of a living tree, with emotions of respect for the past, the strength and balance provided by rootedness, the security of a foundation. Confirming the importance of kinesic simulation as part of metaphorical processing, Jackson argues that 'the living constitution' metaphor is 'oddly disembodied'.[176] Her own imagining of the living tree metaphor is, by contrast, full of affective, sensory and kinesic simulation:

> … the tree metaphor is one that draws attention to origins, to roots, as well as to the possibility of growth. It implies a connection with interpretation in older decisions and a more constrained view of the choices open to later generations – unlike animals that can migrate at will, plants (including trees), must grow from where they begin, and maintain contact with their roots for nourishment and health. Though not without its difficulties, the living tree metaphor embraces the mixed elements of rootedness and change that are so much a part of American constitutional adjudication.[177]

Later, Jackson draws on even more strongly kinetic language:

> [The living tree metaphor] conveys the idea of balance (so the tree will not fall over); it avoids the inflexibility of narrowly grounded historical interpretation (structures that are too rigid break rather than bend under the pressures of time). It embodies the idea of flexibility over time, of the shaping and pruning of a tree through forces of human agency as well as conditions that push in particular directions, without the connotations of untethered, illegitimate decision-making by whoever happens to be the judges. It treats the Constitution as underdetermined, but not entirely indeterminate; there are roots, a trunk and large branches that condition the choices open to claimants, litigants and judges. And it conveys both the possible longevity, and possible fragility, of a constitution.[178]

The point in quoting these passages is to show how metaphorical language enables precisely the kind of imagining that Jackson engages in, and, importantly, how this imagining is valuable to inquiry, ie how it generates normative insight, in this case, as to a constitutional text and the work it does or can do in a certain community. Part of that work is additive, in the sense that it adds novel affectively- and kinesically-loaded images, eg as above, the roots, the idea of balance, to the metaphor. But part of it is also

[174] Ibid, 926.
[175] Ibid.
[176] Ibid, 942.
[177] Ibid, 954.
[178] Ibid, 958–9.

critical. For Jackson, while she nevertheless clearly prefers the 'living tree' metaphor to that of the 'living constitution', there are also difficulties and dangers in the former. Jackson argues, for instance, that 'the tree metaphor understates the effects of major constitutional change and the role of human change in that process.'[179] It is interesting to observe how Jackson engages in the process of critical metaphorical imagining:

> On the other hand, the 'living tree' is only a metaphor and, in some respects, a misleading one. The image that may come to mind – a spreading oak, a graceful maple, the iconic representations of the 'tree of life' – are single-trunked and generally symmetrically branched. Older constitutions, like the United States', however, may have formal amendments that are in some respects more like second trunks. The Civil War Amendments in the United States do not seem entirely like branches but rather like new legal roots of a markedly changed form of constitutionalism. Likewise, in Canada, the Charter of 1982 does not seem so much like a branch as a newly rooted foundation, a joint foundation with the 1867 Act. Can we conceive of a multi-trunked tree? Although there are such trees (banyan trees have multiple trunks and roots; aspens may grow as clones in groves with a common root system), the metaphor now seems strained. Moreover, the natural metaphor understates the role of human agency and the extent of the rupture in the United States from founding premises represented by the Civil War Amendments' outlawing of slavery, abandonment of the 'three-fifths compromise', and extension of federal constitutional rights to limit the state governments.[180]

Jackson's article, then, is an excellent example, as is also the *Same-Sex Marriage* case, of a metaphor being played with interactively and collectively over time. Sometimes, further images, along with affective and kinesic associations, are added to a metaphor; sometimes, a metaphor is criticised for guiding in a particular way. Further judges and scholars respond and interact with the various additions or criticism. In all these ways, a metaphor enables and contributes to inquiry: it serves as language that stimulates and provokes, that remains a little strange, though it is subject, also, to the heavy processes of conventionalisation. That fact that it is contested, ie that scholars and judges, including members of the general public, as per the interveners in the *Same-Sex Marriage* case, contribute different and sometimes opposing images and associations with a metaphor, is a sign that its artefactuality is still working, and that it is still contributing to inquiry.

There is, of course, a long, rich history of the transformation of this particular metaphor to be told. This chapter is not, however, the occasion for this telling; indeed, a number of scholars have engaged with this history already.[181] Some of these scholars have engaged with the legacy of the decision, as understood retrospectively, ie with the transformation in the metaphor already been taken for granted; while others have noted the discrepancies between the metaphors as deployed in *Edwards* and as transformed later, into an icon of progressive constitutional interpretation.[182] Some have engaged with the metaphor, drawing on it to develop an elaborate and sophisticated theory of

[179] Ibid, 926.
[180] Ibid, 959.
[181] In addition to Jackson (2006), see, eg, Waluchow (2015); Horwitz (1993); McBain (1927); Miller (2009) and (2011); Brown (2005); and Langford (2010).
[182] See Miller (2011).

constitutional interpretation,[183] while others have argued that it is unhelpful, misleadingly polarising and caricaturing theoretical options.[184] Tellingly, in terms of the capacity of metaphor to engage parties from opposing political orientations, the metaphor has attracted comment from across the political spectrum. Some have also sought to trace the origins of the metaphor in *Edwards* back, typically to other 'organic' metaphors, and often via the US 'living constitution' metaphor.[185] Finally, many have noted the specific temporalities of the living tree metaphor, observing how, although it surfaced occasionally in the years immediately after *Edwards*, it was not till the late 1970s and early 1980s that it really took off in Canada. As Sharpe and McMahon have observed:

> It was not until the revival of the feminist movement in the 1970s and the approach of the fiftieth anniversary of Viscount Sankey's judgement that Canadians renewed their interest in the case and its legacy. In 1979, Edward Schreyer created the Governor General's Awards in Commemoration of the Persons case to recognise the legal and political fight of the Famous Five, rewarding individuals who have made a long-standing and substantial contribution to the equality of women in Canada. As well, Persons Day celebrations sponsored by the Women's Legal Education and action Fund commemorated the case as a focal point in the struggle for gender equality ... Twenty years after the creation of Sankey's judgement, a statute of the Famous Five, promoted by the Famous Five Foundation and sculpted by Barbara Patterson of Edmonton, was unveiled at Calgary's Olympic Plaza. The same statute sits on Parliament Hill amid the various political dignitaries of Canadian history and was unveiled in Ottawa on 18 October 2000. That year, the Bank of Canada issued a new $50 bill with the Famous Five statute on the reverse.[186]

This history is important, for it suggests not only that different metaphors will have differently temporally-shaped careers, with some potentially lying dormant for a long time, but also that they may have considerably broader audiences than just judges, advocates and legal scholars. Indeed, sometimes metaphors from judicial opinions may be revived first in the broader political culture, where they are expressed in a variety of media, and only subsequently make their way back into legal discourse.

iii. Prospects for Other Histories

If we cast our eye back to the *Edwards* case, we can also say more: as it has been explored thus far, the history of this metaphor has largely been told by reference to its use in Canadian constitutional law, with some reference to comparison with the US and Australia.[187] If, however, we recall its imperial character, there is scope for another kind of history: of imperial metaphors, or metaphors deployed as part of an imperial project.

The Privy Council, and its metaphorical self-styling, would be a fascinating case study for such a history. As Rohit De has observed, the Privy Council 'is a self-conscious

[183] See Waluchow (2006).
[184] See Miller (2009).
[185] See Langford (2010).
[186] Sharpe and McMahon (2007), 201.
[187] See Jackson (2006).

agent in legal history',[188] speaking of itself, for instance, as being 'a body, strictly speaking, without any location', for 'The Sovereign is everywhere throughout the Empire in the contemplation of the law'.[189] Paul Mitchell has also observed how the Privy Council has utilised the language of 'distance', this being another example of a spatially-oriented imperial metaphor.[190]

More broadly, of course, one could consider the metaphors that have been deployed for negotiating relations between legal systems and traditions, eg it is interesting, for example, that the metaphor of the living tree has found its way into the jurisprudence of the European Court of Human Rights. For example, as explained in *Mursic v Croatia*:

> It was in the seminal case of *Tyrer v United Kingdom* (1978) that the Court for the very first time used the leitmotiv of "the Convention as a living instrument", whose interpretation as to take account of evolving norms of national and international law.[191]

Judge Pinto de Albuquerque expressly refers to *Edwards*, saying that according to it, 'the constitution is organic and must be read in a broad and liberal manner so as to adapt it to changing times'.[192] No doubt there will be persuasive uses of such metaphors, aimed, for instance, at injecting authority and legitimacy into the powers of particular courts, eg the Privy Council or the ECtHR, but, as we have seen with the metaphor of the living tree, these metaphors will also take on lives of their own, generating their own kinds of debates and disagreements, and, at once, insights about the values, vulnerabilities and interests at stake, eg with respect to the quality of relations between legal systems and traditions.[193]

Yet another angle on a history of the metaphor of the living tree would be to take the long history of the iconography of trees, and relate them to constitutional, but also more broadly political, debates and changes. Scholars have long been interested in the effects of constitutional and political metaphors, eg in organic and architectural metaphors, examining how these appear not only in official documents, including the jurisprudence of courts, but also beyond in the broader culture.[194] Some have examined specifically how certain metaphors enable political change.[195] Trees would be a fascinating case study for such a comparative constitutional and political metaphorology,[196]

[188] De (2014), 823.

[189] *Hull v McKenna* [1926] IR 402, 406, per Lord Haldane; quoted in De (2014), 834. See also Haldane (1923); Swinfen (1987); Keith (2009); and, on the African context, see Ibhawoh (2013).

[190] See Mitchell (2016).

[191] *Mursic v Croatia* [2016] ECHR 7334/13, 78, para 11, partly dissenting opinion of Judge Pinto de Albuquerque. Subsequent references are to *Mursic* (2016). See also *Tyrer v United Kingdom* [1978] ECHR 2.

[192] *Mursic* (2016), 79, fn 19.

[193] See also, recently, Slaughter (2019), who argues that a specific kind of language, specific both grammatically and rhetorically, arises in the 'contact zones' between cultures and communities. These 'creolised languages', which includes legal languages, eg the language of international law, have their own poetics, and thus their own rhetorical constraints and possibilities. These 'contact zones' are suffused with power imbalances: in other words, the particular poetics that emerges here is a colonial or imperial poetics. On the terminology of 'contact zones', see Pratt (2008) [1992]; and for 'creolised languages', see Glissant (1997) [1990].

[194] See, eg, Saccaro-Battisti (2015); and Anker (2015). On organic metaphors, and their long political and legal history, including in Medieval Wales: see Stacey (2018), ch 3.

[195] See Walzer (1967).

[196] The term 'metaphorology' is used by Blumenberg (2010) [1960].

given not only their long history in the political imaginary, eg Brandon Chao-Chin Yen has explored the political iconography of trees in William Wordsworth's *The Excursion* (1814), specifically by reference to the imagery of 'longevity, rootedness, and strength',[197] but also because of their entanglement with models of knowledge, including legal knowledge.[198]

Many histories are possible, and this is to take just one metaphor, eg I have focused on the living tree, but a similar exercise, just as fascinating, could be done on the metaphor of the 'mistress in her own house', which has also had a political life of its own. For instance, it appears in the Hamlyn Lectures of TB Smith, doing so on behalf of the political autonomy of the Scottish legal system:

> To the wooing of Lord Denning on behalf of English law, therefore, for Scots law I should answer courteously: 'You honour me, my Lord, but I cannot marry you; and will be mistress in my own house. Let us remain good friends and share our thoughts, for we have much in common – but less, perhaps, than you sometimes realise. Though I know you are shy with foreigners, still I want you to get to know my relatives on the Continent and overseas'.[199]

As we have seen above, and as this passage also illustrates, referring not only to the metaphor of the mistress in her own house, but also to friendship and relatives, metaphors often hunt together. Thus, future histories might well take groups or families of metaphor, eg as united, for instance, by a certain common kinesic resonance, such as cutting or pruning,[200] or consider pairs of metaphorical opposites, eg living trees verses frozen concepts. The options thereby multiply, but however such histories are done, it would be vital to see, as I have tried in an inevitably incomplete way above, to show how engagement with a metaphor can enable inquiry, ie can generate normative insight about values, vulnerabilities and interests at stake, doing so not only for individuals in a single case, but also, if not especially, over time, interactively and collectively.

[197] Chao-Chi Yen (2017).

[198] See, eg, Lima (2014).

[199] Smith (1961), 228. On some of the language that has been deployed in relations between English and Scottish legal systems, see Braun (2019).

[200] On the metaphor of crystallisation in international customary law, see Del Mar (2017b).

7

Figures

As many scholars have observed, humans are prone to extend their own understandings of themselves to everything around them. There is, it seems, an almost irrestistable tendency to make sense by ascribing agency,[1] or super-imposing other features of the human: seeing faces in clouds, hearing voices in the dark, making body shapes of trees. As universal as this tendency may be, it manifests itself in different ways in different times and places. After all, what are taken to be the relevant or most important features of the human, the person, or the individual, changes over time and varies across cultures. Intentionality, for instance, and thus treating someone, or anything else, by extension, as having a will, is not a universal feature;[2] neither is the very idea of having a face, voice or name, these being features which we now take for granted.

There is, certainly, a fascinating history to be told of the variety of ways in which we think with figures: projecting differing features of what we take to be human as part of making meaning, orientating ourselves, or communicating with each other. Some scholars have done this by focusing on changes in what has counted as a 'person' or a 'character';[3] others by reference to the very idea of personal names, including the emergence of abstractions such as Somebody or Nobody;[4] and others still by reference to the multi-media expressions of faces and masks.[5] Telling, or re-telling that history is not within the scope of this chapter, though a legally-oriented cultural history of differing ways of appealing to and thinking with figures would be a wonderful project.[6] Instead, what I aim to do in this chapter is to focus on one kind of thinking-with-figures, treating figures as a specific sort of artefact, with related processes of imagining, and trying to see how such figures can enable inquiry.

The example I shall be focusing on, in the second part of this chapter, is the Officious Bystander. This is a figure created in the context of the implication of terms in English contract law. It is used as a test for when terms ought to be implied into a contract. I shall be examining in what sense the Officious Bystander is an artefact, and what processes of imagining it invites and involves. I shall also be examining how, and when, the Officious Bystander enables inquiry in this area of the law: how it assists persons,

[1] See, eg, Currie and Jureidini (2004).
[2] See, eg, Schneewind (1998).
[3] See, eg, Frow (2014).
[4] See, eg, Gallagher (1995).
[5] See, eg, Belting (2017).
[6] I shall be citing some of the relevant literature as we go. For now, let me observe simply that this could be done across a whole range of different areas of the law, eg in international law, see Wheatley (2017) and Slaughter (2019), and in domestic private and public law, see Noonan (1976).

including individually, interactively and collectively, and in the course of a single case as well as over time, to make insights into what values, vulnerabilities and interests may be at stake.

In brief, the Officious Bystander is an artefact because it signals its own artifice. It does so, for instance, through the capitalisation and use of an abstract personal name (the 'Officious Bystander'), and by employing a comic term (officiousness) in a non-comic context. As an artefact, this figure not only signals its own artifice, but it also invites us to do something with it, and it does that because it is highly selective and under-specified: it explicitly evokes only two characteristics (officiousness, and being a bystander), leaving other characteristics to be added, or the present ones to be transformed or understood in a particular way, also requiring us to narratively map out the actions and interactions of this figure.

When it functions as an artefact for us (which it may not, for artefactuality is always contingent, and thus the Officious Bystander may come to simply function as shorthand) it then invites us to imagine. To imagine figurally, in turn, is to enter a distinctive epistemic frame, where we suspend, for instance, our usual reliance on treating proper names as referring to real individuals, or our usual commitment to thinking of persons as more than just placeholders for one or two characteristics. At the same time as entering a distinctive epistemic frame, we also participate actively, eg simulating affects via emotional reactions to the actions and interactions of the figure, constructing mental imagery, and enacting kinesically.

In this sense, to imagine figurally is to engage in a thicker, more involved, process of imagining than, say, imagining fictions, and possibly even metaphors. When we imagine figurally, we participate, in the second limb of imagining, with a high degree of involvement along the affective, sensory and kinesic spectrum, with the kinesic being especially intense in figural imagining. Further, we often do this together with others, eg we swap sometimes opposing imaginings of what the Officious Bystander does, eg what questions he asks (always in the cases I have read a 'he', and that too is significant) and how those he interacts with respond, ie how the parties negotiating the contract respond to the questions posed by the Officious Bystander. Indeed, the swapping, including the discordances between the different imaginings, is an important part of the value of figures.

The figure of the Officious Bystander is helpful and beneficial in adjudication when it enables inquiry. It does so individually, interactively and collectively: individual judges, in part on the back of already imagined accounts by the advocates in the case, imagine the Officious Bystander, and in doing so, make normative insight as to what values, vulnerabilities and interests might be at stake in a particular case, eg how best to balance freedom of contract with protecting vulnerable parties against exploitation by more powerful ones. Avoiding creating a general, non-figural test, can also help make normative insight over time: in the context of implied terms, it can help a legal community to engage with what the proper limits of freedom of contract might be, and whether English law should have something like a good faith requirement. In other words, not only is the Officious Bystander capable of serving as a justification in an instant case, but its value also extends to enabling inquiry over time, ie allowing members of the community, including judges, advocates, scholars, other stakeholders, and citizens, to experimentally probe and tentatively examine, the values, vulnerabilities and interests at stake, eg the authority of the courts in interfering with freedom of contract, or the vulnerability of parties to exploitation by more powerful parties. The Officious Bystander can assist inquiry in this way, but only if it actually functions as an artefact, and only if persons actually imagine it.

This, at least, is what I shall be arguing, and doing so in two parts, as with all the chapters in this second part of the book. In the first, I shall situate my own approach to figures as artefacts, with related processes of imagining, by reference, selectively and inadequately of course, to the literature. I focus mainly on the treatment, within literary theory and history, of personification, character and counterfactual imagining. This part also includes a taxonomy of the different ways in which we draw and project human qualities, including not only figuration, but also personification (and its many varieties: natural, role/status, nominal and performative personification), archetypation and characterisation. In the second part, I then turn to the specific example of the Officious Bystander.

I. Approaching Figures

There are many different ways in which we draw on and project features of the human, which, as above, are socially, culturally and historically contingent, and for a variety of different ends.[7] I therefore begin this section with a rough taxonomy of such different ways, not with a view to covering the possibilities, but primarily with a view to better situating my focus here, namely what I am calling 'figuration' and 'characterisation'. Having done so, and thus having clarified the focus of this chapter, I then turn to three literatures that we can draw on to theorise the work of figures as artefacts and related processes of imagination, namely: first, personification; second, character; and third, counterfactual imagining.

A. A Rough Taxonomy

Without intending to be comprehensive, one way in which we could classify the different ways that we draw on and project features of the human is to employ the following four-fold distinction: personification, archetypation, figuration and characterisation.[8] Within personification, we can make further distinctions between natural, role/status, nominal and performative personification. Let me briefly explain each.

i. Personification and its Varieties

Personification, in general, can be understood to consist in different kinds of ascriptions of qualities and attributes of human personhood. These different kinds of personification include:

- *Natural Personification*: the ascription of qualities and attributes of persons to animals or material objects, including living or non-living things, eg plants or clouds,

[7] See Frow (2014), and see also recently, LoLordo (2019).
[8] For an alternative classification, see Frow (2014); and Rorty (1976).

or abstract objects, eg concepts. In the legal context, this might involve, describing a court-building as being aggressive, speaking of the law itself, or of justice, authority, the state, as, say, male or female, with such-and-such a facial expression or demeanor. Examples of the latter are legion, across both linguistic and visual media: everything from Lady Justice and Our Lady of the Common Law, to the male figure of the authority of law, to gendered personifications of the state, eg Brittania or Uncle Sam, as well as motherlands and fatherlands, and to sources of the law, eg La Doctrine personified as a female person.[9]

- *Status or Role Personification*: the ascription of qualities and attributes of persons, with the status or role they have at a certain time and place, to human beings that have not had such a status or role or to animals, or to material or abstract objects. Status personification may involve the ascription of the status of a person, eg at a certain time and place, this might involve the capacity to own property or to sue in a court, etc to: a) an individual or groups of individuals who have been deprived of such a status, as, for instance, with granting personhood status to those previously deemed slaves, or, in some traditions, to women, or b) to animals, material or abstract objects, such as most obviously corporations, but also rivers or Artificial Intelligence systems. Role personification can be conceived of as a more limited kind of status personification, as in the ascription of the role of being a paterfamilias, or a creditor, owner or employer, or indeed a mixture of these, to a certain person. In this sense, role personification echoes the very etymological origins of personhood – *persona* – as in a mask one wears, and thus a role one plays on a theatrical stage.[10]
- *Nominal Personification*: this involves the ascription of a particular quality or attribute of being a person, namely having a name, to either persons without a name, or to animals, or material or abstract objects. There is a fascinating history awaiting to be told of nominal personification in the legal context, where examples include: John or Emily Doe, Goodtitle, Notitle, Shamtitle, Thrustout, Calvin, and Blackacre (the name given to a fictional place).[11]
- *Performative personification*: related also to the theatrical tradition of wearing masks, but in a different way than in role personification, this kind of personification would involve giving a body and a voice to, as in performing in the name of, another person, whether alive or dead. Performative personification can be linked closely to the old rhetorical figure of *prosopopeia* (literally meaning face or mask making), which involved actors performing, and giving a voice and body to, inter alia, dead

[9] Frederick Pollock once waxed: 'We are here to do homage to Our Lady of the Common Law … Her soul is founded in an order older than the gods themselves, but the joy of strife is not strange to her, nor yet the humours of the crowd. She belongs to the kindred of Homer's gods, more powerful than men but not passionless or infallible': (1912), 2. For more examples and discussion of natural personification see, eg, O'Donoghue (2018); Frow (2020); Kantorowicz (1957); and Stacey (2018). There is a large literature on these personifications in visual form, eg in emblems: see Goodrich (2013); Hayaert (2020); and Haldar (2019).

[10] See eg Naffine (2009); Siraganian (2015) and (2018); Best (2010); and Dayan (2011).

[11] The fictional name Calvin was given to the real person Robert Colville in the famous *Calvin v Smith* case of 1608. A history of fictional legal names overlaps with a history of fictional, including test, cases. For some of the fictional names used in the fiction of ejectment, see Sparkes (2015).

ancestors.[12] This kind of personification may overlap somewhat with the others, but is distinctive given its performative expression. There is a legal context also to this kind of personification, with the practice of advocacy, as well as with certain traditions of legal education, eg the declamations in Ancient Greece and Ancient Rome involved acting as another person in an imaginary scenario.[13]

As broad as these categories are, personification arguably does not exhaust the different ways in which we we draw on and project features of the human. Above, I mentioned in addition archetyptation, figuration and characterisation.

ii. Archetypation

We could delineate archetypation in the following way:

- *Archetypation*: the construction and expression of knowledge in the shape of a person. This is best illustrated with an example: in contract law, in the area of mistaken identity, one might construct and express the knowledge of the cases in that area by creating the following archetypes: the swindler, the rogue, the naïve seller, the circumspect seller, and so on. These archetypes, and the interactions between them, map the various possibilities in this area of the law: eg a swindler charms an overly naïve seller (such that, typically, the contract is not void for mistake), or a rogue cheats a reasonably circumspect seller (this resulting in the contract being void for mistake).[14] Archetypes are sometimes constructed and expressed by judges, and sometimes by scholars who argue that such archetypes are unconsciously influencing decision-making in a certain area of the law.[15] A fascinating project here would be to compare the existence of certain archetypes from literary and cultural history, eg heroes, guardians, heralds, tricksters, martyrs etc, with their role in legal history.

Archetypation is a fascinating aspect of legal reasoning and legal knowledge, but it is not my focus here.

iii. Figuration

Finally, we reach figuration and characterisation. First, figuration:

- *Figuration*: this involves, in the legal context, the construction and expression of a legal test in the form of a figure, with a certain limited range of attributes, qualities or traits. If one must, one could see this as a kind of personification, eg character personification, for the capitalised proper names take the form of character traits. For my purposes here, I shall treat it as a separate category, with its own label.

[12] Another related figure here was that of *ethopoeia*, or 'the making of character', as in, say, the giving of voice to a character. For a discussion, see eg Paxson (2014); Miller (1990); Alexander (2007); and Riffaterre (1985). I return to the theoretical and historical literature on personification below.

[13] On the declamations, and connections to legal advocacy, see eg Russell (1983); and Crook (1995).

[14] See Jackson (1988), ch 4, for a discussion of these cases.

[15] See, eg, Hayes (2016); Robbins (2006); and Sheppard (2009).

> This can be useful because, for instance, if one thought of figuration as, say, the personification of an abstract concept, ie a kind of natural personification, then some figural legal tests may drop out of the picture: eg in the case of the Officious Bystander, it is not clear what is the abstract concept that is being personified. The figures that feature in figural legal tests are sometimes capitalised and sometimes not. When they are, as in the Officious Bystander, they can signal their own artifice especially successfully, for they pretend to be a proper name, replacing proper names with character traits. Even when not, however, figures can still function as artefacts, signaling their own artifice by treating a person as but a vector of one or two character traits. They also, as we shall soon see in more detail, involve related processes of imagination: when we imagine figurally, we enter a distinctive epistemic frame, eg suspending our usual taking of proper names as referring to real persons, while, simultaneously, participating along a high degree of affective, sensory and kinesic involvement.

The common law tradition is packed with such figuration. Lord Justice Reed gave an entertaining list of some of them, himself going on in that case to employ the figural test of the 'reasonably well-informed and normally diligent tenderer':

> The Clapham omnibus has many passengers. The most venerable is the reasonable man, who was born during the reign of Victoria but remains in vigorous health. Amongst the other passengers are the right-thinking member of society, familiar from the law of defamation, the officious bystander, the reasonable parent, the reasonable landlord, and the fair-minded and informed observer, all of whom have had season tickets for many years.[16]

Lord Reed's first line in the above passage equates the 'reasonable man' with the 'man on the Clapham omnibus', and indeed the history of these two expressions are entangled. The origins of the latter are somewhat obscure, with Lord Justice Bowen said to be its author.[17] In *Hall v Brooklands Auto Racing Club*, Lord Justice Greer referred again to the 'man on the Clapham omnibus', grouping it together with a number of other expressions:

> I do not think it can be said that the content of the contract made with every person who takes a ticket is different. I think it must be the same, and it must be judged by what any reasonable member of the public must have intended should be the term of the contract. The person concerned is sometimes described as 'the man in the street,' or 'the man in the Clapham omnibus,' or, as I recently read in an American author, 'the man who takes the magazines at home, and in the evening pushes the lawn mower in his shirt sleeves.' Such a man taking a ticket to see a cricket match at Lord's would know quite well that he was not going to be encased in a steel frame which would protect him from the one in a million chance of a cricket ball dropping on his head. In the same way, the same man taking a ticket to see the Derby would know quite well that there would be no provision to prevent a horse which got out of hand from getting amongst the spectators, and would quite understand that he was himself bearing the risk of any such possible but improbable accident happening to himself.

[16] *Healthcare at Home Ltd v Common Services Agency* [2014] SC (UKSC) 247, [1].
[17] See *McQuire v Western Morning News Company Ltd* [1903] 2 KB 100, where the phrase is attributed to Lord Bowen.

> In my opinion, in the same way such a man taking a ticket to see motor races would know quite well that no barrier would be provided which would be sufficient to protect him in the possible but highly improbable event of a car charging the barrier and getting through to the spectators. The risk of such an event would be so remote that he would quite understand that no provision would be made to prevent it happening, and that he would take the risk of any such accident.[18]

These are early twentieth-century cases, but the deployment of figural tests can be traced back much further. They may have become particularly prevalent in the nineteenth century, travelling across multiple domains of law,[19] and, indeed, the origins of the 'reasonable person' are often traced back to the early nineteenth century decision in *Vaughan v Menlove*,[20] where the Court referred to what a 'man of ordinary prudence' would have done.[21]

However, as Simon Stern has showed, figural tests had been employed in the common law even earlier, drawing sometimes from civil law examples, such as the pater-familias of Roman law, or the 'constantem virum', the firm man, who withstands duress.[22] Thus, for instance, in the very early eighteenth-century case, *R v Jones*,[23] the Court refers to what 'a Cheat or a Person of an ordinary Capacity can't discover'.[24] This reference, in a criminal law context, may itself have borrowed from the famous bailment case of *Coggs v Barnard*,[25] decided just a year earlier, in which Chief Justice Holt spoke of the 'ordinary care, reasonable care, the utmose diligence, such as the most diligent father of a family uses'.[26] Indeed, as Stern has observed elsewhere, the bailment cases appear to have been especially important in the story of figuration in common law reasoning.[27]

A cultural history of these figural tests, even if just confined to England, would be a fascinating project. If such a cultural history of these figures were to be told, and a long view taken of them, it would be interesting to relate their emergence and popularity to the rich tradition of character writing in England.[28] Character writing, to which I will return a little later in this chapter, can be traced back to a student of Aristotle's in Ancient Greece, Theophrastus. It came to enjoy particular popularity in early modern England, arguably thereafter transforming into the tradition of figural periodicals in the eighteenth century, such as *The Tatler* and *The Spectator*, many of which were staffed

[18] *Hall v Brooklands Auto Racing Club* [1933] 1 KB 205, 226.

[19] See Stern (2020).

[20] *Vaughan v Menlove* (1837) 132 ER 490 (CP).

[21] But see *R v Southerton* (1805) 6 East 126, where Lord Justice Ellenborough spoke of a 'man of common firmness', a 'man of ordinary firmness', an 'ordinary free will of a firm man', and of what 'a firm and prudent man might not and ought not to have resisted'. For a discussion, and these examples, see Stern (2017a), 59. See also *Ramsden v Hylton; Hylton v Biscoe* T 1751 2 Ves. 305, in which Lord Chancellor Hardwicke refers to both a 'reasonable man' and 'a reasonable woman'.

[22] Stern (2017b), 60.

[23] *R v Jones* (1703) 5 Mod 105.

[24] Stern (2017b), 60.

[25] *Coggs v Barnard* (1702) 2 L.d. Raym. 909.

[26] Stern (2017a), 64.

[27] See Stern (2020).

[28] See Smeed (1985). It would equally be interesting to consider the connection of figures in law to other developments at the time in literary genre and style, eg in Richardson: see Stern (2017c).

by legally-trained writers, and some of which became well-known lawyers.[29] This is a history that begs to be written, but which I cannot write here.

Figural tests in the law have a long history, and they are also plentiful. Indeed, it is worth observing that they are sometimes thought of as a group.[30] It is common to see them described as passengers on the Clapham omnibus. We saw this in the passage above, per Lord Reed, but there are many such examples. Here is another one, from Lord Justice Hoffmann, writing extra-judicially:

> The horse omnibus service which used to run between Knightsbridge and Clapham was discontinued in 1914. Lord Bowen, who is credited with the invention of its most famous passenger and lived, I think, near the Knighstbridge end of the route, died in 1894. And yet in courts of common law all over the world, the ghostly creak of the wheels and the cracks of the driver's whip are still to be heard. Like the Flying Dutchman, it seems condemned to travel for all enternity, at any rate until some bold judge or legislator has set the passengers free. Let us get on board as it leaves from outside Harvey Nichols and see who is travelling today. The passengers, who used to be distinguished by their ordinariness, have become a rather mixed bunch. There is no difficulty in picking out the reasonable man. He is the one with the bowler hat and umbrella, sitting neither too far forward nor too far back and keeping a look out in case the driver should lose control of the horses. The man sitting next to him, similarly dressed but reading a newspaper, is the right-thinking man, whose views on the libellous nature of an article are always recommended to juries. Both of them have been travelling for many years. But who is that rather distraught-looking shabbily dressed young woman holding a crying baby? She is the reasonable parent deciding whether to consent to the adoption of her child. And who is the man in the top hat and fur-collared overcoat? It is a little surprising to see him travelling by omnibus at all. He is the reasonable landlord, deciding whether to consent to the assignment of a lease. And what about that excitable trio on the rear platform, arguing and gesticulating? Lord Bowen always thought of the passengers as quintessentially English. But two of those men look like foreigners. They are in fact the reasonable Greek ship-owner and the reasonable Indian charterer, who have just been interrupted in their negotiations by an officious bystander.[31]

Sometimes, rather than being passengers on a bus, the various figures are described as living together in the same 'legal village'. Consider the following passage by Lord Justice Hope, from a case in which he applies the 'fair-minded and informed observer' figural test in bias law:

> My Lords, the fair-minded and informed observer is a relative newcomer among the select group of personalities who inhabit our legal village and are available to be called upon when a problem arises that needs to be solved objectively. Like the reasonable man whose attributes have been explored so often in the context of the law of negligence, the fair-minded observer is a creature of fiction. Gender-neutral (as this is a case where the complainer and the person

[29] See Squibbs (2010) and (2014). For instance, Lord Chancellor Hardwicke contributed to *The Spectator* in his youth under the pseudonym of 'Philip Homebred': April 12 (1712), No. 364.

[30] As entertaining it may be to group them together, it can also be misleading to do so, for each of these figural tests perform distinctive functions. Indeed, this goes even for any one such figure, eg as Moran (2003) has shown, the figure of the 'reasonable person' functions quite differently in contexts of tort law and discrimination law, amongst others.

[31] Hoffmann (1995), 127.

complained about are both women, I shall avoid using the word 'he'), she has attributes which many of us might struggle to attain to.[32]

These passages already reveal just how many figural legal tests one can find in the common law. To the above, we can also add: the reasonable juror properly directed, the reasonable recipient,[33] the alert or industrious backbencher,[34] and the person skilled in the art.[35] Some of these figures are more entrenched than others, ie their popularity varies, with some being ad hoc constructions, and others being relied on often. A good example of ad hoc constructions of figures is the entertaining case of *Re Rowland*,[36] where, in determining the meaning of 'coincide with' in a will,[37] the judges, principally Lord Justice Denning, referred to the imaginary interpretations of the term by an 'ordinary man', a 'metaphysician', and a 'grammarian', with these last two being precisely ad hoc figural constructions.

Although no doubt a case could also be made for the pervasiveness of personification and archetypation in the law, my focus here shall be on figuration, which, as above, can be found alive and well in almost all suburbs of the common law.

iv. Characterisation

I mentioned earlier that, in addition to personification, archetypation, and figuration, there was one more category of drawing on and projecting the human: characterisation. We can think of this in the following way:

- *Characterisation*: I shall treat characterisation as a secondary process, ie once one has personified, or created an archetype or figure, one can then go on to characterise it further, either by (re-)interpreting its originally-ascribed qualities and attributes, or by adding or substracting from them. The individual, interactive and collective work of subsequent characterisation is a little-noticed dynamic of legal change. For instance, it is a significant change to add to the figure of 'a man of ordinary firmness' that this is also a man of 'ordinary prudence'. Adding 'prudence' to a figural test is an example of subsequent characterisation. This can be done more or less explicitly or more or less directly, ie one can, as above, explicitly add an extra quality or attribute (being prudent), or one can imply certain qualities or attributes through the way the figure is described as acting or interacting, eg as we shall see with the

[32] *Helow v Secretary of State for the Home Department and another* [2008] UKHL 62, [1].

[33] See *Garston v. Scottish Widows* [1998] 2 EGLR 73.

[34] For the alert backbencher, see *Re DWS (deceased)* [2000] EWCA Civ 282; and for the industrious backbencher, see *Dunnachie v Kingston Upon Hill City Council* [2004] 2 All ER 501.

[35] See *Lilly ICOS v Pfizer* [2001] FSR 16. The following passage has become well known and is also a good example of subsequent characterisation: 'This [the person skilled in the art] is not a real person. He is a legal creation. He is supposed to offer an objective test of whether a particular development can be protected by a patent. He is deemed to have looked at and read publicly available documents and to know of public uses in the prior art. He understands all languages and dialects. He never misses the obvious nor stumbles on the inventive. He has no private idiosyncratic preferences or dislikes. He never thinks laterally. He differs from all real people in one or more of these characteristics', 226, per Laddie J.

[36] *Re Rowland* [1963] Ch 1 (CA).

[37] The issue was whether the deaths coincided or not, with different parties inheriting depending on whether they did.

> Officious Bystander, asking questions in a certain kind of style or being described as 'lurking behind' the negotiating parties, which suggests someone more sinister than a mere busy-body. Characterisation also includes ascribing to the figure a certain background story or background knowledge, eg imagining the Officious Bystander to be a lawyer or being legally trained.

Characterisation also occurs in adjudication in other ways, eg judges engage in characterisation of the parties in the case, but also sometimes counsel, and sometimes even particular rules, principles, doctrines, areas of the law, and whole legal traditions. My focus, however, will be on charactersation as a secondary process, following on from figuration.

v. *The Focus in this Chapter*

We have now identified a possible taxonomy of different ways of drawing on and projecting the human. My focus in this chapter is on the processes of figuration and subsequent characterisation. Thus, when I refer to figure,[38] I mean to refer to the creation and deployment of figural tests in the legal context. Characterisation is important to include in this story, because it is part of what is involved in the 'deployment' of figural tests, ie as they are applied in cases, these figures develop their own histories, precisely in the form of interpretations, additions or subtractions of qualities, attributes or traits, in more or less explicit or direct ways. Further, these characterisations do not form a coherent whole; indeed, they are often inconsistent and incompatable with each other. This is not necessarily something negative: in fact, we can see this experimentation with the subsequent characterisation of an already created figure as part of the process of inquiry.

Indeed, that is my argument: that both the initial act of creating a figure, ie a figural test in a legal context, and the subsequent acts of characterisation, both contribute to the process of inquiry in adjudication. To imagine with figures, which includes characterising them, is a way of making normative insight, individually, interactively and collectively, in single cases and over time. When we imagine with figures, we explore what values, vulnerabilities and interests might be at stake in a certain case and in cases like it in the future. This is a highly casuistic way to make normative insight. As a process of imagining, it is also one involving high degrees of affective, sensory and kinesic involvement.

To get a better grasp of figures as artefacts, with related processes of imagining, it will be helpful to situate them, of course, very selectively and inadequately, in some of the relevant theoretical literature. As indicated above, I shall proceed in three steps: first, I consider some of the literature on personification; second, I look at the literature on character; and third, I turn to the relation between figural imagining and counterfactual imagining. Engaging, even briefly, with these three domains, will, I hope, help clarify the

[38] This is a term that of course itself has such a long and fascinating history, sometimes referring to allegorical interpretation, sometimes to the twists and turns of language as in the idea of 'figural language'. On the history of the term 'figure', see Auerbach (1984) [1938] and see also the essays in Lerer (1996).

sense in which I am thinking of figures as artefacts, with related processes of imagining, as well as why and how I think they can be of value, ie when they enable inquiry.

Important, too, is just how figures are unique artefacts and unique process of imagining, and how uniquely they can enable inquiry, at least when compared to the other case studies. We shall see that like metaphors and scenarios, figures involve a high degree of participation, and that, like scenarios but in this sense less like metaphors, they are also closer to narrative-based cognition. However, at the same time, and in this respect unlike scenarios, figures, or at least many of them, are less ad hoc than scenarios are: they are deployed over and over again in cases, and this diachronically-stretched out process generates its own kinds of resources, although also, inevitably, its own complexities, if not dangers.

B. Personification in Literary Theory and History

i. A Long and Rich History

Personification, both its practice and its theory, has a long and rich history. It is a history that is tied closely to law. As many have observed, if we think of what I have called above 'performative personification', linked as that is to the rhetorical tropes of *prosopopeia* and *ethopoeia*, then we can see the connection to the practice and theory of advocacy. Discussed, for example, in Quintilian's tract on rhetoric, *prosopopeia* involved an advocate 'putting words into the mouth of his client', such that 'the judge seems no longer to be listening to a voice bewailing another's ills, but to hear the voice and feelings of the unhappy victims, men whose appearance alone would call forth tears even though they uttered never a word'.[39]

Advocacy is not the only link. Another key correlation between personification and law occurs in the domain of evidence. As Richard Serjeantson has pointed out in his historical work on testimony:

> One important 'testimonial' figure – one which bears witness, cites authority, or reports a speech – is that of *prosopopeia*. *Prosopopeia* is a figure of rhetorical amplification, defined by the author of the *Rhetorica ad Herennium* (who calls it *conformatio*) as being "when a person not present is feigned in some way as if they were, or when something silent or formless is made to speak". It is as if, says Thomas Wilson, "we imagine a talk for someone to speak". It was a figure that was regarded as having particular force at persuading and inflaming the mind to the emulation of virtue, and its testimonial character is evident, even if its power of proving was less secure.[40]

Of course, this technique of giving life, of animating, has much broader manifestations and implications than in law, with other obvious connections being to theatre and to arguably almost all kinds of literature. For example, there is an important relation between personification and certain kinds of genres or techniques: one of the key issues in the history of personification is which invented persons are given the power of voice

[39] Paxson (1984), 18.

[40] Serjeantson (2007), 187–8; internal references omitted.

or speech, and how this is expressed, eg in dialogue amongst invented persons.[41] In addition to dialogue, it is difficult to imagine the history of lyric without voice-based personification.[42] More broadly, personification, for instance, 'nominal personification', has a prominent role to play in the history of the growth and change of language, including in legal language, eg it may be thought of as one of the techniques of abstraction: giving something a personal name involves turning something difficult to grasp into a tangible and memorable entity, and with which one can interact.[43]

Further, thinking of personification as part of the dynamics of abstraction has also included considering how multiple personifications, eg of ideas, can enable exploration of relations between those ideas, eg as part of a family, or in opposing armies. TBL Webster, for instance, in his survey of personification as a 'mode of Greek thought',[44] analyses personification not only as 'a means of taking hold of things which suddenly appear startlingly uncontrollable and independent: the rolling stone, the blaze of sunrise, the incurable disease, the irresistible desire, or the rule by which men conduct their political affairs',[45] but also as a way of expressing 'a relationship between ideas'.[46] Thus, in Ancient Greek mythology, by relating certain ideas together in a family, one could explore the complexity of the concept that unites them, eg 'in Homer, the war-god Areas has a sister Eris (strife) and a son Phobos (panic); Phobos and Deimos (fear) are Ares' grooms; and Phobos has a companion Phyza (flight)'.[47] This connects a certain event, ie war, with certain movements, eg flight, and with certain emotions, eg panic, fear. Personification, then, might be thought of as a complex way of constructing knowledge of and reflecting upon a certain phenomenon: not only making sense of it, but also exploring its kinesic and affective dimensions.

There is also a fascinating history of emotion that could be anchored around personification, and one which also conveys a certain picture of emotion, ie of 'emotions as something that we do, rather than as something that we have'.[48] Mary Flannery, who has explored some of this history, has observed how important personification has been to the history of emotion: personification, with 'its emphasis on the acting, sensing, feeling body … gives … emotions a body, a face and a personality', and in so doing, 'personification participates in and furthers embodied emotional practice'.[49] Personification, with its affinity with the body and its movements, ie its gestures and postures, but also ways and means of acting and interacting with others, offers a particular way of making sense of emotion, while at the same time shaping the emotions of those who engage with emotions as personifications:

> Personification gives emotions 'an intelligible shape' by giving them bodies; it makes sense of emotions by placing them firmly in the world of the senses. A personified emotion is an

[41] See Paxson (1994).
[42] See Culler (2015).
[43] See Edgecomb (1997).
[44] See Webster (1954).
[45] Ibid, 10–11.
[46] Ibid, 19.
[47] Ibid.
[48] Flannery (2016), 352.
[49] Ibid.

> embodied emotion; as such, it can detect, experience, and respond to sensory stimuli, and it can be depicted as working upon the senses of other bodies, whether of other personifications or of a real or imagined feeling subject. It thus represents embodied emotional practice and also has the capacity to put emotion into practice. Possessed of a body, the personified emotion exhibits the symptoms and performs the gestures associated with that particular emotional state, enabling readers to imagine the sensory experience and practice of that emotion.[50]

In medieval literature, for instance, 'gestures and physical descriptions are key components of the characterisation of personified emotions'.[51]

We can abstract from this personification-based-history-of-emotions to note how personification relates closely the three dimensions of the second limb of imagination: affective, sensory and kinesic. The general point, then, for present purposes, would be that the literature on personification can reveal to us some of the power of figural imagining, for it shows how personification combines together the the emotions, the senses and the body.

ii. Combining the Emotions, the Senses and the Body

Recent theories of personification have ventured precisely down this route, further exploring personification's 'cognitive form and function', and in particular connecting it to affective, sensory and kinesic dynamics.[52] In their introduction to a multi- and inter-disciplinary new collection on *Personification*, Walter Melion and Bart Ramakers insist that personification must be seen to be operating in 'multiple registers: sensory and spiritual, visible and invisible, concrete and abstract', and dealing in 'facts, opinions, and beliefs'.[53] Personification, which they define as 'the rhetorical figure by which something not human is given a human identity or face', 'bodied forth' processes of 'thinking, feeling and experiencing',[54] and did so in many different ways, across many different media and in a bewildering array of forms and genres. Far beyond language, personification can be found in all the arts, visual, sculptural, and architectural, and in objects with wide cultural circulation, such as posters, coins, and banknotes. For many centuries, many of these personifications were, and in many respects remain, highly gendered. Indeed, almost all of them were feminine. As Ernst Gombrich has noted:

> … we tend to take personification for granted rather than to ask questions about this extraordinarily predominantly feminine population which greets us from the porches of cathedrals, crowds around our public monuments, marks our coins and banknotes, and turns up in our cartoons and our posters.[55]

Others, too, such as Marina Warner, have noted the highly feminine character of the history of personification, arguing that this was specifically designed to have persuasive effects on an audience taken to be male.[56] Feminine personifications, Warner says, were

[50] Ibid, 353.
[51] Ibid, 359.
[52] Melion and Ramakers (2016b), 2.
[53] Ibid, 1.
[54] Ibid.
[55] Quoted ibid, 5. See Gombrich (1971).
[56] See Warner (1987).

designed 'to lure, to delight, to appetise, to please'; they were, she adds, 'a weapon of delight', functioning ideally 'as the spur to desire, as the excitement of the senses'.[57]

We see here recognition of the very power of personification, or, for our purposes, figural imagining. We see how, in taking on embodied form, and adopting a certain posture, performing certain gestures, amd interacting in certain physical ways, personification links together, often very powerfully, our emotions, our senses and our embodied knowledge. This is all the more so where the personification is individualised, ie given a name, a face, and a voice. In this sense, and arguably uniquely across the four case studies being examined in this book, figural imagining is most intensively embodied. Out of all the case studies, it relies most on our ability and, arguably, also pleasure, of simulating kinesically, eg postures, gestures, sequences of actions, serving as a foundation for affective and sensory participation.

One scholar who has emphasised the relationship between personification and embodied cognition is Jean Bocharova.[58] According to Bocharova, 'the use of figures', in the sense of invented bodies, 'heightens our limbic response and focuses our attentional resources'.[59] Figural imagining recruits our sensorimotor systems, also being highly memorable, given the close connections between kinesis, especially when supported by emotion and sensory imagery, and memory.[60] Part of the power of figural imagining is that it is so self-involving: it encourages us to either take on the personification ourselves, eg impersonating the personification, and simulating the figure's movements as if we were ourselves that figure, or engaging with it. Giving a literary example of a personification of Despair, crouching over a dead body, Bocharova argues:

> The depiction of Despair in this arrangement – a movement toward and from a location where we see the personified figure himself in a climactic moment – is important because it allows us to remember our encounter with him as an event … The more vivid the memory, the more likely we are to replay it and the more likely it is to become interwoven into our neocortical structures, especially if it is consistent with pre-existing domains … Thus, the Despair episode by directing our attention toward the personified figure and heightening our emotional responses through aesthetic universals, creates a more memorable encounter, an encounter that when recalled could trigger associations with events occurring both earlier and later in the episode … But it is the personified figure of Despair crouched over the body of Terwin that anchors these associations as the reader's corpus of knowledge related to despair is compressed and blended into this vivid image.[61]

It is important that figures are highly memorable. This is important also because they are then more likely to be re-used (more likely, for instance, than fictions, scenarios or perhaps even metaphors). This may well be because they are so kinesically resonant: we can easily identify with them, and we are somehow drawn to either impersonate them, thereby ourselves kinesically simulating them, or to interact with them. One might say that they draw not only on the embodied, but also on the social character of our knowledge: they

[57] Ibid, xx. Quoted in Melion and Ramakers (2016b), 13.
[58] Bocharova (2016).
[59] Ibid, 47.
[60] Ibid.
[61] Ibid, 65–66. The example comes from Spenser's *The Faerie Queen*.

are beings that can accompany our thought. Figural imagining may be so powerful becaue it can serve as a kind of substitute for embodied interaction with others.

We must not think, however, and Bocharova also emphasises this, that the memorability of figural imagining renders it somehow a less complex or flexible mode of thought. Quite the contrary: by rendering a figure, we avoid reducing something that may be quite complex (connecting, as above, affective, sensory and kinesic associations together) into, say, a general proposition that simply cannot bear the burden of that rich meaning. In Spenser's *The Faerie Queen*, for instance, personification provides 'a complex pattern of episodic narrative and allegorical imagery, frustrating attempts to reduce the text to a simple precept'.[62] The above personification of Despair – even just the bare posture of crouching over a dead body – is such a kinesically- and affectively-resonant image and, at once, dramatisation, that it is not only memorable, but also condenses a whole constellation of associations with or meanings of despair, which we could, if we chose to, seek to unpack more explicitly. There is a richness in these personifications, or, in our terms, in figural imagining, that simply cannot be captured by explicit propositions, though we may helpfully use explicit propositions as ways of exploring the condensed, dense meaning of a personification.

Even this briefest of excursions into the literature on personification offers a great deal of illumination, not only on figures as processes of imagining, but also on their potential value for inquiry. Figures are not only, though this is important too, memorable, and thus likely to be re-used, including over time, in multiple cases, but they are also ways of collecting and generating knowledge, and, I would add, in certain contexts, normative insight. This may be because they are so intensively kinesic, which also brings along with it affective simulation and the perspectival construction of mental imagery.

C. Character in Literary Theory and History

To help us delve further into the ability of figures to assist inquiry, especially in the sense of making normative insight, we can draw on the literature on character.[63] This literature, more so than personification, links figural imagining to the practice of judgement, including how thinking-with-character offers a complex and flexible way of evaluating action, as well as how it involves exploring relations between the role of human action and the role of the environment or context within which that action occurs.

Some of the work on character in literary theory[64] has spoken of the way in which readers actively infer character from non-figural aspects of the narrative, including descriptions of physical actions, events or other features of the world, eg the weather. Further, this knowledge and, at once, evaluation of character, can be more or less direct: we can either directly ascribe characteristics to figures, eg precisely by calling them the Officious Bystander, or we can invite readers to infer certain characteristics through descriptions of the context. This is important for present purposes, because it

[62] Bocharova (2016), 47.

[63] There has been a resurgence of interest in character of late, in both literary theory and philosophy: see, eg, Anderson, Felski and Moi (2019); and Masala and Webber (2016).

[64] Especially on character in novels: see Palmer (2004).

offers one way in which we can distinguish between figures and scenarios: figures tend to be more direct and explicit forms of constructing character, ie involving direct and explicit attributions of qualities to imaginary persons, whereas scenarios also connect to figural imagining, but do so through indirect, implicit ascriptions of character to a figure in the scenario. The distinction is not, however, water-tight: for instance, in describing how the Officious Bystander interacts with the negotiating parties, we can also engage in indirect, implicit characterisation.

Nevertheless, generally speaking, whereas scenarios are more anchored to context (precisely because they specify it: we have, in a scenario, not only figure(s) but also the narrative of their actions and interactions), figures are less so. In being less closely tied to contexts, figures thus can be used to explore relations between human action and the contexts in which they occur more flexibly than scenarios. Once we have a figure, we can place them in different contexts, and we have the freedom to describe those contexts ourselves. This is important for figural imagining, and its value in adjudication, for evaluating actions, eg considering whether they are reasonable, often involves deciding how much weight to attribute to human agency, and how much to certain non-agential, ie contextual, features of what occurred, eg culture, folk knowledge, or customary practices in a profession. Of course, this detachment from context also makes figures more transferable, eg as between areas of the law; scenarios, by contrast, are hampered in their travels by being more explicitly narratively thicker or heavier.

When we speak of character, we refer to an imaginary person with certain particular qualities or attributes, where these qualities or attributes are often laden with value, eg we speak, for instance, of 'traits of character'. Further, characters can be more or less developed, ie they vary in degrees of how richly characterised they are. I will be returning to this, and especially to thin, flat or simple characters, including social or moral types, for they, out of the variety of characters that may be found, relate most closely to figures in legal tests. For now, the point is a simpler one, but no less important for that: characterisation is an active process of ascribing, more or less directly, and in varying degrees, qualities or attributes to figures. Again, some figures are created already with, and in a sense only by virtue of, certain attributes or qualities, eg officiousness and being a bystander, or reasonableness, but even then, we have to take into account subsequent processes of characterisation. In the legal context, this subsequent characterisation is manifested by the various uses and applications of the relevant figure in a figural legal test.

i. The Active Reader: Self, Emotion, Evaluation

One key word here is 'activity': aside from any initial explicit acts of ascription of qualities or attributes by the author, as in the creator of the Officious Bystander, the process of subsequent characterisation involves the activity of the reader. Stressing the need for, and importance of, the activity of the reader in the process of characterisation permeates the theoretical literature on character. For example, Alan Palmer, in his excellent *Fictional Minds*, speaks of 'the sheer scale of the input required from readers in constructing minds from novels'.[65] For Palmer, the scale is indeed extraordinary,

[65] Ibid, 3.

because for him reading literature is essentially a process involving the construction of fictional minds. Narrative, Palmer says, 'is the description of mental function.'[66] What the comprehension of any narrative requires is the construction of a fictional mind by reference to the clues and cues in the description provided by a narrative. Further, this is an activity that is stretched out over the entire course of the narrative: characterisation, as Palmer puts it, 'is a continuous process' that 'consists of a succession of individual operations that result in a continual patterning and re-patterning until a coherent fictional personality emerges'.[67] Palmer here quotes Jonathan Culler with approval: 'character is not simply a conglomeration of features … we do not simply add together the actions and attributions of an individual character'; rather, we actively construct character over time, and the role of our own knowledge (including cultural knowledge, but also our knowledge of any one literary genre) is considerable, for in our construction of fictional minds we are 'guided by formal expectations about the roles that need to be filled'.[68]

Of course, this process may be especially complex and involved when confronting a central character in a novel, but the idea is that it is always present, even with quite simple characters. Characterisation always involves the activity of the reader, and the scale of this activity is very considerable. Not only is this because, in the case of a novel, we read all the various aspects of the novel, including desriptions of events and actions, seemingly unrelated to character, as part of our construction of fictional minds, but also because the anticipatory 'filling-in' of characters draws on our own personal stocks of knowledge, and this is not something that can ever be wholly predicted or controlled by an author.

John Frow, one of the other leading scholars in this area, including both on character and personification, also speaks of the importance and extent of the reader's activity. A character must first find a way of engaging our interest, so as to trigger and then sustain the activity of anticipating and predicting the character, as well as our constant revisions of those anticipations and predictions. 'A figural pattern', says Frow, 'asks us to respond to a form of life that we recognise', eg a person in a mid-life crisis, and we ask: 'what happens next, what will its fate be?'.[69] We may, for instance, place ourselves in relation with the character, either impersonating it or interacting with it. We may find familiar and approve of his likes and dislikes. We may identify with his emotional reactions, and the choices he makes. Or, of course, we may not, reacting, instead, with distaste or even disgust, or sheer bafflement. The point is that interest in the character is entangled with our involvement in its world, including possibly participating in the problems and experiences confronted by the character, as well as evaluating the character's responses to them. In constructing and evaluating a character, and its world, our own self is engaged, even if, and importantly, we remain aware of the distance between ourselves and the character. As Frow puts it:

> Learning how to read character is directly bound up with the practice of the self, of recognition of other selves, and of forming an emotional bond with fictional selves, and these practices

[66] Ibid, 12.
[67] Ibid, 40.
[68] Ibid, 42; quoting from Culler (1975).
[69] Frow (2014), 36.

> work in distinctively different ways in different genres and in different historical and cultural formations.[70]

Constructing characters, and we can say, returning to our terminology, figural imagining, is self-involving: part of what it means to characterise is that we relate our characterisation to ourselves, potentially identifying with it and relating to it emotionally in many different ways. In this sense, 'a figural pattern', as Frow calls it, does important 'emotional as well as representational work', and, Frow insists, this is something that occurs not only with thick characters in a rich novel, but arguably even in the case of appeals to figurality in 'discursive prose':

> It's arguable that even discursive prose – a conceptual argument dealing with abstract forces, say – can't be disassociated from our sense of a speaking self onto whom we project characteristics, and perhaps even from our tendency to conceive of abstract forces as actors working at human scale and involved in the fundamental narrative patterns of quest and antagonism.[71]

The work of character in a text involves us, ie it involves ourselves, and thus also our emotions, and, as powerful as this can be, this is not an involvement that the work in question, either fictional or non-fictional, can control. Rather, the activity of the reader in this context is such, and the projection of one's self is so intense, that it relies, to some extent, on our knowledge, which may be tacit, of certain narrative and cultural patterns. As the reader constructs a character, her 'mapping … is integrated with knowledge structures which include scripts, schemata, and stereotypes drawn from both cultural and literary spheres'.[72] This is a complex process, involving the initial interest in a character, construction of the clues and cues of a text, projection of our own selves (identifying or not, approving or not), and engagement of our cultural and literary knowledge. Summarising his work in this area, Frow argues that character can be thought of as 'an apparatus for the mobilisation of subjectivity'.[73] The scale of the activity of the reader in all of this is, again, considerable. As Ralf Schneider articulates it in his work on the cognitive work of character:

> … understanding literary characters requires our forming some kind of mental representation of them, attributing dispositions and motivations to them, understanding and explaining their actions, forming expectations about what they will do next and why, and, of course, reacting emotionally to them.[74]

Many contemporary literary theorists, like Palmer, Frow and Schneider, resist the reduction of character to plot, as, arguably, in Aristotle, and in the tradition of story-analysis, per Vladimir Propp and others in his wake, and speak instead of the complex and dynamic involvement of the reader in the construction of character.

Further, for these theorists, and especially for Palmer, this is a process that constitutes a, if not the, central dimension of experiencing narrative. Patterns, including

[70] Ibid, 54.
[71] Ibid, 36.
[72] Ibid, 20.
[73] Ibid, ix. See also Marta Figlerowicz who speaks of characters as 'forms of condensed knowledge about ourselves and as test cases for what such self-knowledge might be in the first place': (2018), 134.
[74] Schneider (2001), 608.

some of those identified by story-analysis, do play an important role in that process of characterisation, but the process itself is not reducible to them. Characterisation by readers is, as it were, too active and self-involving for that: it is too affectively-rich a process for it to be reducible to our processing of typical narrative patterns. The way we relate emotionally to any character can vary considerably, and, in a complex novel, it can also swing more or less radically in the course of experiencing the novel. The general point is that the process of characterisation is an active, affectively-loaden, self-involving and evaluative process. It is, in many ways, a rich normative experience, of generating and revising hypothetical evaluations of a character, and those she interacts with in a narrative, all the while relating them to ourselves and simulating affectively our relations to them.[75]

ii. Thin, Flat or Simple Characters

A reader keeping in mind the legal context may well ask here: all this talk of activity and complexity may be well and good for richly-expressed characters in complex novels, but this is not what we see with figural tests, which are much thinner, flatter and simpler. Does the above have any relevance for the figures encountered in the legal context? I would urge that it does: the process of characterisation may vary depending on how thinly or thickly figures are characterised, but the basic self-involving, affectively-loaden, and evaluative process is still there. For instance, we might surmise that with the figures we find in the legal context, given the paucity of their, at least explicit, characterisation, eg reasonableness in the case of the Reasonable Person, that more activity of the reader is required.

One might also argue that the role of knowledge of social norms, customs and practices increases: the less thickly-characterised, and in the absence of clues and cues in the text, the more filling-in is needed, with at least some of this filling-in relying on the reader's knowledge of social norms, customs and practices. A thinly-characterised figure, we might say, is an ideal conduit for the changing and dynamic paramaters of this knowledge. It will matter, of course, just what the quality or attribute is, eg reasonableness is considerably different from officiousness, but in both cases, it is likely that readers of such thinly-characterised figures will need to draw heavily on their knowledge of social norms, customs and practices. Indeed, given the social dimensions of inquiry being emphasised throughout this book, one could argue that thinly-characterised figures are excellent platforms upon which to make explicit, as well as swap and debate, our collective knowledge of social norms, customs and practices.

I mentioned earlier that the literature on character has paid attention not only to richly-expressed characters in complex novels, but also to thin, flat and simple characters, eg in complex novels or even adrift of any particular narrative, as in social archetypes. There is, within this scholarship, considerable variety in what is conceived of as a thin, flat or simple character, and in how it is theorised.

[75] For more on this process, especially at the intersection of cognitive science and literary theory, see, eg, Jannidis (2013); Gerrig and Allbritton (1990); Schneider (2001); and Phelan (1989); and Margolin (1983), (1990) and (1995).

Some theorists, for instance, reduce thin characters to something even thinner, eg actants, or vectors in typical plots. They may speak, for instance, of the Hero, the Mentor, the Treshhold Guardian, the Herald, the Shadow, the Trickster, and the Shapeshifter, and again treat them almost as nothing but functions in a plot.[76] No doubt some thin characters in some texts can be captured in this way. Some, but arguably not all: the Officious Bystander, for instance, does not fit easily into any particular category of actant; neither does the Reasonable Person, or indeed any number of figures deployed as part of figural tests in the law. Archetypes, including these plot-determined archetypes, do have an important role to play in structuring and condensing, including transmitting and transforming, legal knowledge (in the taxonomy above, I called this process 'archetypation'), but arguably they are only tangentially related to the figures in these figural tests.

What kinds of thin characters has the literature discussed? Only slightly thicker than the very thin actants are what has become known as 'ficelles'. Ficelle is a French term for 'a string used to manipulate a puppet, or more broadly, any underhand trick'.[77] Henry James deployed it to name:

> … a type of character whose role in a narrative is almost purely functional; an author introduces a ficelle not as a necessary and organic part of the plot but rather as a means of providing necessary exposition, of moving the plot mechanically forward, or of drawing rough and ready thematic antitheses; the ficelle is, indeed, a cheap but effective and maybe unavoidable trick.[78]

Ficelles, then, are 'almost purely functional characters': they are like 'cogs in a narrative machine', and they keep the narrative going. Once the function is fulfilled, they are 'abandoned or forgotten'.[79] Ficelles are in many ways overtly artificial, for the reader can sense, unless this can be hidden well by an author, that the character is there just momentarily to illuminate some feature of the protagonist or perhaps the narrator.[80] Indeed, James is said to have relished the task of hiding the artificiality of ficelles: 'What James loves about a ficelle is the art required to conceal the puppet's strings, the craft needed to make what is avowedly artificial look necessary and natural; he loves it because it allows him to indulge in craft for its own sake and, in fact, to show off a little'.[81]

Are the figures of figural legal tests ficelles? Are they almost purely functional characters, who are then forgotten or abandoned? Figures in figural legal tests do have a sense of artifice, at least when they still function in this way: capitalising the Officious Bystander, and attributing only two characteristics to a personal name, does tend to signal its own artifice. But are such figures soon forgotten or abandoned? As we shall see when we examine the Officious Bystander in the next part, the lives of these figures in the

[76] See, generally, Greimas (1983).

[77] James, quoted by Puckett (2016), 124.

[78] Puckett (2016), 124.

[79] Ibid.

[80] On the idea of 'flat protaginists', see Figlerowicz (2016); but what Figlerowicz appears to have in mind are characters that become thinner over the course of a novel: 'their behaviours are increasingly stereotypical and preditacble, and their means of responsiveness and expression progressively fiinishm until other characters no longer even contradict, but simply disregard, what they say': (2016), 2.

[81] Puckett (2016), 125.

law is not so ad hoc and so dispensable as ficelles in novels: they are carriers of knowledge across cases; they accumulate characteristics as they are applied case after case. Thus, although they may bear some resemblance to ficelles, these do not seem to be a promising analogy.

Another approach in the literature on thin, flat or simple characters has been to refer to 'the sketch of a moral type', eg in James Joyce's *Dubliners*, we encounter 'the spoiled son of a newly wealthy family'.[82] In part, the success of such a 'character sketch' is based on our recognition of it; but in part, it is also generative. Frow refers to Joyce's sketch as one 'filled with a coiled-up narrative time that is ready to unfold: it is a story waiting to happen'.[83] This resonates with the use of figures in the legal context: as recognisable as they may be (some perhaps more than others, eg one might be forgiven for not recognising the 'alert backbencher'), they are also stories waiting to be told, eg what would have the Reasonable Person done, or what will the Officious Bystander ask?

Frow traces the use of these 'moral types' to the Characters of Theophrastus, which I briefly mentioned earlier. These were sketches of a slightly more elaborate type, ie they were not one-line ascriptions of qualities and attributes, but they involved a few paragraphs depicting a certain character with a certain attribute in certain social situations. As Frow notes, 'The pleasure we might take in the sketch is an effect of its sharp, slightly gossipy observation of detail and of our sense of recognition of that type'.[84] This too, resonates, with at least some of the figures in the legal context: although these figures may not be presented along with certain anecdotes told about them, they do nevertheless often give a certain pleasure, and, indeed, often a comic one. In fact, some of these figures, like the Officious Bystander, as we shall see in the second part of this chapter, may be taken as figural forms of comic argument.[85] Their imagining, in company with others, including advocates and judges in the courtroom, is at least sometimes accompanied by laughter. This goes for even some of the more allegedly sober figures like the Reasonable Person: in both judgements and in scholarly work, the character of this figure has often been expressed comically.[86]

Some figures deployed in figural tests are more 'moral' than others, eg the right-thinking member of society in defamation law is arguably more morally-inflected than the Officious Bystander. There is an interesting debate to be had about the Reasonable Person, and whether, or to what extent, the Reasonable Person is held out to be a moral exemplar, a person of virtue, or instead, a representation of a more middling, common, average virtue, more akin perhaps to common sense.[87]

Even, however, in the most morally-inflected figures in the legal context – such as, for instance, the right-thinking member of society in defamation law[88] – the way these

[82] Frow (2014), 108.

[83] Ibid.

[84] Ibid, 109.

[85] There are fascinating overlaps to examine further here between the forms of comic argument in legal contexts, and the comic genre generally, perhaps especially via the notion of figures. Indeed, there may well be historical connections between what is known as 'London Comedy' in the seventeenth century, and after, and the rise of figural legal tests in the common law: see, eg, Hume (2011).

[86] See, eg, Austin (1992).

[87] See, eg, Del Mar (2018c); and Mangini (2019).

[88] See *Sim v Stretch* [1936] 2 All ER 1237.

figures work is probably not going to be exactly like some of the functions of moral types in literature. For instance, the right-thinking member of society surely operates at quite a distance to the models of saints or heroes in Greek, Christian or Renaissance literary cultures, and even probably from 'the forms of moral training disseminated by the *Spectator* and *Tatler*'.[89] Figures in legal contexts seem less to be models of 'moral emulation, a machine for the construction of good moral selves',[90] and more devices for a complex, flexible exercise of normative judgement by the judge. Rather than models to imitate, they are models to think with, as a judge explores what can be attributed to the agency of the person being evaluated, and what to social norms, cultures and expectations.

Another term in this context, possibly related to the 'moral types' in Theophrastus, is that of 'social types'. For instance, Frow argues that there is a 'clear line of connection' from Theophrastan characters, and the French and English tradition of Theophrastan character writing, to 'early eighteenth-century English typologies, particularly the characters of the *Tatler* and *Spectator*'.[91] These, Frow says, 'are either directly professional and social types, or the allegorically named personifications of types', and they too, he insists, are 'stories waiting to be told'.[92]

One scholar who has written about these 'social persons' is Elizabeth Fowler, in her study of *Literary Character*.[93] Fowler defines these as 'models of the person, familiar concepts of social being that attain currency through common use'.[94] They exist as cognitive conventions, ie as 'sets of expectations built in the reader's mind by experience', and they also change over time, as conventions do, and so 'are better regarded as cumulative and changing sets of resemblances than as susceptible to definition by a list of features'.[95]

There is a dynamic relationship between these social persons and characters found in literature. On the one hand, our knowledge of social persons is, in part, gleaned from our reading and processing of these characters; on the other hand, we bring the sets of expectations that social persons collect and condense to our reading practices. In fact, for Fowler, our understanding of 'literary characters' is 'largely cobbled together out of allusions to a number of social persons'.[96] These allusions, ie these opportunities for drawing on, but also building on, our knowledge of social persons, while we read, are multiple in any text. Cues for social persons in texts can be found in:

> … bodily posture and gesture, topos, title, nomination, attribution, built space, mapped space, landscape, allusion, ritual, ceremony, specialised lexis, genre, ethos, ideology, iconography, social relations and bonds, values, virtues and vices, ideals and rules, narratorial attitude and tone, metaphor and other tropes, simile and other figures of speech, habitus, representations

[89] Frow (2014), 64.
[90] Ibid.
[91] Ibid, 111.
[92] Ibid.
[93] Fowler (2003).
[94] Ibid, 3.
[95] Ibid.
[96] Ibid, 17.

> of the passions, allusions to social institutions and historical events, and literary conventions of characterisation.[97]

As we read and process characters, and, crucially, as we also evaluate them, we look for cues to already valenced-social persons, which enable that process of construction and evaluation. This process is a highly affective one. For Fowler, 'human figures make claims upon us through a process fraught with passions and arguments'.[98] It is also a complex one, involving, for instance, balancing between character and social landscape. Figures 'draw us into social landscapes', and it is within a social landscape, ie in a certain social context, involving interactions with other persons, that we both construct and evaluate a character, in part by bringing to bear on that character the various social persons that orient and guide our construction and evaluation of it. Social persons can, in this respect, be said to be 'laboratories to think about intention':[99] we draw upon our knowledge of social persons to attribute different intentions to a character, and we thereby evaluate it. Social persons 'shape our notions of intention'.[100] They are figural thought experiments:

> These chapters [of Fowler's book] show how, as we begin to experience words, images, emotions, and ideas according to the instructions of the text, the authors invite us to undertake figuration as a species of philosophical thought experiment. This is not only a literary experience but a political one. In the experiment of deliberation, we consider what seems good from the position of each social person, always in conjunction with justice as it is exemplified by an entire system of social life. Rather in the way that the demande d'amour leads us to deliberate about the amusing situations hypothesised in romance, all fiction puts its readers in the position of evaluating the social persons that fashion its characters. By means of character, fiction tests the forms, both ethical and political, of social life. This cognitive, moral process … gives fiction its literary shape, its ethical habituation, and its political force.[101]

These social persons may, in some sense, be 'types', and in that sense thin, flat or simple, but they are nevertheless complex condensations of 'values, standards of evaluation, a configuration of attributes, a sense of possible actions and plots, an orientation toward social institutions'.[102] Thus, for example, when a reader of the period read *Chaucer's Pardoner's Tale: A Prologue*, the figure of the Pardoner was constructed and evaluated by attaching to it a whole range of different social persons, including envisaging the Pardoner as 'a eunuch … homosexual, sodomite, queer, preacher, master rhetor, vice figure, philanderer, salesman'.[103] As the reader reads, they draw on multiple social persons. Indeed, it is often 'conflict among social persons', eg seeing the Pardoner as a cross-section of multiple social persons, some seemingly incompatible that 'generates ethical deliberation about the ideals and institutional arrangements of society'.[104]

[97] Ibid, 16.
[98] Ibid.
[99] Ibid, 17.
[100] Ibid, 19.
[101] Ibid, 31.
[102] Ibid, 72.
[103] Ibid.
[104] Ibid, 73.

iii. 'The Ordinary Man of Prudence'

Fowler's is a complex and sophisticated argument, and it is designed to help us understand the process of reading literary character, but I think we can relate it to the use of figures in the legal context. One way to do this would be to treat the figures in figural legal tests as social persons, tagged by the legal community as especially important in evaluating the actions and interactions of the parties that come before them. Thus, the Right-Thinking Member of Society, the Reasonable Person, the Well-Informed and Normally Diligent Tenderer, and the Fair-Minded Observer: all these might be taken to be the law's explicitly-named social persons, each condensing knowledge of social norms, customs and practices, and then brought to bear on the construction and evaluation of the actions and interactions of the parties. Social persons draw us into social landscapes, and thereby enable a specific construction and evaluation of the parties, ie via the balancing of the agency and intention of a person with the circumstances in which the actions and interactions played out. As we construct and evaluate, we draw on social persons to consider what to place on the agency or intention side, and how much weight to attribute to it, and what to place, instead, on the side of the circumstances of the case.

Should we, for instance, in evaluating the actions of a farmer putting haystacks nearby the barns of his neighbour, place more weight on the agency and intentions of that farmer, eg a certain recklessness and thoughtlessness, as someone, say, a risk-taker, a chancer, might do, or should we place more emphasis on the relevant social norms, customs and practices in that community, eg it being, say, common to place haystacks near barns, or it not being conventionally predictable by anyone that such a heavy wind would carry the fire that began in the haystacks to the barn? The point here is that this process in the legal context, of deciding whether someone is responsible (negligent, say), can be understood, on the back of Fowler's approach, to involve the construction and evaluation of character, where this requires deciding on a certain relative distribution of agency and intention on the one hand, and context in the circumstances of the case on the other hand.

This relative distribution of agency/intention and context, in turn, is guided and oriented by knowledge of certain social persons. Of course, the explicit tagging in the social context matters: thus, in the case of negligence, the relevant social person that ought to guide our construction and evaluation of the acts of the defendant is that of the Reasonable Person, with all the knowledge that we have of that figure, as applied in past cases. But the process, in general terms, is similar: the construction and evaluation of literary character, may not be so far away from the construction and evaluation of the character of parties in a case, with both being guided and oriented by our knowledge of social persons.

If we stick, for a moment, with the Reasonable Person, we can see how via this artefact, with its related process of figural imagining, we can generate insight into which values, vulnerabilities and interests may be at stake in a certain case and in cases potentially like it in the future. If we return to the above case of the hay stacks, modelled roughly on *Vaughan v Menlove*,[105] then we see the Court drawing on the figure of the

[105] *Vaughan v Menlove* (1837) 132 ER 490 (CP).

'ordinary man of prudence' to construct and evaluate the character of Menlove, and thereby decide whether he is guilty of negligence in placing haystacks nearby the barns of his neighbour. The figure, or, using Fowler's language, the social person, of the 'ordinary man of prudence' enables a subtle, complex normative judgement: the Court considers whether, in the circumstances, more weight should be placed on the intentions with which Menlove purportedly acted, ie risking or chancing it, despite being warned of the dangers, or more on the social standards prevalent in that community. In that case, one of the arguments made on behalf of the plaintiff appeared to be that he was suffering from less than average intelligence: should that be a relevant consideration? Should the Court place more weight on the social expectations attaching to persons with less than average intelligence, or should more weight be placed, again, on certain intentions with which the plaintiff purportedly acted?

To grapple with the question, it helps to imagine, ie it helps to envisage, not the defendant, but a 'man of ordinary prudence' in the circumstances of the case. We simulate – affectively, senorially, and kinesically – the actions and interactions of the 'man of ordinary prudence': what would he have done? How would he have acted? The point is not that the answer comes immediately: instead, the point is precisely that it is a thought experiment, which takes time to process; we generate possibilities for what the 'man of ordinary prudence' might have done, eg what intentions he might have had, with what corresponding actions, and we draw on them when returning to the actions of the defendant. In doing so, we also make normative insight: we bring into view, for instance: 1) the social function of insurance, eg would the man of ordinary prudence have taken out insurance?; 2) the role of the community vis-à-vis persons of less-than-average intelligence; 3) the general safety of barns, eg are they too prone to fires, the fault not being properly attributable to anyone but to the general standards of building? And so on. The normative judgement here cannot be made in the abstract: it must be made with sensitivity to the norms, customs and practices in the relevant community, as balanced against the agency of and intentions with which the defendant purportedly acted. In this way, figural imagining helps with the exercise of this complex, situated normative judgement.[106]

This process, it should be added, is not all one way: it is not just a matter of bringing to bear our knowledge of a social person, or many social persons, on the character of a party in a case, or a literary character. Rather, our knowledge of the relevant social person(s) is also transformed as a result of our having drawn on it in exercising normative judgement in that case or reading that novel. Our understanding of 'a man of ordinary prudence' is different after *Vaughan v Menlove*. The process, as noted above by reference to Fowler, is dynamic and bi-directional: in part from social persons to characters, and in part from characters to social persons.

[106] For another argument, akin in some ways to Fowler, as to the similarities between reading literary characters and exercising judgement of persons in everyday life, see Hochman (1986). For example, Hochman argues that 'there is a profound congruity between the ways in which we apprehend characters in literature, documented figures in history, and people of whom we have what we think of as direct knowledge in life. In my view, even the clues that we take in and use to construct an image of a person are virtually identical in literature and in life': (1986), 36.

D. Counterfactual Imagining

i. The Significance of Counterfactual Imagining

There is one final domain of the literature that deserves mention here, and that is the idea of the relation between character-based and counter-factual imagining, eg via the notion of 'counterfactual characters'. In the immediate paragraphs above, when referring to the 'man of ordinary prudence' in negligence, I noted that what we do when we imagine figurally is simulate affectively, kinesically, and with the construction of mental imagery, from a perspective, the actions and interactions of someone else, ie someone other than the parties to the case. We ask: 'what would have the man of ordinary prudence done instead?' To ask this question is to engage in counterfactual imagining: we imagine something that might have been done that we know was not done. Why might this be important? What role does it play? Clearly, there is a close relationship between counterfactual imagining and the exercise of judgement: how else can we construct and evaluate the actions of, say, the defendant, without comparing it to what else might have been done? Our ascriptions of intention, it seems, both in understanding and in evaluating the actions of others, and possibly also ourselves, depend, at least sometimes, on counterfactual imagining.

There has been a flowering of work on counterfactual imagining in literary theory in recent years, though there had already been important work on counterfactual imagining in psychology.[107] Literary theorists have argued that it is difficult to see how our attributions of significance to the actions of characters could operate in the absence of some counter-factual imagining, eg as David Herman observes, 'Hamlet's stabbing of Polonius takes on significance when it is contrasted with the way the world would have been had he not slain the officious adviser'.[108] For Albrecht Koschorke, in his rich general theory of narrative, storytelling is itself dependent on the generation, by the reader, of alternative possibilities to what is told in the story: 'The spinning of a tale lives from the background possibility of an alternative linkage, which is to say of another possible sequence, hence of weakened motives and causalities that have been unsettled by countervailing forces'.[109]

For Koschorke, this generation of alternatives, including, as above, alternative evaluations based on different accounts of intentions of characters, remains, even after we have finished a story. He refers to this indeterminate generation of alternative possibilities, which is in tension with what is described as having occurred in the story, as the 'riddle of narrative', and argues that it is an essential part of both the pleasure and the memorability of a story:

> … we can say that a riddle lies embedded in the heart of every good story. Even if the plot usually concludes at the end and the riddle is resolved, the movement into indeterminacy is constitutive for the reception process; indeed, it repeats itself with repeated listening or reading. Through the doubled temporality of stories, their interplay between actual experience in the present and retrospection, the riddle is always both solvable and unsolved; Odysseus'

[107] See, eg, Harris (2000), and Byrne (2007).
[108] Herman (2002), 14.
[109] Koschorke (2018), 56.

wandering and Penelope's waiting have no end, although we know that he made his way home to her, victorious.[110]

As with other kinds of imagining, once we pay careful attention to it, we begin to see it everywhere, its significance growing in our esteem.

ii. The Complexity and Multiplicity of Imagining Counterfactually

The literary scholar who has arguably contributed most, and also most recently, to our understanding of the role of counter-factual imagining, and not only in literature, but also in historiography, is Catherine Gallagher. I cannot do her work justice here: her book-length treatment, *Telling it Like it Wasn't*,[111] is wonderfully rich and complex. I wish only to make a number of observations.

One of these is that counterfactual imagining is often not about imagining one single alternative: once we begin imagining counterfactually, it can sometimes be difficult to stop; we typically generate multiple alternative possibilities even if, when it comes to articulate our evaluation of a character, we contrast it with one especially powerful alternative possibility. This proliferation of alternative possibilities has had some extraordinary examples: eg in the genre of military history, which has made extensive use of counterfactuals, we often see long lists of hypothetical counterfactual possibilities. For instance, Carl von Clausewitz, in his pursuit of the evaluation of Napoloeon's character as a general, generates as many as six orders of hypothetical alternative possibilities. To quote Gallagher:

> I'll summarise a passage in which Clausewitz analyses Napoleon's options after defeating the Archduke Charles on the Tagliamento in 1797. Clausewitz introduced his critique by noting that Napoleon's surprise march across the Alps had been hailed as an act of astonishingly brilliant and successful generaliship, and to demonstrate that it may *not* have been, he subjects Napoleon's campaign to a series of counterfactual tests. Napoleon, he points out, actually arrived too early on the other side of the Alps to rendezvous with the French armies of the Rhine and therefore felt forced to make a strategic armistice. But *should* he have made the armistice? What might have happened if he didn't? The first steps of the analysis unfold like this: from his position after pursuing the Archduke's army into Austrian territory, he negotiates the armistice and goes back to Italy; however, he might have simply waited for the armies of the Rhine, or he might have more actively threatened Vienna. After establishing these two other options, Clausewitz takes us to sixth-order hypotheticals in pursuing them, especially the last one, so that the counterfactuals overwhelm the actual events, which become a small proportion of the possibilities: if Napoleon had not signed the armistice but instead threatened Vienna, the Austrians might have made further concessions or they have might have abandoned the capital, withdrawing into their territory. In that case, there probably would have been a battle on the Rhine, which the French would have probably have won, in which case Napoleon might have pursued his advantage and tried to destroy the Austrian empire, in which case he might have succeeded or, conversely, he might have overextended his forces, but only if the Austrians had continued to resist.[112]

[110] Ibid, 57.
[111] Gallagher (2018).
[112] Gallagher (2011), 324.

The passage is long, but necessarily so, for it conveys something of the complexity and multiplicity of these counterfactual structures in military history. Note, however, that the purpose of these histories is precisely the evaluation of the skill of generalship: in this case, via the evaluation of the character of Napoleon. We learn, in the result, that Napoleon 'might have come away from the campaign with more substantial gains than he actually made',[113] and so we revise our evaluation of Napoleon as a great, brave, risk-prone general, seeing him instead as, say, at least sometimes insufficiently brave, or overly cautious.

Of course, this is a quite extraordinary example, and, outside military history, it is arguably rare to see such complex and multiple counterfactual edifices. Nevertheless, what is clear here is, first, the close relationship between the construction and evaluation of character on the one side, and counterfactual imagining on the other side, and second, the tendency, within counterfactual imagining, to generate multiple alternative possibilities. Once we begin to counterfactually imagine, it can be difficult to stop.

iii. Constraints on Counterfactual Imagining

A question presents itself at this point: why do we stop where we do? Why does Clausewitz not keep going, pushing the hypothetical counterfactuals further back? A cynic might say that we stop when we reach the evaluation we were after: Clausewitz reaches a point at which he can cast doubt on the brilliance of Napoleon as a general, and that for him is enough. But this would suggest that counterfactual imagining is just a way of displaying what one already knew, and not a mode of inquiry: a way of experimentally probing, tentatively examining, what should have happened by way of generating alternatives of what might have.

In the legal context, the constraints on counterfactual imagining may come, in part, from the pragmatics of adjudication. An advocate may well pursue counterfactual imagining only to the extent that it puts her client in the best possible light, and the other party in the worst possible, just as Clausewitz does in the above example. A judge, however, is in a different position: she does not pursue counterfactual imagining with a view to demonstrating an evaluation she has already reached. Instead, the counterfactual imagining engaged in by a judge is a means of experimenting with what values, vulnerabilities and interests might be at stake in this case, and in others potentially like it in the future. In this respect, the judge is helped by having two competing counterfactual imaginings presented by the advocates in the case.

The constraint on counterfactual imagining, in the legal context, then, comes in part from the pragmatics of adjudication: the judges engage in figural imagining, but they do so in ways already illuminated by the exchange of opposing counterfactual imaginings, and with a view not only on the present case, but also on the law's past and its future. In the legal context, unlike in the single-author task of writing, say, a military history, what we see is not just a single judge, on a one-off occasion, counterfactually imagining the actions of, say, a 'man of ordinary prudence', but rather the agonistic exchange of

[113] Ibid, 325.

counterfactual imaginings, all also against the background of previous applications of that figure in past cases, and of potential applications in the future. The judge can, but does not have to, choose one of the two opposing counterfactual imaginings proposed by one or the other advocate; she can also generate her own. Nevertheless, the judge is constrained by what is presented to her as relevant, eg if we keep in mind the complex relationship between figure and context, and thus that when we imagining figurally, incuding counterfactually, that we do not just imagine the actions of a figure in a vacuum, but rather place them within a social landscape, or within the circumstances of the case, then we also see that advocates exercise considerable influence over judges by presenting what circumstances are relevant.

Keeping in mind the pragmatics of adjudication, we can argue that counterfactual figural imagining is not endless, and so only arbitrarily stopped, but is instead to some extent constrained by the social and diachronic dimensions of inquiry in adjudication. Of course, counterfactual figural imagining still retains a certain amount of freedom: in a way, that is its point, namely that it allows us to experiment and explore. Nevertheless, I would suggest, this experimentation and exploration is not such as to be arbitrary, or a mere mode of expression of an already-reached evaluative conclusion.

Like other kinds of imagining, counterfactual imagining has a long history, and one that has close ties to legal practice.[114] We also have to be mindful that it may be deployed in different ways in the legal context, depending on which figural test is being used. Thus, for instance, in the case of the Officious Bystander, we do not imagine what we know did not happen, as we do with the Reasonable Person; we imagine instead what might have happened, ie we imagine a plausible, if not likely, scene of negotiation. Our aim is not to create contrasting possibilities, which then assist us to evaluate the actions of the parties. We are still arguably counterfactually imagining in some sense, eg we may know that the questions asked by the Officious Bystander were not asked at any such negotiation scene. However, we are arguably doing something different from when we imagine how, say, the Reasonable Person would have acted. In making room, then, for the presence of counterfactual imagining in the legal context, and keeping an eye on its relation to the making of normative judgement, we should also bear in mind that counterfactual imagining can, depending on the figural legal test in question, manifest itself in different ways.

E. Summary

Only so much can be said in the abstract about figural imagining. This is, in part, because of the differences between figural legal tests, which have different aims and functions. Bearing this in mind, I have sought to show, by reference to some of the relevant literature, the different kinds of ways in which we draw on and project the human, as well as identifying the sense in which we can speak of figural legal tests as artefacts, with related processes of imagining, which can enable inquiry in adjudication.

[114] See also the essays in Wohl (2014). See also Venzke (2018); and Heller and Venzke (Forthcoming).

As artefacts, figures signal their own artifice in part formally, through the capitalisation of a proper name, though one where the name is supplied by traits of character, as in the Reasonable Person or the Officious Bystander. As an artefact, figures also invite us to do something with them: they are figures waiting to be placed in a context, ie the circumstances of the case, in which their story can be told. In this respect, they are under-specified, and thus call upon us to be active, ie to specify them, to tell their story.

As processes of imagination, figures involve us entering a distinctive epistemic frame, in which we selectively suspend, for instance, otherwise relied-upon epistemic commitments to proper names referring to real persons, or to conceiving of persons as more than vectors of one- or two-character traits. In the second limb of imagining, figural imagining involves a high degree of affective, sensory and kinesic participation. The role of the body is especially important, as the recent literature on personification also emphasises. This heightened kinesic simulation is connected also to our emotions and to the construction of mental imagery from a perspective. The role of the emotions is multi-faceted, eg it may involve simulating the emotion of the figure, as we project their story in a context, as well as evaluating those emotions.

As we have seen by reference to the literature on character, and counter-factual imagining, there is an intimate, but also complex, relation between figural imagining and judgment. Having created a figure, endowed with certain limited character traits, as in figural legal tests, we then imagine the figure in a particular context, ie in the circumstances of the case, but also, given the future-oriented dimension of legal reasoning, in potentially similar cases in the future. In doing this, we often appeal to the character of the figure, ie we explore what officiousness or being a bystander in such-and-such a case may be, or sometimes, as we shall in the second part of this chapter, we add further characteristics, eg imagining the Officious Bystander to be legally trained.

This process, of thinking thorugh the character of the figure in question, is a complex one. It is complex also because in placing the figure in the circumstances of the case, we also generate different ways of balancing the explanatory emphasis, either emphasising the agency/intentionality of the figure or the role of the context in which the figure acts, ie the relevant social norms, customs and practices. Depending on the figure in question, we thereby either evaluate the actions of the figure, and then compare this to the actions of the relevant party, eg the defendant in a negligence case, or we evauate the actions of the parties as they are imagined to interact with the figure, as in the Officious Bystander test. Throughout, again, there is a complex relation between figure and context, ie the circumstances of the case: indeed, part of the role and value of the figure for inquiry in adjudication is that it allows for this flexibility in generating different possible ways of relating the figure and the context.

As artefacts, with related processes of imagination, figures can enable inquiry in adjudication. Figures are typically not one off, ad hoc applications in cases: instead, they are part of legal tests, eg of what counts as defamation, or for negligent liability, or for whether to imply terms into a contract. In this respect, they get re-used and re-imagined case after case. Advocates and judges accumulate knowledge of such figures, drawing on their previous imaginings in other cases. Thus, figural imagining allows not only an individual judge in a single case to justify a decision in that case, eg the defendant is liable because he did not act as the Reasonable Person would have acted, but also allows a legal community to engage in collective inquiry over time. For instance, deploying the Right-Thinking Member of Society test in defamation law is a way of engaging, slowly and casuistically, in an inquiry as to what ought to be the scope of what is defamatory: it is a way of generating, over time, insight as to what values, vulnerabilities and interests might be at stake in cases involving dispute over whether something is capable of being defamatory. The Right-Thinking Member of Society, for example, is a useful way of examining whether statements informing the police are all excluded from being defamatory, or whether they can still be defamatory in certain contexts, and in which. The point is that figural imagining allows for precisely this context-sensitive inquiry. Put another way, figural imagining allows for context-sensitive, casuistic making of normative insight.

II. The Officious Bystander

Although not as old, not as famous, and not as discussed, both positively and negatively, as the Reasonable Person, the Officious Bystander does hold an important position in English contract law. Indeed, it has become one of the key tests for the implication of terms in contract law. Given the link between the implication of terms in contract, and questions concerning the interpretation of contracts in general, the figure has also featured in the much-debated, relatively recent series of cases concerning contractual interpretation. This is a complex and difficult area of the law. My engagement with it below will be necessarily brief and inevitably inadequate. I aim not to summarise and describe this area, but instead to trace the creation and subsequent career of this particular figural legal test.

In what follows, my focus is on the Officious Bystander as an artefact, with related processes of imagining, enabling inquiry. I approach this in two steps. I begin, first, with the origins of the Officious Bystander: how and when, and why, was this figure born? We can ask: why are judges drawn to transforming a non-figural test into a figural one, or, where there is no prior test, figural or non-figural, why introduce a test in the form of a figural one? We can also ask: what various versions of the test were being generated in the period of its creation and initial emergence?

The second step concerns the career of the figure over time: how, in being imagined in particular contexts, have the character traits of the figure being interpreted? Have any further character traits, or other qualities and attributes, been added to the figure in particular cases, and have such additions stuck over time? This second step also concerns attempts, where there are such, and there often are, to kill-off, so to speak, the figure. Have judges and scholars, and if so, how have they, sought to replace the figural legal test with a non-figural one? Why might, at a certain point in time, such attempts be made? Have these attempts been successful, and if not, why not? What do debates over the desirability of a figural legal test reveal about its value?

Throughout, as above, my key concern is to connect the figure as an artefact, with its related processes of imagining, to the practice of adjudication, ie to individual judges deciding and justifying cases, to advocates and judges swapping, exchanging and criticising imagined versions of the figure, and to the community over time drawing on the figure to make insights into what values, vulnerabilities and interests might be at stake in the relevant area of the law.

A. The Origins of the Figure

i. Lords MacKinnon, Scrutton or Loreburn?

It has become somewhat commonplace to trace the origins of the figure of the Officious Bystander to the remarks of Lord Justice Scrutton in *Reigate v Union Manufacturing Co. (Ramsbottom) Ltd.*[115] In that case, also dealing with the question of the implication of terms into a contract, Lord Scrutton said:

> The first thing is to see what the parties have expressed in the contract; and then an implied term is not to be added because the Court thinks it would have been reasonable to have inserted it in the contract. A term can only be implied if it is necessary in the business sense to give efficacy to the contract; that is, if it is such a term that it can confidently be said that if at the time the contract was being negotiated some one had said to the parties, 'What will happen in such a case', they would have both replied 'Of course, so and so will happen; we did not trouble to say that; it is too clear'. Unless the Court comes to some such conclusion as that, it ought not to imply a term which the parties themselves have not expressed.[116]

A number of observations can be made about this famous passage. For a start, it mentions the non-figural test that was the dominant approach to implied terms in contract, namely: is the implication of the term necessary for the business efficacy of the contract? This is known either as 'the business efficacy test' or, after the name of the case in which it was introduced, as 'the *Moorcock* test'.[117] Second, it presents what comes, later, to be called 'the Officious Bystander test', as a way of articulating or applying the business efficacy test, and not as a separate test. As we shall see, the relation between the two tests, including whether there are two tests or they are one and the same, was and has remained a matter of debate. Third, it does not yet give the Officious Bystander a name; instead, Lord Scrutton refers to 'some one'. And, fourth, it imagines a scene taking place, giving the imagined 'some one' a voice, asking, 'What will happen in such a case', and imagining replies made by the parties, 'Of course, so and so will happen …'.

As important as Lord Scrutton's passage is, if one digs a little deeper, it becomes apparent that the origins of the Officious Bystander cannot be traced back to it. Here, it helps to know that the judge credited with introducing 'the Officious Bystander test', ie referring explicitly to an 'officious bystander', is Lord Justice MacKinnon. As we shall see in a moment, Lord Mackinnon was the judge in the Court of Appeal case in *Shirlaw v Southern Foundries*, which was decided in 1939.[118] It also helps to know that

[115] *Reigate v Union Manufacturing Co. (Ramsbottom) Ltd.* [1918] 1 KB 592. Subsequent references to this case are *Reigate* (1918).

[116] *Reigate* (1918), 605.

[117] *The Moorcock* (1889) 14 PD 64, 68, per Bowen LJ. Subsequent references to this case are *The Moorcock* (1889).

[118] *Shirlaw v Southern Foundries* (1926) Ltd [1939] 2 KB 206. Subsequent references to this case are *Shirlaw* (1939).

before MacKinnon became a judge, he served as Scrutton's pupil, when Scrutton was still practising at the Bar as a barrister. Scrutton had an interest in frustration cases, and MacKinnon often served as his junior, going on to develop, especially during the First World War, a considerable reputation as a barrister in contract cases affected by the War.

As it turns out, in 1917, just a year before the 1918 decision in *Reigate*, Lord MacKinnon authored a pamphlet, entitled 'The Effect of War on Contract'.[119] Questions as to whether to imply a term or not arose naturally in cases of frustration, perhaps especially under conditions of war. Should these cases be approached by asking whether the Court should imply a term? And if so, what should be the test for implying terms, at least as part of cases involving claims as to the frustration of a contract because of war? Here is the relevant passage from Lord MacKinnon's pamphlet:

> It is because it involves the question, 'What have the parties impliedly agreed?' that there arises the difficulty in applying the principle to the facts of many particular cases. In all cases of dispute as to contracts the real difficulty is as regards that which the parties have not made clear by expression. Disputes arising out of the most ordinary transactions of daily life would, if worthy of litigation, produce the hardest problems, merely because such contracts are concluded with the minimum of expression and the maximum of implication. Indeed, as to implied terms, the Court must move in a region of artificiality. The truth, in most cases, is that neither party ever thought of the particular matter at all, and were both of one mind about it, since the existence of a contract at all involves essentially the existence of agreement on all points: it must assume that if, while they were concluding their bargain, a third party remarked, 'In the event of so-and-so, of course you are agreed to such and such effect', they would *both* reply, 'Oh, of course!'. The assumption is necessary and is justified; for the parties have declared that they have contracted, and that involves that they are in agreement upon all points. But if permitted to speculate merely as a student of human nature, a judge might well conjecture that in truth the intervention of their more imaginative friend would have revealed such divergence of view among the parties as would have resulted in the conclusion of no contract at all.[120]

It is noteworthy, in this passage, that the relevant figure is first characterised as a 'third-party', and, later in the passage, as a 'more imaginative friend', ie more imaginative than the negotiating parties. Notice, also, that in this passage the third-party does not ask a question of the negotiating parties, but instead makes a statement, and one already involving the expression 'Of course', with both parties simply agreeing with that statement, themselves also replying with 'Oh, of course!'.

At this point in the development of the figural test, there is no capitalised character-based proper name, and also no question being asked, but there is, already, a sense of a figure who is imagined to be present at the original negotiations, and who intervenes in some way (in the above passage, because they are 'more imaginative' than the parties). Further, at this point, the character traits of the figure are that they are not only 'more imaginative', but also a 'friend', and, as we shall see later, although this is not the characterisation that goes on to have such an effect on this area of the law (that honour

[119] MacKinnon (1917).
[120] Ibid, 15–16. Original emphasis.

belongs to the Officious Bystander), nevertheless the figure, in the form of the 'imaginative third-party', though no longer a 'friend', does get repeated at least once.

Let us return to our saga as to the origins of the test. Given that MacKinnon had been Scrutton's pupil, and that they both shared an interest in this area of the law, it is surely not a stretch to hypothesise that MacKinnon sent a copy of his pamphlet to Lord Scrutton in 1917. Perhaps they even met and discussed the pamphlet. After all, the chances of them both coming up with this figural approach to the implication of terms, including both deploying the same expressions, including 'Of course', are pretty slim. Unless we can find further evidence that it was Lord Scrutton who first came up with the figure and the related expressions, and I have been unable to find any such evidence, then we must surely revise the story as to the origins of the Officious Bystander.

We may now be tempted to say that the origins of the figural test ought to be revised in the following way: the test comes not from Lord Scrutton in *Reigate* (1918), and not from Lord MacKinnon in *Shirlaw* (1939); instead, it comes from a pamphlet written by Lord MacKinnon in 1917, who created it by drawing on his extensive experience of pleading as a barrister in war-time frustration cases. When, furthermore, we remind ourselves that *Shirlaw* was heard and decided in 1939, at a time when yet another world war was brewing, it is not surprising, even though *Shirlaw* was not a frustration case, to see Lord MacKinnon returning to his experience as a war-time barrister.

In fact, however, there is more to the story. In 1916, in a case involving questions of frustration of contract, one of the judges also uses, in a similar way, the expression 'Of course!'. In the House of Lords, Lord Justice Loreburn said the following:

> When this question arises in regard to commercial contracts, as happened in *Dahl v. Nelson, Donkin & Co.*, *Geipel v. Smith*, and *Jackson v. Union Marine Insurance Co.* the principle is the same, and the language used as to 'frustration of the adventure' merely adapts it to the class of cases in hand. In all these three cases it was held, to use the language of Lord Blackburn, "that a delay in carrying out a charterparty, caused by something for which neither party was responsible, if so great and long as to make it unreasonable to require the parties to go on with the adventure, entitled either of them, at least while the contract was executory, to consider it at an end." That seems to me another way of saying that from the nature of the contract it cannot be supposed the parties, as reasonable men, intended it to be binding on them under such altered conditions. Were the altered conditions such that, had they thought of them, they would have taken their chance of them, or such that as sensible men they would have said 'if that happens, of course, it is all over between us'? What, in fact, was the true meaning of the contract? Since the parties have not provided for the contingency, ought a Court to say it is obvious they would have treated the thing as at an end?[121]

This passage does not involve the creation of a figure, but it does employ the expression 'of course', and in a very similar way. Should we, then, attribute the origins of the Officious Bystander to Lord Loreburn, deciding a war-time frustration case in 1916? Not so fast: for it turns out that the counsel, both in the Court of Appeal and in the House of Lords, included no one other than MacKinnon! Might it have been MacKinnon, then, who, in his role as an advocate, urged this kind of language on the judges, it finally appealing to Lord Loreburn? This, I have not been able to find out, and neither

[121] *FA Tamplin Steamship Co Ltd vAnglo-Mexican Petroleum Products Co Ltd* [1916] 2 AC 397, 404. Subsequent references to this case are *Tamplin* (1916).

have I been able to find any previous reference to the imagining of the original scene of negotiation between contracting parties in which they deploy the language of 'Of course'. It is possible, then, that we should trace the test back to Lord Loreburn, who inspires Lord MacKinnon to use the expression, with Lord MacKinnon later going on to create the figure of the third-party, the more imaginative friend. On the other hand, it is also possible that it was MacKinnon himself who introduced the expression as an advocate in 1916, with it taking favour with Lord Loreburn, who repeats it. Some mystery remains. Either way, though, clearly Lord MacKinnon does play a major role in this story.

When we turn to *Shirlaw*, in which Lord MacKinnon has often been said to first use the character-based proper name 'the Officious Bystander', Lord MacKinnon cites yet another source for the figural test. He does not refer to his 1917 pamphlet, nor to Lord Scrutton's remarks in *Reigate* (1918), nor indeed to Lord Loreburn's words in the *Tamplin* (1916), but instead to an 'essay I wrote some years ago'.[122] This essay turns out to be a lecture that Lord MacKinnon gave at the London School of Economics in 1926. One can find it on microfilm in the British Library.[123] In the relevant passage, Lord MacKinnon had said this:

> When almost any case arises about the suggested dissolution of a contract under such an implied term, or, under the commercial nickname, by virtue of 'frustration', the truth is that an event has occurred which never entered into the imagination of either party when they made their bargain. Lord Ellenborough's view was simple. "If you did not choose to anticipate this, and provide expressly for it, as with ideal prescience you might have done, the Court has nothing to say; your contract remains effective according to its expressed terms". But the judge nowadays may have to assume, contrary to the obvious fact, that the parties did foresee the event, and did provide for it: but as it is clear they have not agreed expressly they must have done so by implication. So he has to ascertain what is the implied agreement; and this is seldom easy. Prima facie that which in any contract is left to be implied, and need not be expressed, is something so obvious that 'it goes without saying': so that if, while they were making their bargain, an officious by-stander were to suggest some expression provision for it in their agreement, they would testily suppress him with a common 'Oh, of course!'. But in most of these cases the Court has, as a matter of construction to find what is the implied term, if any, ie the obvious common agreement, upon a matter as to which it must have the strongest suspicion that neither party ever thought of it at all, and that, if they had, they would very likely have been in hopeless disagreement what provision to make about it.[124]

It is in this lecture, addressing law students at the LSE in 1926, that Lord MacKinnon first introduces the character-based proper name of 'the officious by-stander'. Incidentally, the language of 'by-standers' appears earlier in the lecture, by reference to the famous inclusion, on the judicial bench, of 'bye-standers', ie non-legally trained merchants, by Lord Justice Mansfield in commercial cases.[125] What Lord MacKinnon

[122] *Shirlaw* (1939), 228.

[123] Andrew Phang has traced a copy to Harvard Law School's basement: see Phang (1998) and (2014).

[124] MacKinnon (1926), 12–13.

[125] Thus, the term 'by-stander' itself, it seems, we owe to Lord Mansfield: see *Bean v Stupart* (1778) 1 Doug. 11, 14, where Lord Mansfield refers to 'The special jury, and the bye-standers'. Quoted in MacKinnon (1926), 6.

is effectively drawing on in this passage is his pamphlet of 1917. This time, however, he develops the test into a fully-fledged figural one, involving an entire scene, with interaction between the 'officious by-stander' and the negotiating parties. As we shall see, it is still not the same scene that he then articulates in *Shirlaw*, but it is the closest previous precursor. For instance, in the above passage, the 'officious by-stander' does not ask a question, instead proposing an express provision to be included in the contract, to which the negotiating parties respond by testily suppressing him with a common 'Oh, of course!'.

ii. Shirlaw

We come, finally, to the *Shirlaw* case, which is the case credited with formally and explicitly introducing the Officious Bystander test. I will be returning to the facts shortly, but let us, first, see how Lord MacKinnon introduces the test. Approaching the case as one involving an issue of an implied term, Lord MacKinnon first mentioned the business efficacy test from *The Moorcock* (1889), casting some doubt on its status (he reminded readers, for instance, that it was 'an extempore judgement'),[126] and then said:

> For my part, I think that there is a test that may be at least as useful as such generalities. If I may quote from an essay which I wrote some years ago,[127] I then said: "Prima facie that which in any contract is left to be implied and need not be expressed is something so obvious that it goes without saying; so that, if, while the parties were making their bargain, an officious bystander were to suggest some express provision for it in their agreement, they would testily suppress him with a common 'Oh, of course!'"
>
> At least it is true, I think, that, if a term were never implied by a judge unless it could pass that test, he could not be held to be wrong.
>
> Applying that in this case, I ask myself what would have happened if, when this contract had been drafted and was awaiting signature, a third party reading the draft had said:
>
>> 'Would it not be well to put in a provision that the company shall not exercise or create any right to remove Mr. Shirlaw from his directorship, and he have no right to resign his directorship?' I am satisfied that they would both have assented to this as implied already, and agreed to its expression for greater certainty. Mr. Shirlaw would certainly have said: 'Of course that is implied. If I am to be bound by this agreement, including the barring of my activities under clauses 11 and 12 when I cease to be managing director, obviously the company must not have, or create, the power to remove me at any moment from the Board and so disqualify me from that post'; and the company, which must be presumed to have been then desirous of binding him to serve them as managing director for ten years, would, I think, with equal alacrity have said: 'Of course that is implied. If you were tempted by some offer elsewhere, it would be monstrous for you to be able to resign your directorship and, by so disqualifying yourself from being managing director, put an end to this agreement.'
>
> In the result, I think that the learned judge came to a right decision and this appeal fails.[128]

[126] *Shirlaw* (1939), 228.
[127] This refers to MacKinnon (1926).
[128] *Shirlaw* (1939), 228–9.

I have set this passage out in full, as it calls upon further analysis, including comparison to the above-cited passages. In case it is not clear, let me observe that Lord MacKinnon finds that a term ought to be implied into the contract, and that, on this basis, the Court ought to find in favour of the plaintiff (who had claimed breach of contract by the defendant). The Officious Bystander test, then, serves here to justify the decision in that case. However, the figural test is not introduced merely to decide the case: it is introduced as a legal test, for use in subsequent cases, and one which 'may be at least as useful' as the business efficacy test. If we recall Lord Scrutton's passage from *Reigate* (1918), where Lord Scrutton appeared to present the 'Oh, of course' test, as he articulated it then, as but a way of articulating or applying the business efficacy test, here, the figural legal test is being proposed by Lord MacKinnon as 'at least as useful'. The phrase is ambiguous, but it surely goes further than Lord Scrutton's, for it is open to being interpreted as introducing either an additional test or an alternative one.

Putting aside, for now, the issue as to the status of the test, and the relations between the tests, let us turn to examining the features of this figural test itself in more detail. There are four such features we can identify.

First, Lord MacKinnon quotes from his above-mentioned 1926 lecture to the LSE, but then goes on to 'apply' the test in a different way. In his application of it to the facts of the case, Lord MacKinnon has a 'third party' reading a draft of the contract. This first feature is one that has rarely been in subsequent applications of the Officious Bystander. It is arguably an important one, for it affects how much knowledge of the contractual circumstances to attribute to the Officious Bystander. The figure, at least in the *Shirlaw* case, appears very well-informed indeed, perhaps more, then, like a Well-Informed and Officious Bystander.

Second, Lord MacKinnon has the figure ask a question, and this, by contrast, has been a feature of this figural legal test that has gone on to become prominent. A number of judges and commentators have subsequently observed that it matters what question the Officious Bystander asks: eg Kim Lewison, in his *Interpretation of Contracts*, has argued that 'it is vital in more complex cases that the question asked be formulated with the utmost care'.[129] Notice, however, that this is not a feature that was present in all the passages pre-*Shirlaw*. In *Reigate* (1918), Lord Scrutton does have 'some one' ask the more open-ended 'What will happen in such a case', and in his 1926 lecture Lord MacKinnon does have the figure propose a provision, but both of these are different from the formulation of a particular question, which at least in *Shirlaw* asks about the potential inclusion of a specific term.

Third, the Officious Bystander is answered by both parties. In the passage above, Lord MacKinnon has both parties answer independently: he actually imagines and reports their answers in direct speech. Only when both answer with an 'of course', and do so with 'alacrity', is the test satisfied.

Fourth, as applied by Lord MacKinnon, the parties do not answer merely with a simple 'of course', but go on to elaborate, and indeed explain, their answer. This is vital, for Lord MacKinnon here arguably imagines the parties acting reasonably. After all,

[129] See Lewison (2011) [6.09].

they give reasoned answers. Notice, though, that the reasonableness of the imagined parties' responses is not moralised, ie the parties are still very much acting in their own interests, eg the company agrees to the implied term not because it then might exercise too much power over the Managing Director, but because it would not want the Managing Director to have such an easy way out of the agreement. Thus, the parties here, in their elaborate, reasoned answers to the question are reasonable, but in a self-interested way. This feature is also vital, for, clearly, what is being imagined is not just the action(s) of a certain figure, ie the Officious Bystander, but also the actions of the parties. The whole scene, one might say, is part of the figural legal test. As we shall see, however, subsequent applications of this figural legal test have not always even had the Officious Bystander ask the question, let alone had both parties answer, and with elaborated reasons.

Here, we can pause to ask: why go to all this trouble of imagining such a scene? How does introducing the figure help? Why not just apply the business efficacy test? When we answer this question, we must remember that what concerns a judge is not only doing justice in the instant case, but also respecting the law's past as well as caring for its future. The judge, in other words, is not only justifying the decision in the present case: mindful of the law's past (in this context, the law's past refers principally to the business efficacy test), the judge is also caring for the future, ie for what ought to be the test for implied terms.

I have been alluding to the facts of *Shirlaw*, but it will be better to have a clearer view of what happened in the case. In an agreement dated 21 December 1933, Mr Shirlaw was appointed by the first defendant, a company of iron-founders, to be their Managing Director for a term of ten years. Under that company's articles of association, it was stated that a Managing Director 'should subject to the provisions of any contract between him and the company be subject to the same provisions as to … removal as the other directors of the company and if he cease to hold the office of director he shall ipso facto and immediately cease to be a managing director' (Article 91). Article 105, in turn, gave the company power to remove a director before the expiration of his period of office. This was relevant, for a Managing Director had first of all to be a director: one could not be a Managing Director without being a director. In 1935, the second defendant, also a company, was formed and took over the first defendant, ie they acquired all their shares. This second defendant passed a special resolution on 17 April 1936 in which they abrogated the existing articles of the first defendant and adopted new ones. Under these new articles, the second defendant was empowered to remove any director of the company. This extended, in effect, to any Managing Director, given that, as already noted, any Managing Director had to also be a director. Then, in the killer blow, so to speak, on 27 March 1937, the second defendant removed Mr Shirlaw, the plaintiff, from his office as a director. As a result, he also immediately ceased to be a Managing Director. Mr Shirlaw duly sued.

As the Court of Appeal approached the issue, the question was whether a term ought to be implied into the agreement (between Mr Shirlaw and the first defendant, the iron-founders company). Mr Shirlaw argued that it ought to, and that the term implied ought to be to the effect that the company had no right to remove Mr Shirlaw as director for ten years, and, likewise, that he had no right to resign his directorship for those ten years. As we know, the Court of Appeal, and ultimately also the House of Lords,[130] found in favour of Mr Shirlaw. In both Courts, it was only Lord MacKinnon and Lord Justice Goddard who approached the case on the basis of an implied term, positively finding that that term ought to be implied.

If one approaches the case on the basis of it raising an issue of the implication of terms, and the above term is proposed, how would one resolve it by reference to the business efficacy test? Here, we immediately see one of the drawbacks of this test. The difficulty is that there may be a large gap between what can be said to be necessary for business efficacy and what can be reasonably be said to have been agreed between the parties. The former test can all too easily be applied in such a manner that it is too distant from what, on any reasonable interpretation, the parties may be said to have agreed. It is, as it were, too unmoored from their intentions, including from the circumstances in which they formed those intentions.

Furthermore, and here perhaps we move beyond respect for the intentions of the parties, and towards something more robustly normative, the business efficacy test offers little protection to vulnerable parties. After all, with the benefit of hindsight (knowing, now, that the Managing Director has not resigned his directorship), it may well be within a company's interests to keep open their own option of removing a Managing Director from his directorship (and, therefore, also removing him as Managing Director). There is, here, a certain injustice that only becomes visible post-facto, or with the benefit of hindsight: a certain exploitation of a vulnerability at time B becomes possible; protection against it may not have been included at time A, and this for all kinds of reasons, including, for instance, that the parties at the time of the negotiation did not wish to spoil the enthusiasm of the agreement with talk of removal or resignation. In this case, nothing was said about the possibility of either resignation or removal of a Managing Director by way of removing them or them resigning as a director. Instead, Mr Shirlaw was appointed for ten years as a Managing Director. This may not have been included for all kinds of reasons, and we can be more or less cynical in how we motivate the parties here. However, whatever may have been the reasons for not having a term (including, of course, not having contemplated the possibility), the point is that, with the passage of time, what we now see is that there existed a vulnerability at time A (the time of entering into the contract), which now, at time B (the time of the dispute, or the case), could be exploited.

There is, then, a certain value or vulnerability that is not being quite captured by the existing test, ie the non-figural test of business efficacy. It is difficult to say that implying a term to the effect that the company will not remove the directorship of the Managing Director (and, equally, that the Managing Director will not resign their directorship), is necessary for business efficacy. The contract could, surely, continue to be efficacious without such a term. But there is a niggling problem, and one that may tug at our normative dissatisfication with such a result. It is a problem, furthermore, that the business efficacy test itself does not seem to help us get at. It may be difficult to articulate – I have referred to the vulnerability of a party at time A, which may be exploited at time B, and this gives a sense of how difficult it is – but we still have a sense that something of normative importance is not being captured by the existing, non-figural test.

[130] *Southern Foundries (1926) Ltd v Shirlaw* [1940] AC 701. Subsequent references to this case are *Southern* (1940).

Here, arguably, is where a figural test becomes valuable. In these circumstances of normative uncertainty, ie where we feel that something of normative importance is at stake, ie some value, vulnerability, or interest, but cannot quite say what it is, the figural test helps us to grope our way towards it. In other words, by imagining figurally we can exercise inquiry, making insight into what values, vulnerabilities and interests might matter in this case and others potentially like it in the future. We place, first, in the original negotiating scene, a figure that we ascribe certain qualities or attributes to. The character traits in this context are those of being a bystander (and thus not someone with a stake in the contract) and being officious. Second, we imagine them interacting with the parties at the time of the negotiation: this Officious Bystander asks the parties a certain question. Then, as a third step, we consider whether the parties would have answered in the affirmative, and what they would have said in reasonabed elaboration of their answer.

It may look as if all we are hunting for is a way to anchor our addition of an implied term to the intentions of the parties. And, in part, we are doing that: we certainly are trying to get closer to the intentions of the parties and the circumstances in which they formed them. Arguably, however, to say that that is all we are doing in employing the figural test is misleading. It is not a mere matter of discerning what may have been obvious to the parties at the time: many things may have been, but they are not being debated. Something of further normative import is at stake, namely: we are seeking to protect a party against the post-facto exploitation of a vulnerability that may either not have been noticed at the time, or, if noticed, was not remarked upon for a whole variety of reasons. We do not need to (cynically) imagine the first defendant being wilfully malicious, ie not stating the term in order to keep their options for removing Mr Shirlaw open. Indeed, in this case, we can see more clearly why that would be stretching plausibility, for here it is the subsequent actions of a second defendant that matter.[131] Whatever the reasons for not including the term in the first place, we now, at time B, can see the possibility of the exploitation of a vulnerability that was at time A, perhaps unwittingly created. We cannot now know if a party is indeed seeking to exploit a vulnerability; but we have a sense, and this is crucial, that there may be circumstances in which we want to protect the vulnerable party against such an exploitation.

My point here is that introducing a figural test may well help us in this inquiry, ie it may help us not only to decide the present case, but also to communicate to future readers, eg members of the legal community, and possibly beyond, that there might be something normatively important at stake, and that we need to work, together, on what that is. This is, of course, not to say that the figural test as presented here, namely the Officious Bystander imagined, as above, to be interacting with the parties, captures what there is to capture normatively. But it does help push the inquiry forward, which can now, in subsequent applications of the figural test, continue to experimentally probe and tentatively examine what values, vulnerabilities and interests may be at stake when implying a term.

[131] This is also the reason why the other judges, including the Lords in the House of Lords, did not approach this case as one of implied terms: instead, they approached it, for instance, as a question of whether the second defendant had any power, as a third party, to alter the contract between Mr Shirlaw and the first defendant: see *Southern* (1940).

One might still ask: why introduce a figural test, and not, say, a fiction or a metaphor? What makes figural imagining so helpful? One possible answer is that imagining a figure, including doing so counterfactually, helps us to evaluate the actions of the parties. After all, our inkling that something is normatively important goes centrally to the characters of the parties, ie it goes to the normative quality of their actions, including both now, potentially exploitating a vulnerability, and then, potentially having acted with the malicious foresight that they could, later, exploit what they can see is a vulnerability. As we have seen, in the first part of this chapter, by reference especially to the scholarly literatures on character and counterfactual imagining, there is an intimate link between constructing and evaluating character, or between imagining counterfactually (which we perhaps do most easily via the actions and decisions of agents rather than, say, events) and evaluating actions or persons. Figural imagining, for example, may be less helpful when what is at stake is constitutional interpretation, which we encountered in the previous chapter. In a case like this, within the domain of private law, when one thing that matters is the quality of relations between the parties, figural imagining appears better suited to the task. Figural imagining, it seems, somehow helps more when what we are pursuing is the normative quality of the actions of persons.

We have now seen how a figural test might come into being, and why it might replace a prior non-figural test. At least in the case of *Shirlaw*, it functions, or so I have argued, to enable inquiry, ie the making of normative insight. It helps the judge, ie Lord MacKinnon, to generate insight as to what values, vulnerabilities and interests might be at stake. However, as noted above, Lord MacKinnon was not simply interested in deciding the case before him. He was also interested in the quality of the law in the future: what should be the test for implication of terms? Lord MacKinnon does not throw out the business efficacy test: he is careful and respectful of the law's past. Nevertheless, he does cast doubt on its sufficiency, and introduces a device – an artefact – which may assist those in the future, including, potentially, he himself in a future case, to inquire further. How did subsequent courts take up the invitation? They did so with enthusiasm, with the test now having been applied in hundreds, if not thousands, of cases, and not only in England, but also in other common law jurisdictions, eg quite prominently, in Singapore.[132]

iii. Towards a Cultural History of the Officious Bystander

Before I turn to the subsequent career of the Officious Bystander, one further remark as to the origins of the Officious Bystander may be made. In a lecture in 1995, Lord Hoffmann, in discussing the Officious Bystander test, noted, as an aside, that:

> Lord Justice MacKinnon was a witty and cultured man, for many years president of the Jane Austen Society. His little scene is plainly based upon the contemporary cartoons of Bateman, in which some unfortunate person is always asking a question which causes general astonishment all round him. But I do not imagine Lord Justice Mackinnon ever thought how seriously this little jeu d'esprit would be taken, how many times it would be cited, analysed, applied or distinguished in courts all over the world.[133]

[132] See Phang (2014).
[133] Hoffmann (1995), 138.

I have contacted the Jane Austen Society, and they have no record of a Sir Frank MacKinnon as a Past President. Lord Hoffmann was right, however, that Lord MacKinnon had interests in literary history: he wrote, for example, on Samuel Johnson.[134]

The reference to the cartoons of Bateman is, indeed, a relishing thought, and a plausible one. HM Bateman (1887–1970) was both proficient and popular as a cartoonist, occasionally also turning to legal themes, eg tax law was a favourite. He was active and proficient at the relevant time, ie the early twentieth century, and many a pleasant hour can be had Bateman-spotting over decades of copies of the *Tatler*, the *Spectator* and *Punch* in the British Library. In a number of these, Bateman does have a character pose all-too-obvious questions, and although these are mostly aimed at showcasing the absurdity of certain social norms and customs and the violence of social normativity, eg the reprobation with which those who break social norms are treated, one could perhaps see how they might have been an inspiration for the invention of the figure of the Officious Bystander.[135]

Another possible source for any future cultural history of this figure is the history of the character trait of officiousness. Earlier in this chapter, I mentioned the Theophrastan tradition, ie the tradition of character writing inspired by Theophrastus. Theophrastus, to recall, after having been a pupil of Aristotle's, became a teacher in Aristotle's Academy in the fourth-century BCE. Theophrastus's character writing was possibly inspired by the comic tradition in Ancient Greece, including mimes[136] and various short literary forms that were often comic in genre, also depicting persons from everyday life. Indeed, there is considerable comic potential in the category of 'officiousness'. And, as it happens, Theophrastus himself created one character who was said to be 'Officious'.[137] Here is the character sketch:

> The officious man will get up and make promises he cannot possibly keep. When an argument is recognised to be just, he has an objection to it and is proved wrong. He will compel the slave to mix more wine than his guests can drink. He will separate two fighters though he does not know them at all. Leaving the high road he will lead you by a short cut and eventually be quite at a loss to know where to go. He will go up to the general and ask when he intends to offer battle and what are the orders for the day after to-morrow. He will come up to his father and tell him his mother is already in bed. When the doctor strictly orders him not to give wine to a sick person he remarks he is anxious to give it a trial and drowns the sick man with it. When a lady dies he inscribes on her tomb her husband's name and her father's and her mother's, and, of course, her own and the place of her birth, adding 'All those named were excellent persons'. At the moment of taking an oath he will remark to those present 'You know, I have often taken oaths before'.[138]

The 'officious man', it seems, is not short on enthusiasm, and this, often, is at the cost of the patience of those around him. The character is introduced by Charles Bennett and

[134] See MacKinnon (1933).

[135] For more on Bateman, see Anderson (1982).

[136] The mimes of Herodas, who was born around 300 BC, often included short comic dialogues with characters from everyday life: see Herodas (1971).

[137] At least that is the way the Greek term was sometimes translated, eg in Thomson-Clerk (1909); and Jebb (1870). At other times, the term was translated as, eg, Impertinence, Diligence, Over-Officiousness, Over-Zealousness, and as referring to a Busybody. See also Boyce (1967).

[138] Thomson-Clerk (1909), 19–20.

William Hammond in an English edition and translation of Theophrastus in 1902 in this way: 'Then as now there existed the officious man, always over-ready to undertake the impossible to interfere in the affairs of others'.[139] Given that, as Lord Hoffmann observed, Lord MacKinnon was a witty and cultured man, he may well have enjoyed reading the comic sketches of character from Theophrastus, perhaps as filtered by the many English versions of character writing. In fact, MacKinnon, as a student, may well have already been exposed to these characters at school.[140]

Although this may seem like nothing but an entertaining tangent, there is a serious point here too. Officiousness does have a comic ring to it, and this is not without importance. Arguably, comic genres have a strong connection to kinesis: we more readily imagine the actions of those that strike us as amusing. Imagining comic figures, then, may well be easier than non-comic ones; it is also, surely, more pleasurable and memorable. It therefore both helps to capture attention, and to maintain it, and this can be important in the life of any institutionally-based exercise of cognition. There is certainly more to mine here at the intersection of figural imagining, the comic genre, and legal thought.

B. The Life of the Figure

Let us turn now to the second step I mentioned I would address above, namely: what has been the subsequent life of the Officious Bystander? What has been its subsequent characterisation, and how has that characterisation, ie interpretations of officiousness and being a bystander, but also addition of further qualities, attributes or character traits, enabled inquiry? Have there been attempts to 'kill off' the Officious Bystander, and what do debates as to the desirability of retaining this figural legal test reveal about its value? A full history of this career is, of course, not possible here.[141] Nevertheless, a brief excursion will be important, for, as with other artefacts, and related processes of imagining, their value must be considered over time.

i. Subsequent Characterisation

The Officious Bystander has certainly had, and continues to have, an outstanding, but also diverse and contested, career. Lord MacKinnon himself, it must be observed, did not necessarily contribute much to its further popularisation. For instance, already in 1940, in *Broome v Pardess*,[142] barely a year after *Shirlaw* (1939), Lord MacKinnon had the opportunity to once again reflect on the proper test for implied terms. Lord MacKinnon

[139] Bennett and Hammond (1902), xv.

[140] See Edmonds and Austen (1904).

[141] It would be wonderful to see more thorough cultural biographies of the figures in figural legal tests.

[142] *Broome v Pardess Co-operative Society of Orange Growers (Est 1900) Ltd* [1940] 1 All ER 603. Subsequent references to this case are *Broome* (1940).

did not, however, here refer to the 'officious bystander', speaking instead of an 'imaginative third party', and referring to Lord Scrutton's formulation in *Reigate* (1918):

> Taking the test as Scrutton LJ applies it, and supposing that, when this contract was being negotiated, a more imaginative friend had said to the plaintiffs, 'You are giving them a rather favourable contract this year with the guaranteed advance of 7*s* 6*d*. What is to happen if there is a very large amount of bad oranges? You know there were 11.96 per cent of bad oranges two years ago. There might be even more,' I am quite unable to come to the conclusion that the plaintiffs and defendants would both have said: 'Of course, if there are more than 5 per cent. of bad oranges, it will have to be made good.' The defendants, I am satisfied, would have said: 'Nevertheless, the whole basis of this contract is that you are to run the risk of the cost of repacking bad oranges. We have provided for that in the contract.' It may be that the result of the imaginative friend's interposition would have been to make the plaintiffs aware that they were running a risk of which they had not formerly been aware. It may be that their eagerness to get the supply of Palestine oranges, for which they thought there would be a tremendous demand owing to Spanish troubles, would have been discounted by the thought that possibly there might be a disastrous number of bad oranges, and that, perhaps, this was not so prudent a contract as they had first thought. It may be that the result of what I have called the imaginative third party's intervention would have been that the parties would have discussed the matter further, and no contract would have been entered into at all, because, for all I know, if the plaintiffs had said, 'We must have this 5 per cent. clause,' the defendants might have said 'No. We will not do that. There is a great demand this year for Palestine oranges. If you are not prepared to give the guaranteed advance of 7*s* 6*d*, and then run the risk of repacking such bad oranges as there are, there are other of your competitors in the market who will give us those terms, and we can go to them, instead of coming to you.' I need not discuss the matter more in detail. I am quite unable to be satisfied that, if this point had, in the words of Scrutton LJ, been suggested to the parties, when they were making this bargain, by a more imaginative third party, as a necessary result they would both have agreed that this implied term about more than 5 per cent of bad oranges would have been inserted expressly in the contract. The result is that I think the plaintiffs fail to establish that there is any such implied term, with the consequence that there has been no breach of contract by the defendants, and the judgment for the plaintiffs for damages for breach of a supposed implied term by the defendants cannot stand. This appeal must be allowed with costs.[143]

I have quoted this passage in full, not only because it shows us the first application post-*Shirlaw* of the figural legal test, but also because it shows us: 1) some differences, already this early, in the application of the test; and 2) that it results in a negative answer.

We see in this passage that the 'more imaginative third party' does not simply ask a question, but in fact offers an observation as to the risks of the contract, in this case, especially, for the plaintiffs. The defendants, though reasonable, elaborate their negative answer by reference to their own interests, eg that they are only contracting with this plaintiff because they can give them the favourable advance, taking on the risk of bad oranges themselves. Of note here, too, is how the figural test is enabling the judge to balance the intentionality of the parties on the one hand, with the contextual circumstances on the other: for instance, the parties are imagined to be taking into account the 'great demand for Palestinian oranges this year', the statistics concerning bad oranges in

[143] Ibid, 612–3.

the past, the Spanish troubles (referring to the Spanish Civil War), and the presence of competition, ie the availability of other suppliers of oranges. Balancing these considerations is how the judge evaluates the actions – we could say, the character – of the parties, and in this case, especially, the defendant. The judge takes a robust approach, looking to see how he can make commercial sense of the actions of the defendant. Finding that he can, the judge does not consider this case to be a proper one for the positive application of the figural legal test: the court will not intervene so far as to protect parties against commercial risks.

What is the difference between this and the *Shirlaw* case? Why was a term implied there, and not here? Did the figural legal test help, and how did it help to differentiate between the two cases? Part of the point is that it is very difficult, in the abstract, to articulate the normative grounds for the distinction, and, perhaps, it is undesirable to do so. It is better, eg for the overall quality of the law, for its ability to keep track of and be responsive to values, vulnerabilities and interests that may be at stake in cases in this area, to stay closer to the circumstances of the cases. Here, one might say, the vulnerability of the plaintiff to the risks of bad oranges does not outweigh the value of the freedom of contract, the value of competition in the marketplace, and the commercial, enterpreunerial interest of the defendant. We might view this conclusion via the filter of the figure, ie we might say that in this case, the figure of 'the more imaginative third-party' goes too far in pointing out commercial risks, that they are being too 'imaginative' or too 'officious'. Or, we might say that the figure's character traits, ie their being 'more imaginative', as per the language in this case, is not really picking up on the values, vulnerabilities and interests that are at stake. What we need, we might say, is not a 'more imaginative third-party', but a bystander that is sensitive to the prospect of exploitation of vulnerabilities that go beyond the usual commercial risk-taking in a certain industry.

The second observation, as mentioned above, is that the application of the figural legal test in the case results in not implying a term. Although I have not undertaken a thorough statistical test, my reading of the cases, since the 1940s, reveals that the figural legal test has, on the whole, not increased the success rate of implied term claims. In fact, success in the test is rare, at least as rare as when the relevant test was business efficacy. In the reported cases, it seems that about two out of ten claims were successful.

After *Shirlaw* (1939) and *Broome* (1940), the test, at least in reported cases, does not seem to arise with great frequency in the 1940s,[144] but picks up again from the 1950s, gaining extra momentum in the 1970s, and then appearing often and regularly in the 1980s, 1990s, and the 2000s. Already by 1950, though, the 'test of the officious bystander' is being described as 'well-known'.[145]

What one is also struck by when reading these cases is just how diverse the 'applications' of the test are. One has to be careful in characteristing some of these

[144] For two examples where the test is applied, see: *Parkinson (Sir Lindsay) & Co. Ltd v Commissions of His Majesty's Works and Public Buildings* [1949] 2 KB 632, and *Kelly v Battershell* (1949) 2 All ER 830. In both of these cases the implied terms claim is unsuccessful. Subsequent references to these cases are: *Parkinson* (1950) and *Kelly* (1949), respectively.

[145] See *E.P. Nelson v Rolfe* [1950] 1 KB 139, 146, per Cohen LJ.

as 'misapplications': after all, who is to say that the test as originally devised by Lord MacKinnon is the right figural test? Nevertheless, some discipline may be required: we are still engaged in an inquiry in which we are trying to generate insight as to which values, vulnerabilities and interests might matter in this area of the law, and, arguably, not all possible formulations of the figural legal test will enable inquiry.

An example of the need for some discipline, to which I shall return below, are instances where, unlike in Lord MacKinnon's treatment of the figure, the answer to the question posed by the Officious Bystander is only given by one party. This appears already early on in the applications of the test, eg in *Kelly v Battershell* (1949), the judge, when applying the figural legal test to a case concerning whether to imply a term which would have required the landlord not to permit the rest of the building to be used for any other purpose than a private dwelling, only has the landlord answer, 'How can I possibly say how I shall use the rest of the building when the war is over?'.[146] The difficulty with having only one party answer the question posed is that it may skew the answer too much in one direction: by not imagining the entire scene, we then miss some of the value of the figural legal test, which, again, as above, allows us to balance the intentionality of the parties with the relevant context, and thereby assess the character of the parties as against the background in which they acted.

This is, however, but one variation in the 'application' of the test, and a relatively mild one. The test has been applied, for instance in the following ways: a) with the Officious Bystander never asking a question, but instead proposing a specific term to the parties;[147] b) the judge imagining himself in the position of the third party,[148] an application which risks losing sight of the situated actions of the parties; c) the Officious Bystander offering an evaluation of some proposed term;[149] d) the Officious Bystander being described as an 'onlooker', who asks why one party has not made something clear to another party;[150] e) the Officious Bystander cross-examining or interrogating

[146] See *Kelly v Battershell* (1949) 2 All ER 830, 838, per Cohen LJ.

[147] *Parkinson* (1950).

[148] 'Supposing I, when the case came before me, had thought of this point and had played the part of the officious bystander': *Re Ley's Will Trusts; Somerset and another v Ley and another* [1964] 2 All ER 326, 330, per Cross J.

[149] 'My Lords, I think the officious bystander uninstructed in the law would say that for an employee to have the use of a brand new car licensed and insured for himself and his family and not at all for the purposes of the employer at a rate in the neighbourhood of £2 to £3 a week would be a valuable perquisite if the employee liked to avail himself of it': *Heaton (Inspector of Taxes) v Bell* [1969] 2 WLR 735, 761, per Upjohn LJ.

[150] 'Mr. Pain has referred more than once, and again finally this morning, to the well-known illustration of the officious bystander. I have endeavoured, following Mr. Pain's line of argument, to attempt to apply that test by imagining an officious bystander watching an interview between a responsible officer of the Railways Board about to engage a highly articulate and intelligent driver or guard and that driver or guard. I have imagined a copy of the rule book being handed over the table and the onlooker asking the former why he has not said to the latter: "You do understand, don't you, that you must not operate these instructions so as to disrupt the entire running of the railways system of the country?" Traditionally it is enough if the answer to that hypothetical question is a testy "of course": Were such a question put I doubt if the driver's or guard's response would have been limited, in MacKinnon LJ 's famous phrase, to such a testy "Oh, of course". I think he might well have been forgiven if he had replied to such a question in more vigorous and less restrained language': *Secretary of State for Employment v Associated Society of Locomotive Engineers and Fireman and Others* [1972] 2 QB 455, 508, per Buckley LJ.

the parties as to their intentions;[151] f) the Officious Bystander looking over the shoulders of the parties, and asking himself a question, and then answering it;[152] g) the Officious Bystander being asked a question either by the parties or by the judge, and seeing in either case whether the Officious Bystander would answer 'of course';[153] h) the Officious Bystander pointing out dangers and risks to the parties;[154] i) seeing whether the Officious Bystander would 'assume' something would be sufficient;[155]

[151] 'If Ocean Island had possessed an officious bystander in 1913 (a gentleman whose functions in relation to implied terms must not be allowed to obscure his utility in other spheres), I suppose that he might have cross-examined the parties as to their intentions. If he had, I would have been very surprised if the upshot had been an expression of intention that land subject to A or C deeds should be bound by two differently expressed obligations to replant, operating in different ways both as to what was to be planted and in other respects': *Tito and others v Wadell and others* [1977] Ch. 106, 285, per Megarry VC. 'Mr Timothy Morshead QC for the appellants submitted in his written case that what was important was "(a) that the risk [of inflation falling and remaining substantially below 10%] would have been obvious to the officious, reasonable bystander who must be imagined interrogating the actual parties and (b) that no reasonable person in the position of the parties, looking at the leases in their entirety and in context, would understand them to have intended that the tenants should assume that risk." He envisaged that in a hypothetical dialogue the officious bystanderwould warn the parties of the risks of their proposed contract and they would make it clear that that was not their intention': *Arnold v Britten and others* [2016] 1 All ER 1, [67], per Hodge LJ, reporting the written submissions of counsel.

[152] 'Various tests have been propounded from time to time with regard to the implication of terms in a contract. The officious bystander is one of the tests which has been used. It seems to me that the officious bystander, looking over the shoulders of Mr. Brodie and Mr. Marchant Lane, as they made the contract which they did, and asking himself whether the defendants could make a contract with Muellers and then break it without incurring any liability to the plaintiffs, would have answered: "No, that cannot be what is intended. It must be intended that, if they make the contract, after having had the buyer introduced to them, they will perform it and enable the agent to earn his remuneration"': *Alpha Trading Ltd v Dunshaw-Patten Ltd* [1981] 2 WLR 169, 180, per Brandon LJ.

[153] Example 1: 'If the officious bystander had been asked whether such a term should be implied, he or she would have said "of course"': *Aberdeen City Council v Stewart Milne Group* (2012) SCLR 114, 123, per Clarke LJ. Example 2: 'The compromise agreement was limited in its terms and effect to the claimant and the second defendant alone. The refusal of the Court of Appeal to imply any reservation of rights against the non-parties to the settlement agreement had been justified in the Gladman case, Mr Harper submitted, because those non-parties were not parties to any existing litigation. In the present case, however, the first and third defendants were parties to existing litigation and the compromise had not in terms extended to them. The officious bystander, in answer to the question: who do you intend to be settling against?, would clearly have answered: the second defendant and no one else. The officious bystander, if asked whom do you intend to be affected by this settlement? would simply have said: the second defendant and no one else. That was said to be reinforced by the terms of the Tomlin order, which was intended to stay proceedings only as between the claimant and the second defendant. There was said to be nothing in the surrounding circumstances to lead the officious bystander to the conclusion that the claim was not to continue against the first defendant. The intention was only to dispose of the claim as between the claimant and the second defendant': *Utilise TDS Limited v Neil Cranstound Davis and others* [2016] EWHC 2127 (Ch) [73], per Hodge, J. See also *Barclays Bank plc v Taylor; Trustee Savings Bank of Wales and Border Counties and another v Taylor and another* [1989] 3 All ER 563, 570, per Croom-Johnson LJ; and *An Informer v A Chief Constable* [2013] QB 579.

[154] 'The weakness, it seems to me, of the implied term theory is that it raises once more the spectral figure of the officious bystander intruding on the parties at the moment of agreement. In the present case, had the officious bystander pointed out to the parties in July 1974 the danger of carrying on the business of a commercial warehouse opposite a listed building of doubtful stability and asked them what they would do in the event of a temporary closure of Kingston Street pending a public local inquiry into a proposal for demolition after the lease had been running for over five years, I have not the least idea what they would have said, or whether either would have entered into the lease at all': *National Carriers Ltd v Panalpina (Northern) Ltd* [1981] AC 675, 687, per Hailsham LJ.

[155] 'An officious bystander would have assumed that annual accounting would be sufficient': *Nelson v Rye* [1996] 1 WLR 1378, 1385, per Laddie J.

j) evaluating how an Officious Bystander would react to a proposed term;[156] k) the Officious Bystanding volunteering an opinion on some proposed term;[157] l) considering whether the Officious Bystander would, when overhearing the parties speaking, agree with some term;[158] and k) seeing whether the Officious Bystander would regard a term as 'obvious'.[159]

In these examples, we see already some subsequent characterisation of the Officious Bystander, but there are also some explicit alternative or additional characterisations: eg a) 'the reasonable bystander';[160] b) someone not instructed in the law;[161] c) someone, by contrast, well-versed in the law, if not actually a lawyer;[162] d) a 'spectral figure', who is imagined to be 'intruding on the parties';[163] e) a 'mythical creature, who lurks in contract law';[164] f) an 'immortal abstraction';[165] and, as above, in various cases, 'a third-party', an 'observer', an 'outsider', or a 'nosy busy-body'.

In addition to the characterisations of the figure itself, there are also alternative characterisations of the parties when they are imagined in conversation with the figure: eg the courts have said that a) it is not the subjective intention of the parties that is to be ascertained, but their reasonable response to the figure's question, where it is recognised that there may be a gap between what a reasonable response might have been and what, in all likelihood, a particular party may have actually answered;[166]

[156] 'The point was made that no officious bystander would regard the MSA as entitling Barclaycard Business to appropriate the gross value of the payments made in respect of the relevant transactions and to retain them permanently. The judge rejected this submission and so would I. As Mr Sutcliffe QC submitted, it is not in fact a question of what an officious bystandermight think, but how the parties would react if such a bystander raised with them the point that the MSA should provide expressly for the making of the payment to the merchant after the expiry of such reasonable time:' *Lancore Services Ltd v Barclays Bank plc* [2010] 2 All ER (Comm) 273, 283 [27–28], per Rimer LJ. This case is another example where the courts have corrected counsel submissions.

[157] 'If the officious bystander had volunteered his opinion on the point, it could have been nothing short of conclusive': *Harding v Wealands* [2006] 3 WLR 83, 106 [80], per Carswell LJ.

[158] 'It seems to me that the reasonable bystander hearing this young couple living together as they were then would have said, "Well of course we envisage that you are going to renovate this property within a reasonable time and you are going to complete the sale within a reasonable time, so that I can get my money back." For my part I can see no reason at all why that term should not have been implied': *Powell v Lowe* [2010] EWCA Civ 1419 [13], per Ward LJ.

[159] 'A term will be implied into a contract when it would be regarded as obvious by any person acquainted with the transaction that it went without saying. That is sometimes called the "officious bystander" test': *Powell v Lowe* [2010] EWCA Civ 1419, [2], per Moore-Bick LJ.

[160] *Powell v Lowe* [2010] EWCA Civ 1419 [13], per Ward LJ.

[161] *Heaton (Inspector of Taxes) v Bell* [1969] 2 WLR 735, 761, per Upjohn LJ.

[162] 'It is impossible, in my judgment, to be sure that if at the time of the contract the officious bystander had asked, "Do you mean to exclude all Moule v Garrett liability?", the petitioner and the company would have answered with a common, "Oh, of course."': *Re Healing Research Trustee Co Ltd* [1992] 2 All ER 481, 485, per Harman J.

[163] *National Carriers Ltd v Panalpina (Northern) Ltd* [1981] A.C. 675, 687, per Hailsham LJ.

[164] 'If one were to introduce the mythical creature who lurks in contract law, the officious bystander, to ask the relevant question in the present case …': *Jones v Kernott* [2010] 1 All ER 947, 959 [33], per Nicholas Strauss QC.

[165] 'Furthermore, if a term is to be implied, it must be such that it would surely have been agreed to both by the reasonable shipowner and the reasonable charterer, not to mention that other immortal abstraction and honorary member of the Baltic Exchange, the maritime officious bystander': *Vardinoyannis v The Egyptian General Petroleum Corporation (The Evaggelos Th)* [1971] 2 Lloyd's Rep 200, 204, per Donaldson J.

[166] See, generally, *Equitable Life Assurance Society v Hyman* [2002] 1 AC 408; *Arla Foods UK plc v Barnes and others* [2009] 1 BCLC 699; and, recently, *Tarmac Trading Ltd v Network Rail Infrastructure Ltd* [2018] CSOH 33.

b) that it matters whether one can easily imagine a number of possible answers that could be given by the parties, for if there are many such possible answers, then the term should not be implied;[167] and c) that it matters how quickly, and in what tone, eg with a 'testy of course', the question posed by the figure is answered by the parties.[168]

My point in mentioning this variability is not to criticise it, though, as above, I do think that some versions of figural imagining in this context will be less helpful than others in enabling inquiry, and thus in generating normative insight. For the moment, observing this variability is itself interesting. On the most generous interpretation, it suggests that a figural legal test like this one, lends itself to being played with counsel and judges exploring and experimenting with slightly different versions of 'applying' the test. On a less generous interpretation, one could say that the test is 'applied' very inconsistently, and without proper critical reflection on whether it is enabling inquiry, ie enabling a court to further tentatively probe what values, vulnerabilities and interests are at stake in this case and others potentially like it in the future.

Before I turn to the attempts to 'kill off' this figure and consider what this debate as to its desirability reveals as to its value, it is worth remarking that the Officious Bystander has also enjoyed a career outside contract law. The figure has found its way into a) tax law;[169] b) family law;[170] c) the interpretation of wills;[171] d) public law;[172] e) maritime law;[173] and f) statutory interporetation.[174] The Officious Bystander has also directly inspired the creation of other figural legal tests: a) the Officious Bystander has been spotted 'intervening in a parliamentary debate', inspiring the creation of the figural legal test of 'an alert backbencher';[175] and b) the reasonable recipient.[176] Such travels across areas of the law, with the creation of 'analogues', are, surely, an important part of any biography of a figural legal test.

[167] See, eg, *Trollope & Colls Ltd v North West Metropolitan Regional Hospital Board* [1973] 1 WLR 601, where there were 'at least four possibilities', 609–610, per Pearson LJ.

[168] This is repeated often, see, eg, *Secretary of State for Employment v Associated Society of Locomotive Engineers and Fireman and Others* [1972] 2 QB 455, 508, per Buckley LJ. Recall also that MacKinnon LJ in *Shirlaw* (1939), 228–9 had referred to answers being made with 'alacrity'.

[169] *Heaton (Inspector of Taxes) v Bell* [1969] 2 WLR 735.

[170] 'I have to put myself in the position of the officious bystander at the family conference which in my judgment is going to take place, probably in seven years time, about what is to be done with Dr Lim when her mother can no longer look after her.': *Lim Poh Choo v Camden and Islington Area Health Authority* [1979] 1 All ER 332, 337, per Bristow J. See also *Cowcher v Cowcher* [1972] 1 All ER 943.

[171] *Re Ley's Will Trusts; Somerset and another v Ley and another* [1964] 2 All ER 326.

[172] 'If an officious bystander at Runnymede in 1215 had asked the Prince-Bishop of Durham whether a prisoner in his gaol was entitled to be transported free of cost to a civil court in London (assuming that the case was not within the local palatinate jurisdiction), I imagine that he would have received a terse and negative reply': *R v Secretary of State for the Home Department, ex parte Wynne* [1992] 2 All ER 301; 315, per Staughton LJ. Here, we see the Officious Bystander being imagined asking questions in the thirteenth century.

[173] *Vardinoyannis v The Egyptian General Petroleum Corporation (The Evaggelos Th)* [1971] 2 Lloyd's Rep 200, 204, per Donaldson J.

[174] *Dunnachie v Kingston Upon Hill City Council* [2004] 2 All ER 501.

[175] *Re DWS (deceased)* [2000] EWCA Civ 282; and 'an industrious backbencher', where the figure was also said to have 'a Parliamentary analogue': *Dunnachie v Kingston Upon Hill City Council* [2004] 2 All ER 501, [43].

[176] *Garston v Scottish Widows* [1998] 2 EGLR 73.

ii. 'Killing Off' the Officious Bystander

One famous early attempt to 'kill off' the Officious Bystander was made by Lord Denning in *Liverpool City Council v Irwin*.[177] This was a case concerning a claim of breach of contract, based on an argument that certain terms should be implied. These terms referred, in particular, to certain landlord obligations, of repair and upkeep of council flats by the Liverpool City Council. Lord Denning first duly listed the two tests for the implications of terms, namely: the *Moorcock* test of what is necessary for business efficacy, and the *Shirlaw* test. Lord Denning described the *Shirlaw* test as one focusing on whether the term 'is so obvious that both parties must have intended it: so obvious indeed that if an officious bystander had asked them whether there was to be such a term, both would have suppressed it testily: "Yes, of course"'.[178] Understood in this way, Lord Denning then went on to criticise both tests. These tests, he said, 'have been repeated so often that it is with some trepidation that I venture to question them. I do so because they do not truly represent the way in which the courts act'.[179] After listing some examples,[180] Lord Denning sought to replace the above tests with another, ie the test of whether it was reasonable in all the circumstances to imply a term:

> If you read the discussion in those cases, you will see that in none of them did the court ask: what did both parties intend? If asked, each party would have said he never gave it a thought: or the one would have intended something different from the other. Nor did the court ask: Is it necessary to give business efficacy to the transaction? If asked, the answer would have been: 'It is reasonable, but it is not necessary.' The judgments in all those cases show that the courts implied a term according to whether or not it was reasonable in all the circumstances to do so. Very often it was conceded that there was some implied term. The only question was: 'What was the extent of it?' Such as, was it an absolute warranty of fitness, or only a promise to use reasonable care? That cannot be solved by inquiring what they both intended, or into what was necessary. But only into what was reasonable. This is to be decided as matter of law, not as matter of fact.[181]

Lord Denning here reminds us of the shortcomings of the business efficacy test: it is simply too restrictive and does not pick up on the circumstances in which, and justifications for which, courts have been willing to imply terms. The Officious Bystander test, however, is barely discussed: it is either mentioned, as above, as concerning what was obvious to the parties, or, it is suggested that it is oriented only towards that which the actual parties intended or might be taken to have intended. Lord Denning appears to think that both tests are too narrow, eg he cites counsel as having 'repeated the old clichés about "necessary to give business efficacy" and the "officious bystander", and said there was no term to be implied at all'.[182] Applying his own test of reasonableness, by

[177] *Liverpool City Council v Irwin* [1976] QB 319. Subsequent references to this case are *Liverpool* (1976).
[178] Ibid, 329.
[179] Ibid, 330.
[180] The examples listed were: *Jones v Just* (1868) LR 3 QB 197; *Asley Industrial Trust Ltd. v Grimley* [1963] 1 WLR 584; *Young & Marten Ltd. v McManus Childs Ltd.* [1969] 1 AC 454; *Hart v Windsor* (1843) 12 M & W 68; *Collins v Hopkins* [1923] 2 KB 617; and *Readhead v Midland Railway Co.* (1869) LR 4 QB 379.
[181] *Liverpool* (1976), 331, per Denning LJ.
[182] Ibid, 330.

contrast, Lord Denning does find that a term, in the case before him, can be implied, though, in the result, he did not think that it was breached.

The two other Lords agreed with the result, but not with Lord Denning's attempts to replace both tests. They thus did not join him in his attempt to 'kill off' the Officious Bystander. However, in their applications of the Officious Bystander test, the other Lords also applied it in a very restricted manner. Here is Lord Justice Roskill's application:

> Applying this test I find it absolutely impossible to believe that the Liverpool City Council, if asked whether it was their intention as well as that of their tenants of these flats that any of the implied terms contended for by Mr. Godfrey should be written into the contract, would have given an affirmative answer. Their answers would clearly have been 'No.'[183]

If we cast our mind back to the test as applied in *Shirlaw* (1939), we see several glaring differences: first, no particular question is asked by an imaginary figure, but instead reference is made to a number of terms proposed by counsel; second, the question is answered only by one party, ie here, the landlord, and thus the side resisting the implication; third, that party, the landlord, is not imagined to be a party acting reasonably, albeit still in their self-interest, but rather as the actual party, not necessarily acting reasonably at all; and fourth, no elaboration and no explanation is offered for the negative answer. We could argue, then, that there is here a failure of imagination: the test is indeed almost whittled down to a cliché, no longer functioning as an artefact, and no longer involving the exercise of imagination, or, at best, involving a very thin exercise, very far from the high degree of affective, sensory and kinesic participation that characterised the application in *Shirlaw* (1939).

It matters whether the Officious Bystander is in fact imagined, and whether, in being imagined, the question is articulated, both parties answering with elaborated, reasoned replies, and with the parties being imagined not as bare, actual parties, but as reasonable, even if still self-interested. Part of the reason for that is that, in the fuller exercise of imagining the Officious Bystander interacting with the parties, we get closer to capturing the dynamics of the negotiation process, including potential power-imbalances, and closer also to taking into account relevant surrounding circumstances. In particular, it is only by imagining that we are able to exercise a more context-sensitive judgement as to whether we can discern an exploitation at time B of a vulnerability created at time A, or whether, this is a matter of typical risk-taking commercial practice.

In his application of his reasonableness test, Lord Denning had implied a covenant to take reasonable care, keeping the lift and the stairs reasonably safe and reasonably fit for use by the tenants and their visitors. Were the Officious Bystander test to be applied in the way it was devised in *Shirlaw* (1939), and thus with a fuller exercise of the imagination, then it, too, may have been sufficient to imply such a term in this case. Put another way: if the Officious Bystander test had been applied well, involving the exercise of imagination, then the more general reasonableness test may not have been needed. The agreement between the tenants and the Liverpool City Council involved no obligations on the landlord, and multiple obligations on the tenant. It is difficult to imagine a negotiating scene where: a) one would ignore the reasonable, even if self-interested, requests of the tenants that the common-access areas be safe and fit for use; and b) the landlord,

[183] Ibid, 339.

again imagined to be reasonable, even if still self-interested, could give an elaborated, reasoned reply to a blanket refusal to have any obligations whatsoever, including the minimal ones above. It is difficult to see in this case anything but an exploitation at time B, of a vulnerability created at time A, ie in this case, the vulnerability of the tenants, given the complete absence of any obligations imposed on the landlord.

When the case went on appeal to the House of Lords, the Officious Bystander did not fare much better.[184] There were no attempts to 'kill him off'. Indeed, the Lords were adamant that any general test of reasonableness was much too broad. Nevertheless, the applications of the Officious Bystander test were again narrow and limited. Thus, for example, Lord Justice Wilberforce, having denounced Lord Denning's attempt 'to extend a long, and undesirable, way beyond sound authority'[185] placed all the emphasis in the test for implication of terms on 'necessity'. The obligation, Lord Wilberforce said, 'should be read into the contract as the nature of the contract itself implicitly requires, no more, no less: a test, in other words, of necessity'.[186] Lord Wilberforce, in effect, ignores the Officious Bystander test.

Lord Justice Cross, in his turn, does not: indeed, he explicitly and critically refers to Lord Denning's attempts to 'kill off' the Officious Bystander.[187] Further, in his abstract articulation of the test, Lord Cross appears to recognise that the Officious Bystander test requires the judge imagining the scene to imagine the parties as 'reasonable men'.[188] Lord Cross also quotes Viscount Simonds in *Lister*,[189] where Viscount Simonds had referred to the 'officious bystander type of case' as one involving attention to 'a term to give efficacy to the contract and make it a workable agreement in such manner as the parties would clearly have done if they had applied their minds to the contingency which has arisen'.[190] Nevertheless, when it came to applying the test, Lord Cross did so as follows:

> The respondent council is a public body … the officials in the council housing's department would know very well that some of the tenants in any given block might subject the chutes and lifts to rough treatment and that there was an ever present danger of deliberate damage by young 'vandals' – some of who might in fact be children of the tenants in that or neighbouring blocks. In these circumstances, if at the time when the respondents were granted their tenancy one of them had said to the council's representative 'I suppose that the council will be under a legal liability to us to keep the chutes and the lifts in working order and the staircases properly lighted', the answer might have well have been – … would have been – 'Certainly not'. The official might have added in explanation: 'Of course we do not expect our tenants to keep them in repair themselves – though we do expect them to use them with care and to co-operate in combating vandalism. The council is a responsible body conscious of its duty both to its tenants and to the general body of rate payers and we will always do our best in what may be difficult circumstances to keep the staircases lighted and the lifts and chutes working, but we cannot be expected to subject ourselves to a liability to be sued by any tenant

[184] *Liverpool City Council v Irwin* [1977] AC 239. Subsequent references to this case are *Liverpool* (1977).
[185] Ibid, 254.
[186] Ibid.
[187] Ibid, 258.
[188] Ibid.
[189] *Lister v Romford Ice and Cold Storage Co. Ltd.* [1957] 1 All ER 125.
[190] Ibid, 144; quoted at *Liverpool* (1977), 258 per Cross LJ.

> for defects which may be directly or indirectly due to the negligence of some of the other tenants in the very block in question'. Some people might that it would have been, on balance, wrong for the council to adopt such an attitude, but no one could possibly describe such an attitude as irrational, or perverse.[191]

The imaginative exercise here is certainly more elaborate, but there is a glaring difference with *Shirlaw* (1939): there is no Officious Bystander asking a question; instead, Lord Cross imagines one of the tenants asking the landlord a question. To imagine that is to imagine a very different scene altogether. Lord Cross does have the landlord give an elaborated, reasoned reply, though one may argue whether it really could not be described as 'irrational or perverse'. However, to imagine the tenant asking the question is already to put the landlord on the defensive and makes a much more self-interested answer sound more reasonable. It is quite another matter to answer with this attitude to an Officious Bystander. To apply the test, and imagine in full, one would need to imagine an Officious Bystander asking both parties what they would do if the state of the common access areas was such that it made it impossible or extremely difficult to access the building? Can one imagine the parties, acting reasonably, even if still in self-interested ways, answering anything but with a 'yes', giving elaborate, reasoned replies to the effect that surely one cannot live in a building one cannot reasonably access? Otherwise, the vulnerability being created, in the absence of any landlord obligations, is simply too great, too stark, and going considerably beyond the usual assumotion of risks in commercial practice.

One may disagree with such an application, and such disagreement is very much part of, and valuable to, common law discourse. One can also argue that there was much more at stake in this case, eg greater policy questions concerning the appropriateness of placing certain burdens on city councils, and perhaps especially in certain parts of the country. However, the broader point for our purposes is that, in not imagining the Officious Bystander interacting with the parties, where they are imagined to be reasonable, even if still self-interested, the judges were depriving themselves of the normative insights that this figural test could generate. In treating the test either as a cliché, or as but a superfluous re-statement of the necessity test, or as restricted to capturing what was obvious to the actual parties, or in applying the test so narrowly and thinly, eg by having one of the parties ask a question, or not having both answer, or not having both give elaborated, reasoned replies, the test was no longer functioning as an artefact, the judges were no longer imagining, and thus the Officious Bystander was no longer enabling inquiry.

There is one more prominent judge, in addition to Lord Denning, who has sought to 'kill off' the Officious Bystander. Both in extra-judicial and in judicial pronouncements, Lord Hoffmann has argued against the use of this figure. Lord Hoffmann's interventions in this respect have been made less in the narrower confines of tests for implied terms, and more in the much broader, and arguably more complex, domain of the interpretation of contracts. To consider this domain with the detail it deserves falls outside the scope of this chapter. I will limit myself only to a few remarks, noting where future work could be undertaken.

[191] *Liverpool* (1977), 258–9.

In his 1995 lecture on figural legal tests, which I have already quoted from in the first section of this chapter, Lord Hoffmann argued as follows:

> The trouble with the Officious Bystander lies not in the character of the Officious Bystander, who is a familiar enough character to anyone who uses public transport, but in the hypothesis of the reasonable contracting parties. The notion that either the Greek ship-owner or the Indian charterer would have said of course to the implication of any terms against their own interests again puts an intolerable strain on the judicial imagination. The vividness of the scene which Lord Justice MacKinnon creates mean that we cannot avoid having our minds and predispositions influenced by what we know of the actual characters of the contracting parties. And yet we know that it is a fundamental principle of the English law of contract that on a question of construction, the characters, minds and subjective intentions of the actual parties are irrelevant and inadmissible.[192]

For Lord Hoffmann, what the Officious Bystander test obscured was 'that the implication of terms into a contract is in essence a question of construction like any other'.[193] It obscured this from view by directing our attention to 'the actual parties': 'By conjuring up the image of the actual parties in such vivid reality, the Officious Bystander distracts the court from the objectivity with which it should interpret the text'.[194]

It has to be said, with respect, that Lord Hoffmann shows little faith in the ability of imagination. Instead, he repeats an age-old criticism of it: it sucks us in, pulling the wool over our eyes, and making us see things we should not be seeing. But is this lack of faith in imagination warranted? Are judges really incapable of imagining not the actual parties, but instead reasonable, even if still self-interested parties? Part of the issue is that Lord Hoffmann sets up too sharp a divide between being reasonable and acting in a self-interested way: as I have sought to suggest above, it is possible to imagine parties acting reasonably, but still in self-interested ways. The Officious Bystander test, when imagined fully, is concentrating our attention on something difficult to grasp and almost impossible to articulate in a general way, which is not surprising given its highly circumstantial character: when does self-interest go too far, going beyond the usual assumption of risks in commercial practice, and result in the post-facto exploitation of a vulnerability? Acting reasonably does not mean acting altruistically, or in a way that is damaging to one's own self-interests. But it might mean not acting in a way that makes post-facto exploitation of a vulnerability possible.

Further, are there not risks in adopting Lord Hoffmann's 'objective' approach? One of the advantages of the Officious Bystander test, perhaps like all figural legal tests, is that they allow for a more subtle, more careful balancing of what I have referred to above as intentionality and the context or the circumstances of the case. Figural legal tests help to situate our judgement: by imagining the scene between the Officious Bystander and the parties, we come closer to the circumstances of the case. When exercised well, this figural imagining is not a matter of allowing one subjectivity to dominate, ie the subjectivity of one party, whether imagined to be entirely self-interested or entirely selfless; instead, it allows for a balancing of multiple subjectivities (where their self-interestedness is

[192] Hoffmann (1995), 139.
[193] Ibid.
[194] Ibid, 140.

tempered by the more inter-subjective notions of reasonableness) with the circumstances of the case (which may include reference to the relevant social norms, customs and practices, eg of what are typical risks in commercial practice). The 'vividness' of the exercise need not result in being trapped in the subjectivity of one of the parties: if we have faith in the capacity of our imaginations, then we can see the possibility of imagining this figural legal test in such a way that allows for the subtle, complex balancing act that judgement in this area of the law requires. When used well, the Officious Bystander test allows a court to proceed delicately, carefully, paying more respect to both the autonomy and vulnerability of the parties and being more mindful of the circumstances of the case, while also being more restricted and more disciplined than they arguably would be, for instance, if applying Lord Denning's reasonableness test.

Of course, Lord Hoffmann also has a point, and especially so when we consider the variety of ways in which the test has been applied (or, in some instances, arguably misapplied), including the above example of the *Liverpool City Council* (1976; 1977) cases. Crafting a figural legal test that can enable inquiry is not easy. Maintaining it and engaging in the imaginative effort its application calls for, is, it seems, even harder. Nevertheless, it is not impossible. Further, it is worth the effort, for, if we sacrifice it, eg for a non-figural test, we may be losing some of what only the figural legal test can generate, namely insights into what values, vulnerabilities and interests might be at stake in a case and in other cases potentially like it in the future. This is not to say that the figural legal test may never be replaced with a non-figural one: indeed, its utility is likely to be diachronically limited, eg it may simply cease at a certain point to function as an artefact, no longer successfully inviting our imaginations. But it is to say that we may want to be careful about dispensing with it. For in losing it, we may also lose a valuable mode of inquiry.

Lord Hoffmann has repeated his attack on the Officious Bystander figure in judicial pronouncements. Most famously, Lord Hoffmann did so when sitting in the Privy Council, in the case of *Belize*.[195] The judgement in that case has generated an extraordinary rich literature, both judicial and scholarly.[196] Some of that literature, again, both judicial and scholarly, has included discussion of the desirability of keeping the Officious Bystander test. In the case of *Marks and Spencer*,[197] for instance, an explicit defence of the Officious Bystander was undertaken by Lord Justice Neuberger, endorsing also the work of members of the Singaporean judiciary.[198] In that case, which involved the interpretation of a lease, and consideration of whether to imply a term into the contract (with no term eventually being implied), Lord Neuberger came to the rescue of the Officious Bystander. Further, Lord Neuberger explicitly noted that when applying the Officious Bystander test, one had to imagine not just the actual parties, but the actual parties acting reasonably. He added that it was also important to be careful in

[195] *Attorney General of Belize v Belize Telecom Ltd* [2009] 1 WLR 1988. Subsequent references to this case are *Belize* (2009).

[196] In terms of the scholarly literature, see, eg, Mitchell (2012); Kramer (2004); McCrachran (2011); Carter and Courtney (2016); Fisher (2016); McCunn (2016); and Hooley (2014).

[197] *Marks and Spencer plc v BNP Paribas Securities Services Trust Company (Jersey) Ltd* [2015] UKSC 72. Subsequent references to this case are *Marks and Spencer* (2015).

[198] See Phang (2014).

articulating the question to be asked by the Officious Bystander.[199] The debate, nevertheless, continues, eg as to whether one should see the various tests for implying terms as independent, alternative tests, or as varying attempts to get at one overall concern, ie to establish what the contract means.[200]

One of the most interesting scholarly interventions into this debate, albeit one that precedes *Belize*, has come from Hugh Collins, who has argued that, in grappling with the implication of terms, 'a court is typically venturing beyond the terms expressed by the parties, even taking into account the possibility of expansive readings of the contract informed by context and commercial common sense',[201] including making judgements as to good faith and fair dealing between the parties. In fact, although Collins does not discuss the Officious Bystander test at length, at one point he does consider the possibility that this figural legal test is the device through which such judgements are enabled:

> The Officious Bystander test has the virtue that it acknowledges the presence of an omission in the allocation of risk, but its appeal to the tacit agreement of the parties fails to address adequately the crucial question whether it would be unjust to leave the loss to lie where it falls or whether the omission should be rectified.[202]

As this quote indicates, the compliment paid to the Officious Bystander is immediately qualified. On the one hand, the Officious Bystander test may help courts turn their minds to what I have called the potential for a post-facto exploitation of a vulnerability; on the other hand, for Collins, the test's 'appeal to the tacit agreement of the parties' leaves too many options open, in particular, 'whether it would be unjust to leave the loss to lie where it falls'. We may, however, also see this alleged bug as a feature. It is true that the figural legal test does withhold direct guidance on where to draw the line. But we could argue that it does so precisely because it enables a more situated and more circumstantial inquiry into what values, vulnerabilities and interests might be at stake in that case, and in others potentially like it in the future. It is very much a casuistic, context-oriented test. It is not one that determines the exercise of judgement. Instead, it enables it, in part by slowing it down, as long as we take the effort to imagine. Collins is, I think, on to something important when, in summarising his view on implied terms, he says:

> In general, without a doubt, the courts should not engage in such a reallocation of risk, but let the loss lies where it falls. But there are a few instances where it is appropriate for a court to intervene. In these case, one party is seeking to take advantage that has not been paid for as part of the consideration of the contract. The contract may omit to regulate this particular advantage or it may apparently permit this advantage to be taken by one party owing to the broad terms in which the contract is written. A court should then ask whether permitting this

[199] *Marks and Spencer* (2015), 7–8 [21], per Neuberger LJ.

[200] Recently, Lord Hoffmann has offered a risposte to the decision in *Marks and Spencer* (2015), saying that 'The Supreme Court in *Marks and Spencer* seems to me, if I may be forgiven for saying so, to have made rather heavy weather of these practical differences between interpreting the meaning given to the document by the use of particular words and interpreting documents as meaning more than its words say': Hoffmann (2018), 564.

[201] Collins (2004), 311.

[202] Ibid, 316.

> advantage to be taken in accordance with the express terms of the contract would be a breach of standards of good faith and fear dealing in the narrow sense of 'unconscionability'. If so, an implied term to fill the omission or qualify the power will be appropriate.[203]

What I have tried to suggest here – mindful, of course, that much more analysis would need to be conducted – is that the figural legal test of the Officious Bystander allows for this inquiry into where the parties have gone beyond the usual assumption of risk in commercial practice, and now seek, instead, to take advantage of the creation of a vulnerability by omission. And it is a considerably more restrained exercise than one which would be guided by some more general, more explicit set of standards concerning good faith, fair dealing or unconscionability. That is, again, because figural imagining helps us to stay closer to the circumstances of the cases: it anchors our inquiry more, in a way that allows us to balance evaluation of the actions of parties with the circumstances of the case, including the context of commercial practice in which it occurs. As a mode of inquiry in this area, it pursues a more relational, more situated judgement than an all-out normative commitment. In that respect, we may see the Officious Bystander as a device for carefully experimenting with and exploring tentatively the prospects of a good faith requirement in English contract law.

We have made our way, now, through the thicket of the history – a most contested history – of the Officious Bystander. Like other figures featuring in figural legal tests, though less than the Reasonable Person,[204] the Officious Bystander has attracted its fair shair of critics, both judicial and scholarly. What I have sought to do is offer a partial defence: partial because it depends on whether the figural legal test in question functions as an artefact, successfully invites us to make the effort to imagine, and is imagined in a way that furthers the process of inquiry. It is certainly a powerful device, but less so because its vividness blinds us, and more so because of the relations between the making of normative insight and imagining, especially in its second limb of affective, sensory and kinesic participation.

Figural imagining involves a high degree of affective, sensory and perhaps especially kinesic participation: insofar as it does so, it emplots us, it situates us, as imaginers, vis-à-vis the parties in the circumstances of that case. But it does more than situate us in this way: it also enables us to generate normative insight, ie to sense which values, vulnerabilities and interests may be at stake in that case and in others potentially like in the future. Figural imagining is not an obstacle to normative judgement, but is, or at least can be, a more careful, more subtle, though also often more difficult, way of exercising it. It is, arguably, the kind of normative judgement that the legal context calls for and requires.

[203] Ibid.

[204] See, eg, Moran (2003); King (2017); and Gardner (2015). For a critique of the well-informed and fair-minded observer in bias law, see Olowofoyeku (2009).

8

Scenarios

As with the other case studies in this second part of the book, a good argument can be made for the foundational character of scenarios to legal thought. It is certainly very familiar to anyone trained in a common law classroom, and it will be familiar, also, to any advocate in a common law court. Both classrooms and courts in the common law tradition are filled with what-ifs in short, fictional narrative form, and the ensuing exchanges between students and teachers, or advocates and judges, are crucial to the dynamics of both education and adjudication.

There is, however, more to the story than that. A long history of this artefact, and its related processes of imagination, could situate it, for instance, at the crossroads of fiction and equitable judgment. As Wesley Trimpi has shown, in his magnificent *Muses of One Mind*,[1] the short narrative form known to the Ancient Greeks as a *hypothesis* (distinguished from the propositional *thesis*), and to the Ancient Romans as a *causa* allowing for the exploration of a *quaestio definito* (a definitive question), was recognised as being useful mainly for exploring the *qualitas* (quality) of an action, ie whether it was right or wrong, appropriate or inappropriate.[2] Thus, these short, fictional narratives were used to exercise what we might call the circumstantial judgement of character, ie the evaluation of an act, in relatively particular circumstances, by reference to the possible intentions and motives that produced it.

These short, fictional narratives lent themselves not only to this circumstantial judgement of character, but also to being played with in the company of others, who could vary the narrative, and thus invite a shift in the judgement of character, and, at once, a shift in the evaluation of their actions. Introducing such changes in the narrative had a label for the Ancients, namely: *colores*, or colours. To introduce a colour was precisely to introduce a narratological change and one that, if successful, resulted in shifts of judgement in one's audience. A successful colour, for instance, might shift one's evaluative perception of what prima facie was an apparently cruel and vicious act, rendering what at first appears bad into something appropriate and justified, eg in the case of a murder, to a necessary means of defending one's life, or the safety of one's community. Facility with colour, in turn, was what animated the training of orators in Ancient Rome, especially via the Roman art of declamation. The importance of these short, fictional narrative forms does not stop there, for according to Trimpi, they, together with the playful and

[1] Trimpi (1983). I return to this book later in this chapter.
[2] For more on hypotheticals in Ancient Greek thought, see Wohl (2014).

interactive invention of colour they invited, were crucial to the history of literature. For instance, one can draw a line, or so Trimpi argues, from the Roman declamations to the practice of sharing tales of lovers in medieval Italy (in Boccaccio, for example).

As the above already suggests, these short, fictional narratives, with their inventive additions of colour, were important not only for the history of literature, but also for law. After all, the students in Ancient Rome were being trained in oratory with a view to potentially enjoying careers as advocates in Roman courts. Further, as a number of scholars have observed, 'the practice of exemplary stories is well established in Roman law'.[3] These often involved 'first person narration or stories about standard figures (Stichus, Titus)'.[4] To give just one example from the *Digest* (26.2.39):

> There are two men called Titus, father and son. Titus is appointed tutor and it is not clear which one was meant by the testator. What is the law on this point, I ask? The reply was: the man appointed is the one intended by the testator. If that cannot be known, the law is not at fault, but proof is lacking. Therefore neither is tutor.[5]

Similar examples, though with important stylistic and generic differences, eg some involving more humour than others, some being more outlandish than others, can be found in other legal traditions, including Jewish,[6] Islamic,[7] and Chinese.[8]

More interconnections between law, rhetoric and literature[9] are available if we work with what André Jolles, in his *Simple Forms*,[10] calls the form of the 'case'.[11] Jolles distinguishes cases from other short forms, such as sagas, myths, legends, riddles,

[3] MacLean (1999), 8.
[4] Ibid.
[5] Ibid.
[6] On short, fictional narrative forms in the Jewish tradition, eg in the form of Rabbinic responsa, see Slepoy (2018); and Bryen (2020). Some of the Rabbinic responsa, especially earlier in the tradition, were based on hypothetical scenarios. Another relevant genre in the Rabbinic tradition were short tales of exemplary deeds by Rabbis: see, eg, Simon-Shoshan (2013). More generally on the role of narratives in Jewish legal thought, see, eg, Bartor (2010); Simon-Shoshan (2012); and Sternberg (2011).
[7] On examples from the Islamic legal tradition, see Berns (2018), Dayeh (2018), and Bori (2018). Generally, on the aesthetics of both Jewish and Islamic legal reasoning, as well as relations between them, see Salaymeh (2016). For a helpful discussion connecting Arabic literary and moral theory and practice, including some reference to Islamic law, see Hogan (2004). There is surely a great deal to explore here as to the historical relations between Roman, Jewish and Islamic legal traditions with respect to fictive legal cases, and related genres. The work of Yan Thomas would be crucial to any such study, see, eg, Thomas (2005) and Thomas (2011), ch 8.
[8] See, eg, Furth, Zeitlin, and Hsiung (2007).
[9] And beyond, eg medicine, including psychiatry: see, eg, Forrester (2017); and, more broadly, the essays in Creagher, Lunbeck and Norton Wise (2007). Gianna Pomata has unearthed some fascinating parallels between the genre of *observationes*, another example of a particular kind of short, fictional narrative, in both law and medicine: 'in the mid-sixteenth century the genre of *observationes* spread to two very status-conscious liberal arts, the law and medicine, in both cases referring to works that contained specialised professional knowledge on how to handle specific cases. The compilations of *observationes legales* or *forenses*, which start to come out in the 1530s and 1540s, had a strong link to judicial practice. They were initially compendia of solutions to hypothetical (fictive) legal cases, based on the jurists' "common opinion"': (2011), 52. Pomata further observes that 'the writing of legal observationes grew rapidly over the course of the seventeenth century, and by the end of the eighteenth century the genre had reached massive proportions': (2011) 73, fn 43. See also Pomata (2010), (2014) and (2018).
[10] Jolles (2017) [1958].
[11] For more historical connections on 'the case', see also Chandler (1998) and (2007); Goldhill (2017); and the essays collected in Passeron and Revel (2005). Literary works, perhaps especially in the early modern period, played with the co-dwelling of case in law and literature, sometimes in extraordinarily complicated ways: see, eg, Altman's discussion of John Heywood's *The Play of Love* (1533), where numerous hypothetical

fairy tales, sayings and *memorabile*. He does so by arguing that what is most distinctive about cases is that they offer occasions for judgement, often precisely for equitable judgement, ie an overall, circumstantial, more merciful, evaluation of an action, and one which often pitted the spirit and the letter of the law against each other, or otherwise invoked a gap or oversight in the written law. Importantly for any future history is Jolles's observation that cases, as occasions for the exercise of circumstantial judgement of character, were by no means confined to the Western tradition. For instance, some of the largest, most influential collections of cases come from India. The *Kathasaritsagara*, for example, is an eleventh century collection of stories-as-cases, compiled by Somadeva in Kashmir and surroundings, with each case concerning a question (of guilt, for example).[12]

For Jolles, what is common across the various examples, including not only these Indian collections, but also examples of fictional cases in nineteenth century German criminal law, in medieval Italian tales, and beyond, is that the case just asks the question, withholding an answer, thereby obliging us to exercise judgement:

> The special character of the case lies in the fact that it asks the question, but cannot give the answer; that it imposes the duty of judgement upon us, but does not itself contain the judgement – what becomes manifest in is the act of weighing, but not the result of the weighing. The weighing Latin device with two bowls is called in Latin *bilanx*, which in the Roman languages produced the terms *balance*, *bilancia*. In German we have from the same source the verb *balancieren*, which also carries the meaning of trying to find the equilibrium. The case presents us with the charms and difficulties of balancing – we could say that the swaying and swinging of the mental disposition of weighing and judging is what becomes manifest in this form.[13]

Then, as now, scales, with their two bowls, are of course a very familiar visual symbol of the law. Balancing and weighing, in turn, are also popular metaphors for the exercise of judgement in the legal context: eg, even today we speak of weighing and balancing principles against each other in hard cases.[14]

Like Trimpi, Jolles too connects the case form to the rise of the novella in medieval Italy, in particular via the courts of love, also involving the evaluations of the acts of lovers.[15] But he also goes beyond Trimpi's account, noting, for instance, the links between these genres of the case and the tradition of casuistry, which he defines as 'the practice of moral theology that has evolved in the Catholic Church, principally since the end of the sixteenth century'.[16] With casuistry, too, says Jolles, 'we have here a morality that weighs norms against each other, a morality with mobile judgement of value,

cases are used by the characters during the course of the play, which is itself a fictional trial: (1978), 112–119. In addition to 'cases', other names for scenarios in any broad-ranging history include 'imago'; 'exemplum'; and 'collatio': see Altman (1978), 116.

[12] Jolles (2017), 150–1. As this reference to the *Kathasaritsagara* suggests, there may well be connections between literary structures of the infinite story and the practice of collecting multiple short, fictional narratives in professional practices, like law and medicine.

[13] Ibid, 153.

[14] For a fascinating history of balance, see Kaye (2014).

[15] See also Goodrich (1996).

[16] Jolles (2017), 158. See Jonsen and Toulmin (1988); and, recently, the essays collected in Ginsburg and Biasiori (2018). For an attempt to relate the tradition of casuistry to common law reasoning, see Paulo (2015).

a morality … that balances'.[17] It is this same weighing and balancing, says Jolles, that we see in the 'psychology of eighteenth and nineteenth century literature – the weighing and measuring of motivations of actions according to inward and outward norms.'[18] For Jolles, it is at the level of the case, and the 'mobile criterion of judgement of characters'[19] that it enables, that we have the meeting place not only of works of literature, but also great moral traditions, like that of casuistry, and we might add, equity.[20]

Jolles also observes, and this too is important for the legal context, that these cases are often copied and travel across time, though also transforming over time. The form of the case, in other words, lends itself to 'countless variants'.[21] It does so, once again, because the case offers a challenge to the exercise of judgement: it 'reveal[s] a sphere in which it is difficult to pass judgement, but where norms are still called for: the sphere of sensory perception, of feeling and taste'.[22] This capacity of the form of the case to generate variations, and at once generate shifts of judgement, is important, and I will be returning to it throughout this chapter.

Even the briefest of dips, then, into the history of short, fictional narratives, shows us just how complex and rich, and wide-ranging in effects and significance, a historical treatment of scenarios could be. I would surmise, though cannot here defend, that such a history would expand considerably beyond the exercise of equitable judgement and include the exercise of judgement in any legal context, even the most seemingly dry and technical. It suffices, for example, to mention that the term 'colour' finds resonance in the term 'gloss':[23] might not the entire tradition of glossing legal texts, as in the tireless labours of the Glossators, working on the Ancient Roman texts, be thought of under the rubric of the circumstantial judgement of character? Is not the circumstantial judgement of character, even if it may sometimes be hidden under a technical language, crucial to the making of law? Is it not, basically, a circumstantial judgement of character that occurs whenever we speak of interpreting the law? Is not the addition of colour what effectively occurs when judges in the common law tradition distinguish past cases presented to them by advocates as precedents governing the present case? One can see how, as with the other case studies, one can quickly come to see scenarios, and the judgement they invite and enable, as foundational to legal thought, eg one could argue

[17] Jolles (2017), 158.
[18] Ibid.
[19] Ibid.
[20] See also Watt (2009).
[21] Jolles (2017), 155.
[22] Ibid.
[23] I am aware that the term 'gloss' does not, in the original Greek *glossa*, have a resonance with the visual, as it does for modern ears. In Ancient Greek, *glossa* referred to 'tongue' or 'language'. Nevertheless, it may be that the activity of glossing can be understood as introducing a variation, the recognition of which is based, effectively, on a change in colour, and therefore also a shift in judgement. For instance, when Gratian in his twelfth century treatise, *A Concordance of Discordant Canons*, glosses the assertion that 'A bishop should not read the books of the heathen' by saying that there is no express prohibition within this assertion as to reading the books of heretics, and thus that the books of heretics may be read 'in order that they [the priests] may know how to speak correctly' (see Berman (1977), 926), he could be understood to be introducing a colour, ie introducing a change, in particular to the possible intentions with which some action is performed, with the effect of inviting a shift in our judgement of that action.

that the narratological dynamics foregrounded in scenarios underlies all processing of fictions, metaphors and figures.

In what follows, my ambitions are considerably more restrained, though I shall draw on some of the literature mentioned above. My focus, as throughout this second part, is on scenarios as distinct kinds of artefacts, with related and distinct processes of imagination. I shall, therefore, pay special attention to the ways that scenarios, as artefacts, signal artifice in particular ways and how they call upon us to participate in particular ways. In this respect, we shall see that scenarios can have different degrees of narrativity, under-specification, particularity (eg using A, B, C instead of proper names), and plausibility (even if most remain highly plausible). In all these ways, and perhaps especially in being under-specified, scenarios call upon us to participate actively, ie to do things with scenarios. And we do many things with scenarios, especially in the company of others. Indeed, scenarios lend themselves to being played with interactively and collectively. We play in different ways, eg by filling them in, by varying them and by introducing alternative or counter-scenarios.

To speak of play, though, is already to venture into the second aspect of scenarios, ie the related process of imagination it invites and involves, at least when the scenario is functioning as an artefact. When we imagine with scenarios, we enter a distinctive epistemic frame where we selectively suspend certain epistemic norms and commitments. Depending on the scenario, this may involve, for instance, suspending certain norms of what is plausible or probable. Further, and this is of great significance with respect to scenarios, we at the same time participate, doing so with a high degree of affective, sensory and kinesic involvement. The role of the emotions is especially crucial, and this, in turn, is connected to the judgement-inviting and judgement-enabling, if not judgement-requiring, function of scenarios. When we imagine a scenario, we typically simulate the emotions of the characters in the circumstances of the scenario, and we also react emotionally to those simulated emotions of the characters. In many respects, we can think of scenarios as 'emotion experiments' rather than 'thought experiments'. Affect, sensory experience, eg as in the construction of mental imagery from a perspective, and kinesis are all closely tied together in imagining scenarios, and all play an important part in inviting and enabling judgement.

Scenarios, as artefacts, with related processes of imagining, can greatly enable inquiry in adjudication. They can do so at all three levels: the level of the individual judge, the level of interaction between advocates and judges, and the level of the community over time. Scenarios are perhaps especially useful at the first two levels: as pointed out in the last chapter, scenarios (because they specify, even if in brief terms, certain circumstances) travel arguably less well over time than figures, which are circumstance-independent. The value of scenarios, then, is sometimes, if not often, confined to particular cases, where, for instance, by being either analogised or contrasted with the facts of the case, they enable the choosing or refining of a particular justification in that case. However, there are also cases of scenarios travelling across time: some scenarios, mentioned only by the by, in obiter, come to have a considerably more important effect on subsequent readers than the case itself. Either way, by imagining with and thanks to scenarios, judges and others involved in the adjudicatory context can generate normative insight: they can generate insight as to what values, vulnerabilities and interests might be at stake in a case and in others potentially like it in the future. In this way, they can come to better balance respect for the law's past, doing justice in the instant case, and caring for the quality of the law in the future.

Or so I shall argue in what follows. As with the other chapters in the second part, I divide the discussion into two: in the first part, I situate my own approach to scenarios as artefacts, with related processes of imagination, in some of the relevant literature, including the above-mentioned literary theoretical and historical scholarship on *hypothesis*, work on hypotheticals in common law reasoning, the philosophy and history of thought experiments, work on consequential reasoning in law and morality, eg John Dewey's notion of dramatic rehearsal, and, more generally, cognitive narratology and exemplarity. In the second part, I then turn to a specific example, and one which not only showcases the role and value of scenarios in a particular case, but which also shows how scenarios can sometimes travel across time, generating important resources for inquiry in adjudication. The example comes from the case of *White & Carter v McGregor*,[24] and involves a scenario of an expert travelling abroad (or, as we shall see, specifically to Hong Kong). We shall see how the scenario, amongst other scenarios, is first introduced by an advocate, and is then played with by the judges in the case. We will also see the effects the scenario has not only within that case, but also across time, and thus how it eventually generates, in the area of repudiation in English contract law, a new test for when such repudiation can be rejected and when it ought to be accepted.

I. Approaching Scenarios

No less, but also, I would say, no more important than fictions, metaphors and figures, scenarios are distinct artefacts, with distinct related processes of imagination. As a result, they can also contribute in distinctive ways to the enabling of inquiry in adjudication. Unlike fictions, for instance, they involve a high degree of affective, sensory and kinesic participation (in the second limb of imagining). Unlike metaphors and figures, scenarios foreground and make explicit their narratological foundations. Although metaphors, figures and scenarios may involve similar levels of affective, sensory and kinesic participation, one could argue that whereas kinesic simulation is higher in figures, and sensory simulation is higher in metaphors, affective simulation is especially extensive and complex in the case of scenarios.

As we shall see, and as was already foreshadowed in the previous chapter, figures and scenarios do have a considerable amount in common. In fact, scenarios could be envisaged as a more-explicitly narratological form of figuration. Certainly, the imagining of figures, including the construction and evaluation of their character, continues to be vital to imagining with scenarios, and I shall be stressing the importance of the circumstantial judgement of character with respect to scenario-imagining. Nevertheless, it is also the case that scenarios are anchored to particular narratives, and this gives them distinct benefits, though also distinct limitations. Scenarios involve explicit articulation of the circumstances of an action, and in so being, they invite, if not require, the exercise of circumstantial judgement. This anchoring, it should be observed,

[24] *White & Carter (Councils) v McGregor* (1962) SC (HL) 1.

although a limitation in a sense, is also a generative one: it lends itself to being played with, amplified, added to, varied or contrasted, most often in the company of others. This simultaneous anchoring and generating, or stable-and-transformative, quality of scenarios is very important to its distinctiveness.

Given the importance of narrative to scenarios, let me make immediately clear that with scenarios, I am referring to a very particular mode of narrative-based thought and experience. Needless to say, there is an abundance of theoretical literature on the relationship between narrative, legal thought and legal form. I will be drawing on some of this literature, but it is important to see that theorising scenarios is not the same as theorising, say, trials as narratives, or precedential reasoning as having narratological dynamics, or the narratological dimensions of proof and evidence.[25] It is also not the same as, say, arguing that all of law, including, for instance, statutory law, has or had a narrative form.[26] Though it connects to various dimensions of narrativity of law and legal thought, imagining with scenarios has its own distinctive formal and cognitive features.

There is another preliminary point to make. There are many theoretical literatures that are in the vicinity of the topic of scenarios, including casuistry, reasoning with hypotheticals, analogical reasoning, consequential reasoning, thought experiments, particularism in moral and legal reasoning,[27] circumstantial rhetoric,[28] equitable judgement, and exemplarity. I shall not be here offering a survey of these various approaches. I shall, instead, draw very selectively on them.

Exemplarity deserves a special mention, especially as it has attracted some attention in recent legal theory.[29] Depending on how it is understood, exemplarity has a long and rich tradition: for instance, one can trace it back to the Greek *paradeigma* or *exemplar* in Latin.[30] The tradition is rich and long in part because of its internal disagreements, eg should one understand an example or a paradigm as an instantiation of a universal (as Plato might), or does one take it as a particular from which one can potentially (if not yet, for it may be a singular particular) infer something general (an approach more akin to Aristotle)? Even if one limits oneself to the first approach, there arise further questions: eg is the example or paradigm merely a typical one, or an especially good one? Is it a model to follow, or is it but an illustration of what is average or usual? Is it a standard or just a sample?

The disagreements are important, but however these questions are answered, to my ears the very terminology of 'example' and 'exemplarity' suggests two dimensions that I do not wish to foreground here: namely, first, an 'example' suggests it is an example of something else, ie something other than it, possibly larger or more important than it, or ontologically prior to it, eg a universal, or a rule or principle; and, second, it connotes something normative, ie either something that is a good example of that something else

[25] On the relations between narrative, proof and evidence, see the essays in Kaptein, Prakken and Verheji (2009).

[26] For an expansive approach to the narrativity of law, see Sternberg (2011).

[27] See, eg, Bańkowski and McLean (2006).

[28] See, eg, Hutson (2015).

[29] See, eg, Lowrie and Ludemann (2015); Condello and Ferrara (2018); and Del Mar and Gordon (2013).

[30] Gelley (1995b), 1.

('typical', too, can be characterised as thinly normative, ie one can be a good example of what is typical), or something to be followed and imitated, eg as in the genre of *exemplum* in the medieval Christian sense, and thus something that teaches and reinforces dogma.

On the way I am conceiving of scenarios, they are not necessarily preceded by, say, a rule or principle: they are not, in that sense, illustrations, instantiations or examples of something else. Neither need they be guides or models to be followed and imitated. Although some scenarios may be devised primarily to persuade, ie they may be strategically constructed by, say, an advocate to persuade a judge to, for instance, dismiss the opposing side's arguments as leading to absurd results, this is not a necessary feature of them. Some scenarios are generated without being preceded by awareness of any particular rule or principle.

Further, far from being followed or imitated, scenarios, on the way I approach them, are prone to be being played with, added to, amplified, varied, and contested. Scenarios can be genuine modes of experimentation, rather than means of repetition or recognition. We construct or confront a scenario, imagine it, and, in the course of imagining it, generate normative insight, eg we come to sense that some value, vulnerability or interest may be at stake that we had not considered before.

Of course, we should probably not make too much of this distinction: as with the other case studies, even where scenarios are first presented strategically, eg by an advocate, seeking to persuade a judge, their meaning is not controlled by the intention with which they are produced. Having some degree of particularity, scenarios always leak beyond that intention, and thus beyond any pre-conceived rule or principle that they may be presented as illustrating, instantiating or exemplifying.

In fact, the theoretical tradition of exemplarity is itself mindful of the reductive dangers in the language of examples and exemplarity, and speaks of exemplarity and exemplification in sophisticated ways, much more akin to the Aristotelian than the Platonic take on them.[31] Alexander Gelley, for instance, in his excellent collection on *Unruly Examples*,[32] speaks of examples that 'serve not as confirmation of a rule, but as an instrument of testing, of possible revision'.[33] One of the aspects of the 'rhetoric of exemplarity' that Gelley seeks to promote is its 'performative and ethical aspect'.[34] As he puts it:

> At the level of praxis there is a continual need to judge in the absence of definitive criteria, whether in aesthetic terms ('is it beautiful?') or in moral terms ('is it right?'). Far from being unconsidered or merely intuitive, this form of judgement operates in the manner of Kant's reflective judgement, that is, by invoking a "general rule that cannot be stated". Though the rule as such cannot be formulated, its point (or *pointing*) emerges from what Lyotard has termed a "symbolisation … through permutations of instances". The example does not stand alone but inaugurates a dynamic that displaces the instance. Each variant or alternative, whether introduced for clarification or for refinement, shifts the direction of the argument, the point of the example.[35]

[31] See also Elgin (2011) on 'exemplification'.
[32] Gelley (1995a).
[33] Gelley (1995b), 12.
[34] Ibid, 13.
[35] Ibid. Original emphasis. Internal references omitted.

Gelley here foregrounds what I have called, in the first chapter of this book, the difficulty of judgement, which is also what makes inquiry so important: we are, as he puts it, 'continually and inescapably called upon to make judgements on insufficient grounds.'[36] Here, the example is understood to be a way of probing possibilities under conditions of uncertainty and insufficiency, including situations where we cannot articulate a 'general rule'. Further, as Gelley observes above, the example understood in this performative sense lends itself to variability and contestation, and in that respect, examples can be part of, if not a means of, the dynamics of shifting and transforming judgement. It is indeed this performative aspect of exemplarity that I seek to further examine under the canopy of scenarios. However, as this is arguably not the first connotation one is likely to have with the language of examples and exemplarity, I prefer the less committal language of scenarios.

A. Scenarios as Artefacts

Our first step is to consider scenario-as-artefacts. This means paying attention to their form: to the distinctive, particular but also different, ways in which they signal their own artifice and call upon us to participate. All scenarios have some degree of narrativity, under-specification, particularity, and plausibility. Depending on how they combine these different dimensions of their form, they may signal artifice in different ways, and call upon us to participate in different ways.

i. Narrativity

Narrativity, at its most minimal, refers to a sequencing of actions or events, with some explicit or implicit causality between them. At the same time, there is an affective phenomenology to narrativity: it affords, as Meir Sternberg has argued, curiosity, suspense and surprise.[37]

Consider the following proverb: 'In the battle between desire and prudence, desire always wins', and now with narrativity: 'Desire battles Prudence. Desire wins. Again'.[38] The latter has sequencing of events, with causality implied between them. It also carries curiosity and suspense: we are told that 'Desire battles Prudence', and this generates interest in, and suspense of, the outcome. It is only in the next sentence that we learn that 'Desire wins' (in this respect, too, some narratives, but arguably not all, include an affective phenomenology of satisfaction, or satisfied expectations). Of course, given the brevity of this particular narrative, the suspense and curiosity are minimal, but they are still there. There is some surprise, too, as we are told at the end that this has happened 'again' (perhaps there is even a flicker of comedy here).

As the above example already indicates, narrativity can be very condensed. There are even more dramatically narratively-condensed examples, eg Caesar's 'Vini, Vidi,

[36] Ibid, 14.
[37] See Sternberg (2001); and for a recent discussion, see Yuan (2018).
[38] Fishelov (2019), 37.

Vici' has narrativity, as of course does the famous six-word story attributed to Ernest Hemingway: 'For Sale: baby shoes, never worn.'[39] Hemingway's story is, in fact, a good example of a narrative that is also highly under-specified: it requires a great deal of unpacking and filling in by readers. Actually, there is a sense in which Hemingway's story is more under-specified than Caesar's: even though the latter is shorter, the former seems to invite more inferential work by the reader. Arguably, it also engages the reader's emotions much more.

ii. Under-Specification

Under-specification is just that: the invitation to inference-making by the reader. Under-specification is relatively independent of brevity: although, obviously enough, under-specification may be easier in short narratives,[40] it is also the case that a narrative can be very long, eg a long, complex novel, but still be quite under-specified (think of the pleasure, but also difficulty, of certain postmodern narratives).

Arguably, every narrative is not only selective, but also, and partly as a result of being selective, always requires considerable inference-work by the reader.[41] We saw how, in the previous chapter, Alan Palmer, in his *Fictional Minds*,[42] emphasised the scale of the work of a reader in reading a novel. Palmer also recognises that an author can make a reader work more or less hard: for instance, with respect to descriptions by a narrator of a character's action, 'the reasons, motives, intentions, purposes, and so on behind the action may be explicitly specified by the narrator, they may be implicit but understood by the reader, or they may remain mysterious.'[43] We shall see that this withholding of explicit descriptions of 'reasons, motives, intentions, purposes' is important to the work of scenarios: precisely by withholding in this way, ie by being under-specified in this manner, they call upon us, the readers, to fill the details in. We do that by simulating the emotions of the character in the scenario, and then ourselves reacting affectively to those emotions. In this way, we exercise circumstantial judgement of character.

Further, given the diversity of persons' affective experiences, we may simulate the emotions of the characters and then react affectively in markedly different ways. Under-specification allows and enables scenarios to be played with interactively and collectively. It also allows and enables the sharing of normative knowledge that takes the form of affective experience. If and when we do react differently to the same scenario, we may also generate variations or alternatives to it, eg sometimes in order to persuade someone else to change their affective reaction to the scenario. Under-specification is, then,

[39] Fishelov suggests that the attribution may be erroneous: see ibid, 43, fn 1. Six-word stories are a flourishing genre, see: www.sixwordstories.net.

[40] For accounts of reader participation in 'miniature fiction' or 'micro fiction', see Trimarco and Hurley (2008); and Irving (2017).

[41] For a quite brilliant account of this activity of the reader, generating hypotheses, often unresolved, in the course of reading, as applied mainly to the Tanakh, see Sternberg (1986).

[42] Palmer (2004).

[43] Ibid, 122.

related to the variability of scenarios. And this too contributes to their social dynamics, and to their capacity to both carry and generate the sharing of normative insight.

iii. Particularity

The degree of particularity of a scenario refers to the extent to which it includes more concrete and even sometimes seemingly superfluous details. It may also refer to the degree to which a scenario is personalised: eg whether it includes proper names of persons and places, and from what perspective it is narrated, eg whether it is narrated in the first person. When Jolles, in his *Simple Forms*, draws on some examples of scenarios (which as we know he calls 'cases') from a 1928 German article on 'The Grotesque and the Tragic in Penal Law', one of them is narrated precisely in the first person:

> A pickpocket steals my wallet in a crowd; the wallet contains a hundred marks in small bills. Sharing his haul with his lover, he tells her of his success. If both should be caught, the woman will be punished as a fence. Suppose that my wallet had contained only a hundred-mark note. The thief has the bill changed and then gives the woman fifty marks; in this case, she is exempt from punishment. For fencing, dealing in stolen goods, is possible only with the objects immediately obtained through the punishable act, not with the exchanged bills.[44]

There are, in fact, two scenarios in this one passage. As a whole, this passage also already includes reflection on the relevant law (on fencing), which this narrative shows to be inadequate (after all, why should the woman be exempt from punishing only because the thief exchanged bills?). But one of the most striking aspects of it is that it is narrated in the first person: as Jolles also observes, 'it was not a wallet, but "my wallet" that is stolen'.[45] Jolles here adds: 'these additions, insignificant in themselves, amplify the feeling of singularity, increase the poignancy of the case'.[46] The apparent superfluity of these details is important: as a result of them, the scenarios resonate more affectively with us.

The addition of particular details can be highly significant, and in surprising ways: someone, at a later time, for example, could process the same particulars in a scenario in a different way. Notice, in this respect, that in the above example, the amount of money stolen is specified: although this does not seem to play an especially significant role for the author of the scenarios, someone later might take this to be important, eg fencing may be said to be punishable only above a certain amount.

[44] Jolles (2017), 138–9. The above example comes from an academic article, and my focus is on judgements in the common law. But it is interesting to observe that this comes from the civil law tradition, where arguably there is little opportunity for judges to include scenarios in their judgements. Might this mean that scenarios are more likely to appear in scholarship, and even then, as in Jolles's example, somewhat surreptitiously, under a pseudonym? Any study of scenarios in the civil law tradition would need to consider Rudolf von Jhering, see, eg, Jhering (1904). To give one example: 'By a hailstorm or an explosion the windows in the dwelling are smashed; who has to mend them, the landlord or the tenant? Is the case the same where windows which have been opened and duly fastened, are shattered by a sudden hurricane? Is it the same where they are broken by the populace, the tenant having given occasion to this by remarks or conduct which enraged them? Is it a point of importance whether the bitter feeling was justified or not, and whether the tenant was rightly or wrongly accused?': see Jhering (1904), 38.

[45] Jolles (2017), 145.

[46] Ibid.

The particular details included can also have the effect of enabling and stimulating a high degree of affective, sensory and kinesic participation. In the above example, the action is said to take place in a 'crowd'; the thief is said to have obtained a 'haul'. This language is strong both in sensory terms and kinesically: it enjoins us to construct mental imagery from a perspective (my wallet stolen in a crowd), and it invites us to simulate certain physical actions and gestures, with their accompanying affective resonances. What Jolles calls 'poignancy', then, we may call a high degree of involvement (in the second limb of imagining), with perhaps special emphasis on affective involvement. The formal features of the scenario (here, some degree of particularity, in addition to narrativity and under-specification), contribute to encouraging us to simulate the emotions of the characters in the scenario, eg the shock of losing that much money, of being robbed in a crowd, and then to react to those simulated emotions, eg with indignation or moral outrage at the woman getting away with it. This, in turn, helps generate normative insight: eg that there is a value, vulnerability or interest at stake that is being missed by the law (of fencing) at present.

Although the above example has some particularity, with first person narration and certain details of the environment being included, it does not have as much particularity as it could: for instance, instead of referring to 'the thief' or 'the woman', one might have given the characters in this scenario a proper name. One could have also described where this scene occurs, eg providing the name of some particular place, even if imaginary. Likewise, though, the above example could also have less particularity: eg instead of referring to 'the thief' and 'the woman' one might have used a symbol, A and B. There is a considerable difference between describing the above actions with 'the thief' and 'the woman' (and a difference, too, between 'the woman' and 'his lover'!) and doing so with symbols: the affective resonance is considerably stronger in the former.

There is a balancing act here: the more a scenario is particularised, the more difficult it may be to generate generalisable normative insight from it; but the less particularised it is, the less effective it may be in inviting us to imagine, especially to participate affectively. Some degree of particularity is needed, but not too much: again, if too much, then the scenario may also lose some of its capacity to signal its own artifice: it gets too close to what we may take to have happened, in some particular place, to some particular persons.

One can signal artifice quite effectively be reducing particularity, eg by using symbols instead of persons (A, B, C), or by using clearly fictional proper names (eg 'Joe Thief'). Consider the following example, which also illustrates how a judge can construct two scenarios and compare them as against each other:

> If a contract has been made between A and B that the latter should go supercargo for the former on a voyage to China, and C, however maliciously, persuades B to break his contract, but in vain, no one, I suppose, would contend that any action would lie against C. On the other hand, suppose a contract of the same kind made, between the same parties to go to Sierra Leone, and C urgently and bona fide advises B to abandon his contract, which on consideration B does, whereby loss results to A. I think no one will be found bold enough to maintain that an action would lie against C. In the first case no loss has resulted – the malice has been ineffectual; in the second, though a loss has resulted from the act, that act was not C's, but entirely and exclusively B's own. If so, let malice be added, and let C have persuaded, not bona fide but mala fide and maliciously, still, all other circumstances remaining the same,

> the same reason applies, for it is *malitia sine damno*, if the hurtful act is entirely and exclusively B's, which last circumstance cannot be affected by the presence or absence of malice in C.[47]

Here, Justice Coleridge in the famous case of *Lumley v Gye* deploys the symbols A, B, C, which reduce particularity, and signal artifice effectively, especially when combined with the explicit language of 'if' and 'suppose'.

Just as decreasing particularity may help with signalling artifice, so increasing it may risk not signalling it. To signal artifice, a scenario needs to bring attention to itself as a means of communication, inviting us, in the process of imagination, to enter a distinctive epistemic frame where we selectively suspend certain epistemic norms and commitments. If, when confronting a scenario, we experience it as describing something that actually occurred, eg in some place, to some particular persons (as we do, for instance, with newspaper stories), then the relevant scenario is no longer functioning as an artefact. In that sense, a high degree of particularity may, in some instances, be an obstacle to a scenario signalling artifice.

iv. Plausibility

The variable of particularity can be related to that of plausibility. A scenario could be described with such particularity that it is taken to be so plausible that, as above, it ceases to signal artifice. Nevertheless, plausibility is also independent of particularity. A scenario could be highly particular, but still be implausible: it could, for example, be completely fantastic or outlandish, involving persons performing unnatural acts, eg flying in the air, living forever, or being part of unnatural events or unlikely states of affairs, eg living in a community that does not have any scarce resources. Utopias, for instance, may be highly particular, but be very implausible.

Introducing some degree of implausibility, or, in other words, lowering the degree of plausibility, can in itself be an effective way of signalling artifice. This can be done, as noted above, by introducing fantastic or outlandish details, or through exaggeration, caricature and hyperbole. One again has to be careful here: the higher the degree of implausibility, the more difficult it may be to generate generalisable normative insight. Sometimes, however, implausibility can be very helpful: it may, for instance, help us isolate some factors that allows us to sense the presence of a value, vulnerability or interest that we otherwise took for granted, eg arguably, certain utopias do precisely that, reminding us, for instance, that we are creatures who are dependent on each other, mutually vulnerable, and that we live in worlds with scarce resources.[48]

Even when, however, scenarios contain a high degree of implausibility in some sense, they often combine this with being highly plausible in other ways, eg utopias are very selective in what they implausibly treat as utopian, either making human beings

[47] *Lumley v Gye* [1843–60] All ER Rep 208, 219, per Coleridge J.

[48] For more on the genre of utopia, and its contextual connections to ethics and politics, see, eg, Frye (1965); and Levitas (2013). To give just a quick sense of this contextualism, Frye observes that 'The Nineteenth century utopia had a close connection with the growth of socialist political thought and shared its tendency to think in global terms': (1965), 327.

into angels while keeping the resources in the world scarce, or the other way around, but not both at the same time.[49] Thus, even if scenarios contain quite fanciful or outlandish elements, reducing plausibility, in some particular respect, to a high degree, imagining with scenarios remains a highly constrained exercise. Scenarios are never highly implausible in every respect.

There is a related debate on whether, and the extent to which, thought experiments in philosophy ought to be fanciful or outlandish, and, equally, the extent to which working with thought experiments remains an exercise of constrained imagination. The issue arises more naturally in philosophy, for thought experiments in this domain are indeed often fanciful and outlandish, involving brains in vats, and all kinds of parallel, impossible worlds.[50]

Given the character of many of philosophy's thought experiments, it is not surprising that many who have been drawn to defending their role in philosophical methodology have also looked to defences of fictional works (mainly literature) and have argued for an analogy between the two.[51] Indeed, some have argued for a continuity between the use of thought experiments in philosophy, and experiments in science and literary fictions. They have done so based, in part, on their common narrative structure:

> Like literary fictions and ordinary experiments, thought experiments have a narrative structure. We perform thought experiments by imagining a scenario in which something happens – a sequence of events with a beginning, middle and end. Thought experiments can be construed as tightly constrained, highly focused, minimalist fictions, like some of the works of Jorge Luis Borges.[52]

As this passage from Catherine Elgin already suggests, those who defend the use of thought experiments in philosophy tend precisely to emphasise how, as narrative forms, they are highly selective, using outlandishness as a means of isolation and emphasis, and how the imagination involved in processing them remains highly constrained. As, again, Elgin states:

> Like an experiment, a work of fiction selects and isolates, contriving situations and manipulating circumstances so that patterns and properties stand out. It may frame or isolate mundane features of experience so that their significance is evident. It may defamiliarize the commonplace, making us aware of how remarkable normal behaviour can be.[53]

The introduction of implausible elements into thought experiments is not a cue for wild, anarchic fantasy: in fact, quite the contrary, the presence of some implausible element often alerts us to the need to exercise care and constraint in imagining that scenario. Again, the implausible element works to help us focus or attend to some particular feature; it is not a licence for arbitrariness.

[49] On some varieties of utopia, and especially by reference to law, but also showing how selectively utopian they are, see Aviles (2000).

[50] Generally, see Sorensen (1992); Stuart, Fehige and Brown (2018); and Gendler (2010); for a history of thought experiments in philosophy, see Fehige and Stuart (2014).

[51] See Elgin (2014); Vidmar (2013); and, for an argument against the analogy, see Egan (2016).

[52] Elgin (2014), 230.

[53] Ibid, 232.

Elgin has also stressed another source of constraint: thought experiments, she has said, 'are not essentially private ... they are publicly articulated, discussed, illustrated and disputed'.[54] Some of the constraint, then, in imagining even (or perhaps, paradoxically, especially) outlandish or fanciful thought experiments comes from the community, ie what is 'recognised, shared, and deemed appropriate by' a community.[55] And, one might argue, these shared norms and practices come to be especially prominent when a thought experiment includes an obviously outlandish or fanciful element.

Of course, the kinds of scenarios one finds in the context of adjudication rarely, if ever, reach the fanciful and outlandish heights of some thought experiments in philosophy. But the point is one of principle: even if they did, and even when they do, contain elements that are less than plausible, this need not be an obstacle to them enabling inquiry.[56]

Be that as it may, there is room for caution too. Even if they do not include outlandish or fanciful examples, scenarios are always necessarily selective. Scenarios are, after all, short narratives. One of the dangers is that they may be too quickly compared to the facts of a present case, thereby oversimplifying the complexity of the present case. The danger of oversimplification arguably increases when some feature of the scenario has an enhanced degree of implausibility, ie when it is exaggerated in some way.

There is a more general point here. It is common to approach scenarios as sources of analogy,[57] and sometimes even as replacement precedents.[58] Although imagining scenarios does have a connection to analogy, my suggestion is that scenarios can be beneficial for inquiry in ways that are not entirely dependent on, and cannot be wholly

[54] Ibid, 227.

[55] Ibid.

[56] For other defences of fanciful or outlandish elements in thought experiments, including in ethics, see Diamond (2002); Stoner and Swartwood (2017); Walsh (2011), and for a critique of thought experiments in ethics, see Davis (2012).

[57] Approaching hypotheticals as sources of analogy is frequent in theories of legal reasoning: eg 'One common form of reasoning from hypotheticals proceeds in the following manner: A court is faced with a case that presents admitted difficulty in choosing between competing rules. The court then states a hypothetical that has, at least in the court's view, three criterial characteristics. First, the hypothetical differs from the case. Second, the hypothetical seems easier to decide than the case – in the hypothetical, one of the competing rules seems clearly preferable. Third, although the hypothetical differs from the case, the case cannot be distinguished from the hypothetical under applicable social propositions. Accordingly, if one of the competing rules should govern the hypothetical, it should govern the case as well': Eisenberg (1988), 99. And for a discussion, see also Bartha (2009); Rissland (1989); Brewer (1996); Ashley (2018); and Ferguson (1982). These theorists are right that advocates and judges do sometimes, if not often, use hypotheticals in this way, and I also agree that this may sometimes be beneficial. I further agree that there is considerable overlap between what I mean by imagining with scenarios and analogical reasoning. Nevertheless, it seems worthwhile to me to pursue the possibility that imagining with scenarios is not entirely explained by analogical reasoning. In his short essay on the topic, Gewirtz (1981) treats hypotheticals as 'test cases' or 'hard cases' and, at least as I read him, does not subsume their value under analogical reasoning. Gewirtz also recognises that hypotheticals can be 'annoying', ie that they generate 'dissonance', which then needs to be resolved in some way, adding that this may sometimes involve rejecting the hypothetical as unhelpful: see (1981), 865. Nevertheless, Gewirtz is not entirely enthusiastic about hypotheticals, especially implausible ones: see (1981), 866.

[58] For a discussion of these issues, see Hurley (1990). As Hurley observes: '... legal reasoning often requires one to discover or construct revealing hypothetical cases', but 'the doctrine of precedent imposes a further constraint on legal deliberation in giving actual settled cases more weight than that of hypothetical settled cases for purposes of determining what counts as treating like cases alike': (1990), 235.

captured by, analogical reasoning. Even if not analogised to the facts of the present case, a scenario can be useful as a device for sensing that some value, vulnerability or interest might be at stake. This also includes implausible scenarios, which may be wildly different to the present case, or any likely future cases: these too may allow us to sense that something normative might be at stake, which we could not see if we did not introduce some greater degree of implausibility into the scenario. Again, scenarios are useful for inquiry not primarily as sources of analogy, and certainly not as replacement precedents, but instead, as means for generating normative insight, especially when caring for the quality of the law in the future. This point is best illustrated with a concrete example, and I do that in the second part of this chapter.

To avoid confusion, as a final point on plausibility, it should also be added that to talk of imagining with plausible scenarios is not to talk of prediction or prophecy. The debate over consequential reasoning in the legal context, for instance, has often centred on it being inappropriate for judges to attempt to predict or prophesise what will happen if they decide in such and such a manner. Judges, it is said, are not trained to make that kind of judgement; nor do courts have the resources to support them in making it. Predictions and prophecies, it is often added, may be appropriate for legislatures, but not for courts. Thus, for some, consequential reasoning, or what is also sometimes referred to as policy-based reasoning, is inimical to adjudication: judges should avoid it, and certainly not let it trump non-consequential considerations, such as rights.[59]

I do not wish to enter into this debate here. My only point is that imagining with scenarios is not the same as reasoning with consequences or policies, and certainly not the same as predicting or prophesising. The confusion arises because some scenarios are constructed with a view to testing how a certain proposed justification in the present case, eg in the form of a rule or principle, might fare in a certain situation in the foreseeable future. Further, an advocate or judge constructing a scenario with such an aim may make every attempt to make the scenario a possible or plausible one, ie one that could happen in the future. But to make a scenario possible or plausible is not to predict or prophesy that it will happen.[60] Constructing a scenario in such a way that it is something that could happen is very different to claiming and approaching it on the basis either that it has happened or that it will happen. When we project a scenario into the future, we are not engaged in probabilistic reasoning about the likely effects of adopting a certain rule or principle. Instead, we are evaluating, by imagining, especially via our affective participation, the action(s) in the scenario, and drawing on this circumstantial judgement of character to generate insight as to which values, vulnerabilities and interests might be at stake in the present case and in other potentially-similar cases in the future. We are engaged not in prediction or prophecy, but in balancing respect for the law's past, doing justice in the instant case, and caring for the quality of the law in the future.

In this respect, imagining with scenarios may resemble, but not be quite the same as what John Dewey had in mind with his notion of dramatic rehearsal.[61] For Dewey,

[59] Most famously, of course, Dworkin (1986).

[60] See MacCormick (1983); and Del Mar (2015c).

[61] See Dewey (1922), 190–209; and for a discussion, see, eg, Caspary (1991) and (2006); Fesmire (2003); Johnson (2018); and Jackson (2009). See also Nanay (2016).

when are we engaged in moral reasoning (about what we ought to do, concerning some decision that we need to make) one of the processes we can engage in involves projecting, into the future, our possible selves, ie those versions of our self that we think are likely to arise if we take such and such a decision. Depending on how we evaluate that imagined, projected self, eg how that self will relate to and interact with others around us, we can then make a better-informed decision in the present.

But to engage in such a process, as important and useful as it clearly can be for an individual making a moral decision, is not the same as to engage in what I am here calling scenario imagining in the context of adjudication. When judges are imagining scenarios, they are not primarily evaluating consequences of what will happen in the future; they are, instead, generating normative insight as part of an exercise of inquiry. When we imagine with a scenario, we are not trying to decide now, on the basis of certain projected consequences, what we ought to do. What we are doing cannot be reduced to a process of decision-making in the present; it is too social, too public, and too diachronically complex for that. We are trying, instead, to ascertain what values, vulnerabilities and interests might be at stake in the difficult task of balancing respect for the law's past, doing justice in the instant case, and caring for the quality of the law in the future. In a sense, we are communicating with those who may come to read us later and generating resources for them. Dramatic rehearsal, then, though it may have some overlap with imagining with scenarios, is too focused on the process of an individual decision-maker deciding in the present.

To say all this, I should clarify, is not to argue against some form of consequential or policy-based reasoning, or even dramatic rehearsal, in the adjudication context. My point, instead, is to make room for something else, ie for inquiry and its artefacts and related processes of imagination. To do that, we need to at least consider the possibility that imagining with scenarios is not the same as either analogical reasoning, consequential reasoning or dramatic rehearsal.

v. *Examples*

Scenarios, then, as short, fictional narrative forms, all contain some narrativity, underspecification, particularity and plausibility, but they also all differ in the degree to which they contain these. I will be looking at an example in some detail in the next section of this chapter, but some further examples may help at this point. In Chapter 5, while discussing fictions, I mentioned a number of scenarios deployed by the judges. One of them, courtesy of Lord Justice Kilbrandon in the *McGhee* case, was as follows:

> Suppose it to be the duty of employers in certain circumstances to supply safety belts. They do not do so, and an employee is injured in a way which would not have happened if the belt had been provided. But he cannot prove that the failure to provide it contributed to the accident, because it is certain that if it had been provided he would not have used it. In the present case, the appellant's body was vulnerable, while he was bicycling home, to the dirt which had been deposited on it during his working hours. It would not have been if he had had a shower. If showers had been provided he would have used them.[62]

[62] *McGhee v National Coal Board* [1972] 3 All ER 1008, 1016.

How does this scenario fare on the above variables? It has some degree of narrativity: there is a sequencing of actions, with explicit causality, and it carries with it an affective phenomenology of suspense, curiosity and surprise (here, will the employee wear the safety belt or won't he?). Its level of under-specification is not especially high, at least not in the initial scenario; it is perhaps only in the comparison that it invites between the scenario and the facts of the case that it requires more inference work from the reader. It is not high in particularity either: it does refer to employers and an employee, and it does refer to 'an accident', but the relationships in question remain relatively abstract, ie they are defined functionally, and the figures in the scenario are functional categories, and not particular persons with fictional names. And it has, arguably, a high degree of plausibility, while still being somewhat speculative: we can imagine an employee not wearing safety belts even if they are provided, though just how plausible we take this to be is likely to depend on our cultural experience of certain employment contexts. We can classify it as a scenario, but we can also suggest that it is not an especially successful artefact: it has relatively low degrees of all four variables, and, as a result, it also does not signal artifice especially strongly, and nor is it likely to successfully invite us to imagine. Instead, the scenario here functions more like a quick analogy: we are invited, quickly, to compare the facts of the scenario with the facts of the present case. This scenario, I would suggest, is not especially valuable for inquiry, and that is, in part, because of its formal features.

Compare the above example to this one:

> It is said that there is a contractual duty of the servant to disclose his past faults. I agree that the duty in the servant to protect his master's property may involve the duty to report a fellow servant whom he knows to be wrongfully dealing with that property. The servant owes a duty not to steal, but, having stolen, is there superadded a duty to confess that he has stolen? I am satisfied that to imply such a duty would be a departure from the well-established usage of mankind and would be to create obligations entirely outside the normal contemplation of the parties concerned. If a man agrees to raise his butler's wages, must the butler disclose that two years ago he received a secret commission from the wine merchant; and if the master discovers it, can he, without dismissal or after the servant has left, avoid the agreement for the increase in salary and recover the extra wages paid? If he gives his cook a month's wages in lieu of notice can he, on discovering that the cook has been pilfering the tea and sugar, claim the return of the month's wages? I think not. He takes the risk.[63]

We have here two multiple scenarios:[64] the short, fictional narratives involving 1) the butler; and 2) the cook. Let us consider their formal aspects: they each have some degree

[63] *Bell v Lever Brothers* [1932] AC 161, 228, per Atkin LJ.

[64] There are some wonderful examples of how multiple scenarios can be, ie how one scenario can suddenly lead a judge to propose another, and then another. A striking example comes from Lord Justice Bramwell in *Honck v Muller*: 'Suppose it was a purchase of 100 yards of silk at so much a yard, and the buyer came for fifty only, could he insist on it? Would it make any difference that fifty yards were to be taken and paid for on Monday and fifty on Tuesday and the Monday's delivery was not taken but refused, and then the Tuesday's was demanded? If there was a charter for an out-and-home voyage, and the charterer refused to load for the outvoyage, could he insist on the ship taking his cargo for the home voyage? Suppose 10,000 tons of coal bought to be delivered at Gibraltar, Aden, and Bombay, in equal quantities – at Bombay in January, at Aden in February, and at Gibraltar in March, and no delivery at Bombay, could the buyer be made to take the other deliveries? Suppose a contract to supply bread to a workhouse for a year from the 1st of January, and the

of *narrativity*, ie sequencing of actions with more or less explicit causality, and with affective phenomenology; they are also both highly *under-specified*, eg we are not told any 'reasons, motives, intentions, purposes' behind the actions of the various parties; they have some degree of *particularity*, arguably more than the previous example, eg here we have not an employer and an employee, but butlers and cooks, and we are given some seemingly superfluous details, eg that the butler 'received a secret commission from the wine merchant', and that 'the cook has been pilfering the tea and the sugar'; and, finally, there is considerable *plausibility*, with it being possible to imagine these events occurring, though we would not mistake them for events that actually occurred to specific persons in a specific place. We could argue, in part based on these formal features, that these scenarios are more successful as artefacts, and that they do invite us to imagine.

However, the capacity of these scenarios to enable inquiry is arguably lessened by their being presented by Lord Atkin as mere examples or illustrations of the general principle that he has already accepted and is now persuading us to accept as well. Right at the outset of the above passage, we are first given the relevant rule or principle, ie that there is no duty by a servant to disclose past faults, and the scenarios are then used to help persuade us to accept the general proposition. In that sense, these scenarios are not enabling inquiry: they are not experimental modes of generating normative insight, at least not in terms of how they are intentionally presented. Of course, although they are presented to us in that manner, we may not treat them so: for example, we may instead, when processing these scenarios, come to simulate emotions of betrayal by the employer, and then react to those emotions with approval, and thus come to think that there is, say, a vulnerability at stake here, eg the employer's, that may require further reflection than Lord Atkin devotes to it. We might think, for instance, that there should be some limits to the extent of the risk we impose on employers. Here, one can see how scenarios can still enable inquiry, even if they are presented, intentionally, as but a means of persuasion by their author.

In the examples above, scenarios were independent short, fictional narratives. Sometimes, however, advocates and judges do not generate scenarios with altogether different facts, but instead explore hypothetical variations of the present facts of the case. It is important to say in this context that doing this is not what I primarily have in mind as examples of scenarios. When I speak of scenarios, I have in mind primarily the construction of short, fictional narratives that are not presented as merely variations on the present facts, but stand, again, relatively independently as narratives in their own right. Here is an example of the practice of hypothetically varying present facts:

> I found great force in the submissions made by Mr. Toulson and agree with much of what he said. Indeed, for much of the hearing I was of opinion that the judge's decision, although fully in accord with the merits as I see them, could not be sustained in principle. But I am

contractor says he will supply and does supply none January, can he insist on supplying in the other eleven months? Suppose he does not supply for eleven months, can he insist on supplying in December? Would it make any difference if he was paid monthly? I hope not – I think not. Suppose a man orders a suit of clothes, the price being 7L-4L for the coat, 2 L for the trousers and 1L for the waistcoat, can he be made to take the coat only, whether they were all to be delivered together, or the trousers and waistcoat first?': *Honck v Muller* (1881) 7 QBD 92, 98–99, per Bramwell LJ. This is certainly an impressive barrage of 'supposes'!

> in the end persuaded that Mr. Toulson's argument proves too much. During the hearing the questions were raised: what if, in a situation such as the present, the council had opened and thereupon accepted the first tender received, even though the deadline had not expired and other invitees had not yet responded? Or if the council had considered and accepted a tender admittedly received well after the deadline? Mr. Toulson answered that although by so acting the council might breach its own standing orders, and might fairly be accused of discreditable conduct, it would not be in breach of any legal obligation because at that stage there would be none to breach. This is a conclusion I cannot accept. And if it were accepted there would in my view be an unacceptable discrepancy between the law of contract and the confident assumptions of commercial parties, both tenderers (as reflected in the evidence of Mr. Bateson) and invitors (as reflected in the immediate reaction of the council when the mishap came to light).[65]

In this passage, Lord Justice Bingham considers hypothetical, counter-factual variations on the present facts, also illustrating some of the interactive dynamics of this practice. This case involved a plaintiff (successfully) suing the Blackpool Borough Council, after they accepted a tender lower than theirs, for their own tender (owing to the negligence of the town clerk's failure to check the mailbox) had not been considered by them. The original judge's decision was in favour of the plaintiff, and Lord Bingham agreed, dismissing the appeal by the defendants. The above hypothetical, counter-factual variations are introduced by counsel for the defendant, in a bid to persuade the judges to see that the Council had not breached any legal obligations, but they are rejected by Lord Bingham. Notice, however, that the hypothetical, counter-factual variations remain close to the facts of the present case. There is no narratively-independent scenario here. This is a common practice, and often involves the consideration of multiple hypothetical, counter-factual variations in one go. Here is another example:

> We have been pressed very much with an ingenious mode of putting the case on the part of the counsel who have argued for the appellants in this case, namely, suppose this fraudulent person had gone himself to the firm from whom he wished to obtain the goods, and had represented that he was a member of one of the largest firms in London. Suppose on his making that representation the goods had been delivered to him. I am very far, at all events on the present occasion, from seeing my way to this, that the goods being sold to him as representing that firm he could be treated in any other way than as an agent of that firm. Or suppose he had said: 'I am as rich as that firm. I have transactions as large as those of that firm. I have a large balance at my bankers'; then the sale would have been a sale to a fraudulent purchaser on fraudulent representations, and a sale which would have been capable of being set aside, but still a sale would have been made to the person who made those false representations; and the parting with the goods in that case might possibly have passed the property. But this case is an entirely different one. The whole case, as represented here, is this: from beginning to end the respondents believed they were dealing with B & S, they made out their invoices to B & S, they supposed they sold to B & S; they never sold in any way to AB; and, therefore, AB cannot by so obtaining the goods have by any possibility made a good title to a purchaser as against the owners of the goods, who had never in any shape or way parted with the property, nor with anything more than the possession of it.[66]

[65] *Blackpool and Fylde Aero Club Ltd v Blackpool Borough Council* [1990] All ER 25, 30, per Bingham LJ.
[66] *Cundy v Lindsay* (1878) 3 App Cas 459, 468–9, per Hatherley LJ.

Here, the 'suppose's' are all hypothetical, counterfactual variations on what happened in the case. In that sense, they remain close to the present facts. They are used, by Lord Justice Hatherley in this case, to help support the justification in the present case: arguably, it adds to the persuasiveness of the justification if it can be shown that it has some limitations, eg that it would not apply to a set of facts relevantly different from those in the present case. I mention this particular example also because it went on, in subsequent cases (of mistake in contract law), to take on considerable significance, it being later said that it does indeed matter, in deciding whether the contract is void for mistake, whether the fraudster comes in person and thus whether the dealings in question are face-to-face (it being presumed, when that is so, that the seller has an intention to deal with the person in front of them).[67] Thus, my argument here should not be taken to mean that I do not think this is an important practice, and one that can have a considerable effect on the law over time. My point, instead, is that there is a difference between the two practices, ie that of generating hypothetical, counter-factual variations on the present case, and constructing scenarios as independent narratives.

The point should perhaps not be pressed too far. The line between the two practices is not always so obvious. Sometimes, what begins as a string of hypothetical, counterfactual variations on the present case also ends up generating scenarios, ie relatively independent short, fictional narratives. Further, the two practices also have some similar features. There is a sense, for instance, in which the practice of generating hypothetical, counterfactual variations also signals artifice: after all, we know that the hypothetical variation being offered is counter-factual, ie we know that it did not happen, and yet we imagine it as if it did. However, arguably, these counter-factual narratives still function somewhat differently from scenarios as I mean the term: because the former retain a connection to the present facts, they have arguably less capacity to invite us to imagine. We remain anchored to our knowledge of what happened in the case, and this is a considerable restraint on our ability to imagine, and thus, also, on our ability to generate normative insight.

What I have in mind with scenarios is subtly different, and, I would suggest, deserves its own analysis. It matters that scenarios create their own fictional world. The connection with the present facts in scenarios is not taken for granted: we may come to relate the scenario to the present facts, and see them as similar, but we may also not. There is, with scenarios, some independence – some autonomy, some freedom – of imagination. And this, or so I would argue, has its own benefits: by taking some distance from the present facts, by quarantining ourselves from them, even if only for a few moments, we are able to generate normative insights that we might not if we stuck to our knowledge of what happened, or even, counterfactually, what might otherwise have occurred.

Before we move on to considering how scenarios involve processes of imagination, there are two more formal features of them as artefacts that deserve mention. The first concerns something signalled already in the previous chapter, and also above: that there is some overlap between scenarios and figures, for in both, the evaluation of character is important. The second concerns the question of genre, and the fact that scenarios can be presented in the guise of different genres or allude to different genres.

[67] See *Shogun Finance Ltd v Hudson* [2004] 1 All ER 215.

vi. Figures-in-Context

Scenarios can be thought of as figures-in-context. The circumstances of a scenario, or the contexts in which actions in a scenario occur, matter, eg they can be played with, added to, varied, and this is part of the uniqueness of scenarios as artefacts. Nevertheless, such changes in circumstances matter, arguably, ultimately because of the different light that they may shed on the character(s) in the scenario. As I have suggested above, imagining with scenarios enables the circumstantial judgement of character. I shall be saying more about this in a moment; for now, I wish simply to observe that the form of scenarios includes description of actions, often withholding further explicit descriptions of the 'motives, reasons, intentions, purposes' with which those actions are done, and often also not including further descriptions of character, eg scenarios say 'the thief' and not 'the greedy thief'. Scenarios work, in part, because they leave this further inferential work to be done by the reader. They also work precisely because different readers may make different inferences, ie they may engage in the active process of circumstantial judgement of character in different ways.

As the theoretical literature on character has discussed, the making of inferences as to character can take its cue from almost any aspect of the narrative. For instance, Palmer has observed, albeit in relation to novels, that 'nearly all physical events in novels are perceived by characters and have an impact on their mental functioning'.[68] It follows, Palmer says, that 'physical events should be considered as character experiences'.[69] Palmer is trying to de-centre the emphasis in some theories of narrative on events, arguing that, for readers, 'events only have significance when they are experienced by actors',[70] ie the characters. For Palmer, this also suggests that, given how important inferences to character are in the experience of narratives by readers, all aspects of narrative can be triggers for on-going character (re)evaluation: 'the whole consciousness of characters', he says, 'can be expanded to include descriptions of aspects of the storyworld that are seen from their perceptual, cognitive and evaluative point of view'.[71]

Extending this to scenarios, we can say that although when confronting scenarios, we may see little explicit evidence of character, eg there may be no reference to adjectives that describe the character of persons, this does not mean that character does not play an important role. In fact, although it may seem as if all the work in scenarios is done by plot, ie by context, event or circumstances, or by sequences and their causal relations, in fact, when scenarios are processed, we experience those circumstances, ie those sequences of events or actions, and their causal relations, as part of an overall construction and evaluation of the characters in the scenarios.

The point here is not that plot and its circumstances do not matter in scenarios: they do, and they probably cannot wholly be subsumed under the construction and evaluation of character, eg our ability to imagine with scenarios may be supplemented with our social and cultural knowledge of archetypal plots or scripts, just as our ability to imagine figures is supplemented by our social and cultural knowledge of figural

[68] Palmer (2004), 31.
[69] Ibid, 49.
[70] Ibid, 30.
[71] Ibid, 49.

archetypes. Nevertheless, at least in the context of inquiry in adjudication, a lot of the significance of plot and its circumstances for scenarios lies in how they enable the circumstantial judgement of character. This includes our capacity to change the plot and its circumstances. As we shall see in the second section of this chapter, it is often by playing with the plot and its circumstances, rather than with explicit descriptions of character, that we can also change the construction and evaluation of character, and, in so doing, generate normative insight.

vii. Genres

The second point mentioned above can be dealt with briefly, though it is infinitely expandable. Scenarios can come in different genres, or they can allude to different genres. Examples of such genres include parable, fable, fairy tales, myth, and utopia/dystopia. It is not inconceivable, for example, for a scenario in an adjudicative context to refer to historical figures, but in a clearly fictional plot. Similarly so with fables,[72] fairy tales,[73] utopias/dystopias,[74] and myths.[75] Arguably, these genres are more popular in scholarship than they are in adjudicative contexts, and a broader study than this one might find interesting results by comparing the use of different short, fictional narrative genres in scholarship and adjudication.

Out of all these different genres, parables are perhaps especially interesting and challenging. Their role in legal reasoning have also received some attention in the legal scholarly literature.[76] Although it may be rare to see parables set out in full in judgements, there are many allusions to them, eg to mention but one, but also perhaps the most famous, example in recent common law memory: the reference to the parable of the Good Samaritan in the case of *Donoghue v Stevenson*.[77] 'Who, in law, is my neighbour'? is one of the most famous questions of the common law, and it comes to us courtesy of a parable.

I include parables as a genre of scenarios because a good argument can be made that they ought not to be reduced to examples of rules or principles, seeking but merely to illustrate them and motivate the reader to follow them.[78] Parables are more self-reflexive and more experimental than this. In that respect, they are more like narrative-based metaphors, linked also to the Ancient genre of the riddle.[79] Further, and this is perhaps what makes parables one of the most interesting genres to study for scenario imagining, they often involve surprising shifts of perspective.

Let us return, for a moment, to the parable of the Good Samaritan: this is a parable that is told by Jesus in response to a question posed by a lawyer, ie as above, 'Who is

[72] See, eg, Pearson (1993); and Stevens (2018).

[73] See, eg, Carpi and Leiboff (2016).

[74] See, eg, Aviles (2000); Almog (2001); and the essays in Sarat, Douglas, and Umphrey (2014).

[75] See, on myths generally, eg Blumenberg (1985).

[76] See, eg, Bańkowski (2001), ch 9; Bell (2013); Burt (1984); and Govier and Ayers (2012).

[77] *Donoghue v Stevenson* [1932] AC 562.

[78] But see Hogan (2016), for a sophisticated version of a view of parables as didactic and motivational, stressing also, as I do here, the importance of the variability of short form narratives.

[79] For more discussion on the relations between parable and metaphor in argumentation, see Bustos (2017). This paper is part of a valuable collection on the relations between narrative and argument: see Olmos (2017).

my neighbour?'. To understand the parable, one must place it in its rhetorical context: Jesus is addressing the parable to the lawyer who asks him the question. As Roger White explains,[80] the standard interpretation of this parable is that it tells us that anyone who is in need of our assistance, even if they are our enemy, is our neighbour. We should be like the Good Samaritan. However, when one remembers that Jesus is addressing a lawyer, and one further remembers 'the deep sectarian hostility between the Samaritans and the Jews',[81] one comes to see that the point of the parable, *for the lawyer*, is to see the *Samaritan* as a neighbour. There is a sense in which the parable is offensive, as is the case with many parables. Parables are meant to be disconcerting, disorientating, often in surprising and self-reflexive ways. In this case, the parable works by confronting the lawyer with his own perspective, ie on Samaritans as non-neighbours. It does so in a roundabout way, ie parabolically, so to speak, via the story of a Samaritan treating the person in need. The parable 'radically challenges the assumed privileged position of the lawyer',[82] ie it invites him, in a roundabout way, to address the question of how neighbours are constituted by his own community. As White says:

> This radical change of perspective is forced by Jesus on the lawyer by the offence implicit in the parable, by taking the last man the lawyer would contemplate as a possible neighbour and forcing the lawyer to acknowledge him as such.[83]

Although we may wish to query the language of 'force' here – the parable seems more invitational to me, though still certainly confrontational – the general point is that parables are not easily subsumed under a simple theoretical frame in which they are but mere didactic examples, used to motivate persons to follow rules or principles with which they are already familiar. They are considerably more exploratory and experimental, and this in distinctive ways: they appear to revel in somewhat inexplicable acts, including trespassing of social norms, and they are often highly self-reflexive, involving surprising shifts in perspective.[84]

My point in mentioning these different genres is simply to observe that these genre-differences can matter: not all scenarios are the same, and each of these different kinds of short fictional narratives deserve their own extended analysis. To do that, however, is not within the scope of this chapter.

B. Imagining Scenarios

I have now examined some of the formal features of scenarios as artefacts. It is time to turn to scenarios as a process of imagining. As already noted above, to imagine with scenarios is to enter a distinctive epistemic frame in which we suspend certain epistemic norms and commitments, which often depend on just how differently the scenario in

[80] See White (1989).
[81] Ibid, 62.
[82] Ibid.
[83] Ibid, 63.
[84] For more on parables, see also Miller (1995); and Landy (2012), ch 2.

question balances the variables above, ie narrativity, under-specification, particularity and plausibility. For instance, where a scenario uses symbols A, B, C we then suspend our usual commitment to treating references to persons as picking out particular individuals, and where scenarios involve exaggeration of some aspect of the plot (say, they make the amount of money stolen to be astronomical) we may suspend certain commitments to realism or plausibility. At the same time as entering a distinctive epistemic frame, when we imagine with scenarios we also participate, and we do so at a high degree of affective, sensory and kinesic involvement. As I have stressed above, affective involvement is especially important with respect to scenarios. When we process scenarios, we often do so by simulating the emotions of the characters, and then ourselves reacting to those emotions. In many ways, it is because scenarios engage us affectively that they can enable the circumstantial judgement of character, which, in turn, can be so beneficial to inquiry in adjudication.

i. The Hypothesis

To help capture some of this processing of scenarios, including not only the affective dimension, but also the social aspect of imagining with scenarios, we can turn to what may seem like an unlikely source: the Ancient Roman practice of declamations. This practice features prominently in Wesley Trimpi's account of the relations between rhetoric, fiction and equity.[85] Before, however, we can ascertain the importance of the declamations to Trimpi's account, and, thereafter for this book, we need to step back a little and consider Trimpi's broader aims.

One of these aims is telling the history of short, fictional narratives. Trimpi's history is incredibly rich, ranging not only across centuries, but also across many different disciplinary domains, eg literature, philosophy, mathematics, and rhetoric. It begins with the Ancient Greeks and the concept of *hypothesis*.[86] A *hypothesis*, associated with the practice of rhetoric, meant a 'specific set of circumstances' or a 'case given to be judged'.[87] *Hypothesis* contrasts with *thesis*; and these terms, in turn, correspond to the later Latin terms, *quaestio definita* (hypothesis) and *quaestio indefinita* (thesis). Where the former involves a specific set of circumstances, with 'facts, persons and times', the latter is a 'proposition', which 'may be argued on either side (*in utrumque partem*) without any reference to any persons or circumstances'.[88] 'Should a man marry?' or 'Should a man enter politics?' were examples of popular action-oriented theses (the former of which was the beginning point for many literary experiments), though there were also more 'scientific' theses, such as 'Is the world governed by providence?'.[89] *Hypotheses*, however, did not articulate a proposition; instead, as above, they offered a case to be judged.

[85] Trimpi (1983). See also Altman (1978).

[86] See also Appendix A, which traces the transformation in meaning from the Ancient *hypothesis* to the medieval *exemplum*: Trimpi (1983), 371–381.

[87] Ibid, 25.

[88] Ibid, 32.

[89] Ibid.

As with a scientific *hypothesis*, which involved postulating or supposing something 'for the purpose of proving something else',[90] in rhetoric, a *hypothesis*, what Trimpi also calls a 'fictional supposition', could also be a 'starting point of proofs'.[91] In a sense, it was a place, an opportunity, to make an argument and to generate arguments. Although part of its history is certainly entangled with scientific practice, perhaps especially geometry, *hypotheses* may also be traced back to the sketches of Ancient comedies and mimes.[92] They were also related to the practice of Ancient drama, eg one could speak of the argument or *hypothesis* of a play, ie something like its general outline. As observed by Trimpi, Aristotle, in the *Poetics*, gives a neat example of such an outline or *hypothesis*, in this case by reference to the drama *Iphigenia*:

> A certain girl has been sacrificed but spirited away from her sacrificers without their seeing how; she has been installed in another country, in which it is the custom to sacrifice all foreigners to the goddess, and has been invested with this priesthood. Some time later the priestess' brother happens to arrive … and having arrived and been captured, is at the point of being sacrificed when he recognises (his sister) and from that comes his salvation.[93]

There is a certain level of abstraction in the *hypothesis*: in the above outline, there is no mention of specific persons, places or times, eg dates. Significantly, there is also no specific mention of motives. One has simply the basic sequence of actions, with causality between them made relatively explicit, eg it being said that the brother is saved because he recognises the priestess as his sister. What we have here, then, is a short, fictional narrative, with some narrativity (including suspense, curiosity and surprise), some level of particularity (but a relatively modest one, for it is bereft of particular persons, places or dates), a high degree of under-specification (ie no description of motives), and some general plausibility but also some modest degree of implausible coincidence (eg it being the sister who is the priestess). We have, then, what we might call a scenario.

At this point, however, it may be unclear how such a short, fictional narrative, or scenario, might be related to practices of evaluation. To see the connection, we need to introduce what was known as the 'status' system, ie the taxonomy of issues or questions one can ask:

> The first kind asks whether something exists or happened (*sitne*) and is to be answered by inference and conjecture (*coniectura*). The second kind asks what the thing is (*quid sit*) and is to be answered by definition (*definitione*). And the third kind asks what its character is (*quale sit*) and is to be answered by distinctions between right and wrong (*iuris et iniuriae distinctione*). This third, or qualitative question … involves what to seek and avoid, what is right and wrong, what is honourable and base.[94]

This third question, in short, is the question of quality, and it calls precisely for the exercise of normative judgement, ie judgement as to what is right or wrong, what is appropriate and inappropriate, what to do and what to avoid doing, and what is virtuous

[90] Ibid, 29.
[91] Ibid, 30.
[92] Ibid.
[93] Aristotle, quoted at ibid, 51.
[94] Trimpi (1983), 252.

and what is vicious. The key connection then becomes that between *hypothesis* (or the *quaestio definita*) and quality (or *qualitas*). How are the two related? Trimpi says as follows:

> … the more detailed the *quaestio definita*, or plot, the more precisely the *quaestiones indefinitae*, which reveal its significance, may be expressed. For the greater the particularity with which one investigates the circumstances of a case, the more he is implicated in motives, choices, and other ethical questions of *qualitas*. The further one hypothesizes in circumstance, in other words, the greater the involvement in quality, and the more qualitative the issues, the more extensive the 'involution' in the generic thesis.[95]

Hypotheses turn out to be the method of inquiry into quality, including both raising the question of what is right and wrong (especially by reference to the actions of a character in the scenario) as well as exploring possible answers to it. One could explore such answers, and thus draw on the *hypothesis* as a mode of inquiry, by both particularising and varying the circumstances. One could make the *hypothesis* particular in specific ways, and in so doing, one could explore possible motivations for the actions of the characters in the *hypothesis*. By doing that, in turn, one could come to evaluate those actions.

Notice, though, that what is built into the *hypothesis* from the beginning is variability: it lends itself to being varied, to being played with. It does that by withholding certain details, ie being under-specified, while also providing sufficient narrativity, particularity and plausibility to, so to speak, whet the appetite of imagination. The *hypothesis* combines all four of the variables I identified above as part of the scenario: for instance, it may introduce some implausibility (while nevertheless retaining general plausibility), thereby signalling artifice and capturing our attention; it also introduces some narrativity and particularity, but not so much that we do not experience it as calling on us to do something with it, eg adding more particularity, and enhancing the narrativity; and it is under-specified, especially in terms of describing motives, which invites us to fill them in and, at the same time, to engage in the evaluation of the actions in question. In so doing, in imagining the *hypothesis*, we thereby generate normative insight: eg as to what values, vulnerabilities and interests might be at stake in judging that this action is right or wrong, virtuous or vicious.

ii. Declamation

At this point, and especially in order to capture some of the social dynamics of this mode of inquiry, we can turn to the Ancient Roman art of declamation. Declamations were rhetorical exercises for aspiring orators. Aspiring orators attended schools of declamation, where one was trained as a declaimer, after which, if one was lucky, one could begin a career as an advocate. Trimpi relies on the declamations as described by Seneca the Elder, from the first century CE. The type of declamation most pertinent for our purposes were the *controversia*, or controversies, ie precisely *hypotheses*, or fictional

[95] Ibid, 255.

cases made for experimental, exploratory, and playful normative judgement. Here is an example from Seneca, as quoted by Trimpi:

> A virgin, captured by pirates and put up for sale, is bought by a prostitutor [we would today say 'pimp'] and put to work. She asks those who wish her favours, however, to pay her fee (which she has to pass on to the prostitutor) without making her earn it. A soldier who refuses to agree to this arrangement tries to rape her, and she kills him. She is charged with murder, acquitted, and returned to her native country, where she applies for the priesthood.[96]

The background law that one must know, and which this *controversia* assumes the audience would know, is that one cannot be a priestess if one is not pure, for purity is a requirement for being a priestess. The question of quality that this *thema* (as a particular *controversia* was called) raises is whether the woman in question can be admitted to the priesthood. Would that be right or wrong, appropriate or inappropriate?

Here is where the training of the declamations kicked in: it was the task of the declaimer – randomly assigned to one or the other side, eg for or against the admission into priesthood by this woman – to further particularise the *thema* in such a way that it would cast light on the character's (here, the woman's) motivations, with a view to evaluating them, and thereby answering the question as to quality. In particularising and varying the *thema*, one had to stay within its broad limits, eg for instance in this case, one could not imagine that she does not kill the soldier, but one otherwise had considerable freedom to 'colour' the circumstances in such a way that they invited certain evaluative inferences as to the motives behind the actions. It was, then, via this technique of colouring the *thema* – by glossing it, so to speak – that one engaged in the circumstantial judgement of character. As Frederick Bonner once described this technique:

> By a slight shift of argument, by an added insinuation, or a guileless plea, they tone down the guilt or represent it in even more flaring colours. The *colores* are the Persian carpet of the declaimer; look at it from one angle and the colours are bright and clear, the pattern simple, but observe it from another angle, and the shade deepens, the pattern changes, and the whole appears in a different light.[97]

Colouring was concerned with motive, but the art involved not doing this too directly. A skilled declaimer coloured the circumstances in such a way that the audience was invited to make an inference, at the same time evaluating the action in the desired way. In the above *thema*, Seneca describes the rhetor Fuscus giving the following colour:

> The immortal gods have wished, with regard to this young girl, to show all their power and to make it perfectly clear that no human force can resist their majesty: they thought that it would be a miracle if one should find liberty in a captive, modesty in one prostituted, innocence in a woman accused of murder.[98]

Notice the increased particularity: the woman in question is now described as a 'young girl'; and notice the specification of motive, here the young girl's own motives being

[96] Seneca (1974), Contr. 1.2; quoted in Trimpi (1983), 308.
[97] Bonner (1949), 56; quoted in Trimpi (1983), 312–3.
[98] Seneca (1974), Contr. 1.2.17; quoted in Trimpi (1983), 313.

downplayed and replaced with the motives of the Gods who are said to have set up this sequence of events as the ultimate test of a potential priestess. Other rhetors coloured by inventing scenes of dialogue between the characters in a *thema*, thereby again inviting certain inferences as to motive by the audience.

Significantly for present purposes, this technique of colouring depended on engaging the emotions of the audience. In fact, the performance of these colours by declaimers often involved high degrees of affectivity, hoping that audiences would share in the simulation of the emotions of the characters and then go on to react emotionally themselves. For instance, in colouring a *thema* involving a man who raped two women in one night, one rhetor exclaimed 'he was on his way to attack a third young lady, had the night not given out!'.[99] The same *thema* might be coloured by a rhetor on the other side by saying that the young man mistakenly believed 'he had raped only one girl', going to that girl and begging her on his knees that she marry him.[100] Again, the art of declamatory colouring involved performing certain actions or events, eg begging on one's knees, that invited the audience to simulate the emotion of the character (here, for instance, the desperation of the young man) and then reacting emotionally to that character (here, by feeling some sympathy for him, and evaluating his actions less harshly).

Notice, that in all of this, normative insights are generated: for instance, in the case of the priestess, we might, thanks to the colour mentioned above, think that the age of a prospective priestess who has undergone such an ordeal matters in deciding whether she can become a priestess: in this case, we might say, thanks to the colour, the prospective priestess was especially vulnerable, as a young girl, and yet she showed particular strength in protecting her own chastity, going as far as to murder for it. Or, in the case of the double rapist, we might, thanks to the colour, consider the willingness of the young man to marry as a factor of mercy in the giving of punishment for this double crime.

Important to this declamatory training, and especially to the technique of colouring, is that it invites the audience to imagine with a high degree of affective, sensory and kinesic participation. The reference to an aspect of visual experience, colour, is not accidental. As Trimpi explains:

> As colours give the picture a lifelike, illusionistic quality, fictional elaboration if plausibly handled gives life … Colour is what deceives the eye. In this sense, it corresponds to the *color* of declamation which puts a certain 'complexion' on the events to be judged.[101]

Questions of quality, it is suggested here, are best encountered precisely via this heightened affective, sensory and kinesic participation, though, all the while, accompanied by an awareness that one is in a distinctive epistemic frame, ie that this is a fictional story, that the *controversia* is made up, not corresponding to any events that actually happened or that one predicts will happen. Indeed, this might be the reason for sometimes quite outlandish, if not also downright cruel and gory, *themata* in the declamatory tradition.

[99] Trimpi (1983), 314.
[100] Ibid.
[101] Ibid, 317.

The art of declamation was so engaging and affectively powerful, and the rhetors were so good at working the audience up, that one had to have a constant reminder of the artifice of the exercise, and having at least some highly implausible elements to the *thema* helped to keep this awareness in mind.

There is one more detail to add to this account, and one which Trimpi himself does not address. This is the highly social, especially interactive, dynamics of declamatory training. For the training in question involved not only two rhetors pitting their wits against each other, offering rival *colores* of a *thema*. Throughout this performance, the audience was very active: not only could they cheer or boo, but they could also, following the performances, offer their own additional colours. The audience, it should be added, included not only the students, but often alumni too, ie past students, now experienced rhetors, who would come to watch the performances, and then offer their own little nuggets of colour. The teacher himself, following all this ruckus, would then also sometimes give his own performance, taking on one or other side, and introducing his own colours. The point is that the *thema* lent itself to this interactive dynamic, to this social exchange of glosses of circumstance, leading to the simulation of different emotions, different emotional reactions, and thereby also different evaluations. The declamatory school was a place of intensely social imagining with scenarios, involving multiple shifts of affective perspective, as one experienced wave after wave of different colours. And these multiple shifts of affective perspectives also generated insight as to potentially relevant values, vulnerabilities and interests at stake in the question of quality posed by the *thema*.

My suggestion here is this: that we draw on this Ancient art of declamation to see how scenarios, in the contemporary adjudicatory context, can enable inquiry. Of course, there will be considerable differences: we are talking of courts, not declamatory schools, and the scenarios that are used in this context are very different in form and style compared to the *themata* of the declaimers. However, the connection, within the declamatory art between the *thema* and the question of quality – but also, more broadly, as Trimpi has shown, between the short, fictional narrative and the equitable judgement – can be similar to that between scenarios and the circumstantial judgement of character they enable. In both, we have groups of persons imagining a short, fictional narrative; in both, that short, fictional narrative can be varied in different ways; in both, we have the simulation of the emotions of the characters, and emotional reactions to those simulations; and in both, we see the generation of normative insight.

Of course, just as there will be distinctive, non-transferable elements of the declamatory practice, there will also be distinctive, non-transferable elements of the use of scenarios in contemporary common law adjudication, eg the latter allows for the generation of alternative, counter-scenarios, whereas the former demanded more discipline from the rhetors in that respect, ie they had to stick to the *thema* rather than invent another. And, needless to say, there is considerably more at stake in the context of a case in the adjudicatory context. These differences are important. Nevertheless, or so I would suggest, they are not so great as to mean that there could not be a similar involvement of imagination, with a similar positive benefit to inquiry, in both practices.

I have barely brushed the surface of the theory and history of imagining with scenarios: so much more remains to be explored. For instance, there is a great deal more to be mined as to the history of inventing and playing with 'circumstances' in rhetorical theory and practice, and especially in drama, including how these link to the making of normative judgement, and indeed to the making of social, moral and legal norms and standards.[102] For now, however, I leave the more abstract engagement with this artefact, and its related processes of imagination, and turn to examine one specific example of it.

II. The Expert Abroad – Or in Hong Kong

In turning to a concrete example of scenarios, I examine the case of *White & Carter v McGregor*.[103] I do so in four steps: first, summarising the facts and the initial proceedings in the Scottish courts; second, considering the role of scenarios in counsel submissions before the House of Lords; third, turning to the judgement in the House of Lords, and in particular to the role of scenarios in the opinions of three of the Lords; and fourth, considering some of the legacy of the scenarios in this case.

A. The Facts and Initial Proceedings

i. The Facts

On 26 June 1957, a salesman for an English advertising company visited the premises of a Scottish garage-business owned by Mr William McGregor. The advertising company – White & Carter Councils (Ltd) – provided bins (also referred to as 'litter baskets') for Councils, and in return, were able to sell advertising space on those bins.

Three years previously, White & Carter had entered into a contract with McGregor, and duly advertised their garage business for three years; McGregor also duly paid. Now, with the expiry of that three-year contract looming (it was to expire on 2 November 1957), the White & Carter salesman visited the premises with a view to renewing the contract for another three years.

Mr McGregor was not on the premises; neither was his accountant, Mr JDS Lockhart. Present, instead, was his sales manager, Mr R Ward. The White & Carter salesman succeeded in persuading Mr R Ward to sign the renewal. Although there was some discussion on the issue, it was eventually conceded that Mr Ward had the ostensible authority to sign and renew contracts on McGregor's behalf.

[102] On this, see, eg, Hutson (2015) and (2006); and Mukherji (2006).

[103] *White & Carter (Councils) v McGregor* (1962) SC (HL) 1. Subsequent references to this case are *White & Carter* (1962).

That afternoon, the accountant, Mr Lockhart, returned back to the garage premises. Mr Ward showed him the renewed contract. By all accounts, Mr Lockhart was furious with Mr Ward: he should not have renewed any contract without speaking to him first. Did he – Mr Ward – not know that Mr McGregor did not want to advertise in this manner anymore? That very day, Mr Lockhart composed a letter to White & Carter. He wrote:

> Dear Sirs,
>
> We regret that our Mr Ward signed an order to-day continuing the lamp post [sic] advertisements for a further period of 3 years. He was unaware that our proprietor Mr McGregor does not wish to continue this form of advertisement. Please therefore cancel the order.
>
> Yours faithfully,
>
> JDS Lockhart

White & Carter were not moved. They did not accept this attempt to cancel the contract (this 'repudiation'). Even though nothing had yet been done – as above, the 1954–1957 contract was still on foot, and the new contract not due to begin till 2 November 1957 – they insisted on it going ahead. They said they would begin advertising, under the new contract, on 2 November 1957. And they duly did so.

The contract had included a clause that the first payment was due one week after the first advertisement. McGregor did not pay. They insisted, as they had done since 26 June 1957, that they did not want this contract. White & Carter, in turn, continued to advertise, and on 7 October 1958, they instituted proceedings, claiming the full amount due under the contract (a sum of almost £200, which was not insignificant in the 1960s, especially for a small Scottish garage business). According to the terms of the contract, they were entitled to do so. They had included a clause which claimed the full payment was due if there was any breach of contract. There had been a breach already, one week after 2 November 1957 when the first payment had been due and not paid. By all accounts, even as the court proceedings were begun and continued, White & Carter continued to advertise McGregor's business and did so until the contract terminated on 2 November 1960.

ii. The Proceedings in Scotland

Meanwhile, on 6 February 1959, the Sheriff-substitute in Scotland heard and dismissed the case by White & Carter. White & Carter appealed to the Court of Session, and after some back and forth concerning proof issues, the Court of Session heard the case in the Second Division on two days in October and November 1960.

It was clear to the Lords in the Second Division that White & Carter were pursuing a particular litigation strategy. They had done this before, with other businesses also being persuaded to sign renewals, their owners attempting unsuccessfully to cancel the unwanted contracts. Knowing their chances were slim in the Scottish courts, White & Carter banked on losing in the Scottish courts, but then winning in the English Court of Appeal. They had done this precisely in *White & Carter v AR Harding* (a decision of the Court of Appeal on 21 May 1958, which went unreported). The reason why they had such slim chances in the Scottish courts was because of a prior case: *Langford & Co v Dutch*.[104] In that case, as explained by Lord Justice Clerk:

> … a firm of advertising contractors entered into an agreement with a person for advertising his business by means of an advertisement film to be shown at a picture house for one year commencing with the first showing. The sum payable for this service was £104 yearly, payable quarterly in advance. Five days after concluding the agreement, the businessman wrote to the contractors asking them to cancel the contract. The contractors proceeded with the execution on their side, and ultimately displayed the film. They later brought an action for the whole figure of £104. The Court held that the proper course for the pursuers to adopt was to treat the defender as having repudiated the contract and as being, on that account, liable in damages.[105]

This Scottish case was a powerful precedent for the Second Division. It seemed to be 'on all fours', as lawyers say, with the facts of the present case. There were two ways one could try to get around it: the first was to challenge it head-on by requesting a full, seven-member bench in Scotland to reconsider it; the second was to bank on losing in front of a smaller bench of the Second Division in Scotland, and then appeal to the English Court of Appeal (where, one might think, the Scottish case might not be so persuasive). As noted above, White & Carter chose the second option. All three of the judges (who wrote their own opinions, the fourth judge simply agreeing) noted this strategy, and they did so clearly with some annoyance.

In the result, the Second Division unanimously decided against White & Carter. They did so primarily by reference to the *Langford* precedent. Of all the judgements, the following passage by Lord Justice Patrick deserves particular mention for present purposes:

> I refer to the case of *Langford* … in which the First Division of the Court decided that a defender could not be compelled to accept a year's advertisement which she did not want, although she might be liable in damages for her breach of contract. We were not asked to reconsider this decision, and, if we had doubts as to its soundness, to refer the matter to a Court of seven Judges. In the circumstances, we must accept the decision as sound, as I readily do. I apprehend that the Court would in many instances refuse to insist on services being performed in order that the servant or contractor might claim the contract price instead of claiming damages for breach of contract. The builder would not be entitled to an order that a house should be built, if it was no longer wanted, nor would the artist be entitled to an order that a portrait should be painted.[106]

The passage is significant for it begins to grapple with some of the values, vulnerabilities and interests that might be at stake in this case, and in others potentially like it in the future. On the one hand, we have a valid contract, which one party is attempting to cancel, ie which it repudiates. We have the value of the freedom and sanctity of contract, ie that one ought to keep one's promises, and that one is free to enter into any contracts, even if they are unfair ones, for the Court does not generally interfere to remedy unfair agreements. According to these values, and according to the law which expressed them,

[104] *Langford & Co v Dutch* (1952) SC 15.
[105] *White & Carter (Councils) v McGregor* (1960) SC 276, 282, per Clerk LJ.
[106] Ibid, 284, per Patrick LJ.

White & Carter were free to either accept McGregor's repudiation (as per the letter on 26 June 1957), and sue for damages, or to continue performing the contract and sue for the amount payable. On the other hand, however, we have another set of values, vulnerabilities and interests, namely ones that may potentially limit the general right to either accept or refuse a repudiation. Just what, however, might those values, vulnerabilities and interests be? The question is not easy. The Court must proceed with care, especially given that any interference into freedom and sanctity of contracts by the Court is likely to be scrutinised, and thus its own legitimacy may be at stake.

In the above passage, Lord Patrick does, even if briefly, grapple with this difficult task. He frames the issue as not one involving the Court interfering with freedom and sanctity of contract, but one where the Court is being asked – by White & Carter – to enforce the performance of unwanted services. What are the limits on the Court to enforce performance? Lord Patrick does not articulate a general rule or principle, but he does provide two short, fictional narratives: the case of the builder who 'would not be entitled to build' an unwanted house, and the case of a painter who would also not be 'entitled to an order that a portrait [now unwanted] should be painted'.

We can see these two short, fictional narratives as scenarios. They are not especially well-developed, and yet, they are short, fictional narratives with some (low) level of narrativity (the builder is first asked to build a house, then is asked not to build it; the artist too is asked to paint a portrait, and then asked not to); there is under-specification (we are not told why the builder or the artist is told not to go ahead); there is some (low) level of particularity; and there is also general plausibility. The artifice is signalled, for instance, by the use of the subjunctive 'would', but also generally by the combination of the above four variables.

Reading these scenarios, we are called upon to do something with them: we are invited, precisely, to imagine. In particular, we are invited to imagine why the house or portrait might be unwanted, and whether any of the possible motivations might help in identifying the values, vulnerabilities and interests at stake in limiting the general right to refuse or accept a repudiation.

Of course, the scenarios are skeletal; they give us little to go on; they are not particularly effective at either signalling artifice or calling on us to participate. Their level of narrativity and particularity is so low that they are unlikely to be especially successful in inviting us to imagine. We may well skip over them quickly when reading. Thus, although they are arguably scenarios, they are not especially good examples of scenarios that can contribute to inquiry. Nevertheless, as we shall see, they were also not entirely ignored in what happened later.

Having lost in the Scottish courts, White & Carter appealed and went straight to the House of Lords. The case was heard before a five-member bench from 17 to 20 July 1961, composed of Lords Reid, Morton, Tucker, Keith and Hodson. The case was a closely fought battle. But, in the result, White & Carter succeeded: their litigation strategy had paid off. They won in the House of Lords with a majority of 3 to 2, with Lords Reid, Tucker and Hodson being in the majority, and Lords Morton and Keith in the minority. The arguments in the House are of special interest for present purposes in part because of the emphasis placed, both in the majority and minority opinions, on scenarios (and, in particular, on one scenario).

B. Counsel Submissions

Before we turn to the opinions, however, we need to examine the submissions of both parties. As we shall see, both submissions were peppered with scenarios, as well as with metaphors and allusions to literary works.

i. *Counsel for White & Carter*

For the appellants, White & Carter, counsel unsurprisingly insisted on the 'innocent party' having 'truly a choice' as to whether to accept or refuse the repudiation.[107] They could not be 'compelled to accept the repudiation'; the 'guilty party could not rid himself of his contractual liability or limit his liability under the contract by repudiating it and insisting that such repudiation be accepted by the innocent party'.[108] The characterisation of the parties here, as 'innocent' or 'guilty', is of course already a significant move, and so is the positioning of the 'guilty party' as the active one, attempting to force the innocent party to accept their repudiation. Throughout, counsel for White & Carter paint them as the victims: if they were forced to accept a repudiation, they would be put at great expense, having to find an alternative advertiser. They were a 'London company with its office in London'; they already had to send 'representatives … from London to the provinces [!] to canvass for advertisers'; surely they should not be forced to 'send a man from London to Clydebank to relet this space'.[109]

Anticipating possible objections, which had already featured in the Scottish courts (as above, per Lord Patrick), counsel for White & Carter sought to quash any potentially problematic scenarios:

> If the innocent party chose not to accept, he might go on and await the date of the performance by the guilty party and, if it was not tendered, his rights, as at that date, were preserved to him. This would not apply to a contract for repairing a house, because a decree of the Court would be needed to get access to the house. That was different from a case of this kind.[110]

Here, we see an echo of the scenario that featured, albeit briefly, in Lord Patrick's opinion. Counsel argued that it need not worry the House: unlike in this case, in the case of the builder, one would require the intervention of the Court. The builder could not simply go to the house and repair it, against the wishes of the owner: the Court would have to force the owner to give access to the house. Thus, counsel here acknowledged one possible limit on the general right to refuse or accept a repudiation, namely when the Court would have to force one of the parties to perform some aspect of the contract, eg give their house over to the builder to be repaired. But this case, counsel argued, is not like this. McGregor did not have to perform anything (apart from paying), and the Court did not have to force the 'guilty party' to do anything. Therefore, although this

[107] *White & Carter* (1962), 3.
[108] Ibid, 4.
[109] Ibid, 7.
[110] Ibid, 4.

was a legitimate limitation on the general right to refuse or accept a repudiation, it did not apply in this case.

Again, counsel insisted, the 'innocent party' had 'truly a choice'. And, again, counsel argued, in this case, there were no alarming implications for other potentially alike cases:

> One did not need to be alarmed at the implications of the principle [of freedom to accept or refuse a repudiation] in the case of a contract to build a large ship, since it was unlikely that it would not contain a clause providing for this matter. As to the case of a person who had been given an article to repair, if the owner brought an action to recover it from him before the work was carried out, he would be held to have a right to be in possession under a lawful contract.[111]

These short, fictional narratives are designed to ward off worries that the Court may have about the potential implications of their decision on other possible cases involving the performance of services. The Court need not worry about these, for it is likely they would either have clauses dealing with them (an arguable point, surely, and quite a speculative one), or because the relevant party would be protected by the law of property (which is not relevant to the present case). There is a sense in which, in these scenarios, counsel for White & Carter does acknowledge that there is something inappropriate about forcing a guilty party to accept unwanted services, but, they quickly add, the Court need not worry, because other areas of the law (or contractual practices in some area of commerce) will protect the party seeking to cancel the contract. It is not stated what the relevant values, vulnerabilities and interest might be (on behalf of the 'guilty party'); perhaps, at best, we can say that the scenarios pick up on some sense in which unwanted services should not be forced onto a party.

There are four further scenarios mentioned by counsel for White & Carter. The first three (involving a picture restorer, a garage proprietor and a scientist) are designed to show how the innocent party may be vulnerable, or what interests of the innocent party would be harmed, were they to be forced, in certain circumstances, to accept a repudiation:

> A picture restorer who was entrusted with a picture to restore or a garage proprietor to whom a motor car had been given for repair might refuse to accept a repudiation of the contract by the owner and insist on retaining the thing and doing the work on it. Apart from the remuneration, there might be the advantage to his reputation in doing the work, and yet, if he accepted the repudiation, he could recover no damages for that.
>
> Taking the case of a picture restorer who had been engaged to restore a famous picture, if the owner repudiated the contract, the restorer could go on and restore it, because no amount of damages could compensation him for the loss of reputation he would suffer in doing the work. A scientist employed to make an elaborate survey would be in the same position.[112]

Here, reference is made, in defence of the principle to have 'truly a choice' as to whether to accept or refuse a repudiation, not to the values of the freedom and sanctity of contract, but instead to the vulnerability of the 'innocent party' and their interests.

[111] Ibid, 7.
[112] Ibid, 5–6.

The relevant interests include not only the monetary interest, but also potential reputational interest in completing the work. No less than three scenarios 'hunt' together, so to speak, in order to generate this normative insight: a picture restorer painting a 'famous' picture, a scientist employed to make an 'elaborate' survey, and (perhaps least persuasively) a garage proprietor repairing a car (unless, say, it was a 'famous' car!). These 'innocent parties', or so the argument goes, should be allowed to complete their work, or not be forced to abandon it, not because of the freedom and sanctity of contract, but because of the potential damage to their reputational interests. Here, then, we have instances of scenarios being drawn on to generate normative insight – in part, through circumstantial judgement of character, eg understanding and feeling sympathy for the motives of the painter, the scientist and the garage proprietor – as to what additional values, vulnerabilities and interests may be at stake in setting limits on the freedom to accept or refuse a repudiation.

The fourth and final scenario is designed to rub further salt in the wounds of the Scottish decision:

> The decision of the Court below was a startling departure from principle. It was unjust to the company to assume that it could easily relet this space. If a parent repudiated his contract to send a boy to a school, the school would be justified in rejecting the repudiation, since it could not get another pupil at a moment's notice.[113]

No mention here is made of the fact that, in the present case, the repudiation was made in June, and the contract was due to begin in November. Nevertheless, it is suggested, the present case is similar to the above scenario: just like a school who is deprived of a pupil, so here the advertisers would be deprived of an advertiser, with it not being easy to find a replacement in either case. This scenario is being used analogically – as scenarios can be – but the scenario, and its utility, can also be treated independently of any analogy to the present case. The scenario here can be understood to be underscoring the financial interests of the 'innocent party', namely that, were they forced to accept a repudiation, they might be seriously harmed financially, possibly losing the opportunity of the business (the advertising spaces) altogether. As if to add an exclamation mark, counsel for White & Carter added that a repudiation, made before any performance was due, was 'writ in water'.[114]

ii. Counsel for McGregor

Counsel for the respondent, ie for McGregor, did not leave the above scenarios unanswered. Quite the contrary, he devised contrary scenarios, which were designed to generate normative insights that might support an argument for the other side, in favour of his client. A party faced with a repudiation did not have complete freedom to refuse a repudiation. The freedom in question was not a blanket one. One well-recognised limitation was where co-operation of the other party was required. This already showed, counsel argued, that the freedom was not absolute, ie that it was limited. But this was

[113] Ibid, 7.

[114] Citing *Howard v Pickford Tool Co Ltd* [1951] 1 KB 417. This is an interesting metaphor in its own right, though not one I shall examine here.

not the only relevant limitation. There were other values, vulnerabilities and interests at stake. It may not be easy to articulate these in abstract terms, but they were there. 'Public policy' considerations, counsel said, might be at stake. And here, counsel gave the scenario that was to play such a large part in the reasoning of the Lords in the House:

> An expert employed by a large company to travel abroad for the purpose of drafting an elaborate report should not be allowed to waste thousands of pounds in preparing it if the company had repudiated the contract before anything had been done under it. A far smaller amount of damages would compensate him for his loss, and any other view would only enable him to extort in settlement far more than reasonable compensation.[115]

There are at least two values, vulnerabilities and interests being generated as relevant by this scenario. One concerns the wastage of resources: should one allow an expert like this to travel abroad and incur thousands of pounds in cost? Should resources be wasted in this way? There is value, surely, this scenario suggests, in not wasting resources unduly. At stake is also something else: if one permits the expert to choose to refuse the repudiation, one creates a vulnerability, namely the vulnerability of the company to possible extortion by the expert, who can, protected as he would be the law, exploit that vulnerability by getting much more compensation than he deserves. Thus, counsel for McGregor suggested, the scenario shows that there is an important value and an important vulnerability at stake in determining whether there should be limitations placed on the freedom to accept or refuse a repudiation.

Notice that the scenario combines the four variables identified in the first part of this chapter: it has some narrativity, it is under-specified (although, in this case, it also involves specifying the potential motive of extortion by the expert), some particularity, and general plausibility. It calls upon readers to do something active with it, ie to fill it in further, possibly considering in what circumstances in might make normative sense to either force the expert to accept the company's repudiation, and in what circumstances it might make normative sense to allow them to refuse it. Although, as above, it does explicitly refer to possible motives (again, the potential extortion by the expert), nevertheless, it is brief and under-specified enough to enable further colouring, ie further additions or changes to the circumstances so as to cast a different light on the motivations of the characters involved. As we shall see, engaging in such colouring (of this precise scenario) is exactly what the majority and minority Lords do in this case.

Counsel for McGregor, however, did not stop there. He also addressed the scenarios introduced by counsel for White & Carter. He did so as follows:

> For example, a painter employed to paint a portrait, and then told not to do so, could not normally paint it if the subject would not sit for him. But suppose the subject was a public man and the painter could paint him without his consent when he appeared in public places? Or take the case of the garage owner employed to repair a car. What if the car were left parked in the street where he could get at it? In neither case should the law allow the unwanted services to be rendered because of such accidental circumstances.[116]

Here, counsel for McGregor sought to flip the scenarios offered originally by counsel for White & Carter. Far from conceding that in the case of the painter, the reputational

[115] *White & Carter* (1962), 9.
[116] Ibid, 9.

interests of the painter would be at stake, counsel suggested that what is also, if not more, at stake is the reputation of the subject of the painting. Should it be allowed that this 'public man' be painted by a painter without the public man's consent? The reasons why, ie the motivations of the public man that would make narrative and normative sense, are not made explicit. We, as readers of the scenario, are invited to fill them in, eg one can imagine it being recently discovered that the painter had been a member of some secret, violent society, perhaps a fascist society of painters, say; in those circumstances, coloured in this way, one can simulate the emotion of the public man, eg anger, disappointment, fear, perhaps, and then react emotionally to it, feeling sympathy for the public man and moral outrage at the painter. The point is that the scenario lends itself to being imagined, ie to being coloured in circumstantially, including simulating the emotions of the characters and then reacting emotionally to them, leading to the circumstantial judgement of character, and, finally, to the generation of normative insight, ie that there are reputational interests on both sides, and that there is vulnerability on the side of the repudiating party.

Not quite satisfied, perhaps, with these two scenarios, counsel for McGregor provided a third one, and one also designed to help generate a similar normative insight, though now arguably with even more at stake:

> Suppose a firm entered into a contract with an advertising agency to advertise a new soap on television and in the newspapers but soon afterwards discovered that it was liable to cause skin disease and took it off the market, cancelling the contract with the advertising agents. The advertising agents would not be entitled to go on with the advertising campaign although the contract was cancelled.[117]

Here, the scenario suggests, not only are the reputational interests of the repudiating party at stake (the soap maker's reputation) but so is the safety of the public. There are, counsel wants to insist, 'public policy' considerations, ones that cannot always be specified in advance (for it depends on the circumstances), and these may be relevant in determining the limits on the acceptance or refusal of a repudiation.

Counsel for McGregor then concluded: 'Justice would be done here simply by a claim for damages for breach of contract'.[118] What White & Carter were doing was seeking, effectively, to impose a penalty on the poor Scottish garage business. Not only, then, might 'the resources of the nation' be 'wasted', and not only might there be 'public policy' considerations, but also, in this case, it ought to be seen that White & Carter were unduly aggressive, seeking but to 'swell [their] own profits', 'manufacturing goods which no one wanted'.[119] They were, in short, doing nothing less than 'seeking … its own pound of flesh':

Portia said in *The Merchant of Venice* (Act IV, Scene 1):

> Of a strange nature is the suit you follow;
> Yet in such rule, that the Venetian law
> Cannot impugn you as you do proceed.

[117] Ibid, 10.
[118] Ibid.
[119] Ibid.

But the law of Scotland could impugn the company.[120]

Counsel for both sides, then, came out swinging in this case. They did so with a mixture of forms of language and cultural allusion. What I have emphasised above is the use, made by counsel, of scenarios. Of course, there is an obvious sense in which the scenarios are being used to persuade: judges are being invited, through the scenarios, to see the present case via the filter of one or another scenario, and thereby to make their judgements on behalf of the relevant party. That use of the scenarios is undeniable. However, that is not their only use. We must remember the pragmatic context of adjudication: counsel for the parties argue strenuously for their clients; they use as many devices of persuasion as they can; but it is then up to the judges to consider both sides, and, to do not only justice in the present case, but also to respect the law's past as well as care for its quality in the future. With that difficult balancing task in mind, the judges approach the scenarios differently: their engagement with them is part of their inquiry into what values, vulnerabilities and interests might be at stake in this case and in cases potentially like it in the future. How did the Lords do that in this case?

C. The Judgement

In what follows, I focus on three of the five opinions: those by Lord Justices Reid, Morton and Keith. Lord Justice Hodson, with whom Lord Justice Tucker agreed, did not address the scenario, choosing simply to reinforce the commitment to the general principle that the party faced with the repudiation had the freedom to choose whether to accept or refuse a repudiation, and that the limitations placed on this freedom were very limited, eg perhaps only extending to situations where the performance of the contract required the co-operation of the other party. The other three Lords, however, engaged in debate and discussion, and especially thanks to and with a scenario, as to what potential values, vulnerabilities and interests were at stake in imposing some limitations on the freedom of the innocent party.

i. Lord Reid

After summarising the facts, Lord Reid began his opinion with an apparently confident statement:

> The general rule cannot be in doubt. It was settled in Scotland at least as early as 1848, and it has been authoritatively stated time and again in both Scotland and England. If one party to a contract repudiates it in the sense of making it clear to the other party that he refuses or will refuse to carry out his part of the contract, the other party, the innocent party, has an option. He may accept the repudiation and sue for damages for breach of contract whether or not the time for performance has come; or he may if he chooses disregard or refuse to accept it and the contract remains in full effect.[121]

[120] Ibid, 11.
[121] Ibid, 11–12.

There were, again, multiple authorities to this effect, stated Lord Reid. In all these authorities, however, no co-operation by the repudiating party was required. Thus, although it is true that there are many cases in which the courts do not interfere, it is also true that in all these cases the co-operation of the repudiating party was not required. This suggests, of course, that the freedom of the party faced with the repudiation is not absolute: there are some circumstances in which the freedom can be curtailed. Then Lord Reid says as follows:

> Developing this argument, the respondent [counsel for McGregor] points out that, in most cases, the innocent party cannot complete the contract himself, without the other party doing, allowing or accepting something, and that it is purely fortuitous that the appellants can do so in this case. In most cases, by refusing co-operation, the party in breach can compel the innocent party to restrict his claim to damages. Then it was said that, even where the innocent party can complete the contract without such co-operation, it is against the public interest that he should be allowed to do so. An example was developed in argument. A company might engage an expert to go abroad and prepare an elaborate report, and then repudiate the contract before anything was done. To allow such an expert then to waste thousands of pounds in preparing the report cannot be right of a much smaller sum of damages would give him full compensation for his loss. It would merely enable the expert to extort a settlement giving him far more than reasonable compensation.[122]

Out of all the scenarios that were introduced, the one that is picked up by Lord Reid, and, as we shall see, also by Lords Morton and Keith, is the scenario of the expert travelling abroad. Lord Reid virtually verbatim repeats the scenario as presented by counsel for McGregor. Lord Reid does not use the language of 'public policy', as counsel had, but instead refers to 'public interest', but otherwise, the wording is almost identical. Both the potentially relevant value (of wastage of resources) and the potentially relevant vulnerability of the guilty party (their being exploited by the expert extracting a settlement beyond reasonable compensation) are mentioned.

Having introduced the scenario, Lord Reid does not immediately discuss it. He goes on, first, to discuss the *Langford* case, which, as above, had loomed so large for the Second Division court in Scotland. Lord Reid is not especially complimentary about it. Aspects of the reasoning, he says, he finds 'difficult to explain'.[123] He concludes that it was wrongly decided.[124] Nevertheless, despite these strong statements, Lord Reid is clearly not entirely convinced that the case is without merit. Similarly, he is not entirely convinced that there is not something in the public interest argument, and thus that there may indeed be certain values, vulnerabilities and interests at stake that render it appropriate to introduce, in certain cases, limitations on the freedom of the party faced with the repudiation to accept or refuse a repudiation. In a long passage, which it will be useful to set out in full, he says the following:

> The other ground [upon which the authority of *Langford* could be defended] would be that there is some general equitable principle or element of public policy which requires this limitation of the contractual rights of the innocent party. It may well be that, if it can be shown

[122] Ibid, 13.
[123] Ibid, 14.
[124] Ibid.

> that a person has no legitimate interest, financial or otherwise, in performing the contract rather than claiming damages, he ought not to be allowed to saddle the other party with an additional burden with no benefit to himself. If a party has no interest to enforce a stipulation, he cannot in general enforce it: so it might be said that, if a party has no interest to insist on a particular remedy, he ought not to be allowed to insist on it. And, just as a party is not allowed to enforce a penalty, so he ought not to be allowed to penalise the other party by taking one course when another is equally advantageous to him. If I may revert to the example I gave of a company engaging an expert to write an elaborate report and then repudiating before anything was done, it might be that the company could show that the expert had no substantial or legitimate interest in carrying out the work rather than accepting damages: I would think that the *de minimis* principle would apply in determining whether his interest was substantial and that he might have a legitimate interest other than an immediate financial interest. But if the expert had no such interest then that might be regarded as a proper case for the exercise of the generable equitable jurisdiction of the court. But that is not this case. Here, the respondent did not set out to prove that the appellants had no legitimate interest in completing the contract and claiming the contract price rather than claiming damages; there is nothing in the findings of fact to support such a case, and it seems improbable that any such case could have been proved. If is, in my judgement, impossible to say that the appellants should be deprived of their right to claim the contract price merely because the benefit to them, as against claiming damages and re-letting their advertising space, might be small in comparison with the loss to the respondent: that is the most that could be said in favour of the respondent. Parliament has on many occasions relieved parties from certain kinds of improvident or oppressive contracts, but the common law can only do that in very limited circumstances. Accordingly, I am unable to avoid the conclusion that this appeal must be allowed.[125]

This long passage is the crucial and final one in Lord Reid's judgement. In it, Lord Reid returns to the above scenario, clearly wrestling with the possible dissonance between it and a decision in favour of White & Carter. One could argue that all the scenario does is that it functions as an analogy for Lord Reid, and one which he distinguishes from the facts of the present case. That may well be part of what the scenario does, and, as I suggested earlier in this chapter, some of the value of scenarios, especially with respect to their role in the justification of present decisions, can be captured by analogical reasoning. Nevertheless, this is not the only value that can be attributed to the scenario.

Arguably, what the scenario also does is acknowledge that there may well be values, vulnerabilities and interests at stake beyond the freedom and sanctity of contract, which courts perhaps ought to take into account when considering whether to place limitations on the general freedom to refuse or accept a repudiation. Lord Reid does not specify what those values, vulnerabilities or interests might be, though he does suggest that it may be unfair to allow one party to penalise another, when they could be compensated by damages. But what Lord Reid does, in order to deal with the scenario first proposed by counsel for McGregor, is to say that, in certain circumstances, it may be that the repudiating party can show that the party faced with the repudiation has no legitimate interest, 'other than an immediate financial interest', in pursuing the continued performance of the contract.

[125] Ibid, 14–15.

Lord Reid is very clear that the circumstances in question do not arise in this case. Here, Lord Reid says, McGregor did not, but also most probably could not, show that White & Carter did not have a legitimate interest. In all likelihood, Lord Reid suggests, White & Carter did have an interest that went beyond 'immediate financial interest' (though, what this might be, is left unexplained). The analogical work, then, might be thought to be poor: the way Lord Reid distinguishes the scenario from the facts of the present case is not entirely persuasive. But, in a sense, that is not the point of the scenario: the point, instead, is to suggest that there may well be values, vulnerabilities and interests at stake, such that there may well be cases where the courts can intervene and limit the freedom of the innocent party.

One cannot, then, see the full value of the scenario when limited solely to the decision in the present case, or to its role as an analogy. Lord Reid is engaging in inquiry, communicating also to future readers, and opening a window of opportunity for advocates of guilty parties to argue that their case fits within those circumstances in which they can show that the party faced with the repudiation only has 'immediate financial interests', and no 'legitimate interests', for refusing the repudiation and continuing with the contract. What is at stake is the quality of the law in the future, and whether it will be capable of doing justice in particular cases. The matter is difficult: it is difficult to tell what those circumstances might be. One will have to wait and see, and collect more cases in which this issue arises.

The scenario helps in this process of inquiry. It may be, Lord Reid says, that in the case of the expert going abroad, the company could show that he had no legitimate interest, beyond an immediate financial one, to go abroad, incur all those expenses, and write the unwanted report. The scenario is not determinative in this respect. As above, one could colour the scenario in such a way that one could see the expert's interests as 'legitimate', eg imagine that his reputational interests were at stake (reverting back to one of the scenarios introduced by counsel: perhaps the expert is a scientist, and his reputation would suffer if he did not write this report). The scenario, again, does not provide the answers: it is, instead, something we can think with; something we can play with (colour with) together, in different ways, in pursuit of the articulation of the relevant values, vulnerabilities and interests at stake in this area.

As noted above, Lord Reid was in the majority in this case. Nevertheless, he was also a minority in that majority, for Lord Tucker agreed explicitly not with him, but instead with Lord Hodson. What Lord Reid said, then, about legitimate interest being a potential limiting factor in the freedom to refuse or accept a repudiation was, strictly speaking, obiter. However, as we shall see, this was yet another example where obiter has gone on to be highly influential, and indeed much more so than the decision on the facts in the case.[126]

ii. *Lord Morton*

The minority in the House, though defeated, did not go down without a fight. Lords Morton and Keith argued forcefully that the decision should go the other way, and that

[126] Not everyone agrees that Lord Reid's remarks are not within the ratio of the case: see *London Borough of Hounslow v Twickenham Garden Developments Ltd* [1970] 3 All ER 326, 343, per Megarry J.

the law should include further limitations (beyond that of cases where co-operation of the other party is required) on the freedom of the party faced with the repudiation. In doing so, they reverted to the scenario that had been introduced by counsel for McGregor, and that had so concerned Lord Reid. Lord Morton said:

> I think that this is a case of great importance, although the claim is for a comparatively small sum. If the appellants are right, strange consequences follow in any case in which, under a repudiated contract, services are to be performed by the party who has not repudiated it, so long as he is able to perform those services without the co-operation of the repudiating party. Many examples of such contracts could be given. One, given in the course of the argument and already mentioned by my noble and learned friend, Lord Reid, is the engagement of an expert to go abroad and write a report on some subject for a substantial fee plus his expenses. If the appellants succeed in the present case, it must follow that the expert is entitled to incur the expense of going abroad, to write his unwanted report, and then to recover the fee and expenses, even if the other party has plainly repudiated the contract before any expense has been incurred.[127]

Here, Lord Morton effectively repeats the scenario as originally given, though this time without reference to the possibility of the exploitation by the expert of the vulnerability of the company (via the extortion of a favourable and unfair settlement).

Lord Morton went on, towards the end of his judgement, to say that 'The course of action followed by the appellants [White & Carter] seems to me unreasonable and oppressive', though he was quick to add that this 'it is not on that ground that I would reject their claim'.[128] That ground, instead, appeared to be that the appellants 'were bound to take steps to minimise their loss'; they could have, and ought to have, attempted to 'procure another advertiser'; instead, they 'deliberately went on to incur expense and perform unwanted services'.[129] For Lord Morton, it seems, the primary ground upon which a decision in favour of McGregor could be justified, and also the primary value at stake in potentially alike future cases, was that of the duty to mitigate resources (and thus, also, the value of not wasting resources unduly). A background consideration, though, which clearly loomed large for Lord Morton, was the behaviour of the appellants: there was something about it, even if it was difficult to articulate exactly what in abstract terms, that rendered it an appropriate set of circumstances in which to intervene and require the acceptance of the repudiation by White & Carter.

iii. Lord Keith

Lord Keith agreed with Lord Morton, but he also went beyond him in his treatment of the scenario. Like Lord Morton, he stresses the importance of the case. At stake was not just justice in the present case, though this case, and, as we shall see, the scenario too, showed that there was something normatively inadequate about the law, especially insofar as it might be said to recognise only the co-operation-requiring limitation on the freedom to accept or refuse a repudiation. But how might we articulate what

[127] *White & Carter* (1962), 16.
[128] Ibid, 17.
[129] Ibid, 16.

this normative inadequacy is, and how might we repair it? How could we generate normative insight here as to what might be the values, vulnerabilities and interests at stake in this case and in other potentially alike cases in the future?

Lord Keith approached this question in a number of ways. One was to tackle it head on by referring to the facts of the case. For instance:

> The contract was to come into operation on the 2nd of November 1957, when the previous contract expired. But it involved, in the absence of other advertising matter supplied by the defender, the display by the appellants of at least the name, business and address of the advertiser. I should hesitate to say that any contractor was entitled to display these particulars of the defender against his wish, even if the withholding of his assent be in breach of contract.[130]

The passage is interesting because it suggests that there might be values, vulnerabilities and interests at stake that, in certain circumstances, trump the value of the freedom and sanctity of contract. Arguably, these are not merely reputational interests, as some of the above scenarios sought to suggest. Some more basic freedom or liberty of persons, if not their dignity (involved in the uses that can be made of their 'name') as well as privacy (the display of their 'address'), could be said, on the facts of this case, to be endangered. Can one party really impose their will on another so blatantly? Can freedom and sanctity of contract really justify one party imposing their will in such a manner on another?

One can see here that engagement with the facts of a present case can also help generate normative insight, ie that one need not necessarily have resource to a scenario. Similarly, one can also have recourse to past cases: and Lord Keith does that, examining a number of past cases where it might be said that allowing a party to refuse a repudiation places certain important values, vulnerabilities and interests at risk. One of these involved the metaphor that had been employed by counsel for White & Carter, namely, that a repudiation before any performance was 'writ in water'. It is interesting to observe, though I shall not further analyse, that Lord Keith goes out of his way to contextualise the metaphor and argue that it does not help counsel in the present case.[131]

In addition, however, to engaging with past cases and with the facts of the present case, it can sometimes be helpful to step aside from facts of cases, and have the freedom to imagine, including vary, and thus play with, the circumstances of short, fictional narratives, ie scenarios. And Lord Keith does exactly that. He does so by not only reverting to the scenario introduced by counsel for McGregor, and engaged with also by Lords Reid and Morton (above), but also by varying it, embellishing or exaggerating it, or we might say, colouring it:

> I find the argument advanced for the appellants a somewhat startling one. If it is right, it would seem that a man who has contracted to go to Hongkong [sic] at his own expense and make a report, in return for remuneration of £10,000, and who, before the date fixed for the start of the journey, and perhaps before he had incurred any expense, is informed by the other contracting party that he has cancelled or repudiated the contract, is entitled to set off

[130] Ibid, 20–21.
[131] Ibid, 21.

> for Hongkong and produce his report in order to claim in debt the stipulated sum. Such a result is not, in my opinion, in accordance with principle or authority, and cuts across the rule that where one party is in breach of contract the other must take steps to minimise the loss sustained by the breach.[132]

Lord Keith adds further details – further particulars – to the scenario. As he does so, he colours it further: the details do not just add particulars for the sake of it, but instead work to invite the reader to infer, even more so than in the scenario as originally described by counsel, that what the expert does here is wrong and inappropriate. The expert is now said to be going to Hong Kong and incurring £10,000 pounds (a very considerable sum). Lord Keith, then, pushes the scenario further, with the extra additions (the extra colours) introducing some more implausibility (how often, after all, especially in the 1960's, would a company employ an expert to fly all the way from London to Hong Kong, and this for £10,000?).

Of course, it is undeniable that Lord Keith deploys the scenario in part in order to persuade: we should find, he says, in favour of the respondents (McGregor); if we do not, we would effectively be allowing for conduct such as that of the expert's. But that is not the only value of the scenario: again, we must remember the pragmatic, especially diachronic and social, dimensions of adjudication. The judges are engaged in the difficult task of balancing respect for the law's past, doing justice in the instant case, and caring for the quality of the law in the future.

For Lord Keith, that first aspect – respecting the law's past – had a personal significance, for, as he admits, he was one of the judges deciding the *Langford* case,[133] which Lord Reid appeared to be (quite disrespectfully one might argue) dismissing as wrongly decided. Clearly, this matters for Lord Keith, but we ought not to be that cynical: as noted above, from the outset of his opinion, he underscores the importance of this case for contract law.

At stake is also justice in the instant case and the quality of the law in future potentially alike cases. Lord Keith's use of the scenario (which also illustrates how prone to, how available for, variability scenarios are) is designed to generate, perhaps more forcefully – for its greater particularity invites more affective, sensory and kinesic engagement from the reader – insight as to the values, vulnerabilities and interests at stake. One such value is clearly the wastage of resources, but there is also a hint that there is something irresponsible, perhaps reckless, something unreasonable, if not oppressive, in the behaviour of the expert; something, one might say, that is too unilateral, not reciprocal enough, too disrespectful of the wishes of the other party. There is, then, perhaps another value at stake here: the value of basic respect for persons and inter-personal decency. Again, this may be something very difficult to articulate, and it may also be undesirable to articulate it in any great generality. Allowing a scenario to speak, instead, may be wiser, and also humbler: it allows future readers, in imagining it, to generate from it further normative insight.

[132] Ibid, 24.
[133] Ibid, 23.

D. The Scenario after *White & Carter*

We see, then, in this case, how scenarios can contribute to inquiry, ie to the experimental generation of insight as to what values, vulnerabilities and interests might be at stake in a case and in others potentially like it in the future. There is, however, more to this story. *White & Carter* generated considerable interest amongst readers, both in academia[134] and in future cases. It did so precisely because of how the judges in this case, and especially Lords Reid, Morton and Keith, engaged in inquiry, and especially with respect to the scenario mentioned above. I cannot give a full account of this more diachronically and socially extended engagement with the normative insights generated by the scenario; but, given the overall argument of this book, namely that we cannot reduce the value of artefacts and related processes of imagination to a single case, a brief discussion is appropriate.

i. *Hounslow v Twickenham*

One striking example of a later case in which explicit acknowledgement was made not only of the above-mentioned scenario, but also of the multiple scenarios, in *White & Carter* is the case of *London Borough of Hounslow v Twickenham Garden Developments Ltd.*[135]

The issue in this case was whether the contractor, Twickenham Garden Developments, could, despite a repudiation by the Borough, 'insist on retaining possession of the site and completing the contract'.[136] Counsel for the contractor, basing his argument on *White & Carter*, insisted that the contractor could refuse to accept the repudiation and continue to perform it, even with the Borough protesting against that.[137] Justice Megarry acknowledged that the majority in *White & Carter* (strictly speaking, Lord's Hodson's judgement), did not qualify the general right to refuse or accept a repudiation. However, he went on to say that such qualifications were present in the judgements of Lord Reid, Morton and Keith. Justice Megarry noted, in particular, both the scenario (in Lord Keith's version) of the expert going to Hong Kong and producing a report for £10,000, as well as the other scenarios in the case. Justice Megarry then reported that, in addition, a number of other scenarios were offered in the course of argument in *Hounslow*. These were ones that extended the *White & Carter* scenarios to others involving land (which were closer to the facts of the case in *Hounslow*):

> A contract to erect buildings on land is let; a few days later the landowner unexpectedly learns that he can obtain a far more advantageous planning permission for developing the land, and he thereupon repudiates the contract; but the contractor insists on performing it, even though the landowner must then either abandon the more valuable development and

[134] See, eg, O'Sullivan (2017); Nienaber (1962); Liu (2011); Rowan (2019); and New Zealand Law Reform Committee (1983).

[135] *London Borough of Hounslow v Twickenham Garden Developments Ltd* [1970] 3 All ER 326. Subsequent references are to *Hounslow* (1970).

[136] Ibid, 341, per Megarry J.

[137] Ibid, 340.

accept the far less profitable buildings or else pull those buildings down when they have been completed and then carry out the more fruitful scheme. Another landowner lets a contract to erect an extravagant building which his wealth can afford; before much work has been done his fortune collapses, and he can pay for the building only by using all that is left to him; yet the contractor insists on performing the contract. A third landowner contracts with an artist to paint extensive frescoes in a new building over a period of two years; the landowner then receives a handsome offer for the unadorned building, provided vacant possession is delivered forthwith; yet the artist insists on painting on for the rest of the two years.[138]

We have here three additional scenarios, now added to the scenarios in *White & Carter*. All of these, said Justice Megarry, 'suggest that there may well be limits to the doctrine'.[139] According to Lords Morton and Keith these limits included 'the duty to mitigate damages', with Justice Megarry adding that 'he who is bound to mitigate can hardly be entitled to insist on aggravating'.[140] They also included, as had already been accepted prior to *White & Carter*, cases where co-operation of the other party is required. But there was more. Here, Justice Megarry referred to Lord Reid's 'cautiously expressed' further limitation:

The other limitation, cautiously expressed, was that 'it may well be' that if a person has no legitimate financial or other interest in performing the contract rather than claiming damages, 'he ought not to be allowed to saddle the other party with an additional burden with no benefit to himself'; and this principle might apply to the example of the expert report. However, no such absence of a legitimate interest in the agents [ie White & Carter] had been established, and so the possible principle did not apply.[141]

Justice Megarry was, also, cautious: 'It seems to me', he said, 'that the decision [in *White & Carter*] is one which I should be slow to apply to any category of case not fairly within the contemplation of their Lordships'.[142] Indeed, he went on to conclude that the *White & Carter* case did not apply to the facts before him. In part, this was because in *Hounslow*, the contract could not really be performed without co-operation from the Borough.

However, Justice Megarry did not stop there. He also suggested that the key point was not whether the repudiating party had to consent to giving access to land. The limitation to the general principle that one could refuse or accept repudiation was not limited solely by active co-operation of this kind (in addition to mitigation). Something else was also doing the normative work of constraining the freedom of choice. Justice Megarry sought to grapple with this with the following scenario:

Suppose that A, who owns a large and valuable painting, contracts with B, a picture restorer, to restore it over a period of three months. Before the work is begun, A receives a handsome offer from C to purchase the picture, subject to immediate delivery of the picture in its unrestored state, C having grave suspicions of B's competence. If the work of restoration is to be done in A's house, he can effectually exclude B by refusing to admit him to the house; without A's 'co-operation' to this extent B cannot perform his contract. But what if the picture stands

[138] Ibid, 341.
[139] Ibid.
[140] Ibid,
[141] Ibid, 342.
[142] Ibid.

> in A's locked barn, the key of which he has lent to B so that he may come and go freely, or if the picture has been removed to B's premises? Can B insist in these cases in performing his contract, even though this makes it impossible for A to accept C's offer? In the case of the barn, A's co-operation may perhaps be said to be requisite to the extent of not barring B's path to the barn or putting another lock on the door; but if the picture is on B's premises, no active co-operation by A is needed. Nevertheless, the picture is A's property, and I find it difficult to believe that Lord Reid intended to restrict the concept of 'co-operation' to active co-operation.[143]

We have here, the return, though in a different version, of one of the multiple scenarios contemplated in *White & Carter*, that of the picture restorer. As with the other scenarios, Justice Megarry constructs it with a view to generating normative insight, ie insight about values, vulnerabilities and interests might be at stake.

Here, although he does not elaborate much on the scenario further, Justice Megarry is arguably inquiring into just what are the normative sources of limitation of choice on the party faced with the repudiation. In the scenario above, this source of limitation cannot be said to be mitigation; nor can it be said to be co-operation, for, in the version with the painting being in the barn, B can access it without A's co-operation (understood in the narrow sense of actively enabling access to the property). But if not any of those, then just what is the normative source of the limitation? What might be the relevant value, vulnerability or interest that suggests to us that B ought not to be allowed to restore the painting, even if B can access it easily in A's barn or indeed on B's own premises? Again, it may be unwise and immodest to attempt a general answer: it is better, in the adjudicative context, to let the scenario be read and imagined by future readers. We could argue, possibly, that were B to insist on restoring the painting, he would be, in some sense, interfering with A's property. But is that the normative rub of the scenario? Something more seems to be at stake: eg B's recklessness about, or total indifference to, A's liberty, ie A's choice, even at some cost, ie damages, not to have the painting restored by B, in order to be able to sell it to C. There is, once more, something too unilateral, too aggressively a-reciprocal in B's conduct vis-à-vis A. Again, it is difficult to articulate, but having the scenario, and imagining it, helps us get at what it might be.

ii. Travelling Scenarios

White & Carter, and especially Lord Reid's remarks, including how he applied them to the scenario of the expert, have been reiterated in innumerable cases since.[144]

[143] Ibid.

[144] See, eg, *Cavendish Square Holding BV v El Makdessi; Parking Eye Ltd v Beavis* [2016] 2 All ER 519; *Stocznia Gdanska SA v Latvian Shipping Co and others* [1998] 1 All ER 883; *Deacons (a firm) v Bridge* [1984] 2 All ER 19; *Clea Shipping Corp v Bulk Oil International Ltd; The Alaskan Trader* [1984] 1 All ER 129; *Bunge Corpn v Tradax SA* [1981] 2 All ER 513; *MSC Mediterranean Shipping Company S.A. v Cottonex Anstalt* [2016] All ER (D) 159 (Jul); *Sunrise Brokers LLP v Rodgers; Reichman and another v Beveridge and another* [2006] All ER (D) 186 (Dec); *Carbopego-Abastecimento de Combustiveis SA v Amci Export Corporation* [2006] All ER (D) 227 (Jan); *Ocean Marine Navigation Ltd v Koch Carbon Inc (The Dynamic)* [2003] All ER (D) 564 (Jul); *The Puerto Buitrago* [1976] 1 Lloyd's Rep 250; *Gator Shipping Corp v Trans-Asiatic Oil Ltd SA and Occidental Shipping establishment (The Odenfeld)* [1978] 2 Lloyd's Rep 357; *Isabella Shipowner SA v Shagang Shipping Co Ltd (The Aquafaith)* [2012] 2 All ER (Comm) 461; *Ministry of Sound (Ireland) Ltd v World Online Ltd* [2003] EWHC 2178 (Ch); *Indian Airlines Limited v GIA International Limited* [2002] EWHC 2361 (Comm).

I do not suggest that the legacy of *White & Carter* is all due to the scenarios in it, including the scenario famously (as it turned out) discussed by Lord Reid. Part of it has to do with the fact that Lord Reid did attempt to generalise, introducing the language of 'legitimate interest', and subsequent courts, and commentators, have certainly engaged with this language more so than they have played with the scenarios in *White & Carter*. Nevertheless, the scenarios, and especially the scenario as discussed by Lord Reid, has certainly played its part in contributing to inquiry in this area of the law, not only in *White & Carter*, but also considerably beyond.

Scenarios travel perhaps less well than the other case studies examined in this book. They do, however, lend themselves to the social dimensions of inquiry: they thrive in variability, which includes not only the construction of variations of a particular scenario, but also the generation of multiple, alternative scenarios. They are, as it were, made for being played with together: whether that be interactively between advocates and judges in a case, or between judges across time, or indeed amongst a wider range of persons, eg academics, law students, law-reformers and perhaps, in some cases, members of the public. They are accessible, and they are fun and pleasurable to process, even if they also often help us with the most difficult, most intractable of normative problems.

Of course, as with the other artefacts and related processes of imagination discussed in this book, scenarios are not inherently beneficial for inquiry; they can also be obstacles to it. This can occur if they are processed too quickly, becoming thereby nothing but means of persuasion. An advocate constructs a scenario and a judge is impressed by it. Having, say, simulated the emotions of the characters in it, and reacted to it in particular ways, thereby also evaluating the actions in the scenario accordingly, the judge goes on to apply it, by analogy, to the facts of the present case. When this happens, judges can be, as it were, overly influenced by a scenario. They can process it too quickly, with too little accompanying reflexivity. That can happen with scenarios, but it does not always. Sometimes, if not often, scenarios are both experienced and reflected on simultaneously: they are imagined, in the sense in which I have urged we can understand that term. They are, as it were, processed with one eye on their being artefacts, signalling artifice and thereby involving us in entering a distinctive epistemic frame, and with one eye on participating in them, ie in the form of affective, sensory and kinesic participation. If they are processed in this way, and especially if they are also played with, with variations introduced, colours invented, circumstances changed, as well as alternative, multiple scenarios considered, then scenarios really can be beneficial to inquiry.

Conclusion

No matter how many plans one makes, and no matter how often one tries out the arguments in front of many different audiences, the course of writing a book still generates its own surprises. This is, or so I have found, both the thrill and the difficulty of writing. Plan as much as you like, but the moment your hands begin typing, the moment they descend to and touch the keyboard, you do not quite know what will come out. In concluding this book, I would like to retrace some of those surprises, especially those which strike me now as offering promising avenues for further work. My beloved high school English teacher always reminded us: conclusions are opportunities to open some windows. Here, then, are some windows onto paths I stumbled upon, but have not been able to take. They will inevitably strike readers as speculative, as indeed they are; but they are also, having now finished the book, what I can see, even if on the distant and indistinct horizon.

I. Legal Techné: Couplings of Form and Cognition

When I began writing this book, my focus was almost entirely on imagination, roughly, as I understood it then, on the cognitive processes that individual persons engage in and experience when they imagine. However, what I found as I kept working was that I had to pay just as much attention to the forms of language that enable and invite such processes. This was crucial, also, to capturing the ways in which imagination is not only, or even mainly, an exercise of an individual mind on a one-off occasion, but is also something we do together, both interactively and collectively, and that we do repeatedly, variably, and sometimes over long stretches of time.

What I did not anticipate until I began to write was just how rich and complex the relations between forms of language and processes of imagination were. The more I wrote, the more I realised that the most interesting discoveries were to be had not when I focused on one of the two, ie either on forms of language or on cognition, or, in the terminology of this book, either on artefacts or on imagination. Rather, the most interesting discoveries were to be found in examining the dynamic relations between them. Hence, when I was writing about features of artefacts, ie the different ways in which they signal artifice, and the different ways in which they call on us to do something with them, I found, much to my surprise, that I was writing as much about cognition as I was about forms of language. This was, of course, 'cognition' in a broad sense, and thus inclusive of its phenomenology, as well as its social and diachronic dimensions. Similarly so when writing about processes of imagination: this required close attention to the forms of language with which we imagine, but also to the forms of language that guide us, to some extend beyond our control, in our imaginings.

In this book, I forced myself to be disciplined and examine only four artefacts, with related processes of imagination: fictions, metaphors, figures and scenarios. However, in view of the importance, as above, of the dynamic relations between artefacts and imagination, an alternative approach would be to construct objects of scholarly attention that are inherently couplings of form and cognition. We can think of such couplings as different *techné*, to recall the Ancient Greek term. Thus, we might call them 'crafts of legal making'. For example: instead of talking about names, one might speak of *naming*. Naming, as a *techné*, is the result of the coupling of both forms and cognition. Naming, we might say, is a craft of legal making; it is something we do actively, and again, not only or even mainly individually, but especially interactively and collectively. Forms of naming, such as capitalised letters as in personal names, assist and guide us, but we also transform those forms as we make with them. In that sense, the forms we use are not tools: to characterise them as such would be to under-estimate their power and to over-estimate ours. We do not control how forms can affect us: they can do so often in surprising ways, and with effects we only come to recognise much later. Naming, then, cannot be entirely explained away as a matter of form; neither can it be understood solely as a mode of cognition. Instead, naming is better approached as a *techné*, and thus a dynamic coupling of form and cognition.

There are surely many other such *techné* that we could identify as important, some of which may be more important to certain legal traditions than others. For instance, we could speak of *alluding* as a *techné*, including the various many ways in which we cite, cross-reference, or hint at the presence of a relevant resource.[1] We could speak of *conversing*, and thus of the different uses to which interactive speech is put to in a legal context, eg including not only the interaction between judges and advocates in a courtroom, but all the various uses of dialogue, including fictional dialogue, in judgements. Other such *techné* might include: *remembering*, and thus drawing on the arts of memory, both linguistically and visually, but perhaps also materially and ritualistically; *plotting*, as when we draw on the temporal and spatial arts of narrative emplotment, including in different generic modes; *archetyping*, as in the arts of creating simplified characters, and relations between them; *distinction-making*, connecting to the ancient art of dialectic; *indexing*, and other modes of finding and labelling; and *taxonomising*, eg as when we create areas of the law, including treating some as central, eg contract, property and tort, and others as marginal, eg succession. It is a slapdash and ad hoc list, certainly. But it may give a sense of the possibilities, and of the importance of the broad idea of *techné*, ie something that captures the dynamic inter-relation between form and cognition, manifested in particular ways, including particular material ways, in particular legal traditions.

II. The Variability of Artefacts and Imagination

Writing this book, I felt again and again the urgent need to historicise artefacts and related processes of imagining. In the second part of this book, I tried, though in a

[1] Citing could itself be related to a broader cultural history of quotation: see, eg, recently Knowles (2018).

very limited way, to occasionally point to how a more historically-sophisticated and historically-sensitive approach to fictions, metaphors, figures and scenarios could be undertaken. Artefacts, and related processes of imagination, change over time. These include quantitative changes, eg the degree of fictionalisation, or the degree to which scenarios are deployed. They also include qualitative changes, eg how do the sources of metaphors change over time (say, from biological to architectural), or what are the changing gender dynamics of figures?

There are also all kinds of links between, on the one hand, the use, and also the degree of use, of such artefacts and related processes of imagination in the legal context, and, on the other hand, other practices, including literary practices, science, technology, political economy,[2] and much else. Literary historians have called for such historicisation with respect to certain kinds of forms, eg Franco Moretti on the clue,[3] or Monika Fludernik on how narratives have relocated attention from one location to another.[4] We could, surely, do the same for artefacts and related processes of imagination. Although legal practices often do develop their own relative autonomy, ie their own relatively autonomous technical languages, knowledge practices as well as professional habits and rituals, these are never completely divorced from changes in other contexts. As a growing number of cultural legal historians have shown, even the most technical of legal forms and operations, eg practices of validity, say, or all kinds of practices of argumentation, are dependent on material forms, eg on genres, styles and rituals of media.[5]

What I found, as I was writing this book, was that there was such richness to be mined, on the histories of both artefacts and imagination. Writing about the imagination, for example, in both of the two limbs of imagination, ie entering a distinctive epistemic frame and participating, I found that there was so much more variety than I could point to. With respect to entering a distinctive epistemic frame, there were clearly many degrees and kinds of reflexivity, doubt, and epistemic norms and commitments that could be temporarily and selectively suspended.

One of the key surprises was being reminded, constantly, of just how complex the overlap was between what we refer to as conscious or less-than-conscious mental processes: one simply could not make a sharp divide between them. As John Searle argued some time ago,[6] there were many degrees of consciousness, and any one cognitive process often swung from being, at certain moments, reflexive of itself, to being placed in the background of one's reflexive awareness. Alan Palmer, who takes inspiration from Searle's recognition of varieties of consciousness, has said:

> There is a wide spectrum of attention along which mental events move, and this movement to and fro along the scale of attention is very fluid. The rigid dichotomy of reflective and non-reflective thought does not reflect the complexity and the fluidity of the mind.[7]

[2] For an example of relations between genre, action and political economy, see Halpern (2017).

[3] Moretti (2000).

[4] Fludernik (2003).

[5] See, eg, Vesting (2018) for an excellent overview of, and contribution to, this literature. See also, recently, the six volumes of Watt (2019).

[6] Searle (1992).

[7] Palmer (2004), 106.

As Palmer also observes, consciousness might not be the right term. One might speak, instead, of varying practices of 'attention', with some things being sometimes in the centre or the foreground, and sometimes in the periphery or the background. If one does insist on speaking of consciousness, then one must speak, at least, of its great variety and variability,[8] including historically.[9] Similarly so with epistemic norms and commitments or, even more generally, epistemic attitudes: there were many different kinds of epistemic moods or tones, and many different related kinds of epistemic practices. There were entire realms of such moods, tones, attitudes and practices that went beyond the regular focus on assertion, as supported by the epistemic attitude of belief, eg a whole variety of tentative, fragile and anxious ones. Many of these may well best be captured by emotions, such as hope, despair, wonder, awe, trepidation, embarrassment, or humility. One could also, in this context, speak of variable speeds of consciousness, and pay close attention to when we proceed slowly, with difficulty, often with some imbalance and disorientation, and when, instead, we plough on, quickly, almost rhythmically and ritualistically. Such variable speeds, in turn, can be closely connected to forms and their effects of language or genre, as indeed the Russian formalists[10] observed long ago and much before the work done in contemporary psychology and philosophy on variable speeds of thought.

Some important work, in this vein, has been done with respect to the imagination. For example, I found the work of Christopher Collins to be especially striking,[11] and I wish I could have engaged with it in this book.[12] Here, we see once again the importance of history to capturing variability: there is only so far we can go by theorising the varieties of consciousness and epistemic practices and attitudes; we can go much further when we attempt to capture some of their historical variability, eg their dependence on certain forms of language, technology, etc. To theorise well, in other words, including to capture the variability of the phenomena we wish to study, we need to also historicise. Or, put another way, to historicise is to theorise better.

I found a similar vertiginous sense of possibilities when examining the second limb of imagination, and thus the various kinds of participation in imagination. I tried to capture some of this by keeping in mind that different artefacts could invite different combinations, as well as different degrees, of affective, sensory and kinesic participation. Imagining with fictions, for instance, was relatively low on the scale, connecting to our affective participation, and not containing much, if any, sensory or kinesic participation. Imagining with metaphors, figures and scenarios, on the other hand, involved high degrees of all three, but with still important differences, eg although kinesis was important to metaphors and scenarios, figures scored especially high on that dimension of participation. Throughout, however, I had the distinct feeling I was skating on the

[8] See, eg, Kriegel (2015).

[9] See, eg, Bruhn and Wehrs (2014).

[10] For a recent discussion, see Kalinin (2018), especially on the importance of mobility and movement in Shklovsky.

[11] Collins (2013) and (2016). See also Mithen (2001).

[12] There is much to explore at the intersections of legal reasoning, historical pragmatics and cognitive history. One fascinating dimension of this is the history of our ways of representing the mind, including in theory and in literary practice: see, eg, Fletcher (1991); and Pasanek (2015). This history, in turn, has implications for legal practice: eg see Blumenthal (2016).

surface: there was so much more to say about the role of affective, sensory and kinesic experience. There would be even more to say if one found a way of historicising these experiences.

III. Kinesic Legal Theory and History

One of the most striking discoveries for me in the course of writing this book was that of the kinesic dimension. Time and again, re-reading the examples I decided to focus on, but also some others that did not make it, I kept being struck by the highly kinetic language of legal discourse. Equally, a re-occurring thought was that so many, if not all, processes of imagination were somehow about movement. Put another way: I was repeatedly struck by how much movement matters to thought. In fact, we signal this in our theoretical language, eg within rhetorical theory, we speak precisely of 'tropes', or twists and turns of language. Our labels for some of our most cherished forms of language wear the importance of movement on their sleeves, eg mention could be made just of metaphor (or transfer), parable (or placing side-by-side), or allegory (or something veiled, beneath which one can find something else). The relations between reflexivity, experience, emotion, form and, crucially, movement, deserve more attention. All this, of course, would have to connect strongly with embodiment, including bodies interacting with each other.

The mobility of thought is surely crucial, and this, in turn, makes forms of language that invite it, including invite us to simulate actions, gestures and postures, crucial too. As a result of important recent work in cognitive literary studies,[13] we know that simulated kinesis is important to our processing of literature. What I have found, and what I think I probably did not express as strongly and clearly as I could have, is that this matters also very much for legal thought. To do this properly, however, we would, once again, have to historicise forms that invite kinesic simulation and pay attention to how these change over time.

Given the many links between legal thought and narrative, the history of narrative would clearly be vital to any such task: we would need to look, for example, at the history of temporal aspects of narrative, eg delay, deferral, flashbacks, flashforwards, repetition, acceleration, deceleration, re-arrangement of chronology, and the history of its spatial aspects, eg digression, indirection, diversion, expansion, condensation, threading, and distortion.[14] These changes in narrative practices are connected to kinesis and movement, because they also make us move, as readers, in different ways: to read, we might say, is to move, but we can be invited to move in many different ways, corresponding, for instance, to the different patterns of temporal and spatial narrative structures. We could connect, I surmise, changes in these various narrative practices to changes in certain key dynamics of legal thought, eg construction of circumstances, as in fact patterns of past cases; construction and evaluation of action and character; construction of forms

[13] I discussed this literature in ch 3. A good starting point is the work of Guillemette Bolens, Terence Cave, and Ellen Spolsky.

[14] See, eg, Barthes (1975).

and degrees of abstraction and taxonomisation, and much else besides. Such a history of narrative, would, of course, need to be deeply political: as many feminist and postcolonial scholars have argued, changes in narrative practices are also changes in what we emphasise as important, in who is given voice and who is excluded.[15]

IV. The Politics of Artefacts and Imagination

The political dimension of artefacts and related processes of imagination is, indeed, another dimension I would have liked to have engaged with much more. For certain reasons, which I articulated briefly in the introduction, I wanted to focus in this book on inquiry, ie the process of generating insight into what values, vulnerabilities and interests might be at stake in a case and in others potentially like it in the future. The difficulty with placing the politics of legal form and cognition in the foreground is that it can all too easily slide into a cynical exercise in which we see all such forms and processes via a filter of suspicion, of masked domination, of camouflaged power. I am not denying that this is important: without doubt, legal form and cognition are inextricably bound up with power, domination, violence, and exclusion. However, I struggled with paying equal attention to this dimension and to the ways that the forms and processes of legal practice can enable inquiry. Given the lack of defences of artefactual language and imagination in adjudication, I erred on the side of being upbeat and positive about the capacity of these forms and processes to contribute to the making of normative insight, and thus to doing justice. I acknowledge, however, that I have probably been too generous, and not sensitive enough to the dark side of these forms and processes.

Further work would certainly need to return to the table and think more critically: just what are, for instance, the artefacts and related processes of imagination that are valuable politically and which ones are dangerous? Which of them, for example, are connected best to what Robert Cover called juris-generative practices and which ones are especially good at killing off other normative traditions, ie the juris-pathic ones?[16] Or, are all of them necessarily juris-generative in some respects, and juris-pathic in others, it being perhaps at best possible to be vigilant and make room for the former rather than the latter? I do not know, but I know I would like to investigate such questions further.

One vital context for this investigation would be the link between these forms and processes, ie artefactual language and related processes of imagination, and the theory and history of political economy. It would be fascinating to investigate the relations, for instance, between fictions, metaphors, figures and scenarios and, say, capitalist or feudal forms and practices. In addition, a number of scholars have also shown how certain practices of the legal imagination are connected with certain forms and practices of capitalism.[17] There is no doubt that capitalism has its own aesthetics, or perhaps

[15] See, eg, Hunter, McGlynn, Rackley (2010); and Guha (1997).

[16] See Cover (1983).

[17] See, eg, Pistor (2019); and Keenan (2016) and (2020).

distinct traditions of aesthetics, and these must surely percolate down into legal forms and processes, or indeed, to some extent, be influenced by them. These are matters calling out for further reflection and research.

Another vital context would have to be colonial and imperial legal history.[18] Writing Chapter 6, on metaphor, I had to resist the urge to hunt down further colonial and imperial metaphors, used, eg to buttress the legitimacy and authority of the Privy Council. There is an opportunity and need for a discipline of colonial and imperial legal poetics.[19] We could ask, for instance: how many of the now-familiar fictions, metaphors, and figures, were first crafted by courts exercising colonial or imperial jurisdictions, eg the courts of Admiralty? How many other features of legal language are vestiges, echoes or remains of colonial and imperial imaginations?[20] Theorists of legal reasoning, including of common law reasoning, have largely neglected colonial and imperial contexts,[21] and yet there is a case to be made for the idea that not only are there distinct modes and styles of legal reasoning and argumentation in such contexts, but that many of the modes and styles found in domestic courts originated there. This research is all the more pressing given the rise of international and transnational, including regional, courts.

I am also conscious that I have been insufficiently sensitive to the gender, racial and class dimensions of artefacts and related processes of imagination. I did try to be sensitive, especially to the gender dimensions of the case studies I examined, but I am conscious of just how much more can be and ought to be done. Some of the best work on the rhetoric of science was done through the looking-glass of gender,[22] and equally so for the rhetoric of philosophy.[23] I sought to draw on this research, but I am painfully aware that there is so much more to the gender, racial and class dynamics of fictions, metaphors, figures and scenarios in legal discourse than I have paid attention to in this book.

V. Varieties of Play in Legal Education

There is one final window I would like to open. When I began this book, I wanted desperately to make room for the importance of educating the imagination. Several times when presenting some of the arguments in this book, I was asked why I have focused on and spoken of imagination, and not, say, play, or at least not both play and imagination? Play, one can argue, is connected not only to how we imagine, but also

[18] See, eg, Koskenniemi (2005); the essays in Orford (2006); and, more recently, Motha (2018); and Slaughter (2019).

[19] Ruskola's work on *Legal Orientalism* (2013) might be read in this way. Work on the historical poetics and stylistics of international law would of course be vital here: see, eg, Warren (2015); Simpson (2019); and Tang (2018). This would be a discipline that could draw on, but also contribute to, the study of colonial or imperial poetics generally, see, eg, Mulholland (2013), Cheyfitz (1991); More (2012); and Boehmer (2018).

[20] See, eg, Stoler (2016).

[21] This is the case, of course, generally for legal theories, not only of theories of legal reasoning. A starting point would be to situate existing legal theories in colonial and imperial contexts, eg as has been done recently by Coel Kirkby (2018). See also Pitts (2018).

[22] See Keller (1985); Haraway (1976); and Hayles (1984).

[23] Le Doeuff (1989); and La Caze (2002).

to how we learn to do so. Further, is it really possible to separate out how we imagine from how we learn to do so? Is not imagination itself a skill, and, thus, any attempt to articulate how it works involves attention to the differing degrees of skill with which it can be exercised?

Right from the outset, one of my ways into the topic of imagination was via education: working with Zenon Bańkowski in Edinburgh during my doctorate, the principal reason I was drawn to examining the relations between ethics and the imagination was because of what I felt was the pedagogical potential of the imagination. Encountering the work of Martha Nussbaum and James Boyd White was also important in this respect. And, over the years, I have indeed sought to articulate the importance of the imagination to legal education.[24] Further, I have also found that one effective way of theorising something was to see it as an ability that required development: with the imagination, we could understand more about it if we thought about its very first stirrings in very young children,[25] and then reflected further on how it grows and develops, or how its growth and development may be thwarted.[26] In this respect, one of the obvious sources of theoretical literature was one that I was already drawn to, though also for other reasons, namely pragmatism. It was no accident, I thought, that John Dewey combined interests in both education and in the moral dimensions of imagination, eg via his concept of dramatic rehearsal.[27]

Further, much of the value I have come to see in artefacts and related processes of imagination came to me from observing their value in the legal classroom: how fun it was, for example, to consider variations of what the reasonable person, or, indeed, the unreasonable person, would do in such-and-such a case, or the endless play of what-if scenarios one could engage in during discussion of a certain case. Whenever I succumbed to the temptation to delve more into play and pedagogy, especially historically, I found ever more fascinating examples, which I wish I could have spent more time on: one such example, which did find its way briefly into the book, is that of the Ancient Roman pedagogical practice of the declamations. But there are so many more varieties of play to capture in the history of legal education: the play of memory, for example, or the play of dialogue, as in mooting, or the play of character, as in oratory and advocacy. This was not just interesting and important for historians of education; it was also vital for anyone who wants to theorise law and legal thought. It was artificial, and probably misleading, to separate out practice from pedagogy. In the end, however, I realised that I could not do justice to the pedagogical, and to the many contexts and varieties of play within legal education, in this book.

Those, then, are some of the surprises I have experienced in the course of writing this book, as well as some regrets, having now completed it. As one writes one book, one does not write so many other possible ones. I hope, though, to have also opened some windows onto vistas beyond this one: may a thousand flowers bloom.

[24] See, eg, Del Mar (2018a); and see also Fisher (forthcoming).
[25] See Harris (2000).
[26] See, eg, Egan (1992).
[27] For a discussion, see Fesmire (2003).

BIBLIOGRAPHY

Cases and Statutes

Aberdeen City Council v Stewart Milne Group (2012) SCLR 114.
Alpha Trading Ltd v Dunshaw-Patten Ltd [1981] 2 WLR 169.
An Informer v A Chief Constable [2013] QB 579.
Angus v Dalton (1877) 3 QBD 83.
Arla Foods UK plc v Barnes and others [2009] 1 BCLC 699.
Arnold v Britten and others [2016] 1 All ER 1.
Asley Industrial Trust Ltd. v Grimley [1963] 1 WLR 584.
Attorney General of Belize v Belize Telecom Ltd [2009] 1 WLR 1988.
BAI (Run Off) Ltd v Durham [2012] 1 WLR 867.
Baker v Corus [2006] 2 AC 572.
Barclays Bank plc v Taylor; Trustee Savings Bank of Wales and Border Counties and another v Taylor and another [1989] 3 All ER 563.
Bean v Stupart (1778) 1 Doug 11.
Bell v Lever Brothers [1932] AC 161.
Blackpool and Fylde Aero Club Ltd v Blackpool Borough Council [1990] All ER 25.
Bonnington Castings Ltd v Wardlaw [1956] AC 613.
British North America Act 1867.
Broome v Pardess Co-operative Society of Orange Growers (Est 1900) Ltd [1940] 1 All ER 603.
Bunge Corpn v Tradax SA [1981] 2 All ER 513.
California v Carney 471 US 386 (1985).
Canadian Charter of Rights and Freedoms 1982.
Carbopego-Abastecimento de Combustiveis SA v Amci Export Corporation [2006] All ER (D) 227.
Cavendish Square Holding BV v El Makdessi; Parking Eye Ltd v Beavis [2016] 2 All ER 519.
Clea Shipping Corp v Bulk Oil International Ltd; The Alaskan Trader [1984] 1 All ER 129.
Coggs v Barnard (1702) 2 Ld Raym 909.
Collins v Hopkins [1923] 2 KB 617.
Cundy v Lindsay (1878) 3 App Cas 459.
Deacons (a firm) v Bridge [1984] 2 All ER 19.
Donoghue v Stevenson [1932] AC 562.
Dunnachie v Kingston Upon Hill City Council [2004] 2 All ER 501.
E.P. Nelson v Rolfe [1950] 1 KB 139.
Edwards v Attorney-General of Canada (1928) SCR 291.
Edwards v The Attorney General of Canada [1930] AC 124.
Equitable Life Assurance Society v Hyman [2002] 1 AC 408.
FA Tamplin Steamship Co Ltd v Anglo-Mexican Petroleum Products Co Ltd [1916] 2 AC 397.
Fairchild v Glenhaven Funeral Services Ltd [2003] 1 AC 32.
Garston v Scottish Widows [1998] 2 EGLR 73.
Gator Shipping Corp v Trans-Asiatic Oil Ltd SA and Occidental Shipping establishment (The Odenfeld) [1978] 2 Lloyd's Rep 357.
Hall v Brooklands Auto Racing Club [1933] 1 KB 205.
Harding v Wealands [2006] 3 WLR 83.
Hart v Windsor (1843) 12 M & W 68.

Healthcare at Home Ltd v Common Services Agency [2014] SC (UKSC) 247.
Heaton (Inspector of Taxes) v Bell [1969] 2 WLR 735.
Helow v Secretary of State for the Home Department and another [2008] UKHL 62.
Honck v Muller (1881) 7 QBD 92.
Howard v Pickford Tool Co Ltd [1951] 1 KB 417.
Hull v McKenna [1926] IR 402.
Indian Airlines Limited v GIA International Limited [2002] EWHC 2361 (Comm).
Isabella Shipowner SA v Shagang Shipping Co Ltd (The Aquafaith) [2012] 2 All ER (Comm) 461.
Jones v Kernott [2010] 1 All ER 947.
Jones v Just (1868) LR 3 QB 197.
Kelly v Battershell (1949) 2 All ER 830.
Lancore Services Ltd v Barclays Bank plc [2010] 2 All ER (Comm) 273.
Langford & Co v Dutch (1952) SC 15.
Lilly ICOS v Pfizer [2001] FSR 201.
Lim Poh Choo v Camden and Islington Area Health Authority [1979] 1 All ER 332.
Lister v Romford Ice and Cold Storage Co. Ltd. [1957] 1 All ER 125.
Liverpool City Council v Irwin [1976] QB 319.
London Borough of Hounslow v Twickenham Garden Developments Ltd [1970] 3 All ER 326.
Lumley v Gye [1843–60] All ER Rep 208.
Marks and Spencer plc v BNP Paribas Securities Services Trust Company (Jersey) Ltd [2015] UKSC 72.
McGhee v National Coal Board (1972) SLT (Notes) 61.
McGhee v National Coal Board [1972] 3 All ER 1008.
McQuire v Western Morning News Company Ltd [1903] 2 KB 100.
Ministry of Sound (Ireland) Ltd v World Online Ltd [2003] EWHC 2178 (Ch).
MSC Mediterranean Shipping Company S.A. v Cottonex Anstalt [2016] All ER (D) 159.
Mursic v Croatia [2016] ECHR 7334/13.
Nadan v The King (1926) AC 482.
National Carriers Ltd v Panalpina (Northern) Ltd [1981] AC 675.
Nelson v Rye [1996] 1 WLR 1378.
Nicholson v Atlas Steel Foundry and Engineering Co Ltd [1957] 1 WLR 613.
Ocean Marine Navigation Ltd v Koch Carbon Inc (The Dynamic) [2003] All ER (D) 564.
Parkinson (Sir Lindsay) & Co. Ltd v Commissions of His Majesty's Works and Public Buildings [1949] 2 KB 632.
Powell v Lowe [2010] EWCA Civ 1419.
R v Jones (1703) 5 Mod 105.
R v Secretary of State for the Home Department, ex parte Wynne [1992] 2 All ER 301.
R v Southerton (1805) 6 East 126.
Ramsden v Hylton; Hylton v Biscoe T (1751) 2 Ves. 305.
Re DWS (deceased) [2000] EWCA Civ 282.
Re Healing Research Trustee Co Ltd [1992] 2 All ER 481.
Re Ley's Will Trusts; Somerset and another v Ley and another [1964] 2 All ER 326.
Re Rowland [1963] Ch 1 (CA).
Readhead v Midland Railway Co. (1869) LR 4 QB 379.
Reference re Same-Sex Marriage (2004) 19 BHRC 658.
Reigate v Union Manufacturing Co. (Ramsbottom) Ltd. [1918] 1 KB 592.
Secretary of State for Employment v Associated Society of Locomotive Engineers and Fireman and Others [1972] 2 QB 455.
Shirlaw v Southern Foundries (1926) Ltd [1939] 2 KB 206.
Shogun Finance Ltd v Hudson [2004] 1 All ER 215.
Sienkiewicz v Greif [2011] 2 WLR 523.
Sim v Stretch [1936] 2 All ER 1237.
Southern Foundries (1926) Ltd v Shirlaw [1940] AC 701.
St Aubyn v Attorney-General [1952] AC 15.
Stocznia Gdanska SA v Latvian Shipping Co and others [1998] 1 All ER 883.
Sunrise Brokers LLP v Rodgers; Reichman and another v Beveridge and another [2006] All ER (D) 186.
Tarmac Trading Ltd v Network Rail Infrastructure Ltd [2018] CSOH 33.

The Moorcock (1889) 14 PD 64.
The Puerto Buitrago [1976] 1 Lloyd's Rep 250.
Tito and others v Wadell and others [1977] Ch. 106.
Trollope & Colls Ltd v North West Metropolitan Regional Hospital Board [1973] 1 WLR 601.
Tyrer v United Kingdom [1978] ECHR 2.
Utilise TDS Limited v Neil Cranstound Davis and others [2016] EWHC 2127 (Ch).
Vardinoyannis v The Egyptian General Petroleum Corporation (The Evaggelos Th) [1971] 2 Lloyd's Rep 200.
Vaughan v Menlove (1837) 132 ER 490 (CP).
Wardlaw v Bonnington Castings (1955) SLT 320.
White & Carter (Councils) v McGregor (1960) SC 276.
White & Carter (Councils) v McGregor (1962) SC (HL) 1.
White & Carter v AR Harding, Court of Appeal, 21 May 1958, unreported.
Wilsher v Essex Area Health Authority [1988] 1 AC 1074.
Young & Marten Ltd. v McManus Childs Ltd. [1969] 1 AC 454.
Zurich Insurance Plc UK Branch v International Energy Group Ltd [2016] AC 509.

Articles and Books

Alexander, G (2007) 'Prosopopoeia: The Speaking Figure' in Adamson, S, Alexander, G and Ettenhuber, K (eds) *Renaissance Figures of Speech* (Cambridge: Cambridge University Press) 96.
Allan, TRS (2018) 'Principle, Practice and Precedent' 77(2) *Cambridge Law Journal* 269.
Almog, S (2001) 'Literary Legal Utopias: Alexander's Visit to Kasiah and Law at the End of Days' 12(2) *Utopian Studies* 164.
Altman, J (1978) *The Tudor Play of Mind: Rhetorical Inquiry and the Development of Elizabethan Drama* (Berkeley: University of California Press).
Amaya, A and Del Mar, M (eds) (2020) *Virtue, Emotion and Imagination in Law and Legal Reasoning* (Oxford, Hart).
Anderson, A (1982) *The Man Who Was HM Bateman* (Exeter: Webb & Bower).
Anderson, A, Felski, R and Moi, T (2019) *Character: Three Inquiries in Literary Studies* (Chicago: Chicago University Press).
Anderson, B (1996) *'Discovery' in Legal Decision-Making* (Dordrecht: Kluwer Academic Publishers).
Anderson, M, Cairns, D and Sprevak, M (eds) (2018a) *Distributed Cognition in Classical Antiquity* (Edinburgh: Edinburgh University Press).
Anderson, M, Cairns, D and Sprevak, M (2018b) 'Distributed Cognition and the Humanities' in Anderson, M, Cairns, D and Sprevak, M (eds) *Distributed Cognition in Classical Antiquity* (Edinburgh: Edinburgh University Press) 1.
Ando, C (2015a) *Roman Social Imaginaries: Language and Thought in Contexts of Empire* (Toronto: Toronto University Press).
Ando, C (2015b) 'Fact, Fiction and Social Reality in Roman Law' in Del Mar, M and Twining, W (eds) *Legal Fictions in Theory and Practice* (Dordrecht: Springer) 295.
Anker, E (2015) 'Rebuilding the Nation: On Architecture and the Aesthetics of Constitutionalism in South African Literature' 2 *Cambridge Journal of Postcolonial Literary Inquiry* 73.
Anscombe, GEM (1958) 'Modern Moral Philosophy' 33(124) *Philosophy* 1.
Appiah, A (2010) *The Honour Code: How Moral Revolutions Happen* (New York: W&W Norton).
Appiah, A (2017) *As If: Idealization and Ideals* (Cambridge, MA: Harvard University Press).
Aristotle (1908) *The Parva Naturalia*, trans. Beare, JI (Oxford: Clarendon Press).
Aristotle (1987) *De Anima (On the Soul)*, trans. Lawson-Tancred, H (London: Penguin).
Aristotle (2018) *Rhetoric*, trans. Reeve, CDC (Indianapolis: Hackett).
Arcangeli, M (2018) *Supposition and the Imaginative Realm: A Philosophical Inquiry* (London: Routledge).
Arendt, H (1963) *Eichmann in Jerusalem: A Report on the Banality of Evil* (New York: Viking Press).
Arendt, H (1982) *Lectures on Kant's Political Philosophy* (Chicago: University of Chicago Press).
Ashley, K (2018) 'Precedent and Analogy', in Bongiovanni, G, Postema, G, Rotolo, A, Sartor, G, Valentini, C, and Walton, D (eds) *Handbook of Legal Reasoning and Argumentation* (Dordrecht: Springer) 673.

Atiyah, P (1987) *Pragmatism and Theory in the Common Law* (London: Sweet & Maxwell).
Auerbach, E (1984) [1938] 'Figura' in Auerbach, E, *Scenes from the Drama of European Literature* (Minneapolis: University of Minnesota Press) 11.
Augustine (1925) *Confessions* (Paris: Les Belles Lettres).
Austen, GEV and Edmonds, JM (1904) *The Characters of Theophrastus* (London: Blackie and Son).
Austin, R (1992) 'Better Off with the Reasonable Man Dead or the Reasonable Man Did the Darndest Things' *Brigham Young University Law Review* 479.
Aviles, MAR (2000) 'The Law-Based Utopia' 3(2–3) *Critical Review of International Social and Political Philosophy* 225.
Bacon, F (1803) *Maxims of the Law*, The Works of Francis Bacon, Vol. IV (London: Crowder and Hemfled).
Bailey, ML and Knight, KJ (eds) (2017) 'Special Issue: Emotions in Legal History' 38(2) *The Journal of Legal History*.
Baker, J (2001) *The Law's Two Bodies: Some Evidential Problems in English Legal History* (Oxford: Oxford University Press).
Balganesh, S and Parchomovsky, G (2015) 'Structure and Value in the Common Law' 163 *University of Pennsylvania Law Review* 1241.
Ball, M (1985) *Lying Down Together: Law, Metaphor and Theology* (Madison: University of Wisconsin Press).
Bańkowski, Z (2001) *Living Lawfully: Love in Law and Law in Love* (Dordrecht: Springer).
Bańkowski, Z (2006) 'In the Judgement Space: The Judge and the Anxiety of the Encounter' in Bańkowski, Z and MacLean, J (eds) *The Universal and the Particular in Legal Reasoning* (Abingdon: Ashgate) 25.
Bańkowski, Z (2013) 'The Space to See: Law and the Ethical Imagination' in Bańkowski, Z and Del Mar, M (eds) *The Moral Imagination and the Legal Life* (Abingdon: Ashgate) 11.
Bańkowski, Z, Del Mar M and Maharg, P (eds) (2013) *The Arts and the Legal Academy* (Abingdon: Ashgate).
Banks, K (2018) 'Metaphor, Lexicography and Rabelais' Prologue to *Gargantua*' in Banks, K and Chesters, T (eds) *Movement in Renaissance Literature: Exploring Kinesic Intelligence* (London: Palgrave MacMillan) 81.
Banks, K and Chesters, T (eds) (2018a) *Movement in Renaissance Literature: Exploring Kinesic Intelligence* (London: Palgrave MacMillan).
Banks, K and Chesters, T (2018b) 'Introduction' in Banks, K and Chesters, T (eds) *Movement in Renaissance Literature: Exploring Kinesic Intelligence* (London: Palgrave MacMillan) 1.
Barfield, O (1947) 'Poetic Diction and Legal Fiction' in Lewis, CS (ed) *Essays Presented to Charles Williams* (London: Oxford University Press) 127.
Barsalou, L (2008) 'Grounded Cognition' 59 *Annual Review of Psychology* 617.
Bartha, P (2009) *By Parallel Reasoning: The Construction and Evaluation of Analogical Arguments* (Oxford: Oxford University Press).
Barthes, R (1975) 'Introduction to the Structural Analysis of Narratives' 6(2) *New Literary History* 237.
Bartor, A (2010) *Reading Law as Narrative: A Study in the Casuistic Laws of the Pentateuch* (Atlanta: Society of Biblical Literature).
Bate, J (2019) *How the Classics Made Shakespeare* (Princeton: Princeton University Press).
Bayne, T and Montague, M (eds) (2011) *Cognitive Phenomenology* (Oxford: Oxford University Press).
Bell, J (2006) *Judiciaries within Europe* (Cambridge: Cambridge University Press).
Bell, J (2013) 'Analogy and Parable in Legal Reasoning' in Del Mar, M and Michelon, C (eds) *The Anxiety of the Jurist: Legality, Exchange and Judgement* (Abingdon: Ashgate) 241.
Bell, J (2016) 'Is Comparative Law Necessary for Legal Theory?' in Del Mar, M and Lobban, M (eds) *Law in Theory and History: New Essays on a Neglected Dialogue* (Oxford: Hart) 127.
Belting, H (2017) *Face and Mask: A Double History*, trans. Hansen, TS and Hansen, AJ (Princeton: Princeton University Press).
Bender, J and Marrinan, M (2010) *The Culture of Diagram* (Stanford: Stanford University Press).
Bennett, C and Hammond, W (1902) *The Characters of Theophrastus* (New York: Green and Co).
Berger, B (2002) 'Trial by Metaphor: Rhetoric, Innovation and the Juridical Text' 39(3) *Court Review: The Journal of the American Judges Association* 1.
Berger, L (2004) 'What is the Sound of a Corporation Speaking? How the Cognitive Theory of Metaphor Can Help Lawyers Shape the Law' 2 *Legal Communication and Rhetoric Journal* 169.
Berger, L (2007) 'Of Metaphor, Metonymy, and Corporate Money: Rhetorical Choices in Supreme Court Decisions on Campaign Finance Regulation' 58 *Mercer Law Review* 949.

Berger, L (2013) 'Metaphor and Analogy: The Sun and Moon of Legal Persuasion' 22 *Journal of Law and Policy* 147.

Berger, L and Stanchi, K (2017) *Legal Persuasion* (London: Routledge).

Berger, L and Stanchi, K (2018) 'Gender Justice' in Hanne, M and Weisberg, R (eds) *Narrative and Metaphor in the Law* (Cambridge, Cambridge University Press) 157.

Berman, H (1977) 'The Origins of Western Legal Science' 90 *Harvard Law Review* 894.

Berns, A (2018) '"I Signed but I Did Not Say": The Status of Chess in Early Modern Judaism' in Ginsburg, C and Biasiori, L (eds) *A Historical Approach to Casuistry: Norms and Exceptions in a Comparative Perspective* (London: Bloomsbury) 101.

Berthoz, A (2000) *The Brain's Sense of Movement* (Cambridge, MA: Harvard University Press).

Best, S (2010) *The Fugitive's Properties: Law and the Poetics of Possession* (Chicago: University of Chicago Press).

Beynon-Jones, S and Grabham, E (eds) (2018) *Law and Time* (London: Routledge).

Binnie, I (2007) 'Interpreting the Constitution: The Living Tree vs Original Meaning' 10 *Options Politique* 104.

Bottici, C (2014) *Imaginal Politics: Images Beyond Imagination and the Imaginary* (New York: Columbia University Press).

Birks, P (1986) 'Fictions Ancient and Modern' in MacCormick, N and Birks, P (eds) *The Legal Mind: Essays for Tony Honoré* (Oxford: Clarendon Press) 83.

Bjerre, CS (1999) 'Secured Transactions Inside Out: Negative Pledge Covenants Property and Perfection' 84 *Cornell Law Review* 305.

Black, M (1955) 'Metaphor' 55(1) *Proceedings of the Aristotelian Society* 273.

Black, M (1962) *Models and Metaphors: Studies in Language and Philosophy* (Ithaca: Cornell University Press).

Blackstone, W (1829) *Commentaries on the Laws of England*, 18th edn (Sweet: London).

Bloch, D (2007) *Aristotle on Memory and Recollection: Text, Translation, Interpretation, and Reception in Western Scholasticism* (Leiden: Brill).

Blum, L (1991) 'Moral Perception and Particularity' 101(4) *Ethics* 701.

Blumenberg, H (1985) *Work on Myth*, trans. Wallace, R (Cambridge, MA: MIT Press).

Blumenberg, H (2010) [1960] *Paradigms for a Metaphorology* (Ithaca: Cornell University Press).

Blumenthal, S (2016) *Law and the Modern Mind: Consciousness and Responsibility in American Legal Culture* (Cambridge, MA: Harvard University Press).

Bocharova, J (2016) 'Personification Allegory and Embodied Cognition' in Melion, W and Ramakers, B (eds) *Personification: Embodying Meaning and Emotion* (Leiden: Brill) 43.

Boehmer, E (2018) *Postcolonial Poetics: 21st Century Critical Readings* (London: Palgrave).

Bolens, G (2012) [2008] *The Style of Gestures: Embodiment and Cognition in Literary Narrative* (Baltimore: Johns Hopkins University Press).

Bolland, WC (1925) *A Manual of Year Book Studies* (Cambridge: Cambridge University Press).

Bonner, FS (1949) *Roman Declamation in the Late Republic and Early Empire* (Liverpool: University Press of Liverpool).

Boquet, D and Nagy, P (ed) (2018) *Medieval Sensibilities: A History of Emotions in the Middle Ages* (Cambridge: Polity).

Bori, C (2018) 'The Many Roads to Justice: A Case of Adultery in Sixteenth Century Cairo' in Ginsburg, C and Biasiori, L (eds) *A Historical Approach to Casuistry: Norms and Exceptions in a Comparative Perspective* (London: Bloomsbury) 113.

Bosmajian, H (1992) *Metaphor and Reason in Judicial Opinions* (Carbondale: Southern Illinois University Press).

Bowdle, B and Gentner, D (2005) 'The Career of Metaphor' 112 *Psychological Review* 193.

Boyce, B (1967) *The Theophrastan Character in England to 1642* (London: Frank Cass & Co Ltd).

Boyd, B (2009) *On the Origin of Stories* (Cambridge, MA: Harvard University Press).

Brady, M and Fricker, M (eds) (2016) *The Epistemic Life of Groups: Essays in the Epistemology of Collectives* (Oxford: Oxford University Press).

Brann, E (2017) [1991] *The World of the Imagination: Sum and Substance* (Lanham, Rowman & Littlefield Publishers).

Braun, A (2019) 'The Value of Communication Practices for Comparative Law: Exploring the Relations between Scotland and England' 72(1) *Current Legal Problems* 315.

Brewer, S (1996) 'Exemplary Reasoning: Semantics, Pragmatics, and the Rational Force of Legal Argument by Analogy' 109 *Harvard Law Review* 925.

Bricker, A (2019) 'Is Narrative Essential to the Law? Precedent, Case Law Judicial Employment' 15(2) *Law, Culture and the Humanities* 319.

Broackes, J (ed) (2011) *Iris Murdoch, Philosopher* (Oxford: Oxford University Press).

Brooks, P (2003) 'Inevitable Discovery: Law, Narrative, Retrospectivity' 15 *Yale Journal of Law and Humanities* 71.

Brosch, R (2018) 'What We "See" When We Read: Visualization and Vividness in Reading Fictional Narratives' 105 *Cortex* 135.

Brown, D (2005) 'Tradition and Change in Constitutional Interpretation: Do Living Trees Have Roots?' 19 *National Journal of Constitutional* 44.

Brown, V (1992–3) 'The Dialogic Experience of Conscience: Adam Smith and the Voices of Stoicism' 26(2) *Eighteenth-Century Studies* 233.

Bruhn, M and Wehrs, D (eds) (2014) *Cognition, Literature, and History* (New York: Routledge).

Bruhn, MJ (2009) 'Romanticism and the Cognitive Science of Imagination' 48(4) *Studies in Romanticism* 543.

Brun, G, Doguoglu, U and Kuenzle, D (eds) (2008) *Epistemology and Emotions* (Abingdon: Ashgate).

Bryen, A (2020) 'Responsa' in Stern, S, Del Mar, M and Meyler, B (eds) *The Oxford Handbook of Law and Humanities* (Oxford: Oxford University Press).

Buber, M (1958) [1923] *I and Thou*, trans. Smith, RG (New York: Scribner).

Burazin, L, Himma, K and Roversi, C (ed) (2018) *Law as an Artefact Kind* (Oxford: Oxford University Press).

Burgers, CF (2016) 'Conceptualizing Change in Communication through Metaphor' 66(2) *Journal of Communication* 250.

Burke, M and Troscianko, E (eds) (2017) *Cognitive Literary Science: Dialogues between Literature and Cognition* (Oxford: Oxford University Press).

Burt, R (1984) 'Constitutional Law and the Teaching of the Parables' 93 *Yale Law Journal* 455.

Bustos, E (2017) 'Parables: Crossroads Between the Cognitive Theory of Metaphor and Argumentation Theory' in Olmos, P (ed) *Narration as Argument* (Dordrecht: Springer) 83.

Byrne, R (2007), *The Rational Imagination: How People Create Alternatives to Reality* (Cambridge, MA: MIT Press).

Cameron, L (2011) *Metaphor and Reconciliation: The Discourse Dynamics of Empathy in Post-Conflict Conversations* (New York: Routledge).

Camp, E (2006) 'Metaphor and That Certain "Je Ne Sais Quoi"' 129(1) *Philosophical Studies* 1.

Camp, E (2009) 'Two Varieties of Literary Imagination: Metaphor, Fiction, and Thought Experiments' *Midwest Studies in Philosophy: Poetry and Philosophy* 107.

Camp, E (2013) 'Slurring Perspectives' 54(3) *Analytic Philosophy* 330.

Camp, E (2015) 'Metaphors in Literature' in Carroll, N and Gibson, J (eds) *The Routledge Companion to Philosophy of Literature* (London: Routledge) 334.

Camp, E (2017) 'Why Metaphors Make Good Insults' 174 *Philosophical Studies* 47.

Camp, E (Forthcoming) 'Imaginative Frames for Scientific Inquiry: Metaphors, Telling Facts, and Just-So Stories' in Levy, A and Godfrey-Smith (eds) *The Scientific Imagination: Philosophical and Psychological Perspectives* (Oxford: Oxford University Press).

Campbell, K (1983) 'Fuller on Legal Fictions' 2(3) *Law and Philosophy* 339.

Caracciolo, M (2013) 'Blind Reading: Toward an Enactivist Theory of the Reader's Imagination' in Bernaerts, L, de Geest, D, Herman, L and Vervaeck, B (eds) *Stories and Minds: Cognitive Approaches to Literary Narrative* (Lincoln: University of Nebraska Press) 81.

Caracciolo, M (2014) *The Experientiality of Narrative: An Enactivist Approach* (Berlin: de Gruyter).

Cardozo, B (1925) 'Law and Literature' 14 *Yale Law Review* 699.

Carpi, D and Leiboff, M (eds) (2016) *Fables of the Law: Fairy Tales in a Legal Context* (Berlin: de Gruyter).

Carruthers, M (1998) *The Craft of Thought: Meditation, Rhetoric, and the Making of Images, 400–1200* (Cambridge: Cambridge University Press).

Carruthers, M (2008) *The Book of Memory*, 2nd edn (Cambridge: Cambridge University Press).

Carston, R (1998) 'Informativeness, Relevance and Scalar Implicature' in Carston, R and Uchida, S (eds) *Relevance Theory: Applications and Implications* (Amsterdam: John Benjamins) 179.

Carston, R (2010) 'Metaphor: Ad Hoc Concepts, Literal Meaning and Mental Images' 110(3) *Proceedings of the Aristotelian Society* 295.

Carter, A, Clark, A, Kallestrup, J, Palermos, O and Pritchard, D (eds) (2018) *Socially Extended Epistemology* (Oxford: Oxford University Press).

Casey, E (2010) *Imagining: A Phenomenological Study*, 2nd edn (Bloomington: Indiana University Press).

Caspary, W (1991) 'Ethical Deliberation as Dramatic Rehearsal: John Dewey's Theory' 41(2) *Educational Theory* 175.

Caspary, W (2006) 'Dewey and Sartre on Ethical decisions: Dramatic Rehearsal Versus Radical Choice' 42(3) *Transactions of the Charles S. Peirce Society* 367.

Castoriadis, C (1987) *The Imaginary Institution of Society*, trans. Blamey, K (Cambridge: Polity).

Cavanagh, E (2019) 'Flowers of the Crown in English Legal Thought: Metaphorical Assessments of Royal Power in Transitional Periods of Monarchy' 6(1) *Royal Studies Journal* 38.

Cave, T (2016) *Thinking with Literature: Towards a Cognitive Criticism* (Oxford: Oxford University Press).

Cave, T (2018a) 'Towards a Passing Theory of Literary Understanding' in Cave, T and Wilson, D (eds) *Reading beyond the Code: Literature and Relevance Theory* (Oxford: Oxford University Press) 167.

Cave, T (2018b) 'Chiastic Cognition: Kinesic Intelligence Between the Reflective and the Pre-reflective in Montaigne and Scève' in Banks, K and Chesters, T (eds) *Movement in Renaissance Literature: Exploring Kinesic Intelligence* (Cham: Palgrave MacMillan) 13.

Cave, T and Wilson, D (eds) (2018a) *Reading beyond the Code: Literature and Relevance Theory* (Oxford: Oxford University Press).

Cave, T and Wilson, D (2018b) 'Introduction' in Cave, T and Wilson, D (eds) *Reading beyond the Code: Literature and Relevance Theory* (Oxford: Oxford University Press) 1.

Chan, T (ed) (2014) *The Aim of Belief* (Oxford: Oxford University Press).

Chandler, J (1998) *England in 1819: The Politics of Literary Culture and the Case of Romantic Historicism* (Chicago: Chicago University Press).

Chandler, J (2007) 'On the Face of the Case: Conrad, Lord Jim, and the Sentimental Novel' 33(4) *Critical Inquiry* 837.

Chao-Chi Yen, B (2017) 'The Political Iconography of Trees in The Excursion' 31(7) *Textual Practice* 1253.

Charteris-Black, J (2012) 'Forensic Deliberations on Purposeful Metaphor' 2(1) *Metaphor and the Social World* 1.

Chesters, T (2018) 'Scève's Denominal Verbs' in Banks, K and Chesters, T (eds) *Movement in Renaissance Literature: Exploring Kinesic Intelligence* (London: Palgrave MacMillan) 55.

Cheyfitz, E (1991) *The Poetics of Imperialism: Translation and Colonization from The Tempest to Tarzan* (Philadelphia: University of Pennsylvania Press).

Chiassoni, P (2019) *Interpretation without Truth: A Realistic Enquiry* (Dordrecht: Springer).

Chico, T (2018) *The Experimental Imagination: Literary Knowledge and Science in the British Enlightenment* (Stanford: Stanford University Press).

Chowdhury, T (2017) 'Temporality and Criminal Law Adjudication's Multiple Pasts' 38(2) *Liverpool Law Review* 187.

Chowdhury, T (Forthcoming) *Time, Temporality and Legal Judgement* (London: Routledge).

Clark, A (1997) *Being There: Putting Brain, Body, and World Together Again* (Cambridge, MA: MIT Press).

Clark, A (2003) *Natural-Born Cyborgs: Minds, Technologies and the Future of Human Intelligence* (Oxford: Oxford University Press).

Cocking, JM (1984) *Imagination: A Study in the History of Ideas* (London: Routledge).

Code, L (1984) 'Toward a 'Responsibilist' Epistemology' 45(1) *Philosophy and Phenomenological Research* 29.

Cohen, LJ (1992) *An Essay on Belief and Acceptance* (Oxford: Clarendon Press).

Cohen, T (1978) 'Metaphor and the Cultivation of Intimacy' 5(1) *Critical Inquiry* 3.

Cohen, T (2012) *Thinking of Others: On the Talent for Metaphor* (Princeton: Princeton University Press).

Cohn, D (1999) *The Distinction of Fiction* (Baltimore: Johns Hopkins University Press).

Coliva, A and Moyal-Sharrock, E (eds) (2016) *Hinge Epistemology* (Netherlands: Brill).

Collins, C (2013) *Paleopoetics: The Evolution of the Preliterate Imagination* (New York: Columbia University Press).

Collins, C (2017) *Neopoetics: The Evolution of the Literate Imagination* (New York: Columbia University Press).

Collins, H (2004) 'Implied Terms: The Foundation of Good Faith and Fair Dealing' 67 *Current Legal Problems* 297.

Colombetti, G (2017) *The Feeling Body: Affective Science Meets the Enactive Mind* (Cambridge, MA: MIT Press).

Colombetti, G and Krueger, J (2015) 'Scaffoldings of the Affective Mind' 28(8) *Philosophical Psychology* 1157.

Conaghan, J (2013) *Gender and Law* (Oxford: Clarendon Press).

Condello, A and Ferrara, A (eds) (2018) 'Special Issue: Exemplarity and its Normativity' 30(3) *Law and Literature*.

Conrad, S (1988) 'Metaphor and Imagination in James Wilson's Theory of Federal Union' 13(1) *Journal of Law and Social Inquiry* 1.

Constable, M (2014) *Our Word is our Bond: How Legal Speech Acts* (Stanford: University of Stanford Press).

Coplan, A (2011) 'Understanding Empathy' in Coplan, C and Goldie, P (eds), *Empathy: Philosophical and Psychological Perspectives* (New York, Oxford University Press) 3.

Cordell, S (2017) 'Group Virtues: No Great Leap Forward with Collectivism' 23(1) *Res Publica* 43.

Cotterill, A (2004) *Digressive Voices in Early Modern English Literature* (Oxford: Oxford University Press).

Cover, R (1983) 'The Supreme Court 1982 Term Foreword: Nomos and Narrative' 97 *Harvard Law Review* 4.

Cover, R (1986) 'Violence and the Word' 95 *Yale Law Journal* 1601.

Cox, V (1992) *The Renaissance Dialogue: Literary Dialogue in Its Social and Political Contexts, Castiglione to Galileo* (Cambridge: Cambridge University Press).

Creagher, A, Lunbeck, E and Norton Wise, N (eds) *Science without Laws: Model Systems, Cases, Exemplary Narratives* (Durham: Duke University Press).

Crook, JA (1995) *Legal Advocacy in the Roman World* (London: Duckworth).

Crowe, J (2019) *Natural Law and the Nature of Law* (Cambridge: Cambridge University Press).

Culler, J (1975) *Structuralist Poetics: Structuralism, Linguistics, and the Study of Literature* (Ithaca: Cornell University Press).

Culler, J (2015) *A Theory of the Lyric* (Cambridge, MA: Harvard University Press).

Currie, G (1990) *The Nature of Fiction* (Cambridge: Cambridge University Press).

Currie, G and Jureidini, J (2004) 'Narrative and Coherence' 19(4) *Mind & Language* 409.

Currie, G and Ravenscroft, I (2002) *Recreative Minds: Imagination in Philosophy and Psychology* (Oxford: Oxford University Press).

Daston, L (1998) 'Fear and Loathing of the Imagination in Science' 134(4) *Daedalus* 16.

Daston, L (2011) 'The Empire of Observation' in Daston, L and Lunbeck, E (eds) *Histories of Scientific Observation* (Chicago: Chicago University Press) 81.

Davis, D (2020) 'Legal Maxims' in Stern, S, Del Mar, M and Meyler, B (eds) *The Oxford Handbook of Law and Humanities* (Oxford: Oxford University Press).

Davis, M (2012) 'Imaginary Cases in Ethics: A Critique' 26(1) *International Journal of Applied Philosophy* 1.

Dayan, C (2011) *The Law is a White Dog: How Legal Rituals Make and Unmake Persons* (Princeton: Princeton University Press).

Dayeh, I (2018) 'Islamic Casuistry and Galenic Medicine: Hashish, Coffee and the Emergence of the Jurist-Physician' in Ginsburg, C and Biasiori, L (eds) *A Historical Approach to Casuistry: Norms and Exceptions in a Comparative Perspective* (London: Bloomsbury) 132.

De Jaegher, H, & Di Paolo, E (2007) 'Participatory Sense-Making' 6(4) *Phenomenology and the Cognitive Sciences* 485.

De Paul, M and Zagzebski, L (eds) (2003) *Intellectual Virtue: Perspectives from Ethics and Epistemology* (Oxford: Oxford University Press).

De Sousa, R (2008) 'Epistemic Feelings' in Brun, G, Doguoglu, U and Kuenzle, D (eds) *Epistemology and Emotions* (Abingdon: Ashgate) 185.

De, R (2014) '"A Peripatetic World Court": Cosmopolitan Courts, Nationalist Judges and the Indian Appeal to the Privy Council' 32(4) *Law and History Review* 821.

Del Mar, M (2010a) 'Beyond Text in Legal Education: Art, Ethics and the Carnegie Report' 56 *Loyola Law Review* 101.

Del Mar, M (2010b) 'Normativism, Anti-Normativism and Humanist Pragmatism' 33(2–3) *Human Studies* 305–323.

Del Mar, M (2011) 'Legal Understanding and the Affective Imagination', in Maughan, C and Maharg, P (eds), *Affect and Legal Education* (Surrey: Ashgate) 177.

Del Mar, M (2012) 'Relational Jurisprudence: Vulnerability between Fact and Value' (2012) 2 *Law and Method* 63.

Del Mar, M (2013a) 'The Education of Attention and Encounter in the Legal Academy' Bańkowski, Z and Del Mar, M (eds) *The Moral Imagination and the Legal Life* (Abingdon: Ashgate) 33.

Del Mar, M (2013b) 'Thinking in Images in Legal Theory' in Del Mar, M and Michelon, C (eds) *The Anxiety of the Jurist: Legality, Exchange and Judgement* (Abingdon: Ashgate) 43.

Del Mar, M (2014) 'Judging Virtuously: Developing an Empathic Capacity for Perceptual Sensitivity' 5(1) *Jurisprudence* 177.

Del Mar, M (2015a) 'Legal Fictions and Legal Change in the Common Law Tradition', in Del Mar, M and Twining, W (eds) *Legal Fictions in Theory and Practice* (Dordrecht: Springer) 225.

Del Mar, M (2015b) 'Introducing Fictions: Examples, Functions, Definitions and Evaluations' in Del Mar, M and Twining, W (eds) *Legal Fictions in Theory and Practice* (Dordrecht: Springer) ix.

Del Mar, M (2015c) 'The Forward-Looking Requirement of Formal Justice: Neil MacCormick on Consequential Reasoning' 6(3) *Jurisprudence* 429.

Del Mar, M (2016a) 'Learning How to Read a Case: Resources and Activities from the Visual and Dramatic Arts', in van Klink, B and de Vries, B (eds) *Academic Learning in Law: Theoretical Positions, Teaching Experiments and Learning Experiences* (Cheltenham: Edward Elgar) 244.

Del Mar, M (2016b) 'The Natural and the Normative: The Distinction, not the Dichotomy between Facts and Values in a Broader Context', in Taekema, S, van Klink, B and de Been, W (eds) *Facts and Norms in Law: Interdisciplinary Reflections on Legal Method* (Cheltenham: Edward Elgar) 224.

Del Mar, M (2017a) 'Imagining by Feeling: A Case for Compassion in Legal Reasoning' 13(2) *International Journal of Law in Context* 143.

Del Mar, M (2017b) 'Metaphor in International Law: Language, Imagination and Normative Inquiry' 86(2) *Nordic Journal of International Law* 170.

Del Mar, M (2017c) 'Legal Reasoning in Pluralist Jurisprudence: The Practice of the Relational Imagination', in Halpin, A and Roughan, N (eds), *In Pursuit of Pluralist Jurisprudence* (Cambridge: Cambridge University Press) 40.

Del Mar, M (2018a) 'Educating the Legal Imagination' *Law & Method*, available online: www.lawandmethod.nl/tijdschrift/lawandmethod/2018/10/lawandmethod-D-18-00007.

Del Mar, M (2018b) 'Emotion Experiments in Legal Thought' 5(2) *Critical Analysis of Law*, available online: https://cal.library.utoronto.ca/index.php/cal/article/view/32054.

Del Mar, M (2018c) 'Common Virtue and the Perspectival Imagination: Adam Smith and Common Law Reasoning' 9(1) *Jurisprudence* 58–70.

Del Mar, M and Gordon, R (eds) (2013) 'Special Issue: Exemplary Narratives in Law and Legal Reasoning' 25(3) *Law and Literature*.

Del Mar, M and Lobban, M (eds) (2014) *Legal Theory and Legal History* (Abingdon: Ashgate).

Del Mar, M and Lobban, M (eds) (2016) *Law in Theory and History: New Essays on a Neglected Dialogue* (Oxford: Hart).

Del Mar, M and Michelon, C (eds) (2013) *The Anxiety of the Jurist: Legality, Exchange and Judgement* (Abingdon: Ashgate).

Del Mar, M and Twining, W (eds) (2015) *Legal Fictions in Theory and Practice* (Dordrecht: Springer).

Delgado, R (1989) 'Storytelling for Oppositionists and Others: A Plea for Narrative' 87 *Michigan Law Review* 2411.

Demos, R (1923) 'Legal Fictions' 34 *International Journal of Ethics* 37.

Deonna, J and Rodogno, R (2011) *In Defense of Shame* (Oxford: Oxford University Press).

Devlin, A and Bokulic, A (eds) (2015) *Thomas Kuhn's Scientific Revolutions 50 Years On* (Dordrecht: Springer).

Dewey, J (1922) *Human Nature and Conduct* (New York: Henry Holt & Co).

Diamond, C (2002) 'What If x Is the Number of Sheep? Wittgenstein and Thought Experiments in Ethics' 31(3) *Philosophical Papers* 227.

Dor, D (2015) *The Instruction of Imagination: Language as a Social Communication Technology* (Oxford: Oxford University Press).

Dor, D (2017) 'From Experience to Imagination: Language and its Evolution as a Social Communication Technology' 43(B) *Journal of Neurolinguistics* 107.

Dorsch, F (2014) *The Unity of Imagining* (Berlin: de Gruyter).

Dowling, A (2003) 'The Doctrine of Lost Modern Grant' 38 *Irish Jurist* 225.

Duff, D (2014) 'Melodies of Mind: Poetic Forms as Cognitive Structures' in Bruhns, M and Wehrs, D (eds) *Cognition, Literature and History* (New York: Routledge) 17.

Durkheim, E (1995) [1912] *The Elementary Forms of the Religious Life*, trans. Fields, K (New York: Free Press).

Dworkin, R (1982) 'Law as Interpretation' 9 *Critical Inquiry* 179.

Dworkin, R (1986) *Law's Empire* (Cambridge, MA: Harvard University Press).
Dworkin, R (2011) *Justice for Hedgehogs* (Cambridge, MA: Harvard University Press).
Eden, K (1986) *Poetic and Legal Fiction in the Aristotelian Tradition* (Princeton: Princeton University Press).
Eden, K (2001) *Friends Hold All Things in Common: Tradition, Intellectual Property, and the Adages of Erasmus* (New Haven: Yale University Press).
Edgecombe, RS (1997) 'Ways of Personifying' 31 *Style* 1.
Edlin, D (2016) *Common Law Judging: Subjectivity, Impartiality and the Making of Law* (Ann Arbor: University of Michigan Press).
Edlin, D (ed) (2007) *Common Law Theory* (Cambridge: Cambridge University Press).
Edwards, L (2010) 'Once Upon a Time in Law: Myth, Metaphor and Authority' 77 *Tennessee Law Review* 883.
Egan, D (2016) 'Literature and Thought Experiments' 74(2) *Journal of Aesthetics and Art Criticism* 139.
Egan, K (1992) *Imagination in Teaching and Learning: Ages 8–15* (London: Routledge).
Eilan, N (ed) (2016) *The Second Person: Philosophical and Psychological Perspectives* (London: Routledge).
Eisenberg, M (1988) *The Nature of the Common Law* (Cambridge, MA: Harvard University Press).
Elgin, C (1996) *Considered Judgement* (Princeton: Princeton University Press).
Elgin, C (2008) 'Emotion and Understanding' in Brun, G, Doguoglu, U and Kuenzle, D (eds) *Epistemology and Emotions* (Abingdon: Ashgate) 33.
Elgin, C (2011) 'Making Manifest: The Role of Exemplification in the Sciences and the Arts' 15(3) *Principia* 399.
Elgin, C (2014) 'Fiction as Thought Experiment' 22(2) *Perspectives on Science* 221.
Elgin, C (2017) *True Enough* (Cambridge, MA: MIT Press).
Elias, N (1994) [1939] *The Civilising Process: Sociogenetic and Psychogenetic Investigations* (Oxford: Blackwell).
Etxabe, J and Watt, G (eds) (2014) *Living in a Law Transformed: Encounters with the Works of James Boyd White* (Ann Arbor: University of Michigan Press).
Fahnestock, J (1999) *Rhetorical Figures in Science* (New York: Oxford University Press).
Faucionnier, G and Turner, M (2003) *The Way We Think: Conceptual Blending and the Mind's Hidden Complexities* (New York: Basic Books).
Fehige, Y and Stuart, M (2014) 'On the Origins of the Philosophy of Thought Experiments: The Forerun' 22(2) *Perspectives on Science* 179.
Ferguson, M (1983) *Trials of Desire: Renaissance Defenses of Poesy* (New Haven: Yale University Press).
Ferguson, RB (1982) 'The Horowitz Thesis and Common Law Discourse' 3(1) *Oxford Journal of Legal Studies* 34.
Ferraris, M (1996) *L'immaginazione* (Bologna: Il Mulino).
Fesmire, S (2003) *John Dewey and the Moral Imagination* (Bloomington: Indiana University Press).
Feteris, E (1997) 'A Survey of 25 Years of Research on Legal Argumentation' 11(3) *Argumentation* 355.
Figlerowicz, M (2016) *Flat Protagonists: A Theory of Novel Character* (Oxford: Oxford University Press).
Figlerowicz, M (2018) 'Novels and Characters' in Bulson, E (ed) *The Cambridge Companion to the Novel* (Cambridge: Cambridge University Press) 123.
Fine, A (1993) 'Fictionalism' 18(1) *Midwest Studies in Philosophy* 1.
Finnis, J (1981) *Natural Law and Natural Rights* (Oxford: Clarendon Press).
Fish, S (1982) 'Working on the Chain Gang' 9 *Critical Inquiry* 201.
Fishelov, D (2019) 'The Poetics of Six-Word Stories' 27(1) *Narrative* 30.
Fisher, J (2016) 'Implied Terms Again, or How Lord Hoffmann Got Treated in *Marks & Spencer*' 45(2–3) *Common Law World Review* 236.
Fisher, L (Forthcoming) 'Legal Imagination and Teaching International Environmental Law', in Rajamani, L and Peel, J (eds) *The Oxford Handbook of International Environmental Law*, 2nd edn (Oxford: Oxford University Press).
Fitzpatrick, P (1992) *The Mythology of Modern Law* (London: Routledge).
Flannery, M (2016) 'Personification and Embodied Emotional Practice in Middle English Literature' 13(6) *Literature Compass* 351.
Fletcher, A (1964) *Allegory: The Theory of a Symbolic Mode* (Princeton: Princeton University Press).
Fletcher, A (1991) *Colors of the Mind: Conjectures on Thinking in Literature* (Cambridge, MA: Harvard University Press).
Fludernik, M (2003) 'The Diachronization of Narratology' 11(3) *Narrative* 331.
Fludernik, M (2018) 'The Fiction of the Rise of Fictionality' 39 *Poetics Today* 67.

Fludernik, M (2019) *Metaphors of Confinement: The Prison in Fact, Fiction and Fantasy* (Oxford: Oxford University Press).

Forrest-Thomson, V (2016) *Poetic Artifice: A Theory of Twentieth Century Poetry* (Bristol: Shearsman).

Forrester, J (2017) *Thinking in Cases* (Cambridge: Polity).

Fowler, E (2003) *Literary Character: The Human Figure in Early English Writing* (Ithaca: Cornell University Press).

Fraser, RE (2018) 'The Ethics of Metaphor' 128(4) *Ethics* 728.

Fricker, M (2010) 'Can There Be Institutional Virtues?' in Gendler, TS and Hawthorne, J (eds) *Oxford Studies in Epistemology*, Vol. 3 (Oxford: Oxford University Press) 235.

Frow, J (2014) *Character and Person* (Oxford: Oxford University Press).

Frow, J (2020) 'Personhood' in in Stern, S, Del Mar, M and Meyler, B (eds) *The Oxford Handbook of Law and Humanities* (Oxford: Oxford University Press).

Frye, N (1965) 'Varieties of Literary Utopias' 94(2) *Daedalus* 323.

Fuller, L (1930–31) 'Legal Fictions' 25 *Illinois Law Review* 363, 513, 877.

Furtak, R (2018) *Knowing Emotions: Truthfulness and Recognition in Affective Experience* (Oxford: Oxford University Press).

Furth, C, Zeitlin J, and Hsiung, P-C (2007) *Thinking with Cases: Specialist Knowledge in Chinese Cultural History* (Honolulu: University of Hawaii Press).

Fusaroli, R, Gangopadhyay, N, and Tylen, K (2014) 'The Dialogically Extended Mind: Making a Case for Language as Skilful Intersubjective Engagement' 29–30 *Cognitive Systems Research* 31.

Gaakeer, J (2019) *Judging from Experience: Law, Praxis, Humanities* (Edinburgh: Edinburgh University Press).

Gallagher, C (2005) *Nobody's Story: The Vanishing Acts of Women Writers in the Marketplace 1670–1920* (Berkeley: University of California Press).

Gallagher, C (2007) 'The Rise of Fictionality' in Moretti, F (ed) *The Novel*, Vol. 1 (Princeton: Princeton University Press) 336.

Gallagher, C (2011) 'What Would Napoleon Do? Historical, Fictional, and Counterfactual Characters' 42 *New Literary History* 323.

Gallagher, C (2018) *Telling it Like it Wasn't: The Counterfactual Imagination in History and Fiction* (Chicago: Chicago University Press).

Gallagher, S (2005) *How the Body Shapes the Mind* (Oxford: Oxford University Press).

Gallagher, S (2013) 'The Socially Extended Mind' 25–26 *Cognitive Systems Research* 4.

Gallese, V (2014) 'Bodily Selves in Relation: Embodied Simulation as Second-Person Perspective on Intersubjectivity' 369(1644) *Philosophical Transactions of the Royal Society B* 201301770.

Gama, R (2015) 'Presumptions and Fictions: A Collingwoodian Approach' in Del Mar, M and Twining, W (eds) *Legal Fictions in Theory and Practice* (Dordrecht: Springer) 347.

Gamwell, L (2016) *Mathematics and Art: A Cultural History* (Princeton: Princeton University Press).

Gardner, J (2015) 'The Many Faces of the Reasonable Person' 131 *Law Quarterly Review* 563.

Garratt, P (ed) (2016) *The Cognitive Humanities: Embodied Mind in Literature and Culture* (London: Palgrave MacMillan).

Gauker, C (2018) 'Imagistic Cognition', *The Junkyard*, available online: https://junkyardofthemind.com/blog/2018/8/13/imagistic-cognition.

Gelley, A (ed) (1995a) *Unruly Examples: On the Rhetoric of Exemplarity* (Stanford: Stanford University Press).

Gelley, A (1995b) 'Introduction' in Gelley, A (ed) *Unruly Examples: On the Rhetoric of Exemplarity* (Stanford: Stanford University Press) 1.

Gendler, TS (2000) 'The Puzzle of Imaginative Resistance' 97(2) *The Journal of Philosophy* 55.

Gendler, TS (2010) *Intuition, Imagination and Philosophical Methodology* (Oxford University Press).

Geng, P (2019) 'Jurisprudence by Aphorisms: Francis Bacon and the "Uses" of Small Forms' *Law, Culture and the Humanities* 1.

Gentner, D, Bowdle, B, Wolff, P and Boronat, C (2001) 'Metaphor is Like Analogy' in Gentner, D, Holyoak, K and Kokinov, B (eds) *The Analogical Mind: Perspectives from Cognitive Science* (Cambridge, MA: MIT Press) 199.

Gerrig, R and Allbritton, D (1990) 'The Construction of Literary Character: A View from Cognitive Psychology' 24(3) *Style* 380.

Gewirtz, P (1981) 'The Jurisprudence of Hypotheticals' 67(7) *American Bar Association Journal* 864.

Gibbs, R (2005) *Embodiment and Cognitive Science* (Cambridge: Cambridge University Press).

Gibbs, R (2017) *Metaphor Wars: Conceptual Metaphors in Human Life* (Cambridge: Cambridge University Press).
Gibbs, R (2018) 'Embodied Metaphor in Persuasive Legal Metaphor' in Hanne, M and Weisberg, R (eds) *Narrative and Metaphor in the Law* (Cambridge, Cambridge University Press) 90.
Giere, R (1999) *Science without Laws* (Chicago: Chicago University Press).
Ginsburg, C and Biasiori, L (eds) (2018) *A Historical Approach to Casuistry: Norms and Exceptions in a Comparative Perspective* (London: Bloomsbury).
Giudice, M (2015) *Understanding the Nature of Law: A Case for Constructive Conceptual Explanation* (Cheltenham: Edward Elgar).
Glenberg, A and Kaschak, M (2002) 'Grounding Language in Action' 9(3) *Psychonomic Bulletin & Review* 558.
Glenn, P (2007) *On Common Laws* (Oxford: Oxford University Press).
Glenn, P (2013) *The Cosmopolitan State* (Oxford: Oxford University Press).
Glenn, P (2014) *Legal Traditions of the World: Sustainable Diversity in Law*, 5th edn (Oxford: Oxford University Press).
Glissant, E (1997) [1990] *Poetics of Relation*, trans. Wing, B (Ann Arbor: University of Michigan Press).
Godfrey-Smith, P (2009) 'Models and Fictions in Science' 143(1) *Philosophical Studies* 101.
Golder, B (2019) 'Thinking Human Rights Through Metaphor' *Law and Literature*, Latest Articles, available online: https://doi.org/10.1080/1535685X.2018.1558756.
Goldhill, S (2017) 'The Limits of the Case: Exemplarity and the Reception of Classical Literature' 48(3) *New Literary History* 415.
Goldie, P (2000) *The Emotions: A Philosophical Exploration* (New York: Oxford University Press).
Golding, M (1984) *Legal Reasoning* (Peterborough: Broadview Press).
Goldman, A (1983) 'Epistemology and the Theory of Problem Solving' 55 *Synthese* 21.
Goldman, A (1992) *Liaisons: Philosophy Meets the Cognitive and Social Sciences* (Cambridge, MA: MIT Press).
Goldman, A (2006) *Simulating Minds: The Philosophy, Psychology, and Neuroscience of Mindreading* (Oxford: Oxford University Press).
Gombrich, E (1971) 'Personification' in Bolgar, R (ed) *Classical Influences on European Culture, AD 500–1500*, Vol. 1 (Cambridge: Cambridge University Press) 247.
Goodrich, P (1984) 'Law and Language: An Historical and Critical Introduction' 11(2) *Journal of Law and Society* 173.
Goodrich, P (1986) *Reading the Law: A Critical Introduction to Legal Method and Techniques* (Oxford: Blackwell).
Goodrich, P (1994) 'Antirrhesis: Polemical Structures of Common Law Thought', in Sarat, A and Kearns, T (eds) (1994) *The Rhetoric of Law* (Ann Arbor: University of Michigan Press) 57.
Goodrich, P (1996) *Law in the Courts of Love: Literature and Other Minor Jurisprudences* (New York: Routledge).
Goodrich, P (2013) *Legal Emblems and the Art of Law* (Cambridge: Cambridge University Press).
Goodrich, P (2015) 'The Example: Of the Infinite Particulars of Early Modern Common Law' in Lowrie, M and Ludemann, S (eds) *Exemplarity and Singularity: Thinking Through Particulars in Philosophy, Literature and Law* (New York: Routledge) 140.
Goodwin, C (2000) 'Action and Embodiment within Human Social Interaction' 32(10) *Journal of Pragmatics* 1489.
Gordley, J (2013) *The Jurists: A History* (Oxford: Oxford University Press).
Gordon, R (1986) 'Folk Psychology as Simulation' 1 *Mind and Language* 158.
Gosetti-Ferencei, JA (2018) *The Life of Imagination: Revealing and Making the World* (New York: Columbia University Press).
Govier, T and Ayers, L (2012) 'Logic, Parables and Argument' 32(2) *Informal Logic* 161.
Grabham, E (2016) *Brewing Legal Times: Things, Form and the Enactment of Law* (Toronto: Toronto University Press).
Grant, B (2016) *The Aphorism and Other Short Forms* (London: Routledge).
Greco, J (2010) *Achieving Knowledge: A Virtue-Theoretic Account of Epistemic Normativity* (Cambridge: Cambridge University Press).
Greenawalt, K (1977) 'Policy, Rights, and Judicial Decision' 11 *Georgia Law Review* 991.
Gremas, A (1983) *Structural Semantics: An Attempt at a Method* (Lincoln: University of Nebraska Press).
Grethlein, J and Huitink, L (2017) 'Homer's Vividness' 137 *Journal of Hellenic Studies* 67.
Guha, R (1997) *Dominance without Hegemony* (Cambridge, MA: Harvard University Press).

Gurnham, D (ed) (2016) 'Special Issue: Law's Metaphors: Interrogating Languages of Law, Justice and Legitimacy' 43(1) *Journal of Law and Society*.

Haack, S (2014) 'Do Not Block the Way of Inquiry' 50(3) *Transactions of the Charles S. Peirce Society* 319.

Haldane, Lord (1923) 'The Work for the Empire of the Judicial Committee of the Privy Council' 1 *Cambridge Law Journal* 143.

Haldar, P (2019) 'Arguments: The Visual Mediation of Arguments in the Renaissance' in Goodrich, P (ed) *A Cultural History of Law in the Early Modern Age* (London: Bloomsbury) 99.

Halliday, P (2014) 'Authority in the Archives' 1 *Critical Analysis of Law* 1.

Halliwell, S (1987) *The Poetics of Aristotle: Translation and Commentary* (Chapel Hill: University of North Carolina Press).

Halliwell, S (2002) *The Aesthetics of Mimesis: Ancient Texts and Modern Problems* (Princeton: Princeton University Press).

Halpern, R (2017) *Eclipse of Action: Tragedy and Political Economy* (Chicago: Chicago University Press).

Hanne, M and Weisberg, M (eds) (2018) *Metaphor and Narrative in the Law* (Cambridge: Cambridge University Press).

Haraway, D (1976) *Crystals, Fabrics and Fields: Metaphors of Organicism in Twentieth-Century Developmental Biology* (New Haven: Yale University Press).

Hare, RM (1952) *The Language of Morals* (Oxford: Clarendon Press).

Harpham, G (1982) *On the Grotesque: Strategies of Contradiction in Art and Literature* (Princeton: Princeton University Press).

Harris, P (2000) *The Work of the Imagination* (Oxford: Blackwell).

Harris, RA (2019) 'The Fourth Master Trope, Antithesis' 22(1) *Advances in the History of Rhetoric* 1.

Haverkamp, A (2017) *Productive Digression: Theorizing Practice* (Berlin: de Gruyter).

Hawhee, B (2004) *Bodily Arts: Rhetoric and Athletics in Ancient Greece* (Austin: University of Texas Press).

Hawhee, D (2011) 'Looking into Aristotle's Eyes: Toward a Theory of Rhetorical Vision' 14(2) *Advances in the History of Rhetoric* 139.

Hayaert, V (2020) 'Emblems' in Stern, S, Del Mar, M and Meyler, B (eds) *The Oxford Handbook of Law and Humanities* (Oxford: Oxford University Press).

Hayes, L (2016) *Stories of Care: A Labour of Law* (London: Palgrave Macmillan).

Hayles, K (1984) *The Cosmic Web: Scientific Field Models and Literary Strategies in the Twentieth Century* (Ithaca: Cornell University Press).

Heal, J (1998) 'Co-Cognition and Off-line Simulation' 13 *Mind and Language* 477.

Heller, J and Venzke, I (eds) (Forthcoming) *Situating Contingency in International Law* (Oxford: Oxford University Press).

Helm, B (2007) *Emotional Reason: Deliberation, Motivation and the Nature of Value* (Cambridge: Cambridge University Press).

Henkin, L (2005) 'War and Terrorism: Law or Metaphor' 45 *Santa Clara Law Review* 817.

Herman, B (1993) *The Practice of Moral Judgement* (Cambridge, MA: Harvard University Press).

Herman, D (2002) *Story Logic: Problems and Possibilities of Narrative* (Lincoln: University of Nebraska Press).

Herman, D (ed) (2003) *Narrative Theory and the Cognitive Sciences* (Chicago: Chicago University Press).

Herman, MJ (1976) 'The Founding of the Supreme Court of Canada and the Abolition of the Appeal to the Privy Council' 8(1) *Ottawa Law Review* 7.

Herodas (1971) *Mimiambi*, ed. Cunningham, IC (Oxford: Clarendon Press).

Hesse, M (1963) *Models and Analogies in Science* (London: Sheed and Ward).

Hibbits, B (1994) 'Making Sense of Metaphors' 16 *Cardozo Law Review* 229.

Higgins, L and Leps, MC (1998) '"Passport, Please": Legal, Literary, and Critical Fictions of Identity' 25 *College Literature* 94.

Hildesheimer, W (1984) *Marbot: Eine Biographie* (Frankfurt: Suhrkamp).

Hills, D (2017) 'The What and the How of Metaphorical Imagining, Part One' 174(1) *Philosophical Studies* 13.

Hochman, B (1986) *Character in Literature* (Ithaca: Cornell University Press).

Hoffmann, Lord (1995) 'Anthropocentric Justice: The Reasonable Man and his Friends', 29 *Law Teacher* 127.

Hoffmann, Lord (2018) 'Language and Lawyers' 134 *Law Quarterly Review* 553.

Hogan, PC (2004) 'Stories and Morals' in Spolsky, E (ed) *The Work of Fiction: Cognition, Culture and Complexity* (Aldershot: Ashgate) 31.

Hogan, PC (2016) 'Jesus's Parables' 24(2) *Narrative* 113.
Holmes, OW (1995) *The Collected Works of Justice Holmes*, ed. Novick, SM (Chicago: Chicago University Press).
Holmes, R and Johnson, T (eds) (2018) 'Special Issue: In Pursuit of Truth: Law and Emotion in Early Modern Europe' 54(1) *Forum for Modern Language Studies.*
Honoré, T (1993) 'The Dependence of Morality on Law' 13 *Oxford Journal of Legal Studies* 1.
Hookway (2008) 'Epistemic Immediacy, Doubt and Anxiety: On a Role for Affective States in Epistemic Evaluation' in Brun, G, Doguoglu, U and Kuenzle, D (eds) *Epistemology and Emotions* (Abingdon: Ashgate) 51.
Hookway, C (1998) 'Doubt, Affect States and the Regulation of Inquiry' 28(1) *Canadian Journal of Philosophy* 203.
Hooley, R (2014) 'Implied Terms after *Belize Telecom*' 73(2) *Cambridge Law Journal* 315.
Hope, Lord (2003) 'James McGhee: A Second Mrs Donoghue?' 62 *Cambridge Law Journal* 587.
Horwitz, MJ (1993) 'Foreword: The Constitution of Change: Legal Fundamentality Without Fundamentalism' 107 *Harvard Law Review* 32.
Hoyningen-Huene, P (1987) 'Context of Discovery and Context of Justification' 18(4) *Studies in History and Philosophy of Science Part A* 501.
Huitink, L (2018) 'Enargeia, Enactivism, and the Ancient Readerly Imagination' in Anderson, M, Cairns, D and Sprevak, M (eds) *Distributed Cognition in Classical Antiquity* (Edinburgh: Edinburgh University Press) 169.
Huizinga, J (1996 [1919] *The Autumn of the Middle Ages*, trans. Payton, R and Mammitzsch, U (Chicago: Chicago University Press).
Hui, A (2019) *A Theory of the Aphorism: From Confucius to Twitter* (Princeton: Princeton University Press).
Hume, D (1978) [1739] *A Treatise of Human Nature*, ed. Nidditch, PH (Oxford: Oxford University Press).
Hume, R (2011) 'The Socio-Politics of London Comedy from Jonson to Steele' 74(2) *Huntington Library Quarterly* 187.
Hunter, R, McGlynn, C and Rackley, E (eds) (2010) *Feminist Judgements: From Theory to Practice* (Oxford: Hart).
Hurley, S (1990) 'Coherence, Hypothetical Cases, and Precedent' 10 *Oxford Journal of Legal Studies* 221.
Hutchinson, A (2005) *Evolution and the Common Law* (Cambridge: Cambridge University Press).
Hutson, L (2006) 'Forensic Aspects of Renaissance Mimesis' 94 *Representations* 80.
Hutson, L (2015) *Circumstantial Shakespeare* (Oxford: Oxford University Press).
Hutson, L (ed) (2017) *The Oxford Handbook of Law and Literature 1500–1700* (Oxford: Oxford University Press).
Ibhawoh, B (2013) *Imperial Justice: Africans in Empire's Court* (Oxford: Oxford University Press).
Irving, D (2017) 'Storytelling in Miniature: Microfiction and Reader Participation' (2017) 18 *Enthymema* 150.
Iser, W (1993) *The Fictive and the Imaginary: Charting Literary Anthropology* (Baltimore: Johns Hopkins University Press).
Jackson, B (1988) *Law, Fact and Narrative Coherence* (Liverpool: Deborah Charles).
Jackson, N (2009) 'Moral Particularism and the Role of Imaginary Cases: A Pragmatist Approach' 8(1) *European Journal of Pragmatism and American Philosophy* 237.
Jackson, V (2006) 'Constitutions as Living Trees? Comparative Constitutional Law and Interpretive Metaphors' 75 *Fordham Law Review* 921.
Jaffey, P (2017) 'Two Ways of Understanding the Common Law' 8(3) *Jurisprudence* 435.
Jannidis, F (2013) 'Character', *The Living Handbook of Narratology*, available online: www.lhn.uni-hamburg.de/node/41.html.
Jarratt, S (1991) *Re-Reading the Sophists: Classical Rhetoric Refigured* (Carbondale: Southern Illinois University Press).
Jeannerod, M (2006) *Motor Cognition: What Actions Tell of the Self* (Oxford: Oxford University Press).
Jebb, RC (1870) *The Characters of Theophrastus* (London: Macmillan).
Jefferson, T (2019) *Jefferson's Legal Commonplace Book*, ed. Konig D and Zuckert, M (Princeton: Princeton University Press).
John, E (1998) 'Reading Fiction and Conceptual Knowledge' 56(4) *Journal of Aesthetics and Art Criticism* 331.
Johnson, M (2007) 'Mind, Metaphor, Law' 58 *Mercer Law Review* 845.

Johnson, M (2018) *The Aesthetics of Meaning and Thought: The Bodily Roots of Philosophy, Science, Morality and Art* (Chicago: Chicago University Press).

Jolles, A (2017) [1958] *Simple Forms: Legend, Saga, Myth, Riddle, Saying, Case, Memorabile, Fairytale, Joke*, trans. Schwartz, P (London: Verso).

Jonsen, A and Toulmin, S (1988) *The Abuse of Casuistry: A History of Moral Reasoning* (Berkeley: University of California Press).

Kalinin, I (2018) 'The Body of the Plot: Victor Shklovsky's Theory of Narrative' in Garrett, M (ed) *The Cambridge Companion to Narrative Theory* (Cambridge: Cambridge University Press), 46.

Kang, HY and Kendall, S (2020) 'Legal Materiality' in Stern, S, Del Mar, M and Meyler, B (eds) *The Oxford Handbook of Law and Humanities* (Oxford: Oxford University Press).

Kaptein, H, Prakken, H and Verheji, B (eds) (2009) *Legal Evidence and Proof: Statistics, Stories and Logic* (Farnham: Ashgate).

Kantorowicz, E (1957) *The King's Two Bodies: A Study in Medieval Political Theology* (Princeton: Princeton University Press).

Kaufmann, L (2011), 'Social Minds' in Jarvie, I and Zamora, J (eds) *The Sage Handbook of the Philosophy of Social Sciences* (London: Sage) 153.

Kaye, J (2014) *A History of Balance, 1250–1375: The Emergence of a New Model of Equilibrium and Its Impact on Thought* (Cambridge: Cambridge University Press).

Kayman, M (1997) 'The Reader and the Jury: Legal Fictions and the Making of Commercial Law in Eighteenth-Century England' 9(4) *Eighteenth-Century Fiction* 373.

Kearney, R (1988), *The Wake of Imagination: Towards a Postmodern Culture* (London: Routledge).

Keenan, S (2016) 'Smoke, Curtains and Mirrors: The Production of Race Through Time and Title Registration' 28(1) *Law and Critique* 87.

Keenan, S (2020) 'Property: Changing Formations of Having and Being' in Stern, S, Del Mar, M and Meyler, B (eds) *The Oxford Handbook of Law and Humanities* (Oxford: Oxford University Press).

Keith, K (2009) 'The Interplay with the Judicial Committee of the Privy Council' in Blom-Cooper, L, Dickson, B and Drewry, G (eds) *The Judicial House of Lords 1876–2009* (Oxford: Oxford University Press) 315.

Keller, EV (1985) *Reflections on Gender and Science* (New Haven: Yale University Press).

Kelsen, H (2015) 'On the Theory of Juridic Fictions. With Special Consideration of Vaihinger's Philosophy of the As-If', trans. Kletzer, C in Del Mar, M and Twining, W (eds) *Legal Fictions in Theory and Practice* (Dordrecht: Springer) 3.

Kendon, A (2004) *Gesture: Visible Action as Utterance* (Cambridge: Cambridge University Press).

Kennedy, D (2008) *Legal Reasoning: Collected Essays* (Aurora: The Davies Group).

Kertzer, J (1988) *Poetic Argument: Studies in Modern Poetry* (Montreal: McGill-Queen's University Press).

Kind, A (2001) 'Putting the Image Back in Imagination' 62(1) *Philosophy and Phenomenological Research* 85.

Kind, A (2017) 'Imaginative Vividness' 3(1) *Journal of the American Philosophical Association* 32.

Kind, A (2018) 'How'd Imagination Become So Hot', *The Junkyard Blog*, available online: https://junkyardofthemind.com/blog/2018/5/8/howd-imagination-become-so-hot.

Kind, A (2020) 'Empathy, Imagination and the Law' in Amaya, A and Del Mar, M (eds) *Virtue, Emotion and Imagination in Law and Legal Reasoning* (Oxford: Hart).

Kind, A (ed) (2016) *The Routledge Handbook of the Philosophy of Imagination* (London: Routledge).

Kind, A and Kung, P (eds) (2016) *Knowledge Through Imagination* (Oxford: Oxford University Press).

King, M (2017) 'Against Personifying the Reasonable Person' 11(4) *Criminal Law and Philosophy* 725.

Kirkby, C (2018) 'Law Evolves: The Uses of Primitive Law in Anglo-American Concepts of Modern Law, 1861–1961' 58(4) *American Journal of Legal History* 535.

Knauer, N (2010) 'Legal Fictions and Juristic Truth' 23 *St. Thomas Law Review* 70.

Kneller, J (2007) *Kant and the Power of Imagination* (Cambridge: Cambridge University Press).

Knowles, E (2018) *'And I Quote …': A History of Using Other People's Words* (Oxford: Oxford University Press).

Kobow, B (2014) 'How to Do Things with Fictions: Reconsidering Vaihinger for a Philosophy of Social Sciences' 44(2) *Philosophy of the Social Sciences* 201.

Korda, N (2013) 'Coverture and its Discontents: Legal Fictions on and off the Early Modern Stage' in Stretton, T and Kesselring, K (eds) *Married Women and the Law: Coverture in England and the Common Law World* (Montreal: McGill-Queen's University Press) 45.

Koschorke, A (2018) *Fact and Fiction: Elements of a General Theory of Narrative* (Berlin: Walter de Gruyter).

Koskenniemi, M (2005) *From Apology to Utopia: The Structure of International Legal Argument* (Cambridge: Cambridge University Press).
Kramer, A (2004) 'Implication in Fact as an Instance of Contractual Interpretation' 63(2) *Cambridge Law Journal* 384.
Krenmayr, T (2011) *Metaphor in Newspapers*, Doctoral Thesis, Vrije Universiteit Amsterdam, available online: https://research.vu.nl/en/publications/metaphor-in-newspapers.
Kriegel, U (2015) *The Varieties of Consciousness* (Oxford: Oxford University Press).
Kripke, S (1980) *Naming and Necessity* (Cambridge, MA: Harvard University Press).
Krisch, N (2010) *Beyond Constitutionalism: The Pluralist Structure of Postnational Law* (Oxford: Oxford University Press).
Kuhn, T (1970) [1962] *The Structure of Scientific Revolutions* (Chicago: Chicago University Press).
Kukkonen, K (2014) 'Presence and Prediction: The Embodied Reader's Cascades of Cognition' 48(3) *Style* 367.
Kukkonen, K (2018) 'A Moving Target: Cognitive Narratology and Feminism' 32(6) *Textual Practice* 973.
La Caze, M (2002) *The Analytic Imaginary* (Ithaca: Cornell University Press).
Laden, A (2002) *Reasoning: A Social Picture* (Oxford: Oxford University Press).
Lahroodi, R (2007) 'Collective Epistemic Virtues' 21(3) *Social Epistemology* 281.
Lakoff, G and Johnson, M (1980) *Metaphors We Live By* (Chicago: Chicago University Press).
Lakoff, G and Turner, M (1989) *More than Cool Reason: A Field Guide to Poetic Metaphor* (Chicago: Chicago University Press).
Lamond, G (2005) 'Do Precedents Create Rules?' 11 *Legal Theory* 1.
Landy, J (2012) *How to Do Things with Fictions* (Oxford: Oxford University Press).
Langer, U (2018) 'Turning to the Beloved (Virgil, Petrarch, Scève)' in Banks, K and Chesters, T (eds) *Movement in Renaissance Literature: Exploring Kinesic Intelligence* (London: Palgrave MacMillan) 31.
Larsson, S (2013) 'Metaphors, Law and Digital Phenomena: the Swedish Pirate Bay Court Case', 21 *International Journal of Law, Information and Technology* 354.
Le Doeuff, M (1989) *The Philosophical Imaginary*, trans. Gordon, C (Stanford: Stanford University Press).
Leeuwen van, N (2013) 'The Meanings of "Imagine". Part I: Constructive Imagination' 8(3) *Philosophy Compass* 220.
Leiter, B (2007) *Naturalising Jurisprudence: Essays on American Legal Realism and Naturalism in Legal Philosophy* (Oxford: Oxford University Press).
Lerer, S (ed) (1996) *Literary History and the Challenge of Philology: The Legacy of Erich Auerbach* (Stanford: Stanford Univ. Press).
Levenbook, B (2000) 'The Meaning of a Precedent' 6 *Legal Theory* 185.
Levi, EH (1949) *An Introduction to Legal Reasoning* (Chicago: University of Chicago Press).
Levi, EH (1965) 'The Nature of Judicial Reasoning' 32(3) *University of Chicago Law Review* 395.
Levinas, E (1991) *Totality and Infinity* (Dordrecht: Kluwer).
Levitas, R (2013) *Utopia as Method* (London: Palgrave Macmillan).
Levy, A and Godfrey-Smith (eds) (Forthcoming) *The Scientific Imagination: Philosophical and Psychological Perspectives* (Oxford: Oxford University Press).
Lewison, K (2011) *Interpretation of Contracts*, 5th edn (London: Sweet and Maxwell).
Lima, M (2014) *The Book of Trees: Visualising Branches of Knowledge* (Princeton: Princeton Architectural Press).
Lind, D (2015) 'The Pragmatic Value of Legal Fictions' in Del Mar, M and Twining, W (eds) *Legal Fictions in Theory and Practice* (Dordrecht: Springer) 83.
Little, OM (1995) 'Seeing and Caring: The Role of Affect in Feminist Moral Epistemology' 10(3) *Hypatia* 117.
Liu, Q (2011) 'The *White & Carter* Principle: A Restatement' 74 *Modern Law Review* 171.
Llewellyn, K (1960) *The Common Law Tradition: Deciding Appeals* (Boston, MA: Little Brown & Co).
Lloyd, G (2013) *Enlightenment Shadows* (Oxford: Oxford University Press).
Lloyd, GER (1999) *Magic, Reason and Experience: Studies in the Origins and Development of Greek Science* (Cambridge, MA: Hackett).
Lobban, M (1991) *The Common Law and English Jurisprudence* (Oxford: Oxford University Press).
LoLordo, A (ed) (2019) *Persons: A History* (Oxford: Oxford University Press).
Lowrie, M and Ludemann, S (eds) (2015) *Exemplarity and Singularity: Thinking Through Particulars in Philosophy, Literature and Law* (New York: Routledge).
Lucy, W (2017) *Law's Judgement* (Oxford: Hart).

MacCormick, N (1978) *Legal Reasoning and Legal Theory* (Oxford: Clarendon Press).
MacCormick, N (1983) 'Legal Decisions and their Consequences: From Dewey to Dworkin' 58 *New York University Law Review* 239.
MacCormick, N (1995) 'The Relative Heteronomy of Law' 3(1) *European Journal of Philosophy* 69.
MacCormick, N (2005) *Rhetoric and the Rule of Law* (Oxford: Oxford University Press).
MacCormick, N (2009) *Practical Reason in Law and Morality* (Oxford: Oxford University Press).
MacCormick, N and Summers, R (eds) (1991) *Interpreting Statutes: A Comparative Study* (Aldershot: Ashgate).
MacCormick, N and Summers, R (eds) (1997) *Interpreting Precedents: A Comparative Study* (Aldershot: Ashgate).
MacDonald, V (1951) 'The Privy Council and the Canadian Constitution' 29 *The Canadian Bar Review* 1021.
Mack, P (2011) *A History of Rhetoric in the Renaissance 1380–1620* (Oxford: Oxford University Press).
MacKinnon, FD (1917) *The Effect of War on Contract* (Oxford: Clarendon Press).
MacKinnon, FD (1926) *Some Aspects of Commercial Law: A Lecture*, Delivered at the London School of Economics on 3 March 1926 (London: Humphrey Milord / Oxford University Press).
MacKinnon, FD (1933) 'The Law and the Lawyers' in Tuberville, AS (ed) *Johnson's England: An Account of the Life and Manners of His Age*, Vol. 2 (Oxford: Clarendon Press), 307.
Macklem, T (2015) *Law and Life in Common* (Oxford: Oxford University Press).
Maclean, I (1999) 'Legal Fictions and Fictional Entities in Renaissance Jurisprudence' 20(3) *Legal History* 1.
Maclean, I (2002) *Logic, Signs and Nature in the Renaissance* (Cambridge: Cambridge University Press).
MacLean, J (2012) *Rethinking Law as Process: Creativity, Novelty, Change* (London: Routledge).
Maine, H (1931) [1861] *Ancient Law* (London: Oxford University Press).
Makela, F (2011) 'Metaphors and Models in Legal Theory' 52 *Les Cahiers de Droit* 397.
Mangini, M (2019) 'Is the Reasonable Person a Person of Virtue?' *Res Publica*, First Online, available online: https://doi.org/10.1007/s11158-019-09432-5.
Margolin, U (1983) 'Characterisation in Narrative: Some Theoretical Prolegomena' 67 *Neophilologus* 1.
Margolin, U (1990) 'Individuals in Narrative Worlds: An Ontological Perspective' 11 *Poetics Today* 843.
Margolin, U (1995) 'Characters in Literary Narrative: Representation and Signification' 106 *Semiotica* 373.
Markova, I (2017) 'From Imagination to Well-Controlled Images: Challenge for the Dialogical Mind' in Zittoun, T and Glaveanu, V (eds) *Handbook of Imagination and Culture* (Oxford: Oxford University Press) 319.
Marsh, D (1980) *The Quattrocento Dialogue* (Cambridge, MA: Harvard University Press).
Marshall, D (1984) 'Adam Smith and the Theatricality of Moral Sentiments' 10 *Critical Inquiry* 592.
Masala, A and Webber, J (eds) (2016) *From Personality to Virtue: Essays on the Philosophy of Character* (Oxford: Oxford University Press).
Matlock, T (2004) 'Fiction Motion as Cognitive Simulation' 32(8) *Memory & Cognition* 1389.
Matsuda, M (1989) 'When the First Quail Calls: Multiple Consciousness as Jurisprudential Method' 11 *Women's Rights Law Reporter* 7.
McArthur, N (2004) 'David Hume's Legal Theory: The Significance of General Laws' 30(4) *History of European Ideas* 149.
McBain, HL (1927) *The Living Constitution: A Consideration of the Realities and Legends of Our Fundamental Law* (New York: The Workers Education Bureau Press).
McCaughran, J (2011) 'Implied Terms: The Journey of the Man on the Clapham Omnibus' 70(3) *Cambridge Law Journal* 607.
McGinn, C (2004) *Mindsight: Image, Dream, Meaning* (Cambridge, Mass: Harvard University Press).
Medina, J (2013) 'An Enactivist Approach to the Imagination: Embodied Enactments and "Fictional Emotions"' 50(3) *American Philosophical Quarterly* 317.
Melion, W and Ramakers, B (eds) (2016a) *Personification: Embodying Meaning and Emotion* (Leiden: Brill).
Melion, W and Ramakers, B (2016b) 'Personification: An Introduction' in Melion, W and Ramakers, B (eds) *Personification: Embodying Meaning and Emotion* (Leiden: Brill) 1.
Mendenhall, A (2017) *Oliver Wendell Holmes Jr., Pragmatism, and the Jurisprudence of Agon: Aesthetic Dissent and the Common Law* (Lewisburg: Bucknell University Press).
Merleau-Ponty, M (2002) *Phenomenology of Perception*, Trans. Smith, C (London: Routledge).
Michelon, C (2012) 'Practical Wisdom in Legal Decision-Making' in Amaya, A and Ho, L (eds) *Law, Virtue and Justice* (Oxford: Hart) 29.
Michelon, C (2018) 'Lawfulness and the Perception of Legal Salience' 9(1) *Jurisprudence* 47.

Miller, B (2009) 'Beguiled by Metaphors: The "Living Tree" and Originalist Constitutional Interpretation in Canada' 22 *Canadian Journal of Law and Jurisprudence* 331.

Miller, B (2011) 'Origin Myth: The Persons Case, the Living Tree, and the New Originalism' in Huscroft, G and Miller, B (eds) *The Challenge of Originalism* (Cambridge: Cambridge University Press) 120.

Miller, JH (1990) *Versions of Pygmalion* (Cambridge, MA: Harvard University Press).

Miller, JH (1995) 'Parabolic Exemplarity: The Example of Nietzsche's *Thus Spoke Zarathustra*' in Gelley, A (ed) *Unruly Examples: On the Rhetoric of Exemplarity* (Stanford: Stanford University Press) 162.

Milsom, SFC (2003) *A Natural History of the Common Law* (New York: Columbia University Press).

Mitchell, C (2012) 'Obligations in Commercial Contracts: A Matter of Law or Interpretation?' *Current Legal Problems* 455.

Mitchell, P (2016) 'Privy Council and the Difficulty of Distance' 36 *Oxford Journal of Legal Studies* 26.

Moglen, E (1998) 'Legal Fictions and Common Law', available online http://moglen.law.columbia.edu/publications/fict.html.

Mootz III, FJ (2006) *Rhetorical Knowledge in Legal Practice and Critical Legal Theory* (Tuscaloosa: University of Alabama Press).

Mootz III, FJ (2010) *Law, Hermeneutics and Rhetoric* (London: Routledge).

Moran, M (2003) *Rethinking the Reasonable Person: An Egalitarian Reconstruction of the Objective Standard* (Oxford: Oxford University Press).

Moran, R (2017) *The Philosophical Imagination: Selected Essays* (Oxford: Oxford University Press).

More, AH (2012) 'Colonial Poetics' in Greene, R et al (eds) *The Princeton Encyclopedia of Poetry and Poetics* (Princeton: Princeton University Press) 278.

Moretti, F (2000) 'The Slaughterhouse of Literature' 61(1) *Modern Language Quarterly* 207.

Morgan, E (2004) 'The Crying of Rule 49' 54 *University of Toronto Law Journal* 45.

Morton, A (2012) *Bounded Thinking: Intellectual Virtues for Limited Agents* (Oxford: Oxford University Press).

Morton, A (2013) *Emotion and Imagination* (Cambridge: Polity).

Morton, A (2014) 'Shared Knowledge from Individual Vice' 2(1) *Philosophical Inquiries* 163.

Moscovitz, L (2002) *Talmudic Legal Reasoning: From Casuistics to Conceptualization* (Tubingen: JCB Mohr).

Moscovitz, L (2015) 'Rabbinic Legal Fictions' in Del Mar, M and Twining, W (eds) *Legal Fictions in Theory and Practice* (Dordrecht: Springer) 325.

Moss, A (2011) *Printed Commonplace-Books and the Structuring of Renaissance Thought* (Oxford: Oxford University Press).

Motha, S (2018) *Archiving Sovereignty: Law, History, Violence* (Ann Arbor: University of Michigan Press).

Motyka, K (2007) *Leon Petrażycki: Challenge to Legal Orthodoxy* (Lublin: Towarzystwo Naukowe Katolickiego Uniwersytetu Lubelskiego Jana Pawła II).

Mukherji, S (2006) *Law and Representation in Early Modern Drama* (Cambridge: Cambridge University Press).

Mulholland, J (2013) *Sounding Imperial: Poetic Voice and the Politics of Empire 1730–1820* (Baltimore: Johns Hopkins University Press).

Murdoch, I (1956) 'Vision and Choice in Morality' 30 *Proceedings of the Aristotelian Society Supplementary Volumes* 32.

Murdoch, I (1970) *The Sovereignty of Good* (London: Routledge and Kegan Paul).

Musolff, A (2000) 'Political Imagery of Europe: A House without Exit Doors?' 21(3) *Journal of Multilingual and Multicultural Development* 216.

Musolff, A (2006) 'Metaphor Scenarios in Public Discourse' 21(1) *Metaphor and Symbol* 23.

Musolff, A (2014) 'Metaphorical Parasites and "Parasitic" Metaphors: Semantic Exchanges Between Political and Scientific Vocabularies' 13(2) *Journal of Language and Politics* 218.

Naffine, N (2009) *Law's Meaning of Life: Philosophy, Religion, Darwin and the Legal Person* (Oxford: Hart).

Nanay, B (2016) 'The Role of Imagination in Decision-Making' 31(1) *Mind & Language* 127.

Nenad Miscevic, N (2019) 'Imaginative Enactments in Thought: Locating Thought Experiments', *The Junkyard Blog*, available online: https://junkyardofthemind.com/blog/2019/4/28/imaginative-enactments-in-thought-locating-thought-experiments.

Netz, R (1999) *The Shaping of Deduction in Greek Mathematics: A Study in Cognitive History* (Cambridge: Cambridge University Press).

Netz, R (2009) 'Imagination and Layered Ontology in Greek Mathematics' 17(1) *Configurations* 19.

New Zealand Law Reform Committee (1983) 'The Rule in *White & Carter v McGregor*: A Report by the Contracts and Commercial Law Reform Committee', 5 May 1983.

Nichols, S (ed) (2006) *The Architecture of the Imagination: New Essays on Pretence, Possibility and Fiction* (Oxford: Oxford University Press).

Nichols, S and Stich, S (2003) *Mindreading: An Integrated Account of Pretence. Self-Awareness, and Understanding Other Minds* (New York: Oxford University Press).

Nickles, T (1989) 'Heuristic Appraisal: A Proposal' 3 *Social Epistemology* 175.

Nickles, T (ed) (1980) *Scientific Discovery: Case Studies* (Dordrecht: Springer).

Nienaber, PM (1962) 'The Effect of Anticipatory Repudiation: Principle and Policy' 20(2) *Cambridge Law Journal* 213.

Noe, A (2004) *Action in Perception* (Cambridge, MA: MIT Press).

Noonan, J (1976) *Persons and Masks of the Law: Cardozo, Holmes, Jefferson, and Wythe as Makers of the Masks* (New York: Farrar, Straus and Giroux).

Novikoff, A (2013) *The Medieval Culture of Disputation; Pedagogy, Practice and Performance* (Philadelphia: University of Pennsylvania Press).

Novitz, D (1987) *Knowledge, Fiction and Imagination* (Philadelphia: Temple University Press).

Nussbaum, M (1986) *Aristotle's De Motu Animalium* (Princeton: Princeton University Press).

Nussbaum, M (1997) *Poetic Justice: The Literary Imagination and Public Life* (New York: Beacon Press).

Nussbaum, M (2001) *Upheavals of Thought: The Intelligence of Emotions* (Cambridge: Cambridge University Press).

O'Connell, P (2017a) 'Enargeia, Persuasion, and the Vividness Effect' 20(3) *Advances in the History of Rhetoric* 225.

O'Connell, P (2017b) *The Rhetoric of Seeing in Attic Forensic Oratory* (Austin: Texas University Press).

O'Donoghue, A (2018) '"The Admixture of Feminine Weakness and Susceptibility": Gendered Personifications of the State in International Law' 19(1) *Melbourne Journal of International Law* 227.

O'Gorman, TE (2005) 'Aristotle's Phantasia in the Rhetoric: Lexis, Appearance, and the Epideictic Function of Discourse' 38(1) *Philosophy and Rhetoric* 16.

O'Sullivan, J (2017) 'Repudiation: Keeping the Contract Alive' in Virgo, G and Worthington, S (eds) *Commercial Remedies: Resolving Controversies* (Cambridge: Cambridge University Press) 51.

Ogden, CK (1932) *Bentham's Theory of Fictions* (New York: Kegan Paul).

Olivier, P (1975) *Legal Fictions in Theory and Practice* (Rotterdam: Rotterdam University Press).

Olmos, P (ed) (2017) *Narration as Argument* (Dordrecht: Springer).

Olowofoyeku, A (2009) 'Bias and the Informed Observer: A Call for a Return to Gough' 68 *Cambridge Law Journal* 388.

Olson, G (2018) 'On Narrating and Troping the Law: The Conjoined Use of Narrative and Metaphor in Legal Discourse' in Hanne, M and Weisberg, M (eds) *Metaphor and Narrative in the Law* (Cambridge: Cambridge University Press) 19.

Orford, A (ed) (2006) *International Law and its Others* (Cambridge: Cambridge University Press).

Ossa-Richardson, A (2019) *A History of Ambiguity* (Princeton: Princeton University Press).

Ovid (2010) *Metamorphoses*. Trans. Lombardo, S (Indianapolis: Hackett Publishing Co Ltd).

Palmer, A (2004) *Fictional Minds* (Lincoln: University of Nebraska Press).

Palmer, A (2010) *Social Minds in the Novel* (Ohio: Ohio University Press).

Paolo, N (2015) 'Casuistry as Common Law Morality' 36(6) *Theoretical Medicine and Bioethics* 373.

Pasanek, B (2015) *Metaphors of Mind: An Eighteenth-Century Dictionary* (Baltimore: Johns Hopkins University Press).

Passeron, JC and Revel, J (eds) (2005) *Penser par cas* (Paris: Éditions de l'École des Hautes Études en Sciences Sociales).

Paxson, J (1994) *The Poetics of Personification* (Cambridge: Cambridge University Press).

Peacocke, C (1985) 'Imagination, Possibility and Experience' in Foster, J and Robinson, H (eds) *Essays on Berkeley* (Oxford: Oxford University Press) 19.

Pearson, R (1993) *The Fables of Reason: A Study of Voltaire's "Contes Philosophiques"* (Oxford: Oxford University Press).

Perelman, C and Olbrechts-Tyteca, L (1969) *The New Rhetoric: A Treatise in Argumentation* (Notre Dame: University of Notre Dame Press).

Perelman, J and Young, K (2010) 'Rights as Footprints: A New Metaphor for Contemporary Human Rights Practice' 9(1) *Northwestern Journal of International Human Rights* 27.

Petrażycki, L (1955) *Law and Morality*, trans. Babb, HW (Cambridge, MA: Harvard University Press).

Petroski, K (2018) *Fiction and the Languages of Law* (New York: Routledge).

Phang, A (1998) 'Implied Terms, Business Efficacy and the Officious Bystander: A Modern History' 1 *Journal of Business Law* 1.

Phang, A (2014) 'The Challenge of Principled Gap-Filling: A Study of Implied Terms in a Comparative Context' *Journal of Business Law* 263.

Phelan, J (1989) *Reading People, Reading Plots: Character, Progression, and the Interpretation of Narrative* (Chicago: Chicago University Press).

Picciuto, E (2009) 'The Pleasures of Suppositions' 22(4) *Philosophical Psychology* 487.

Pitts, J (2018) *Boundaries of the International: Law and Empire* (Cambridge, MA: Harvard University Press).

Plato (1875) *The Theaetetus*, trans. Paley, FA (London: George Bell and Sons).

Plett, H (2012) *Enargeia in Classical Antiquity and the Early Modern Age: The Aesthetics of Evidence* (Leiden: Brill).

Pollock, F (1912) *The Genius of the Common Law* (New York: Columbia University Press).

Polvinen, M (2017) 'Cognitive Science and the Double Vision of Fiction' in Burke, M and Troscianko, E (eds) *Cognitive Literary Science: Dialogues between Literature and Cognition* (Oxford: Oxford University Press) 135.

Polvinen, MK (2016) 'Enactive Perception and Fictional Worlds' in Garratt, P (ed) *The Cognitive Humanities: Embodied Mind in Literature and Culture* (London: Palgrave MacMillan) 19.

Pomata, G (2010) 'Sharing Cases: The Observationes in Early Modern Medicine' 15 *Early Science and Medicine* 193.

Pomata, G (2011) 'Observation Rising' in Daston, L and Lunbeck, E (eds) *Histories of Scientific Observation* (Chicago: Chicago University Press) 45.

Pomata, G (2014) 'The Medical Case Narrative: Distant Reading of an Epistemic Genre' 32(1) *Literature and Medicine* 1.

Pomata, G (2018) 'The Medical Case Narrative in Pre-Modern Europe and China: Comparative History of an Epistemic Genre' in Ginsburg, C and Biasiori, L (eds) *A Historical Approach to Casuistry: Norms and Exceptions in a Comparative Perspective* (London: Bloomsbury) 15.

Popper, K (1959) *The Logic of Scientific Discovery* (London: Hutchinson & Co).

Postema, G (2002) 'Classical Common Law Jurisprudence I' 2(2) *Oxford Commonwealth Law Journal* 155.

Postema, G (2003) 'Classical Common Law Jurisprudence II' 3(1) *Oxford Commonwealth Law Journal* 1.

Postema, G (ed) (2017) *Matthew Hale: On the Law of Nature, Reason and Common Law* (Oxford: Oxford University Press).

Pound, R (1959) *Jurisprudence* (St. Paul: West Publishing).

Pound, R (1999) [1963] *The Spirit of the Common Law* (New Brunswick: Transaction Publishers).

Powell, J (ed) (2013) *Heidegger and Language* (Bloomington: Indiana University Press).

Pratt, ML (2008) [1992] *Imperial Eyes: Travel Writing and Transculturation* (New York: Routledge).

Priel, D (2017) 'Conceptions of Authority and the Anglo-American Common Law Divide' 65(3) *American Journal of Comparative Law* 609.

Prinz, J (2007) *The Emotional Construction of Morals* (Oxford: Oxford University Press).

Puckett, K (2016) *Narrative Theory: A Critical Introduction* (Cambridge: Cambridge University Press).

Quintilian (2002) *Institutio Oratoria*, trans. Russell, D (Cambridge, MA: Harvard University Press).

Railton, P (1994) 'Truth, Reason, and the Regulation of Belief' 5 *Philosophical Issues* 71.

Raz, J (1980) *The Concept of a Legal System* (Oxford: Clarendon Press).

Reichenbach, H (1938) *Experience and Prediction: An Analysis of the Foundations and the Structure of Knowledge* (Chicago: Chicago University Press).

Richard, I (2014) 'Metaphors in English for Law: Let Us Keep Them!' 8 *Metaphor Studies in the English Language*, available online: https://journals.openedition.org/lexis/251.

Richards, IA (1936) *The Philosophy of Rhetoric* (Oxford: Oxford University Press).

Richards, R and Daston, L (eds) (2016) *Kuhn's Structure of Scientific Revolutions at Fifty: Reflections on a Science Classic* (Chicago: Chicago University Press).

Richardson, A (2011) 'Defaulting to Fiction: Neuroscience Rediscovers the Romantic Imagination' 32(4) *Poetics Today* 663.

Richardson, A (2014) 'Imagination: Literary and Cognitive Intersections' in Zunshine, L (ed) *The Oxford Handbook of Cognitive Literary Studies* (Oxford: Oxford University Press) 225.

Riffaterre, M (1985) 'Personification' 69 *Yale French Studies* 107.

Riffaterre, M (1990) *Fictional Truth* (Baltimore: Johns Hopkins University Press).

Rissland, E (1989) 'Dimension-Based Analysis of Hypotheticals from Supreme Court Oral Arguments' *Proceedings of the 2nd International Conference on Artificial Intelligence and Law* 111 (ACM: New York).

Ritchie, D (2010) '"Everybody Goes Down": Metaphors, Stories and Simulations in Conversations' 25 *Metaphor and Symbol* 123.

Robbins, RA (2006) 'Harry Potter, Ruby Slippers and Merlin: Telling the Client's Story Using the Characters and Paradigm of the Archetypal Hero's Journey' 29 *Seattle University Law Review* 767.

Roberts, R and Wood, WJ (2007) *Intellectual Virtues: An Essay in Regulative Epistemology* (Oxford: Oxford University Press).

Roeser, S (2018) 'Socially Extended Moral Deliberation about Risks' in Carter, A, Clark, A, Kallestrup, J, Palermos, O and Pritchard, D (eds) *Socially Extended Epistemology* (Oxford: Oxford University Press) 157.

Rogoff, B (1990) *Apprenticeship in Thinking: Cognitive Development in Social Context* (Oxford: Oxford University Press).

Roland, A (2007) 'Appeals to the Judicial Committee of the Privy Council: A Canadian Perspective' 32(4) *Commonwealth Law Bulletin* 569.

Rorty, A (1976) 'A Literary Postscript: Characters, Persons, Selves, Individuals' in Rorty, A (ed) *The Identities of Persons* (Berkeley: University of California Press) 301.

Rorty, A (2014) 'The Ethics of Collaborative Ambivalence' 18(4) *The Journal of Ethics* 18 391.

Roth, P (2006) 'Naturalism without Fears' in Turner, S and Risjord, M (eds), *Philosophy of Anthropology and Sociology* (Amsterdam: Elsevier) 683.

Ross, R (1969) *Law, Reason, and Justice* (New York: New York University Press).

Rowan, S (2019) 'The "Legitimate Interest in Performance" in the Law of Penalties' 78(1) *Cambridge Law Journal* 148.

Rundle, K (2012) *Forms Liberate: Reclaiming the Jurisprudence of Lon L Fuller* (Oxford: Hart).

Ruskola, T (2013) *Legal Orientalism: China, the United States and Modern Law* (Cambridge, MA: Harvard University Press).

Russell, DA (1983) *The Greek Declamations* (Cambridge: Cambridge University Press).

Saccaro-Battisti, G (2015) 'Changing Metaphors of Political Structures' 44(1) *Journal of the History of Ideas* 31.

Salaymeh, L (2016) *The Beginnings of Islamic Law: Late Antique Islamicate Legal Traditions* (Cambridge: Cambridge University Press).

Samuel, G (2003) *Epistemology and Method in Law* (Abingdon: Ashgate).

Samuel, G (2015) 'Is Legal Reasoning Like Medical Reasoning?' 35 *Legal Studies* 323.

Samuel, G (2017) 'Should Jurists Take Interests More Seriously?' *Law and Method*, available online: http://dx.doi.org/10.5553/REM/.000023.

Samuel, G (2018a) *Rethinking Legal Reasoning* (Cheltenham: Edward Elgar).

Samuel, G (2018b) 'What Is (Or Perhaps Should Be) the Relationship between Legal History and Legal Theory?'6(1) *Comparative Legal History* 97.

Sarat, A and Kearns, T (eds) (1994) *The Rhetoric of Law* (Ann Arbor: University of Michigan Press).

Sarat, A, Douglas, L and Umphrey, M (eds) (2014) *Law and the Utopian Imagination* (Stanford: Stanford University Press).

Sartre, J-P (1972) *The Psychology of Imagination* (London: Metheun).

Scanlon, L (2007) *Narrative, Authority and Power: The Medieval Exemplum and the Chaucerian Tradition* (Cambridge: Cambridge University Press).

Scarry, E (1999) *Dreaming by the Book* (Princeton: Princeton University Press).

Schaeffer, JM (1999) *Why Fiction?* (Lincoln: University of Nebraska Press).

Schank, RC and Abelson RP (1977) *Scripts, Plans, Goals and Understanding: An Inquiry into Human Knowledge Structures* (Hilsdale, NJ: Erlbaum, 1977).

Scharffs, B (2001) 'Law as Craft' 54(6) *Vanderbilt Law Review* 2245.

Schauer, F (1987), 'Precedent' 39 *Stanford Law Review* 571.

Schauer, F (2009), *Thinking Like a Lawyer: A New Introduction to Legal Reasoning* (Cambridge, MA: Harvard University Press).

Schelly, JM (1985) 'Interpretation in Law: The Dworkin-Fish Debate (or, Soccer amongst the Gahuku-Gama)' 73 *California Law Review* 158.

Schickore, J and Steinle, F (eds) (2006) *Revisiting Justification and Discovery: Historical and Philosophical Perspectives on the Context Distinction* (Dordrecht: Springer).

Schilbach, L, Timmermans, B, Reddy, V, Costall, A, Bente, G, Schlicht, T, and Vogeley, K (2013) 'Toward a Second-Person Neuroscience' 46(4) *Behavioral and Brain Sciences* 393.

Schlag, P (2002) 'The Aesthetics of American Law' 115(4) *Harvard Law Review* 1047.

Schneewind, JB (1998) *The Invention of Autonomy: A History of Modern Moral Philosophy* (Cambridge: Cambridge University Press).

Schneider, R (2001) 'Towards a Cognitive Theory of Character: The Dynamics of Mental-Model Construction' 35(4) *Style* 607.

Searle, J (1992) *The Rediscovery of the Mind* (Cambridge, MA: MIT Press).

Sellers, M (ed) (2017) *Law, Reason and Emotion* (Cambridge: Cambridge University Press).

Sellevold, K (2018) 'On the Borders of the Ostensive: Blushing in Edith Warton's *House of Mirth*' in Cave, T and Wilson, D (eds) *Reading beyond the Code: Literature and Relevance Theory* (Oxford: Oxford University Press) 93.

Seneca, The Elder (1974) *Controversiae*, trans. Winterbottom, M (Cambridge, MA: Harvard University Press).

Serjeantson, R (2007) 'Testimony: The Artless Proof', in Adamson, S, Alexander, G and Ettenhuber, K (eds) *Renaissance Figures of Speech* (Cambridge: Cambridge University Press) 179.

Shah, N (2003) 'How Truth Governs Belief' 112(4) *Philosophical Review* 447.

Shanto, T (2019) 'Imaginative Resistance and Empathic Resistance' *Topoi*, First Online, available online: https://doi.org/10.1007/s11245-019-09642-9.

Sharpe, R and McMahon, P (2007) *The Persons Case: The Origins and Legacy of the Fight for Legal Personhood* (Toronto: University of Toronto Press).

Shaw, J (2012) 'The Continuing Relevance of Ars Poetica to Legal Scholarship and the Modern Lawyer' 25(1) *International Journal for the Semiotics of Law* 71.

Shaw, J (2017) 'Aesthetics of Law and Literary License: An Anatomy of the Legal Imagination' 38(1) *Liverpool Law Review* 83.

Sheets-Johnstone, M (2011) *The Primacy of Movement*, 2nd edn (Amsterdam: John Benjamins).

Sheppard, J (2009) 'Once Upon a Time, Happily Ever After, and in a Galaxy Far, Far Away: Using Narrative to Fill the Cognitive Gap Left by Overreliance on Pure Logic in Appellate Briefs and Motion Memoranda' 46 *Willamette Law Review* 255.

Shklovsky, V (2015) 'Art as Device' 36(3) *Poetics Today* 151.

Shmilovits, L (2019) *Deus ex Machina: Legal Fictions in Private Law*, Doctoral Thesis, University of Cambridge, available online: https://doi.org/10.17863/CAM.33535.

Sidney, P (1868) [1595] *An Apologie for Poetrie* (London: Alex Murray and Son).

Siegel, H (1980) 'Justification, Discovery and the Naturalising of Epistemology' 47 *Philosophy of Science* 297.

Silveira, L (2014) 'Discovery and Justification of Judicial Decisions: Towards More Precise Distinctions in Legal Decision-Making', *Law and Method*, available online: www.bjutijdschriften.nl/tijdschrift/lawandmethod/2014/09/RENM-D-14-00003.

Simon-Shoshan, M (2012) *Stories of the Law: Narrative Discourse and the Construction of Authority in the Mishnah* (Oxford: Oxford University Press).

Simon-Shoshan, M (2013) '"People Talking Without Speaking": The Semiotics of the Rabbinic Legal Exemplum as Reflected in Bavli *Berakhot* 11a' 25(3) *Law and Literature* 446.

Simpson, B (1973) 'Common Law and Legal Theory' in Simpson, AWB (ed), *Oxford Essays in Jurisprudence*, 2nd series (Oxford: Oxford University Press) 77.

Simpson, G (2019) 'Imagination' in D'Aspremont, J and Singh, S (eds) *Fundamental Concepts for International Law* (Cheltenham: Edward Elgar) 413.

Simpson, MC (2015) 'Participation and Immersion in Walton and Calvino' 29(2) *Philosophy and Literature* 321.

Siraganian, L (2015) 'Theorizing Corporate Intentionality in Contemporary American Fiction' 27 *Law & Literature* 99.

Siraganian, L (2018) 'Dreiser's Anti-Corporate Tools: Veil-Piercing and the Novel of Corporate Agency' 30 *American Literary History* 249.

Slaughter, J (2019) 'Pathetic Fallacies: Personification and the Unruly Subjects of International Law' 7(1) *London Review of International Law* 3.

Slepoy, VZ (2018) 'Form and Function of Rabbinic Responsa: Comparative Law Perspectives' *Ancilla Juris* 123, available online: www.anci.ch/articles/2018Ancilla_Slepoy_123.pdf.
Smeed, JW (1985) *The Theophrastan Character: The History of a Literary Genre* (Oxford: Clarendon Press).
Smith, A (2002) [1759] *The Theory of Moral Sentiments*, ed. Haakonssen, K (Cambridge: Cambridge University Press).
Smith, J (1917) 'Surviving Fictions' 27(2) *Yale Law Journal* 147.
Smith, J (1918) 'Surviving Fictions II' 27(3) *Yale Law Journal* 317.
Smith, M (2007) 'Levels of Metaphor in Persuasive Legal Writing' 58 *Mercer Law Review* 919.
Smith, M (2011) 'On the Twofoldness of Character' 42 *New Literary History* 277.
Smith, TB (1961) *British Justice: The Scottish Contribution*, Hamlyn Lectures (London: Stevens and Sons Limited).
Soifer, A (1986) 'Reviewing Legal Fictions' 20 *Georgia Law Review* 871.
Sorensen, R (1992) *Thought Experiments* (Oxford: Oxford University Press).
Sparkes, P (2015) 'Ejectment: Three Births and a Funeral' in Del Mar, M and Twining, W (eds) *Legal Fictions in Theory and Practice* (Dordrecht: Springer) 275.
Spaulding, N (2012) 'The Enclosure of Justice: Courthouse Architecture, Due Process, and the Dead Metaphor of Trial' 24 *Yale Journal of Law & the Humanities* 311.
Spolsky, E (1996) 'Elaborated Knowledge: Reading Kinesis in Pictures' 17(2) *Poetics Today* 157.
Spolsky, E (2015) *Contracts of Fiction: Cognition, Culture and Community* (Oxford: Oxford University Press).
Spolsky, E (2018) 'How Do Audiences Act?' in Banks, K and Chesters, T (eds) *Movement in Renaissance Literature: Exploring Kinesic Intelligence* (London: Palgrave MacMillan) 225.
Squibbs, R (2010) 'The Artful Templar: Law and the Periodical Essay in Eighteenth-Century Britain' 108(1) *Modern Philology* 89.
Squibbs, R (2014) *Urban Enlightenment and the Eighteenth-Century Periodical Essay* (London: Palgrave Macmillan).
Stacey, R (2018) *Law and the Imagination in Medieval Wales* (Philadelphia: University of Pennsylvania Press).
Stanchi, K (2002) 'Feminist Legal Writing' 39 *San Diego Law Review* 387.
Steel, S (2015) *Proof of Causation in Tort Law* (Cambridge: Cambridge University Press).
Steen, G (2008), 'The Paradox of Metaphor: Why We Need a Three-Dimensional Model of Metaphor' 23(4) *Metaphor and Symbol* 213.
Stein, P (1966) *Regulae Iuris: From Juristic Rules to Legal Maxims* (Edinburgh: Edinburgh University Press).
Sterelny, K (2010) 'Minds: Extended or Scaffolded?' 9(4) *Phenomenology and the Cognitive Sciences* 465.
Stern, S (2017a) 'Legal and Literary Fictions' in Anker, E and Meyler, B (eds) *New Directions in Law and Literature* (Oxford: Oxford University Press) 313.
Stern, S (2017b) '*R. v. Jones* (1703): The Origins of the Reasonable Person' in Handler, P, Mares, H, and Williams, I (eds) *Landmark Cases in Criminal Law* (Oxford: Hart) 59.
Stern, S (2017c) 'Samuel Richardson and the Law' in Sabor, P and Schellenberg, B (eds) *Samuel Richardson in Context* (Cambridge: Cambridge University Press) 231.
Stern, S (2020) 'The Legal Imagination in Historical Perspective' in Amaya, A and Del Mar, M (eds) *Virtue, Emotion and Imagination in Law and Legal Reasoning* (Oxford: Hart).
Sternberg, M (1986) 'The King Through Ironic Eyes: Biblical Narrative and the Literary Reading Process' 7(2) *Poetics Today* 275.
Sternberg, M (2001) 'How Narrativity Makes a Difference' 9(2) *Narrative* 115.
Sternberg, M (2011) 'If-Plots: Narrativity and the Law-Code' in Pier, G, Landa, G and Angel, J (eds) *Theorizing Narrativity* (Berlin: de Gruyter) 29.
Stevens, K (2018) 'Trump, Snakes and the Power of Fables' 38(1) *Informal Logic* 53.
Stjernfelt, F (2007) *Diagrammatology: An Investigation on the Borderlines of Phenomenology, Ontology, and Semiotics* (Dordrecht: Springer).
Stock, K (2007) 'Sartre, Wittgenstein, and Learning from Imagination' in Goldie, P and Schellekens, E (eds), *Philosophy and Conceptual Art* (Oxford: Oxford University Press), 171.
Stokes, D (2019) 'Mental Imagery and Fiction' 49(6) *Canadian Journal of Philosophy* 731.
Stoler, A (2016) *Duress: Imperial Durabilities in Our Times* (Durham: Duke University Press).
Stone, J (1985) *Precedent and Law: The Dynamics of Common Law Growth* (Sydney: Butterworths).
Stone, M (1985) 'Dickens, Bentham, and the Fictions of the Law: A Victorian Controversy and Its Consequences' 29 *Victorian Studies* 125.

Stonebridge, L (2011) *The Judicial Imagination* (Edinburgh: Edinburgh University Press).
Stoner, I and Swartwood, J (2017) 'Fanciful Examples' 48(3) *Metaphilosophy* 325.
Strawson, PF (1970) 'Imagination and Perception' in Foster, L and Swanson, JW (eds) *Experience and Theory* (Amherst: University of Massachusetts Press) 31.
Stuart, M (2019) 'Towards a Dual Process Epistemology of Imagination' *Synthese*, First Online, available online: https://doi.org/10.1007/s11229-019-02116-w.
Stuart, M, Fehige, Y, and Brown, JR (eds) (2017) *The Routledge Companion to Thought Experiments* (London: Routledge).
Sunstein, C (1999) *One Case at a Time* (Cambridge, MA: Harvard University Press).
Swaminathan, S (2019) 'Mos Geometricus and the Common Law Mind: Interrogating Contract Theory' 82(1) *Modern Law Review* 46.
Swinfen, DB (1987) *Imperial Appeal: The Debate on the Appeal to the Privy Council 1833–1986* (Wolfeboro: Manchester University Press).
Taekema, S, van Klink, B and de Been, W (eds) (2016) *Facts and Norms in Law: Interdisciplinary Reflections on Legal Method* (Cheltenham: Edward Elgar).
Tamen, M (2004) *Friends of Interpretable Objects* (Cambridge, MA: Harvard University Press).
Tang, C (2018) *Imagining World Order: Literature and International Law in Early Modern Europe, 1500–1800* (Ithaca: Cornell University Press).
Tappolet, C (2016) *Emotions, Values and Agency* (Oxford: Oxford University Press).
Taylor, C (2003) *Modern Social Imaginaries* (Durham: Duke University Press).
Temple, K (2010) 'Manley's Feigned Scene: The Fictions of Law at Westminster Hall' 22(4) *Eighteenth-Century Fiction* 573.
Terry, R (1992) 'Transitions and Digressions in the Eighteenth-Century Long Poem' 32(3) *Studies in English Literature, 1500–1900* 495.
Thagard, P (2002) 'The Passionate Scientist: Emotion in Scientific Cognition' in Carruthers, P, Stich, S and Siegal, M (eds) *The Cognitive Basis of Science* (Cambridge: Cambridge University Press) 235.
Thomas, Y (2005) 'L'extrême et l'ordinaire. Remarques sur le cas médiéval de la communauté disparue' in Passeron, JC and Revel, J (eds) *Penser par cas* (Paris: Éditions de l'École des Hautes Études en Sciences Sociales) 45.
Thomas, Y (2011) *Les opérations du droit* (Paris: Le Seuil).
Thomson-Clerk, R (1909) *The Characters of Theophrastus, the Mimes of Herodas, the Tablet of Kebes* (London, George Routledge & Sons).
Thornburg, E (1995) 'Metaphors Matter: How Images of Battle, Sports and Sex Shape the Adversary System' 10 *Wisconsin Women's Law Journal* 225.
Tiersma, P (1999) *Legal Language* (Chicago: Chicago University Press).
Tiersma, P (2007) 'The Textualisation of Precedent' 82 *Notre Dame Law Review* 1187.
Trimarco, P and Hurley, U (2008) 'Less is More: Completing Narratives in Miniature Fiction' 1(1) *21: A Journal of Contemporary and Innovative Fiction* 82.
Trimpi, W (1983) *Muses of One Mind: The Literary Analysis of Experience and its Continuity* (Princeton: Princeton University Press).
Troscianko, E (2013) 'Reading Imaginatively: The Imagination in Cognitive Science and Cognitive Literary Studies' 42(2) *Journal of Literary Semantics* 181.
Tschacher, W and Bergomi, C (eds) (2011) *The Implications of Embodiment: Cognition and Communication* (Exeter: Imprint Academic).
Turner, S (2010), *Explaining the Normative* (Cambridge: Polity).
Turri, J, Alfano, M and Greco, J (2017) 'Virtue Epistemology' *Stanford Encyclopaedia of Philosophy*, available online: https://plato.stanford.edu/entries/epistemology-virtue/.
Twining, W (1984) 'Taking Facts Seriously' 34(1) *Journal of Legal Education* 22.
Twining, W (2019) *Jurist in Context* (Cambridge: Cambridge University Press).
Twining, W (ed) (1986) *Legal Theory and Common Law* (Oxford: Wiley-Blackwell).
Twining, W and Miers, D (1976) *How to Do Things with Rules* (London: Weidenfeld & Nicolson).
Tye, M (1991) *The Mental Imagery Debate* (Cambridge, MA: MIT Press).
Tylen, K, Weed, E, Wallentin, M, Roepstorff, A, & Frith, CD (2010) 'Language as a Tool for Interacting Minds' 25(1) *Mind & Language* 3.

Vaihinger, H (1925) [1911] *The Philosophy of 'As if': A System of the Theoretical, Practical and Religious Fictions of Mankind*, trans. CK Ogden (London: Kegan Paul).

Valverde, M (2015) *Chronotopes of Law: Jurisdiction, Scale and Governance* (New York: Routledge).

van der Burg, W and van Willigenburg, T (eds) (1998) *Reflective Equilibrium: Essays in Honour of Robert Heeger* (Dordrecht: Springer).

van Domselaar, I (2020) 'All Judges on the Couch? On Iris Murdoch and Legal Decision-Making' in Amaya, A and Del Mar, M (eds) *Virtue, Emotion and Imagination in Law and Legal Reasoning* (Oxford: Hart).

van Eck, C (2007) *Classical Rhetoric and the Visual Arts in Early Modern Europe* (Cambridge: Cambridge University Press).

van Klink, B (2009) 'Facts and Norms: The Unfinished Debate between Eugen Ehrlich and Hans Kelsen' in Hertogh, M (ed) *Living Law: Reconsidering Eugen Ehrlich* (Oxford: Hart), 127.

Veitch, S (2007) *Law and Irresponsibility: On the Legitimation of Human Suffering* (New York: Routledge).

Venzke, I (2018) 'What If? Counterfactual (Hi)Stories of International Law' 8(2) *Asian Journal of International Law* 403.

Vesting, T (2018) *Legal Theory and the Media of Law* (Cheltenham: Edward Elgar).

Vickers, B (1988) *In Defense of Rhetoric* (Oxford: Clarendon Press).

Vidmar, I (2013) 'Thought Experiments, Hypotheses and Cognitive Dimension of Literary Fiction' 55–56 (1–2) *Synthesis Philosophica* 177.

Viehweg, T (1993). *Topics and Law: A Contribution to Basic Research in Law*, trans. Durham, WCJ (Frankfurt: Lang).

von Jhering, R (1904) *Law in Everyday Life* (Oxford: Clarendon Press).

Vygotsky, LS (1978), *Mind in Society* (Cambridge, MA: Harvard University Press).

Waddams, S (2003) *Dimensions of Private Law: Categories and Concepts in Anglo-American Legal Reasoning* (Cambridge: Cambridge University Press).

Waithe, M (2012) 'Empson's Legal Fictions' 62(3) *Essays in Criticism* 279.

Waldron, J (2011) 'Ius Gentium: A Defence of Gentili's Equation of the Law of Nations with the Law of Nature' in Kingsbury, B and Straumann, B (eds) *The Roman Foundations of the Law of Nations: Alberico Gentili and the Justice of Empire* (Oxford: Oxford University Press) 283.

Waldron, J (2012), 'Stare Decisis and the Rule of Law: A Layered Approach' 111 *Michigan Law Review* 1.

Walker, Lord (206) '"As If …" – The Wonderland of Statutory Hypotheses' 37(3) *Statute Law Review* 183.

Walker, N (2014) *Intimations of Global Law* (Cambridge: Cambridge University Press).

Walsh, A (2011) 'A Moderate Defence of the Use of Thought Experiments in Applied Ethics' 14(4) *Ethical Theory and Moral Practice* 467.

Walsh, R (2007) *The Rhetoric of Fictionality* (Ohio: Ohio State University Press).

Walton, D (2013) *Methods of Argumentation* (Cambridge: Cambridge University Press).

Walton, K (1990) *Mimesis as Make-Believe* (Cambridge, MA: Harvard University Press).

Waluchow, W (2006) *A Common Law Theory of Judicial Review: The Living Tree* (Cambridge: Cambridge University Press).

Waluchow, W (2015) 'Constitutions as Living Trees: An Idiot Defends' 18 *Canadian Journal of Law and Jurisprudence* 207.

Walzer, M (1967) 'On the Role of Symbolism in Political Thought' 82(2) *Political Science Quarterly* 191.

Warner, M (1987) *Monuments and Maidens: The Allegory of the Female Form* (Berkeley: University of California Press).

Warren, C (2015) *Literature and the Law of Nations 1580–1680* (Oxford: Oxford University Press).

Wasserstrom, R (1961) *The Judicial Decision: Toward a Theory of Legal Justification* (London: Oxford University Press).

Watt, G (2009) *Equity Stirring: The Story of Justice Beyond Law* (Oxford: Hart).

Watt, G (ed) (2019) *A Cultural History of Law*, 6 Vols. (London: Bloomsbury).

Webb, R (2009) *Ekphrasis, Imagination, and Persuasion in Ancient Rhetorical Theory and Practice* (Surrey: Ashgate).

Webster, TBL (1954) 'Personification as a Mode of Greek Thought' 17(1–2) *Journal of the Warburg and Courtauld Institutes* 10.

Wechsler, H (1959) 'Toward Neutral Principles of Constitutional Law' 73 *Harvard Law Review* 1.

Weinrib, E (2005) *Legal Reason: The Use of Analogy in Legal Argument* (Cambridge: Cambridge University Press).

Weisberg, M (2013) *Simulation and Similarity: Using Models to Understand the World* (Oxford: Oxford University Press).
Wertsch, JV (1985) *Vygotsky and the Social Formation of Mind* (Cambridge, MA: Harvard University Press).
West, R (1985) 'Jurisprudence as Narrative: An Aesthetic Analysis of Modern Legal Theory' 60(2) *New York University Law Review* 145.
Wheatley, N (2017) 'Spectral Legal Personality in Interwar International Law: On New Ways of Not Being a State' 35(3) *Law and History Review* 786.
White, A (1990) *The Language of Imagination* (Oxford: Blackwell).
White, EK (2020) 'On Emotions and the Politics of Attention in Judicial Reasoning' in Amaya, A and Del Mar, M (eds) *Virtue, Emotion and Imagination in Law and Legal Reasoning* (Oxford: Hart).
White, JB (1985a) *Heracles Bow: Essays on the Rhetoric and Poetics of Law* (Madison: University of Wisconsin Press).
White, JB (1985b) 'Law as Rhetoric, Rhetoric as Law: The Arts of Cultural and Communal Life' 52(3) *University of Chicago Law Review* 684.
White, JB (2018) [1973] *The Legal Imagination* (New York: Wolters Kluwer).
White, R (1989) 'MacKinnon and the Parables', in Surin, K (ed) *Christ, Ethics and Tragedy: Essays in Honour of Donald MacKinnon* (Cambridge: Cambridge University Press) 49.
Williamson, T (2016) 'Knowing by Imagining' in Kind, A and Kung, P (eds) (2016) *Knowledge Through Imagination* (Oxford: Oxford University Press) 113.
Wilson, KJ (1995) *Incomplete Fictions: The Formation of English Renaissance Dialogue* (Washington: The Catholic University Press of America).
Winter, S (2001) *A Clearing in the Forest: Law, Life and Mind* (Chicago: University of Chicago Press).
Wittgenstein, L (1980) *Remarks on the Philosophy of Psychology*, ed. von Wright, GH and Nyman, H (Oxford: Blackwell).
Wohl, V (ed) (2014) *Probabilities, Hypotheticals and Counterfactuals in Ancient Greek Thought* (Cambridge: Cambridge University Press).
Wollheim, R (1987) *Painting as an Art* (London: Thames and Hudson).
Yanal, R (1994) 'The Paradox of Fiction and Emotion' 75 *Pacific Philosophical Quarterly* 54.
Young, J (1996) 'Inquiry in the Arts and Sciences' 71(276) *Philosophy* 255.
Yuan, Y (2018) 'Framing Surprise, Suspense, and Curiosity: A Cognitive Approach to the Emotional Effects of Narrative' 45 *Neohelicon* 517.
Zagzebski, L (1996) *Virtues of the Mind: An Inquiry into the Nature of Virtue and the Ethical Foundations of Knowledge* (Cambridge: Cambridge University Press).
Zetterberg Gjerlevsen, S (2016a) 'A Novel History of Fictionality' 24(2) *Narrative* 174.
Zetterberg Gjerlevsen, S (2016b) 'Fictionality' in the *Living Handbook of Narratology*, available online: www.lhn.uni-hamburg.de/node/138.html.
Zittoun, T and Glaveanu, V (eds) (2017) *Handbook of Imagination and Culture* (Oxford: Oxford University Press).
Zunshine, L (ed) *The Oxford Handbook of Cognitive Literary Studies* (Oxford: Oxford University Press).

INDEX

CPSIA information can be obtained
at www.ICGtesting.com
Printed in the USA
LVHW041703290322
714724LV00004B/101

9 781509 955046